ALLE ZEIT WACH 1842

Rudolf Richter

Money

Lectures on the Basis of General Equilibrium Theory and the Economics of Institutions

Translated from the German by
Wolfgang F. Stolper

With 38 Figures

Springer-Verlag Berlin Heidelberg New York
London Paris Tokyo Hong Kong

Professor Dr. Rudolf Richter
Department of Economics
Universität des Saarlandes
6600 Saarbrücken 11, FRG

Translator:

Wolfgang F. Stolper
Professor Emeritus
Department of Economics
University of Michigan
Ann Arbor
Michigan, USA

ISBN-13:978-3-642-74039-8 e-ISBN-13:978-3-642-74037-4
DOI: 10.1007/978-3-642-74037-4

Library of Congress Cataloging-in-Publication Data
Richter, Rudolf, 1926-
[Geldtheorie. English]
Money : lectures on the basis of general equilibrium theory and the economics of institutions / Rudolf Richter : translated from the German by Wolfgang F. Stolper.
p. cm.
Translation of: Geldtheorie.
Bibliography: p.
Includes indexes.
ISBN-13:978-3-642-74039-8 (U.S.)
1. Money. 2. Equilibrium (Economics) I. Title.
HG221.G41313 1988
332.4--dc 19

Softcover reprint of the hardcover 1st edition 1989

Typesetting: ASCO Trade Typesetting Ltd., Hong Kong

2142/7130-543210

To my wife

Introductory Remarks

> Nowadays every exposition of the problems of the money economy should really begin with a theory of price and distribution.
>
> *J. A. Schumpeter (1917/18, 631; English translation 1956, 150)*

> Economics comes closer to being a 'science of contract' than a 'science of choice'.
>
> *J. M. Buchanan (1975, 229)*

The theory of money is the theory of exchange involving the use of money. Both exchange and the use of money are social phenomena. Both can only be explained within the framework of a social model. For exchange considered in isolation there exists such a model: the theory of general equilibrium. As far as the use of money is considered matters are somewhat more complicated. Nevertheless, the theory of general equilibrium is in the process of being supplemented by a theory of exchange by means of money. At the same time, the institutional basis of a money economy, i.e. the economics of institutions, is once again being stressed. However, a systematic joint analysis of both is still missing. This book, too, will not succeed in presenting a complete synthesis. We will, however, try to direct the attention of the reader in this direction. Neoclassical equilibrium analysis will be understood as the ideal result of a specific institutional framework, as a system of consistent contracts between individuals which are carried out exactly. How these contracts are reached will not be analyzed. A stationary equilibrium model will serve as a reference system. Deviations from stationary equilibrium are interpreted as the result of slack within the institutional framework. A description or explanation of the process of adaptation to equilibrium is not of interest in this context.

No analysis of market processes will be given. The analysis of evolutionary processes is confined to the evolution of currency orders where "order" is defined as a system of social norms or rules. Monetary theory is understood as a theory of the currency order. This approach permits not only clearer access to problems of monetary theory, it also gives a total view of monetary theory that is otherwise impossible.

The book consists of two parts. Part I presents, in elementary form and tailored to our purposes, the basic skeleton of the theory in so far as it is relevant to our subsequent considerations: general equilibrium theory and the economic theory of institutions. In Part II we develop monetary theory on the basis of these fundamental considerations.

Part I consists of three chapters. Chapter 1 presents the general theory of competitive equilibrium for one period. The chapter limits itself to exchange or purchase transactions where both sides of the exchange occur simultaneously. The second chapter deals with the theory of general equilibrium over several periods. Loans in kind and forward purchases are now possible. A model of stationary equilibrium and the theory of overlapping generations are presented. The overlapping generations model will later be used as the basic model of monetary theory. Chapter 3 deals with the economic theory of institutions in general, not merely with the theory of the institution of money. The concepts of "property rights" and of "transaction costs" will be introduced. The model of a transactions firm will be described which will be used later to explain the holding of cash balances and the theory of the banking firm. We finally deal with the theory of the market as an institution and, in this context, the concept of a market community.

Part II consists of Chapters 4 to 8. Chapter 4 presents approaches to the economic explanation of the institution of money. In the older literature this was called the analysis of the "nature of money", a term which we also will use. We introduce the concepts of a "currency community" and of an "elementary currency order". The core of this chapter is the description and economic explanation of the regulatory objects of an elementary currency order. Chapter 5 deals first with the concept of "payment" applied to exchange by means of money. Next we describe an economy without transaction costs. In such an economy the holding of cash balances does not pay even if exchange involves the use of money. Money is "qualitatively" perfectly neutral; that is, it makes no difference whether exchange involves the use of money or not, whether we deal with money purchases or barter transactions, whether loans are made in kind or involve money, or which currency is used in accounting. The conditions of arbitrage equilibria, which play a pervasive role in neoclassical theory, are described; the significance of the arbitrage logic is illustrated. Chapter 6 introduces transaction costs and their effects. We develop a stationary overlapping generations model in which the holding of cash balances is worthwhile because the exchange of cash for interest-bearing assets and vice versa involves cost. The quantity theory of money applies: the amount of money and the prices of goods are related in a strictly proportional manner. Money is "quantitatively" neutral. Chapter 7 deals with problems of the various institutional solutions to the problem of safeguarding the value of money on the basis of the overlapping generations model which has been developed in the preceding chapter. The two basic types of a currency order, the commodity standard and the paper standard, are discussed, both for the case of a single country (i.e. on a "national" basis) and for the case of two countries (i.e. on an "international" basis). Freely fluctuating exchange rates are discussed in this context, as are the arguments for and against the commodity and the paper standard. Chapter 8 discusses financial intermediaries, particularly banks, using the concept of a "transactions firm" which was introduced in Chapter 3. We return to the problem of how to safeguard the value of money and discuss the problems of public regulation of the central bank and the commercial banks.

The book has grown out of a series of lectures which the author gave during the past fifteen years and which he continuously revised. It is a mixture of monograph and textbook. Its central idea is the importance of the currency order. The currency order determines the why and how of the use of money. The individuals who negotiate purchase or loan agreements orient themselves on such an order. It is the currency order which is the basis of the trust in a currency which in turn is the precondition for the proper functioning of money. It has been our intention to interpret the theory of money as the theory of a currency order. We have done so on the simple assumptions of a stationary overlapping generations model whose primary function has been to help organize our thoughts. We deviate from this model in our interpretations whenever this seems appropriate. We have not tried to formulate an exact model for the economic analysis of institutions as applied to money.

The theory of money is such a vast subject matter that it is impossible to discuss all of the relevant literature even when limiting oneself to a particular point of view. On the other hand, an intensive and extensive study of the literature is essential for an understanding of the theoretical topics which we treat. To help the student, we have appended to each chapter suggestions for further reading together with brief comments.

The English version is a translation of the first German edition which went to the printer in January 1987 and which appeared during the summer of 1987. The references to the literature have been extended for the English reader, and a few important later contributions have been incorporated. Tables and Charts were updated to 1987 inclusive. Several paragraphs were revised and it is hoped, improved, among them in particular the end of Chapter 6. Two errors were corrected: an unjust criticism of Patinkin in Appendix 3 to Chapter 6 which was pointed out to me by U. Schlieper and a wrong subscript in equation (3) of Appendix 1 to Chapter 8 which was discovered by one of my students. This correction made the results of equation (8-3) more complicated and also affected the arguments in Sections 8.2 and 8.4. All told, the English translation may be considered a revised and enlarged second edition of the German book.

My debts of gratitude are extensive. My first debt is to the University of the Saarland for maintaining good working conditions despite difficult budgetary problems. The University of Michigan extended two invitations for longer periods as guest professor which were most stimulating and helpful. My thanks are also due to the Deutsche Forschungsgemeinschaft and the Wissenschaftliche Gesellschaft des Saarlandes for financial help with two shorter visits to the USA. To the same foundations, the Fritz Thyssen Stiftung and the Kultusminister of the Saarland go my thanks for providing the major part of the costs of the international seminars on the New Institutional Economics organized by Eirik G. Furubotn and myself which gave me insights into new and interesting directions of research. Mr. Hans Gliem, President of the Landeszentralbank für das Saarland, and Mr. Herbert Weber, Chairman of the executive board of the Landesbank Saar, Girozentrale, provided contacts with actual practice.

Numerous discussions with colleagues of the Faculty of Law and Economics of the University of the Saarland stimulated the work on the manuscript. The discussion of early versions of Chapters 3 and 4 in a working group on law and economics with Georg Rees, Dieter Schmidtchen and Dietrich Schultz should be specially mentioned. It was a beautiful experience. Elke Schäfer-Jäckel read and criticised in particular early versions of Chapters 2 and 6. Wolfgang Stützel helped with questions and answers to Chapter 5. My former assistant Peter Dittus discussed with me the various drafts of the last three chapters and the whole conception of the book.

I am greatly obliged to Emil Baltensperger, Eva Bössmann, Ekkehard Schlicht and Ulrich Schlieper for critically reading the final version of the manuscript. Individual parts of the manuscript were presented and discussed at Washington University St. Louis, Texas A&M University, College Station, the University of Texas at Arlington and several times at the University of Michigan, Ann Arbor. In this connection I owe particular thanks to Eirik G. Furubotn, Douglas C. North, Steven Wiggins, Aquiles Almansi, David Aschauer and Jeffrey Miron for their critical comments.

My friend Wolfgang F. Stolper translated the manuscript from the German, not without frequent substantive objections and proposals for improvement. Occasionally, I have even listened to him – after lengthy and animated discussions. His openness to arguments, patience and labor intensity deserve many thanks.

My assistants and selected graduate students helped in many ways both with the preliminaries and the final version of the German and English manuscripts. Frank Diener made the calculations and the computer plotted figures and drew the graphs. Ralf Maurer compiled and improved the German manuscript including the list of references. With great patience and perseverance Barbara Thimm-Maldener typed the German version and Eva Schneider and Detlef Karges typed the English version. Claudia Korf and Thomas Büsch made the index, provided the English references and helped with the final proofs of both versions. David Andrews helped with the editing of the English translation and Joan Kmenta with editorial advice.

To my wife my thanks are due for her patience, moral support and help with the final work on the manuscript. The English version was finished in March 1988.

Rudolf Richter

Contents

Part I
Theoretical Foundations: An Elementary Overview

Chapter 1
General Equilibrium Theory: An Outline

The theory of money is a special theory of exchange. Since as we confine ourselves in this book to the case of a general economic equilibrium, the necessary foundations are provided by general equilibrium theory. It is generally said that money cannot be found in it. That is not quite correct. We have become accustomed to regard prices in terms of money also in general equilibrium, i.e., to regard money as an accounting unit, and it needs not much imagination to imagine in this model money used also as a means of payment. However in the traditional version of general equilibrium theory there are no cash holdings. They can only be explained if transaction costs are taken into consideration, which usually is not the case in general equilibrium theory. The appearance of transaction costs leads us into the midst of the problems discussed later in this book; they are of a fundamental nature.

To clear up the terminology for the next chapters this chapter repeats briefly the main ideas of general equilibrium theory. We interpret the notions of general equilibrium theory for purposes of monetary theory and explain what is to be understood by the purchasing power of money. Cash holdings are introduced and it is explained how the purchasing power of money may be determined to a first approximation within the framework of general equilibrium theory. In this context we shall meet the problem of the classical dichotomy of the general equilibrium model, i.e., the division of the economic system into a real and a monetary part. Finally we shall talk about the Patinkin controversy which deals with the question of whether this dichotomy is valid or not.

We are not concerned with the problem of the existence of a general equilibrium.[1] We simply assume that an equilibrium solution exists. This is sufficient for our purposes. We are only interested in the interpretation of general equilibrium theory from the standpoint of monetary theory and institutional economics.

1.1 General Equilibrium Theory Without Production

We start with a pure exchange economy without production which consists only of households. The households negotiate barter or sales contracts with each other. For simplicity's sake we assume only two households and two goods. Each of the households starts with a given positive amount of each good, its initial endowment. There exists a central accounting system through which all final barter or purchase agreements are cleared, either in real exchange relations π or in money prices p.

Let good 1 be wheat and good 2 oats. The monetary unit is the mark. The real exchange ratio π_{21} is measured in the following units or, using a physicists' notion, has the *dimension*

[1] See on this point, e.g., H. Varian (1987, Ch. 6).

$$\dim[\pi_{21}] = \frac{\text{kg oats available here and now}}{\text{kg wheat available here and now}} \ .$$

The price p_1 has the dimension

$$\dim[p_1] = \frac{\text{mark payable today by crediting an account in the central accounting system}}{\text{kg. wheat available here and now}} \ .$$

We assume that there are two possibilities: barter in kind as well as exchange by means of money. In the latter case we assume that the use of money possesses two characteristics:

- abstract money[2], i.e., money of account[3], and
- concrete money[2], i.e., means of payment, money proper[3,4].

The only concrete money (means of payment) in the model under discussion is an entry in an account with the central accounting system, i.e., a deposit in the banking system (this will be illustrated more extensively in Chapter 5). We deal, as it were, with a supermodern money economy in which all payments are made without cash.

The relative money prices p_1/p_2 have, as can easily be seen, the same dimensions as the real exchange ratio π_{21}, since the money units cancel. We also assume that there are no cost involved in using the market. On this assumption the barter transaction "exchange of good 2 against good 1" amounts to the same thing as two purchasing transactions:

(a) Purchase of good 1 available here and now at price p_1,
(b) Sale of good 2 available here and now at price p_2.

In the simple neo-classical world without transaction costs arbitrage transactions (see below Section 4.3) ensure that $\pi_{21} = p_1/p_2$.

We make the usual assumptions of consumer theory, in particular that each household has a system of preferences formalized by the utility function

$$U_k = U_k(x_{1k}, x_{2k}) \ ; \qquad k = 1, 2$$

---

[2] We use J.G. Koopman's (1933, 247) terminology. We emphasize that money in this sense is "on principle a dualistic phenomenon": "there exists *both* a concrete (or real) money *and* abstract (or ideal) money, which in their appearance *may* coincide, e.g., the accounting unit with 'Reichsmark' on one side, and coins, notes and bank accounts made out in terms of Reichsmark on the other side, but which *need not* do so." (Translated by W.F. Stolper).

[3] This is J.M. Keynes's (1930, 5) terminology: "We have seen that the introduction of a *money-of-account* gives rise to two derived categories – offers of Contracts, Contracts and Acknowledgsments of Debt, which are in terms of it, and *money-proper* answering to it, delivery of which will discharge the Contract or Debt." (Italics in the original). See also, e.g., W.S. Jevons (1875, 69 ff.) or D. Patinkin (1965, 15).

[4] This will be discussed in detail in Chapter 4.

where x_{ik} denotes the amount of good i consumed by household k. Each household k wants to realize its consumption plan (x_{1k}, x_{2k}) through barter or exchange by means of money, which will bring it a higher utility than its original endowment $(\bar{x}_{1k}, \bar{x}_{2k})$. In order to achieve this end the two households trade with each other. We shall consider only the case of exchange by means of money. We also assume perfect competition, i.e., we assume that no household has an influence on the equilibrium exchange relationships. The prices p_i are given from the individual's point of view, i.e., we assume that households are price takers. As a rule we imagine negotiations between the households by means of an auctioneer. The auctioneer calls out a certain pair of prices (p_1, p_2). The households determine the consumption plans (x_{1k}, x_{2k}) which will maximize their utilities at this pair of prices. They inform the auctioneer of the amounts which they wish to buy or sell. The auctioneer investigates for each good whether the amounts offered equals the amounts demanded. If this is not the case no transaction is concluded. The auctioneer then calls out a new pair of prices $(p_{1'}, p_{2'})$ and continues to do so until a general equilibrium has been reached, i.e., until both markets are cleared. The purchase contracts arrived at in this manner are then executed. The optimizing procedure of each household (assuming rational behavior by households) occurs in this case of exchange by means of money and under conditions of pure competition as follows: each household k determines its consumption plan (x_{1k}, x_{2k}) which maximizes its utility U_k, subject to the condition that it cannot consume more than the money value of its original endowment.

Under the usual assumptions of the theory of consumer behavior, the optimization problem is therefore:

Max $U_k = U_k(x_{1k}, x_{2k})$ (i.e., the utility function of k)

s.t. $p_1 x_{1k} + p_2 x_{2k} = p_1 \bar{x}_{1k} + p_2 \bar{x}_{2k}$ (the budget constraint or budget equation of k)[5] .

Under certain simplifying assumptions the marginal utilities of the optimal consumption plan (x_{1k}, x_{2k}) are proportional to their prices:

$$\frac{\partial U_k}{\partial x_{1k}} : \frac{\partial U_k}{\partial x_{2k}} = p_1/p_2 \ .$$

(The precise derivation of this proposition is given in Appendix 1 of this chapter).

The optimal amounts consumed depend on the original endowment and the relative prices p_1/p_2, not on the absolute prices. The equations determining the optimal amounts consumed are, therefore, functions of the following general type:

$$x_{ik} = x_{ik}(p_1/p_2, \bar{x}_{1k}, \bar{x}_{2k}) \ , \qquad k = 1, 2$$

[5] Note: a household may, of course, chose not to utilize part of its original endowment ("throw it away"). In this case the $\bar{x}$ are simply smaller than originally assumed. This does not happen in our example because we have for simplicity's sake implied insatiability of consumers (see G. Debreu 1959, 55).

The relative goods prices p_1/p_2 are equal to the real ratio of exchange of the two goods. The dimension "mark payable here and now for each good through an entry into an account with the central accounting system" cancels out. The optimal consumption plan remains unchanged as long as the relative prices remain constant, regardless of their absolute levels. The households penetrate the veil of money, so to speak, in their real planning. In the last analysis they plan with respect to the real exchange rate of the goods. They are free of money illusion[6].

In addition to the relative prices, the equation determining the optimal amounts consumed also contain, of course, as arguments the original endowments of the households. Since by assumption they do not vary during the period under consideration, they are usually not written explicitly into the equation.

A household may be a demander or a supplier of goods, depending whether its optimal amount of consumption x_{ik} is greater or smaller than its original endowment $\bar{x}_{ik}$. Hence

$$\hat{x}_{ik}(p_1/p_2) = x_{ik}(p_1/p_2) - \bar{x}_{ik}$$

is the *demand function* for $\hat{x}_{ik} > 0$, and the *supply function* for $\hat{x}_{ik} < 0$, where x denotes the so-called excess demand.

A market equilibrium exists for good i when the amount supplied equals the amount demanded of good i. In the assumed case with two households, equilibrium for good i is defined by

$$\hat{x}_{i1} + \hat{x}_{i2} = 0 \ .$$

A *competitive equilibrium* is a special case of market equilibrium. It exists in the market for good i, when at a particular price of good i (which the individual economic unit cannot influence) every economic unit realizes ceteris paribus its optimal plan, in the present case when it maximizes its utility.

In our example competitive equilibrium on the market for good 1 exists at that price p_1 which, with a given price $p_2 = \bar{p}_2$, fulfills the condition for competitive equilibrium

$$\hat{x}_{11}(p_1/\bar{p}_2) + \hat{x}_{12}(p_1/\bar{p}_2) = 0 \ .$$

General market equilibrium exists when for each of the n goods, the amount supplied equals the amount demanded.

General competitive equilibrium or briefly "general equilibrium" for a pure exchange economy without production means a general market equilibrium in which at competitive prices (which no individual economic unit can influence) every household realizes its optimal consumption plan. Household 1 chooses and realizes

---

[6] This is true also when as a result of cost incurred in using the market $\dfrac{p_1}{p_2} \neq \pi_{21}$.

a consumption plan which maximizes its utility function

$$U_1(x_{11}, x_{21})$$

subject to

$$p_1 x_{11} + p_2 x_{21} = p_1 \bar{x}_{11} + p_2 \bar{x}_{21}$$

and mutatis mutandis the same for household 2. Expressed differently, the following system of equations must be fulfilled

$$\hat{x}_{i1}(p_1/p_2) + \hat{x}_{i2}(p_1/p_2) = 0 \ , \quad i = 1, 2 \ . \tag{1-1}$$

Exchange takes place only when the equilibrium values of the exchange relations (here the relation p_1/p_2) have been found through a somehow organized process of negotiation, e.g., with the help of an auctioneer. General (competitive) equilibrium is in this elementary version (without uncertainty) an idealized state of the economy in which all exchange contracts are completely realized, viz. at competitive prices which, by assumption, the individual economic unit cannot influence. (A more detailed discussion will be found in Section 3.5).

Equation system (1-1) is a special case of the so-called Walrasian system, which has one more equation than unknowns. In the present case it consists of two equations in one unknown. It can be shown that one of the market equilibrium conditions (one market equation) is linearly dependent on the others. If the markets for $n - 1$ goods are in equilibrium then the market for the nth good is in equilibrium as well.

We reason as follows: if every household k chooses a plan which, at current market prices (p_1, p_2), meets its individual budget equation

$$p_1 \hat{x}_{1k} + p_2 \hat{x}_{2k} = 0 \ ,$$

then the sum of individual plans fulfills simultaneously the budget equation for the economy as a whole:

$$\sum_{k=1}^{m} (p_1 \hat{x}_{1k} + p_2 \hat{x}_{2k}) = 0 \ , \quad (m = 2) \ . \tag{1-2}$$

Equation (1-2) is the formulation of Walras's law under our conditions.[7]

Walras's law viewed ex ante refers to the individual planning of "future" consumption. Ex post each individual consumption plan satisfies an individual budget equation and therefore a budget equation for

---

[7] This term was introduced by O. Lange (1942, 50) because Walras was the first to recognize the importance of this basic relation for general equilibrium theory. Lange assumed that one of the n goods was at the same time the medium of exchange, i.e., money in the sense of commodity money. The logic of the theoretical considerations remains the same.

the economy as a whole. Ex post, i.e., for realized plans, the individual and aggregate budget equations are always fulfilled. Ex ante, i.e., for intended plans, they are not necessarily fullfilled. Ex post the individual budget equations and with them the budget equation for the economy as a whole are budgetary identities.[8] Ex ante they are budgetary constraints.

In words, and generally, Walras's law may be expressed as follows: in a system of n goods, and hence of n markets, the sum of the excess demands of the individual planned quantities valued of any arbitrary market price vector $\{p_1\}$ is equal to zero, provided that all economic units choose consumption plans at prices of the vector $\{p_i\}$ which are internally consistent, i.e., lie on the budget line.[9]

We reason as follows: if $n-1$ markets are in equilibrium then

$$(1\text{-}3) \qquad \sum_{i=1}^{n-1} p_i\hat{X}_i = 0 \ ; \qquad \hat{X}_i = \sum_{k=1}^{m} \hat{x}_{ik} \ .$$

Now, Walras's law is valid:

$$(1\text{-}4) \qquad \sum_{i=1}^{n} p_i\hat{X}_i = 0 \ .$$

Hence

$$p_n\hat{X}_n = 0 \ ,$$

i.e., if $p_n \neq 0$

$$\hat{X}_n = 0 \ ;$$

that is, the market for good n is also in equilibrium.

It follows therefore from Walras's law that of the n goods markets of the general equilibrium model, only $n-1$ markets can be (linearly) independent of each other.

---

[8] The *ex ante* or *ex post* budget equation may at the same time also be interpreted as a definitional equation of an *ex ante* or *ex post* surplus or deficit. If all items of a balance sheet are planned *ex ante* except for a residual (= a balance), then it follows automatically what residual must be planned for the balance sheet of a particular period. If all items in an ex post balance sheet are explained except for a residual (= a balance), the "causation" of the balance is thereby also "explained." In the case of an *ex post* analysis, the balance sheet identity plays an analogous role in the "causal" explanation of the individual balance sheet items. If the causes of all balance sheet items but one are explained, then the balance sheet identity gives also a purely formal explanation for the residual (= the balance). This says, however, nothing about the direction of real causality. For, the choice of the residual is entirely arbitrary. On thinking in terms of balance sheets, in particular, the *ex post* "balance mechanics" (Saldenmechanik), see W. Stützel (1958), particularly Chapter 3.

[9] Note that Walras's Law does not imply that all markets are in equilibrium, i.e., the p_i may also be disequilibrium prices. The law of one price, though, necessarily holds.

1.2 General Equilibrium Theory With Production

We now expand the model to include production. There is a new economic unit, the firm, whose technical aspects are characterized by a production function. Every firm is owned by private households.

The simplest case is the socalled Robinson Crusoe economy which only consists of one household and one firm. The firm Robinson is totally owned by the household Robinson. With two goods, the Robinson economy may be easily pictured graphically. We shall examine in considerable detail the explanation of this figure which helps in understanding monetary theory on the basis of general equilibrium theory.

The Robinson economy is constructed as follows [9a]: the household Robinson chooses a consumption plan (x_1, x_2), the firm Robinson a production plan (y_1, y_2). Good 1 is labor, good 2 is wheat. The same good "labor" (No. 1) may be used for consumption (x_1) and production (y_1). Consider first the firm Robinson. It possesses a given technical knowledge, limited by the production function $y_2 = f(y_1)$. The production function relates to each quantity of labor input $(y_1 < 0)$ a maximum quantity of good 2 (wheat) that can be produced with it $(y_2 > 0)$. We assume that wheat is produced only with labor. The graph of the production function is shown in Fig. 1-1.

The slope of the production curve $\left|\frac{dy_2}{dy_1}\right|$ expresses the marginal productivity of labor. It decreases with increasing amounts of labor used. The profit Q of the firm is defined as revenues minus costs, i.e.,

$$Q = p_1 y_1 + p_2 y_2 \ ;$$

where: $y_1 < 0$ input ,
$y_2 > 0$ output .

All production plans yielding the same profit $\bar{Q}$ lie on a straight line on the (y_1, y_2) diagram. This is the socalled iso-profit curve (Fig. 1-2). It is more easily understood when we solve the profit equation for y_2:

$$y_2 = \frac{\bar{Q}}{p_2} - \frac{p_1}{p_2} y_1 \ .$$

The greater Q, the higher the iso-profit line. There is a family of parallel iso-profit lines, with one iso-profit line corresponding to each of the different values of Q.

The profit maximizing production plan which can be realized with the price (p_1, p_2) called out by the auctioneer is given by the tangency point P of the production curve and the iso-profit line (Fig. 1-3).

In this manner we can picture graphically the optimizing problem of the firm Robinson, i.e., the maximization of profits Q under conditions of perfect competition

[9a] Since we have only one firm and one household, the subscripts refer only to the goods.

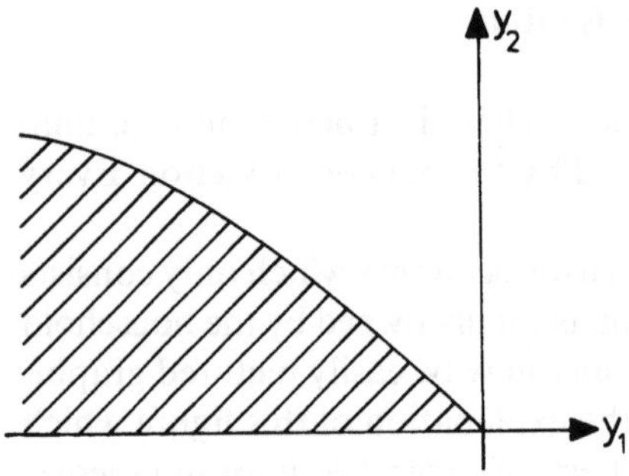

Fig. 1-1. The Production Curve

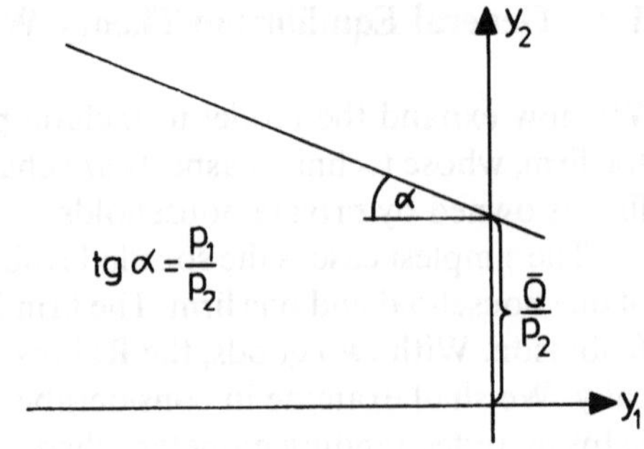

Fig. 1-2. The Iso-profit Curve

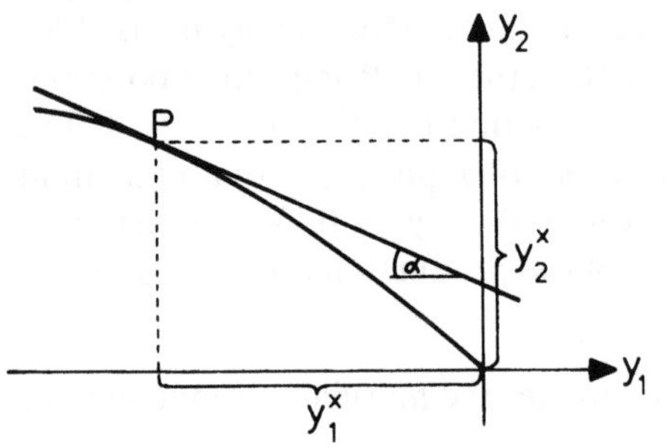

Fig. 1-3. The profit-maximizing Production Plan *P*

subject to the existing technical knowledge. Expressed in symbols, the problem, is:

$$\text{Max} \quad Q = p_1 y_1 + p_2 y_2$$
$$\text{s.t.} \quad \phi(y_1, y_2) = 0$$

using the implicit form $\phi(\cdot)$ of the production function $y_2 = f(y_1)$. The necessary condition for a profit maximum is

$$\frac{\partial\phi}{\partial y_1} : \frac{\partial\phi}{\partial y_2} = p_1 : p_2$$

or (according to the rules of implicit differentiation):

$$-\frac{dy_2}{dy_1} = \frac{p_1}{p_2} \; ;$$

$\left|\frac{dy_2}{dy_1}\right|$ is the marginal rate of transformation of good 1 (input) into good 2 (output). It is equal to the slope of the production curve. It also expresses the marginal productivity of good 1. (For the precise derivation see Appendix 2 of this chapter.) In this manner we can derive the equations determining the optimal quantities of input and output $y_1 = y_1\left(\frac{p_1}{p_2}\right)$; $y_2 = y_2\left(\frac{p_1}{p_2}\right)$ which in our example are the demand function for labor $y_1(\cdot)$ and the supply function of wheat $y_2(\cdot)$. As can be seen, the firm as well as the household are free of money illusion.

The household Robinson has a certain preference system expressed by the utility function

$$U = U(x_1, x_2) \ .$$

It has a positive original endowment of labor $\bar{x}_1$; that is, $\bar{x}_1 > 0$, $\bar{x}_2 = 0$. Since we are here interested only how much the household demands and supplies of each good, we can picture Robinson's system of preferences in the $\hat{x}_1$, $\hat{x}_2$ system of coordinates (Fig. 1-4).

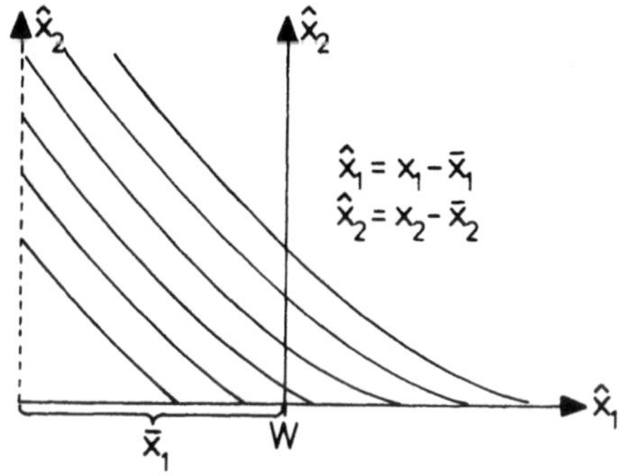

Fig. 1-4. Preference System

$W = (\bar{x}_1, 0)$ is the original endowment of the household. In addition to the original endowment of labor, the household Robinson receives 100% of the profits Q of the firm Robinson. The budget equation is therefore:

$$p_1 x_1 + p_2 x_2 = p_1 \bar{x}_1 + Q \ .$$

It is graphically determined in a $\hat{x}_1$, $\hat{x}_2$ coordinate system in Fig. 1-5 for an

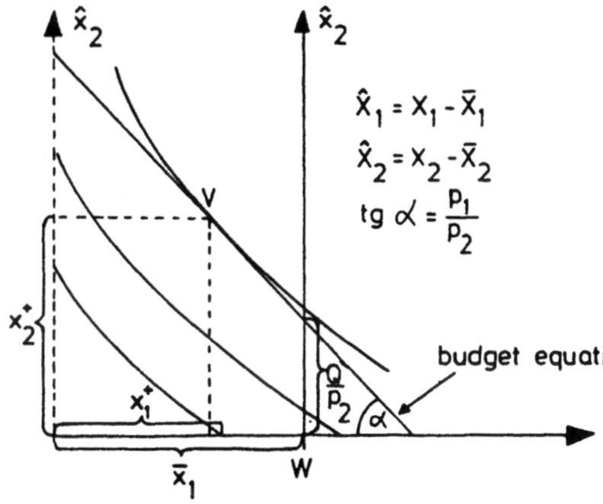

Fig. 1-5. The Optimal Consumption Plan V

arbitrarily chosen pair of prices (p_1, p_2) and a particular system of indifference curves derived from the household's utility function $U(x_1, x_2)$.

In this manner we can determine the optimal consumption plan $V = (x_1^+, x_2^+)$ graphically, where x_1 is the own use of labor. In other words, the household must solve the maximization problem:

$$\begin{aligned} &\text{Max} \quad U = U(x_1, x_2) \\ &\text{s.t.} \quad p_1 x_1 + p_2 x_2 = p_1 \bar{x}_1 + Q \end{aligned}$$

We already know the necessary condition

$$\frac{\partial U}{\partial x_1} : \frac{\partial U}{\partial x_2} = \frac{p_1}{p_2}$$

or

$$-\frac{dx_2}{dx_1} = \frac{p_1}{p_2} ,$$

where $\left|\frac{dx_2}{dx_1}\right|$ is the marginal rate of substitution of good 2 for good 1. It is expressed by the slope of the indifference curve. The solutions are the equations

$$x_1 = x_1\left(\frac{p_1}{p_2}\right) , \quad x_2 = x_2\left(\frac{p_1}{p_2}\right) .$$

In general equilibrium all markets are in equilibrium at the same prices called by the auctioneer. Therefore:

$$\hat{x}_1\left(\frac{p_1}{p_2}\right) = y_1\left(\frac{p_1}{p_2}\right) .$$

$$\hat{x}_2(\cdot) = y_2(\cdot) , \quad \text{where } \hat{x}_i = x_i - \bar{x}_i .$$

We have once again two equations in one unknown p_1/p_2. But because of Walras's Law, only one has to be considered, e.g., the first.

The derivation of *Walras's Law* is now as follows: The budget equation for the economy as a whole as seen by the households is identical with the budget equation of the household Robinson:

$$p_1 x_1 + p_2 x_2 = p_1 \bar{x}_1 + p_2 \bar{x}_2 + Q .$$

By definition

$$Q = p_1 y_1 + p_2 y_2 ,$$

so that we can derive the following budget equation for the economy as a whole:

$$p_1 x_1 + p_2 x_2 = p_1 \bar{x}_1 + p_2 \bar{x}_2 + p_1 y_1 + p_2 y_2$$

or $$p_1(x_1 - \bar{x}_1) + p_2(x_2 - \bar{x}_2) = p_1 y_1 + p_2 y_2$$

or $$p_1 \hat{x}_1 + p_2 \hat{x}_2 = p_1 y_1 + p_2 y_2$$

or $$p_1(\hat{x}_1 - y_1) + p_1(\hat{x}_2 - y_2) = 0$$

or $$\sum_{i=1}^{2} p_i(\hat{x}_i - y_i) = 0 \ .$$

Every one of these equations exhibits Walras's Law. When $\hat{x}_1 - y_1 = 0$, then $\hat{x}_2 - y_2 = 0$, provided $p_i \neq 0$. That is, if the market for good 1 is in equilibrium, Walras's Law states that the market for good 2 must also be in equilibrium.

We can solve thc system graphically by superimposing Fig. 1-1 on Fig. 1-4 so that the origin of Fig. 1-1 coincides with point W and the y_1 axis coincides with the x_1-axis, the y_2-axis coincides with the $\hat{x}_2$-axis (Fig. 1-6).

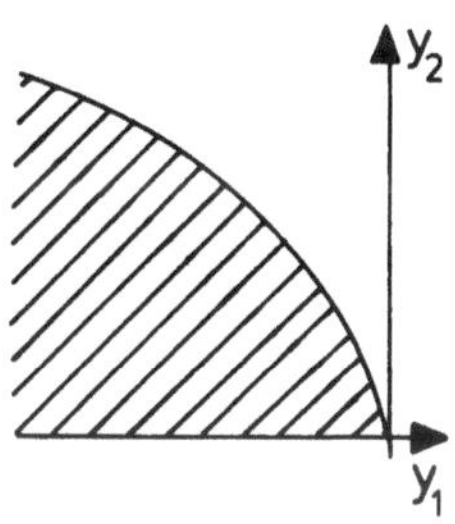

Fig. 1-1

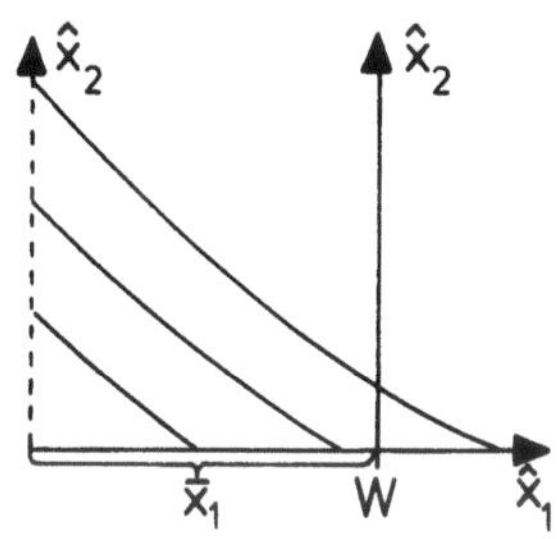

Fig. 1-4

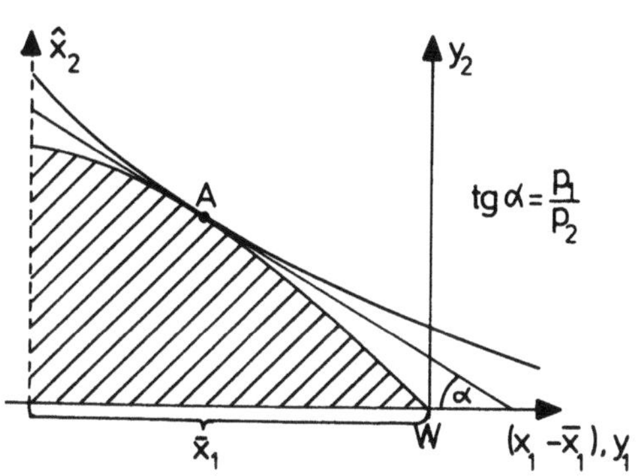

Fig. 1-6. Robinson Diagram

In Fig. 1-6, every point in the hatched area is a state of general market equilibrium that may be realized. Robinson will always bring about the general market equilibrium of his one-man economy by "central planning." He will, if he wants to maximize his utility, immediately choose point A. In order, however, to illustrate general equilibrium theory we shall assume that Robinson chooses his production and consumption plans separately on the basis of the prices (p_1, p_2) called out by an autioneer as described above.

The auctioneer alone is not sufficient to keep Robinson from influencing the equilibrium value of the prices (p_1, p_2). The household Robinson can achieve this easily by arbitrarily holding back or "embezzling" part of his original endowment of wheat. In the case of one household this makes no sense but if there were two or three it might (see below Chapter 3). To exclude this possibility we assume in the model of perfect competition a large number of households of approximately equal size which, for whatever reasons, do not form coalitions. Because of this assumption the Robinson diagram has to be used with caution.

Point A represents a general equilibrium of the economy. The slope $(= tg\alpha)$ of the line tangent to the production curve at point A and the corresponding indifference curve of Robinson (which has determined where A will be) expresses the general equilibrium value of the exchange ratio p_1/p_2. The tangency line at point A is simultaneously the iso-profit line of the firm Robinson and the budget line of the household Robinson. Thus it can be seen that in general equilibrium the marginal rate of transformation of good 1 for good 2 is equal to the marginal rate of substitution of good 2 for good 1 and to the price ratio p_2/p_1.

We now leave our Robinson world. With an arbitrary number of households $(k = 1, \ldots, m)$ and an arbitrary number of firms $(j = 1, \ldots, s)$ the following must be true in general equilibrium:

$$\text{(1-5)} \qquad \hat{X}_i\left(\frac{p_i}{p_n}, \ldots \frac{p_{n-1}}{p_n}\right) = Y_i(\cdot),\ i = 1, \ldots, n\ .$$

$$\text{where: } \hat{X}_i \equiv \sum_{k=1}^{m} \hat{x}_{ik}\ ,$$

$$Y_i \equiv \sum_{j=1}^{s} y_{ij}\ .$$

In this case, Walras's Law is:

$$\text{(1-6)} \qquad \sum_{i=1}^{n} p_i(\hat{X}_i - Y_i) = 0\ .$$

For the derivation see Appendix 3 of this chapter.

If equilibrium prevails on the first $n - 1$ markets, then it must be true that

$$\text{(1-7)} \qquad \sum_{i=1}^{n-1} p_i(\hat{X}_i - Y_i) = 0\ .$$

By substracting equation (1-7) from equation (1-6) we get:

$$p_n(\hat{X}_n - Y_n) = 0$$

or for $p_n \neq 0$:

$$\hat{X}_n - Y_n = 0 \ .$$

In words, according to Walras's Law the nth market will also be in equilibrium.

Note: recall that the profit Q is defined by what is left after all costs have been deducted, including the interest cost of the firm's own capital and the entrepreneurial wage. Q is the "surplus profit" (revenues minus all factor costs). We do not discuss here the allocation function of surplus profits. It consists in drawing resources into industries the demand for whose products has increased and to withdraw resources from industries the demand for whose products has declined (when $Q < 0$). In long-run equilibrium, profits Q must be zero. But this presupposes a different production function from the one we have assumed. In general, we do not consider the dynamics of the rise and fall of firms. The firms are simply assumed to exist. We do not consider the question why they exist. Chapter 3 will have more to say on this point.

We now begin an elementary discussion of problems of the theory of money by considering a few questions which arise in connection with the discussion of the theory of general equilibrium.

1.3 The Purchasing Power of Money: Definition

The so-called purchasing power of money plays an important role in the discussion of monetary theory. By purchasing power of money we mean a measure intended to answer the question: What can one mark buy? What is the exchange value of money? The question refers to a basket of commodities $Wk = \{x_i^*\}$ with a money value P. Thus

$$P = \sum_i p_i x_i^* \ ; \qquad x_i^* \geqq 0 \ . \tag{1-8}$$

The magnitude x_i^* refers to the amount of good No. i which, experience has shown, is demanded by a particular economic unit during a particular period of time, say a month or a year. As a rule we normally consider a basket of goods Wk which is suitable for a particular purpose or type of business, e.g., consumption, wholesale etc.; p_i is the average price of good i during a particular period. P has the dimension "units of money per basket of commodities" (mark/Wk).

The purchasing power of money refers to a particular basket of commodities Wk^0; it is the reciprocal $1/P$ of the money value P of the particular basket of commodities Wk^0.[10] It has the dimension "basket of goods per monetary unit" (Wk/mark).

[10] I. Fisher (1911, 13) did not think initially of a specific basket of goods. He writes simply: "The purchasing power of money is indicated by the quantities of other goods which a given quantity of money will buy."

Thus, if $P = \frac{10 \text{ mark}}{Wk_0}$ then the purchasing power of the mark is

$$1/P = \frac{1/10\ Wk^0}{\text{mark}} .$$

In this example, one mark buys one tenth of the commodity basket Wk^0. The larger P is, the smaller the fraction of Wk^0 is which a mark can buy. The purchasing power of the mark falls as P increases, assuming a constant commodity basket. However, no single objective exchange value of money exists.[11] We can operate only with averages.

As a rule, the literature refers to the purchasing power of money in terms of consumption goods. J.M. Keynes (1930, 54) referring to Alfred Marshall, says on this point:

"We mean by the Purchasing Power of Money the power of money to buy the goods and services on the purchase of which for purposes of consumption a given community of individuals expend their money income. That is to say, it is measured by the quantity of such goods and services, weighted according to their importance as objects of consumption, which a unit of money will buy; and the appropriate index-number is of the type sometimes designated as the Consumption Index. It follows that Purchasing Power must always be defined with reference to a particular set of individuals in a given situation, namely those whose actual consumption furnishes us with our standard, and has no clear meaning unless this reference has been given."

A demand for the stability of the purchasing power of money corresponds to a demand for the (approximately) constant money value P of a particular commodity basket Wk. For two arbitrary periods $t-1$, and t, it is desired that

$$\frac{P_t}{P_{t-1}} = 1$$

or, using the formula of equation (1-8) that

$$\text{(1-9)} \qquad P_t^* = \frac{P_t}{P_{t-1}} = \frac{\sum_i p_{it} x_{it-1}^*}{\sum_i p_{it-1} x_{it-1}^*}$$

with $P_t^* = 1$.

Equation (1-9) is a Laspeyres Price Index with the base period $t-1$. Thus $P_t^* = 1.05$ says that the money value P_t of a particular commodity basket Wk is in period t 5% greater than it was in base period $t-1$. This is one possible way of measuring the stability of the value of money. An example is the cost of living index

[11] Fundamentally on this point G. Haberler (1927).

for private households.[12] The general rule is: the construction of a price index should depend on the purpose which it is to serve.[13]

1.4 The Determination of the Purchasing Power of Money

How can the purchasing power of money be determined? This is one of the central questions of the theory of money. Chapters 7 and 8 will discuss these questions in detail. Here we propose to give an elementary answer. We start with the general market equilibrium and assume that the equilibrium values of the relative prices

$$\mathbb{L} = \left\{\frac{p_1}{p_n}, \dots, \frac{p_{n-1}}{p_n}\right\}$$

are known and uniquely determined. In this case, the question becomes:

How may the equilibrium value of the absolute goods prices $p_1, \dots, p_n$ expressed in an abstract unit of account be determined? In principle by giving the unit of account some "real content." Two typical methods have been applied for that purpose: the commodity standard and the paper standard. In the commodity standard the abstract unit of account is defined as a certain amount of a concrete commodity or a commodity basket (one mark = 0.358423 gramme gold fine), guaranteed either directly by using the money commodity as a means of payment or else by the use of means of payment which are redeemable into the money commodity at a fixed rate. On the other hand, with the paper standard, there exists in general only a rough connection between the unit of account (the currency unit) and goods, i.e., only a rough determination of the money value in the sense of the purchasing power of money. The money value is safeguarded by keeping the amount of paper money scarce.

We shall deal with the commodity and the paper standard in greater detail in later chapters. At present we consider two extreme cases: for the commodity standard a pure gold coin standard, for the paper standard a pure paper circulation. The only means of payment applied in the first case are gold coins, in the second case inconvertible banknotes. In the first case the unit of account is defined by the determination of a fixed gold price p_n, in the second case the currency authority is supposed to vary the quantity of money in such a way as to aim at a certain money value P of a commodity basket Wk_0 of consumer goods. The dimension of the p_i's is:

in the first case:

$$\dim[p_i] = \frac{\text{currency units payable here and now in the form of gold coins}}{\text{unit of good } i \text{ available here and now}},$$

[12] See, e.g., R. Dornbusch and S. Fischer (1987, 41 f.).

[13] G. Haberler (1927, 75).

in the second case:

$$\dim[p_i] = \frac{\text{currency units payable here and now in the form of bank notes}}{\text{unit of good } i \text{ available here and now}}.$$

1.4.1 *The Case of a Commodity Standard: The Pure Gold Coin Standard*

Suppose a gold standard in which only minted gold is used as a means of payment. For obvious reasons no such case has ever existed. But the assumption facilitates the exposition of the principle underlying the institutional guarantee of the value of money under a gold standard. A central authority determines the standard of coinage, i.e., the number of currency units per ounce of gold of a certain purity.

For example: during the period of the German gold standard, between 1876 and 1914, the standard of coinage was 1395.0 marks per half kilo of fine gold.

If good n is gold, then $p_n = \mu$ is the exogenously determined standard of coinage. We may understand it as a price target. If the price target is to exist not only on paper, there must be a suitable institutional arrangement to guarantee adherence to it. In the case under discussion, there must be a regulation of the minting of coins which ensures the circulation of unadulterated coins. Gold will be demanded for cash holdings (in form of gold coins) as well as for other purposes. Once we know the equilibrium values of the relative prices in general equilibrium, then we know also the equilibrium values of the absolute prices $p_1, \ldots, p_{n-1}$, when $p_n = \mu$ is given.

At the same time, it is easily seen that in general equilibrium the money value P of an arbitrary commodity basket Wk is equally determined and with it the purchasing power of money $1/P$. To be sure, it will be "subject to the caprices of the production and consumption of gold, and the demand for the circulation of coins."[14,15] What monetary unit, i.e., which number $\mu = p_n$, is chosen as the standard of coinage is irrelevant. Money is perfectly neutral (on the neutrality of money see below Section 6.6).

1.4.2 *The Case of a Paper Standard: A Pure Paper Circulation*

We now assume that the only means of payment are particular pieces of paper on which their nominal value, expressed in currency units (e.g., mark) has been printed.

---

[14] K. Wicksell (1936, 194).

[15] We know all p_i/p_n. Hence we also know

$$\tilde{P} = \frac{P}{p_n} = \sum_i \frac{p_i}{p_n} x_i^*$$

where $1/\tilde{P}$ is the purchasing power of the monetary *commodity* (e.g., gold) and hence also of money. The money value of a bundle of consumption goods depends on how they exchange against the monetary commodity.

Cash is held only in the form of bank notes. In a paper money economy there is then, besides real goods, the further good "paper money," which is demanded and supplied.

With this additional good, there is an additional price (the price of paper money expressed in terms of paper money is one) as well as an additional market equilibrium condition (the money market equation (1-11)).

Assume that a certain amount of real cash holdings M/P is planned; P is the money value of a particular commodity basket Wk. The demand for real cash holdings is of the form

$$(1\text{-}10^*) \qquad \frac{M}{P} = L^*\left(\frac{p_1}{P}, \ldots, \frac{p_{n-1}}{P}\right)$$

with

$$(1\text{-}8) \qquad P = \sum_i p_i x_i^*$$

Because of (1-8) the variables $\frac{p_1}{P}, \ldots, \frac{p_n}{P}$ and the variables $\frac{p_1}{p_n}, \ldots, \frac{p_{n-1}}{p_n}$ are uniquely related. Therefore, we may also write

$$(1\text{-}10) \qquad \frac{M}{P} = L\left(\frac{p_1}{p_n}, \ldots, \frac{p_{n-1}}{p_n}\right).$$

The demand for real cash holdings is free of money illusion. It depends, exactly as the demand for goods, only on relative prices.

The nominal demand for money M is confronted by a particular supply of money $\overline{M}$. The market for money is in equilibrium when $M = \overline{M}$.

In other words, equilibrium on the market for money exists when the economic units wish to hold the existing quantity of paper money, i.e., if the equilibrium equation for the money market

$$(1\text{-}11) \qquad \frac{\overline{M}}{P} = L\left(\frac{p_1}{p_n}, \ldots, \frac{p_{n-1}}{p_n}\right)$$

is fulfilled.

If the equilibrium values of the relative prices

$$\frac{p_i}{p_n}, \qquad i = 1, \ldots, n-1$$

are known, we can also calculate P. The purchasing power of money $1/P$ is therefore determined. Finally, by use of (1-8), we can determine p_n provided the money supply $\overline{M}$ is exogenously fixed. Since the equilibrium values of relative prices are already known we can find the equilibrium values of the absolute prices $p_1, \ldots, p_{n-1}$. The preceding consideration leads us to the following *basic theorem of the determination of the purchasing power of paper money*:

> In general equilibrium, in a paper money economy, the equilibrium value of the purchasing power of money is determined when the nominal supply of paper money is exogenously given.

In this form the theorem applies to models without interest rates. It is important to recognize that the theorem relates only to the solution of a general equilibrium model. It does not describe the process of exchange through the use of money. This is never described by equilibrium theory (see below Section 3.5). One has to distinguish between the process of exchange by the use of money and its ideal result, the equilibrium in all markets as expressed by the mathematical solution of a system of equations. With regard to the latter it is mathematically correct to argue that we must first solve the real part of a general equilibrium system to determine the demand for real cash holdings, and then to calculate, using a nominally fixed money supply, the price P of the commodity bundle Wk in which the real cash holdings are expressed. Yet, as has been mentioned, the manner in which a system of equations is to be solved has nothing to do with the actual social process of searching for a system of market clearing prices (or for a single equilibrium price). If we assume money to be economically relevant, i.e., not to be merely a veil, we cannot assume that individuals will begin to negotiate exchange contracts by the use of money without any knowledge of some price, e.g., the standard of coinage μ or the money value P of a commodity basket.

E.F. Fama is correct to argue that the decisive problem "is not 'rendering a monetary system determinate' (Patinkin 1961, 116), but rather giving content to a pure nominal unit of account (a dollar) as a separate, welldefined economic good." (E.F. Fama 1980, 55). However, Fama incorrectly goes on to view the process also as a description of a search for the set of equilibrium prices, arguing that in the case of a definite paper standard "the numéraire is currency" (E.F. Fama 1983, 18). What is implicitly assumed is that the individuals know in advance the money value P of some commodity basket Wk which they don't. Of course, viewed as the mathematical solution of a system of equations for the purpose of determining the equilibrium value of P, Fama would be right; but, as was shown, this is a different problem.

1.5 The Classical Dichotomy and the Patinkin Controversy

Our considerations have now reached the stage from which we can deal with a money theoretic issue which today is only of interest as an episode in the history of economic thought: the so-called Patinkin controversy. It starts from the possibility of splitting a general equilibrium model into a real goods part and a monetary part. We consider the case of the paper standard. If we add the equation for the money market (1-11) to the Walrasian system as expressed in equation (1-5) for n goods, we must add the endowments of real cash balances, equal to $\overline{M}/P$ in the aggregate, to the endowment of goods $\bar{x}_i$. As previously discussed in Section 1.1 the original endowments are also arguments of the equations determining the equilibrium consumption plan. They must now be supplemented by the real cash balances.

Given suitable assumptions,[16] and neglecting the fixed original endowment with goods $\bar{X}_i$, we can write the total demand for good i as follows:

$$\text{(1-12)} \qquad \hat{X}_i\left(\frac{p_1}{p_n},\ldots,\frac{p_{n-1}}{p_n},\frac{\bar{M}}{P}\right) \quad \text{where } P = \sum_i p_i x_i^* \ .$$

The demand function for money (1-10) must therefore be expanded to read:

$$\text{(1-10')} \qquad \frac{M}{P} = L^0\left(\frac{p_1}{p_n},\ldots,\frac{p_{n-1}}{p_n},\frac{\bar{M}}{P}\right) .$$

The money market equation reads now as

$$\frac{\bar{M}}{P} - L^0\left(\frac{p_1}{p_n},\ldots,\frac{p_{n-1}}{p_n},\frac{\bar{M}}{P}\right) .$$

or, if we bring $\bar{M}/P$ to the left side of the equation

$$\text{(1-11)} \qquad \frac{\bar{M}}{P} = L\left(\frac{p_1}{p_n},\ldots,\frac{p_{n-1}}{p_n}\right) .$$

Explicitly then, the case of the paper money economy requires the solution of the following system of equations

$$\text{(1-13)} \qquad \hat{X}_i\left(\frac{p_1}{p_n},\ldots,\frac{p_{n-1}}{p_n},\frac{\bar{M}}{P}\right) = Y_i\left(\frac{p_1}{p_n},\ldots,\frac{p_{n-1}}{p_n}\right)$$

$$\text{(1-11')} \qquad \frac{\bar{M}}{P} = L\left(\frac{p_1}{p_n},\ldots,\frac{p_{n-1}}{p_n}\right) .$$

We have therefore $n + 1$ equations in n unknowns.

Walras's Law can be expressed in this case as:

$$\text{(1-14)} \qquad \sum_{i=1}^{n} p_i(\hat{X}_i - Y_i) = \bar{M} - M \ .$$

Expressed in words: the sum of the excess demands for goods at particular prices is equal to the excess supply of money. Because of Walras's Law there are now (at most) n independent equations. It is irrelevant which equations are used to solve for the n unknowns. If a solution exists the exogenously given quantity of $\bar{M}$ allows us to determine the equilibrium values of the goods prices $p_1, \ldots, p_n$.

---

[16] Neutral *distribution effects* (see D. Patinkin 1965, 74) and a *neutral manner of changes in the quantity of money* (see below Section 6.7).

Conceived as a tâtonnement process, we can consider the process of searching for equilibrium prices as follows. The auctioneer calls out an arbitrary price vector $\{p_i\}$, $i = 1, \ldots, n$. The households determine their optimal consumption and (nominal) cash balance plans, considering their shares in the profits (or losses), their original endowments with goods (which for the economy as a whole are fixed as $\bar{X}_i$) and their cash holdings (which for the economy as a whole are fixed as $\bar{M}$). The firms determine their optimal production plans. All economic units report their corresponding demands and supplies of goods, and in addition their desired nominal cash holdings, to the auctioneer (who does not necessarily have to know the total amount of money $\bar{M}$ available). The auctioneer will vary the prices until there is equilibrium in the markets of all goods. Because of Walras's Law it is then necessarily true that the desired cash holdings as a whole equal the existing amount of money, i.e.,

$$M = \bar{M} \ .$$

Mathematically the system of equations (1-11) and (1-13) is solved by the following steps:

We first enter (1-11′) into the n equations (1-13), i.e., we assume the market for money is in equilibrium. We get then a system of n goods market equations with the only unknowns being the relative prices p_i/p_n:

$$(1\text{-}13') \qquad X_i^*\left(\frac{p_i}{p_n}, \ldots, \frac{p_{n-1}}{p_n}\right) = Y_i^*(\cdot) \ , \qquad i = 1, \ldots, n \ .$$

Because of the assumption that the market for money is in equilibrium (i.e. $M = \bar{M}$), which has been made solely to facilitate the solution of the system of equations, Walras's Law can now be expressed as:

$$(1\text{-}15) \qquad \sum_{i=1}^{n} p_i(\hat{X}_i - Y_i) = 0 \ .$$[17]

Of the n equations for the goods market, only $(n - 1)$ are independent. We solve for the $n - 1$ exchange relations and use the equilibrium values of the money market equation (1-11) to determine the equilibrium value of P and afterwards p_n via (1-8) and all the other absolute prices.

The model of general equilibrium is thus divided in two parts purely to facilitate its mathematical solution. There is the real-goods-market part (1-13) and the

[17] In O. Lange's (1942, 52) terminology, (1-15) is written as an *identity*

$$\sum_{i=1}^{n} p_i(\hat{x}_i - y_i) \equiv 0$$

which is called "Say's Law." In this case the supply of money is *identically* equal to the demand for money. O. Lange (1942, 53) continues: "Thus Say's Law implies a peculiar nature of the demand for money, namely, that the individuals in our system, taken together, are *always* satisfied with the existing amount of money and never wish to hold either more or less." In this view holding cash balances is not an equilibrium problem. If we understand equation (1-13) as a station on the path to the solution (by substitution) of the system of equations (1-13), (1-11′) then Lange's interpretation is wrong. The lack of clarity on this point contributes to the Patinkin controversy which is described below.

monetary part (1-11′). The literature talks of a dichotomy into a real and a monetary part (Patinkin 1965, 622ff.): the real part, in this sense, is used to calculate the equilibrium conditions of the relative prices; the monetary part determines the absolute prices. The dichotomy must not be understood as a causal relation; it must be understood purely as a method of solving the whole system of equations.

As can be seen, in the case under consideration, paper money is quantitatively neutral. The amount of money $\overline{M}$ has no influence on the equilibrium exchange relations. It thus has no influence on the equilibrium quantities of goods demanded and supplied. This postulate of neutrality, however, does not imply that the amount of money $\overline{M}$ is not considered during the earlier process of negotiations which leads to the equilibrium values of the absolute prices p_i. On the contrary, the tâtonnement process described includes a consideration of $\overline{M}$. That is, we do not assume a dichotomy of the process by which prices are determined.[18]

Since the equilibrium values of the relative prices p_i/p_n are independent of $\overline{M}$, and because we have implicitly assumed that a change in the amount of money changes the original cash holdings of the individual households and firms proportionately, we are now also in a world in which the quantity theory of money is valid: a doubling of $\overline{M}$ immediately doubles P as equation (1-11) shows; and because of (1-8) and the unchanged equilibrium (real) exchange ratios p_i/p_n, a doubling of $\overline{M}$ also results in a doubling of all p_i. There exists a strict proportionality between M and p_i.

Note on the History of Thought of the Consistent Dichotomy Problem

The problem of the consistency between the real and the monetary part of general equilibrium was first raised by Lange (1942) and then taken up by Don Patinkin (1948, 1949). This problem has later been referred to as the *Patinkin Controversy*.[19] The discussion concerned to the following question: according to Patinkin (1965, 174), neoclassical monetary theory argues as follows: given a purely "real" Walrasian system with $n-1$ independent goods market equations of the type (1-4), i.e., without real cash holdings, by which $n-1$ linear independent equilibrium exchange relations can be determined, the mere introduction of a money market equation of the type (1-11) is asserted to suffice to determine the level of money prices p_i. According to Patinkin, this manner of introducing money is not without internal contradictions. Patinkin *expressis verbis* limits his considerations to the case of paper money,[20] and further, as he emphasizes later, to the case of a pure outside money economy[21] (The definition of outside money will be discussed below, Section 4.2). His proof proceeds as follows:[22]

---

[18] This is, however, conceivable, as J. Niehans (1978, 9) has shown. Unfortunately, Niehans neglects in this connection the magnitude $\overline{M}/P$ in the demand function and so the underlying behavioral hypothesis remains unclear. See Review of J. Niehans (1978) by S. Fischer (1979b, 287).

[19] See e.g., B. Hansen (1966) or E.-M. Claassen (1980), Ch. VIII.

[20] D. Patinkin (1948, 140).

[21] D. Patinkin (1965, 15, 174).

[22] D. Patinkin (1965, 475f.).

We assume for the sake of simplicity that real cash holdings are measured in units of good No. n and consider as one system the equations

$$(1\text{-}13') \qquad \hat{X}_i\left(\frac{p_i}{p_n},\ldots,\frac{p_{n-1}}{p_n}\right) = Y_i(\cdot)\ , \qquad i = 1,\ldots,n \text{ ("real part")}\ ,$$

$$(1\text{-}11') \qquad \frac{\overline{M}}{P} = L\left(\frac{p_i}{p_n},\ldots,\frac{p_{n-1}}{p_n}\right)\ , \quad \text{with } P = \sum_i p_i x_i^* \text{ ("money part")}\ .$$

Walras's Law is:

$$(1\text{-}14) \qquad \sum_{i=1}^{n} p_i(\hat{X}_i - Y_i) = \overline{M} - M\ .$$

The real part determines equilibrium values of the relative prices p_i/p_n without regard for the level of absolute prices. This makes the left side of equation (1-14) equal to zero regardless of the prices p_i. This, however, means that the right side of equation (1-14) also becomes zero independent of the absolute prices p_i, i.e., $\overline{M} = M$. There is, therefore, equilibrium on the money market regardless of the level of the prices p_i, and hence also regardless of the level of p_n. But this contradicts the equilibrium equation for the market for money (1-11′).

Patinkin is correct insofar as that if paper money is used, the real cash holdings $\overline{M}/P$ in (1-13) must be explicitly considered, as we have done above in equation (1-13). The argument is completed in the following manner:

Walras's Law has to be applied to the system of equations (1-13) and (1-11′). The unknowns of the model are then the $n - 1$ relative prices and the real value of the existing or supplied balances $\overline{M}/P$. The left side of (1-14) becomes zero, if both the equilibrium values of the $(n - 1)$ relative prices and the equilibrium value of the real balances have been determined. But in this case the absolute prices p_i are also determined, since $\overline{M}$ has been assumed to be exogenously given.

Patinkin is wrong if he rejects the dichotomization of the process of price determination as "invalid." As Niehans (1978, 9ff.) has shown, it may be considered a meaningful tâtonnement process. Besides, equilibrium analysis does not offer an analysis of processes. Only questions regarding the mathematical solution of the system may be considered (in the present case, as illustrated above, a two-step approach). In this sense, a logically correct dichotomy of the model into a real part (1-13′) and a monetary part (1-11′) is possible.

The confusion has a double origin. It arises from two distinct causes: Oskar Lange's discussion of Say's Law, which he defined in a particular manner and the introduction of dynamic elements into an essentially static discussion.[23] Instead of clearing up the role of the real cash balances $\overline{M}/P$ as a variable in his model, Patinkin (1965, 175ff.) expressly considers the effect of real cash balances which he calls the "real balance effect":

"This is a crucial point. The dynamic groping of the absolute price level towards its equilibrium value will – through the real-balance effect react back on the commodity markets and hence on relative prices. And it is precisely the constant failure to find this point explicitly recognized... that is the basis of our original contention that the roots of the invalid dichotomy are to be found in the neoclassical analysis of Walras, Fisher, Pigou, and Cassel." (Patinkin 1965, 183)

However, as we have seen, it is not necessary to entertain quasi-dynamic considerations in order to solve the system (1-13′), (1-11′).

---

[23] This has been worked out in detail by K. Nagatani (1978, 13ff.). Nagatani gives also a survey of the decisive objections to the results of the quasi-dynamic considerations of Patinkin.

Appendix to Chapter 1

1 The Determination of the Optimal Consumption Plan of a Household

Omitting the subscript k, the optimization procedure of Section 1.1 is:

(1) $$\text{Max} \quad U = U(x_1, x_2)$$

(2) $$\text{s.t.} \quad p_1 x_1 + p_2 x_2 = p_1 \bar{x}_1 + p_2 \bar{x}_2 \ .$$

Using the Lagrange multiplier, we maximize the following function:

(3) $$V = U(x_1, x_2) - \lambda(p_1 x_1 + p_2 x_2 - p_1 \bar{x}_1 - p_2 \bar{x}_2) \ ; \qquad \lambda > 0 \ .$$

For a maximum the necessary condition is that the first derivatives with respect to x_1, x_2, and λ are equal to zero:

(4) $$\frac{\partial V}{\partial x_1} = \frac{\partial U}{\partial x_1} - \lambda p_1 = 0 \ ,$$

(5) $$\frac{\partial V}{\partial x_2} = \frac{\partial U}{\partial x_2} - \lambda p_2 = 0 \ ,$$

(6) $$\frac{\partial V}{\partial \lambda} = p_1 \bar{x}_1 + p_2 \bar{x}_2 - p_1 x_1 - p_2 x_2 = 0 \ .$$

Equation (6) is the budget equation (2). Equations (4) and (5) can be reduced to:

$$\lambda = \frac{\partial U}{\partial x_1} : p_1 = \frac{\partial U}{\partial x_2} : p_2 \ .$$

From this it follows that

(7) $$\frac{\partial U}{\partial x_2} : \frac{\partial U}{\partial x_1} = p_2 : p_1 \ .$$

For an interior utility maximum, subject to the condition (2) it is necessary that the ratios of the marginal utilities of the goods are equal to their price ratios.

The sufficient condition for utility maximization is given by the following determinant

$$\begin{vmatrix} U_{11} & U_{12} & -p_1 \\ U_{21} & U_{22} & -p_2 \\ -p_1 & -p_2 & 0 \end{vmatrix} > 0 \ ,$$

where

$$\frac{\partial\left[\frac{\partial U(x_1,x_2)}{\partial x_1}\right]}{\partial x_1} \equiv U_{11} \quad \text{etc.}$$

Alternatively, equating $U_{21} = U_{12}$, and solving for the last column:

$$2U_{12}p_1p_2 - U_{22}p_1^2 - U_{11}p_2^2 > 0 \ . \tag{8}$$

We next determine the shape of the indifference curve

$$\bar{U} = U(x_1,x_2) \ .$$

Its slope (using the rules of implicit differentiation) is

$$\frac{dx_1}{dx_2} = -\frac{\partial U}{\partial x_2} : \frac{\partial U}{\partial x_1} \quad \text{or}$$

$$\frac{dx_1}{dx_2} = -U_2 : U_1 = -\frac{U_2(x_1(x_2),x_2)}{U_1(x_1(x_2),x_2)} \tag{9}$$

In order to determine the curvature of the indifference curve we must find the second derivation of equation (9) with respect to x_2:

$$\frac{d^2x_1}{dx_2^2} = -\frac{1}{U_1^2}\left[\left(U_{21}\frac{dx_1}{dx_2} + U_{22}\right)U_1 - \left(U_{11}\frac{dx_1}{dx_2} + U_{12}\right)U_2\right]$$

or, since $\frac{dx_1}{dx_2} = -\frac{U_2}{U_1}$, we can write

$$\frac{d^2x_1}{dx_2^2} = -\frac{1}{U_1^2}\left[-U_{21}U_2 + U_{22}U_1 + \frac{U_{11}U_2^2}{U_1} - U_{12}U_2\right]$$

or (when $U_{21} = U_{12}$)

$$\frac{d^2x_1}{dx_2^2} = \frac{1}{U_1^3}2U_{12}U_2U_1 - U_{22}U_1^2 - U_{11}U_2^2) \ .$$

According to equation (7)

$$U_2 = \frac{p_2U_1}{p_1} \ .$$

Substituting this expression into the preceding equation, we get

$$\frac{d^2x_1}{dx_2^2} = \frac{1}{U_1^3}\left[\frac{2U_{12}U_1^2p_2}{P_1} - U_{22}U_1^2 - U_{11}U_1^2\right] \quad \text{or}$$

(10) $$\frac{d^2x_1}{dx_2^2} = \frac{1}{U_1p_1^2}[2U_{12}p_1p_2 - U_{22}p_1^2 - U_{11}p_2^2]$$

Because of (8), equation (10) is always positive. Hence the indifference curves which fulfill equation (8), will be concave from above.
We shall assume this throughout.

2 *The Determination of the Optimal Production Plan of a Firm*

The optimization problem of Section 1.2 is

$$\begin{aligned} &\text{Max} \quad Q = p_1y_1 + p_2y_2 \\ &\text{s.t.} \quad \phi(y_1, y_2) = 0 \ . \end{aligned}$$

We use once more the Lagrange multiplier and maximize the function

$$W = p_1y_1 + p_2y_2 - \lambda\phi(y_1, y_2) \ ; \qquad \lambda > 0 \ .$$

The necessary conditions for profit maximization are

$$\frac{\partial W}{\partial y_1} = p_1 - \lambda\frac{\partial\phi}{\partial y_1} = 0 \ ,$$

$$\frac{\partial W}{\partial y_2} = p_2 - \lambda\frac{\partial\phi}{\partial y_2} = 0$$

and

$$\frac{\partial W}{\partial\lambda} = \phi(y_1, y_2) = 0 \ .$$

For an (interior) profit maximum it is also necessary that

$$\partial\phi_1 : \partial\phi_2 = p_1 : p_2$$

or, alternatively, that

$$-\frac{dy_2}{dy_1} = \frac{p_1}{p_2} \ .$$

For an interior profit maximum it is sufficient that the yield curve is convex from above.

3 Walras's Law with Any Number of Households and Firms

Let there be m households and s firms. The share in the profits received by household k in firm j is θ_{kj}. The budget equation for the economy as a whole expresses Walras's Law and can be written as:

$$\text{(a)} \qquad \sum_{i=1}^{n}\sum_{k=1}^{m} p_i x_{ik} = \sum_{i=1}^{n}\sum_{k=1}^{m} p_i \bar{x}_{ik} + \sum_{k=1}^{m}\sum_{j=1}^{s} \theta_{kj} Q_j \ .$$

Let

$$\sum_{k=1}^{m} x_{ik} \equiv X_i \ ,$$

$$\sum_{k=1}^{m} \bar{x}_{ik} \equiv \bar{X}_i \ ,$$

$$\sum_{k=1}^{m} \theta_{kj} \equiv 1 \ .$$

Thus (a) can be written as:

$$\sum_{i=1}^{n} p_i X_i = \sum_{i=1}^{n} p_i \bar{X}_i + \sum_{j=1}^{s} Q_j \ .$$

By definition

$$Q_j = \sum_{i=1}^{n} p_i y_{ij} \quad \text{and}$$

$$\sum_{j=1}^{s} Q_j = \sum_{i=1}^{n} p_i Y_i \quad \text{with } Y_i \equiv \sum_{j=1}^{s} y_{ij} \ ,$$

so that (a) becomes:

$$\sum_{i=1}^{n} p_i X_i = \sum_{i=1}^{n} p_i \bar{X}_i + \sum_{i=1}^{n} p_i Y_i$$

or

$$\sum_{i=1}^{n} p_i (\hat{X}_i - Y_i) = 0 \ .$$

Suggested Readings to Chapter 1

1 Theory of General Equilibrium

The reader who is already somewhat familiar with microeconomics is referred immediately to *G. Debreu* (1959). Debreu has completed the static theory of pure competition put forward by *L. Walras* (1872) (English translation 1954). The Walrasian tradition was continued by *V. Pareto* (1927) (English translation 1971).

In the anglophone countries, *J.R. Hicks* (1946) has made general equilibrium theory accessible to wider professional circles. An older text in this tradition is *J.M. Henderson* and *R.E. Quandt* (1958, 1980). Since then numerous microeconomic texts have appeared, see, e.g., *H. Gravelle* and *R. Rees* (1981) or *H. Varian* (1978).

On the history of the term "neoclassical," which we occasionally use in this book, see *J. Niehans* (1987, 410).

2 The Purchasing Power of Money

About the technique and problems of the calculation of price indices, see, e.g., *R.G.D. Allen* (1975).

The basic books discussing the problems of index numbers are *G. Haberler* (1927), *J.M. Keynes* (1930) Book 2. For the nature of the value of money, see *L.V. Mises* (1924) pp. 73ff. (English translation 1953, 97ff.)

3 Determination of the Purchasing Power of Money

For a discussion with special reference to general equilibrium, see *J.H.G. Olivera* (1970). For a discussion with attention to paper money in particular, see *D. Patinkin* (1961), pp. 111–116. The earlier discussion was dominated by *I. Fisher* (1911). For additional literature, see the suggested readings to Chapter 7.

Chapter 2
Capital Theory

Money and credit are seen to be closely connected with each other: exchange by the use of money on the one hand, and simultaneously money loans on the other. The central problem of the former is the explanation of (nominal) goods prices, of the latter the explanation of the money rate of interest. In the end, individuals are only interested in the consumption of goods. This has always to be kept in mind when dealing with monetary theory. It is capital theory which provides the "real" foundation (in this sense) of the theory of money loans or financial markets. Its basic features can be derived in a simple manner from the theory of general equilibrium. We just have to change the one-period neo-classical model into a multi-period theory. This allows us to develop a theory of the optimal allocation of resources over time. This is precisely what capital theory in its micro-economic formulation does.[1] Capital theory and the theory of interest rates are closely connected; indeed, the explanation of the role of the rate of interest is the central problem of the (micro-economic) theory of capital. We limit ourselves to a brief and elementary description of capital theory, just enough to provide a goods-market basis for our discussion of the theory of money. First, we shall develop the basic determinants of the real rate of interest on the assumptions of rational behavior of individuals and perfect competition. Next, we shall develop a long term model, the overlapping generations model, which will be the basis for the subsequent analysis of the theory of money.

We start with some comments on the concept of capital. For a long time, it was "the apple of discord for theorists."[2] "Capital" is here defined in a double sense: "real capital" and "capital value."

Specifically, *physical capital* is the real endowment with production goods, the collectivity of "produced means of production" or capital goods[3] (machinery, seeds, other real assets). An example would be the amount of wheat used today as seed. The *value of capital* is the sum of the net returns of future periods, discounted back to a particular period.[4] An example would be the future wheat harvest valued at the present value of future prices, less the value at present prices of the seed used; i.e., the present value of the profit.

---

[1] The conept of capital theory pertains immediately to growth theory. See F.A. Lutz (1963, 3). E. Helmstädter (1969, 4) talks in this connection of the accumulation theory of capital.

[2] On the discussion of the concept of capital, see E.v. Böhm-Bawerk (1930, 24 ff.) and I. Fisher (1912, 53 ff.).

[3] "Capital goods at time *t* include everything that has been made in preceding periods and is transferred to period *t* for further production. This definition is the old produced means of production." E. Malinvaud (1953, 235).

[4] This is all meaningful only if all future net incomes are absolutely certain and known and the rate of interest remains constant. "With these provisos it is very simple to derive the capital-value of the income to be yielded by any article of wealth or item of property; .... That value is simply the present worth of the future income from the specified capital." I. Fisher (1912, 202).

What we have called "real capital" and "capital value," Hicks, e.g., has called "volume of capital" and "value of capital." He distinguishes between economists who use the first definition of capital, whom he calls "materialists," and those who apply the second definition, whom he calls "fundists". However, his historical interpretation of individual authors is disputed.[5]

We mention briefly two further concepts of capital which, however, we shall not use futher in this book:

Money capital, liquid means available for investment purposes. The terms "earning assets" or "financial assets" are synonyms of money capital. In common every day usage capital is usually understood in this manner.[6]

Capital as a fund of means of subsistence (Jevons, Böhm-Bawerk, Wicksell): the concept of a subsistence fund is based on the idea that workers and land owners must utilize it for consumption while production proceeds.[7]

2.1 The General Approach

The transition from a one-period to a multi-period theory of the allocation of resources is very simple. The two theories are formally equivalent. The only difference is that in the case of the multi-period theory, the time dimension is explicitly introduced into the definition of a good; for example, wheat available today and wheat available tomorrow are considered to be two different goods.[8] Let x_{it} be the amount of good i consumed ($i = 1,\dots,n$) during period t ($t = 1,\dots,T$). The consumption plan is then a vector with $n \times T$ elements. The change from a one-period to a multi-period allocation model consists simply in rewriting the one-dimensional model into a nT-dimensional model – a trivial substitution because n and T may be any numbers.[9] The prices are provided with corresponding subscripts: p_{it} is the price of good i available in period t which is paid today in period 1. ("Period" is always to be understood as a moment of time at the "beginning of the period.") As described in Chapter 1, we may once again imagine two kinds of transactions which are economically equivalent as long as there are no costs of using the market, which is the assumption made in this chapter:

1. *Barter transactions* without the use of money, which can be understood here as loans in kind. This is an exchange of good i available in period $t + 1$ for good i available in period t at the exchange ratio $\pi_{it+1,it}$. Loans in kind are negotiated on the (real) capital market.

[5] J.R. Hicks (1974, 307–316).

[6] "Capital value and liquid capital are both measured in units of current funds; but the latter is a sum of current while the former is only a present valuation of future elements." J. Hirshleifer (1970, 154).

[7] See, e.g., E.v. Böhm-Bawerk (1930, 322).

[8] Whether they are considered to be different will be expressed in the utility function. If they are considered as different goods, the indifference curves will not be declining 45° lines.

[9] See E. Malinvaud (1961, 145).

2. *Purchase transactions*; instead of a loan in kind, good i may be purchased with money today and sold on the forward market. A loan in kind may thus be split into two purchase transactions:
   (a) a spot transaction: purchase of good i available in period t for mark available in t_0 at the price p_{it};
   (b) a forward transaction: sale of good i available in period $t + 1$ for mark available in period t_0 at the price p_{it+1}.

A further division of loans in kind is possible, viz. into a spot transaction today, a money-loan transaction today and a spot transaction tomorrow. We deal with this case further in Chapter 5 below which deals among other things with the explanation of the money rate of interest.

Spot transactions are negotiated on the spot market, future transactions on the futures market. By assumption payments are made through entries into the books kept by a central authority. Under our assumptions, the effects of both transactions are the same. An arbitrage equilibrium

$$\pi_{it+1,it} = \frac{p_{it}}{p_{it+1}}$$

exists.

Assuming perfect competition, consider the case of purchase transactions. An auctioneer calls "today" the prices of "wheat available today," "tomorrow" etc. The economic units report their corresponding amounts supplied and demanded until a general equilibrium is found through tâtonnement. At that moment all negotiated sales contracts for "today" at point of time 1 and for "all further dates" until point of time T become legally valid. In order to simplify the discussion we assume that all payments are made "today." The purchased goods are delivered as agreed upon "today," "tomorrow" etc. In this sense, all transactions for periods $t = 1, \ldots, T$ are concluded "today" in the form of spot or forward contracts. J.R. Hicks (1962, 140) calls this model a "Pure Futures Economy."

On real world spot markets, the two sides of each transaction are carried out immediately, while on real forward markets the two sides of each transaction are (differently from our model) agreed upon now and carried out later.[10]

We shall, however, maintain the assumption that the price of a forward transaction, which results from the tâtonement process, refers to "today" and is payable "today," that is, at the beginning of the period under consideration.

2.2 A Simple Robinson Economy

Even though the individual steps in the development of our capital theory are very simple, the theory as a whole is not so easily grasped. We shall therefore construct a simple model of the theory of capital using the Robinson model of Chapter 1.

[10] On forward markets in reality, see the article "Futures" in Encyclopaedia Britannica (1982).

To start with: the real exchange ratio $\pi_{it+1,it}$ may be expressed differently. Consider first its dimension:

$$\dim[\pi_{it+1,it}] = \frac{\text{quantities of good } i \text{ available in } t+1}{\text{quantities of good } i \text{ available in } t} .$$

For example:

$$\frac{\text{1.2 kg wheat available tomorrow}}{\text{1 kg wheat available today}} .$$

The borrower has promised to return tomorrow to the lender 20% more wheat than he has borrowed today. The numerical value 1.2 of the exchange ratio may also be written as the sum

$$1 + 0.2$$

or, generally,

$$1 + \rho_1 .$$

The number $0.2 = \rho_1$, is called the own rate of interest[11] of wheat. In our model with only one good ρ_1 is, at the same time, simply "the" real rate of interest ρ. The real exchange ratio π is equivalent to the sum $1 + \rho$. Arbitrage equilibrium implies

$$\frac{p_{11}}{p_{12}} = 1 + \rho_1 .$$

The dimension of $1 + \rho_1$, is the same as that of $\pi_{12,11}$. We assume one household, one firm, and only one good "wheat." Planning relates to two periods "today" and "tomorrow."

Assume that Robinson has a certain amount of land of uniform quality and an original endowment with wheat $\bar{x}_{11}$. He also knows his utility function $U(x_{11}, x_{12})$ which formally is assumed to have the same properties as a utility function for two goods in the one-period case. Note that we assume that Robinson considers goods with the subscripts 11 and 12 to be two different goods, i.e., the principle of the difference of needs over time is valid.[12] This principle is satisfied when the indifference curves are, for example, concave from above (Fig. 2-1).

[11] See, e.g., J.M. Keynes (1936, 223); originally P. Sraffa (1932, 50).

[12] This is one possible interpretation of Böhm-Bawerk's "First Reason" for a positive interest rate: it seems plausible that goods available today are valued more highly than goods available tomorrow. Böhm-Bawerk reaches the same result even if future income is lower by assuming that goods can be stored costlessly and by relaxing the assumption that today's goods are equal to today's consumption. See E.v. Böhm-Bawerk (1930, 249–252).

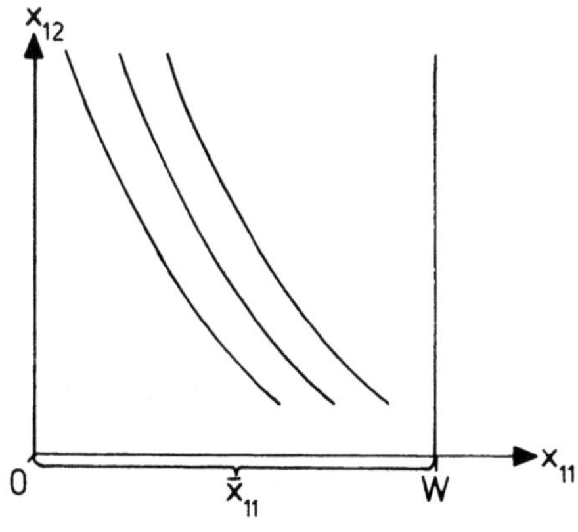

Fig. 2-1. Intertemporal Indifference Curves.

The amount of the slope of the indifference curves $\frac{dx_{12}}{dx_{11}}$ expresses the intertemporal marginal rate of substitution of the future good with subscript 12 for the present good with subscript 11. Roughly speaking, it gives the amount of future wheat which Robinson is ready to exchange for an additional unit of present wheat while maintaining the same level of utility. Following Irving Fisher, we call the expression

$$\left|\frac{dx_{12}}{dx_{11}}\right| - 1$$

the time preference for wheat.[13] If the time preference is greater than zero a unit of wheat today is evidently worth more to Robinson than a unit of wheat tomorrow. This is the *principle of underestimating future needs.*[14]

If the time preference is zero, present and future wheat are for Robinson equally desirable goods. The indifference curve is in this case a negatively sloped 45° line.

We now consider the firm Robinson. Suppose Robinson stores the wheat which he does not consume today with no storage losses. In this case the production curve of the firm Robinson is a 45° line through the origin. Let the production plan of the firm be (y_{11}, y_{12}). As discussed in Chapter 1, $y_{ij} > 0$ is an output, $y_{ij} < 0$ is an input. The case discussed above is illustrated in Fig. 2-2.

If Robinson not only stores his wheat but sows it, i.e., if he uses it productively, he can get more wheat tomorrow than he has sown today – at least within certain limits. Within these limits, the production curve will lie above the 45° line. We can visualize the production curve under these conditions as on Fig. 2-3.

---

[13] Or "degree of impatience," see I. Fisher (1930, 62).

[14] This is Böhm-Bawerk's terminology. Applied strictly, this principle demands that the time preferences are everywhere greater than zero. (See P.A. Samuelson, 1967). This principle is included in Böhm-Bawerk's "Second Reason" for a positive interest rate: "We systematically underestimate future wants and the goods which are to satisfy them." E.v. Böhm-Bawerk (1930, 253). See also J. Rae (1905, 52–59).

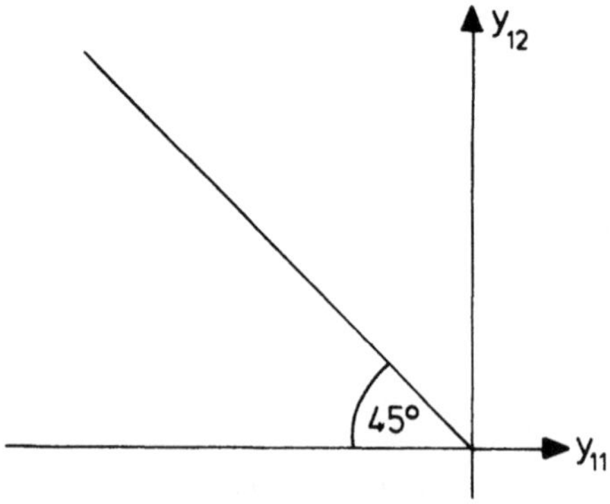

Fig. 2-2. The Intertemporal Production Curve: The Case of Costless Storage.

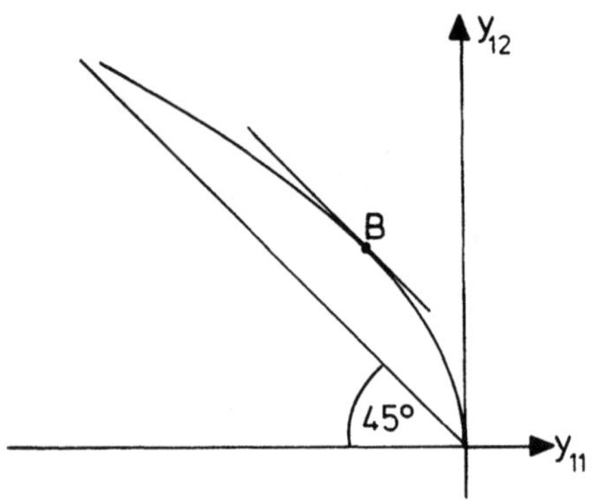

Fig. 2-3. The Intertemporal Production Curve: The Case of a Positive Net Product.

The wheat used as seed is here capital in the sense of physical capital: the quantity of produced goods which is used productively.

The intertemporal production curve represents the production function $\phi(y_{11}, y_{12}) = 0$; or written in explicit form: $y_{12} = f(y_{11})$. We assume that the firm Robinson knows its production function perfectly.

The *gross marginal productivity of capital* of the wheat sown today is represented by $\left|\frac{dy_{12}}{dy_{11}}\right|$. It corresponds to the amount of the slope of the production curve. The marginal input of capital is 1. The *net marginal productivity of capital* is

$$\left|\frac{dy_{12}}{dy_{11}}\right| - 1 \ .$$

The net marginal productivity of capital declines in Fig. 2-3. With increasing inputs of wheat it starts with positive values, at B it is zero and after B negative.

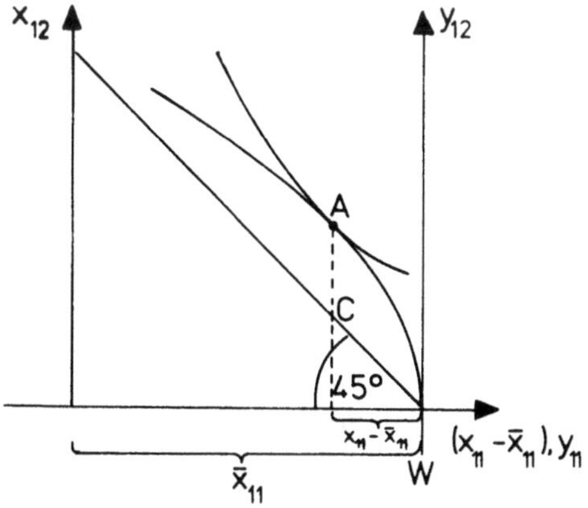

Fig. 2-4. Robinson Diagram for Two Periods.

We now superimpose Fig. 2-3 upon Fig. 2-1 so that point *W* coincides with the origin of Fig. 2-3. We get in this manner a Robinson diagram analogous to the one in Chapter 1.[15]

The Robinson diagram permits us to picture in a simple manner the lending transaction "wheat available today for (more) wheat available tomorrow." *AC* is the amount of wheat harvested in period 2 above the amount sown in period 1. The lender receives tomorrow *AC* more wheat from the borrower than he has lent today. In this example, *AC* is the net social product in period 2.

At point *A* the gross marginal productivity of capital (the marginal rate of transformation of present for future goods) is equal to the marginal rate of substitution of the future for the present goods: $\left|\frac{dy_{12}}{dy_{11}}\right| = \left|\frac{dx_{12}}{dx_{11}}\right|$. The amount $|x_{11} - \bar{x}_{11}|$ corresponds to the amount of physical capital employed (the capital stock); $\bar{x}_{11}$ denotes the original endowment and x_{11} is the amount of wheat consumed during period 1. Wheat is now used in two ways: it is on the one hand a consumption good to the extent to which it is immediately consumed, and on the other hand a capital good. The use of a particular amount of wheat as seed (i.e., capital good), combined with a given amount of land and a given technical knowledge, yields a particular output in the next period.[16] In Fig. 2-4, the net product *AC* is smaller than the technically possible maximum output. The net marginal productivity of capital is greater than zero. If Robinson were to save more wheat today and were to use it productively, he could get tomorrow (in period 2) a larger net product (and thus, in this case, a larger net social product).

$$\text{Maximum output is reached when } \left|\frac{dy_{12}}{dy_{11}}\right| = \left|\frac{dx_{12}}{dx_{11}}\right| = 1.$$

---

[15] See Chapter 1, Fig. 1-6. This is an analogy to the "Crusonia Plant" of F. Knight (1944, 26–47); discussed by D. Dewey (1965, Ch. 6). Samuelson speaks of the "Fisher-interest diagram" (*Economics*, 8th ed., p. 587). For a substantively very similar exposition, see E. Sohmen (1976, 170ff.).

[16] We assume that Robinson has a life expectancy of two periods and that he therefore plans only for those two periods. If he were to plan for more than two periods we could maintain the production side of the model with a recursive formulation of capital theory. The endowment, which Robinson finds in

If the principle of underestimating future needs applies generally, Robinson will never realize his maximum possible net product. But even if this principle does not apply generally, Robinson may prefer the smaller net product in period 2 to the maximum obtainable, given his original endowment $\bar{x}_{11}$. If Robinson plans for more than the two periods and if the principle of underestimating future needs does not apply generally, it is conceivable that he will approach in the course of time this maximum net social product. This problem is dealt with by the theory of growth in the context of the so-called theory of optimal growth[17]. (On this point, see Section 2.5).

Thus it is clear: up to a certain point it is worthwhile to increase the use of capital. The net product increases with increasing use of capital. We have here an analogy to the *principle of the advantageousness of capitalistic production.*[18] Where "capitalistic" means only that production involves capital goods.

We can consider the Robinson diagram as a simple model of perfect competition. We limit ourselves to the case in which exchange proceeds with the use of money. Household Robinson and firm Robinson negotiate with each other through an auctioneer who calls out spot and future prices in mark. The prices called out are taken by the economic units as parameters. The household and the firm Robinson solve their economic optimization problems as described in Chapter 1.

Household Robinson:

(2-1) Max $U = U(x_{11}, x_{12})$

(2-2) s.t. $p_{11}x_{11} + p_{12}x_{12} = p_{11}\bar{x}_{11} + Q$.

Firm Robinson:

(2-3) Max $Q = p_{11}y_{11} + p_{12}y_{12}$

(2-4) s.t. $\phi(y_{11}, y_{12}) = 0$.

---

each period, is the output which was produced with the amount of wheat sown in the preceding period. Malinvaud greatly prefers this recursive method which goes back to Walras, to the Böhm-Bawerkian hypothesis of the round-about processes of production or time required for maturation (Ausreifungszeit), because the latter requires the attribution, in practice impossible, of the capital services to the original factors of production, labor and land. Malinvaud continues: "One frequently objects to the recursive approach that it assumes fixed delay periods between input and output. This is formally true of each elementary operation. But, if the length of the productive process may actually vary, nothing prevents us from representing this process by many elementary operations, each one describing the conditions corresponding to a definite production period. Thus, the concrete features of the technology will be present in our recursive model." See E. Malinvaud (1961, 159). "A productive transformation which requires a long time between the main inputs and the output may be viewed as a sequence of shorter operations." (Ibid. p. 152). On Böhm-Bawerk, see R. Dorfman (1958/1959) and (1959), T. Haavelmo (1960). See also W. Seyfert (1985a, 75–99).

[17] For a survey, see E.S. Phelps (1967).

[18] Böhm-Bawerk's "Third Reason" for a positive interest rate (1930, 260–272). However, he really had something else in mind, viz. "the greater fruitfulness of lengthy methods of production." (See E.v. Böhm-Bawerk 1930, 273). The "Third Reason" is the real *characteristicum* of Böhm-Bawerk's theory, which deals with the *process* of interest rate formation and not merely with the equilibrium state. This was from the very beginning subject to animated scientific debate. See on this point, W. Seyfert (1985a, 57f.).

For equilibrium the following conditions must be fulfilled in the *markets for goods*:

$$
\text{(2-5)} \qquad \begin{aligned} x_{11} - \bar{x}_{11} &= y_{11} \\ x_{12} &= y_{12} \ . \end{aligned}
$$

In words: on the market for wheat today, the supply of wheat as seed available today $(x_{11} - \bar{x}_{11})$ must be equal to the amount of wheat as seed demanded today y_{11}. On the market for wheat available tomorrow, the demand for wheat available tomorrow x_{12} must be equal to the supply of wheat available tomorrow y_{12}. As mentioned above, all prices refer to period 1 ("mark payable today").

For the household, the solution of the optimization problem (2-1), (2-2) gives the marginal condition for an interior optimum:

$$
\text{(2-6)} \qquad \frac{\partial U}{\partial x_{11}} : \frac{\partial U}{\partial x_{12}} = p_{11} : p_{12} \ .
$$

The equations determining the optimal consumption plan are thus:

$$
x_{11} = x_{11}\left(\frac{p_{11}}{p_{12}}\right) , \qquad x_{12} = x_{12}\left(\frac{p_{11}}{p_{12}}\right) .
$$

Hence, household Robinson is free of money illusion. For the *firm* we get the following marginal condition for an interior optimum on the basis of equations (2-3) and (2-4):

$$
\text{(2-7)} \qquad \frac{\partial \phi}{\partial y_{11}} : \frac{\partial \phi}{\partial y_{12}} = p_{11} : p_{12} \ .
$$

The equations determining the optimal production plan are

$$
y_{11} = y_{11}\left(\frac{p_{11}}{p_{12}}\right) , \qquad y_{12} = y_{12}\left(\frac{p_{11}}{p_{12}}\right) .
$$

We substitute the two determining equations into the two market equations (2-5). This yields the following conditions for a general intertemporal equilibrium:

$$
\text{(2-8)} \qquad x_{11}\left(\frac{p_{11}}{p_{12}}\right) = y_{11}\left(\frac{p_{11}}{p_{12}}\right) + \bar{x}_{11} \quad \rightarrow \text{spot market for wheat}
$$

$$
\text{(2-9)} \qquad x_{12}\left(\frac{p_{11}}{p_{12}}\right) = y_{12}\left(\frac{p_{11}}{p_{12}}\right) \qquad \rightarrow \text{forward market for wheat} \ .
$$

By Walras's law the two equations are dependent upon each other (see Chapter 1). We therefore have only one independent equation in one unknown, the unknown being the relative price of p_{11} in terms of p_{12}

$$\frac{p_{11}}{p_{12}} .$$

We can determine the equilibrium value of $\frac{p_{11}}{p_{12}}$ graphically in the same manner as shown in Chapter 1 (Fig. 1-6), by drawing the line tangent to the production curve at point A where Robinson's indifference curve is tangent to the production curve (Fig. 2-5).

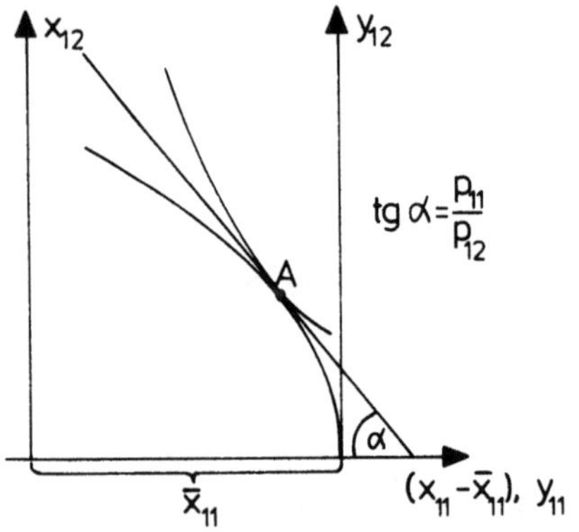

Fig. 2-5. Own Rate of Interest in the Two-Period Robinson Diagram.

The slope of this tangent line, $tg\,\alpha$, represents the general equilibrium value of p_{11}/p_{12}. Since we have also assumed an arbitrage equilibrium we have also

$$\frac{p_{11}}{p_{12}} = 1 + \rho_1 .$$

We may therefore rewrite (2-6), using the rules of implicit differentiation, as

$$\text{(2-6')} \qquad \left|\frac{dx_{12}}{dx_{11}}\right| - 1 = \rho_1 .$$

In words: when the individual household is in equilibrium, the time preference for wheat is equal to the own rate of interest of wheat.[19]

We can rewrite (2-7) correspondingly as

$$\text{(2-7')} \qquad \left|\frac{dy_{12}}{dy_{11}}\right| - 1 = \rho_1 .$$

[19] See Irving Fisher (1930, 106).

In words: when the individual firm is in equilibrium, the net marginal productivity of wheat is equal to the own rate of interest of wheat. Alternatively, the present value of profits is maximized when the yield of the last unit of seed used is just sufficient to replace the last unit of capital (i.e., the last kg of seed) and to cover the interest cost equal to the own rate of interest. The utility of the owner of the firm (in this case simply Robinson) is maximized when the present value of the firm, i.e., the capital value or market value, is maximized. This is the so-called market value criterion,[20] a term from the theory of finance.

In the case of the Robinson economy the total (physical) capital input is financed through equity. In the case of more than one household, things may look different. Household No. 1, e.g., may be the owner of the firm (the owner of the residual profits) while household No. 2 may have hired out the total (physical) capital to the firm at a previously agreed upon (real) rate of interest ρ_1. But we could just as well assume that the capital input of the firm is financed partly with own funds or equity (i.e., by household No. 1), partly with outside funds or debt (i.e., by household No. 2). However, the mix of equity and debt has no influence on the equilibrium value of the own rate of interest.

In order to find a condition for intertemporal general equilibrium we may combine equations (2-6′) and (2-7′):

$$\text{(2-10)} \qquad \left|\frac{dx_{12}}{dx_{11}}\right| - 1 = \left|\frac{dy_{12}}{dy_{11}}\right| - 1 = \rho_1 \ .$$

The absolute amount of the goods prices p_{11}, p_{12} is therefore without influence on the equilibrium value of the real rate of interest. In other words, the (real) loan contract is free of money illusion. Here we have a purely real theory of interest involving only goods.

In general, equation (2-10) implies the following: on our assumptions, the *fundamental theorem of the theory of the real rate of interest* for an arbitrary time horizon T and an arbitrary number of goods n is valid. That theorem can be stated thus:

In intertemporal general equilibrium the own rate of interest of every type of good is in every period $t = 1, \ldots, T-1$ equal to

1. the rate of time preference of the goods; and
2. the net marginal productivity of the type of good involved.

In the final period T no loan contracts are concluded. The assumption that arbitrage equilibrium obtains at all times permits us to read equations (2-8) and (2-9) also as functions of ρ_1. We can find the equilibrium value of the own interest rate of wheat ρ_1 by solving one of the two market equations, e.g., (2-8).

[20] We maximize not the profit during a period (which is a flow variable) but the present value of the sum of the present and all future profits of the firm. This is in our model equal to the market value of the firm. The theory of finance speaks therefore of a "market value criterion." See E.F. Fama and Merton H. Miller (1972, 69 ff.); see also below Section 2.3. This approach is from I. Fisher (1930) and was later taken up again by J. Hirshleifer (1959). Problems arise if a firm is not managed by its owners and the costs of monitoring the management (the agency costs) are accounted for. For a survey see E.G. Furubotn and S. Pejovich (1972, 1148 ff.), H. Gravelle and R. Rees (1981, 335 ff.).

Equation (2-8) may now be expressed in the following form:

$$(2\text{-}8') \qquad |x_{11}(\rho_1) - \bar{x}_{11}| = |y_{11}(\rho_1)| \ .$$

The left side represents the planned real assets of the household or its supply of capital K^s; the right side represents the planned input of real capital of the Robinson economy or the demand for capital K^d. Therefore we can also write:

$$K_1^s(\rho_1) = K_1^d(\rho_1) \ \rightarrow \text{(real) capital market} \ .$$

Generalizing in a simple manner we can regard wheat as the national product, and the own rate of interest of wheat as the own rate of interest of the national product, or "the" real rate of interest. The fundamental theorem of the theory of the real rate of interest implies therefore: at the equilibrium value of the real rate of interest

the planned supply of real capital = the planned demand for real capital .

In equilibrium, the real rate of interest ensures that the real supply of capital is equilibrated exactly with the real demand for capital. This is the essential content of the classical theory of interest.[21] It is obvious that with a given state of technical knowledge the real stock of capital can be enlarged only when there are increased savings.[22] It is also clear that in general equilibrium the level of planned saving is equal to the level of planned investment. In this case Say's law also holds, according to which real exchange transactions (including loans in kind) are at all times balanced. In particular, it is certain under these conditions that planned supply of real capital equals planned demand for real capital. Adam Smith and the other classics (excepting Malthus) argue in this manner, while J.M. Keynes, for example, has his doubts on this point. Thus, Adam Smith (1976, 338) writes

"That portion which he [the rich man] annually saves, as for the sake of the profit is immediately employed as a capital, is consumed in the same manner, and nearly in the same time too, but by a different set of people, by labourers, manufacturers, and artificers, who reproduce with a profit the value of their annual consumption."

J.M. Keynes (1936, 210f.), on the other hand, argues:

"An act of individual saving means – so to speak – a decision not to have dinner today. But it does *not* necessitate a decision to have dinner or to buy a pair of boots a week hence... Thus it depresses the

---

[21] E.g., K. Wicksell (1935, 190):
"It is a well recognized principle of this kind that in the last analysis the money rate of interest depends upon the supply of and demand for *real capital* or, as Adam Smith, and later Ricardo, expressed it, that the rate of profits from the employment of capital itself and not by the number or quality of the pieces of metal which facilitate the turnover of its products."

[22] "Capitals are increased by parsimony, and diminished by prodigality and misconduct." A. Smith (1976, 337).

business of preparing today's dinner without stimulating the business of making ready for some future act of consumption."

"In any case, ..., an individual decision to save does not, in actual fact, involve the placing of any specific forward order for consumption, but merely the cancelation of a present order."

To summarize the preceding discussion: the topic of (microeconomic) capital theory is the explanation of the own or real rates of interest ρ. The intertemporal optimal allocation of resources for T periods has been analyzed under the assumptions of perfect competition and that all economic units have complete information about their own preference orderings, their own technical knowledge and their original endowments during each period. The model is formally identical to the model of the theory of general equilibrium for a single period, as briefly described in Chapter 1. It is simply a more general interpretation of this theory, viz. in the sense of a theory of an intertemporal general equilibrium. From this point of view interest theory and price theory are formally equivalent.[23] This analogy aside, we are interested in this chapter in the explanation of real interest rates. The money rates of interest and their level will be dealt with below, Chapters 5 and later.

2.3 Two Present and Two Future Goods: Does "*the*" Real Rate of Interest Exist?

The own rates of interest of different goods need not be the same. To show this we expand the Robinson economy to two present and two future goods, i.e., to four goods. As before there are only endowments of present goods. Future goods do not fall from heaven like Manna. They must be "transported" into the future by storage or production.

We assume, as before, two kinds of transactions:
- barter, and
- purchase.

We use the following subscripts:

11: wheat available today,
21: oats available today,
12: wheat available tomorrow,
22: oats available tomorrow.

Household Robinson and firm Robinson solve their individual optimization problems in a manner analogous to the procedure described above in equations (2-1) to (2-4). We will not repeat the derivations of the solutions. We find the

[23] "The theory of interest bears a close resemblance to the theory of prices, of which, in fact, it is a special aspect. The rate of interest expresses a price in the exchange between present and future goods." I. Fisher (1930, 61). This was clear to him already in 1907, see I. Fisher (1907, 88).

equations determining the optimal plans of the household and the firm and substitute them into the market equilibrium conditions. For four goods there are four market equilibrium conditions. We obtain a Walrasian system of four equations in three unknown exchange ratios.

Because of Walras's law any one of the equations is linearly dependent on the other three. If a solution exists, we get a vector of solutions of the type

$$\mathbb{L} = \left\{\frac{p_{11}}{p_{12}}, \frac{p_{21}}{p_{22}}, \frac{p_{11}}{p_{21}}\right\} . \tag{2-11}$$

Assuming that arbitrage equilibrium obtains at any moment, so that barter and purchase always have the same real end result, the vector of solutions for barter transactions is identical to (2-11); here it is merely expressed in different symbols:

$$\mathbb{L} = \{1 + \rho_1, 1 + \rho_2, \pi_{21}\} . \tag{2-12}$$

The two own rates of interest ρ_1, ρ_2 will in general not be equal to each other. Hence, in general the theory of the real rate of interest supplies *various* different own rates of interest; "the" real rate of interest does not generally exist.

The two own rates of interest of wheat and of oats will be equal to each other when the rates of time preference and the net marginal productivities for the two goods are equal to each other. However, this need not be so: "... there is no reason ... why the wheat-rate of interest should be equal to the copper-rate of interest." (J.M. Keynes 1936, 223).

If however the exchange ratio π of the two goods remains the same in each period ("If no change is expected in the relative value of two alternative standards, ..." (Keynes 1936, 224)) all own rates of interest are equal to each other. For, in our terminology, as spot and forward prices we have

$$\frac{p_{11}}{p_{12}} = \frac{p_{21}}{p_{22}} ,$$

from which it follows that

$$\frac{p_{11}}{p_{12}} = \frac{p_{21}}{p_{22}} \quad \text{or} \quad \rho_1 = \rho_2 .$$

This is so in *stationary equilibrium.*[24] For the rest of this chapter, we will deal only with stationary equilibria.

[24] "... contrary to the belief of most economists since the time of Böhm-Bawerk, no single real interest-rate is implied for a capitalist or socialist state. Equality would be a necessity only in the highly unusual case where relative prices of all goods remain the same over time." P.A. Samuelson (1947, 233, n. 30).

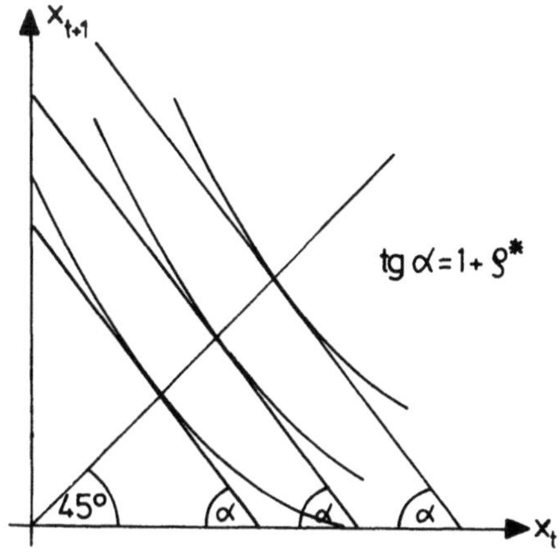

Fig. 2-6. Robinson's Intertemporal Indifference Curves.

2.4 The Robinson Economy in Stationary Equilibrium

In a stationary equilibrium, the stock of seed in our Robinson economy will have the same magnitude in each period. It is a capital stock equilibrium. The planned stock of capital in this case has the *same* magnitude in each period, the net investments are zero.[25] We assume a constant population, constant preferences, constant technical knowledge, and no uncertainty about the future.[26] This case may also be described by means of a Robinson diagram. Planning occurs over an unlimited stretch of time from which we take any two successive periods. We assume, therefore, that Robinson lives infinitely long.

We first consider the system of indifference curves of the household Robinson as a "rolling two-period model" (Fig. 2-6). The locus of all stationary consumption plans ($x_t = x_{t+1}$) is the 45° line through the origin. We call it the stationary consumption line. The magnitude

$$\left|\frac{dx_{t+1}}{dx_t}\right| - 1$$

(for all t) is the long term or stationary rate of time preference. We assume it to be constant along the stationary consumption line.

[25] The stationary state has analytical rather than practical interest. It deals with the fiction of a state of rest of the economy with unchanged underlying conditions – which exists no more than an absolute vacuum or a frictionless pendulum. Just the same, the concept of a stationary equilibrium is indispensable as a means of explaining the workings of an economy. J.A. Schumpeter stressed the importance of the stationary economic model for economic analysis. He writes: the theory "of the stationary flow, gives us, as it were, the bare bones of economic logic which, however abstract or remote from real life it may be, yet renders indispensable service in clearing the ground for rigorous analysis." See J.A. Schumpeter (1939, 68).

[26] This is a special case. See W. Seyfert (1985a, 128ff.) where may also be found further considerations about stationary equilibrium.

In stationary equilibrium for any two successive periods t, $t+1$ and for any arbitrary level of consumption $x_t = x_{t+1}$, the following is true:

$$-\frac{dx_{t+1}}{dx_t} = \frac{U_t}{U_{t+1}} = 1 + \rho^* \; ; \qquad U_t \equiv \frac{\partial U}{\partial x_t} \text{ etc.}$$

If we assume that individual households with infinitely long lives engage in long term planning with perfect foresight, as is appropriate to the idea of long run equilibrium, then the assumption that individuals will underestimate their future needs may be inappropriate. Assuming a certain minimal original endowment it seems plausible that there will not be a systematic underestimation of future needs.[27] The stationary rate of time preference of Robinson is then zero. For stationary consumption plans there is time neutrality of the utility function.[28] This may be the proper interpretation of Milton Friedman's assertion that a rational household would not discount the future, because the household already knows today that tomorrow it would have to be satisfied with a smaller consumption level than it could obtain. This contradicts a feature of rational behavior, viz. not to behave today in a manner which one would regret tomorrow.[29]

Intertemporal indifference is thus a sensible assumption to make for a household with an infinitely long life in a stationary state. 100 kg wheat today are as good or as bad as 100 kg wheat tomorrow. The stationary rate of time preference in such a case is zero; the slope of all indifference curves along the stationary consumption line is 45°:

$$\text{(2-13)} \qquad \frac{dx_{t+1}}{dx_t} = \frac{U_t}{U_{t+1}} = 1 \; .$$

We now turn to the firm Robinson whose production curve is as follows:

---

[27] I. Fisher (1930, 246f.).

[28] T.C. Koopmans (1960) and T.C. Koopmans, P.A. Diamond, and R.E. Williamson (1964) show that no utility function exists which is simultaneously time-neutral at all utility levels and fulfills other reasonable postulates. However, Koopmans et al. use a different concept of time neutrality from the one used here. They also define decision alternatives in a way that under our assumptions cannot be efficient at the same time. In addition, parts of their postulates may presume "impatience," the measure here used to quantify the "distance" between different programs. To this extent the results of Koopmans et al. do not contradict the assumption of time neutrality in our special case.

[29] In Friedman's words, Robinson would say to himself: "Had I been sensible enough to make a temporary sacrifice years ago, it would be long past by now, but I would be enjoying today, and *forever after* a higher level of consumption. I was a fool not to have made a sacrifice then." Friedman then continues: "And this retrospective judgement does not involve any knowledge the individual did not have available at time t_0. His failure to make a temporary sacrifice then therefore conflicts with one characteristic it is natural to assign to 'rational' behavior: behaving in a way that one does not later regret on the basis of data initially available." M. Friedman (1969, 22). For this reason an individual who lives forever will not discount his future consumption. (*op. cit.* p. 21). Things are different when life is limited (*op. cit.* p. 22).

By sowing *OD* wheat today, *OE* wheat will be produced tomorrow, i.e., *EF*, more than was sown. In the stationary case the stock of capital is constant, so that the same amount of wheat will be sown tomorrow as today ($OF \equiv OD$). The net product or "net national product" *EF* is entirely consumed. The division of the gross product *OE* into stationary reinvestment (here equal to the capital stock $OD = OF$) and stationary consumption *EF* may be simply determined on Fig. 2-7 by means of the 45° line.

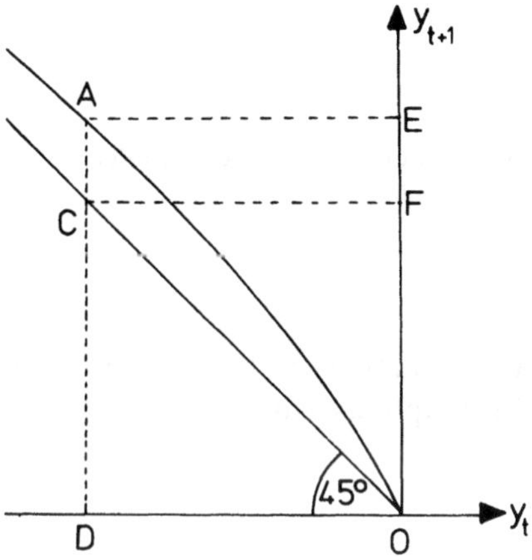

Fig. 2-7. Robinson's Intertemporal Production Curve.

Robinson's stationary equilibrium may be easily shown graphically under these assumptions: it is where the slope of the production curve (i.e., the gross marginal productivity of capital) is equal to the slope of the indifference curves along the stationary consumption line.[30] Under our assumptions it is equal to 1.

Let *A* be that optimum. Then *EF* is the stationary level of consumption which is here identical with the stationary net national product. *OE* corresponds to the value of the stationary gross national product.

We now superimpose Fig. 2-6 on Fig. 2-7 so as to allow for the stationary level of the capital stock and of consumption. This gives us the graphic solution of the problem on Fig. 2-8:

The household Robinson harvests in each period the gross quantity $EO = GF$. It plans to consume *GC* and to reinvest *CF*, i.e., to lend to the firm Robinson *CF* as seed.

The profit *Q* equals the consumption *CG*; it can be understood as Robinson's real wages. Since the slope of the indifference curves along the stationary consumption line is, on our assumption, equal to 1, the rate of interest will be in the stationary equilibrium, i.e., long term equilibrium, equal to 0. In our model world Robinson always reaches his highest possible level of consumption in long term equilibrium (point *A*).[31] At this point, the economy is saturated with capital.[32] Of course, it will

[30] See, e.g., W. Leontief (1958).

[31] "bliss": F.P. Ramsey (1928, 545).

[32] T.C. Koopmans (1957, 122ff.).

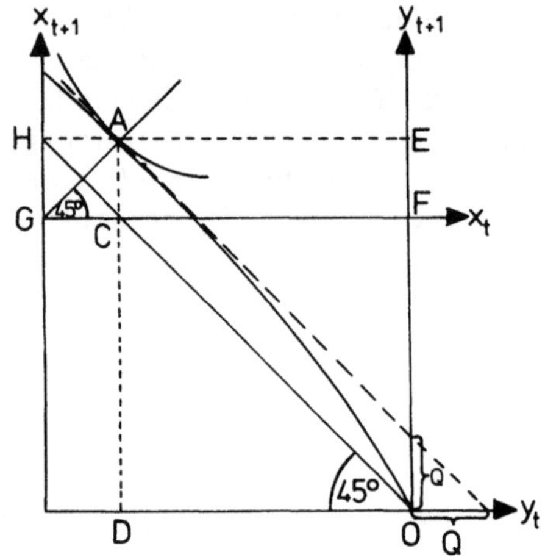

Fig. 2-8. Robinson's Diagram for Two Periods: A Stationary Equilibrium.

be realized in this case only if the *net* marginal productivity is 1. As Koopmans rightly stresses, this is an empirical question. We simply assume this for the case under discussion.[33]

With reference to the production function

(2-14) $$\phi(y_t, y_{t+1}) = 0$$

the case of capital saturation implies that

(2-15) $$\frac{\partial\phi/\partial y_t}{\partial\phi/\partial y_{t+1}} = -\frac{dy_{t+1}}{dy_t} = 1 \ .$$

Because of equations (2-13) and (2-15) it must also be the case that in stationary equilibrium

(2-16) $$\frac{\partial U/\partial x_t}{\partial U/\partial x_{t+1}} = \frac{\partial\phi/\partial y_t}{\partial\phi/\partial y_{t+1}} = 1 \ , \qquad t = 0, 1, 2, \ldots \ .$$

In the limiting case of such a stationary equilibrium the real rate of interest will be zero, and the stock of capital remains unchanged at the level of saturation. If the existing capital stock is below the saturation level (and if for that reason the supply of consumption goods to the stationary population is suboptimal), then the real rate of interest will be positive. Savings and (in this case simultaneously) real capital

[33] Technical progress is not considered in the stationary model. With technical progress the level of consumption in long term equilibrium with population constant will be maximized not when $\rho = 0$, but at a positive rate of interest. This follows from the so-called "golden rule of accumulation," a concept that plays an important role in the theory of growth. See E. Phelps (1961), C.C.v. Weizsäcker (1962), T.W. Swan (1956). For a survey, see A. Takayama (1974, particularly p. 441). See also E. Phelps (1967), C.J. Bliss (1975, 61–91).

accumulation are stimulated until a stationary equilibrium is reached. This corresponds to the classical theory.[34]

In principle it is possible that the supply of consumer goods of the stationary population is suboptimal because the existing capital stock is greater than its saturation level. In such a case the real rate of interest would be negative, and the stock of capital would be reduced until its stationary equilibrium level has been reached. Viewed in this fashion, the real rate of interest steers the household plans of capital formation towards a stationary equilibrium. The problem of the stability of the stationary equilibrium is, under the assumption of complete information in the deterministic model, irrelevant.[35] What matters is that a stationary equilibrium solution exists.[36] In stationary equilibrium the interest rate is zero. This is, at the same time, the optimal rate of interest.[37]

J.M. Keynes (1936, 376) speaks in this connection of the "euthanasia of the rentier" and writes: "I see, ..., the rentier aspect of capitalism as a transitional phase which will disappear when it has done its work." However, Keynes (1936, 379) doubts the effectiveness of the invisible hand and defends, therefore, a governmental intervention into the process of savings and investments in order to achieve or maintain in this manner full employment.[38] Keynes defends the implied necessity of expanding the tasks of the state with the argument that he sees in it the only practical means "of avoiding the destruction of existing economic forms in their entirety and as the condition of the successful functioning of individual initiative."[39]

Capital accumulation as such is the subject matter of the theory of growth.[40] It differs from the stationary model in two ways:

- it assumes that the basic underlying conditions change continuously: population increases, technical knowledge improves; and
- it does not allow for the time preferences of the households explicitly. The current level of savings is independent of the rate of interest, instead savings are assumed to be a constant fraction of income.[41]

---

[34] See, e.g., A.H. Hansen (1941, 288): "The classicals were quite right when they argued that without technological progress, the price system, including the rate of interest, would progressively drive the economy to the point at which there would be no net investment." Hansen, however, continues along Keynesian lines: "They were wrong in assuming that the price system could also ensure a propensity to consume compatible with this investment situation, so as to provide full employment."

[35] See W. Seyfert (1985a, 135).

[36] See W. Seyfert (1985a, 143 ff.) for a proof under the assumption of our model.

[37] Our result is reminiscent of Schumpeter's dynamic interest theory: "... without development, ..., there would be no interest." J.A. Schumpeter (1951, 174). To be sure, his theory of interest is different from the one we have expounded. On this point, P.A. Samuelson (1982, 11) writes that Schumpeter had seen the "golden rule state", i.e., maximum per capita availability of consumption goods, before Ramsey, Meade, Allais, Phelps, v. Weizsäcker and other theorists, that "his zero-rate equilibrium would maximize the aggregate steady state real consumption of fixed-supply primary factors of production."

[38] J.M. Keynes (1936, 378) writes: "I conceive, therefore, that a somewhat comprehensive socialization of investment will prove the only means of securing an approximation to full employment; ... ."

[39] J.M. Keynes (1936, 380).

[40] A survey is found in F.H. Hahn and R.C.O. Matthews (1964); J.R. Hicks (1965), (1977); J. Cornwall (1979).

[41] The corresponding stationary case but without time preference (i.e., with $S_t = sY_t$) is expounded in R. Richter, U. Schlieper, W. Friedmann (1981).

The neglect of the time preference function in growth theory seduces the analyst to the erroneous conclusion that government intervention is always necessary in order to reach the optimal consumption level of the individuals. As we have shown, however, one can also imagine the long term optimal consumption level to be reached without governmental steering of growth.

2.5 The Young and the Old Robinsons: The Stationary Theory of Overlapping Generations

The stationary theory has so far assumed that Robinson lives forever. We now assume that the individual dies, but that successive generations of Robinsons go on forever. This brings us to a stationary model of overlapping generations which plays an important role, among others, in modern monetary theory. It is the basis for our money-theoretical argumentation from Chapter 6 onward. A justification will be given at the end of this section.

At any moment of time t, there live two generations: the young Robinson (generation t) and the old Robinson (generation $t-1$). Generation t works. Generation $t-1$ has left the work force. Each generation lives exactly 2 periods so that in each period there are precisely two overlapping generations (Fig. 2-9).

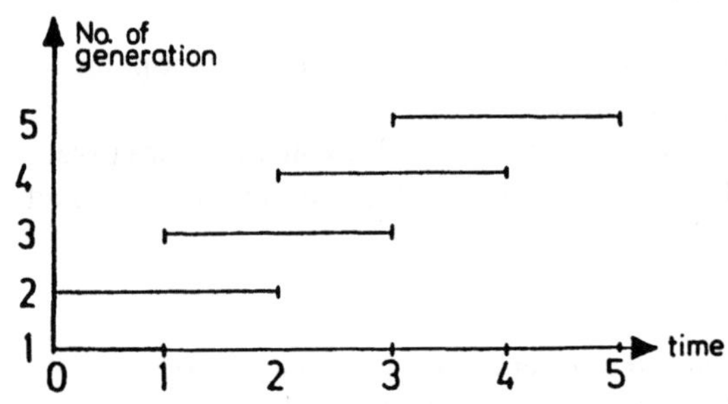

Fig. 2-9. Overlapping Generations.

We consider first a model without production, then one with production.

2.5.1 *An Overlapping Generations Model Without Production*

In this model only the household side of the sequence of generations plays a role;[42] the production side is excluded. Imagine that a perishable good is produced in each period solely by the use of labor. As stated previously, only the young Robinson works. His quantity of work remains constant over time and may thus be neglected in the version of the household theory under consideration here. As before, the household consumes only one good, say, wheat, which cannot be stored. Robinson receives during his working life a certain amount of wheat $\bar{x}_t^t$ as wage. The super-

[42] The exposition of this section follows P.A. Samuelson (1958).

script t refers to the young generation born in period t; $\bar{x}_t^t$ corresponds to the lifetime income of generation t. Since wheat cannot be stored the young Robinson cannot take care for his old age through storing wheat. The wheat harvested today must be consumed today.

We restrict ourselves to the stationary case. Population remains constant (=2). The net savings of the economy are zero, however this does not exclude the possibility that the individual savings of the young and the old Robinson may differ from zero. In particular, it is possible that the young generation saves part of its income and leaves it to the old generation for consumption. How big this fraction is will depend on the time preference of the young generation. The young Robinson will not necessarily divide his real lifetime income $\bar{x}_t^t$ in the ratio 1 : 1 between his youth and his old age. He might prefer a ratio of 2 : 1. Whatever the case, the stationary consumption line (Fig. 2-7) need not longer be a 45° line. It may, for example, have the slope as on Fig. 2-10. In other words, it is compatible with stationary equilibrium that Robinson consumes different amounts in his youth and his old age. Only total consumption must be the same in each period in stationary equilibrium, and must be equal to the stationary national product.

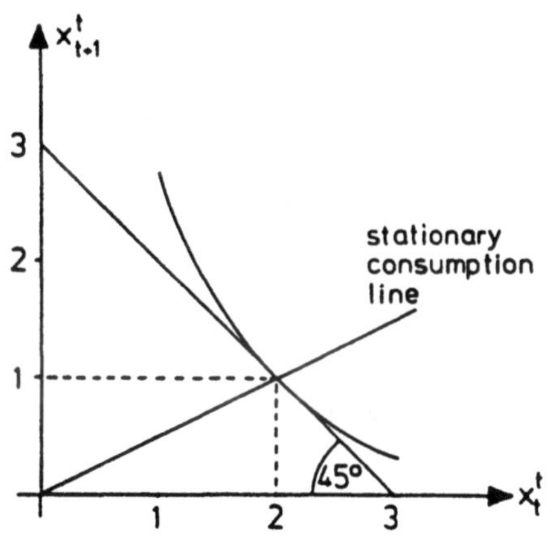

Fig. 2-10. A Stationary Consumption Line.

On the assumption of perfect competition the optimization problem for a particular young generation t looks as follows:

$$\text{(2-17)} \qquad \begin{aligned} &\text{Max} \quad U^t = U^t(x_t^t, x_{t+1}^t) \\ &\text{s.t.} \quad p_t x_t^t + p_{t+1} x_{t+1}^t = p_t \bar{x}_t^t \ . \end{aligned}$$

The equations determining the optimal consumption plan of generation t are:

$$x_t^t = x_t^t\left(\frac{p_t}{p_{t+1}}\right), \qquad x_{t+1}^t = x_{t+1}^t\left(\frac{p_t}{p_{t+1}}\right).$$

The long term market equilibrium conditions ("equilibrium over time" conditions) of the model are:

$$x_t^t\left(\frac{p_t}{p_{t+1}}\right) + x_{t-1}^t\left(\frac{p_{t-1}}{p_t}\right) = \bar{x}_t^t \quad \text{for all } t \ ,$$

or

(2-18) $$x_{t-1}^t(\cdot) = \bar{x}_t^t - x_t^t(\cdot) \quad \text{for all } t \ .$$

If, with a constant endowment of $\bar{x}_t$ goods in the economy as a whole, the old generation wishes to consume more, then the young generation must reduce its consumption correspondingly (and *mutatis mutandis* if the old generation wishes to consume less).

We assume once more that

$$\frac{p_t}{p_{t+1}} = 1 + \rho_t \ .$$

In the special case of a stationary equilibrium it must be true that

$$\rho_{t-1} = \rho_t = \cdots = \rho \ .$$

The stationary rate of interest may be zero, but it need not be (see appendix to this chapter).

Furthermore, in stationary equilibrium all young Robinsons save the same amount of wheat, i.e.,

$$\cdots = \bar{x}_t^t - x_t^t = \bar{x}_{t+1}^{t+1} - x_{t+1}^{t+1} = \cdots = \bar{x}^t - x^t \ ,$$

and all old Robinsons consume the same amount of wheat, i.e.,

$$\cdots = x_t^{t-1} = x_{t+1}^t = \cdots = x^{t-1} \quad .$$

Therefore

(2-19) $$x^{t-1}(\cdot) = \bar{x}^t - x^t(\cdot) \ .$$

One possible solution of (2-19) is evidently $\rho = 0$, for a real interest rate of zero suffices, because of $x_t^{t-1} = x_{t+1}^t$, also the budget equation (2-17). The real rate of interest of zero is in this case simultaneously the optimal rate.

P.A. Samuelson (1958, 471) illustrates this result in the following manner:

"In a stationary system, everyone goes through the same life-cycle, albeit at different times. Giving over goods now to an older man is figuratively giving over goods to yourself when old. At what rate ... does one give over goods to one's later self? ... To answer this, note that chocolate today is chocolate today ..." Samuelson continues by noting that when the young man does today give chocolate to the old man, then this is indeed a physical transfer in the ratio one-to-one.

We can illustrate this with the following numerical example: Let $\bar{x}_t^t = 3$. Each generation t consumes 2 units of wheat in the first period of its life, and one unit of wheat in the second. Graphically, the stationary optimal consumption plan is shown in Fig. 2-10 (assuming linear homogeneous utility functions).

However, the overlapping generations model presents a particular problem: it is impossible to exchange "wheat tomorrow against wheat today" directly between two living persons. The "today-young" Robinson cannot conclude a contract today with the as yet unborn "tomorrow-young" Robinson and thus obtain the property right in a certain amount of wheat tomorrow. But, what cannot be done directly may be done through the creation of appropriate institutions. Two solutions are possible:

1. making arrangements for one's old age through voluntary exchange agreements (free exchange),
2. making arrangements for one's old age through mandatory legal mechanisms (compulsory exchange).

Both solutions bring out more clearly what we also had to assume in the case of a simple direct exchange: the existence of and confidence in a system of order, which is guaranteed by convention or law,[43] or which allows us to expect a certain uniformity of particular social actions. It implies the existence of a community, e.g., of a market community[44] or, as in the present case, a community of provision.[45]

Ad 1. Old Age Provision by Voluntary Contract

In the overlapping generations model it may be brought about, for example, by an exchange by means of money. Young Robinson sells old Robinson wheat today against payment in money (in form of paper money, deposit money, gold coins, or gold bars) in the confident expectation that the young Robinson of tomorrow will sell him the same amount of wheat for the money he has received today. As opposed to our previous considerations, there is now a rational reason for indirect exchange by means of money in place of the direct exchange: the indirect exchange is the only possible one; the direct exchange is impossible. Whatever objects are used as concrete money, the essential condition for the continuing existence of the system is the trust of the "investors" in the administration of the institution (e.g., no fraudulent variation in the quantity of money) and the continuance of the living habits from generation to generation (the young people of tomorrow must provide to the same extent for the old people of tomorrow).

G. Simmel (1978, 178f.) writes on this point: "Without the general trust that people have in each other, society itself would disintegrate, for very few relationships are based entirely upon what is known with certainty about another person, and very few relationships would endure if trust were not as strong

[43] M. Weber (1968, 29ff.).

[44] M. Weber (1968, 635ff.).

[45] W. Seyfert (1985b, 174).

as, or stronger than, rational proof or personal observation. In the same way, *money transactions would collapse without trust.*" (Italics added)[46]

Another possible contractual provision for old age is the creation of a private or public insurance institution. Young Robinson exchanges with the insurance institution a certain amount of wheat available today (when he is young) against the right to be supplied the same amount of wheat tomorrow when he is old. Unlike with a funded system the "trick" consists here in the creation and mediation of a legal person as "faithful broker" which uses its present income from contributions by the young to cover its obligations towards the old.

With perfect foresight about demographic changes and the future availability of goods and with consumption preference systems unchanged over every generation during youth and old age, such an institutional arrangement on a private basis could work perfectly.[47]

Ad 2. Old Age Provision by Mandatory Law

We disregard here solutions involving family law (the legal obligation to pay maintenance or alimony) and limit ourselves to the case of the creation of an insurance institution by public law. This institution collects from the young Robinson compulsory contributions which, let us say, are always just sufficient "that the income will finance the payments due during the period."[48] Such a case is called pay-as-you-go system of financing the provision of old age by mandatory law; it has been applied in social security systems.[49] This situation is also one of indirect exchange, the only difference from the earlier case being that the indirect exchange is mandatory. The young generation acquires by exchange of present goods a right enforceable by public law to provision in old age, an old age social security claim.[50] Confidence continues to play an essential role, including confidence in a just adaptation of the right of present possession to a setback in per-capita income.

The legal protection of the public social security claim – however founded – cannot at the same time be a claim for a legally and ex ante determined payment. "A Government ... cannot be constrained from changing claims on property assets when this is necessary. Otherwise the old age insurance through an intergenerational agreement would be an entirely unilateral enterprise in favor of the beati possidentes at the expense of those who are not yet members of that group."[51]

---

[46] Simmel does not think only of confidence in next year's harvest but also of "... a further element of social-psychological quasi religious faith. The feeling of personal security that the possession of money gives is perhaps the most concentrated and pointed form and manifestation of confidence in the socio-political organization and order." (1978, 179).

[47] Random fluctuations could, of course, be counteracted by buffer stocks.

[48] H. Lampert (1985, 149f.).

[49] An alternative form of financing legal old-age insurance is through a funded system. "According to this system, enough capital is accumulated from the incoming premia that the yields of the invested capital in real values and stocks and bonds as well as the accumulated capital cover the claims of the insured." H. Lampert (1985, 149; translated by W.F.St.).

[50] F. Klanberg and A. Prinz (1983) speak of "social titles."

[51] D. Katzenstein (1982, 189). This article deals with the question whether and in how far claims under social legislation are guaranteed as property by the constitution of the Federal Republic of Germany.

When it is considered further that the level of old age insurance is politically determined, so that it depends in practice on the demographic situation, it becomes uncertain which method of insuring for old age is the more trustworthy, a provision through freely entered-upon agreements or one regulated by mandatory law, a free or an enforced exchange. In addition a question may be raised concerning the relative efficiencies of the two systems; however, we shall not deal with it.

We have thus far assumed that a certain quantity of goods $\bar{x}_t$ is somehow produced in each period. We will now explicitly introduce production into our Robinson model.

2.5.2 *An Overlapping Generations Model With Production*

Consider now the case in which production takes time and requires both labor and capital. The current gross production $\bar{x}_t$ is now used to pay both for the services of labor and for those of capital. As previously assumed, only the young generation works, and it does so for a fixed period of time, namely one period. It receives a real wage $\bar{x}_t^t$. The young generation now establishes a firm FM_t to which it contributes a certain amount of seed $-y_t$ as capital out of its income $\bar{x}_t^t$. In return the firm "promises" to pay x_{t+1}^t in period $t+1$ when generation t has grown old. The real interest on the invested capital is:

$$x_{t+1}^t : (-y_t) = 1 + \rho_t \ .$$

Firm FM_t uses the amount of seed which maximizes its profit Q_t'. We assume a linear homogeneous production function. The maximum profit $Q_{t,\max}'$ is then zero (see below). In the following period $t+1$ the firm FM_t buys or barters the labor services of the young generation $t+1$ against a wage payment of $\bar{x}_{t+1}^{t+1}$. The remainder of the harvest $(\bar{x}_{t+1} - \bar{x}_{t+1}^{t+1})$ is paid according to the "agreement" to the supplier of the capital fund, the old generation. After this transaction the firm FM_t is dissolved.

In contrast to the previous discussion, generation t has an immediate right to wheat today (the wage $\bar{x}_t^t$) and wheat tomorrow, i.e., the production $\bar{x}_{t+1}$ of its firm FM_t. However, it cannot ensure by agreement a property right over the labor input by tomorrow's young generation. Thus, confidence into the continued existence of the present economic order and the way of life of the future generations are just as important as in the preceding example.

Every young generation negotiates with the new firm FM about the level of its capital investment, i.e., how much of its income $\bar{x}_t^t$ it consumes today (x_t^t) and how much wheat it leaves to be sown by the firm. What decision will it make?

The answer depends on the kind of utility function of each generation. There are two extreme cases:

1. Every generation thinks only of itself and maximizes only its own individual utility. This is a case of strict generational egotism. The utility function is

$$U^t = U^t(x_t^t, x_{t+1}^t) \ .$$

2. Every generation thinks of itself and all future generations (as member of a community of men, e.g., a family, in which a certain level of wealth is generated and, by bequeathing, preserved and further accumulated). The utility function is then

$$U^t = U^t(x_t^t, x_{t+1}^t; x_{t+1}^{t+1}, x_{t+2}^{t+1}; \ldots).$$

The second case results in the same optimization problem as does the case of an economic unit with infinitely long life. Thus planning proceeds analogously to the case of Robinson who lives forever (see above Section 2.5). Under certain assumptions we approach a stationary equilibrium with an interest rate of zero, in which the quanitities of wheat consumed by the individual generations are at their maximum feasible level. Every generation acts, as the literature has called it, "super-rationally" though the term would perhaps be better "super-morally" in the sense that it feels morally obliged and forced by social sanctions to maximize its own utility together with that of all future generations.[52]

The intergenerational transfer is, in this case, not a pure exchange, i.e., not a pure *quid pro quo*; it is in part a gift.

In the first case every generation thinks only of itself. If it did not sow any wheat at all, i.e., if it were to consume its whole income today, it would be without any means in old age when it is unable to work. It is therefore only rational that the young people save and invest part of their income, that is that they sow some quantity of the wheat $(-y_t)$ directly or indirectly. What are in this case the optimizing considerations of each individual young generation? We continue to assume perfect competition and the conclusion of purchase agreements between the young household of period t and the firm FM_t.

For the household Robinson of generation t, i.e., for the household Robinson that will be young in period t, the optimization problem is:

$$\begin{aligned} \text{Max} \quad & U^t = U^t(x_t^t, x_{t+1}^t) \\ \text{s.t.} \quad & p_t x_t^t + p_{t+1} x_{t+1}^t = \bar{x}_t^t \ . \end{aligned}$$

The budget equation of the young Robinson household contains the following variables: its consumption of wheat planned for today and tomorrow x_t^t, x_{t+1}^t and its wage income $\bar{x}_t^t$. We obtain the marginal condition

$$U_t^t : U_{t+1}^t = p_t : p_{t+1}$$

and the equations determining the optimal consumption plan

$$x_t^t = x_t^t\left(\frac{p_t}{p_{t+1}}\right), \qquad x_{t+1}^t = x_{t+1}^t\left(\frac{p_t}{p_{t+1}}\right) .$$

[52] "Current generations act effectively as though they were infinitely-lived when they are connected to future generations by a chain of operative intergenerational transfers." R. Barro (1974, 1097).

The young household of period t and the firm FM_t may also agree on a loan in kind at the real rate of interest ρ_t. By assumption an arbitrage equilibrium always exists where

$$\frac{p_t}{p_{t+1}} = 1 + \rho_t \ .$$

Note: unlike in the preceding case there is now the possibility of working out a direct barter agreement between two parties (the household and the firm of generation t) of wheat tomorrow for wheat today.

But it is impossible for the firm which negotiates today the delivery of wheat tomorrow to also negotiate a wage for tomorrow's workers who are not yet born. This point has already been stressed.

As for the firm Robinson of generation t, we argue as follows:

The firm FM_t produces wheat with a quantity of seed y_t in period t and a constant quantity of labor in period $t + 1$ in exchange for a real wage $\overline{x}_t^t$ which is determined already in period t.

The total profit of the firm, Q', is therefore

$$Q_t' = p_{t+1}(\overline{x}_{t+1} - \overline{x}_{t+1}^{t+1}) + p_t y_t \ .$$

By assumption the production function is linear homogenous in both factors so that the maximum (total) profit

$$Q_{t,\,\max} = 0 \ .$$

Since the amount of labor used and its wage are assumed to be constant, and since therefore only the amount of seed used is variable, it is sufficient to maximize the gross profit on the capital input

$$\begin{aligned} \text{Max} \quad & Q_t = Q_t' + p_{t+1}\overline{x}_{t+1}^{t+1} \\ \text{s.t.} \quad & \phi(\overline{x}_{t+1}, y_t) = 0 \ . \end{aligned}$$

On the assumptions made the maximum gross profit is

$$Q_{t,\,\max} = p_{t+1}\overline{x}_{t+1}^{t+1} \ .$$

The optimization problem is in this case as follows

$$\begin{aligned} \text{Max} \quad & Q_t = p_{t+1}\overline{x}_{t+1} + p_t y_t \\ \text{s.t.} \quad & \phi(\overline{x}_{t+1}, y_t) = 0 \ . \end{aligned}$$

The marginal conditions are:

$$\phi_t : \phi_{t+1} = p_t : p_{t+1}$$

and the equations which determine the optima are

$$\bar{x}_{t+1} = \bar{x}_{t+1}\left(\frac{p_t}{p_{t+1}}\right) ; \quad y_t = y_t\left(\frac{p_t}{p_{t+1}}\right) \quad \text{where} \quad \frac{p_t}{p_{t+1}} = 1 + \rho_t \ .$$

The condition for *temporary* market equilibrium in period t is given by equation

(2-20) $$x_t^t(\rho_t) + x_t^{t-1} = \bar{x}_t + y_t(\rho_t)$$

or

(2-21) $$\bar{x}_t - x_t^{t-1} - x_t^t(\rho_t) = -y_t(\rho_t)$$

so that, in analogy to (2-8), we can understand this relation also as "supply of capital = demand for capital in period t":

$$K_t^s(\rho_t) = K_t^d(\rho_t) \ .$$

The equilibrium real rate of interest ρ_t is found by solving either equation (2-20) or equation (2-21).

Long term general equilibrium for all periods t is described by the following system of equations:

(2-22) $$x_t^t(\rho_t) + x_t^{t-1}(\rho_{t-1}) = \bar{x}_t(\rho_{t-1}) + y_t(\rho_t) \ ; \qquad t = 1, 2 \ldots \ .$$

In stationary equilibrium

$$\rho_{t-1} = \rho_t = \cdots = \rho \ .$$

The system of equations (2-22) then reduces to a single equation

(2-23) $$x^t(\rho) + x^{t-1}(\rho) = \bar{x}(\rho) + y(\rho) \ .$$

Thus we are left with one equation in one unknown. Equation (2-23) may also be read as follows: in stationary equilibrium and in each period we have

(2-24) $$\bar{x}(\rho) - x^{t-1}(\rho) - x^t(\rho) = -y(\rho)$$

or $$K^s(\rho) = K^d(\rho) \ .$$

The quantity of wheat sown in each period remains the same, i.e., the stock of capital remains unchanged over time.

The question remains whether the equilibrium rate of interest differs from zero in the case of generational egotism. In other words, if the different generations plan individually, is it possible that no optimal stationary equilibrium may be realized?

This may indeed be the case as Diamond has shown[53]. The stationary interest rate may differ from zero even when the utility and production functions in principle permit an equilibrium rate of interest equal to zero. This will be shown in the appendix to this chapter.

We have seen that the overlapping generations model is suitable to deal with problems of old-age provision. Yet, the idea of an endless time horizon is also important for monetary theory, viz. for the explanation of a positive purchasing power of definitive paper money[54].

The overlapping generations model permits a consistent examination of this problem. In addition, it is suitable, as we shall show in Chapter 7, to describe an economy in which paper money redeemable into a commodity is used. Therefore, the overlapping generations model is a meaningful approach to deal with the problems of monetary theory with which we are concerned. This is not to say that the model can provide a satisfactory explanation of the use or the nature of money. Tobin (1980a) remarks quite correctly: "... overlapping generations of mortal agents do not constitute either a sufficient or necessary explanation for money." He continues by concerning that the model does capture

> "one feature of money that any theory of money must confront: its value to me today depends on its value to you tomorrow, which depends on its value to someone else the next day, and so on into the endless future. But the model does not capture other essential attitudes of money connected with its use as a transaction medium and unit of account."

Still, the property of the overlapping generations model valued by Tobin is important enough to make it useful as a basic approach to monetary theory.

Appendix to Chapter 2

The Stationary Rate of Interest May be Different from Zero

We show by an algebraic example that the stationary rate of interest may be different from zero.

We simplify our symbols: let (x_1, x_2) be the consumption plans of a generation when young (subscript 1) and when old (subscript 2). Correspondingly let $(y_1, \bar{x}_2)$ be the production plan of the firm belonging to this generation. The optimization calculation for the household of the young generation is as follows, assuming a Cobb-Douglas utility function:

---

[53] P.A. Diamond (1965, 1134).

[54] There must be no final period. "The reason is obvious. Money is worthless at the end of the final period. Consequently, in the next-to-last period individuals desire to dispose of money holdings in order to avoid capital losses. This drives the price of money to zero at the end of the next-to-last period. And so on. Individuals with foresight drive the price of money to zero in each period, i.e., the 'general price level' in equilibrium must be infinite." Y. Balasko and K. Schell (1981, 13).

$$\text{Max} \quad U = x_1^{\alpha} x_2^{1-\alpha}, \quad \text{where} \quad 0 < \alpha < 1$$

$$\text{s.t.} \quad p_1 x_1 + p_2 x_2 = Q_0^1 .$$

Q_0^1 is the labor income of the young generation. It is formally equal to the present value of the profits of the firm founded in the preceding period.

The marginal condition is:

$$\frac{\partial U}{\partial x_1} : \frac{\partial U}{\partial x_2} = p_1 : p_2 .$$

Since

$$\frac{\partial U}{\partial x_1} = \alpha \left(\frac{x_2}{x_1}\right)^{1-\alpha} \quad \text{and} \quad \frac{\partial U}{\partial x_2} = (1-\alpha)\left(\frac{x_1}{x_2}\right)^{\alpha} ,$$

it follows that

$$\frac{\partial U}{\partial x_1} : \frac{\partial U}{\partial x_2} = \frac{\alpha}{1-\alpha} \frac{x_2}{x_1}$$

or

$$\frac{\alpha}{1-\alpha} \frac{x_2}{x_1} = \frac{p_1}{p_2} .$$

We solve these and the budget equation for the optimal quantities consumed x_1, x_2. For x_1 we get

(1) $$x_1 = \alpha \tilde{Q}_0^1 ; \quad \tilde{Q}_0 \equiv \frac{Q_0^1}{p_1} .$$

Equation (1) is the consumption function of the young generation for the period when it is young, α is the marginal or average consumption propensity to consume. The corresponding savings function, or more precisely, capital supply function is:

(2) $$K_1^s = (1-\alpha)\tilde{Q}_0^1 .$$

For the *firm* of the young generation we assume the production function

$$\bar{x}_2 = (-y_1)^{\beta} , \quad 0 < \beta < 1 .$$

The graph of this function, the production curve, is of the type shown in Fig. 2-3. The corresponding optimization problem is

$$\text{Max} \quad Q_1^1 = p_1 y_1 + p_2 \bar{x}_2$$

$$\text{s.t.} \quad \bar{x}_2 = (-y_1)^{\beta} ; \quad 0 < \beta < 1 .$$

Q_1^1 is the present value of the profit of the firm established by the young generation today.

The marginal conditions are

$$\frac{d\bar{x}_2}{dy_1} = \frac{\bar{x}_2}{(-y_1)} = \frac{p_1}{p_2}$$

or

$$\beta\frac{\bar{x}_2}{(-y_1)} = 1 + \rho$$

or

$$(3) \qquad -y_1(1 + \rho_1) = \beta\bar{x}_2 \ .$$

The left side of the equation is the repayment due tomorrow which has been agreed upon in the loan contract. It corresponds to the fraction $\beta\bar{x}_2$ of the harvest planned for tomorrow, $\bar{x}_2$, i.e., of tomorrow's gross national product. The remainder $(1 - \beta)\bar{x}_2$ of $\bar{x}_2$ equals the real wages paid tomorrow ($\equiv\tilde{Q}_1^2$).

We may therefore write

$$(4) \qquad \tilde{Q}_1^2 = (1 - \beta)\bar{x}_2 \ .$$

Today's demand for capital K^d by the firm estabished by the young generation is found by solving (3) for $-y_1$:

$$(5) \qquad K_1^d = \frac{\beta}{1 + \rho_1}\bar{x}_2 \quad \text{where} \quad K_1^d \equiv -y_1 \ .$$

K_1^s is

$$(6) \qquad K_1^s = (1 - \alpha)(1 - \beta)\bar{x}_1$$

because of (2) and, because, analogously to (4),

$$\tilde{Q}^1 = (1 - \beta)\bar{x}_1 \ .$$

In temporary equilibrium (5) is equal to (6) so that

$$\frac{\beta}{1 + \rho_1}\bar{x}_2 = (1 - \alpha)(1 - \beta)\bar{x}_1 \ .$$

In stationary equilibrium $\bar{x}_1 = \bar{x}_2 = \bar{x}$ and $\rho_1 = \cdots = \rho$. We get therefore

$$\frac{\beta}{1 + \rho}\bar{x} = (1 - \alpha)(1 - \beta)\bar{x} \ ,$$

or, solved for $(1 + \rho)$

$$1 + \rho = \frac{\beta}{(1-\alpha)(1-\beta)} \gtreqless 1 \ .$$

Hence stationary equilibrium may be achieved with a real rate of interest different from zero. This will generally be the case unless we assume "super-rational" utility maximization. In the course of our later discussion we shall deal with stationary states of equilibrium with a positive real rate of interest. We shall therefore not assume super-rationality.

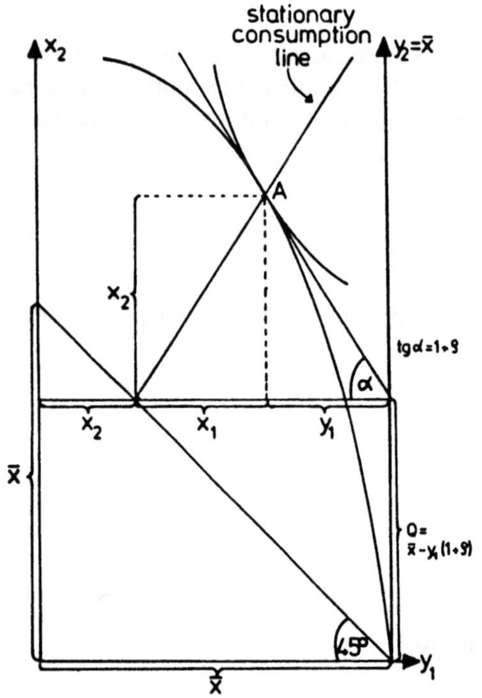

Fig. 2-11. A Stationary Rate of Interest Greater Zero.

The picture of such a case is represented in Fig. 2-11, where x_1 is the consumption of the young and x_2 the consumption of the old generation. As can be seen, at the optimum A the old Robinson is repaid the amount of wheat x_2 which, as a young man, he has handed over to his firm plus interest accrued at the rate of ρ. Every young Robinson receives the amount of wheat $\bar{x} - x_2$ which he divides according to his preference ordering between his two life periods.

As a rule the stationary rate of interest will not be zero.

Suggested Readings to Chapter 2

1 The Robinson Economy

Similar graphic representations are now fairly common. They may be found, e.g., in *D. Dewey* (1963), *J. Hirshleifer* (1970). *E.F. Fama* and *M.H. Miller* (1971), *E. Sohmen* (1976), Ch. 6. A clear graphic treatment of Irving Fisher's considerations compared to Böhm-Bawerk's is found in *P.A. Samuelson* (1967).

2 The General Case

E. Malinvaud (1953) has clearly demonstrated that the neo-classical theory of capital is a special case of the theory of general equilibrium, see also *Malinvaud* (1961). *Koopmans* (1957, 105–125) provides a clear presentation of this reasoning. A careful study of the whole Koopmans article is highly recommended.

3 The Optimal Capital Stock of an Economy

F.P. Ramsey's (1928) contribution has become a classic. There are more recent contributions as, e.g., by *D. Cass* (1965), and a survey by *A. Takayama* (1974), which also gives a very good exposition of the connection between this question and growth theory. *E. Sohmen* (1976) Chapter 6, pp. 178–216 is also very readable. A simplified graphic presentation may be found in *T.C. Koopmans* (1967).

4 Two Approaches to Capital Theory

The first approach was dealt with in this chapter: capital appears in the form of capital goods, i.e., produced means of production. This is the neoclassical approach. All capital theories belong to this group which deal with a production function in which capital and labor are separate inputs. In its purest form this approach is found in *E. Malinvaud* (1953, 1961) and *T.C. Koopmans* (1957).

The other approach emphasizes the role of time and the intertemporal structure of capital. Capital, in this view, is understood as a subsistence fund. To this group belongs *E.v. Böhm-Bawerk*'s (1888, English transl. 1930 of the edition of 1891) theory of the roundabout processes of production. *K. Wicksell* (1934), *E.R. Lindahl* (1929), and *F.A. Hayek* (1941) use the same approach. More recently it has enjoyed increased attention and has been further developed, by, among others, *C.C.v. Weizsäcker* (1971), *J.R. Hicks* (1973) and *P. Bernholz* and *M. Faber* (1978). A survey may be found in *E. Burmeister* (1974). The two approaches are not mutually exclusive, however, some phenomena are better explained with one, while different phenomena are better explained with the other. See, e.g., *C.C.v. Weizsäcker* (1972). For a critical view, see *E. Burmeister* (1974).

To some extent, *I. Fisher* (1907, 1930) occupies an intermediate position. Fisher has violently attacked Böhm-Bawerk's concept of the period of production without ever using the neoclassical capital concept. He viewed capital as discounted future consumption (in general Fisher defined income as consumption).

5 General Discussion of Capital and Interest Theory

About the general interrelationship between neoclassical capital theory and the theory of finance, see *E.F. Fama* and *H. Miller* (1971). *W. Stützel* (1954) gives a brief survey of the discussion of the question how the capitalist gets his interest income. For an exhaustive discussion of the older debate of this question, see *E.v. Böhm-Bawerk* (1884, English transl. 1959 of the edition of 1921a). *W. Seyfert* (1985a) deals with the representatives of the main points of view in the controversies about interest and its role in economic development from a modern standpoint. A survey of the older disputes on the notion of capital is found in *Böhm-Bawerk* (1888, English transl. 1930 of the edition of 1891). The debate has been revived in the socalled Cambridge controversy, though with different foci, e.g., the measurement of the capital stock in the aggregate production function. For an overview see *C.J. Bliss* (1975). The period of the canonical prohibition of interest is of particular interest. For a survey, see *Böhm-Bawerk* (1884, English transl. 1959 of edition of 1921a), Chs. II and III. See also *T. Sommerlad* (1911). A detailed account of the views of the canonical writers is found in *W. Endemann* (1863).

6 The Model of Overlapping Generations

P.A. Samuelson introduced this model in 1958. Its basic idea has since become the standard approach to the microeconomic foundations of a longer term macroeconomic analysis. It is used, for example, in the analysis of the financing of provisions for old age, in the discussion about the problem of the long term effects of tax vs. loan financing of public expenditures, and in particular in monetary theory (see below Ch. 6). Samuelson's model does not take production into account.

P.A. Diamond (1965), in an important contribution, made production endogenous by means of a neoclassical production function in which capital and labor appear as arguments. Diamond analysed with his model the long term effects of public debts. His result that public obligations are part of private net assets has been rejected by *R.J. Barro* (1974), who used the same approach with the inheritance motivation included. Barro supplies with his contribution a modern theoretical basis of the so-called equivalence theorem of *David Ricardo* (1817), Ch. XVII. On the other side of this controversy are, among others, *A. Drazen* (1978), *W.H. Buiter* (1979), *W.H. Buiter* and *J. Tobin* (1979). The Buiter and Tobin contribution also has a survey of the history of the theories concerned with this problem. Further literature on this topic will be suggested at the end of Ch. 6.

Chapter 3
The Economics of Institutions*

To understand monetary theory one not only has to understand its "real" foundation, i.e., the theory of the allocation of present and future goods as analyzed by the model of general equilibrium theory; it is also necessary to understand the relevant institutional framework. "Money" is an institution par excellence; therefore, monetary theory – the economic analysis of the use of money – cannot stop short of the analysis of money as an institution. Yet the institution of money, for its part, is closely associated with the institutions of a "market" and of a "financial intermediary." It is indeed difficult to find an exact boundary of where the one institution ends and the other begins.

Since the economic analysis of institutions itself does not depend on the type of institution analyzed, we deal first of all in this chapter – in keeping with the abstract character of Part I of this book – with the economic analysis of institutions in general. The answers to the following questions are of particular interest to us:

1. How can one model the fact that the use of the market has costs in terms of resources? As we shall see it is not too difficult to get an answer using the apparatus of general equilibrium theory. The model we are going to deal with here is central to our further money theoretic considerations. We will apply it in order to explain the level of individual cash holdings as well as the behavior of banking firms. In both activities the costs of using the market play a central role.
2. What kind of rational account can be given for the existence of economic institutions – in particular, markets, firms, contractual relations, public regulation, and, of course, money? We shall only attempt to answer this question in an argumentative fashion; no general models will be constructed. This should be sufficient for a basic understanding of these institutions, and that is all we are aiming at in this book.

3.1 Topics of Modern Institutional Economics

Although institutions play an important role in economic life they are not analyzed in depth within neoclassical theory. They are assumed to be given and are frequently described only in a rather superficial manner. Theoretical research during the past 30 or 40 years has concentrated on the greatest possible precision of microeconomics on the basis of an elementary institutional framework. The importance of this

*I would like to thank my colleagues Georg Ress, Dieter Schmidtchen, and Dietrich Schultz as well as Eva Bössmann, Professor of Economics, University of Cologne, for valuable advice, numerous suggestions and a critical reading of this and the next chapter. I am, of course, solely responsible for any errors.

institutional framework for the conclusions of the model may have been noticed, yet as a rule has not been considered rigorously and in depth.

In the last two or three decades a new development in economics can be observed: in the '60s economic theorists began to pay attention to the economic analysis of the institutional framework itself. Granted that economists (particularly representatives of the German historical school such as Roscher, Hildebrand or, later, Schmoller) had dealt with institutional problems before. The German historical school, though, was a reaction against English classical economics; it was basically hostile to abstract theoretical work. The same is true for American institutionalists such as Commons. The representatives of modern institutional economics, however, try to explain institutions as they are or should be by using the analytic apparatus of modern economic theory, specifically that of neoclassical theory. Three hypotheses are particularly relevant in this context.

Methodological individualism, in the sense that "society," "the state," "the firm," "the political parties" etc. are not dealt with as if they were autonomous beings which act as *individual* agents. Rather, a theory of social phenomena has to proceed from the views and behaviors of the individual members from whom such phenomena are composed.

The assumption of consistent and stable individual preferences or utility functions, as we know it from household theory, with the difference that individual utility functions are also applied to the behavior of firm managers, bureaucrats, representatives of the state, public institutions etc..

The ideal type of economic purposeful rational behavior of individuals, in the sense of individual utility maximization subject to constraints, either in pure form or in its weaker variant expressed in Herbert Simon's hypothesis of bounded rationality.

Representatives of modern institutional economics supplement these well-known neoclassical hypotheses with various additional hypotheses, of which the following two in particular should be emphasized:

The concept of economic incentives and their social application through suitable institutional arrangements in the form of the allocation of property rights, as reflected in the so-called *property rights approach.*

The concept of transaction costs (the old idea of "frictions"), e.g., in the case of a purchase, the potential buyer's search costs, the cost of concluding contracts and of supervising or enforcing the execution of those contracts.

These two hypotheses, as well as other hypotheses which are in part derived from them, lead to a new view of economics which at first was hardly noticed but today attracts increasing attention. Hans Albert speaks of an "institutional revolution in pure economics" (W. Meyer 1983, 3).

Thinking in terms of contracts plays a central role in modern institutional economics. This contrasts with traditional microeconomics as dealt with in the first two chapters, where contracts are seldom if at all mentioned. The difference in the method of thinking may be illustrated by the example of the definition of general equilibrium. In the manner of microeconomics of the last 30 years we say: General equilibrium exists in an abstract economy of *m* households, *s* firms, *n* goods if, at a certain system of prices (the equilibrium prices) each household chooses an optimal consumption plan and each firm an optimal production plan, and if in this state of the economy the demand equals the supply in each market. In terms of modern institutional economics one speaks, instead, not simply of "goods" but of "property rights in goods and services." Also, one does not simply say each household "chooses" a consumption plan but the households or firms conclude contracts about the exchange of property rights over goods and services with or without the use of money. From this point of view a general equilibrium is a state of the economy in which all exchange contracts are exactly fulfilled.

Such a view implies that one must explicitly consider the institutional framework of the general equilibrium model. In particular, an elementary legal order is to be assumed regulating

- The *property rights* of individuals (according to the principle of private property) and
- The *transfer of these rights* by contract (according to the principle of freedom of contract).[1]

The rules of the elementary legal order are assumed to be strictly observed.

In our zero-transaction-costs world (ZTC world), the organization of the institutional framework beyond the elementary legal order is somehow developed by the individuals themselves according to the principle of *Privatautonomie* (the principle that each individual is free to regulate the circumstances of his life by himself). How this additional legal framework appears in the end is economically irrelevant for our model economy because the use and transfer of property rights do not generate transaction costs. Individuals are assumed to negotiate with each other until they reach a state of the economy in which no one can improve himself without hurting anybody else, i.e., until Pareto efficiency is achieved. Since under the assumption of perfect competition all individuals are equally "strong" or "weak," the principle of free contracting described here is also the optimal means to achieve a fair conciliation of interests: the assumption that many independent suppliers and demanders of each good do not cooperate is a guarantee that contracts are not simply dictated by the more powerful. The exchange contract corresponds perfectly to the ideal of the fair compromise. The principle of freedom of contract can be applied without any restrictions (see D. Schultz 1967, 32).

[1] The individual has the right to regulate his contractual relations with a freely chosen partner in a mutually binding agreement. The creation of law (Recht) is decentralized in that way, "so that the legal order appears largely to be generated not as a 'compulsory order' (Zwangsordnung) of the state but as a 'voluntary order' (Freiheitsordnung) built up from below" (E.v. Hippel 1963, 27, English translation by W.F. Stolper). The principle of freedom of contract is the legal or institutional counterpart of the principle of decentralization of economic decisions to single economic units which characterizes typical market models. This freedom of contract does not, of course, exist without preconditions and limits. The feasibility of the contract principle indispensably requires inherent validity measures and freedom of will, as well as objective restrictions to protect third party interests or prevailing societal demands (see, e.g., K. Larenz 1982, 41 ff.). For a discussion of the principles involved see, e.g., F.v. Hippel (1936).

The elementary legal order of the model of perfect competition is a special case of the concept of "order." It is the social order which steers individual action in a particular direction. The concept of order provides the necessary bridge from the model of individual action to the theory of the behavior of a system of individuals; it aids in the understanding of the nature of institutions. An order can be a bilateral, self-policed governance structure; it can be some other private arrangement, self-policed or policed by a third party; and of course, it can be a legal system enforced by the state. An order may come into existence in various ways, e.g., through coercion, through explicitly negotiated contracts between private persons, or without negotiations, simply as a result of the economic interests of individuals.[2] The concept of order does not imply that a central authority, the state, is involved in its development. The opposite may be the case. An order may develop "spontaneously" (F.A. Hayek) as the "unintended result of individuals pursuing their own self-interest" (C. Menger 1892).

The three concepts – property rights, transaction costs and order – are connected with each other in the following way. The order regulates the type of property right and its mode of transfer, the use and transfer of property rights generate transaction costs, therefore, the institutional organization of an economy is not without influence on its total product.

Among modern institutionalists, various groups and schools of thought have developed, of which the following four may be mentioned.

1. *Public choice or new political economy*: the application of economic analysis to political science (the theory of the state, voting rules, voter behavior, party politics, the bureaucracy etc.) and is represented by Downs, Buchanan, Tullock, Niskanen, Bernholz, B. Frey, D.C. Mueller et al.
2. The *new institutional economics*: the application of economics to the analysis of economic institutions of both capitalist and noncapitalist systems (the theory of the firm, vertical integration, vertical market restrictions, labor union organization, regulation etc.) and is represented by Coase, Alchian, Demsetz, O.E. Williamson, Furubotn, North et al.
3. The *economic analysis of law*: the application of economics to questions of legal interpretation and policy (the economic theory of property rights, of contract rights and remedies, of tort rights, of criminal sanction and criminal law, etc.) as represented by Coase, Posner, Calabresi, Becker, Polinsky et al.
4. The (*neo*-) *Austrian school*: the application of the spontaneous order approach, in the tradition of C. Menger (1883, 1963), to the explanation of economic and other social institutions. Representatives of this line of thought are, of course, Mises and Hayek as well as Lachmann, Kirzner, O'Driscoll, Mario Rizzo, Littlechild, L.H. White et al.

---

[2] We use the concept of "order" in a wider sense than M. Weber's (1968, 31) "legitimate order," viz. in the sense of an order which results simply from certain uniformities of orientation (op. cit. 29). Such an order may be determined by self-interest, "if and insofar as the actors' conduct is instrumentally (*zweckrational*) oriented toward identical expectations." (op. cit. 29).

Currency problems have only been dealt with by representatives of the first and the last groups. Representatives of the public choice group, such as Bernholz (1983, 1986), stress the importance of the currency constitution as a foundation of stable money. Representatives of the Austrian school like Hayek and White, support free banking, i.e., they are opponents of national central banks. The representatives of the other two groups have been unconcerned with monetary issues. Yet it is the transaction cost approach, so heavily applied in the new institutional economics, which is particularly interesting for monetary theory. The concept of transaction costs has been applied for a long time to explain the superiority of the money economy *vis-à-vis* the barter economy. It has also been applied to explain the existence of cash holdings, banks and other financial intermediaries etc.. However, the concept of economic incentives and their social control through the allocation of property rights to financial assets is also of interest for monetary theory. Property rights and transaction costs are closely connected with each other; in particular, the level of transaction costs depends on the formation of property rights. Both concepts are important for monetary theory, especially the concept of transaction costs, at which we will now take a closer look.

3.2 What are Transaction Costs?

By transaction costs, we understand those costs which occur by the transfer and the use of property rights. First of all, they include the costs of using the market, i.e., the costs arising by the exchange of goods with or without the use of money.

Even in a market economy, goods are not allocated by the market alone, but in part by administrative action. This is the case, for example, within an enterprise by the use of predetermined contractually agreed upon rights of direction. Costs arising in this connection we shall call the costs of exercising the rights to give orders.

Beyond this there exist additional and more general transaction costs: the costs of making an organization of a basic governmental community available. For simplicity we assume them to be independent of the costs of using the market and of exercising the rights to give orders. We distinguish thus between three types of transaction costs:

(a) the costs of using the market;
(b) the costs of exercising the right to give orders within a firm;
(c) the costs of producing a minimal political organization.

We shall now explain these three variants in greater detail. To simplify the discussion we shall allocate all constant transaction costs to category (c).

a) Transaction Costs as Costs of Using the Market

"In order to carry out a market transaction it is necessary to discover who it is that one wishes to deal with, to inform people that one wishes to deal and to what terms, to conduct negotiations leading up to a bargain, to draw up the contract, to undertake the inspection needed to make sure that the terms of the contract are being observed, and so on."[3]

The costs of exchange in a market consist primarily of information costs and negotiating costs. The costs of negotiating should not be underestimated.[4] Thus Dahlman (1979, 148) probably goes too far when he says that one need speak of only one kind of transaction costs: "resource losses incurred due to imperfect information." On the other hand, the complete absence of transaction costs as in neoclassical models is connected with the assumption of complete information while in reality information is, of course, very incomplete. There exists *market uncertainty*.[5] No one knows immediately and automatically who will buy or sell each commodity under what conditions.

Once interested parties have found each other they must try to find out who the other party is, whether it is willing and able to live up its agreement. Negotiations are needed to find an efficient exchange relationship and to determine the detailed conditions of the exchange. There may be a need to provide for legal safeguards. The fulfillment of the contract must be supervised. Errors are possible. It may be necessary to enforce the fulfilment of contractual obligations by legal means etc.

The costs of using the market may be classified in more detail as follows:

1. the costs of preparing contracts: search and information costs narrowly defined;
2. the costs of concluding contracts: costs of negotiating and decision making, etc.;
3. the costs of supervising and enforcing the contractual obligations.

These three types of transaction costs may be characterized briefly as follows:

1. Search and Information Costs

These are costs of searching for another party to the transaction which may arise to the individual directly (e.g., through advertising, visiting prospective customers, etc.) or indirectly through the creation of organized markets (e.g., stock exchanges, fairs, weekly markets). Also included are the costs of communication among prospective parties to the exchange, such as postage, telephone expenses, expenses of sales representatives as well as the costs of gathering information about prices demanded by different suppliers for the same good.[6] There are also the costs of testing: quality control by the purchaser before the purchase, e.g., expert testing, but also simple inspection, control of weight and measures, or the quality control by a consumer organization. In the case of services: control of the suitability of the person, e.g., certification by appropriate institutions such as universities.[7] Such

[3] R.H. Coase (1960, 15).

[4] They also play a role under "perfect information" since in this context "perfect information" or "perfect foresight" means only perfect information about all traded goods and their prices (J. R. Hicks 1946, 140). The principle of unlimited privacy is assumed to be valid (see below Section 3.4).

[5] On this concept, see J. Hirshleifer and J.G. Riley (1979, 1376).

[6] The problem is a typical one for search theory which has been developed on the basis of an article by G. Stigler (1961). For a survey, see: S.A. Lippman and J.J. McCall (1976).

questions are dealt with in one form or another by the special field of the economics of information.[8] The use of resources to get information helps, among other things in avoiding mistakes.[9]

2. Costs of Negotiations and Decisions

These include the costs related to the negotiation of a contract among the concerned parties, e.g., the time required, legal advice, etc.. Depending on the particular case a contract may be legally more or less complicated and correspondingly more or less difficult to negotiate. The decision costs are closely connected with the costs of making the information gathered usable.

3. Costs of Control

Costs of control involve monitoring the agreed-upon delivery times, quality, amounts, prices etc.. In such cases, costs of information play an important role. There are costs involved in ensuring through legal processes that obligations are enforceable and actually correctly fulfilled.[10]

b) *Transaction Costs as Costs of Exercising the Right to Give Orders in Firms*

The issue here is the cost of utilizing service contracts between the firms and their employees. We assume that the contracts have already been concluded. According to our scheme, these costs belong to the costs of the exchange of goods in markets (Case (a)).

Representatives of modern institutional economics reason as follows: the firm (the "organization") "is a legal entity that serves as a nexus for a complex set of contracts (written or unwritten) among disparate individuals."[11] Together, these contracts specify the particular organization of the firm. It specifies which particular tasks are to be fulfilled by which individual employees, and how the coordination of the division of labor within the firm is to be accomplished.[12] The organization of the firm determines among other things the interrelationship of the rights to give orders. We think in this connection exclusively of a hierarchical structure[13] for

[7] We mention the concept of "market signalling": "... higher quality workers signal by acquiring education (even if education does not contribute to productivity), on the hypothesis that employers know that higher quality workers can more easily and cheaply undergo the educational ordeal." M. Spence, quoted by J. Hirshleifer (1973, 37).

[8] For a survey, see: J. Hirshleifer (1973, 37 ff.) as well as J. Hirshleifer and J.G. Riley (1979), E. Bössmann (1977).

[9] One might imagine that the costs of getting information are minimized by a suitable contractual arrangement.

[10] See M. Adams (1981).

[11] M.C. Jensen (1983, 326).

[12] See W.R. Scott (1981).

[13] There are good reasons for this. See O.E. Williamson (1980).

which there exists a number of basic forms. The organization of the firm determines also how the exchange of information is to be accomplished, i.e., what system of communications is to be used. It regulates the manner in which the execution of the individual tasks within the framework of an appropriately developed control system is to be monitored etc.. It is in this connection that the opportunism of individuals is to be taken into account. Williamson means by opportunism an effort to realize individual gains through deliberately incomplete or distorted transmission of information, obscuring or suppressing of facts, etc..[14]

The costs of managing a firm, working up of information, of the communications within, and supervision of a firm belong to the transaction costs of the type "costs of exercising the right to give orders." Our enumeration gives a series of examples and is not intended to be complete. The application of the transaction costs approach is also new to the theory of the organization of the firm, and is only now being developed.[15]

c) *Transaction Costs as Costs of Supplying the Minimal Organization of a Political Community*

The exchange of goods and the exercise of the right to give orders presuppose a certain local, national, or international order or organization of the political community or communities, which we have assumed to have the character of a market economy. The furnishing of such an order also involves costs. The costs increase with increasing development ("civilization") of the community, a point which Adam Smith made.[16] His classification allows three sets of tasks for the state (the "duties of the sovereign"): expenditure for defense, for administration of justice and for "public works and public institutions" such as transport investment or education. In addition the government itself must be financed (A. Smith 1776/1976, 814). In modern terminology these are the costs of the supply of public goods. Musgrave speaks in this connection of the allocation function of budgetary policy and lists in addition two further tasks: the distributional function and the stabilization function of budgetary policy.[17]

In general, the tasks of the state are nowadays seen to be wider than 200 years ago, and with different emphasis. This is also true of the regulation of money and monetary policy. Thus far, however, virtually no attention has been paid to the transaction costs approach in the discussion of the role of the state. Thus, the costs of governmental intervention have only been taken into account in a few theoretical discussions,[18] although they may be considered to be implicit in cost-benefit analysis.[19] No empirical analysis exists.

[14] O.E. Williamson (1975b, 258f.).

[15] On this point, see O.E. Williamson (1981), A. Picot (1981).

[16] A. Smith (1776/1976, 689, 709, 723).

[17] R.A. Musgrave (1959), Chap. 1.

[18] For a survey, see R. Richter (1978).

[19] For a survey, see R.A. Musgrave (1969), N. Andel (1977).

It is important to see that the level of transaction costs depends essentially on the behavior of individuals. Transaction costs are low if mutual trust predominates, property rights are respected and comparatively uniform ideas exist about fair solutions in cases of conflict. Yet, such a situation may be unstable. Regularities in individual behavior may result in their exploitation. Therefore, individuals may try to protect themselves against exploitation which can increase transaction costs.

The type of social order and the form of its guarantee influence the level of transaction costs. Not only the possibility of legal enforcement is to be thought of here, but also, above all, the evolution of social routines which provide more certainty in social life.[20]

The nature and development of morals and with it confidence and trust must be seen in this light.[21] Thus Arrow (1971, 22) argues:

> "It is useful for individuals to have some trust in each other's word. In the absence of trust, it would become very costly to arrange for alternative sanctions and guarantees, and many opportunities for mutually beneficial cooperation would have to be foregone. Banfield (1958) has argued that lack of trust is indeed one of the causes of economic underdevelopment."

In other words: the development of trust reduces the uncertainty in which we live and thus transaction costs. It is the function of institutions to make social actions easier to anticipate. A. Schotter (1981, 11) defines:

> "Social institution is a regularity in social behavior that is agreed to by all members of society, specifies behavior in recurrent situations and is either self-policed or policed by some external authority."

The concept of transaction costs has been used in the literature in connection with two questions, both of which are of interest to us:

1. How can one model transaction costs, given the level of organizational technique of an economy?
2. How can one give an account of the institutions of an economy as transaction costs minimizing devices?

The first question is of interest in the explanation of the holding of cash balances and the existence of the banking firm, questions with which we are dealing in later chapters. With regard to the second question we make general arguments which we shall briefly illustrate in this chapter with examples of the institutions of the market, the firm, the contractual relation and public regulation. In the next chapter we shall apply these arguments more extensively to explain the institution of money.

3.3 Transaction Costs in General Equilibrium Theory: A Simple Example

We take the technique of organization as given and ask: how can one model transaction costs in general equilibrium theory? More precisely: how can one allow

---

[20] But never perfect certainty. "The best we can attain ... is not certainty but the elimination of avoidable uncertainty ..." F.A. Hayek (1976a, 125).

[21] See, e.g., H. Albach (1980).

for the costs of the use of markets and the supply of the organization of a political community? Part of the transaction costs is independent of the volume of transactions; this is true for the costs of setting up a governmental organization, as well as for the so-called set-up costs of the market exchange of goods. Another part depends on the volume of transactions. In this section we shall deal explicitly only with the transaction costs that vary with the volume of transactions. We shall follow D.K. Foley (1970) in this: transaction costs are included in the model of perfect competition by adding the activity of conducting transactions or, in short, the activity of "transaction" analogously to the activity of "production." This new activity reflects the assumed state of the organizational technique. It may be performed by existing economic units, households or firms, or by new economic units such as brokers or other intermediaries. We shall discuss both possibilities, continuing to assume the model of the Robinson economy with one good (wheat) and two periods, today and tomorrow, and a household and a firm.

We start with the exchange between future and present goods (see Chapter 2). This is to be understood for the present as a loan in kind. The household Robinson lends the firm Robinson 1 kg wheat available today against the promise that the firm Robinson will repay the loan of wheat in the next period including interest (in the form of wheat), e.g., if the interest rate is 20%, it will repay 1.2 kg wheat tomorrow. The initiation, conclusion and monitoring of this loan contract produce transaction costs, which we assume to be in terms of wheat available today.[22] Assume then the transaction costs are paid by the household. Suppose Robinson saves today 1 kg wheat which he intends to give to the firm Robinson as a loan in kind. The firm receives, however, only 0.9 kg, i.e., the (real) cost C of the transaction amounts to 0.1 kg or 10% of 1 kg wheat available today. Assuming that the own rate of interest continues to be 20% the firm will repay tomorrow $0.9 + 0.18 = 1.08$ kg wheat available tomorrow.

The general formulation of this relationship looks as follows: the activity "transaction" defined as "loan in kind made today" may, in analogy with the production function, be represented by a transaction function:[23]

$$\varphi(y_{1H}, y_{1U}) = 0 \ ,$$

where the subscripts

$1H$ denotes wheat available today to the household,

$1U$ denotes wheat available today to the firm.

Graphically the transaction function is shown in analogy with the production function on Fig. 3-1

[22] We assume that the quantity of wheat applied to transaction costs is necessary to pay for the labor input in the activity "transaction."

[23] We assume that the activities "production" and "transaction" are independent of each other.

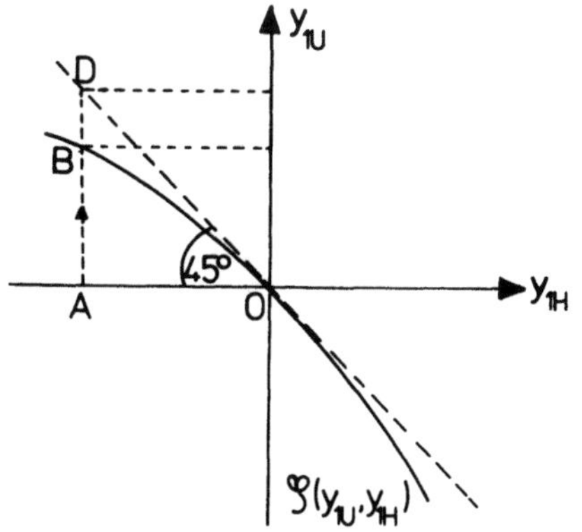

Fig. 3-1. The Transaction Curve.

The distance OA is the amount sold by the household, i.e., the "transaction input." The distance AB is the corresponding amount bought by the firm, the "transaction output." The transaction costs $C = -(y_{1H} + y_{1U})$ are represented by the distance BD. As can be seen, the transaction function is here interpreted exactly like a production function. Its picture, the transaction curve, must lie below the 45° line if there are positive transaction costs.

The slope of the transaction curve will be called the marginal rate of transactions

$$\left|\frac{dy_{1U}}{dy_{1H}}\right| ;$$

we could also speak of the marginal productivity of the transaction process. It shows here, roughly speaking, how many additional kg of wheat the firm Robinson will receive if the household Robinson supplies an additional kg of wheat. On our assumptions the marginal rate of transactions is less than 1 and declines with increasing volume of transactions.

We now include the transaction costs into the optimization calculus. It now makes a difference which economic unit is assumed to undertake the activity "transaction": the (production) firm, the household or a special transaction firm. Because of our interest in money theoretic issues, we will examine the latter two cases in considerable detail. Yet, the first mentioned case [the activity "transaction" as part of the (production) firm] is of such fundamental interest that we will discuss it first, albeit only graphically.

To attribute the activity "transaction" to the (production) firm is very easy. In this case, all that is necessary is to deduct the appropriate transaction cost from the maximum gross product achievable with the given technique of production. The curve of net production lies correspondingly below the gross production curve (Fig. 3-2). All optimizing considerations relate to the net-production curve (or function). We continue to argue precisely as before in the theory of the firm.

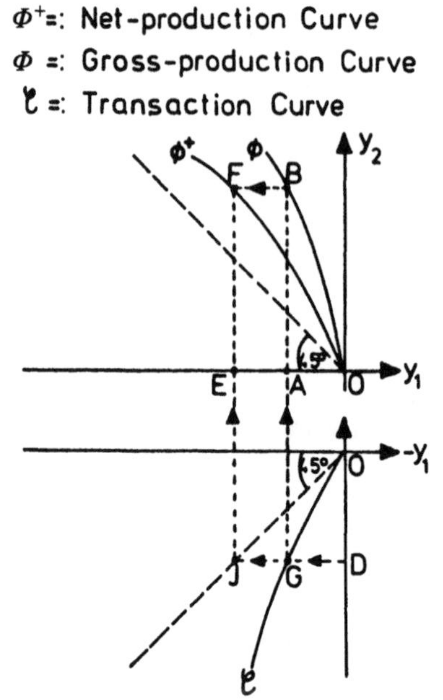

Fig. 3-2. The Activity "Transaction" Attributed to the Production Firm.

To further clarify Fig. 3-2:

If the firm Robinson wants to sow the amount OA of wheat available today, the household Robinson must lend it the amount $OD = OE$; AE represents the associated real transaction costs. They are unavailable for either consumption or production. As a consequence, a particular output, e.g., AB, now requires, because of transaction costs, a greater amount of factor inputs (in our example at least OE). The curve of net production Φ^+, i.e., the gross production curve minus transaction costs, lies therefore correspondingly lower. Its slope, the net marginal productivity, is at each point y_1 smaller than the gross marginal productivity.

Thus, the higher the transaction costs, the lower the net production curve Φ^+ with a given state of technical knowledge. This consideration may be applied to the aggregate production function. With a given level of technical knowledge the net production curve is lower the less efficient is the coordination of economic activities in society. It may, for example, happen that governmental activity (e.g., through poor legislation) may lead to substantially lower net production curves Φ^+ in one economy compared to another even with the same technological knowledge.

In an extreme case high transaction costs may prevent any production from taking place; i.e., no real capital (wheat) is lent to the firm for productive use even though from a purely technological standpoint the sowing of wheat would yield a considerable return. In our example this would be the case if the net production curve Φ^+ were to lie throughout its whole range below the 45° line. In such a case it would be more advantageous for the household to transform present into future wheat simply through storage, provided that costs of storage are sufficiently low, rather than to lend the wheat to a firm for production. The market for loans in kind collapses because of too high transaction costs. We have a case of "market failure." Such a market failure may be avoided by proper changes in the institutional framework, in the "order" of the economy, which in German is referred to as "Ordnungspolitik." Conversely, a high level of technological knowledge may be rendered economically ineffective by a bad institutional policy.

If therefore, the economic development of a country is to be stimulated, it is necessary to pay attention to both the development of production and of organizational technique. Legislation which increases transaction costs may, even if it costs "nothing" directly, offset an increase of productivity based on technical progress and may even reduce the total productivity of an economy. On the other hand, legislation which reduces transaction costs may increase productivity even with unchanged technical knowledge. Economic stagnation may therefore be the result as much of poorly thought through organizational (institutional) measures as of the absence of innovations in the technique of production or in the world of goods. The rejuvenation of a stagnating economy does not therefore always require the use of new technical achievements (steam engine, electric motor, internal combustion engines). Institutional policy, either in the sense of creating or recreating an efficient monetary economy so as to reduce transaction costs, or in the sense of diminishing institutional obstacles to the demand for labor or the use of capital, may in some circumstances be more effective and cheaper than a quantitative economic policy. Examples might be the West German currency and economic reform of 1948, or deregulation and efforts at tax reform in the United States in the '80s. Thus a role for an "entrepreneurial politician" in rejuvenating an economy, analogous to the Schumpeterian economic entrepreneur, becomes apparent.

So much for the fundamental importance of transaction costs regarding the theory of the production function. We proceed now to attribute the activity "transaction" to the household or to a particular transaction firm placed between the household and the production firm.

First let us consider the assignment of the activity "transaction" to a special *transaction firm* (commercial enterprise). We limit ourselves to the case of the conclusion of spot and future sales contracts. For the sake of simplicity we assume that the transaction firm mediates only on the spot market for wheat. It buys wheat at price p_{1H} from the household and sells it at price p_{1U} to the production firm. In general the transaction firm is owned by households, in case of the Robinson economy by household Robinson.

In our example the optimizing approaches of the three economic units household, transaction firm and production firm are as follows:

Household

$$\begin{aligned} \text{Max} \quad & U = U(x_1, x_2) \\ \text{s.t.} \quad & p_{1H}x_1 + p_2x_2 = p_{1H}\bar{x}_1 + Q + R \ ; \end{aligned}$$

Transaction firm

$$\begin{aligned} \text{Max} \quad & R = p_{1H}y_{1H} + p_{1U}y_{1U} \\ \text{s.t.} \quad & \varphi(y_{1H}, y_{1U}) = 0 \ ; \end{aligned}$$

Production firm

$$\begin{aligned} \text{Max} \quad & Q = p_{1U} y_1 + p_2 y_2 \\ \text{s.t.} \quad & \Phi(y_1, y_2) = 0 \ . \end{aligned}$$

We derive the following equations determining the optimal plans of the firms and the household:

$$x_1 = x_1\left(\frac{p_{1H}}{p_2}, \frac{p_{1H}}{p_{1U}}\right), \qquad x_2 = x_2\left(\frac{p_{1H}}{p_2}, \frac{p_{1H}}{p_{1U}}\right),$$

$$y_{1H} = y_{1H}\left(\frac{p_{1H}}{p_{1U}}\right), \qquad y_{1U} = y_{1U}\left(\frac{p_{1H}}{p_{1U}}\right),$$

$$y_1 = y_1\left(\frac{p_{1U}}{p_2}\right), \qquad y_2 = y_2\left(\frac{p_{1U}}{p_2}\right).$$

The conditions for market equilibrium are:

$$\begin{aligned} x_1 - \bar{x}_1 &= y_{1H} \\ 0 &= y_{1U} + y_1 \\ x_2 &= y_2 \ . \end{aligned}$$

We substitute the equations determining the optimal plans into the market equilibrium conditions and solve for the two unknowns $\frac{p_{1H}}{p_2}, \frac{p_{1H}}{p_{1U}}$.

For the transaction firm we get the marginal condition

$$-\frac{dy_{1U}}{dy_{1H}} = \frac{p_{1H}}{p_{1U}} \qquad \text{(see Fig. 3-3)} \ .$$

On our assumptions the slope of the transaction curve in the fourth quadrant will everywhere be less than 1 so that $-\frac{dy_{1U}}{dy_{1H}} < 1$ and in the equilibrium of the

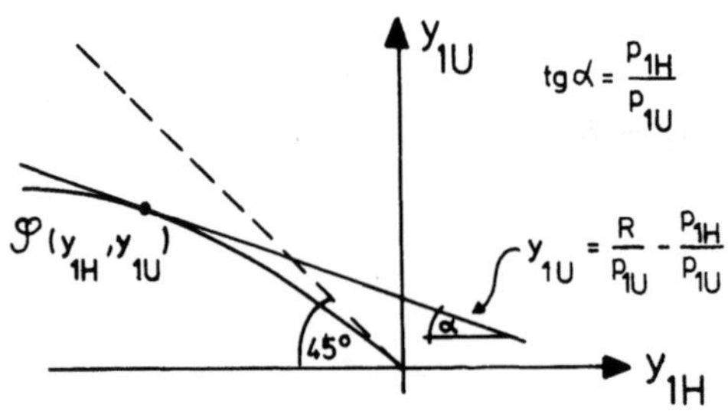

Fig. 3-3. The Profit-maximizing Transaction Firm.

individual firm:

$$\frac{p_{1H}}{p_{1U}} < 1 \ , \quad \text{or} \quad p_{1H} < p_{1U} \ .$$

The production firm pays, therefore, more for the seed it has purchased than the selling household receives. The difference is due to the transaction costs. The reason for the difference between purchase and sales prices becomes obvious. The profit of the transaction firm is R. We shall use this approach in Chapter 8 in our discussion of the theory of banks.

We shall finally consider the case where the transaction activity φ is carried out by the household. We continue to restrict ourselves to the conclusion of spot and futures contracts on the assumption of perfect competition. For our example we then get the following

Optimization Problem for the Household, Including the Activity of Transaction:

$$\begin{aligned}
\text{Max} \quad & U = U(x_1, x_2) \\
\text{s.t.} \quad & p_1 x_1 + p_1 y_{1U} - p_1(y_{1H} + y_{1U}) = p_1 \bar{x}_1 + Q \\
& p_2 x_2 = p_1 y_{1U} \\
& x_1 = \bar{x}_1 + y_{1H} \\
& \varphi(y_{1H}, y_{1U}) = 0 \ .
\end{aligned}$$

For an interior optimum we get the marginal condition

$$\frac{U_1}{U_2} \cdot \frac{\varphi_{1U}}{\varphi_{1H}} = \frac{p_1}{p_2}$$

or

$$\frac{dx_2}{dx_1} \cdot \frac{dy_{1H}}{dy_{1U}} = \frac{p_1}{p_2} \qquad (= 1 + \rho)$$

(see appendix to this chapter).

We now may write the real transaction costs pictured on Fig. 3-1, viz.

$$C = -(y_{1H} + y_{1U})$$

as a function of the net quantity of wheat loaned today to the firm, as a transaction costs function

$$C(y_{1U}) = f(y_{1U}) - y_{1U} \qquad \text{(see Fig. 3-4)} \ ;$$

$f(y_{1U}) = -y_{1H}$ is an explicit form of the transaction function φ with $f' > 1$.

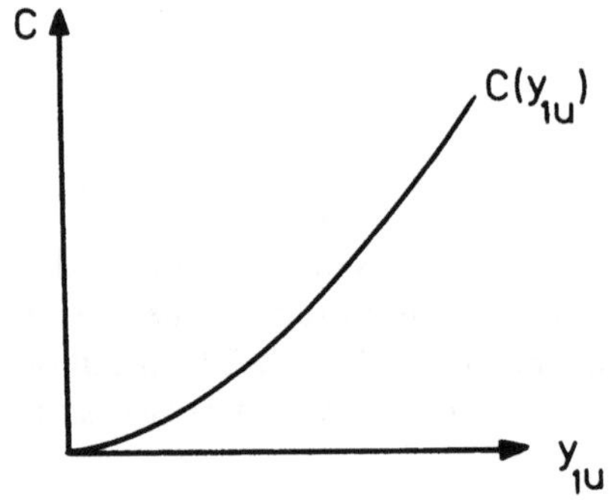

Fig. 3-4. The Transaction-Costs Curve.

The real *marginal costs of transaction* are

$$C'(y_{1U}) = f'(y_{1U}) - 1 > 0 \ .$$

They increase with the increasing volume of loans in kind y_{1U}.

The following is an algebraic example of

$$-y_{1H} = f(y_{1U}) \ , \quad f' > 1 \ .$$

Let:

$$-y_{1H} = (y_{1U})^2 + y_{1U} \ .$$

Because

$$C = -y_{1H} - y_{1U}$$

we get the transaction costs function

$$C(y_{1U}) = (y_{1U})^2 \ .$$

The marginal cost of transaction

$$C' = 2y_{1U} > 0$$

is positive in the relevant range:

$$0 \leqq y_1 < \infty \ .$$

If we assume profits Q to be zero, as, e.g., in the overlapping generations model of Section 2.5.2, we can write $y_{1U} = \frac{p_2}{p_1} x_2$, i.e., the real present value of a loan in kind is equal to the quantity of wheat supplied today to the production firm. The optimization problem of the household applies the transaction costs function $C(\cdot)$

$$\text{Max} \quad U = U(x_1, x_2)$$

$$\text{s.t.} \quad p_1 x_1 + p_2 x_2 + p_1 C\left(\frac{p_2}{p_1} x_2\right) = p_1 \bar{x}_1 + Q \ .$$

For an interior optimum the marginal condition is:

$$\frac{U_1}{U_2}(1 + C') = \frac{p_1}{p_2} .$$

(On this point see the appendix to this chapter).

Since $C' = f' - 1$, and $f' = -\frac{dy_{1H}}{dy_{1U}}$, we get the same marginal condition:

$$\frac{dx_2}{dx_1} \cdot \frac{dy_{1H}}{dy_{1U}} = \frac{p_1}{p_2} .$$

We shall come back in Chapter 6 to the transaction costs function $C(\cdot)$ when explaining the optimal real cash balances of a household (see Section 6.2).

To summarize: we have modelled transaction costs in this section in the form of a convex transaction function as a simple extension of general equilibrium theory by the activity "transaction," which is characterized by the assumption that parts of the resource inputs are used up in the transaction, so that the marginal conditions of the model look different. Apart from that the general equilibrium remains unaffected.[24] In particular, the extended general equilibrium as described in this section remains pareto efficient.

3.4 Why Economic Institutions?

We turn now to the second kind of transaction costs analysis, i.e., the economic justification of the institutions of an economy.

To begin with, what do we mean by institutions? We follow in principle the definition given by A. Schotter (1981, 11) as quoted above in Section 3.2:

"A social institution is a regularity in social behavior that is agreed to by all members of society, specifies behavior in recurrent situations and is either self-policed or policed by some external authority."[25]

Hence, certain behavioral norms and their enforcement, i.e., a system of incentives and disincentives, play an important role. M. Weber's notion of "legitimate

[24] C.J. Dahlman (1979, 144ff.). From a purely formal point of view, the approach expounded here corresponds to the one of a general equilibrium model with transport costs.

[25] A similar description of the concept of an institution is given by D.C. North (1986, 231): "..., institutions are regularities in repetitive interactions among individuals. They provide a framework within which people have some confidence as to how outcomes will be determined. ... institutions are not persons, they are customs and rules that provide a set of incentives and disincentives for individuals. They entail enforcement either of the self-enforcing variety, through codes of behavior, or by third party policing and monitoring." North adds in the next sentence: "Because ultimately a third party must always involve the state as the source of coercion, a theory of institutions also inevitably involves an analysis of the political structures of a society and the degree to which that political structure provides a framework of effective enforcement."

order" or "guarantee of the legitimacy of an order" are relevant in this connection (M. Weber 1968, 31 ff.). According to Weber the guarantee can be realized either "purely subjectively" (rein innerlich), e.g., "affectual; resulting from emotional surrender," and/or "by the expectation of specific external effects" (by convention or law). "Monitoring" plays an important role in this connection.

The principles of private property and freedom of contract, which are central to the model of perfect competition, can presumably also be accounted for using the concept of transaction costs. We are not going to do this here. Rather, we will start with the elementary legal order described in Section 3.1. We assume, without going into detail, that all individuals strictly observe the rules of the elementary legal order. The assumption of perfect information ("costless monitoring") may help in understanding this assumption. Yet, perfect information of "everybody about everybody and anything else" is not assumed in our model of perfect competition. On the contrary, perfect information means in this model only perfect information about all traded goods and their prices. Otherwise, there exists the principle of unlimited privacy.[26] During the negotiations of exchange contracts no individual needs to reveal his order of preference or the extent of his original endowment or his shares in firm ownerships. No firm needs to reveal its technical knowledge. All communications relate only to goods and their prices.

How an economy is organized, based upon our elementary legal order, has, in a world without transaction costs, no influence on the Pareto efficiency of general equilibrium:

"since any advantages one mode of organization appears to hold over another will be simply eliminated by costless contracting ..."[27]

In a zero-transaction costs world (ZTC) Pareto efficiency is always realized. The ZTC-world is, in this sense, perfectly neutral with respect to institutions. We shall make clear by means of some examples precisely what this means. We hope that these examples will contribute to a better understanding of the role of the institutional framework of the goods and financial markets which underly monetary theory.

3.4.1 The Market as an Institution: Auction Markets or Direct Negotiations?

General equilibrium theory is a static theory. It describes the conditions of general equilibrium; it does not describe how this general equilibrium comes about. Normally one thinks of an auction market, but this is only an auxiliary construct and not an essential part of general equilibrium theory. The imagined negotiations might be organized in a totally different manner. In particular, with zero transaction costs general equilibrium might come about as the result of everybody negotiating

---

[26] The fact that the disclosure of personal information is a potential interference with one's personal freedom, shows that this principle is an essential liberal principle.

[27] O.E. Williamson (1979, 233).

directly with everybody else. The number of contracting parties is irrelevant in a ZTC world. What is important to realize is that individuals negotiate continuously directly or indirectly until equilibrium is reached. This is also true for the case of so-called "perfect competition."

Within a framework of general equilibrium theory the process of negotiations is irrelevant. It suffices, therefore, to recognize that in principle a total competitive equilibrium may be reached even with direct negotiations. To see this, imagine a two-person pure exchange economy without production. The individuals negotiate not about a particular state of the economy but about an exchange relationship. In graphic terms, they negotiate about a price line in the Edgeworth box, not about a particular point. This means that the coordination of the plans is achieved only through prices. Each party then considers which point, i.e., which consumption plan, on the price line mentioned in the negotiations is optimal for it. Then both see whether desired purchase and sales plans agree. If they do, i.e., if the plans are consistent, an exchange will take place. If not, they start new with a different negotiating price until a competitive equilibrium has been found.

Of course, this kind of coordination of individual economic plans in which the parties negotiate first about prices and then about the quantities is implausible in the case of only a few market participants. For in such a case each individual could influence the equilibrium price and could therefore try to improve his position. For example, an individual household needs only to destroy part of its original endowment in order to improve its situation.[28] With only a few parties it is therefore reasonable to assume that both prices and quantities are negotiated, i.e., that negotiation concerns a set of points in the Edgeworth box. In this case the quantities agreed-upon are a certain section of the contract curve which contains also the competitive equilibrium. This section becomes the smaller the greater the number of the market parties. Under certain assumptions it may be shown that the solution will converge towards the total competitive equilibrium as the number of exchange partners approaches infinity.[29] Total competitive equilibrium is the limiting case.

The precise manner in which the negotiations of everyone with everyone are organized in a ZTC world is irrelevant. This is not so if transaction costs are taken into consideration. In this case the way the market is organized, i.e., the particular kind of market order and the manner in which it is guaranteed, does play a significant role. The problems are as follows: which goods (more precisely which property rights) are traded on the market and under which conditions? How are the property rights combined? Does exchange take place with the use of money or not? What kind of money is used? Who supplies and guarantees the particular market order (i.e., a private entrepreneur, a private organization, the government)?

It is the differences in transaction costs which determine the different kinds of market organization in a world with private property and freedom of contract: the auction of antiques or objects of art, the trade of securities or of (fungible) commodities at the stock or the commodity exchange, the trade in real estate

---

[28] See, e.g., W. Hildenbrand and A.P. Kirman (1976, 13f.).

[29] For a survey see: W. Hildenbrand and A.P. Kirman (1976), or H. Gravelle and R. Rees (1981), Ch. 10.

through the intermediation of a broker, the sale of products through an independent commercial agent, the wholesale or retail trade in its different forms etc. Transaction costs may also be a reason, as already mentioned, why "market failure" is occasionally observed.

3.4.2 Why Do Firms Exist?

We usually consider "production" for the market and "consumption" to be the characteristic activities of two distinct types of economic units: the firm and the household. If we look more closely, such a distinction is to be understood in a ZTC world as at most functional. There is no reason why two such distinct institutions should exist.

We may interpret the usual assumptions of general equilibrium theory as follows: each household always consists of only one person. Every individual has a certain original endowment of goods and technical knowledge expressed in a production function. In our hitherto applied terminology this reads: each household owns 100% of some firms characterized by certain production functions. Using the household's utility function, its technical knowledge and its original endowment, it formulates a consumption *and* a production plan. The coordination of these individual consumption and production plans is achieved only through the market.

> "An economist thinks of the economic system as being coordinated by the price mechanism ... The economic system 'works itself'."[30]

R.H. Coase, whom we have just quoted, continued by noting that this is a very incomplete picture of the real world. For the coordination of plans within a firm, the picture is not applicable. He continues:

> "For instance, in economic theory we find that the allocation of factors of production between different uses is determined by the price mechanism. The price of factor *A* becomes higher in *X* than in *Y*. As a result, *A* moves from *Y* to *X*, until the difference between the prices in *X* and *Y*, except in so far as it compensates for other differential advantages, disappears. Yet in the real world, we find that there are many areas where this does not apply. If a workman moves form department *Y* to department *X*, he does not go because of a change in relative prices, but because he is ordered to do so." (R.H. Coase 1937, 387).

What causes this difference? Evidently, transaction costs play a role here too. In a ZTC world it is irrelevant for the consumption level of households whether production plans are formulated by the individuals and executed and coordinated by the market, or whether this is done through separate organizations called "firms," in which several individuals exercise different functions. With ZTC it is impossible

---

[30] Coase quoting Hayek. Coase continues: "But this theory assumes that the direction of resources is dependent directly on the price mechanism. Indeed, it is often considered to be an objection to economic planning that it merely tries to do what is already done by the price mechanisms." Here, too, Coase refers to Hayek. See R.H. Coase (1937, 387).

to explain economically why firms exist, which are "non-markets of a special kind," hierarchically organized spheres within a national economy in the style of a centrally planned economy. In a ZTC world they would not increase production.[31]

Thus, transaction costs also explain why firms exist, which we have so far simply assumed. Beyond this, the idea of transaction costs helps us to understand why firms grow only to a certain level. It helps us to understand their specialization, their size structure in different economic branches, their different legal forms, their internal organization. And for us it is important that transaction costs will allow us to show in a simple manner why transaction firms exist (trading firms, banks, etc.). The existence of such firms is elucidated by the concept of transaction costs in a twofold manner – by the specific consideration of the activity "transaction" and by its use in differentiating the "transaction firm."

3.4.3 Why Relational Contracts?

In the ZTC world of a pure futures economy no "personal preferences" for particular contracting parties exist. An individual who orders something for delivery in period t is indifferent just who will make the delivery. The supplier may in each period be a different firm. Every individual purchase agreement is a discrete transaction, "sharp in by clear agreement; sharp out by clear performance."[32] Macneil speaks in this context of a classical contract.

With uncertain expectations one can by analogy imagine the conclusion of contingent contracts which take into account all contingencies. That is not possible in a world with transaction costs (i.e., also with information costs). An alternative to forming a contingent contract is to form a relational contract. From an economic point of view this is a rational thing to do with transactions which are frequently repeated and which require comparatively large specific investments. Examples are contracts for the supply of otherwise difficult to sell intermediate products which require the investment of special machinery and specific training of workers; or labor contracts which require that the employees make firm specific investments, e.g., to acquire special skills which they otherwise cannot use etc. Characteristic of relational contracts or what is also referred to as "contractual relations" are two properties: first, gaps are left in the agreements, i.e., one does not make agreements for all future contingencies, because this is simply impossible; and secondly agreement exists between the parties about the manner in which they intend to rearrange themselves in whatever new situation may arise.

The adaptation to new circumstances necessarily leads to problems of profit reallocation. O.E. Williamson (1985b, 76) writes on this point:

> "What is needed, evidently, is some way for declaring admissible dimensions for adjustment such that flexibility is provided under terms in which both parties have confidence. This can be accomplished partly by (1) recognizing that hazards of opportunism vary with the type of adaptation proposed and (2)

[31] See R.H. Coase (1937); L. Putterman (1986).

[32] I.R. Macneil, as quoted by V.P. Goldberg (1976a, 49).

restricting adjustments to those where the hazards are least. But the spirit within which adaptations are effected is equally important (Macaulay 1963, p. 61)."

We are interested in the concept of relational contracts mainly for the analysis of transactions between banks and non-banks and between commercial banks and central banks. Both are typical relational contracts formed in view of uncertain expectations, which necessitate larger amounts of specific investments, viz. informations about debtors.

A note on the history of thought:

The interest of economists in the concept of relational contracts dates back to the work of S. Macaulay (1963) and I.R. Macneil (1974). In connection with a widely regarded empirical analysis on "Non-Contractual Relations in Business" S. Macaulay (1963, 62) argues: "... while detailed planning and legal sanctions play a significant role in some exchanges between businesses, in many business exchanges their role is small." Macaulay submits as a possible reason for the omission of a precisely planned contract and its legal enforcement the desire to maintain a reputation as a good business partner, which can easily be lost due to the violation of the spirit of a contract, and thereby to secure the material advantages of a long term relationship (op. cit. p. 63). Carefully worked out contracts indicate a lack of trust and blunt the demand for friendship, "turning a cooperative venture into a antagonistic horse trade." (p. 64). The loss of flexibility which results from this is likewise to be valued negatively. "Businessmen may welcome a measure of vagueness in the obligations they assume so that they may negotiate matters in the light of actual circumstances." (p. 64).

Subsequent to Macaulay's work, Ian R. Macneil analyses thoroughly in a series of articles (1974, 1978, 1980, 1983) the relational character which is typical for many contractual commitments. A system of "discrete" contracts is supposed to secure a smooth realization of transactions by including the highest possible degree of completeness in the drafting of a contract ("discreteness") and, connected with that, the most precise "presentiation" possible of future developments which are relevant to the contract (see Macneil 1978, 862ff.). Opposed to that, modern contractual business relationships are characterized by the following elements:

"... primary personal relations; multiple participants; some utility that is difficult or impossible to measure or to specify; internal sources of solidarity among participants; extended periods of commencement, duration and termination; much planning of very different kinds from that of discrete transactions – planning for change, for example – but often incorporating very precise and binding planning as well; circumstances where future cooperation will be essential to the relation; sharing as well as dividing of benefits and burdens; obligations – general as well as specific – arising from the relation itself and also arising externally; in some ways not transferable to others, but transferable 'en masse' (as in the case of the workforce in a corporate takeover); different attitudes of participants to conflict of interest, unity, time, and trouble; complex power relations, including hierarchical." (Macneil 1983, 345).

A third external party which a system of "discrete" contracts cannot dispense with, is not necessarily needed in the described system of relational contracts. Rather, mechanisms internal to the contract serve to secure the bilateral fulfillment of a contract.

The concept of "relational contracts" was "discovered" for economics by V.P. Goldberg (1976b) and O.E. Williamson (1976). They used the concept in the analysis of public regulation. We will deal with this problem in the next section.

3.4.4 *Why Public Regulation?*

Public regulation has been justified with the argument that the market is unable to solve certain structural problems on its own. Such problems include among others:

natural monopolies,
externalities,
difficulties arising in getting information,
cutthroat competition,
unequal bargaining power,
other problems of protecting certain groups, e.g., protection of consumers, workers and employees, patients etc.

These problems do not arise in the ZTC world of the model of perfect competition. The inefficiencies associated with the first two problems will be eliminated through contracting. The third problem does not arise because information costs are zero in the ZTC world. Cutthroat competition does not occur because by assumption the bargaining power of all individuals is the same, special measures of protection are not necessary since everybody is assumed to be fully informed about the qualities and risks of all the property rights and, as for the rest, because everybody exactly knows what he wants.

We will now briefly look more closely at the first two problems.

1. If externalities exist, it may be objected, general equilibrium will not be Pareto efficient; this provides a rationale for government intervention.
   This argument is at least inexact. According to a well-known theorem by R. Coase (1960), externalities can be internalized. In a ZTC world it is irrelevant whether this is done "by the market" (through direct negotiations between the persons concerned)[33] or "by the government." The conclusion "more market is always better than more government" does not follow from this consideration. Coase did not draw this conclusion.[34]
2. Natural monopolies emerge if average costs decrease continually as quantity produced increases. Eventually, only one firm will be left in a market under such circumstances. Government intervention, it is said, would be unavoidable also in this case, because the remaining single firm would otherwise demand monopoly prices, i.e., market forces would not lead to a Pareto optimum. Again, the argument is not quite clear. Monopolistic inefficiencies are unknown to the ZTC world in which negotiation costs are zero as well. Buyer and seller negotiate with each other until neither benefits from further negotiations (i.e., until a Pareto optimum is reached).[35] Public regulation is not necessary in this world. Only in a world with transaction costs can public regulation become relevant. Representatives of the Chicago School doubt this too (G.J. Stigler 1971; S. Peltzman 1976; R.A. Posner 1974). In their opinion, public regulation is no more than

[33] For a formal exposition see E. Sohmen (1976, 236ff.).

[34] V.P. Goldberg (1976a, 46).

[35] H. Demsetz (1968b, 61). Demsetz continues: "If a monopolistic structure exists on one side of the market, the other side of the market will be organized to offset any power implied by the monopolistic structure. The organization of the other side of the market can be undertaken by members of that side or by rivals of the monopolistic structure that prevails on the first side. The coexistence of monopoly power and monopoly structure is possible only if the costs of negotiating are differentially positive, being lower for one set of sellers (or buyers) than it is for the rival sellers (or buyers)."

a form of cartelization of firms using political forces. It appears where private cartelization is impossible or too expensive while government intervention is easily achieved or inexpensive (R.A. Posner 1974, 345f.). V.P. Goldberg (1976b) argues against the Chicago view that this view is only concerned with discrete transactions. In case of long-term business relationships (relational contracts) as, e.g., between an electric power supply company and its customers, public regulation can be justified on economic grounds as being in the interest of both sides. The regulatory agency can, in this case, be interpreted as the agent of the customers. In the initial state, the agent negotiates for a fair protection of the rights of both sides – the right to serve and to be served – and administers afterwards the established contractual relationships.

In the case of the discrete exchange paradigm, parties to a contract deal only with prices and clearly specified goods (or property rights) which enter as arguments in the optimizing calculus of the parties as households and firms. In the initial state of a long term business relationship the agent faces a much more complex problem. Goldberg (1976b, 432) writes on this point: "The longer the anticipated relation and the more complexity and uncertainty entailed in that relation, the less significance will be placed on the price and the quantity variables at the formation stage. The emphasis will instead be on establishing rules to govern the relationship: rules determining the appropriate length of the relationship; rules determining the process of adjustment to unexpected factors that arise in the course of the relationship; and rules concerning the termination of that relationship."

As we have seen, Goldberg applies two concepts for the economic explanation of the institution of public regulation: the institution of relational contract and the institution of the principal-agent relation. Regarding the latter the problem of agency costs needs to be considered, i.e., the cost of monitoring the agents by their principals.[36] Public regulation may be more advantageous than private regulation because the agency costs may be lower in the first case than in the second, though not equal to zero. The problem of monitoring a governmental agent is certainly not insignificant. With this in mind we agree with Goldberg when he writes:

"... the administered contracts [relational contracts] framework opens up new areas of search for innovations in regulatory institutions." (Goldberg 1976b, 445).

We further agree with him that, in the case of regulation by the granting of monopoly rights, the shape of the long-run average cost curve should not be decisive (very often we don't know it anyway); rather what is of primary importance is the consideration of

"... the complexities involved in devising and administering such a contract." (Goldberg 1976b, 431).

Our primary interests in the issue of public regulation are with regard to government regulation of money and credit in general, and the regulation of central banks and commercial banks in particular.

So much for the economic explanation of the market, the firm, the relational contract and public regulation. Our examples have illustrated the transaction costs

[36] See M.C. Jensen and W.H. Meckling (1976).

approach of which A. Picot (1982) aptly remarks that it is a very simple, almost simplistic instrument of analysis which allows clarifying insights ("Aha-experiences") into important organizational relationships by maintaining a connection with traditional economic theory.

3.5 General Equilibrium and Institutional Economics: Some Conceptual Considerations

The central concern of modern microeconomics of the past two or three decades had been the logical existence of a general equilibrium. The fact that equilibrium prices are determined by negotiations is allowed for in the theory of the core, though only in a very general form. Difficulties arise in the explicit modeling of the process of price formation, i.e., the manner in which the "invisible hand" actually works, or, in other words, the dynamics of the "market mechanism" proper.[37] The process of price determination in the sense of the Arrow-Debreu world plays no role in general equilibrium theory. It happens, so to speak, in a black box connected beforehand. All we see is the end result: the state of general equilibrium.[38] Representatives of the Viennese school have criticized this defect of neoclassical theory, and they were misunderstood as the well-known debate between Böhm-Bawerk and Irving Fisher shows.[39] The criticism of the later "Neo-Austrians"[40] of the "Anglo-Saxon" economic theory follows along the same lines (genetic-causal theory[41] vs. equilibrium theory).

In this respect the modeling of the process of price formation (process of tâtonnement) by a dynamic approach, viz. by the development of an appropriate system of differential or difference equations is more precise.[42] Yet, to this end assumptions about individual adaptive behavior are necessary which cannot be justified in the pure style of neoclassical theory, i.e., in the manner of a strict ideal-typical rational behavior directed towards achieving a specific aim. Ad-hoc assumptions become necessary. These play an even more important role in modeling

[37] To this extent general equilibrium theory is not a "science of contract" which J.M. Buchanan would like economics to be. J.M. Buchanan (1975, 229).

[38] The process of tâtonnement is not part of general equilibrium theory.

[39] See I. Fisher (1930, 473 ff.) and the literature cited there. Compare in particular p. 484 note 39, where Fisher objects to the "causal-process" approach of Böhm-Bawerk with the argument: "The advance of all science has required the abandonment of such simplified conceptions of causal relationship for the more realistic conception of equilibrium: the mathematical solution of the problem of interest by means of simultaneous equations recognizes the mutual interdependence of all the factors in the interest problem and, at the same time, yields a determinate solution for the problem." This is, of course, a rather crude misunderstanding.

[40] A group of economists in the United States and in the German speaking literature under the aegis of Kirzner, Lachmann and Rothbard, who want to continue the "Austrian tradition" as developed by Menger, Mises and Hayek. For a survey, see: N. Moldofsky (1982), S. Böhm (1980).

[41] H. Mayer (1932, 148).

[42] For a survey, see T. Negishi (1962).

the so-called non-tâtonnement processes which underlie disequilibrium theory.[43] The multiplication of the possible models is boundless, resulting in an unsatisfactory state of affairs which gets us further and further away from a cleancut modeling of social systems on the basis of ideal-typically rationally acting individuals.[44]

It is possible, of course, that we have simply reached the limits of this ideal-typical style of thinking and that there is no other way out than to model human behavior on an ad-hoc basis. This view is certainly not entirely wrong, since obviously every ideal type, in fact, every model, has limits. The question is merely whether one should give up so soon. We do not think so because we believe that the question of the processes of price formation and the stability of general equilibrium has been posed in a wrong manner. The analogy to mechanics does not meet the central question. The problem of modeling a social system consists in finding a bridge from the model of individual action (e.g., the Robinson Crusoe economy) to the theory of the behavior of a system of individuals.[45] This means that the institutional framework must be allowed for. In our case the analysis has to include the elementary legal order and the concrete organization of the market. This inolves in part questions about whether exchange takes place by use of money or not, whether the individual plans are coordinated via the market, whether they are considered within firms or by relational contracts, whether public regulation of the economy is necessary etc. Institutional economics starts with these questions. The concept of transaction costs helps us to understand why under certain conditions certain institutions make economic sense. The concepts of a legitimate order and its guarantee help us to explain how each single institution works. Individual actions are steered by social orders and corresponding control mechanisms. In our model, for example, they are steered towards a general (competitive) equilibrium. Whatever the imagined final point is, we envisage the limiting case as an equilibrium, i.e., a state of the economy in which all individual plans and thus all contracts can be and are fulfilled to the letter. How the equilibrium is achieved, what the process of negotiations looks like, does not interest us. From the viewpoint of institutional economics all that is of interest is the question of the results of individual actions within a certain institutional framework, i.e., within certain orders and related control mechanisms (O.E. Williamson 1985b, speaks in this connection of the existence of a certain "governance structure"). In this context it is important to realize that there exists beside a general order (e.g., the general legislation) a network of specific orders, e.g., orders within firms or contractual relations. Some of these

---

[43] Which deals also with equilibrium analysis, though with a different concept of equilibrium. See E. Malinvaud (1977, 5ff.).

[44] It is characteristic of this development that the question of Pareto optimality of this disequilibrium-equilibrium is frequently forgotten, e.g., in the Keynesian underemployment equilibrium. These theories also assume rationally acting individuals. Why do these individuals not continue to negotiate until a Pareto optimum has been found? R. Weintraub (1977, 16) undertakes considerations in this direction. On the prove of a Drèze equilibrium, see P.R. Hayak (1980).

[45] See J.S. Coleman (1984, 86). Coleman writes that the central intellectual problem of the social science "is the problem of moving from a model of individual behavior to a theory of the behavior of a system composed of these individuals, taking social organization explicitly into account in making this transition, rather than assuming it away."

orders come into existence through coercion, others are the result of contractual agreements or simply of individual self-interest, i.e., they "may be said to be 'determined by self-interest,' if and insofar as the actors' conduct is instrumentally (zweckrational) oriented toward identical expectations." (M. Weber 1968, 29)

Borrowing freely from M. Weber's (1968, 636) terminology we call a system of prospective buyers and sellers together with the prevailing institutional framework (the prevailing general and specific orders inclusive of their control mechanism) a *market community.*[46]

A market community is a mixture of cooperation with respect to the prevailing institutional framework and competition according to the rules of the framework. Time plays a role in that business, transactions are seen to recur and relational contracts to develop. The actors' experiences with regard to business practices of others matter. They contribute essentially to the observation of the rules. One aspect of the just mentioned arguments is illustrated by M. Weber (1968, 637) as follows:

> "It is normally assumed by both partners to an exchange that each will be interested in the future continuation of the exchange relationship, be it with this particular partner or with some other, and that he will adhere to his promises for this reason and avoid at least striking infringements of the rules of good faith and fair dealing. It is only this assumption which guarantees the law-abidingness of the exchange partners. Insofar as that interest exists, 'honesty is the best policy.' This proposition, however, is by no means universally applicable, and its empirical validity is irregular; naturally, it is highest in the case of rational enterprises with a stable clientele."

We summarize: two theoretical approaches are available to analyze the "real" foundations of monetary theory:

- the concept of *economic equilibrium* together with the concept of transaction costs, e.g., in form of general equilibrium theory inclusive of the activity "transaction" and
- the *economic theory of institutions* in particular with the concepts of "transaction costs", "order" and "guarantee of an order".

Both approaches may be applied to the same object. The first approach provides us with the conditions under which individual economic plans are consistent, e.g., the conditions under which all contracts can be carried out. The second approach illustrates how individual actions can be steered towards a state of equilibrium. The first approach is static, the second dynamic. Only the first approach will be explicitly modelled in our book, the second approach will be applied in an argumentative style as a complement to the first. Much more than an argumentative treatment of the latter seems out of reach, given the present state of institutional economic

---

[46] The title of the (unfinished) Chapter VI of the German edition of M. Weber's "*Wirtschaft und Gesellschaft*" (M. Weber 1980) used here is "*Marktvergesellschaftung.*" In the chapter itself Weber uses the term "*Marktgemeinschaft*" which is translated (in M. Weber 1968, 636) as "market community." On M. Weber's definition of "*Vergemeinschaftung*" (communal relationship) and "*Vergesellschaftung*" (associative relationship) see M. Weber (1968, 40f.). We let this question rest and use the term "market community" as defined above in the text.

research, at least for the analysis of such a general and large field as that of monetary theory. It is an advantage of the argumentative style of the institutional economic parts of this book that we may occasionally leave the narrow and strict world of equilibrium theory and thus are able to better explain the implications of equilibrium analysis. We restrict ourselves completely to the working style of institutional economics in the rational justification of the use of money, e.g., the treatment of the "nature of money". This is the topic we are going to deal with in the next chapter.

Appendix to Chapter 3

Utility Maximization of the Household Including Transaction Costs

The optimizing approach of the household including transaction costs is:

$$\begin{aligned} \text{Max} \quad & U = U(x_1, x_2) \\ \text{s.t.} \quad & p_1 x_1 + p_1 y_{1U} - p_1(y_{1H} + y_{1U}) = p_1 \bar{x}_1 + Q \\ & p_2 x_2 = p_1 y_{1U} \\ & x_1 = \bar{x}_1 + y_{1H} \\ & \varphi(y_{1H}, y_{1U}) = 0 \ . \end{aligned}$$

We optimize according to Lagrange:

$$\begin{aligned} L = U(x_1, x_2) & - \lambda_1(p_1 x_1 + p_2 y_{1U} - p_1(y_{1H} + y_{1U}) - p_1 \bar{x}_1 - Q) \\ & - \lambda_2(p_2 x_2 - p_1 y_{1U}) \\ & - \lambda_3(x_1 - \bar{x}_1 - y_{1H}) \\ & - \lambda_4 \varphi(y_{1H}, y_{1U}) \ . \end{aligned}$$

Necessary conditions for an optimum are:

$$U_1 - \lambda_1 p_1 - \lambda_3 = 0 \ , \tag{1}$$

$$U_2 - \lambda_2 p_2 = 0 \ , \tag{2}$$

$$-\lambda_1 p_1 + \lambda_1 p_1 + \lambda_2 p_1 - \lambda_4 \varphi_{1U} = 0 \ , \tag{3}$$

$$\lambda_1 p_1 + \lambda_3 - \lambda_4 \varphi_{1H} = 0 \ . \tag{4}$$

From (1) and (4) follows

$$\frac{U_1}{\varphi_{1H}} = \lambda_4 \ . \tag{5}$$

from (2) follows

(6) $$\frac{U_2}{p_2} = \lambda_2 \ .$$

Because of (3)

(7) $$\frac{\varphi_{1U}}{p_1} = \frac{\lambda_2}{\lambda_4} \ .$$

We put (5) and (6) into (7) and get

$$\frac{U_2}{p_2} : \frac{U_1}{\varphi_{1H}} = \frac{\varphi_{1H}}{p_1}$$

or

$$\frac{U_1}{U_2} \cdot \frac{\varphi_{1U}}{\varphi_{1H}} = \frac{p_1}{p_2} \ .$$

Using the transaction costs function

$$C(y_{1U}) \quad \text{with} \quad C = -(y_{1H} + y_{1U}) \quad \text{and}$$

$$Y_{1H} = f(y_{1U}) \quad \text{with} \quad y_{1U} = \frac{p_2}{p_1} x_2 \ ,$$

we can argue as following

$$y_{1U} = \frac{p_2}{p_1} x_2 - \frac{Q}{p_1} \quad \text{with} \quad y_2 = x_2$$

because

$$Q = -p_1 y_{1U} + p_2 y_2 \ .$$

The optimization approach reduces then to

$$\text{Max} \quad U = U(x_1, x_2)$$

$$\text{s.t.} \quad p_1 x_1 + p_2 x_2 + p_1 C\left(\frac{p_2}{p_1} x_2 - \frac{Q}{p_1}\right) = p_1 \bar{x}_1 + Q \ .$$

We optimize following Lagrange

$$L = U(x_1, x_2) - \lambda\left(p_1 x_1 + p_2 x_2 + p_1 C\left(\frac{p_2}{p_1} x_2 - \frac{Q}{p_1}\right) - p_1 \bar{x}_1 - Q\right) .$$

Neglecting that Q depends on y_2 $(=x_2)$ or assuming $Q = \text{const.}$ (as in Section 2.5.2 and later in Section 6.2), we receive the following necessary conditions for an optimum:

$$(8) \qquad U_1 - \lambda p_1 = 0 \; ,$$

$$(9) \qquad U_2 - \lambda p_2 - \lambda p_1 C' \frac{p_2}{p_1} = 0$$

$$\Rightarrow \frac{U_1}{U_2}(1 + C') = \frac{p_1}{p_2} \; .$$

since

$$C' = -f' - 1 \; ,$$

so that

$$\frac{U_1}{U_2}(-f') = \frac{p_1}{p_2}$$

or

$$\frac{dx_2}{dx_1} \cdot \frac{dy_{1H}}{dy_{1U}} = \frac{p_1}{p_2} \; .$$

Suggested Readings to Chapter 3

1 Property Rights and Transaction Costs in General

As an overview of the role of property rights see *E.G. Furubotn* and *S. Pejovich* (1974).

As a general explanation of the concept of transaction costs and overview of this topic see *E. Bössmann* (1982) and *J. Hirshleifer* (1975).

2 Transaction Costs in General Equilibrium Theory

In principle there are two approaches:

a) the case of a single market date (one "day"), at which all exchange contracts are concluded for "all times to come" (as in the Arrow-Debreu world). For the fundamentals of this approach see *D.K. Foley* (1970). Other relevant contributions are, e.g., *M. Kurz* (1974a) and *S. Honkapohja* (1978); or
b) the case of sequential market dates ("sequence economy"), in which the market is re-opened in each new period of time; for the fundamentals of this approach see *F.H. Hahn* (1971). Further contributions are, among others, *M. Kurz* (1974b), *F.H. Hahn* (1973), *D.A. Starret* (1973). In the foreground of the discussion is an

efficiency problem, which can be solved by the introduction of money. Overview: *A.M. Ulph* and *D.T. Ulph* (1975).

The benefit to monetary theory from these works is disputed. *J. Niehans* (1978, 19), e.g., writes: "It is fair to say that this literature has not progressed to the subject matter of monetary theory."

On the criticism of the inclusion of transaction costs in general equilibrium analysis see, e.g., *C.J. Dahlman* (1979).

3 Why Economic Institutions?

On the irrelevance of the organization of a ZTC economy see *O.E. Williamson* (1979).

a) *Auction Markets or Direct Negotiations?*
E. v.Böhm-Bawerk (1930, 193–197) gives an illustrative description of the "fundamental law of price formation" in case of direct negotiations between the parties "under the hypothesis that all who take part in the exchange act *exclusively* from the motive of pursuing their immediate economical advantage in it." (p. 193). The concept of the core and its reduction to a point by an unlimited increase in the number of demanders and suppliers is also in *Böhm-Bawerk* (1930, 215; much more pronounced in the German original (1821b, 266–292)). See also *F.Y. Edgeworth* (1881). For proof of the limit theorem of the core see the lucid exposition of *W. Hildenbrand* and *A.P. Kirman* (1976) or *H. Gravelle* and *R. Rees* (1981), Ch. 10. A historic exposition of the concept of the core is found in *M. Shubik* (1982) Ch. 6.

b) *Why Do Firms Exist?*
R.H. Coase was the first to discuss this problem (1937). The more recent advances come primarily from *O.E. Williamson* (1975a, 1979, 1984, 1985a). The different opinions positions of a number of authors are found in *R. Richter* (ed.) (1981). For a survey of the literature on the economic nature of the firm see *L. Putterman* (1986).

c) *Why Relational Contracts?*
I.R. Macneil (1974, 1978) posed the problem in the form which we have used. It was taken up for economics by *V.P. Goldberg* (1976a, 1976b) and *O.E. Williamson* (1976). On the legal consequences, see *P.-C. Müller-Graff* (1973). Overview: *V.P. Goldberg* (1980), *P.L. Joskow* and *R. Schmalensee* (1983,25–32); on the more recent discussion see *A.A. Alchian* and *R. Richter* (eds.) (1985), *O.E. Williamson* (1985b), *E.G. Furubotn* and *R. Richter* (eds.) (1988).

d) *Internalization of External Effects*
The relevant theorem of *R.H. Coase* (1960) is explained by, among others, *H. Demsetz* (1968b) and proven formally by *E. Sohmen* (1976). *V.P. Goldberg*'s criticism is interesting (1976a). For a game theoretic discussion of the Coase theorem see *U. Schweizer* (1988).

e) *Why Public Regulation?*
H. Demsetz (1968b) points out that in the ZTC world a natural monopoly would not cause inefficiencies. Prominent representatives of the Chicago School are *G.J. Stigler* (1971), *R. Posner* (1974) and *S. Peltzman* (1976). The contribution by Posner provides a good survey of the views of the Chicago School. *H. Demsetz* (1968b) suggests the auctioning of property rights; critical on this point is *O.E. Williamson* (1976) with a paper which also applies the concept of contractual relations to the problem of public regulation. On this "argument against the argument for public regulation" see *V.P. Goldberg* (1976b). General overview: *P.L. Joskow* and *R.C. Noll* (1981), *C.C.v. Weizsäcker* (1982).

4 On the Economic Theory of Institutions

The discussed theory of the market as an institution is a special case of the so-called economic theory of institutions. An excellent introduction which is at the same time a basic contribution to the history of ideas is *C. Menger* (1883, English transl. 1963) who develops a theory of the "organic" origin of social structures, including money, in the form of a "constructed history;" see also *J.R. Commons* (1934), particularly his discussions of the concept of "institution" and "transaction." In contrast to Menger, Commons represents a "collectivist" position. *M. Weber* (1968, Ch. I) describes the basic sociological terms applied in this chapter, in particular, the concept of legitimate order and the guarantee of the legitimacy of an order. *W. Eucken* (1952) should be read on the role of order as an instrument for the control of the economic process. *R.H. Coase* (1937) drew attention to the analytic possibilities of the transaction costs approach for the analysis of organizations, especially the firm. *F.A. Hayek* (1945) works out the importance of a decentralized organization for optimal utilization of knowledge of a society. See also *K.J. Arrow* (1969, 1974) on the problems of information and of market failures. *A. Schotter* (1981) presents further developments in the tradition of *C. Menger* by the use of game theory.

O.E. Williamson (1975a, 1984, 1985a, 1985b) is an important representative of the economics of institutions, being the first to use the concept of the "new institutional economics" (*Williamson* (1975a, 1). The *new institutional economics* deals with among other things, the analysis of transaction costs and property rights (*O.E. Williamson* 1985b, Ch. 1). For surveys of the different subject matters and approaches of the new institutional economics see also *E.G. Furubotn* and *R. Richter* (eds.) (1984) and *D.C. North* (1986). On the relationship between the approach of the German *Ordnungspolitik* and the new institutional economics see *D. Schmidtchen* (1984).

Part II
Monetary Theory

Chapter 4
The Nature of Money

This chapter deals with two problems: the economic justification of the use of money and the institutional framework of a money economy. The two are closely interrelated. We shall analyze both in terms of the concepts of institutional economics developed in the preceding chapter. In particular, we shall use, in addition to the traditional transaction costs approach, the concepts of a legitimate order and its guarantee to explain the use of money. First it will be useful to describe and systematize the institutional framework of a money economy. Next we shall give reasons for the use of money and the existence of its institutional framework – the currency order. Finally we shall deal with the guarantee of the currency order, i.c., with the relation between the state and the currency.

4.1 The Elementary Currency Order: Some Basic Considerations

Exchange by means of money involves two social activities: the exchange of goods and the use of money. A one-person model, such as a Robinson economy, can explain neither exchange nor the use of money. We need a theory of the behavior of a system of individuals. We must therefore allow explicitly for the institutional framework together with the network of general and specific orders including a control mechanism. In Section 3.5 we introduced the concept of a market community for this purpose. For the case of exchange by means of money we expand this concept to that of a *currency community*. This we understand to be an open community of individuals who enter into purchase and loan agreements with each other by the use of a particular "currency," i.e., a particular kind of money. The exchange of goods is regulated by, among other things, an elementary legal order of the kind described in Chapter 3. The use of money requires, implicitly or explicitly, the existence of an *elementary currency order*. What should such an order regulate? The answer to this question is closely conncected with the question: what is money? The common answer to this seemingly innocuous question is: money is what money does! It serves as a general unit of account, as a general means of exchange and as a store of value, to name just the three most obvious functions of money. The first two functions refer to calculation and payment in money; the third function, though, is not a function of money alone. However, only that which has value is suitable as an accounting unit and a means of exchange.

We start with the first two functions. The elementary currency order determines the unit of account and the form of the means of payment of the currency community; i.e., it "determines" the form of calculating in money and the manner in which payments are made. With J.A. Schumpeter (1970) we imagine payments to consist of bookkeeping entries in an imaginary or actual "social ledger."[1] The word "determined" is not intended to imply that a currency order is created solely by legislation, that money is always "a creature of law" (in the sense of G.F. Knapp (1924, 1)). The currency order may develop spontaneously from the self-interest of individuals. We shall come back to this aspect at the end of this section.

The elementary currency order must regulate the following:

1. The bookkeeping or *accounting unit* in which debts and prices are expressed in terms of a cigarette, a D-mark, a dollar etc., understood to be abstractions;
2. The bookkeeping technique or, in other words, the *means of payment* with the help of which debt contracts and purchase contracts are discharged:

(a) "Bookkeeping" through the transfer of pieces, such as cigarettes, or DM-coins or dollar notes; or
(b) Bookkeeping by crediting or debiting particular accounts.

Both (a) and (b) are to be understood as actual (concrete) events.

The imagined creation of a social bookkeeping system, however, does not yet describe completely the nature of exchange by means of money. We must also have a method of safeguarding the value or the purchasing power of money. For, exchange by means of money presupposes confidence in the value of money, or differently expressed, presupposes the applicability of money (the means of payment) as a store of value.

We have shown in Section 1.4 that the value of money, i.e., the money value P of a commodity basket Wk (of cost of living goods) may be made determinate in two ways:

- By setting and guaranteeing the price p expressed in accounting units of a particular good or basket of goods, e.g., the standard of coinage of 1395 mark for 500 g of fine gold. This is characteristic for a commodity standard, or
- By supplying and guaranteeing a certain amount of means of payment M, as with a paper standard.

We have also argued that we must distinguish between the determination of a general equilibrium on the one side and the description of the process of exchange involving the use of money by which equilibrium is reached on the other. Here we are concerned with the latter. More precisely, we are concerned with the basic conditions for such a process to work satisfactorily, i.e., with the elementary cur-

[1] Schumpeter (1970, 206) writes: "The book transfers in the social ledger also reflect the meaning of the real process in those cases ... where in reality other methods than book transfers are used. This is the basic case for all types of payments. All other kinds of payments are only technical variations on this one case of book transfers. Any difficulties in this basically very simple matter are merely due to our habit of regarding as the basic case of payments the transfer of "pieces of money" and to build all other methods on this case or to try to derive them from it" (translated by W.F. St.). This point was also worked out by G.F. Knapp (1924, 152f., 1st. German edition 1905): "Payment then in its more comprehensive definition does not require the actual delivery of pieces, but a legal transfer of claims and counter-claims in units of value directed to a Central (Clearing) Office. Such transfer may or may not be made by means of actual delivery of chartal pieces, that is, of money; ... ."

rency order. We have argued in Section 1.4 that in the case of exchange by means of money we cannot assume that the individuals will enter into purchase or loan transactions without the knowledge of a price expressed in accounting units. With a commodity standard they know from the very start one price: the standard of coinage. With a paper standard the individuals need also some price information before they enter a transaction, for example, information about the level of the price index P which the currency authority aims at, such as the "unavoidable increase" in prices compared to the preceding period which the German Bundesbank published for a number of years (see Section 7.3). For want of a better expression we shall use the term "price target" of the currency order for the standard of coinage in the case of a commodity standard or for the announced money value P of a commodity basket of cost of living goods with a paper standard. The guarantee of the price target is achieved through the manner in which the supply of the means of payment is regulated.

In order to safeguard the value of money the elementary currency order thus needs two particular regulations: the connection of the accounting unit to specific amounts of goods or baskets of goods, i.e., the price target, and an appropriate regulation of the supply of money. The currency community can, however, freely choose only one of the two elements of its currency order. If it fixes the price target, e.g., the standard of coinage with the commodity standard, it must take care to have the appropriate supply of the means of payment. If it predetermines the supply of means of payment, e.g., the supply of money with a paper standard, it must accept the appropriate price target, i.e., the purchasing power of money. In order to safeguard the value of money, the elementary currency order must determine the following:

1) *The price target*
   (a) The money value of a good (e.g., the standard of coinage) or of a basket of goods (e.g., of the cost-of-living goods);
   (b) The foreign exchange value of another currency or a basket of currencies, for which a price target for goods exists;
2) *Organization of the supply of the means of payment*, i.e., the particular organization of "money creation" and "money destruction."

The elementary currency order of a currency community may thus be split into two suborders: a bookkeeping order and an order to safeguard the value of money. These must be understood as a unit. This is schematized in the following table.

Scheme of an Elementary Currency Order

Bookkeeping order determines	*Value safeguarding order* determines
1. Unit of account	1. Price target
2. Means of payment	2. Supply of means of payment

The elementary currency order contains the minimum regulations of a currency constitution, which "somehow" evolves in each functioning currency community through an "invisible hand," through private contracts, government regulation or a mixture thereof. To clarify this point, take a primitive means of payment of the recent past, the *cigarette currency*. In its pure form it was found, for example, in reasonably well-supplied prisoner-of-war camps (see, e.g., R.A. Radford 1945). In such a case, cigarettes simultaneously perform the service of a good (they are smoked) and the services of money.

We have the following

Elementary Order of a Cigarette Currency

Bookkeeping order	*Value safeguarding order*
1. Accounting unit: one cigarette (abstract)	1. Price target: one $\frac{\text{cigarette (abstract)}}{\text{cigarette (concrete)}}$
2. Means of payment: one cigarette (concrete)	2. Supply of means of payment: supply of cigarettes

The example may *mutatis mutandis* be applied to other money goods, such as silver or gold. G.F. Knapp calls currency orders in which goods for exchange are measured in physical units (counted, weighed etc.) *Autometallism.*[2] Max Weber calls the means of payment used in such cases "*natural means of payment*."[3] Imagine a silver standard in which the accounting unit is a certain weight of silver of a certain quality [e.g., 1 mine (=546.6 g) of fine silver[4]]. The means of payment is fine silver in ingot form of arbitrary size and without stamp. The price target is

$$1\,\frac{\text{mine of silver (abstract)}}{\text{1 mine of fine silver (concrete)}}\,.$$

In this case, the supply of means of payment is identical with the silver supply of the currency community. The example is not as primitive as it may seem. It already implies that standards of weight for silver have been developed. In addition, a standardized form of silver might already exist, such as a standard ingot or the development of silver rings to simplify the circulation of silver.[5]

Just the same, the actual payment transactions remain rather cumbersome. With each individual payment, the parties must verify the weight, genuineness or quality

---

[2] "The quantity of the material is measured in a merely physical manner; in the case of metal, by weighing. The exchange-commodity is always weighed out to the creditor." (G.F. Knapp 1924, 5).

[3] M. Weber (1968, 76).

[4] Babylonian measure of weight for silver.

[5] Cf., e.g., E. Meyer (1910, 825).

of silver. The introduction of coins substantially eases transactions because weight and quality of the metal are certified.[6]

The step from unminted to minted metal, from the simple "fine silver according to weight" means of payment to a *reliable* certified silver coin that may be used with confidence in its weight and quality without testing is very big. In the first case we deal with a currency community which can arise spontaneously in response to the common interest of the users without an actual agreement or legal coercion. In the second case a (public or private) *central agent* must become active. The central agent of the currency community – here the mint – frees the users of money from the necessity of constantly verifying the weight and genuineness of the currency metal.[7] The concept of public regulation mentioned in Chapter 3 becomes relevant in this context. The activity of the central agent must be supervised in an appropriate manner. Agency costs arise. This is certainly true for the regulation of the quality of the coins, while everybody may verify the weight with the proper mint scales. This does not yet mean that we have to have a public mint. However, private mints have not stood the test of time.[8]

Only when the cost of minting, together with the agency cost, are less than the cost of the individual's use of money, for his verification of the weight and quality of the metal, is it economical to use coined instead of ingot metal as a means of payment. The level of the agency cost depends among other things on the general level of the cultural development of a society. The high agency cost may possibly have been responsible for the relatively late development of coinage in the Lydian state in the 7th century B.C..

Once a currency community uses minted metals as a means of payment, the bookkeeping part of the elementary currency order determines, besides the unit of account, the kind of coins, how they are to look, which metal is to be used (in our example silver), what fineness is to be minted, which alloy is to be produced etc.. The value safeguarding part of the elementary currency order determines the standard of coinage as the price target, whether the silver content of the coin must be equal to the standard of coinage, whether free mintage is allowed, what the seigniorage is and so on.

As far as the bookkeeping order is concerned, i.e., from the standpoint of book transfers of the imagined "social ledger," it is irrelevant whether the unit of account (one thaler or one dollar) is printed on a silver plate of a certain weight and fineness or on pieces of paper with little intrinsic value. From the standpoint of bookkeeping, the means of payment are merely data chips. Their intrinsic material value may be arbitrarily small. The only relevant property is that they can fulfill their function.

---

[6] C. Menger (1909, 572): "Only because the monetary metals can be divided ... within technical limits into *identical* pieces is it possible ... *to represent, pay and receive particular amounts of precious metal by the mere addition of the coined pieces.*" (Italics in the original; transl. by W.F. St.).

[7] The users of the coins can at any moment of time directly check whether the central agency works cleanly or not, and whether its seal of quality is credible or not.

[8] On private coinage, see, e.g., C. Menger (1909, 574, col. 2 n. 2). Thus the privately minted coins in California in the 1850's turned out to be substandard and were after 1854 more and more displaced by the coins of the national mint in San Francisco.

As far as their use as means of payment is concerned, both full-bodied coins and pieces of paper, are merely *paytokens* or tickets used as means of payment. Thus G.F. Knapp (1924, 32) correctly subsumes the two cases under one category which he calls the *chartal form* of the means of payment (from the Latin word *charta* which Knapp translates as "ticket or token"). The fact that in our example minted silver plates are used as tokens has therefore nothing to do with the bookkeeping technique: "book entries" are made by a transfer of tokens. The bookkeeping order depends only on the chosen organization of securing or safeguarding the value of money: determination of a standard of coinage as the price target which the coin itself embodies.

The fixed relation of an accounting unit to a particular currency metal, e.g., silver, may exist without the use of full-bodied silver coins, e.g., by the use of paper money as the means of payment. The order of safeguarding the value of money must only be appropriately organized, e.g., by means of the central bank which must exchange its notes at a fixed rate (the standard of coinage) into the currency metal and vice versa. The organization of the currency community including the control of the central agent, is in this case, of course, still more complicated. This will be expressed in the cost of such a currency system, in particular in the agency cost, whose level will in turn depend on the level of development of society. Here, too, we may say that the transition to paper money redeemable in currency metal is economic when it reduces transaction costs. A consistent train of thought leads us finally to the world of paper money proper which is not further redeemable into any money commodity.

In this book we shall deal primarily with models of currency communities within free market economies which use chartal or bank money. Each currency community has its (private or public) central agent[9] which either is part of a predetermined elementary currency order or which determines the currency order itself. All currency aspects are well ordered and the activities of the central agent are successfully controlled by the users of money. We shall later discuss in greater detail the most important variants of a currency community and we will explain them economically.

A Note on the History of Thought of These Ideas:

We have pointed out in this chapter that money need not be a "creature of law." It may also be "determined by the self-interest" of the actors (M. Weber 1968, 29). Or, as C. Menger (1963, 154) writes, it may even develop "without any agreement, without any legislative compulsion, *even without any consideration of public interest*."[10] This is true for the very first beginnings of a currency with natural means of payment. But chartal means of payment need, as we have just seen, a central agency which need not be governmental. Sooner or later, however, in the history of money, the state has become an actor, though not necessarily at the very beginning. C. Menger (1909, 574) expresses this as follows:

---

[9] J.A. Schumpeter (1970, 219): "social authority." With Schumpeter, this includes social usage. For simplicity's sake we assume that the central agent determines the whole currency order which is accepted by the users and thereby becomes social usage.

[10] Italics in the original.

"Money has not arisen by law; its origin is not governmental but a social phenomenon. The sanction of it by governmental authority is foreign to the general concept of money. However, the institution of money ... has been perfected by governmental acceptance and regulation in a manner similar to ... customary law having been perfected by legislation ... ."[11]

With this argumentation Menger argued against G.F. Knapp (1905/1921, English translation 1924), who defended the view that the origin of money could not be explained without a consideration of the state. According to Knapp the attempt to deduce the monetary system without the idea of the state "is not only out of date, but even absurd, however widely these views may still obtain" (G.F. Knapp 1924, VIII). His theory dominated the theoretical discussion in Germany after its publication, despite its incompleteness. For Knapp dealt only with the first half of the currency order, namely the bookkeeping order. This he treated very thoroughly, indeed. Yet he completely omitted what we called the "value safeguarding order" of the currency. He simply ignored what determines the purchasing power of money. The problem of guaranteeing the value of money did not exist for him. For these reasons, Knapp has been justly criticized, devastatingly so, by J.A. Schumpeter (1970, 84).

4.2 Further Discussion of the Elementary Currency Order

In the preceding section we have become acquainted with the concept of the elementary currency order and we have begun to comment on it. We shall now make the comments more precise and thorough. To this end we will start with the bookkeeping part, and then go on to the value-safeguarding part.

4.2.1 The Bookkeeping Order

The concept of money involves both elementary regulations of the bookkeeping order, i.e., the unit of account and means of payment, although in different ways. As already noted at the very beginning of Chapter 1, money in its function as a unit of account is *abstract money*[12] (money of account[13]). In its function as means of payment it is *concrete money* (money proper[13]). Abstract money is the accounting unit in terms of any currency: cigarettes, pounds of fine gold, mark, dollar.[14]

Concrete money represents accounting units which are actually used as means of payment.[15] We assume that abstract and concrete money are expressed in terms of the same unit of account. This need not always to be the case.[16] The following pages relate to the actual forms and properties of concrete money. In the economic literature "money" is regularly understood as "concrete money," i.e., as the normal

---

[11] Translated by W.F. St. – In truth, the origin of money becomes understandable to us "only by our learning to understand the *social* institution discussed here as the unintended result, as the unplanned outcome of specifically *individual* efforts of members of a society." (C. Menger, 1963, 155; italics in the original).

[12] J.G. Koopmans (1933, 247); see above Chapter 1, n. 2.

[13] J.M. Keynes (1930, 5); see above Chapter 1, n. 3.

[14] The "ideal unit," in the literature also called "monetary unit," "unit of account," "unit of value." See A. Nussbaum (1950, 15f.).

[15] Data carrier (metal plate, note, filing card, magnetic tape) plus number of accounting units.

[16] Among many examples see, e.g., W. Eucken (1950, 185ff.)

means of payment of a currency community.[17] The actual means of payment are determined – in our terminology – by the bookkeeping order of the currency community. At the same time it regulates how payments are actually made, i.e., the transfer in the "social ledger." To this extent the value safeguarding order is irrelevant. In particular, there need not exist any physical connection between the means of payment and a particular money good as determined by the value safeguarding order. The only thing relevant for the actual payment is the transfer of units of account by crediting the payee and debiting the payer. How this is actually done depends on the state of the arts in general, and of the level of the "organizational technique" in particular.

The actual transfer of the units of account must be as *reliable* as possible. To this extent the choice of the operational scheme and with it of the units of account (the data carriers) play a role, given the state of technical knowledge and of the "organizational technique" of the currency community. What must be organized flawlessly is first the guarantee of access to particular accounts of the "social ledger," i.e., the ability to make payments and secondly the data processing, i.e., the input, transport, transformation, backing-up and protection of the data.

We group the techniques of bookkeeping transactions in the "social ledger" into three types: payment by transfer of pieces of money; payment by crediting and debiting a bank account; payment by transfer of a money debt.[18] Thus we distinguish the following forms of concrete money:

- piece money,
- book money (bank money),
- credit money.[19]

In the particular case, cigarettes, silver coins, bank notes are piece money. Book money consists, e.g., of deposits with commercial banks or the central bank ("Giralgeld"). Credit money includes all other claims for money which are not payable on demand and not absolutely secure (L.v. Mises 1953, 61) such as bills of exchange.

Piece money may, as a we already pointed out, be either natural or chartal means of payment. The latter may be coins or paper money, and the coins may be full-bodied or not.

The forms of money which we have listed have the following interrelationships:

[17] For the case of natural means of payment, i.e., the commodities which have become means of exchange (cattle, shells, salt) see C. Menger (1909, 561).

[18] Payment by *direct* transfer of "primary securities," the latter as understood by J.G. Gurley and E.S. Shaw (1960, 93). "Primary securities include all debt and equity issues of nonfinancial spending units." For these authors, however, primary securities are not "money," not even partially money.

[19] L.v. Mises (1953, 61) understands credit money to be "... that sort of money which constitutes a claim against any physical or legal person. But these claims must not be both payable on demand and absolutely secure; ..." On the problem to what extent, e.g., bank notes or bank deposits must be claims on something and hence must be understood to be credit money, see below Section 4.5.

Forms of Money and their Interrelationships

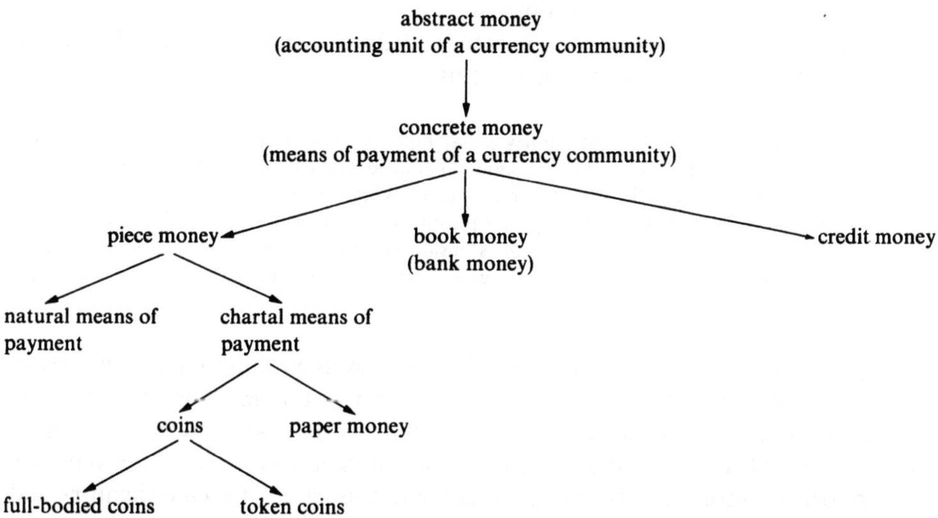

Means of payment may also be classified according to their redeemability. We speak of "redeemable" and "definitive" money.

Definitive money includes all non-redeemable means of payment such as full-bodied silver or gold coins in a silver or gold standard, or central-bank notes in the case of paper money proper.[20] Definitive bank money can be imagined, but as far as we know has nowhere been observed. The currency order determines which means of payment are definitive.

How may definitive money be recognized? Knapp (1924, 102) defines as follows:

> "Money is definitive if, when payment is made in it, the business is completely concluded: first for the payer, secondly for recipient, and thirdly for the issuer of the money. The payer is no longer under any obligation [as, e.g., in the case of bills of exchange, R.R.], the recipient has no further rights either against the payer or against the State, if the State has issued the money."

If the payment is made in *redeemable* ("provisional") *money*, at least the recipient still has a claim against the issuer.

There are legal difficulties with definitive paper money. Bank notes which are redeemable into gold or foreign exchange may be understood as a claim of the owner on the issuer of the money to pay in gold coins to the same extent, or the payment of, say, US-dollars at a fixed rate of exchange. But, where is the subject of the claim of definitive paper money? K. Duden (1968, 7) observes:

> "... our legal concept of claims and debts fits very badly the law of bank notes ever since they have ceased to be redeemable into other money (in Germany since the law of August 4, 1914)." (Translated by W.F. St.)

[20] See G.F. Knapp (1924, 69). There may be more than one kind of definitive money, e.g., in France before 1914 where both gold pieces and silver five-franc pieces were definitive money (ibid., 104).

Duden proposes to supplant the figure of "claims" by the legal figure of "membership": "the owner of money (as) member of a community,"[21] a thought which fits our concept of a currency community.

In the more recent American literature, definitive money is called "outside money," and redeemable money "inside money."

"The distinguishing feature of outside money is that it does not constitute a redeemable claim to any physical asset.... The world has known both commodity outside money – gold and silver coins provide the most familiar example – and fiat outside money." (L.H. White 1984b, 703).

The concepts of inside and outside money were introduced by J.G. Gurley and E.S. Shaw (1960, 73), though with a different meaning. They call liabilities "inside the private sector" inside money, and outside money claims "against the world *outside* the private sector." We use in this book the two concepts in the sense of White.

Finally, means of payment may be classified by their suitability as means of repayment of money debts, i.e., those which, when in doubt, must be used to satisfy a money debt, and those for which this is not the case. Clarification of this issue serves to reduce transaction costs, but it does presuppose governmental recognition of the particular money. A distinction is made in this case between obligatory and facultative money.[22]

Obligatory money, or legal tender (in German: gesetzliches Zahlungsmittel) are such means of payments which the creditor is not privileged to refuse if it is offered ("tendered") by a debtor in payment of his debt.[23]

On the *Historical development of legal tender* see A. Nussbaum (1950, 45ff.). He gives also a brief survey on the legal theory and practice of the refusal to accept legal tender. Common law and Roman law differ in this respect. Penalties for the non-acceptance of legal tender have not existed in Central European or in Anglo-American law at least since the nineteenth century (A. Nussbaum, 1950, 53f.). Yet, history knows of cases of severe penalties for the non-acceptance of legal tender. "From Marco Polo we learn that, in the 13th century, Chinese law made rejection of imperial paper money punishable by death, and twenty years in chains or, in some cases, death was the penalty provided for the refusal to accept French assignates. Early English law punished repudiation as lèse-majesté. At the time of the American Revolution, non-acceptance of Continental notes was treated as an enemy act and sometimes a forfeiture of the debt. The Latin Codes still preserve, although in a very attenuated form, penalties for the non-acceptance of legal tender." (A. Nussbaum 1950, 53; references can be found there)

According to the Currency Act (Währungsgesetz) of the Federal Republic of Germany, the only unlimited legal tender are the notes of the German Bundesbank. (The original law referred to the Bank Deutscher Länder, Art. 1, Sec. 2. No. 1 Währungsgesetz). Federal coins are legal tender only within limits. Mark-coins denominated in mark must be accepted up to mark 20,–; coins denominated in pfennige up to mark 5,– (Art. 14 Deutsche Bundesbank Act; Art. 5 Münzgesetz).

Legal tender need not at the same time be definitive money of the currency community. "Provisional" (redeemable) money may also be legal tender: the notes of

[21] K. Duden (1968, 7, n. 12a).

[22] G.F. Knapp (1924, 97).

[23] A. Nussbaum (1950, 45f.).

the Bank of England after 1833 and of the Deutsche Reichsbank after 1909 were also legal tender. Legal practice in the Federal Republic of Germany has raised doubts

"that the creditor of claims going into the millions must accept notes rather than a transfer on his bank account."[24]

A Note on the History of Thought:

The older economic or legal literature frequently limits the concept of money to legal tender. "The other money is called 'imperfect,' 'not real' [*uneigentlich*], 'customary' or it is simply not called money."[25] C. Menger (1909, 602) observes that the clarification of which means of payment are legal tender is part of the system of governmental regulations which serve the simplification of transactions and simultaneously meet the needs of the administration of justice; i.e., which lower transaction costs. By designating certain means of payment as obligatory money, the state "undoubtedly" improves (from the standpoint of the administration of justice) this kind of money *in its property as a means of payment.* The assignates and mandates of the French Revolution, whose fixed exchange was enforced by the guillotine and a number of legal regulations which were intended to prevent any attempt of the creditors to escape the effects of the enforced rate of exchange, were from the standpoint of the administration of justice and perhaps also from that of the debtor, who had already satisfied all their credit needs, without any doubt the ideal "means of payment." But were they also the ideal *money*? This is not a legal but an economic question which the history of money has answered, ..." (Italics in the original, translation by W.F.St.)

4.2.2 The Order of Safeguarding the Value of Money

As discussed, we distinguish between two methods of determining the general value of money, the commodity and the paper standard.

1. With the *commodity standard* the price p of a particular good or bundle of goods expressed in accounting units is given and guaranteed. The means of payments are either full-bodied coins or paper money (or token coins) redeemable into the money commodity (or a basket of money commodities).
2. With the *paper standard* a particular amount of M is given and guaranteed. The means of payment are paper money or token coins. There is no promise of redemption.

Furthermore, we have seen that also in the case of the paper standard, individuals must have an idea, from the very beginning of contractual negotiations, of what the according units represent in real terms. In our terminology: they must in this case also have an idea of the price target. The price target may refer to a particular good (e.g., gold) or a basket of goods (e.g., cost-of-living goods).

With a commodity standard the price target is precisely predescribed to the central agent by contract or the state. The power of discretion to create and destroy

[24] K. Duden (1968, 8) translated by W.F.St.

[25] A. Nussbaum (1925, 24) translated by W.F.St.

means of payment is, as a rule, very narrowly limited. With a paper standard the corresponding agreements or regulations are considerably less strict.

The question: "rules or authority" is a central problem for the safeguarding of the value of money. Simplifying we can distinguish between the following two limiting cases:

1. *Strict rules*, i.e., a strict tying of the central agent by private contract or the state to unambiguously formulated fixed rules, to which the central agent must strictly adhere in supplying the currency community with means of payment. An example is the Peel's Bank Act of July 19, 1844 which permitted the Bank of England to issue notes against certain money claims up to 14 million pounds, beyond this only against gold and silver ingots at a fixed price with the further restriction that the silver ingots could not exceed more than a quarter of the gold or silver ingots held by the issuing department.
2. *Freedom from all rules*, or more precisely, more discretion on the part of the central agent concerning the regulation of the supply of means of payment, or the determination of the price target of the currency community respectively.[26] For example the Deutsche Bundesbank Act (BBkG) limits the discretion of the Bundesbank in only a very general manner.

According to Article 3 of the Deutsche Bundesbank Act the Deutsche Bundesbank regulates "... the amount of money in circulation and of credit supplied to the economy, ..., with the aim of safeguarding the currency, ..." It is responsible for the proper handling by banks of domestic and external payments. Art. 12 BBkG obliges the Bundesbank "to support the general economic policy of the Federal Government subject to safeguards in performing its own tasks. In exercising the power conferred on it by this Act it shall be independent of instructions from the Federal Government." The legislator does not determine a particular price or quantity-of-money target. (We use the English translation of the Bundesbank Act in Deutsche Bundesbank Special Series No. 7, 1987.)

Our two examples have referred to governmental central agencies. Yet, the central agent may also be a private firm, e.g., a private bank of issue, which commits itself legally vis-à-vis its money users to obey certain rules. In other words, the obligation to obey certain regulations may have the character of civil or public law.

Thus we get the following scheme for the value safeguarding part of a chartally organized currency order:

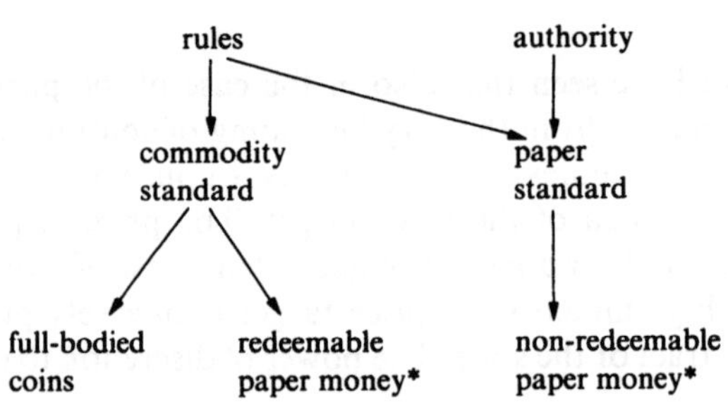

[26] On this point see the classic article by H.C. Simons (1936).

* Paper money which is or is not redeemable into a money commodity at a fixed rate of exchange; non-redeemable paper money may, however, be redeemable into means of payment of orther currency orders.

To simplify we did not mention token coins or bank money. They belong in this case to the category of "paper money."

The regulation of money debts must be seen in the context of the construction of a value safeguarding order. In particular it must specify what in doubtful cases is the *content of a money debt.* An unambiguous answer to this question facilitates money payments; it lowers transaction costs. Two answers are imaginable and both are found in reality, the "metallistic" and the "nominalistic" principle. According to the *metallistic* (or valoristic) principle the debt consists either of a certain amount of the money good (e.g., fine silver) or that amount of paper money which is necessary to buy a certain amount of the money good. According to the *nominalistic* principle the debt consists merely of a certain quantity of accounting units.

While the metallistic principle is applicable only to the commodity standard, the nominalistic principle is applicable both to the paper standard and the commodity standard.

This was apparently the case in the German Reich at the time of the gold standard before 1914. The creditors were at the time either unaware of this fact, or they were confident that the mark would continue to be redeemed into gold at the standard of coinage of 1395 mark per 500 g fine gold, or that the suspension of redeemability at the outbreak of war was expected to be temporary and be reversed after the war. The hyperinflation led to bitter disappointments. Since then, nominalism in Germany has a bad reputation. Yet, it is a reasonable principle of organization which needs not lead to injustices – provided the purchasing power of money is kept reasonably stable.

Consider the *nominalistic* principle further. It treats money debts as debts of a certain nominal value. The principle "mark = mark" prevails. The accounting unit is also the *standard of deferred payments.* The obligation to pay 30 thaler is the obligation to pay what the currency order at the time of payment recognizes as 30 thaler. The creditor bears the risk of devaluation, the debtor that of appreciation. Neither party can sue at the courts for unexpected losses. "It is fundamental that contracting ... in terms of any currency involves an element of speculation and it is of the essence of nominalism ... that neither party can complain about the outcome of a speculation which has miscarried."[27] The parties to the contract may, if they wish, protect themselves, e.g., by an index clause, provided no legal regulations prohibit such agreements; "if they fail to do so, although they anticipate disarrangements of monetary value, they must be taken to have accepted the risks involved."[28]

It is in principle possible to substitute private clauses for the guarantee of money debts for the lack of public guarantees. This is, however, likely to be more expensive than if the central agent itself guarantees the value of money. Consider the private

[27] F.A. Mann (1971, 273).

[28] F.A. Mann (1971, 76).

guarantee of the value of money further. The bookkeeping part of the elementary currency order is applied as before. The accounting unit and the means of payment continue to be used. However, the sum of a money claim is not fixed at the time of entering the debt but only when it is due. An index clause determines unequivocally how the owed sum, expressed in accounting units, is to be determined by the price of fine gold or of other goods and services, or by a cost of living (or any other) index (hence the expression "index clause" or "indexation"), or by the exchange rate of a foreign currency. Depending on the basis for valuation one speaks of a foreign exchange clause, a gold clause, a commodity price clause, a fixed salary clause etc.

Index clauses are in the Federal Republic of Germany permissible only to a limited degree (see Art. 3 Währungsgesetz, also the article "Value guarantee clauses, synopsis of the Bundesbank's policy in granting permits," Monthly Report of the Deutsche Bundesbank, April 1971, pp. 24ff.).

4.3 Economic Explanation of an Elementary Currency Order: The Bookkeeping Order

The preceding two sections have discussed the concepts of a currency community and an elementary currency order. We will now deal with their economic explanation. We consider first the bookkeeping order, that is, the economic explanation of the accounting unit and the means of payment of a currency community and with it the use of money. This is an ancient theme of monetary theory, for which the concept of transaction costs has been used implicitly or explicitly for a long time. The typical procedure is to start with a barter economy and to show that it is in everyone's interest to use a particular good as a unit of account and general means of exchange (or means of payment). It describes how the use of money might have developed from the barter economy on the basis of the idealtypical rational behavior of individuals, even though it might not have developed in reality in this way. We will proceed analogously.[29] Our considerations deal with simultaneous purchase and sales transactions ("pari passu" transactions). We will deal with the economic justification of other transactions, such as money loans, further below in Section 4.5.

4.3.1 An Illustration of the Advantages of a General Unit of Account

Assume a barter economy. How many exchange relations in one direction do exist with two goods? Of course, only one: good one for good two. What about four

[29] C. Menger uses this "causal-genetic" style of explanation. He writes (1963, 225): "The knowledge thus obtained is not historical in the empirical-realistic sense of this word. However, it is knowledge which, in contrast to the phrases 'originality,' 'primeval nature,' 'organic origin' of law etc., indicates at any rate a significant advance in the theoretical understanding of that process by which law" – [he discusses in this context the social institution of law, but his argument applies equally to money] – "came into being in its most original form. Indeed it has the advantage of offering us not only the superficial picture of the development under discussion, but also of revealing the motivating forces which led to the genesis of law with the growing insight of man into his interests."

goods? Consider the following transactions matrix:

	1	2	3	4
1	●	•	•	•
2		●	•	•
3			●	•
4				●

In both directions (1 for 2, 2 for 1 etc.) there are twelve exchange relations, in one direction six:

$$\pi_{12}\ ,\quad \pi_{13}\ ,\quad \pi_{14}\ ,\quad \pi_{23}\ ,\quad \pi_{24}\ ,\quad \pi_{34}\ .$$

The exchange relations π_{12} etc. indicate how many units of good 1 are exchanged against one unit of 2, etc. With n goods there are $\frac{n(n-1)}{2}$ exchange relations in one direction. Thus, with ten goods, there exist 45 exchange relations.

In a pure barter economy, each good can be exchanged *directly* against any other goods. But it may also be exchanged *indirectly*. There exists, therefore, an arbitrage problem of direct exchange compared to indirect exchange. The following example will clarify this on the assumption that transaction costs are zero.

Suppose a household has good 3 and would like to exchange it against good 2. There are now two possibilities. It can exchange $\frac{\text{good 3}}{\text{good 2}}$ *directly*; but it can exchange also *indirectly*, e.g., via good 1.

$$\frac{\text{good 3}}{\text{good 1}}\ ,\quad \frac{\text{good 1}}{\text{good 2}} \rightarrow \frac{\text{good 3}}{\text{good 2}}\ .$$

With many goods the chains of indirect exchange may be rather long. Assume that indirect exchange is more profitable than direct exchange. In our example this means

$$\pi^0_{31} \cdot \pi^0_{12} > \pi^0_{32}\ ,$$

e.g., $$\frac{1\text{ kg wheat}}{3\text{ kg barley}} \cdot \frac{2\text{ kg barley}}{1\text{ kg oats}} > \frac{1\text{ kg wheat}}{3\text{ kg oats}}\ .$$

In such a case the individual households may become arbitrageurs. They need have no goods in the initial situation. In the given example the arbitrageur may enter into the following two exchange transactions: by way of direct exchanges he promises to deliver 1/3 kg wheat (good 3) per kg oats (good 2). He gets the wheat by a profitable indirect exchange, namely by trading 2/3 kg wheat for 1 kg oats. He uses 1/3 kg wheat to pay his direct exchange debt; another 1/3 of wheat is his arbitrage profit. This is analogously true for all households.

With the assumed exchange relations π_{ij}^0 all households will notify the imagined Walrasian auctioneer of arbitrage transactions beyond all limits or they will try in any way whatever to enter into arbitrage contracts with each other. This will lead to an accelerated conversion of the direct and indirect exchange relations wheat/oats until, with transaction costs zero,

$$\pi_{31} \cdot \pi_{12} = \pi_{32} \ .$$

This is the *arbitrage equilibrium.*

Note that the arbitrage equilibrium in principle may also be reached without any actual arbitrage transactions. It suffices that arbitrage is *possible* and that the *expectation* of possible arbitrage transactions enters into the calculation of the negotiating parties.

The arbitrage problem may be visualized in the following graph:

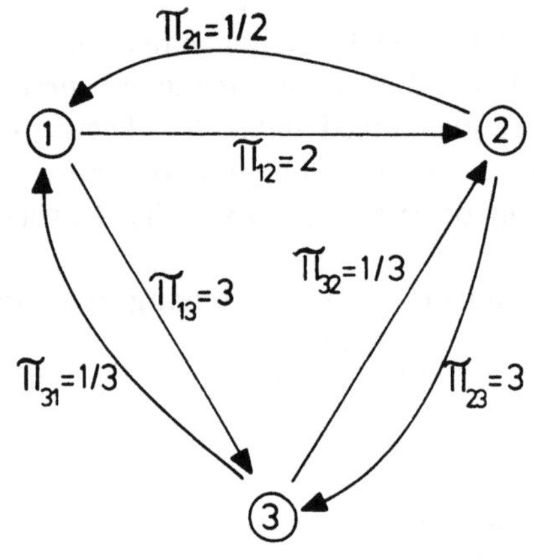

The corners 1, 2, 3 are the three goods; the numbers besides the arrows are the relevant exchange relations π_{ij} expressed in quantity units, e.g., kg wheat/kg barley etc.

In the present example we have

$$\frac{1}{3}\frac{(\text{good } 3)}{(\text{good } 1)} \cdot 2 \frac{(\text{good } 1)}{(\text{good } 2)} > \frac{1}{3}\frac{(\text{good } 3)}{(\text{good } 2)} \ .$$

In *arbitrage equilibrium*, on the other hand:

$$\frac{1}{3}\frac{(\text{good } 3)}{(\text{good } 1)} \cdot 2 \frac{(\text{good } 1)}{(\text{good } 2)} = \frac{2}{3}\frac{(\text{good } 3)}{(\text{good } 2)} \ .$$

This case is pictured as follows

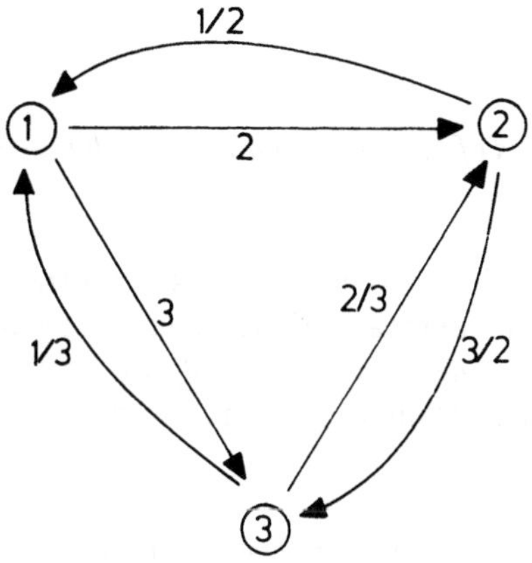

If all parties calculate only in terms of good 1, we are left with only two exchange relations:

$$\frac{\text{good 1}}{\text{good 3}}, \quad \frac{\text{good 1}}{\text{good 2}}.$$

Good 1 is simultaneously applied as the measure of value in the case of direct exchange of good 2 for good 3. The *arbitrage problem* of direct exchange vis-à-vis all possibilities of indirect exchange disappears.

If the parties to the exchanges use, as members of a currency community, only quantities of *one* good as the *general accounting unit*, then the discussed arbitrage problem of direct compared to indirect exchange does not arise. All transactions take place only at the $n - 1$ exchange relations expressed in the general unit of account. The partners to the market transactions need now to know only the particular "announced" or "existing" $n - 1$ exchange relations, instead of the $\frac{n(n-1)}{2}$ relations. This is evidently an enormous simplification and thus a lowering of cost in a world with transaction costs. With transaction costs it is thus profitable for all contracting parties to use a particular good (abstractly) as a common unit of account. One might imagine that money has originated that way, i.e., that a traded good was first used as accounting unit and only later became the general means of exchange. J. Laughlin, for example, believes that money has indeed developed in such a manner.[30]

[30] J. Laughlin (1903, 7) quoted in P. Einzig (1951, 369): "So natural is this operation of the human mind that the evolution of the standard concept must have preceded the concept of the medium of exchange." For a survey, see P. Einzig (op. cit. 264).

In principle one might use a basket of goods instead of a single good as the general unit of account. This would however increase the cost of calculation. Therefore it should be economically more reasonable to stick to a single money commodity.

4.3.2 An Illustration of the Advantages of General Means of Exchange as a Means of Payment

The so-called *coincidence problem* of direct exchange plays a central role in the rational explanation for the use of a general means of exchange, that is the problem of the mutual agreement of the exchange wishes ("wheat for barley/barley for wheat"). C. Menger (1909, 557) quotes from the report of the Africa explorer V.L. Cameron to illustrate this point.

> "To obtain boats to proceed on my Tanganyika cruise was my first consideration; but the owners of two promised me by Said ibn Salim at Unyanyembé were away, and therefore I could not procure them. I discovered a good one, however, belonging to Syde ibn Habib – who had met Livingstone both in Sékélétu's country and in Manyuéma – and managed to hire it from his agent though at an extortionate rate.
>
> The arrangement at the hiring was rather amusing. Syde's agent wished to be paid in ivory, of which I had none; but I found that Mohammed ibn Salib had ivory, and wanted cloth. Still, as I had no cloth, this did not assist me greatly until I heard that Mohammed ibn Gharib had cloth and wanted wire. This I fortunately possessed. So I gave Mohammed ibn Gharib the requisite amount in wire, upon he handed over cloth to Mohammed ibn Salib, who in his turn gave Syde ibn Habib's agent the wished-for ivory. Then he allowed me to have the boat."[31]

Menger adds: "Such a difficult exchange process hinders also the occupational division of labor, and might make it even impossible."[32] In other words, the transaction costs are very high, and might be sufficiently high to prevent any trade. "Market failure" is the result (K.J. Arrow 1969).

If the trading parties of a market community use a general means of exchange which they use regularly for *indirect* exchange the coincidence problem becomes the substantially simpler problem of selling offered goods against the general means of exchange, or to buy the demanded goods for the general means of exchange. This reduces transaction costs.

As a rule, though not necessarily, the general means of exchange (or more precisely: its unit of measurement) will serve at the same time as the general unit of account.

It may be supposed that those goods become general means of exchange which cause the lowest transaction costs,[33] or, which have the highest degree of saleableness as C. Menger (1892, 242) would say.[34] It can not be said in general which goods

[31] V.L. Cameron, Across Africa, (1877, I. 246ff.).

[32] C. Menger (1909, 557) translated by W.F. St.

[33] J. Niehans (1969, 717); for further literature, see Suggested Readings to this chapter.

[34] C. Menger (1892, 243) stresses this point: "*the theory of money necessarily presupposes a theory of the saleableness of goods.*" (Italics in the original).

that will be. In fact, primitive societies used very different goods as means of exchange. Here a few examples from a varied list given by H. Wagenführ (1959, 33):

agate (Borneo)	mahagony wood (Honduras)
fish hooks (Indochina)	mats (Hebrides)
antimony powder (Sudan middle)	mulberry bark (Polynesia)
axes (Kongo)	mussles (South Sea)
bread grain (Egypt)	needles (Gold Coast)
butter bricks (Tibet)	nephrites (Carribean)
dates (Oasis Siwa)	opium (Hainan)
peanuts (Niger)	mother-of-pearl (New Guinea)
feathers (Melanesia)	pepper corns (Peru)
dried fish (Island)	rice (Korea)
flint (Melanesia)	rum (New South Wales)
fish teeth (New Caledonia)	sago (East Indonesia)
glas goods (West Africa)	salt (Abyssinia)
resin balls (Malay Archipelago)	silk (China)
deer leather (China)	tea (Mongolia)
millet (Somalia)	jaspis (Udschidschi)
jadeit (China)	animal teeth (Fidji Islands)
camphor (Middle Sudan)	onions (Sudan middle)
cowrie mussles (Siam)	

Menger (1892, 248) argues in this context as follows: "With the extension of traffic in space and with the expansion over ever longer intervals of time of prevision for satisfying material needs, each individual would learn, from his own economic interest, to take good heed that he bartered his less saleable goods for those special commodities which displayed, beside the attraction of being highly saleable in the particular region, a wide range of saleableness both in time and place. These wares would be qualified by their costliness, easy transportability, and fitness for preservation ..., to ensure to the possessor a power, not only 'here' and 'now,' but as nearly as possible unlimited in space and time generally over all other market-goods at economic prices." (Similarly C. Menger 1909, 561). Menger (1909, 561) continues: in addition, we have the properties important for exchange transactions of *divisibility* and *fungibility*. This explains why precious metals became the general means of exchange beyond all local borders.

C. Menger (1909, 600) considers the use of a general means of exchange to be the essential feature of money. What the general concept of money and, with that, its nature determines is its function of serving as a general means of the exchange. This is, according to Menger, the original function of money. Its function of serving as a measure of value and its other functions would be "consecutive functions of the medium-of-exchange function of money" (599).

We have so far illustrated the economic advantages of the use of natural means of payment compared to (direct) barter. Further savings in transaction costs are thinkable if the currency community proceeds to the use of chartal means of payment. The first step of this transition from the natural means of payment consists in minting full-bodied coins. As shown in Section 4.1, this is an important step. It requires the introduction of a central agent of the currency community which among other things issues the chartal means of payment. The agency problem, which we have also hinted at in Section 4.1, arises and must be dealt with.

The history of the further development of chartal money might be imagined as follows: the first central agents are one or more mints. At some later stage private banks arise which issue notes redeemable into gold. Later the note issue becomes a monopoly of the central bank. Finally, the redeemability of notes and the price target with respect to a money good is given up: the paper standard with bank notes as definitive means of payment has come into existence. Check payments and bank transfers already exist before that step. With the progress of information technique a clearing traffic in credit cards is developed to the "point of sale system" in retail trade or by the home banking procedure.

Note: in this evolutionary process the accounting unit is always linked with the definitive means of payment; there exists no "ghost money" (see L.H. White 1984b, 704).

4.4 Economic Explanation of the Elementary Currency Order: The Value Safeguarding Order

We deal in this section with the economic explanation of the first partial regulation of the order to safeguard the value of money: the price target. The second partial regulation of the value safeguarding order, i.e., the regulation of the supply of the means of payment is one of the main topics of our book and will be discussed in later chapters.

By "price target" we understand, in connection with a currency order the given or desired money value of a good or a basket of goods. The monetary value P of a basket of goods Wk of cost of living goods (or its inverse, the purchasing power of money as defined by the cost of living) is a special case of such a price target. Once the monetary value of a particular good is determined, the monetary value of any commodity basket of cost of living goods, or the purchasing power of money, is determined in general equilibrium. If the monetary value of a single good is held constant, and if the real exchange relationships among all goods remain constant, as is the case in a stationary equilibrium, the purchasing power of money remains constant. This is a theoretical limiting case. In general we cannot count on this happening, and we must be aware of whether a constant price target is defined as the price of a single good or as the purchasing power of money.

As discussed, exchange by means of money is imaginable only if the individual traders connect the general accounting unit with something real. It is simplest if they all count on a fixed monetary value of a particular good when engaging in transactions, i.e., if the price target of a currency community refers only to a single good. The arbitrage problem discussed in the preceding section does then not arise. Transaction costs are saved.

With only a single transaction it becomes irrelevant to which good the price target refers, i.e., which good is in fact used as a unit of account. This is not so when exchanges occur time after time. In such a case the fact that the real exchange relationships may change must be considered. In such a case it becomes advisable that the currency community selects for its price target a commodity whose exchange relation vis-à-vis other goods fluctuates as little as possible, e.g., gold instead of green salad (Niehans 1978, 123). A good will be selected whose demand and supply has only little seasonal or other known variations. Random fluctuations ("real shocks") may be accepted except if the price target is directed towards a combination of several goods, i.e., a commodity basket *Wk*, instead towards a single good. With a commodity basket the random fluctuations of individual prices may in part cancel each other out. The commodity currency suggested by B. Graham (1937) is based on this idea.

It would be ideal if there existed a money good whose supply and demand function are perfectly stable, so that changes in, say, the price of wheat (expressed in this monetary commodity) can at least not be reduced to changes in the demand for or supply of the monetary commodity. The older literature refers in this connection to an "intrinsic exchange value" of the money good. The ideal is a money commodity with "unalterable intrinsic exchange value."[35] Carl Menger writes on this point:

"With the help of such a money good we could ... correctly estimate the local differences and the movement in the exchange relations. For, if the exchange relation between the former (i.e., the good with a stable intrinsic exchange value!) and any other good were to change, we should know a priori and without any further investigation, that this difference or change refers back to explanations of price formation which are on the side of the particular good."[36]

This ideal case is of course illusory.

In choosing the monetary commodity, or as we might say, the accounting good, a further consideration plays a role: the ultimate goal of all economic activities is consumption. Why not, therefore, choose a commodity basket Wk^0 which corresponds to the annual needs of an average family? Random fluctations of supply and demand of the individual components of the basket may partially offset each other so that the "intrinsic exchange value" of Wk^0 is likely to be relatively constant. In such a case the price target of a currency community might be the monetary value P of the commodity basket Wk^0 of cost of living goods. The individuals now use for their negotiations units of Wk^0 instead of, say, gold. If we allow for a series of transactions it becomes rational to hold the monetary value P of the commodity basket constant. In the case of a commodity standard this presupposes an appropriate variation in the standard of coinage (an idea of I. Fisher 1911, 348) or an appropriate public intervention in the market for the monetary commodity. With a paper standard, the monetary value P of the commodity basket Wk^0 may, in principle, be regulated precisely by an appropriate variation in the volume of money M.

What is the connection between a constant standard of coinage, say, of gold, and the purchasing power of money (here of gold)?

Consider the following example:

The commodity basket of cost of living goods Wk^0 consists, in a n-good economy only of goods 1 and 2 in the following quantities:

$$Wk^0 = \{x_1^0, x_2^0\} \ .$$

[35] C. Menger (1909, 594).

[36] C. Menger (1909, 594).

The monetary value of this commodity basket is

$$P = p_1 x_1^0 + p_2 x_2^0 \; . \tag{4-1}$$

The price of gold p_n is known by assumption and is constant. In general equilibrium the relative prices $p_1/p_n, \ldots, p_{n-1}/p_n$ are determined and with it the value in terms of gold of the commodity basket of cost of living goods Wk^0:

$$\frac{P}{p_n} = \frac{p_1}{p_n} x_1^0 + \frac{p_2}{p_n} x_2^0 \; . \tag{4-2}$$

As a result, the absolute ("money") prices $p_1, \ldots, p_n$ and the nominal monetary value P of Wk^0 are also determined. In calculating a cost of living index the monetary value of a commodity basket of cost of living goods Wk in current prices P_t is compared with the monetary value P_0 of the same Wk-value in the basis year. In the case of the gold standard considered here, in which p_n is constant, the price index P_t/P_0 measures both the development in the purchasing power of money $(1/P)$ and that of gold (p_n/P).

From (4-2) it can immediately be seen that P/p_n is relatively stable when the p_i/p_n are relatively stable.

Is it necessary that our reasoning also holds if, with a paper standard, the monetary value P of the commodity basket Wk^0, i.e., the inflation rate, is to be kept constant? Will not an a priori known inflation rate of whatever magnitude serve as well? In a world without transaction costs this question must be answered with "yes;" but when transaction costs arise the answer to the question is "no." As is well known, in such a case many prices remain temporarily constant ("rigid"). The period of time over which individual prices p_i remain constant differs with different goods. It follows that the relative prices p_i/P will fluctuate even with an approximately constant rate of inflation, and will do so the more, the greater the rate of inflation of P is.[37]

This will continue until a definite upper limit of the inflation rate P is reached, after which all goods prices p_i will rise practically simultaneously. This is the case of a hyperinflation.[38]

A more limited rate of inflation will therefore lead to fluctuations in relative prices which are superimposed on real changes. In this case, it becomes more difficult for the individuals to recognize the real influences which alone are relevant for economic decisions.[39] Even a perfectly anticipated inflation causes, therefore, additional cost of information. These costs and the associated unavoidable inefficiencies may even be greater than the losses in the real value of cash balances caused by inflation.

But even if it were possible to keep the projected value of P more or less constant, the paper standard is not without problems. If the arbitrage problem discussed in

[37] Numerous empirical investigations justify this hypothesis. See, e.g., M.D. Bordo (1980) and S. Fischer (1982).

[38] F.D. Graham (1930).

[39] M. Friedman (1977, 467) says on this point in his Nobel lecture: "The more volatile the rate of general inflation, the harder it becomes to extract the signal about the relative prices from the absolute prices: the broadcast about relative prices is, as it were, being jammed by the noise coming from the inflation broadcast ...."

Section 4.3.1 is to be eliminated the individuals must agree on the real definition of the unit of account, in the present case on the precise content of the commodity basket *Wk*. But this will hardly be the case.[40] In practice the exact calculation of a cost of living index is known only to a few experts. Beyond this it is frequently unclear which index expressses the target of the currency authority at all. Moreover, the cost of living vary from location to location and for each individual. For this reason it must be supposed that the arbitrage problem remains unsolved with a paper standard, at least to a certain degree.

If the rate of inflation is not prefectly anticipated and if its changes are substantial, the contracting parties may help themselves by index clauses (see above, Section 4.2).

If all members of the currency community index their money claims or debts in terms of the same commodity or a bundle of commodities, the arbitrage problem mentioned disappears. One could imagine a development in this direction based only on the self-interest of the individuals without any agreement or any legislative compulsion.

In addition to the argument that a stabilization of the value of money minimizes calculation and transaction costs, there is in the older literature also the not generally accepted argument that a stabilization of the value of money would lead to a smoothing of economic development. I. Fisher or R.G. Hawtrey are representatives of this view.[41] On the other hand Wicksell (1936, 194) and Hayek (1931a, 105ff.) warned against such a policy. Hayek points out that an active monetary policy might lead to a destabilization of business cycles rather than to its stabilization.[42]

The discussion of the Philipps curve trade-off is part of the relevant modern discussion, a discussion which was in general resolved against a monetary policy oriented on employment considerations.[43]

To summarize this section: to allow exchange by means of money it suffices to define the accounting unit in terms of a *single* good. This is the case with a commodity standard. In order to reduce the cost of calculation it is in this case advisable to use a monetary commodity, e.g., gold, whose exchange relation with respect to the other goods fluctuates as little as possible. The purchasing power of money is, however, in this case subject to the "caprices of the production and consumption of gold or of the demand for the circulation of coins." (K. Wicksell, 1936, 194).

---

[40] Because of the costs of information involved. Of course, information about the precise content of a cost-of-living commodity basket are available and the weights of the index are only infrequently changed. But such commodity baskets are rather complicated and awkward.

[41] See, e.g., I. Fisher (1911, Chapter 5) or the writings of R.G. Hawtrey. For a survey of Hawtrey's writings see G. Haberler (1958, 15).

[42] He saw in the attempt to stabilize the price level one of the most important causes of the crisis of 1931 and of the price collapse at that time. See F.A. Hayek (1931b, V).

[43] The Phillips curve relates the rate of change of money wages (or prices) to the level of unemployment. The lower the unemployment rate, the more rapid the rate of wage or price increase (see R. Dornbusch and S. Fischer 1987, 467). M. Friedman (1968) and E. Phelps (1972) argued, on theoretical grounds, that a long-run trade-off between inflation and unemployment was illusory. Modern empirical analysis broadly supports this view (op. cit. 170). For West Germany see, e.g., R. Richter and F. Diener (1987).

With a paper standard, on the other hand, a stable purchasing power of money may be, at least theoretically, easily achievable. All that is necessary is to turn "the" value of money itself, i.e., the monetary value P of a basket of, say, cost of living goods Wk, into the price target. If this is done it becomes useful to keep the value of P as stable as possible in order to save transaction costs, in analogy to keeping the standard of coinage constant with a gold standard. By making the purchasing power of money itself the price target, that target necessarily becomes vague. No clear real anchoring or definition of the accounting unit exists. On the users' side this may contribute to the need to employ resources for otherwise unnecessary arbitrage transactions. On the supply side the control problems become more complicated. The resulting problems and difficulties are the subject matter of later chapters (see below Chapters 7 and 8).

4.5 Money Loans

In Section 4.3 we dealt with the economic explanation of exchange with the use of money in a one-period economy, i.e., in a world in which there is only a single and simultaneous exchange by means of money. In reality, however, exchange by means of money over several periods of time plays a most significant role: purchase on credit, bank loans etc. What is the economic explanation for the use of money in this case?

We need first to expand our concept of a currency community: the currency community ceases now to be just a "payments community." It becomes now a "credit community" or perhaps even several "credit communities." Individual experiences of doing business with others in their capacities as creditors or debtors become relevant.[44] The members of the credit community give each other money loans for limited periods of time which are denominated in the accounting unit of a particular currency community. A central agent decides what the "measure of debt" and what the "manner of payment" are. The transaction costs are lower if it is established which currency is, for ambiguous cases, the "money of contract" (see A. Nussbaum 1950, 376ff. for examples). Transaction costs are also lowered by the ruling that, unless another agreement is reached, units of account are owed (nominalistic principle) which must be payed in the form of definitive money or legal tender.

Relevant in this context is the role of the state, viz. the importance of the law concerning money debt, even though it can be observed that regularities in behavior are only "to a small extent the result of an orientation toward legal rules. To the extent that the regularities are consciously oriented towards rules at all and do not merely spring from unreflected habituation, they are of the nature of 'custom' and 'convention;' often they are predominantly rational maxims of purposeful self-interested action, on the effective operation of which each participant is counting for his own conduct as well as that of all others."

[44] On this point see the explanations given by H. Bonus (1986, 318) for the rural credit associations (Darlehenskassenvereine) of Raiffeisen and Schultze-Delitzsch. These institutions utilized the intimate knowledge of the personal and family situations of the credit seeking clients in their immediate neighborhoods. This enabled them to charge considerably lower interest than the local money lenders.

(M. Weber 1968, 324). In this sense the order of a credit community is mainly guaranteed or enforced by the members themselves.

The transaction-costs-reducing advantages of the nominalistic principle are fully realized only if the individual participants have confidence in the currency community and its policy to safeguard the value of money.

The economic advantages of intertemporal exchange using money are the same as those of simultaneous transactions by means of money: the use of a single accounting unit as a measure of the debt (with a given price target) eliminates the arbitrage problem of the exchange which has been described in Section 4.3; the use of the same means of payment in discharging money debts eliminates the coincidence problem of exchange. With money loans the use of a single accounting unit also facilitates control of the business activities of the debtor, reducing the supervisory cost of loan transactions. Beyond this, a currency community may reduce the level of the cost of control and other transaction costs even further by allowing a more efficient organization of the loan business.

Note in this context the difference between debt and other obligations. While the latter may be terminated by a subsequent impossibility of performance this is not the case "where a money debtor, even by the most deplorable accident, becomes financially unable to pay his debts" (A. Nussbaum 1950, 144). Monetary debt is an "indestructible obligation."

The lower the transaction costs associated with loans expressed in money the more marketable or liquid is the relevant title. This is true for all property rights. Demand deposits are more liquid than bonds and in general bonds are more liquid than real assets. Hence it is generally true that a property right is the more *liquid* the less the expected value of the loss involved in changing it within a specified period (an hour, a day) into definitive money.[45]

The expected value of the loss involved in a quick sale is a measure of the level of all transaction costs associated with the sale of a property right – including search, negotiation and control costs. These three elements of transaction costs are not independent of each other. For example, high control costs probably imply high costs of search. High control costs are typical of money loans. They can be reduced by the use of financial intermediaries but they cannot be avoided altogether. The activity "control of money debtors" must be taken over by some members of the currency community. The better the control functions the greater may be the volume of intertemporal exchange with the use of money, as measured for example, by the relation of the sum of all money loans to the sum of all real assets of an economy.

A money claim is, as a rule, a bundle of property rights in one of any number of arrangements. Bank deposits, for example, do not only give one the right to demand certain sums of interest-bearing money, but also, e.g., the right to write checks as often as desired and over arbitrarily small amounts, to use a check card (in Europe), and even to overdraw the bank account up to a certain limit. Also acquired with a

[45] Following Keynes, J.R. Hicks defines "more liquid" as follows: "One thing is more liquid than another if it is '*more certainly*' realisable at short notice without loss." See J.R. Hicks (1962, 790); J.M. Keynes (1930, II. 67). See also W. Stützel (1959).

bank deposit may be a deposit insurance to a certain limit, the activity of the banking supervisory authority etc.. With a bill of exchange, the endorser acquires at the same time the right of recourse against all previous endorsers (to the acceptor, drawer, or to previous endorsers). The supplier of commodities, who sells on account, owns not only a money price against his customer but acquires also an additional name to his list of customers (which has a market value).

It is in the interest of expanding intertemporal exchange with the use of money to bundle property rights associated with claims on money in such a manner that the bundle contains sufficiently attractive incentives to reduce the control cost of money loans. Relational contracts, i.e., relationships in which the contracting parties for a multiplicity of reasons supervise and control each other, should be seen in this context. They are peculiarly suitable to monitor or "control" (in the technical sense of the word) money debts. A currency community contains an interconnected system of credit communities in the small, e.g., communities of merchants who trade with each other and frequently issue, accept or endorse trade bills of exchange or who, as a rule, buy and sell on credit etc. The liquidity of money claims and their eligibility to lend money on them depends, among other things, on the "liquidity" of the members of these credit communities, i.e., their ability to satisfy demands for payment more or less easily (W. Stützel, 1959, 622). This is most easily seen in the example of a bill of exchange.

To become part of such a credit community involves costs which are not necessarily marketable. This is particularly true for personal business relationships. We may therefore assume that there exists a non-marketable "fee" for the membership in a particular credit community which is reflected in the conditions and the liquidity of money loans.

Banks and their customers and depositors form another type of credit community. The claims on a bank, particularly demand deposits, are very liquid property rights. They are so liquid that one considers them in macroeconomics to be part of the quantity of money of an economy. A substantial part of modern money transactions goes through the transfer system of commercial banks. The customers of a commercial bank may therefore be understood to form a combination of a payments and a credit community, i.e., as a particular "*secondary*" *currency community* (e.g., the customers of the Dresdner Bank or the Chase Manhattan Bank etc.) which are connected in a particular manner with a superior or "*primary*" *currency community* (e.g., the currency community of the Deutsche Bundesbank or the Federal Reserve System).[46] The commercial bank in question is at the same time the central agent of the secondary currency community, whose elementary currency order looks as follows:

The unit of account is, e.g., the Deutsche mark. The means of payment are the mark book entries of the *A*-bank (the particular commercial bank). The price target is the exchange rate 1 (1 mark of the *A*-bank currency community = 1 mark of the

---

[46] B. Klein (1974, 441) speaks of "dominant money" and "nondominant money."

Bundesbank currency community). The A-bank is obliged to redeem its deposits at the fixed exchange rate 1 into means of payment of the Deutsche Bundesbank.[47]

The supervisory or control cost of credit transactions are decentralized by the formation of secondary credit communities. In this manner the limits of a primary currency community may be expanded further and further. This rests on the following reasoning: if we assume that at least part of monetary circulation of a currency community enters the economy through loans by the central agency we may suppose that the marginal control cost of the central agent increase after a certain point. This sets limits to the efficient size of a single central agency. These limits may possibly be pushed outward by, e.g., a two-tiered organization for the control of loans: the central agents of the secondary currency communities supervise the ultimate debtors; the central agent of the primary currency community supervises the agents of the associated secondary currency communities. Instead of a hierarchically structured monopoly bank we get an organizational principle combining both market and hierarchy. Incentives to reduce transaction costs are created by allowing private ownership of the central agencies of the competing secondary currency communities (i.e., of the commercial banks). A market exists on which bank shares are traded. The price of the shares is one determinant regulating the activity of the management of the banking firms. The question arises whether the same principle – competition among private enterprises – may also be applied to primary currency communities. We shall discuss this question in the next section.

A Note on the History of Thought:

What we have called *secondary currency communities* G.F. Knapp calls "*Unstaatliche Zahlgemeinschaft*" (G.F. Knapp 1921, 131) translated into English in G.F. Knapp (1924, 145) as: "a pay-society or group which is not the State." The concept of the payments community ("pay-society") is used by Knapp analogously. He writes:

"Payment is a transaction which in any case implies a society, whether it be the State or the customers of a bank or any other kind of association of payers. It might even extend beyond the State, ..." "In any case, chartal payment communities need a central agent." "It must have a center from which it is managed. In the case of State money, this means the authority of the State; in the case of private methods of payment, it means, for example, a bank." (G.F. Knapp 1924, 152).

4.6 Competition in Currencies

F.A. Hayek (1976c, 101) concludes his provoking book *denationalisation of money* with the following proposal: "What we now need is a Free Money Movement comparable to the Free Trade Movement of the 19th century ..."

Hayek continues that the abolition of the currency monopoly of the state and the introduction of private competing currencies would end acute inflations and

[47] In the Federal Republic of Germany the *Gesetz über das Kreditwesen* as amended on May 3, 1976, Art. 3, No. 3 expressly states: "Forbidden are ... 3. credit or deposit transactions when agreement or business habits exclude or make considerably difficult to dispose over the credit or the deposits by cashing them."

deflations. Private, unregulated firms, should found currency communities and be allowed to offer means of payment. Hayek thinks evidently of the founding of primary currency communities of a paper standard type.[48]

This thesis stands the traditional doctrine on its head. In the traditional view with the paper standard in which the supply of the means of payment is regulated according to the principles of a private economy, either the price level is indeterminate[49] or an inflation must be expected.[50]

Hayek's argument against this view is the following: if private banks of issue do not ensure the determinateness and stability of the money produced by them, they would lose out to a competitor, because the stability of the value of money is of central importance to the user of money. The competing issuing banks would, therefore, take pains to realize as accurately as possible their announced price target, as long as they wish to maximize their own market value. This they can do only by regulating appropriately the quantity of money they supply.

In this manner profit maximizing banks of issue would serve the public interest much better than "any institution has ever done or could do that supposedly aimed at it." (Hayek 1976c, 79).

In terms of our elementary currency order, Hayek's construction looks as follows. Private persons may found a private central agency (a firm). They may in this context choose their own accounting units ("ducats"), their own means of payment (bank deposits, bank notes, coins etc.), their own price targets. The government protects the name of the accounting unit like any trade mark against illegal use. It protects also bank notes, coins etc. against forgeries, exactly as it protects any document. Since the cost of living vary interlocally, Hayek recommends a price target as a basket of various widely traded products (such as raw materials, agricultural food stuffs and certain standard semi-finished industrial products), similar to the case of a commodity reserve standard (Hayek 1976c, 63). However, the central agent is not obliged to redeem its money into the basket of goods which in any case would not be feasible. They must therefore try to achieve their price targets indirectly by an appropriate regulation of the supply with means of payment, i.e., the supplied quantity of money. This could be done relatively accurately provided there would be no unanticipated changes in the real demand for money, which Hayek assumes (op. cit. p. 41).

Hayek writes that his proposal would turn out to be a more practical method to achieve all the aims of a commodity reserve standard or some other kind of "tabular standard."

"At the same time it would remove the necessity of making it fully automatic by taking the control from a monopolistic authority and entrusting it to private concerns. The threat of the speedy loss of their whole business if they failed to meet expectations (and how any government organisation would be

---

[48] "Convertibility is a safeguard necessary to impose upon a *monopolist*, but unnecessary with *competing* suppliers who cannot maintain themselves in the business unless they provide money at least as advantageous to the user as anybody else." (F.A. Hayek 1976c, 84. Italics in the original).

[49] So, e.g., D. Patinkin (1961, 95–116).

[50] See, e.g., F.A. Lutz (1936), H.G. Johnson (1968).

certain to abuse the opportunity to play with raw material prices!) would provide a much stronger safeguard than any that could be devised against a government monopoly. Competition would certainly prove a more effective constraint, forcing the issuing institutions to keep the value of their currency constant (in terms of a stated collection of commodities), than would any obligation to redeem the currency in those commodities (or in gold). And it would be an infinitely cheaper method than the accumulation and the storing of valuable materials." (Hayek 1976c, 40f.).

The financial newspapers would observe the results of the efforts of the (primary) banks of issue very carefully and report daily to what extent the currencies would deviate from their announced price targets. Of course, the formation of secondary currency communities would have to be expected. (Hayek talks of "parasitic currencies," op. cit. p. 53f.) This would be, however, unobjectionable, provided the parasitic issues are "clearly labelled as debts to be paid in the currency of the issuer." The original issuers should refuse rigorously to buy the secondary or parasitic currencies at par in order to avoid the possibility that their currency might lose value due to the activities of the secondary issuers. If it is made clear a priori that the primary issuers are not willing to supply their currency to the secondary issuers at a fixed exchange ratio, the secondary issuers would be forced "to practice something very close to '100 per cent banking'" (op. cit. p. 55).

Even if the private banks of issue or central agents do not promise to redeem their money into the chosen real definition of their accounting unit, they would have to satisfy some promise of redemption. Their creditors, i.e., the depositors or users of their money, will demand this. The latter will be only willing to hold money of a bank of issue if they have a criterion of solvency. For this reason Hayek proposes the "single legal obligation" that the "ducats" of the private (primary) issuers have to be redeemed on demand and at the choice of the owner into, say, 5 Swiss franc, or 5 mark or 2 dollar.

"This redemption value would however be intended only as a floor below which the value of the unit could not fall because I would announce at the same time my intention to regulate the quantity of the ducats so as to keep their (precisely defined) purchasing power as nearly as possible constant." (op. cit. p. 39).

Hayek, therefore, presupposes, at least at the beginning, the existence of governmental money to which private money attaches itself in the described manner. As long as this is true, the central agent of a private currency community may become insolvent. To that extent its business practices are subject to a guaranteed "stop rule." This ceases to be true if no obligation to redeem its notes exists. It can then issue its money to any desired extent. But in such a case it will find no customers for its money. Whoever makes the initial payment (here the depositors or money users) demands protection against exploitation, against a "hold-up." A guarantee of the price target that depends only on the private interest of the issuer is too weak. It does not exclude that the owner of the central agency (a bank) decides suddenly for a rip-off and liquidates its banking business altogether even if he has pursued it thus far in a generally satisfactory manner (see P. Bernholz 1978, 139). Nor does it exclude less extreme forms of exploitation, in particular: inflationary practices.

An elementary and very effective protection against exploitation is the demand of the depositor to give something as collateral. Full-bodied coins may in such a case be considered as collateral of the issuing central agency to maintain the promised price target. The threat of an enforcement or "execution" (by writ) is an analogous guarantee. All individuals in a market economy are subject to this discipline.

It is a characteristic of a free market economy that all promises of supply, including promises to pay, must be kept, and that, if necessary, they are enforced by the powers of the state. "This fact gives the requirement of liquidity its true character, compared, e.g., with the demand for maximum profitability, optimal productivity, etc." (W. Stützel, 1959, 625; translated by W.F.St.).

A private bank which in the ordinary sense of the word cannot become illiquid must thus be subject to another kind of "stop rule." One regulation that suggests itself is that the government forbids the bank to issue more than a certain quantity of money. But such a regulation is not really consistent with the idea of *competing* private banks of issue. Whatever is done, a bank which issues definitive paper money is imaginable only as a special institution which the members of the currency community accept. In such a case, a particular governmental supervision of the business practices of these social institutions seems inevitable.

As we have seen, Hayek did not go so far as to propose the creation of private banks of issue with the right to issue non-redeemable paper money. He thought of a legal obligation of private suppliers of money to redeem their money into some already existing governmental money at a stated minimum rate of exchange. Other authors, however, such as B. Klein (1974) go further. In their view, no governmental money, in the sense of non-redeemable paper money, anywhere in the world is necessary.

Our considerations suggest that a world-wide competition among private commodity standards may be imagined. However, the direction of such a development, determined purely by self-interest, is likely to go towards a single money good used by everyone, such as gold, i.e., a natural means of payment, which is used as world money. In such a case the central agents of individual currency communities could become illiquid. In this sense a state based purely on the upholding of public order and committed to absolute laissez faire is conceivable, in which even the control of the monetary system is entirely by private enterprise (M. Weber 1968, 52). Such an extreme assumption about the state may be, at most, consistent with the limiting case of zero transaction costs. But in such a case the use of money is economically irrelevant, and this makes the question irrelevant also whether a currency community exists and how big it is.

The situation is different if we allow for transaction costs. In this case, the use of money is profitable and so is the unification of monetary institutions of a closed area. Money is a natural monopoly good not only as an accounting unit and means of payment but also in the sense of being a characteristic of a currency community. Not only goods and services but also institutions are produced. In both cases there exist "natural monopoly goods." They are characterized not only by diminishing average costs of production but also (at least in case of a currency community) by diminishing average costs to use the money. Furthermore: a substantial part of the use of money takes place not within the framework of discrete transactions but within relational contracts. This is particularly true for money loans.

Relational contracts arise on two levels: in the small, between debtors and creditors, in the large, between the users of money and the central agent of the currency community. The relational contracts in the small rest on particular expectations about the future of the currency in which transactions are concluded and balance sheets calculated. This results in the need for regulation of relational contracts in the large, particularly when the transaction-cost saving nominalist principle is applied. The required regulations refer both to the accounting order and to the value-safeguarding order. As far as the accounting order is concerned, the users of the money assume that the accounting unit at the time when a contract is being concluded will continue to exist, or at least that when the accounting unit is changed the appropriate connection between the old and the new units is clearly stated. There must also be certainty about the means of discharging the money debt. As for the value-safeguarding order, the users of money need to know as precisely as possible how the price target of the currency community develops over time (e.g., maintenance of a particular standard of coinage in the case of a commodity standard, or the rate of inflation announced by the central agent in the case of a paper standard).

The specific investments of the "first choice" of a currency might be negligible; the cost of a change of the currency in which books are kept is not. Thus a change in the currency in which books of a firm are kept raises the cost of control or supervision for its creditors and shareholders[51] and creates exchange-rate risks.

There are thus two concepts which play a role in the characterization of currency communities: the concept of a natural monopoly in the sense that it is advantageous to use the same original currency in as large an area as possible; and the concept of relational contracts with large specific investments. Both concepts speak for government intervention when a currency community is created, both in its capacity as legislator and as the public regulating authority. In this case it is not necessary to wait until an "organic" development (e.g., the evolution of common law) has led to a situation recognized beforehand as meaningful, i.e., until a single currency is used over a certain area. This would be a very expensive, time-consuming and uncertain procedure which might never reach its goal. Transaction costs are saved if the state or an international public authority anticipates this result. C. Menger speaks in this connection of the "perfecting of the money and coinage system by the state" (1909, 574).[52]

No strict currency monopoly which excludes the use of other currencies is required. It suffices that a particular currency is used in a particular area for particular purposes.[53] Transaction costs are saved, if the government makes clear

[51] P. Bofinger (1985, 44ff.) discusses the confusion which may arise for creditors and shareholders of a firm if the firm is entirely free to choose the currency in which its balance sheets are published.

[52] Menger does not think much of an entirely spontaneous or automatic development of money; it would, so Menger, lead easily by its very nature to an intolerable multiplicity of monetary forms. (C. Menger, 1909, 575).

[53] The question of the size of an "optimal currency area" is discussed in the literature. Mundell (1961) was the first to define the problem in these terms. J. Niehans (1984, 291) comments on this problem: "... it is a prohibitively difficult problem and it is therefore not surprising that twenty years of academic efforts have brought little progress towards its solution." We shall not enter into this subject matter at this point.

in which accounting unit money debts are denominated in ambiguous cases; which means of payment are, if in doubt, to be used; which currency is to be used in the case of legal debt relationships (damage payments, payments obligations in cases of unjustified enrichment, obligations to pay maintenance such as alimony etc.); which currency is to be used to draw up financial statements, e.g., in order to determine the profits to be paid to share holders; which currency is to be used to state prices etc. All such measures are likely to make for the general use of a currency designated by the state. In addition the state itself needs revenues and, therefore, must determine which currency is to be used for the payment of taxes and other compulsory levies. For the modern tax state with expenditure quotas of 40% and more of GNP this alone determines unequivocally which money is overwhelmingly used in a national territory, even when the inhabitants are free in which currency they wish to conclude private transactions, such as purchase, rental, labor or loan contracts.[54] What remains is at best a competition among currencies "at the border lines" of the systems, a certain competition among currencies and means of payment at the conclusion of private contracts.

As for the public regulation of the monetary system, we must distinguish between secondary and primary currency communities. The central agents of secondary currency communities (the commercial banks) compete with each other, at least on the assumptions of our model. The public interest is limited to maintaining the competition among the commercial banks and to protect the creditors. For the central agent of a primary currency community (the central bank) matters are different. The central bank has a monopoly position within its area. Monopolistic practices are conceivable: inflationist manoeuvers which we shall describe in Sections 8.4 and 8.6. Public regulation must exclude such practices or at least limit them. This is especially true for the paper standard in which the central bank has an exceptional position: it cannot become insolvent. The value safeguarding order of the currency must in this case be guaranteed by public regulation.

The discussion of currency competition suggests interesting thought experiments about the problem of the economic explanation of public regulation of a primary currency community. The present section is limited to a brief illustration of the problem. The eighth chapter will present further thoughts about this subject matter. A comprehensive discussion for and against currency competition is not possible within the framework of this book (but see the enumerated literature at the end of this chapter). In reality there exist certainly no private competing primary currency communities, though the governmental currency communities compete with each other. Among them there may be competition over which currency or currencies are used as world money of the first, second or third order. In this context we still can observe that "primordial" state which C. Menger described as the

[54] A.P. Lerner (1947, 313) writes: "The modern state can make anything it chooses generally acceptable as money ...." "If the state is willing to accept the proposed money in payment of taxes and other obligations to itself the trick is done. Everyone who has obligations to the state will be willing to accept the pieces of paper with which he can settle the obligations, and all other people will be willing to accept these pieces of paper because they know that the tax payers etc. will accept them in turn." This is correct in more or less normal circumstances. It was not quite true, e.g., in Germany after World War II before the currency reform.

beginning of the history of the evolution of money: certain currencies are used as international money, though only because of the economic self-interest of the trading individuals "without agreement, without legal compulsion, even without any consideration of a common interest" (C. Menger, 1909, 558, translated by W.F. St.).

Appendix to Chapter 4

The Black-Fama-Hall System

The literature describes a number of currency orders besides the commodity and paper standard, among them one constructed by F. Black (1970), E.F. Fama (1980) and R.E. Hall (1982b), which R.L. Greenfield and L.B. Yeager (1983) combine under the name of the Black-Fama-Hall (BFH) system (see also Readings to this chapter). In the BFH-system the state or some other central agent determines the accounting unit and the price target without however determining the means of payment expressed in terms of the accounting unit. The state is prohibited from issuing bonds because they might be used as money. It is also prohibited from declaring any titles to be legal tender.

"No longer would there be any such thing as money whose purchasing power depended on limitation of its quantity. No longer, then, could there be too much of it, causing price inflation, or too little, causing depression, or a sequence of imbalances, causing stagflation. A wrong quantity of money could no longer cause problems because money would not exist." (R.L. Greenfield and L.B. Yeager 1983, 305).

The price target might refer to one good or a basket of goods. Greenfield and Yeager assume the latter in their exposition of the BFH-system. The money goods need not be storable (in contradistinction to the commodity standard), for they serve only as an abstract definition of the accounting unit and do not serve as concrete money.

The BFH-system fits perfectly the model of general equilibrium with perfect foresight, i.e., with no transaction costs. The elementary currency orders of the commodity and the paper standard are fused in the currency order of the BFH-type. We have here a world without cash balances and, indeed, without cash, which we shall consider in Chapter 5. As soon as there are also transaction costs and therefore imperfect foresight, the picture is considerably changed.

Cash balances become worthwhile. To this purpose there must be some means of payment, either currency or bank money. Of course, the abstract accounting unit need not be identical with the accounting unit of concrete money. When currency situations are unclear and uncertain, the two do indeed differ, so e.g., during the Middle Ages (see e.g., W. Eucken 1950, 243). If, on the other hand, the price target is clearly defined, as is assumed in the BFH-system, it must be presumed that competition among means of payment will result in a means of payment expressed in terms of the general accounting unit which is redeemable into the money good or the basket of money goods (the latter would be quite impractical if not impossible).

Justification: In the world of Greenfield and Yeager, to which we limit ourselves, shares in mutual funds are used as money. The mutual funds might be denominated in accounting units, though not in a fixed amount. The customer can dispose over his fund by check.

"Apart from his adding to it or drawing it down, his holding would rise or fall in value as his fund received earnings and made capital gains, or as it suffered losses on its asset portfolio." (R.L. Greenfield and L.B. Yeager 1983, 307).

It is obvious that with this construction only non-banks might experience liquidity problems; banks would not. There would be no run problem. Banks might perhaps acquire claims on money, i.e., they would give credits expressed in terms of accounting units, but they themselves would not issue debts denominated in accounting units. The bank depositors share the risk of the bank just (or almost just) as do the shareholders of the bank. It is doubtful whether all depositors really would want this. Rather, a certain number of them might try to make their deposits more secure. To this end they would get deposit insurance or, perhaps better, investment insurance. If in doubt, the bank itself would go into the business of investment insurance for the full or at least for a substantial amount. After all, it knows its own business policy best. This amounts, however, to the bank also accepting deposits denominated in accounting units in addition to shares in the mutual fund.

From there to the use of deposits or bank notes of a particular bank as a general means of payment which can be used to settle clearing balances is but a small step (see, e.g., G.A. Selgin and L.H. White, 1986). The definitive means of payment offered by private money producers would be used only if it were redeemable into the money goods to which the price target refers (for an explanation, see Section 4.6). With competition the world of the BFH-system would therefore lead to a private commodity standard.

Greenfield and Yeager have not thought through their system. They do not investigate the question how the BFH-system will develop under the competitive conditions which they assume. Regardless of which regulations are reserved to the state, all four parts of the elementary currency order must somehow be determined. If the government determines only the accounting unit and the price target and leaves the rest to the free play of the market, the appropriate definitive means of payment will appear by themselves – if this currency succeeds at all. An appropriate supply of the means of payment will be determined by itself by the workings of the invisible hand on the basis of individual self-interest or by contract. C. Menger's (1883) mode of thinking applies *mutatis mutandis* (see L.H. White, 1984b). For references see Suggested Readings to this chapter and to Chapter 8.

Suggested Readings to Chapter 4

The newer literature takes only scant notice of the problem of the nature of money in the sense of an economic explanation of the social organization of the use of money.

Modern monetary theory is a theory of the value of money in the first place. In the older German monetary theory, on the other hand, the theory of the "nature of money" played a prominent role. However, the older literature confined itself mostly to description rather than analysis. For a survey of the older literature on the nature of money, see *W. Ehrlicher* (1981, 374–378); *E. and M. Streissler* (1984, 317–323). For an example of the theory of the nature of money, see *L. v. Mises* (1953, Part One) or *F. Bendixen* (1908). The posthumously published work of *J. A. Schumpeter* (1970) is an eye-opener on this subject matter. It was finished in its published form about 1929/1930.

1 The Elementary Currency Order

Concerning thinking in terms of orders, see *M. Weber* (1968) and *W. Eucken* (1952). Our considerations about monetary orders were especially stimulated by *J.A. Schumpeter* (1970) Chapter IX, and *C. Menger* (1909; English summary of parts of this important article in *C. Menger* 1892). The work of *G.F. Knapp* (1905, 1921, English translation 1924) also deserves attention though with considerable qualifications. He was the first to describe clearly the bookkeeping side of the use of money, however, he completely neglected the value safeguarding aspects of the elementary currency order. He overemphasized the role of the state as a producer of money. On his famous dictum: "money is a creature of the State," see *C. Menger* (1909, 574ff.), *M. Weber* (1968, 78f., 184ff.), *A.P. Lerner* (1947). Knapp's theory of money was sharply criticized by *J.A. Schumpeter* (1970, 82ff; 1955, 1090f.).

On the sociology of money, see *G. Simmel* (1907; 1930, 164ff., English translation 1978). Simmel's work has been appraised from a modern point of view by *D.E.W. Laidler* and *N. Rowe* (1980).

2 The Economic Explanation of the Use of Money

C. Menger [1883 (English translation 1963), and 1909 (English summary of parts of it 1892)] is still worth reading. A simple formalization of Menger's approach is found in *K. Nagatani* (1978, 118ff.), which in turn is based on *R.A. Jones* (1976). Menger's causal-genetic style of argument has been applied to the paper standard by *L.H. White* (1984b). Most of the analytical literature on this subject is new. *J. Niehans* (1969) investigates optimal payments arrangements in a world with transaction costs. *K. Brunner* and *A. Meltzer* (1971, 799) hypothesize that for an individual, cash balances are an "investment in information." Lack of information ("ignorance") leads to the use of money. For work in the same direction see *A.A. Alchian* (1977).

3 The Economic Explanation of the Order of Safeguarding the Value of Money

On the concept of the purchasing power of money, see the Suggested Readings to Chapter 1, No. 2. For a clarification of the role of money as a "measure of price," see *C. Menger* (1909, 582ff.). On the problem of computation cost with perfectly anticipated inflation see *J. Niehans* (1978, 127f.) and *P. Dittus* (1987).

On the rational explanation of temporarily fixed prices, see *A.A. Alchian* (1970), *M.L. Wachter* and *O.E. Williamson* (1978), *A.M. Okun* (1981). About the relation between variability of inflation rates and the average inflation rate see *J.B. Taylor* (1981). On the dependence of the variability of relative prices on the inflation rate see the empirical investigations by *M.D. Bordo* (1980) and *S. Fischer* (1982).

The problem of the cost of inflation has been investigated by, e.g., *M.J. Bailey* (1956). For the newer debate, see *S. Fischer* (1981).

4 The Early History of Money

The book by *P. Einzig* (1951) is very informative. In contrast to the economic explanation of money in the sense of *C. Menger* which has been dealt with in this chapter, *G. Laum* (1924), for example, believes, that money arose first in the sacral area. *W. Gerloff* (1944, 1947) also gives a non-economic, cultural-sociological explanation for the origin of money. An overview of the whole history of money from antiquity to the end of the gold standard is found in *K.E. Born* (1980). On the history of paper money before 1914, see *W. Lexis* (1893). For the older literature about money with primitive peoples and the oldest forms of money, see *C. Menger* (1909, 560, n. 1). Menger also gives an excellent survey of the origin of the word "*Geld*" ("money") (ibid. 561, n. 1). The German and Dutch word *Geld* (verbal noun from "*Gelten*" = pay, to give something in exchange or to give something as a substitute) originally meant payment or return ("*Vergeltung*") of any kind.

5 The Law of Money

In order to understand the currently dominant nominalistic principle, a general study of the legal doctrines of money is advisable. We limit ourselves to a few suggestions. Foremost we mentioned the comparative study by *F.A. Mann* (1971), a very detailed and clearly written monograph or, more briefly, *E. Krispis* (1967). For the interwar period, we mention the book of *A. Nussbaum* (German edition 1925; completely revised English edition 1950). The English edition provides an excellent international historical overview of the law of money. A summary of the German law of money for the period before the first world war is found in *M. Wolff* (1917). *H. Fögen* (1969) gives the outline of the modern (West) German law of money. On the transformation or metamorphosis of money and its legal consequences for West Germany, see *K. Duden* (1968). For the legal problems around cashless payments transactions, see *W. Möschel* (1986).

A comparative survey of central banking law is provided by *H. Aufricht* (1965). For more literature on central bank law, see below Suggested Readings to Chapter 8, No. 9.

6 On Currency Competition

The old subject matter of "money and the state" is nowadays discussed under this heading. The newer debate started with *B. Klein* (1974) and *F.A. Hayek* (1976b, 1976c, 1978). For the further development of this idea see *R. Vaubel* (1977, 1978, 1985). For an overview on private-money theories see *R.G. King* (1983). *P. Bofinger* (1985) has criticized Hayek's position and at the same time clarified what may be understood by "currency competition" and what institutional problems arise with the different variants of currency competition. *M. Hellwig* (1985) is critical of Vaubel and Hayek. For a criticism of the whole approach, see *S. Fischer* (1986). On the "stop rule" with a paper standard, see *M. Friedman* (1960, 6), where may also be found a brief justification for the necessity of public regulation of money (op. cit., 8).

Other forms of competition among means of payment have been suggested by *E.F. Fama* (1980), *R.E. Hall* (1982b), *R.L. Greenfield* and *L.B. Yeager* (1983). For a survey, see *L.H. White* (1984b) and the Appendix to this chapter. Similar ideas are expressed by *W. Engels* (1977, 1981). We shall return to this approach in Chapter 8 in the context of the public regulation of money (see also the Suggested Readings to Chapter 8, No. 7).

Chapter 5
An Abstract Book-Money Economy

What role does the price target of a currency order play in determining the money prices of goods, the money (or nominal) rate of interest and the exchange rates? What are the consequences of variations in the price target over the course of time? To what extent is it possible to replace it by interest or exchange rate targets? How does a consistent price-, interest-, exchange-rate-target bundle look, provided such a thing exists? We deal with these elementary questions in this chapter under assumptions which are as simple as possible, viz. those of the model of general equilibrium with zero transaction costs (the Pure Futures Economy or ZTC-world).

Money is not needed in such a world. Still, one can imagine that it is used by interpreting all transactions as exchanges by the use of money, assuming that all payments are made through a central bookkeeping system. That is, of course, an abstract borderline case. Yet, it is extremely well suited for showing the pure "market logic" consequences which a currency community would have to accept if it chose a particular price target. In the long run, no economic policy maker can ignore the inherent logic of a market economy.

We now imagine that money is being used in the ZTC world. Currency communities exist; their currency orders determine among other things the specific units of accounts and price targets. The means of payment are book money: credits or debits in the individuals' accounts of the central bookkeeping system. Cash balances do not pay in the ZTC-world because it costs nothing to transfer book money into interest bearing assets and back again into book money. There exists no "quantity of money" in the sense of "stocks of book money" or any other meaning (see J.A. Schumpeter 1970, 235). The regulation of the supply of means of payment relates only to the willingness of the central agent to carry out the transfers in the central ledger as desired by the individuals. This willingness is imagined to be based on the certainty of absolute honesty and reliability of all individuals.

The price target may be related to the price of a single good or to a bundle of goods; it may also be directed to interest rates or exchange rates. How it is determined and guaranteed in our abstract book-money economy is left open in this chapter. We will deal with this question later on (see below Section 8.5).

In principle there are two possible ways to determine the price target: to fix it the "direct way," e.g., as standard of coinage, discount rate, "fixed" exchange rate, or to determine it the "indirect way" by an appropriate fixing of a nominal quantity, e.g., the volume M of paper money. Which path is taken does not concern us in this chapter. Yet, it assists our imagination to assume that the central agent determines the "direct way" as a price target the price p of a specific good, the money-interest rate i or the exchange rate e without being worried about the manner in which the price target is guaranteed.

We proceed in this chapter as follows. First we describe the handling of the payment transactions in the central bookkeeping system, for purchase as well as money loan transactions. Next we deal briefly with the neoclassical theory of the money rate of interest, which may be understood as the monetary interpretation of the theory of the real interest rate as presented in Chapter 2. In this connection we raise the central problem of this chapter, the problem of consistent price targeting. The basis of this discussion is the hypothesis that arbitrage equilibrium is always automatically established in a market economy. That is true for the real as well as for the borderline case of the ZTC-world. In the latter arbitrage equilibria are of a particularly simple kind. The relevant "laws," e.g., the law of one price, are here 100 percent valid. On this elementary foundation of "market logic" we will discuss step by step the problem of consistent price targeting.

At first we deal with price and interest rate targets of a closed currency community and after that with price, interest rate and exchange rate targets of open currency communities illustrated by the case of two currency communities. The model underlying these considerations is the world of perfectly neutral money. At the end of this chapter we enter briefly into the history of thought of the concept of neutral money.

5.1 A Central Accounting System

Consider exchange by the use of money. How do the corresponding bookkeeping entries in the central accounting system of the monetary community look? For each economic agent there exists an account. If, in the course of a purchasing transaction, the buyer offers p_1 mark per kg of wheat available today, that implies in this context that he promises to pay the seller a bookkeeping deposit of $|p_1 \hat{x}_1|$ mark available today on the seller's account as the purchase sum. The buyer can assure the seller of his ability to pay without cost, since there are no transaction costs.

There is thus the rule: "*ein Mann – ein Wort*." If the debtor promises the payment of mark 30 through a bank deposit on the account of his creditor at the end of the market day, the creditor takes this promise literally like "cash." The entries of the central bookkeeping system always balance. None of its users is ever disappointed.

All credits and debits are executed only after general equilibrium has been found. At that time the amount of $|p_1 \hat{x}_1|$ is credited to the wheat seller's account; he receives a *payment*. The same amount is entered as a debit on the account of the buyer; he "pays" this amount; we have a *disbursement*.

We assume, as we have done so far, that no economic units suffer from money illusion. Applied to our example this means that the wheat seller will consider the *real* value of the "p_1 mark per kg of wheat available today" which the potential buyer has offered. He can do this, since we assume here that the unit of account has a real definition. The central agent of the currency community has fixed in this case a certain price target, the price p of a particular good, e.g., gold.

Thus, if in the case of a one-period model, the price p_n has been fixed from the beginning in abstract monetary units, the wheat seller can calculate during the negotiations the value of the offered amount of money p_1 in terms of units of good n, i.e., p_1/p_n (kg of good n per kg of good 1). And he can compare this price ratio

p_1/p_n with the end result of an alternative barter transaction π_{n1}. This is so because with ZTC there exists always an arbitrage equilibrium between a direct exchange and exchange by means of money. Book money has all the money properties discussed in Chapter 4: it serves as the unit of account ("mark"), as a means of payment and – in principle – as a store of value. However, in a ZTC-world it is not used as a store of value. In such world, only interest bearing claims on money are kept. Book money is completely exchanged against securities, e.g., bills of exchange, because an exchange into interest bearing assets and vice versa into book accounts does not cost anything.

We continue our considerations: if p_n has been fixed by the central agent and if general equilibrium exists, we know with p_n all equilibrium values of all other prices expressed in terms of the accounting unit of the currency community. As soon as the equilibrium values of the absolute prices $p_1^0, \ldots, p_{n-1}^0$ are determined our central bookkeeping system begins to operate. All book entries are made, as it were, instantaneously.[1] At the same time all transactions are promptly fulfilled as agreed upon.

Since in the Pure Futures Economy all real transactions are effectuated definitely for all times, it is determined for each period of the final period T what the payments and disbursements are used for. Neither insolvency nor illiquidity exist. No money debt exists whose real utilization is not exactly determined; nor is there any money oligation whose fulfillment is not precisely determined by the proceeds from the sales of goods. *Say's law* is valid

> "whose core is, as is well known, the thesis that goods and services are initially paid in money, but that they are basically paid with other goods or services." (J.G. Koopmans 1933, 256; translated by W.F. St.).

Open debt claims or liabilities exist only if the economic units do not determine by contract their real consumption or production plans "for all times" at the market day, but if they prefer to leave their future dispositions over real goods open. In such a case Say's law does not necessarily hold. This case will be discussed in the next chapter.

We now will describe the bookkeeping transactions of this elementary currency order, i.e., the central bookkeeping system, for the elementary case of our Robinson example with one good "wheat" and two periods, "today" and "tomorrow." Good 1 is wheat available today, good 2 is wheat available tomorrow. Contracts expressed in money are concluded today and for all times. Payments are made through bookkeeping transactions today. In this case the bookkeeping system looks as follows:

[1] In our model world without errors and frauds there are no wrong book entries through fraudulent computer manipulations, forgeries of bank notes, theft of bank notes which are destined for destruction etc.

5.1.1 *The Account of the Household Robinson*

Equilibrium on all goods markets is assumed, i.e., $x_1 = x_1^0$, $x_2 = x_2^0$, where the x_i^0 are the equilibrium amounts.

The equilibrium exchange relation $\pi_{21}^0 = (p_1/p_2)^0$ is known. The price p_2 of good 2 is fixed by the central agent of the currency community as the value of the price target p_2^0:

$$p_2 = p_2^0 \ .$$

Because of the known equilibrium exchange relationship $(p_2/p_1)^0$ the price p_1 is also determined:

$$p_1 = p_1^0 \ .$$

By assumption, the household Robinson *sells* wheat to the firm Robinson payable today through credit to his account. His account will reflect the following amount paid to the household:

$$p_1^0(x_1^0 - \bar{x}_1) = p_1^0(-\hat{x}_1^0) \ \rightarrow \text{credit entry} \ .$$

As a further payment, the household Robinson receives the equilibrium value (Q^0) of the present value of the profit of the firm Robinson which he owns in full:

$$Q = Q^0 \ \rightarrow \text{credit entry} \ .$$

We remind the reader once more: all payments in this example are made *today*.

Furthermore, the household Robinson *buys* from the firm Robinson wheat available tomorrow but payable today through a credit to the firm's account. On the household account the following amount paid by the household must be entered:

$$p_2^0 x_2^0 \ \rightarrow \text{debit entry} \ .$$

The entries on the account are therefore as follows:

Household Robinson

$p_2^0 x_2^0$	$p_1^0(-\hat{x}_1^0)$
	Q^0

or $$p_2^0 x_2^0 = p_1^0(-\hat{x}_1^0) + Q^0$$

or $$p_1^0 x_1^0 + p_2^0 x_2^0 = p_1^0 \bar{x}_1 + Q^0 \quad \text{(budget equation of the household)} \ .$$

The account "Household Robinson" of the central bookkeeping system is thus simply another form of the budget equation of the household. It can be interpreted also as follows:

The household Robinson has a money debt of the present value $p_2^0 x_2^0$ as the result of its forward purchase contract "wheat to be delivered tomorrow from the firm to the household, payable today through a book transaction." The debt is expressed in the accounting unit of the currency community. At the same time, the household Robinson receives a credit entry from the firm of $p_1^0 \hat{x}_1^0 + Q^0$ because of his spot purchase contract "wheat to be delivered today from the household to the firm, payable today through a book transaction," and because he owns 100% the firm Robinson. There are no unsettled money credits or debits (see above).

5.1.2 *The Account of the Firm Robinson*

In equilibrium, the inputs of factors and the outputs of goods are, respectively:

$$y_1 = y_1^0 \ , \quad y_2 = y_2^0 \ ,$$

where $$y_1^0 = \hat{x}_1^0 \ , \quad y_2^0 = x_2^0 \ .$$

We have already discussed prices.

The firm Robinson *buys* wheat available and payable today through a book credit on the account of the household Robinson. The account of the firm shows the following amount paid by the firm:

$$p_1^0 y_1^0 \ \rightarrow \text{debit entry} \ .$$

The firm Robinson sells wheat available tomorrow and payable today through a book credit. The following payment is charged to the account of the firm

$$p_2^0 y_2^0 \ \rightarrow \text{debit entry} \ .$$

In addition, the firm Robinson will pay today to the household Robinson the present value of the (certain) profit Q^0; a corresponding debit entry is made on its account.

Thus, the entries to its account look as follows:

Firm Robinson

$p_1^0(-y_1^0)$	$p_2^0 y_2^0$
Q^0	

or $$p_1^0(-y_1^0) + Q^0 = p_2^0 y_2^0$$

$$Q^0 = p_1^0 y_1^0 + p_2^0 y_2^0 \quad \text{(profit equation of the firm)} \ .$$

As can be seen, the account of the firm Robinson is merely another form of its *profit equation*.

Thus far we have assumed that both spot and forward purchase contracts were payable today. It is, however, also possible to imagine a direct exchange without the use of money (here a loan in kind). In our ZTC-world, there exists a zero transaction cost arbitrage equilibrium between the two kinds of doing business, i.e., between the money and barter transactions.

Thus, in a ZTC-world the combination of spot and forward purchase results in the same real rate of interest as a barter agreement:

$$1 + \rho_1 = \frac{p_1}{p_2} \, .$$

We now turn our attention to the manner in which money loan transactions are to be treated.

5.2 Money Loan Transactions

The combination of spot and forward purchases both payable today may be separated into three individual transactions when a money loan is inserted:

1. *A Spot Transaction*
The exchange of wheat available today *payable today* through a book credit at the price p_1;

2. *A Money Loan Transaction*
An exchange of money payable tomorrow against money payable today at the money or nominal rate of interest i, i.e., book entries at the central bookkeeping system available tomorrow against book entries available today.

3. *A Forward Transaction* (*Payable Tomorrow*)
An exchange of wheat available tomorrow against money *payable tomorrow* by means of a book transaction, at the price p_2^*.

Note: the transaction is concluded *today*, but effectuated tomorrow.

We have now two payment methods for today's forward transactions: mark payable *tomorrow* per kg of wheat delivered tomorrow (p_2^*); and mark payable *today* per kg of wheat delivered tomorrow (p_2). In our model world without transaction costs there exists the following zero transaction cost arbitrage equilibrium between the two methods of payment:

$$p_2 = \frac{p_2^*}{1 + i} \, .$$

As before, all means of payment consist of book transactions at the central bookkeeping system. Thus a money credit transaction looks as follows:

The borrower promises the lender the payment of a sum of money of B accounting units ("mark") available tomorrow in the form of a book credit in favor of the lender (available tomorrow) in return for a sum of money today of $B/(1 + i)$ accounting units ("mark"), i.e., if he receives a corresponding bank credit today. We have therefore an exchange of, e.g.,

$$\frac{1.2 \text{ mark available tomorrow}}{1 \text{ mark available today}} = \frac{B}{B}(1 + i) = (1 + i) = 1 + 0.2 \ .$$

The term i is *the own rate of interest of money*, or simply the money or *nominal rate of interest*. Its dimension is "i mark payable tomorrow per 1 mark repayment tomorrow," i.e., it is a pure number without dimension.

Since ZTC-arbitrage equilibrium obtains throughout we have also

$$1 + \rho_1^0 = \left(\frac{p_1}{p_2^*}\right)^0 = \left(\frac{p_1}{p_2}(1 + i)\right)^0 .$$

We imagine throughout that money loans take the form of bonds made out to bearer whose quality is assured.

Each individual title represents one unit of money (1 mark) available "tomorrow." The number of bonds is B. The present value (quotation) of a one-period title is

$$\gamma = 1/(1 + i) \ .$$

To explain further: a money loan transaction concluded today at the rate of interest of 8% per period ($i = 0.08$) and for the sum of $B = 100$ has the following content: the borrower receives today a money loan of $\gamma B \approx 92.60$ mark. He owes tomorrow 100 mark book money. This debt is in the form of 100 titles called "bonds," each of which has the nominal value of 1 mark available tomorrow. We imagine that the bonds are traded on the market under conditions of perfect competition, and that, therefore, their quotation or price γ (and with it the nominal rate of interest i) is determined exactly as the price p of any other good.

In order that the parties may negotiate the agreed upon nominal rate of interest i without money illusion it is necessary that they know, at least in principle, the purchasing power of money of today *and* tomorrow, or that they at least have an approximate idea of the purchasing power. In this case, it is therefore not sufficient that the central agent of the currency community fixes the price target only for the *one* period t either in the form of the value of money P_t of a basket of goods or the price p_{1t} for a particular good No. i. The central agent must also determine a price target (or interest target) for every future period (see below). Thus in our extremely simple example the central agent must fix p_1 and p_2^* as his price targets. If a general equilibrium exists, the equilibrium value of the exchange relation is known. It is

$$\pi_{21}^0 = \left(\frac{p_1}{p_2^*}(1 + i)\right)^0 .$$

The equilibrium value of the nominal rate of interest i is determined once p_1 and p_2^* are assumed.

We now turn to the bookkeeping aspects of the combination "spot transaction payable today—money loan transaction today—forward transaction payable tomorrow" for the Robinson example.

There are now two accounts for each economic unit, one for period 1 ("today") and a second one for period 2 ("tomorrow"). In addition a distinction is made in each period between the current account and the asset account of each economic unit.

As before we continue to assume equilibrium on all markets without using the superscript zero. Specifically the book entries are as follows:

Period 1

We start with the *household* Robinson:

Current Account of Household Robinson ($t = 1$)

M_{H1}	$p_1(-\hat{x}_1)$

In words: the household Robinson sells wheat available today for a credit on its bank account available today of $p_1(-\hat{x}_1)$. The credit or deposit corresponds to the amount of book money M_{H1}. In addition the household has an asset account with the central accounting system which in the present case shows the following changes:

Asset Account of Household Robinson ($t = 1$)

$\dfrac{B^d}{1+i}$	M_{H1}

In words: the household Robinson buys bonds with the present value $B^d/(1 + i)$, for the amount of money M_{H1} available today, i.e., it invests its money in the bond market. The symbol B^d denotes the *demand* for bonds (the supply of money loans).

If we consolidate the current and the asset accounts of the household Robinson we get for period 1

$$\frac{B^d}{1+i} = p_1(-\hat{x}_1) .$$

Because $\hat{x}_1 = x_1 - \bar{x}_1$, we can write the previous equation as

$$p_1 x_1 + \frac{B^d}{1+i} = p_1 \bar{x}_1 \ ; \tag{5-1}$$

this is the budget equation of the household Robinson for period 1.

For the *firm* Robinson the following book entries are made for period 1:

Current Account of Firm Robinson ($t = 1$)

$p_1(-y_1)$	M_{U1}

In words: the firm Robinson buys wheat available today against a bank debit on its account available today of $p_1(-y_1)$. Its payment corresponds to the sum of book money M_{U1}. Its asset account is charged as follows:

Asset Account of Firm Robinson ($t = 1$)

M_{U1}	$\frac{B^s}{1+i}$

In words: the firm Robinson gets the amount of money M_{U1} by selling bonds at their present value $B^s/(1 + i)$. Or, differently expressed, the firm goes into debt to the bond market for the same amount. The symbol B^s denotes the *supply* of bonds (the demand for money loans).

If we consolidate the current and the asset accounts of the firm Robinson, we get for period 1

$$p_1(-y_1) = B^s/(1 + i) \quad (5\text{-}2)$$

The *spot transaction* "exchange of wheat available today against money payable today through credit to his account" is made apparent by means of the current account of the household and the firm for period 1. The book entries in the asset accounts of the household and the firm make apparent the corresponding *money loan transaction B* mark available tomorrow against $B/(1 + i)$ mark available today. The money loan transaction is thus presented as related to "today," for our account refers to period 1.

Since we assume equilibrium on all markets, $\hat{x}_1 = y_1$ and $B^d = B^s$.

We continue in an analogous manner for period 2 (tomorrow).

Period 2

Again, we begin with the *household* Robinson:

Current Account of Household Robinson ($t = 2$)

$p_2^* x_2$	M_{H2}

Household Robinson purchases today for future delivery wheat available tomorrow and payable tomorrow by a book entry debiting his account. He receives the claim to a delivery of wheat in the value $p_2^* x_2$. The debiting of his account, i.e., the disbursement, corresponds to the amount of book money of M_{H2}. The household ensures the receipt of the needed amount of money of M_{H2} in the following manner:

Asset Account of Household Robinson ($t = 2$)

M_{H2}	B^d $Q(1 + i)$

In words: the household Robinson offers a money loan today which in turn gives him the claim to the payment of B^d mark, including interest, available tomorrow. In addition as owner of the firm Robinson he has a claim to the payment of the profit of the firm Robinson which will accrue tomorrow at its value tomorrow of $Q(1 + i)$.

By consolidating the current and the asset accounts of the household Robinson we get for period 2:

(5-3) $$p_2^* x_2 = B^d + Q(1 + i) \ .$$

Household Robinson pays its money debt due tomorrow of $p_2^* x_2$ with its claim to receive tomorrow the amount of money of $B^d + Q(1 + i)$. It is already today determined how tomorrow's money receipts are to be used. There are no open positions.

For the *firm* Robinson we get the following book entries:

Current Account of Firm Robinson ($t = 2$)

M_{U2}	$p_2^* y_2$

In words: the firm Robinson sells tomorrow's wheat harvest today for future delivery against a bank loan M_{U2} on its account available tomorrow to the amount of $p_2^* y_2$.

The utilization of the amount of money M_{U2} by the firm Robinson looks as follows:

Asset Account of Firm Robinson ($t = 2$)

B^s $Q(1 + i)$	M_{U2}

Firm Robinson repays its money debts due tomorrow to the extent of B^s currency units (including interest which is here included with B^s) and, according to agreement, distributes its entire profit whose value tomorrow is $Q(1 + i)$.

By consolidating the current and asset accounts of the firm Robinson, we get for period 2:

(5-4) $$B^s + Q(1 + i) = p_2^* y_2 \ .$$

The two current accounts of the household and the firm Robinson in $t = 2$ illustrate the bookkeeping procedures for the forward transaction (payable tomorrow). The intermediation of the money-loan transactions does not change the validity of Say's law. If the household were to save today an additional 1 mark and were to invest it at the same time in interest-bearing bonds, it would be simultaneously determined which additional goods and in what amounts it will buy tomorrow. In the words of Keynes from the beginning of the 16th Chapter of his *General Theory* this means:

the decision not to have lunch today *does* here "necessitate a decision to have dinner or to buy a pair of boots a week hence or a year hence or to consume any specified thing at any specified date." (J.M. Keynes 1936, 210).

The lender knows exactly which transaction is being financed by his money loan. The borrower knows with certainty which transaction will allow him to repay the loan.

We now consolidate equations (5-1) to (5-4) so that the money loan remains visible. We get

1. *For the Household Robinson*

(5-1) $$p_1 x_1 + B^d/(1+i) = p_1 \bar{x}_1 \qquad \text{for } t = 1 \ ,$$

(5-3) $$p_2^* x_2 = B^d + Q(1+i) \qquad \text{for } t = 2 \ .$$

2. *For the Firm Robinson*

(5-2) $$p_1(-y_1) = B^s/(1+i) \qquad \text{for } t = 1 \ ,$$

(5-4) $$B^s + Q(1+i) = p_2^* y_2 \qquad \text{for } t = 2 \ .$$

As can be seen there are no cash holdings (M). Cash (=money) does not appear as an instrument to transfer assets into the future. This would be uneconomic since we have assumed that the exchange of cash against bonds and vice versa does not entail any cost. The cash M appears only as a transitory item in each individual period.

Equations (5-1) and (5-3) show in a different manner the total budget equation of the household Robinson for period 1

$$p_1 x_1 + p_2 x_2 = p_1 \bar{x}_1 + Q \ .$$

This representation does not show, however, the possible insertion of money loans.

Analogously, equation (5-2) and (5-4) are another way of writing the profit equation of the firm Robinson for period 1

$$Q = p_1 y_1 + p_2 y_2 \ .$$

To repeat: in the case of a Pure Futures Economy it makes no difference

- whether the contracting parties agree on a real loan with the exchange relation $1 + \rho_1$; or
- whether they conclude spot and forward purchase agreements, payable today, at prices p_1, p_2; or
- whether they conclude two purchase agreements at prices p_1, p_2^* with the intermediation of a money-loan transaction at the money or nominal rate of interest i.

ZTC-arbitrage equilibrium exists among all three possibilities, i.e.,

$$1 + \rho_1 = p_1/p_2$$

and $$\frac{p_1}{p_2} = \frac{p_1}{p_2^*}(1 + i) \ .$$

p_1, p_2^* are here by assumption fixed by the central agent. The nominal rate of interest i must be determined on the market. The market system which is relevant for our example consists therefore of two goods market equations:

$$\hat{x}_1(i) = y_1(i) \quad \text{spot market for wheat today} \ ,$$

$$x_2(i) = y_2(i) \quad \text{forward market for wheat tomorrow, but payable today} \ .$$

The equation for the bond market can be derived from either of the two equations for the goods markets, e.g., from the equation for the spot market, by using equations (5-1) and (5-2).

$$\tilde{B}^d(i) = \tilde{B}^s(i) \quad \text{market for money loans or bond market} \ ,$$

$$\tilde{B} \equiv \frac{1}{p_1}\frac{B}{1 + i} \ .$$

It is $$\frac{B^d}{1 + i} = p_1(-\hat{x}_1) \quad \text{and} \quad \frac{B^s}{1 + i} = p_1(-y_1)$$

or $$\tilde{B}^d = -\hat{x}_1 \quad \text{and} \quad \tilde{B}^s = -y_1 \ .$$

The equilibrium value of i, if it exists, may be calculated from any one of the three equations. Because of *Walras's law*, equilibrium on the forward market for wheat exists (e.g.) if there is equilibrium on the spot market. The equation for the bond market may be simply substituted for the equation for the spot or forward market in order to calculate the equilibrium rate of interest i.

We have shown in this section how one might think of money loan transactions for an economy with only one good (wheat) under the ideal conditions of an intertemporal equilibrium. The money or nominal rate of interest i was introduced and explained. We have shown which assumptions about price goals are necessary for the money rate of interest to be determined in general equilibrium.

5.3 The Neo-Classical Theory of the Money or Nominal Rate of Interest: A Simple Case

We continue our considerations of the preceding section by asking how one can explain the determination of the equilibrium value of the nominal rate of interest from the standpoint of the individual firm. We stick to the elementary case of a Robinson economy with only one good (wheat) and two periods (today and tomorrow).

For the *household* Robinson we assume maximization of utility in analogy to (2-3), (2-4). The constraint (2-4) is at first broken down into (5-1), (5-3).

The optimization problem of the household is:

$$\text{Max}\, U = U(x_1, x_2)$$

subject to

(5-1) $$p_1 x_1 + B^d/(1+i) = p_1 \bar{x}_1 \;,$$

(5-3) $$p_2^* x_2 = B^d + Q(1+i) \;.$$

If we consolidate the constraints (5-1), (5-3) into one equation, we can rewrite the optimization problem of the household as:

(5-5) $$\text{Max} \quad U = U(x_1, x_2)$$

(5-6) $$\text{s.t.} \quad p_1 x_1 + \frac{p_2^*}{1+i} x_2 = p_1 \bar{x}_1 + Q \;.$$

For the optimal consumption plan we have under the usual assumptions of an interior optimum the marginal condition

$$\frac{U_1}{U_2} = \frac{p_1}{p_2^*}(1+i)$$

or

(5-7) $$\frac{U_1}{p_1} = \frac{U_2}{p_2^*}(1+i) \;.$$

The dimension of the left side (5-7) is

$$\dim\left[\frac{U_1}{p_1}\right] = \frac{\text{marginal utility today}}{\text{kg good 1}} \cdot \frac{\text{kg good 1}}{\text{mark today}} = \frac{\text{marginal utility today}}{\text{mark today}} \;.$$

The same is true for the right side of (5-7). In other words, today's *marginal utility of money* appears on both sides.

The meaning of equation (5-7) is, in words: with an interior optimum of the household, today's marginal utility of money when used for present goods is equal to today's marginal utility of money when used for future goods. (Gossen's second law: law of the equalization of the marginal utility of money).

We know already that

$$\frac{U_1}{U_2} = -\frac{dx_2}{dx_1} .$$

We may thus reformulate (5-7) to read:

$$\text{(5-8)} \qquad \frac{p_2^*}{p_1}\left|\frac{dx_2}{dx_1}\right| - 1 = i .$$

In words: with an interior optimum the rate of time preference of money is equal to the money (or nominal) rate of interest.

I. Fisher (1930, 46) assumes in this connection that $p_2^* = p_1$ so that the nominal rate of interest is equal to the own rate of interest ($i = \rho_1$). Under his assumptions this is true for all goods. (This is also true in the stationary case).

Differences between the nominal and the real rates of interest are, according to Fisher, a monetary phenomenon rather than a problem of explaining the rate of interest.[2]

The equations which determine the optimal consumption plan (x_1, x_2) are thus:

$$\text{(5-9)} \qquad x_1 = x_1\left(\frac{p_1}{p_2^*}(1+i)\right) ,$$

$$\text{(5-10)} \qquad x_2 = x_2(\cdot) .$$

The equation which determines the optimal demand for bonds follows from equation (5-1). It is

$$\text{(5-11)} \qquad \tilde{B}^d = \tilde{B}^d\left(\frac{p_1}{p_2}(1+i)\right) = x_1 - \bar{x}_1 , \qquad \text{where } \tilde{B}^d = \frac{B^d}{1+i}\frac{1}{p_1} .$$

We now consider the *firm* Robinson.

The optimization problem for the firm corresponds to (2-5), (2-6), with $p_2 = p_2^*/(1+i)$:

$$\text{(5-12)} \qquad \text{Max} \quad Q = p_1 y_1 + \frac{p_2^*}{1+i} y_2 ,$$

[2] I. Fisher (1930, 45): "While the deviations of the money rate of interest from the real rate are of tremendous practical importance, they may be regarded as belonging more to the problem of money than to the problem of interest, ..."

(5-13) s.t. $\phi(y_1, y_2) = 0$.

For the optimal production plan we get under the usual conditions of an interior optimum:

$$\frac{\phi_1}{\phi_2} = \frac{p_1}{p_2^*}(1 + i) \ ,$$

or, because $\phi_1/\phi_2 = -dy_2/dy_1$

$$\left|\frac{dy_2}{dy_1}\right| = \frac{p_1}{p_2^*}(1 + i)$$

or, alternatively

$$\frac{p_2^*}{p_1}\left|\frac{dy_2}{dy_1}\right| - 1 = i \ . \quad \text{(5-14)}$$

In words: with an interior optimum of the firm the *marginal efficiency of capital*[3] equals the nominal rate of interest.

To explain: the left side of (5-14) may be read as the net return which results from an additional mark invested related to just this additional mark invested (marginal internal rate of interest).

By using the rate of change of the price of wheat v_1, which is defined as

$$p_2^* = (1 + v_1)p_1 \ ,$$

we can rewrite (5-14) as

$$\left|\frac{dy_2}{dy_1}\right| = \frac{1 + i}{1 + v_1}$$ (= $1 + \rho_1$, because there is ZTC-arbitrage equilibrium)

or as

$$\left|\frac{dy_2}{dy_1}\right| - 1 = \frac{i - v_1}{1 + v_1} \quad \text{(5-15)}$$ (= ρ_1, because of ZTC-arbitrage equilibrium) .

In words: with an interior optimum of the firm the net marginal productivity of capital is equal to the nominal rate of interest, corrected for the rate of change of the price. Thus, there are two versions of the marginal conditions for the profit maximizing capital stock. Both are found in the literature.

---

[3] "i.e., the relation between the prospective yield of one more unit of [a capital asset] and the cost of producing that unit, ..." (J.M. Keynes 1936, 135). I. Fisher (1930, 159f.) speaks in this connection of the "marginal rate of return over cost."

We get the supply of bonds of the firm

$$\tilde{B}^s = \frac{\tilde{B}^s}{1+i}\frac{1}{p_1}$$

from (5-2) as

$$\text{(5-16)} \qquad \tilde{B}^s = \tilde{B}^s\left(\frac{p_1}{p_2^*}(1+i)\right) = -y_1(\cdot)\ .$$

In intertemporal general equilibrium it follows from equations (5-8) and (5-14) that

$$\frac{p_2^*}{p_1}\left|\frac{dx_2}{dx_1}\right| - 1 = \frac{p_2^*}{p_1}\left|\frac{dy_2}{dy_1}\right| - 1 = i\ .$$

Corresponding to the main theorem of the theory of the real rate of interest (Section 2.2) we get the following

Fundamental Theorem of the Neoclassical Theory of the Nominal Rate of Interest: In intertemporal general equilibrium the nominal (or money) rate of interest in each period $t = 1, \ldots, T$, is equal to

1. the rate of time preference of money,
2. the marginal efficiency of capital.

From (5-11) and (5-16) it follows for the bond market that

$$\text{(5-17)} \qquad \tilde{B}^d\left(\frac{p_1}{p_2^*}(1+i)\right) = \tilde{B}^s\left(\frac{p_1}{p_2^*}(1+i)\right)\ .$$

As can be seen immediately the prices p_1, p_2^* must be fixed exogenously by the central agent (or the currency order) if the nominal rate of interest i is to be a free variable. At the equilibrium value i^0 of the nominal rate of interest, it follows from (5-17) that the real present value of the supply of money loans ($\tilde{B}^d$) is equal to the real present value of the demand for money loans ($\tilde{B}^s$) (Fig. 5-1). Demand for and supply of loanable funds are in equilibrium. We have here a simple form of the so-called loanable funds theory of the nominal (or money) rate of interest, i.e., the classical or neoclassical theory of the nominal rate of interest.[4] It is a strictly real theory of the rate of interest.[5]

---

[4] For a survey, see D. Patinkin (1965, 366ff.). There one will also find the quotation from J.S. Mill: "the rate of interest ... depends essentially and permanently on the comparative amount of real capital offered and demanded in the way of loan."

[5] "The classical theory ... is a non-monetary or real theory of interest ... ." See L.A. Metzler (1951) as quoted in the reprint in R. Thorn (1966, 329).

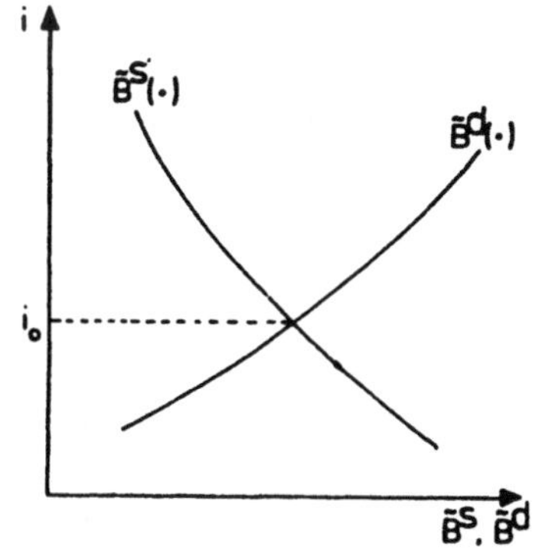

Fig. 5-1. Demand for and Supply of Money Loans

This is the manner in which we think of money-loan transactions which are interposed between two corresponding purchase agreements. The money interest rate i is negotiated. The relevant equilibrium relationship is the equation for the bond market:

$$(5\text{-}17) \qquad \tilde{B}^d\left(\frac{p_1}{p_2^*}(1+i)\right) = \tilde{B}^s\left(\frac{p_1}{p_2^*}(1+i)\right) .$$

In words: the planned supply of money loans (in real terms) is equal to the planned demand for money loans. The prices p_1, p_2^* are assumed to be given exogenously.

In the case of a loan in kind, the level of the real rate of interest ρ_1 is an object of negotiations. The relevant equilibrium condition is one of the two equations for the goods market, e.g., of the market for wheat available today. It can be in the form of (2-8) or

$$(2\text{-}10) \qquad K^s(\rho_1) = K^d(\rho_1) .$$

In words: the planned supply of real capital is equal to the planned demand for real capital (see Section 2.2).

All lending is effected in the form of "real capital goods" (Wicksell). The equilibrium value of ρ_1 is, in Wicksell's (1936, 102) terminology, "the current value of the *natural rate of interest on capital*." In a world without transaction costs, loans in kind and in the form of money have exactly the same result; there is arbitrage equilibrium in the sense of

$$(5\text{-}18) \qquad 1 + \rho_1 = \frac{p_1}{p_2^*}(1+i) .$$

The exogenous determination of p_1, p_2^* and i amounts to the exogenous determination of the real rate of interest ρ. This is incompatible with the conditions of a free market economy in which there is no government intervention. One of the three terms p_1, p_2^* or i must remain a free variable – in the present case only one! At the moment we assume this to be the nominal interest rate i.

For exogenously fixed prices with $p_1 = p_2^*$ we get for our simple Pure Futures Economy in general equilibrium

$$\rho_1 = i \ ,$$

i.e., the own rate of wheat is in equilibrium equal to the nominal rate of interest.

In Wicksell's terminology, the natural rate of interest on capital equals the rate of interest on loans.

There is no difference between the results of the direct exchange of real capital goods and of the indirect exchange through the interposition of loans.

With reference to a pure book money system, Wicksell (1936, 104) writes: "Now if money is loaned at this same rate of interest, it serves as nothing more than a cloak to cover a procedure which, from the purely formal point of view, could have been carried on equally well without it. The conditions of economic equilibrium are fulfilled in precisely the same manner. In such a case, there is no occasion for any alternation in the level of prices." (The last sentence refers to Wicksell's theory of price level changes; see below).

We can visualize by means of a simple diagram (Fig. 5-2) which transactions are possible in our simple case and which exchange relations are equal to each other in ZTC-arbitrage equilibrium.[6]

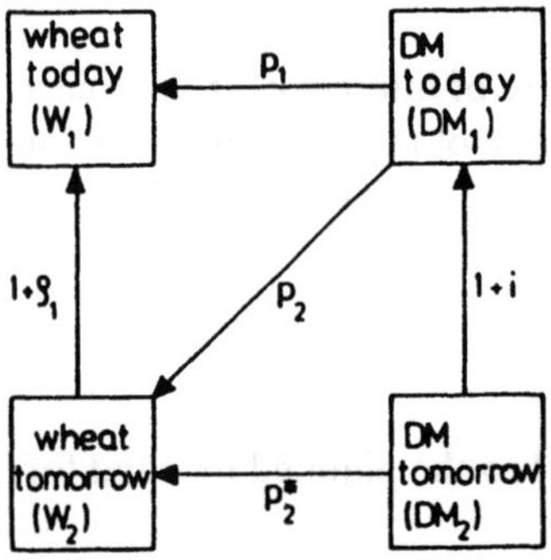

Fig. 5-2. ZTC-Arbitrage Diagram: two Goods, one Currency, two Periods

The boxes show the particular objects of the exchange. The arrows indicate the direction of the exchange relationships. The diagram can be read as follows:

Arrow p_1: the exchange of p_1 mark payable today (DM_1) per kg wheat available today (W_1). For the reverse transaction we use the reciprocal price $1/p_1$, i.e., the exchange of $1/p_1$ kg wheat for 1 mark payable today, etc.

We get the relevant ZTC-arbitrage equations when we choose any two objects of the exchange, e.g., W_1 and W_2. All paths which lead from W_1 to W_2 and vice versa refer to equivalent exchange relationships in ZTC-arbitrage equilibrium. The ex-

[6] I owe this figure and the idea of its application to H. Jäckel.

change relationships of multiple transactions are found by multiplication of the (possibly reciprocal) exchange relationships of the individual transactions.

$$
\begin{aligned}
& W_2 \to W_1 && = 1 + \rho_1 \\
\Leftrightarrow\ & W_2 \to \mathrm{DM}_1 \to W_1 && = p_1 \cdot \frac{1}{p_2} \\
\Leftrightarrow\ & W_2 \to \mathrm{DM}_2 \to \mathrm{DM}_1 \to \mathrm{W}_1 && = p_1(1+i)\frac{1}{p_2^*}
\end{aligned}
$$

In ZTC-arbitrage equilibrium,

$$1 + \rho_1 = \frac{p_1}{p_2}$$

and

$$1 + \rho_1 = \frac{p_1}{p_2^*}(1+i) \ ,$$

where

$$p_2 = \frac{p_2^*}{1+i} \ .$$

5.4 The Neo-Classical Theory of the Money or Nominal Rate of Interest: Some Extensions

We now extend our simple model to more than one good and to money loans subject to different time stipulations. The idea is to thus get a base for a more extensive discussion of the interrelationship between interest and prices than our simple model offered. For that purpose we look at two smaller extensions of our simple model:

- the case of two present and two future goods; and
- the case of one good and three periods.

5.4.1 *Two Present and Two Future Goods*

We limit our discussion to the vector of solutions $\mathbb{L}$ of general equilibrium. Assuming spot and forward purchase transactions we get:

$$\mathbb{L} = \left\{\frac{p_{11}}{p_{12}}, \frac{p_{21}}{p_{22}}, \frac{p_{11}}{p_{21}}\right\}$$

(see Section 2.3).

We have assumed that arbitrage equilibrium exists at all times. Hence, the vector of solutions for barter transactions

$$\mathbb{L} = \{(1+\rho_1), (1+\rho_2), \pi_{21}\}$$

is numerically equal to the case of spot and forward purchases. The same holds for the case of a combination of purchase and money loan transactions

$$\mathbb{L} = \left\{\frac{p_{11}}{p_{12}^*}(1+i), \frac{p_{21}}{p_{22}^*}(1+i), \frac{p_{11}}{p_{21}}\right\}$$

or, written differently,

$$\mathbb{L} = \left\{\frac{1+i}{1+v_1}, \frac{1+i}{1+v_2}, \frac{p_{11}}{p_{21}}\right\} .$$

In the present context we are interested mainly in the third case, i.e., the case of a purchase with the intermediation of money loan transactions.

The *conditions for a market equilibrium* are found using the corresponding equations which determine the optimal consumption and production plans:

$$\left.\begin{aligned} \hat{x}_{11}\left(\frac{p_{11}}{p_{12}^*}(1+i), \frac{p_{21}}{p_{22}^*}(1+i), \frac{p_{11}}{p_{21}}\right) &= y_{11}(\cdot) \\ \hat{x}_{21}(\cdot) &= y_{21}(\cdot) \end{aligned}\right\} \quad \text{spot markets}$$

$$\left.\begin{aligned} x_{12}(\cdot) &= y_{12}(\cdot) \\ x_{22}(\cdot) &= y_{22}(\cdot) \end{aligned}\right\} \quad \text{forward markets}$$

$$\tilde{B}^s(\cdot) = \tilde{B}^d(\cdot) \qquad \text{bond market}$$

Note that in this case the real demand for bonds is found by adding two quantities of goods demanded (which must, of course, have the same dimensions). The same is true for the supply of bonds. For example:

$$\tilde{B}^d = -\hat{x}_{11} + \frac{p_{21}}{p_{11}}(-\hat{x}_{21}) ,$$

$$\tilde{B}^s = -y_{11} + \frac{p_{21}}{p_{11}}(-y_{21}) .$$

Because of Walras's law, only three of the four goods market equations are independent of each other. The three basic variables of the model are

$$\frac{p_{11}}{p_{12}^*}(1+i) , \quad \frac{p_{21}}{p_{22}^*}(1+i) , \quad \frac{p_{11}}{p_{21}} .$$

The system can in principle be solved for these three variables by using three of the four goods market equations, or by using two of the goods market equations (e.g., of spot and forward wheat) and the bond market equation, as defined above. The prices p expressed in accounting units are determined. So is the nominal rate of interest i if we assume the prices of one of the present goods (e.g., p_{11}) and of one of the future goods (e.g., p_{12}^*) to be fixed as price targets by the central agent. Note: in a Pure Futures Economy, all transactions are concluded today for all time to come and with complete certainty. This is true even when money loan transactions are inserted. Hence all forward prices payable tomorrow (p^*) are known with perfect certainty to all parties in the market. In this sense we have perfect foresight.[7]

We now return to our model.

In the stationary case we have:

$$\frac{p_{11}}{p_{21}} = \frac{p_{12}^*}{p_{22}^*}$$

$$\Rightarrow \frac{p_{11}}{p_{12}^*} = \frac{p_{21}}{p_{22}^*}$$

$$\Rightarrow v_1 = v_2 = v \ .$$

The v_1, v_2 are the rates of price changes $p_{12}^* = (1 + v_1)p_{11}$; $p_{22}^* = (1 + v_2)p_{21}$.

In stationary general equilibrium the relative prices remain constant over time. Absolute prices change only by the same multiple v for *all* goods. We speak of a general increase or decrease of prices, of *inflation* or *deflation* (=negative inflation). The variable v is thus the expected *rate of inflation* between today and tomorrow which in our case is known exactly because we have assumed perfect foresight.

We have shown in Section 2.3 that in stationary equilibrium

$$\rho_1 = \rho_2 = \rho \ .$$

It is also true for all periods that

$$1 + \rho = \frac{1 + i}{1 + v}$$

or

$$\rho = \frac{1 - v}{1 + v} \ . \tag{5-19}$$

[7] Thus defined, e.g., by J.R. Hicks (1946, 140). Hicks stresses the *theoretical* usefulness of the unrealistic concept of the Pure Futures Economy as follows: "By examining what system of prices would be fixed up in a futures economy, we can find out what system of prices would maintain equilibrium over time under a given set of changing conditions. Economists have often toyed with the idea of a system where all persons trading have 'perfect foresight.' This leads to awkward logical difficulties, but the purpose for which they have invented such systems can be met by our futures economy."

For small values of v it is approximately true that

$$\rho \approx i - v \quad \text{or} \quad i \approx \rho + v \ .$$

This is the form in which the so-called *Fisher relation* is usually written.[8] It is, in words:

With zero transaction costs the nominal rate of interest i is approximately equal to the equilibrium value of the real rate of interest ρ plus the rate of inflation v. Thus, the Fisher relation is the consequence of a certain ZTC-arbitrage equilibrium.

For $\quad v = 0 \quad$ (the case of price stability)

$$\rho = i \ ,$$

i.e., the real and the nominal rates of interest are equal.

In the case of inflation, i.e., a general increase in prices,

$$v > 0$$

and $\quad \rho < i \ .$

"The fact that interest expressed in *money* is high, say 15%, might conceivably indicate merely that general prices are expected to rise ... at the rate of 10%, and that the rate of interest expressed in terms of *goods* is not high, but only about 5%."[9]

With perfect foresight (which exists in the Pure Futures Economy) future price increases are completely anticipated and the changes in purchasing power in all money claims are completely compensated for via an increase in the nominal rate of interest. We can understand this as the limiting case of the so-called *fully anticipated inflation*, a concept which is used among others, by D.E.W. Laidler and M. Parkin (1975, 794).

"If inflation was fully anticipated by all parties the economy could operate consistently at full employment, and there would be no redistribution of income and wealth except between the holders of non-interest-bearing cash balances and those whose liabilities include such balances."

The ZTC-arbitrage equations for the previous example may be graphically presented for wheat W and oats H as follows:

[8] So named after I. Fisher who emphasized this particular connection. See I. Fisher (1896/1926, 55–58; 1930, 37–42). Fisher, however, thought of the use of a cost of living index to determine his real rate of interest, not of the academic case of a stationary general equilibrium (see I. Fisher 1930, 42).

[9] I. Fisher (1930, 41 f.). For the real world, it is argued that the real rate of interest cannot, at least in the long run, be influenced by a change in the rate of inflation. For literature for and against, see, e.g., J. Fried and P. Howitt (1983, 968 f.).

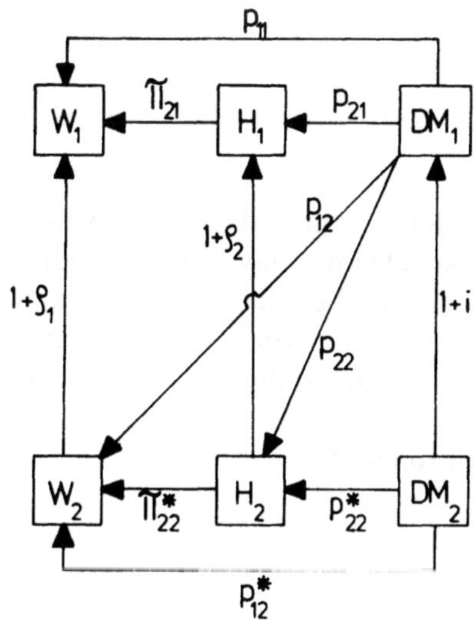

Fig. 5-3. ZTC-Arbitrage Diagram: one Good, one Currency, two Periods

We could compose very different arbitrage equations, e.g.,

for $W_2 \to W_1$

for example: $1 + \rho_1 = \dfrac{p_{11}}{p^*_{12}}(1 + i)$,

for $H_2 \to H_1$,

for example: $1 + \rho_2 = \dfrac{p_{21}}{p^*_{22}}(1 + i)$

and for $W_1 \to H_1$,

for example: $\pi_{21} = \dfrac{p_{11}}{p_{21}}$.

5.4.2 *One Good and Three Periods*

Here, too, we will discuss only vectors of solutions $\mathbb{L}$ for general equilibrium. We use the following subscripts:

11: Wheat available today,
12: Wheat available tomorrow,
13: Wheat available the day after tomorrow.

The vector of solutions $\mathbb{L}$ is now for the case of a spot and future purchase

$$\mathbb{L} = \left\{\frac{p_{11}}{p_{12}}, \frac{p_{11}}{p_{13}}\right\} .$$

If we insert money loans, it becomes

$$\mathbb{L} = \left\{\frac{p_{11}}{p_{12}^*}(1 + {}_1i_2), \frac{p_{11}}{p_{13}^*}(1 + {}_1I_3)^2\right\}$$

where ${}_1i_2$ is the rate of interest for "short-period" loans from today to tomorrow, and ${}_1I_3$ is the rate of interest for "long-period" loans from today to the day after tomorrow. Correspondingly there are now two kinds of bonds, short-term and long-term bonds. If the interest rates ${}_1i_2$, ${}_1I_3$ are to be determined through free negotiations on the market, the p_{11}, p_{12}^*, p_{13}^* are the magnitudes which are to be exogenously fixed by the central agent.

It is the second variant of $\mathbb{L}$ which is of interest to us. We have:

$$(1 + {}_1I_3)^2 = (1 + {}_1i_2)(1 + {}_2i_3) \tag{5-20}$$

and therefore

$${}_1I_3 = \sqrt{(1 + {}_1i_2)(1 + {}_2i_3)} - 1$$

or approximately

$${}_1I_3 \approx \frac{{}_1i_2 + {}_2i_3}{2} .$$ [10]

We speak in this case of the *equal rate of return principle* (see, e.g., E.F. Fama and M.H. Miller 1972, 79). It follows from the assumption of a general ZTC-arbitrage equilibrium: equation (5-20) must be valid since there are markets for all three forms of money loans (the two short-period loans and the long-period loan) at the time of planning. Otherwise it would be possible to realize perfectly certain profits from interest arbitrage; the three markets would not be in an arbitrage equilibrium. Thus it is here irrelevant whether one concludes one money-loan contract for two periods or two money-loan contracts for one period each, one after the other. All investments yield the same return.

The interest rates for short loans ${}_1i_2$ and for long loans ${}_1I_3$ form the *term structure of interest rates of the model.* Equation (5-20) and its variants correspond to the so-called expectations hypothesis of the theory of the term structure of interest rates. It plays an important role in the explanation of the term structure in the real world.[11]

For the interest rate differential ${}_1I_3 - {}_1i_2$, the so-called *spread*, we distinguish the following three cases:

(1) The spread is zero (${}_1I_3 - {}_1i_2 = 0$). The rate of interest i for short loans is expected to be constant: ${}_1i_2 = {}_2i_3$.

[10] J. R. Hicks (1946, 145f.).

[11] See, e.g., B.G. Malkiel (1966, 17ff.); for empirical measurements, see C.R. Nelson (1972).

(2) The spread is positive ($_1I_3 - {}_1i_2 > 0$). The short rate of interest i is expected to rise:

$$_1i_2 < {}_2i_3 \ .$$

(3) The spread is negative ($_1I_3 - {}_1i_2 < 0$). The nominal rate of interest i is expected to fall:

$$_1i_2 > {}_2i_3 \ .$$

The curves of the term structure of interest rates look correspondingly. The interest rate structure is not independent of the development of the rate of inflation, the so-called inflation rates structure. Consider the case in which the real rate of interest or short loans ρ is constant:

$$_1\rho_{12} = {}_2\rho_{13} = \rho \ .$$

Because of the ZTC-arbitrage equilibrium conditions, we have:

$$\text{(5-21)} \qquad 1 + \rho = \frac{p_{11}}{p_{12}^*}(1 + {}_1i_2) = \frac{p_{12}^*}{p_{13}^*}(1 + {}_2i_3)$$

or for $p_{12}^* = (1 + {}_1v_2)p_{11}$ and $p_{13}^* = (1 + {}_2v_3)p_{12}^*$

$$1 + \rho = \frac{1 + {}_1i_2}{1 + {}_1v_2} = \frac{1 + {}_2i_3}{1 + {}_2v_3} \ .$$

As is immediately apparent, for $_1v_2 = {}_2v_3 = 0$, we get

$$\rho = {}_1i_2 = {}_2i_3 \ .$$

The rate of interest for money loans is constant and equal to the "natural" rate of interest.

For a positive but constant rate of inflation ($v > 0$) we get:

$$\rho < {}_1i_2 \ ; \qquad {}_1i_2 = {}_2i_3 \ .$$

The rate of interest for loans is constant but higher than the "natural" rate of interest, whose level is independent of the rate of inflation.

For a positive but increasing rate of inflation ($_1v_2 < {}_2v_3$) we get

$$\rho < {}_1i_2 \ ; \qquad {}_1i_2 < {}_2i_3$$
$$\Rightarrow {}_1I_3 - {}_1i_2 > 0 \ .$$

The rate of interest for loans increases and is higher than the "natural" rate of interest.

In the stationary case, therefore, a positive spread implies the expectation of an increasing rate of inflation, an expectation which in our case is assumed to be certain. *Mutatis mutandis*, the conclusions apply to the case of diminishing rates of interest for loans.

For the case of short- and long-term loans in kind the ZTC-arbitrage condition (5-20) reads as follows:

$$(1 + {}_1R_{13})^2 = (1 + {}_1\rho_{12})(1 + {}_2\rho_{13}) \; .$$

R designates the value of the real rate of interest related to the unit period of the long-term loan made in kind. In arbitrage equilibrium with zero transaction costs it is

$$1 + {}_1\rho_{12} = \frac{p_{11}}{p_{12}^*}(1 + {}_1i_2) \; ,$$

$$(1 + {}_1R_{13})^2 = \frac{p_{11}}{p_{13}^*}(1 + {}_1I_3)^2 \; .$$

The diagram for the arbitrage equilibria looks as follows:

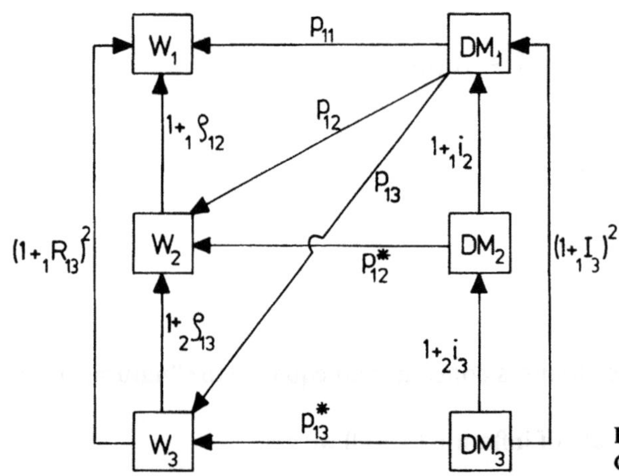

Fig. 5-4. ZTC-Arbitrage Diagram: one Good, one Currency, three Periods

Here, too, it is possible to formulate the most diverse arbitrage equations. For example,

for $W_2 \rightarrow W_1$ we might use

$$1 + {}_1\rho_{12} = \frac{p_{11}}{p_{12}^*}(1 + {}_1i_2) \; ;$$

and for $W_3 \rightarrow W_1$ we might use

$$(1 + {}_1R_{13})^2 = \frac{p_{11}}{p_{13}^*}(1 + {}_1i_2)(1 + {}_2i_3) = \frac{p_{11}}{p_{13}^*}(1 + {}_1I_3)^2 \; .$$

5.5 Interest and Prices

We have so far assumed that the central agent determines for each period as its price target the price of a particular good or basket of goods. However, the price target may also contain target values of nominal rates of interest. Consider, for example, the case of two present and two future goods. The relevant vector of solutions is:

$$\mathbb{L} = \left\{\frac{p_{11}}{p_{12}^*}(1 + i), \frac{p_{21}}{p_{22}^*}(1 + i), \frac{p_{11}}{p_{21}}\right\} .$$

The equilibrium values of the absolute prices and with them the purchasing power of money are determined, if, e.g., p_{11} and i are exogenously fixed. The exogenous determination of the nominal rate of interest does not, however, suffice to determine the purchasing power of money. The central agent must, in addition, fix the price of at least one good. It is generally true: interest rate targets do not suffice to determine the purchasing power of money. The value of the currency requires a *real anchoring* by the exogenous fixing of the price of at least one good. For the case of T periods, this means that the central agent must fix not only the rates of interest for $t - 1$ periods but the price of one good as well, in order to make the equilibrium values of the absolute price determinate. There is thus a "$(T - 1)$ *problem of interest rate policy.*"

We have seen that the purchasing power of money is determined only if the central agent fixes price targets which may include interest rates. It is, however, not entirely free in this. It must observe certain consistency conditions.

In order to show this, consider the stationary equilibrium of our examples. We have in this case:

$$\mathbb{L} = \left\{\frac{p_{11}}{p_{12}^*}(1 + i), \frac{p_{21}}{p_{22}^*}(1 + i), \frac{p_{11}}{p_{21}}\right\}$$

where $$\frac{p_{11}}{p_{12}^*}(1 + i) = \frac{p_{21}}{p_{22}^*}(1 + i) \quad (= 1 + \rho)$$

or $$\frac{1 + i}{1 + v_1} = \frac{1 + i}{1 + v_2} ; \quad v_1 = v_2 = v .$$

Because of ZTC-arbitrage equilibrium we get

$$\text{(5-22)} \qquad \frac{1 + \rho}{1 + i} = \frac{1}{1 + v} ;$$

p_{11} and i are exogenously fixed. The choice of i determines simultaneously the equilibrium value of the rate of inflation v.

From (5-22) follows:

(1) If in stationary equilibrium the central agent of the currency community fixes the nominal rate of interest precisely at the level of the equilibrium value of the real rate ($i = \rho$), the inflation rate will be zero ("Wicksell's theorem"). Wicksell, who also thought of the process of adaptation, expressed himself as follows:

"There is a certain rate of interest on loans which is neutral in respect to commodity prices, and tends neither to raise nor to lower them. This is necessarily the same as the rate of interest which would be determined by supply and demand if no use were made of money and all lending were effected in the form of real capital goods. It comes to much the same thing to describe it as the current value of the *natural rate of interest on capital*." (K. Wicksell 1936, 102; italics in the original).

Wicksell, however, overlooked that the (absolute) prices and with them the purchasing power of money are determined only if the $(T - 1)$ problem of the interest rate policy is allowed for, that is, only if the price of one good is exogenously fixed in addition.

(2) If the central agent of the currency community does not fix the nominal rate of interest i at the equilibrium level of the real rate ρ ($i \neq \rho$), the fixed nominal rate of interest is consistent with a stationary equilibrium only if the currency community accepts the according to (5-22) matching rate of inflation or deflation: if $i < \rho$, $v < 0$; if $i > \rho$, $v > 0$.

In the present model, the central agent cannot fix the nominal rate of interest at any arbitrary level and *simultaneously* aim at a certain rate of inflation, e.g., $v = 0$. It certainly could not do this in the long run. M. Friedman (1968, 7) stresses this point:

"Paradoxically, the monetary authority could assure low nominal rates of interest ... by engaging in a deflationary monetary policy. Similarly, it could assure high nominal interest rates by engaging an inflationary policy... ."

We consider here only models with perfect foresight and flexible prices. Wicksell's theory of the process of price changes refers, however, to the case of imperfect foresight or of inflexible prices. Referring to a stationary equilibrium, Wicksell asks which rate of inflation v results from an exogenous change in the nominal rate of interest, i, if the producers expect constant prices despite a change in the nominal rate of interest? His answer is:

"If prices remain unchanged, entrepreneurs will in the first instance [if the rate of interest on loans is lower than the natural rate of interest on capital, R.R.] obtain a surplus profit (at the cost of the capitalists) over and above their real entrepreneurial profit or wage [more precisely it should be said: entrepreneurs will *calculate* for themselves a surplus profit, R.R.] ... They will inevitably be induced to extend their businesses in order to exploit to the maximum extent the favourable turn of events. And the number of people becoming entrepreneurs will be abnormally increased. As a consequence, the demand for services, raw materials, and goods in general will be increased, and the prices of commodities must rise."[12]

Hence Wicksell concludes, that the difference between the money and the natural rate of interest cannot persist. The central agent of the Wicksellian currency

---

[12] K. Wicksell (1936, 105f.). Wicksell describes this clearly on p. 90, where he speaks only of a *tendency* for production to expand. "...; but this does not in any way imply that production will *in fact* increase. There will in general be no such increase, or only a relatively small one, if the available means of production, labour and so on, are already almost fully occupied." (Italics in the original).

community is not, or not necessarily, the central bank which issues paper money proper. Wicksell rather thinks of a gold standard and deposit banks which must ensure their liquidity by holding gold or central bank notes. If they fix their interest rate below the natural rate they will loose gold reserves or central bank notes. They must therefore finally raise again their bank rate of interest.

"It is thus confidently to be expected that the Bank rate, or more generally the money rate of interest, will always coincide eventually with the natural capital rate, or rather that it is always tending to coincide with an ever-changing natural rate. But whether this result is achieved with sufficient rapidity to prevent a continual rise in prices at times when the capital rate is rising (so that the money rate is left below the natural rate), or to obviate a gradual fall in prices at times when the capital rate is falling (and consequently the money rate is left higher than the natural rate), seems a priori very doubtful. This question involves a survey of various complications which unfortunately requires a far more intimate insight into the secrets of banking technique than is at my disposal...." (K. Wicksell 1936, 117).

And a little later Wicksell stresses again in view of the competition of the deposit banks:

"The open market may perhaps seem to present a somewhat more lively picture, but it is practically certain that the lending rate of interest never follows directly on movements of the natural rate, and usually follows them only very slowly and with considerable hesitation. During the period of transition, the deviation between the two rates has full play ..." (K. Wicksell 1936, 119).

These remarks may suffice to illustrate the Wicksellian process of adaptation to which we shall not return in this book.

We have shown in this chapter that the central agent must in any case determine *one* (commodity) price target, if the purchasing power of money is to be determined. Beyond this it can also fix certain interest rate targets ("in the long term"), provided it accepts the corresponding equilibrium values of the rates of inflation.

The consistency of economic policy goals may be simply clarified, for example, by means of the arbitrage equilibrium condition (5-22) assuming a general equilibrium. Thus, it is immediately obvious that a policy of cheap money (meaning $i < \rho$) *and* of stable prices ($p_{11} = p_{12}^*$) are inconsistent with the condition of general equilibrium (the efficient version of full employment). Alternatively, it can be seen, that it is in any case problematic to try to achieve simultaneously general equilibrium in the sense of efficient full employment, a stable value of money, a certain level of money wages, *and* a determinate low rate of nominal interest, for example, in order to reduce the burden on the government budget.

5.6 The Case of Two Currencies: Some Elementary Arbitrage Calculations

We now turn to the simplest case of a ZTC-world with only one good (wheat), two periods (today and tomorrow), but with two currencies, mark and dollar. We have two currency communities; each has a central agent which, among other things, fixes the accounting unit (mark, dollar) and the means of payment (mark-book money and dollar-book money). Every currency community has a clearing office which manages all payments. We do not consider spatial differences. We assume that there is only one location where trade takes place (a "punctiform" market) and for every good both the mark- and dollar-price are quoted.[13]

The number of goods and the spatial differences are irrelevant for our purposes. We may as well understand our ZTC-world with two currencies as a vast common market in which many goods are traded day in day out and where all goods are quoted in the two currency units mark and dollar.

The foreign exchange market, on which mark-book money is exchanged against dollar-book money at the exchange rate e, is a free market.[14]

We use the following symbols:

p_1^1: price of wheat available today, payable today by a credit in the mark-book money system (currency community No. 1). The superscript refers to the currency → spot price in mark;

p_1^2: price of wheat available today, payable today by a credit in the dollar-book money system (currency community No. 2) → spot price in dollar;

p_2^{1*}: price of wheat available tomorrow, and payable tomorrow through a credit in the mark-book money system (currency community No. 1) agreed-upon today: → forward price in mark;

p_2^{2*}: price of wheat available tomorrow, payable tomorrow by a credit in the dollar-book money system (currency community No. 2) agreed-upon today → forward price in dollar;

i^1: mark nominal rate of interest for loans;

i^2: dollar nominal rate of interest for loans;

e_1: rate of exchange of "mark available today per dollar available today" (spot rate of exchange);

e_2: rate of exchange of "mark available tomorrow per dollar available tomorrow" (the expected rate of exchange for tomorrow, here at the same time the forward rate of exchange.).

Transaction and transport costs are assumed to be zero. In this case the following direct connection exists between the wheat prices expressed in dollar and in mark (law of one price, arbitrage equilibrium for goods):

$$p_1^1 = e_1 p_1^2 \ , \quad p_2^{1*} = e_2 p_2^{2*} \ .$$

As before, all payments are made through crediting or debiting particular accounts. In the case involving two currencies, e.g., of mark in the dollar-book money

[13] To that extent we may speak of a pure theory of multiple currencies. Girton and Roper use this expression. They write: "Just as the pure theory of international trade abstracts from monetary phenomena, the pure theory of multiple currencies can be investigated independently of the number of countries or regions." See L. Girton and D. Roper (1981, 12).

[14] G.F. Knapp (1924, 216) calls e "*the inter-valuta relations.*" He argues, this expression is better, "as excluding the notion of a bill of exchange, here unimportant." At present, the major means of international payments are transfers and checks.

system, the credit is entered in dollar in the dollar-book-money system, the debit is entered in mark in the mark-bookkeeping system.[15] The conversion involves e_1 or e_2.

The mark-book-money system receives the dollar-credit in the dollar-bookkeeping system by the exchange of book money, i.e., by offering to the dollar-bookkeeping system a corresponding mark-credit per dollar-credit (in the case of paper money: units of mark-notes per unit of dollar-notes). A currency transaction (foreign exchange transaction) is agreed upon. Because we have assumed the law of one price (ZTC-arbitrage equilibrium for goods) the exchange rates satisfy the following conditions:

$$e_1 = \frac{p_1^1}{p_1^2}\,, \tag{5-23}$$

$$e_2 = \frac{p_2^{1*}}{p_2^{2*}}\,.\text{[16]} \tag{5-24}$$

This is the hypothesis of *absolute purchasing power parity* (PPP) between two currencies. (This refers here to the price of the single good wheat assuming zero transport and transaction costs).[17]

Since interlocal differences are not considered, the preceding example does not refer to currency areas but to different currencies at the same location. "This condition means that neither money is discriminated against or discounted relative to the other, when used as a medium of exchange." (L. Girton and D. Roper 1981, 15).

We remember from 2.1 that all transactions for periods $t = 1, 2, \ldots, T$ are concluded "today" in the form of spot or forward contracts. In other words: in our Pure Futures Economy or ZTC-world there exist complete forward markets for the unlimited future for all goods and services, all types of loans of any duration and all foreign exchange transactions. In particular international currency risks associated with trade and investment can be perfectly hedged. (We shall return to this last point further down in Section 5.7.1).

---

[15] On the practice of internationally active credit institutions (which is roughly similar to our description) see L.E. Chalmovsky (1984, 28 ff.).

[16] On agreeing on the rate of exchange e, the imagined central bookkeeping systems ("foreign exchange dealers") regularly anticipate the known result of the goods arbitrage equilibrium. See D.N. McCloskey and R.J. Zecher (1976).

[17] For any number of goods and for period 1 we have:

$$e_1 = \frac{p_{i1}^1}{p_{i1}^2}\,, \qquad i = 1, \ldots, n$$

and correspondingly for period 2:

$$e_2 = \frac{p_{i2}^{1*}}{p_{i2}^{2*}}\,, \qquad i = 1, \ldots, n\,.$$

A Note on the History of Thought:

The concept of purchasing power parity (PPP) is due to Gustav Cassel (1918, 413). He uses the concept in the context of his theory of the rate of exchange to explain the actual exchange rates. He does, however, not use, as we do here, the prices of individual goods expressed in the one or the other currency, but the *general price levels* of two freely fluctuating currencies:

"... the rate of exchange between ... two countries will be determined by the quotient between the general levels of prices in the two countries." (G. Cassel 1916, 62).

Very quickly Cassel noticed considerable deviations of the actual rates of exchange from the theoretical exchange rate calculated by means of the purchasing power parity theory which had been observed and which can still be observed (see below Chapter 7, Figure 7-6). The deviation may be explained by, among other reasons, the fact that in the real world arbitrage transactions frequently are not worthwhile. The sunk cost of the development of new export markets are frequently too high to allow profit making from short term price differentials between two currencies. The paradigm of the economic exchange between two parties which conclude a contract – the classical concept of a discrete contract – is only rarely applicable. It would be applicable, e.g., for precious metals such as gold or silver, or with other fungible goods[18] which are typically traded on commodity exchanges.[19] In the majority of cases, international trade requires close and durable business connections (relational contracts, see Chapter 3) which are terminated only at great cost in time and money. These are not suitable for taking advantage of merely short term arbitrage profits.[20] Thus, price differentials which are considered to be merely transitory are presumably not taken advantage of. For sufficiently long term price differentials, on the other hand, the arbitrage operation may conceivably pay off. We must, therefore, suppose a certain connection between the exchange rate and purchasing power parity but certainly not a perfect connection.

We agree therefore with J.A. Frenkel (1978, 188):

"The relationship embodied in the traditional formulations of PPP, should not be viewed as a theory of the determination of exchange rates. Rather, it describes an equilibrium relationship between two endogenous variables. As such, the PPP relationship should be viewed as a short-cut rather than a substitute for a complete model of the determination of prices and exchange rates. It is with this perspective that one should assess the policy usefulness of the doctrine. Its main usefulness is in providing a guide as to the general trend of exchange rates rather than the day-to-day fluctuations. It might be useful as a guide for setting exchange rates in the face of monetary disturbances after a period of massive dislocations (like that of World War I). As for the conduct of macroeconomic policy, the PPP relationship serves as a reminder that the exchange rate and the price level cannot be divorced from each other and therefore, policy targets concerning these two variables should be consistent."

We will now describe different possible interpretations of the vector of solutions of a general equilibrium model as they apply to the case under discussion. For loans

[18] "*Fungible goods* are goods such as grain, any unit or post of which can replace another unit, ..." (Webster's Deluxe Unabridged Dictionary, 2nd ed. New York 1983).

[19] As, e.g., corn or oats at the Chicago Board of Trade.

[20] One should not, however, overlook that the world is steadily becoming smaller. The argument in the text does not apply to multinational firms. As the world economy develops further an expansion of the effective area of the direct price connection (or the law of one price) must be expected.

in kind the vector of solutions of our two-good model is a number

$$\mathbb{L} = \{1 + \rho_1\} \ .$$

Under our assumptions it is equal to the solution in the case with spot and forward transactions

$$\mathbb{L} = \left\{\frac{p_1^1}{p_2^1}\right\} = \left\{\frac{p_1^2}{p_2^2}\right\}$$

and equal to the vector of solutions with the insertion of DM- or $-credit transaction:

$$\text{(5-25)} \qquad \mathbb{L} = \left\{\frac{p_1^1}{p_2^{1*}}(1 + i^1)\right\} = \left\{\frac{p_1^2}{p_2^{2*}}(1 + i^2)\right\} \ .$$

The term (5-25) may also be read as the equation for the parity of real interest rates.

If we use the rates of change of prices ("rates of inflation") v^1, v^2, where

$$p_2^{1*} = p_1^1(1 + v^1) \ ,$$

$$p_2^{2*} = p_1^2(1 + v^2)$$

we can rewrite the equation for the parity of real rates of interest (5-25) as:

$$\frac{1 + i^1}{1 + v^1} = \frac{1 + i^2}{1 + v^2}$$

or

$$\frac{i^1 - v^1}{1 + v^1} = \frac{i^2 - v^2}{1 + v^2} \ .$$

For small v's the equation for the parity of real rates of interest is approximately

$$\text{(5-26a)} \qquad i^1 - v^1 = i^2 - v^2 \ .$$

Note: while ρ_1 is the *agreed upon* real rate of interest for a loan in kind, $i - v$ is an (approximately) *calculated* real rate.

We may, therefore, rewrite equation (5-26a) as

$$\text{(5-26b)} \qquad i^1 - i^2 = v^1 - v^2 \qquad \text{("real-interest-rate parity")} \ .$$

The v^1, v^2 are to be understood as *expected* rates of change of prices which, by assumption, are also realized here.

In *stationary equilibrium*, in which there is only *one* real rate of interest ρ and for each currency community only one rate of inflation v^j $(j = 1, 2)$, we get the following approximative *theorem*: the difference between the nominal rates of interest of two currencies is equal to the difference between their rates of inflation.

Now, in ZTC-arbitrage equilibrium we have at the same time[21]

$$(5\text{-}27) \qquad \frac{p_1^2}{p_2^{2*}}(1+i^2) = \frac{\frac{1}{e_1}p_1^1}{\frac{1}{e_2}p_2^{1*}}(1+i^2) = \frac{(1+\varepsilon)(1+i^2)}{(1-v^1)} ,$$

where ε is the expected rate of change in the exchange rate from today to tomorrow which in the present case is known with certainty. Hence

$$e_2 = (1+\varepsilon)e_1 ,$$

or

$$\varepsilon = \frac{e_2}{e_1} - 1 .$$

The rate of change of the exchange rate is in the Pure Futures Economy equal to the *swap rate*[22] as quoted on the foreign exchange market.

Note: in a Pure Futures Economy perfect foresight obtains. The forward rate agreed upon today, e_2, is with complete certainty the spot rate tomorrow. The swap rate ε (the ex ante rate) is equal to the swap rate ex post. Because of uncertainty, however, reality is quite different!

In ZTC-arbitrage equilibrium the following is also true:

$$(5\text{-}28) \qquad \frac{p_1^1}{p_2^{1*}}(1+i^1) = \frac{1+i^1}{1+v^1} .$$

If we substitute (5-27), (5-28) into (5-23) we get the following condition for the ZTC-*arbitrage equilibrium of the rate of interest*:

$$1 + i^1 = (1+\varepsilon)(1+i^2)$$

or

$$1 + i^1 = \frac{e_2}{e_1}(1+i^2)$$

or

$$(5\text{-}29) \qquad i^1 = i^2 + \varepsilon + i^2\varepsilon .$$

---

[21] See below Fig. 5-4:

$$W_1 \to \$_2 \to W_2 = W_1 \to \mathrm{DM}_1 \to \$_1 \to \$_2 \to \mathrm{DM}_2 \to W_2$$

[22] The technical terms are "contango rate" if $e_2 < e_1$ and "deport rate" in the opposite case.

For small ε we can write approximately:

$$(5\text{-}30) \qquad i^1 - i^2 \approx \varepsilon \qquad (\text{"nominal interest rate parity"}) \ .$$

In words: the difference between the rate of interest for money loans is approximately equal to the swap rate. Applied to the forward market for foreign exchange one speaks therefore of the interest parity theory of forward exchange.[23]

P. Einzig (1937, 151) names J. M. Keynes as the first writer to have scientifically formulated this relation between interest rates and forward rates of foreign exchange which every dealer in foreign exchange has (empirically) known. He writes: "The Interest Parity theory of Forward Exchange must be regarded, therefore, as one of his many contributions to the progress of Economic Science "..." The most detailed explanation and analysis of the Interest Parity theory is to be found in J.M. Keynes's Tract on Monetary Reform (pp. 122–132)."

The general idea is, however, already in, among others, D. Ricardo's "Reply to Mr. Bosanquet's Practical Observations on the Report of the Bullion Committee," London 1811, pp. 9f.

In a stationary general equilibrium using (5-26) and (5-30) the following equation holds approximately for two currencies ("inter-valuta equilibrium"[24]).

$$(5\text{-}31) \qquad i^1 - i^2 = \varepsilon = v^1 - v^2 \ .$$

The arbitrage equilibrium equations which we have assumed to be fulfilled in our example, may be represented in the following arbitrage diagram:

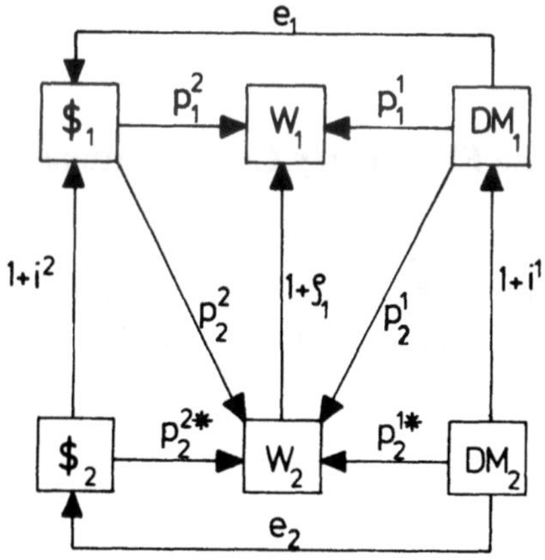

Fig. 5-5. ZTC-Arbitrage Diagram: one Good, two Currencies, two Periods

As before, the different relevant arbitrage equations may be easily derived: thus the exchange relation of wheat today for wheat today ($W_1 \to W_1$) is, for example, equal to one. Hence for the chain of exchanges:

$$W_1 \to \mathrm{DM}_1 \to \$_1 \to W_1$$

[23] See P. Einzig (1937, 150).

[24] In German: multivalutarisches Gleichgewicht; W. Stützel (1969, 16).

we get the following condition for an arbitrage equilibrium:

$$\frac{1}{p_1^1} e_1 p_1^2 = 1$$

or

$$e_1 = \frac{p_1^1}{p_1^2} \quad \text{(PPP)} \ .$$

Alternatively: wheat tomorrow exchanged directly for wheat today ($W_2 \rightarrow W_1$) gives $1 + \rho_1$. Allowing for the indirect chain of exchange through mark

$$W_2 \rightarrow \text{DM}_2 \rightarrow \text{DM}_1 \rightarrow W_1$$

we get the following condition for an arbitrage equilibrium:

$$\frac{1}{p_2^{1*}}(1 + i^1)p_1^1 = 1 + \rho_1$$

or

$$\frac{p_1^1}{p_2^{1*}}(1 + i^1) = 1 + \rho_1 \ .$$

5.7 Fixed or Flexible Exchange Rates? Some Elementary Considerations

In the preceding section we said nothing about the purchasing power of the two currencies. In order to do so, on the assumption that the central agents fix certain price targets, we look again at the equation of the real interest rate parity

$$\text{(5-25)} \qquad \frac{p_1^1}{p_2^{1*}}(1 + i^1) = \frac{p_1^2}{p_2^{2*}}(1 + i^2)$$

together with the conditions of the law of one price

$$p_1^1 = e_1 p_1^2 \ ; \quad p_2^1 = e_2 p_2^2 \ .$$

It is obvious that in this case four nominal quantities have to be fixed by the two central agents. With respect to the exchange rate we have to distinguish two important borderline cases:

1. Neither central agent desires a fixed exchange rate: this is the case of "flexible exchange rates."

2. Both central agents agree upon and realize a specific target for the exchange rate: this is the case of "fixed exchange rates."

In the first case, the rate of exchange is a "purely mercantile phenomenon."[25] In the second case we think of the exchange rate as fixed through the central agents by contract and guaranteed by law.

5.7.1 *Flexible Exchange Rates*

Initially, the central agent of each currency community fixes the price p of one good in each community, deliverable and payable today. It further fixes the current price p^* of the same good deliverable and payable tomorrow. In the present case we will therefore assume that p_1^1, p_2^{1*}, p_1^2, p_2^{2*} are exogenously given. The interest rates i^1 and i^2 and the rates of exchange e_1, e_2 are freely variable ("flexible"). The exchange rates which are formed on the market are, because of the hypothesis of the law of one price, equal to the parity rates

$$(5\text{-}23) \qquad e_1 = \frac{p_1^1}{p_1^2} \ ,$$

$$(5\text{-}24) \qquad e_2 = \frac{p_2^{1*}}{p_2^{2*}} \ .$$

In our ZTC-world without spatial extension (no transport cost) the freely determined (market-) exchange rates are perfectly determined by (5-23), (5-24). More realistically, we suppose that the price targets of the central agents relate to the same good for which there is practically always an arbitrage equilibrium (gold, silver ...). In such a case the mere *possibility* of perfect commodity arbitrage suffices to keep the fluctuations of the exchange rates around their parities within very narrow limits which are determined by transport and transaction costs.

The calculations made by individuals concerning the nominal interest rates i are similar to those developed in Section 5.3. The loanable funds theory of the nominal rate of interest is now applied to the two kinds of money claims: for mark-loans and for \$-loans. If the central agents choose for each currency the same rates of change for their respective price targets, i.e., the same rates of inflation $v^1 = v^2$, the interest rate i^1 will be equal to i^2, and $e_1 = e_2$. In other words: in a ZTC-world in general equilibrium the nominal rates of interest will, with the same rates of inflation, be equal to each other in all currency communities, and the exchange rates of two currencies will remain constant over time. The exchange rates are thus in effect "fixed" without being exogenously fixed through agreed upon exchange rate targets.

With unequal inflation rates ($v^1 \neq v^2$) the equilibrium rates of exchange will not be constant over time because of the inter-valuta equilibrium conditions (5-31) $e_1 \neq e_2$. Thus, if $v^1 = 0$, $v^2 > 0$, i.e., if $v^1 < v^2$, then (5-31) shows that $\varepsilon < 0$, i.e., $e_2 < e_1$.

[25] G.F. Knapp (1924, 217).

In words: the exchange rate e [mark/dollar] will, in general equilibrium be lower tomorrow than it was today (the mark is revaluated compared to the dollar) if a lower rate of inflation is chosen for the mark-currency than for the dollar-currency. If both currency communities are willing to accept the rate of change of the exchange rate ε as determined by (5-31), and with it the interest rate differential $i^1 - i^2$, the central agents may fix the relevant price targets entirely independently of each other.

Now we have several kinds of goods (wheat, oats, ...) so that, e.g., for currency 1 the money price of wheat (or gold), for currency 2 the price of oats (or silver) may be fixed. In a ZTC-world and in *stationary* equilibrium we also get fixed exchange rates ($e_1 = e_2$) provided the two central agents fix the same rates of change for their respective price targets. For, in stationary equilibrium all real exchange relations are constant over time:

$$\pi_{21} = \frac{p_{11}^1}{p_{21}^1} = \frac{p_{12}^{1*}}{p_{22}^{1*}} = \frac{p_{11}^2}{p_{21}^2} = \frac{p_{12}^{2*}}{p_{22}^{2*}} .$$

Moreover, in the ZTC-world we always have arbitrage equilibrium on the goods market so that in the case of a punctiform market

$$e_1 = \frac{p_{11}^1}{p_{11}^2} = \frac{p_{21}^1}{p_{21}^2} , \qquad e_2 = \frac{p_{12}^{1*}}{p_{12}^{2*}} = \frac{p_{22}^{1*}}{p_{22}^{2*}}$$

and $\qquad e_1 = e_2$.

On the other hand, with a *non-stationary* general equilibrium, the exchange rate will, as a rule, not be constant even in a ZTC-world ($e_1 \neq e_2$) if the money prices of *different* goods are exogenously fixed and constant in each currency community, e.g., gold for mark and silver for dollar. In such a case, the relative prices of gold and silver will not necessarily be constant. If it is desired that the (freely variable) exchange rates are constant over time ($e_1 = e_2$), the price of some good (e.g., gold) or of some basket of goods must be fixed and kept constant by the central agents of *all* currency communities and, e.g., over *all* periods ($v = 0$).

In the real world there exists, beyond this, the problem of transaction costs. This implies: if the exchange rates which are freely determined by the market are to remain within a narrow band of the parity rate (5-23), (5-24), the price targets must relate to goods for which the law of one price holds as closely as possible due to arbitrage operations, as is the case, e.g., for gold or silver.

If the price targets relate to baskets of cost-of-living goods, however, the situation is different. For most goods of daily consumption the law of one price does not apply, either because of the transaction costs which we have described before (see Section 5.6) or because they are not traded internationally. In such a case, the freely fluctuating exchange rates on the currency market will not be kept within narrow limits by actual or potential goods arbitrage operations. This is true even if the central agents of the two currency communities publish the prices of identical baskets of goods of daily consumption and in addition aim at the same rates of inflation. We must expect the phenomenon of "*overshooting*" of the parity rates of exchange (5-23), (5-24) (or a clearly delimited band around the parity rates). At best, some stabilization of the exchange rates through speculation may be expected. The theory of the stabilizing effect of speculation on the nominal exchange rate e disregards the possibility of speculative bubbles due to the rather lose relationship between exchange rates and the goods' markets[26] (on this point see below Section 7.4). These international currency risks could be avoided if we had complete forward markets for all foreign exchange transactions. This is not the case in real life. Firms, e.g., "investing in physical plant or human capital find they have substantial exchange risk which *cannot* be hedged as long as exchange rates are free to fluctuate." (Kindleberger 1972, 1985; quoted from R.I. McKinnon 1988, 89; emphasis in the original).

McKinnon (ibid.) continues: "The problem lies not so much with any inadequacy in the forward markets for foreign exchange, but rather is rooted in the incompleteness of forward contracting in markets for goods and services. We know that a manufacturer contemplating a new investment cannot make all his future production and sales decisions before the plant is built – then lay off the economic risks with a complete set of forward commodity contracts contingent on various uncertain states of nature. ... (This is impossible) because the transaction costs and moral hazard associated with contract enforcement of such contingent futures are generally prohibitive." (See K.J. Arrow 1974, 8; E. Greenwald and J. Stiglitz 1986). McKinnon argues that because of these incomplete forward markets for commodities producers of internationally tradeable goods and services cannot hedge their investments effectively against most foreign exchange risk. He calls the lack of complete forward markets the "Arrow-Debreu Dilemma" (loc. cit 88).

Our discussion in this chapter refers, however, only to a ZTC-world, in which the spot and future exchange rates are freely formed on the corresponding markets, and are kept within narrow limits by the PPP, irrespective of whether the price of a particular commodity or of a commodity basket is chosen as a price target.

We now look at the price targets more closely: the magnitudes fixed by the central agents need not (necessarily) be goods' prices. They could, for example, fix all nominal rates of interest (here i^1, i^2), as well as the money price of only *one* good in a *single* period in both currencies, here, e.g., the price for wheat p_1^1, p_1^2. The free variables are in this case, in (5-25), the money prices of the remaining goods: here for wheat available tomorrow p_2^{1*}, p_2^{2*} and according to (5-23) and (5-24) the exchange rates e_1, e_2. Note that because of the $(T-1)$ problem the purchasing power of money is indeterminate unless one money price in each currency community is exogenously fixed (see above Section 5.5).

The coordination problem for the two central agents is now shifted to the different possible interest rates. Thus $i^1 = i^2$ must be chosen if $p_1 = p_2^*$ are planned in each currency and also $e_1 = e_2$ (in the ZTC-world). In the case of several goods, in the ZTC-world, the constancy of the rate of exchange requires (except, of course, in the stationary case) that the money price of the same good or basket of goods must be fixed as a price target in both currencies. Finally: the movements of the exchange

[26] The question of destabilizing vs. stabilizing effects of foreign exchange speculation has been intensively discussed. However, this refers only to the volatility of the time series of exchange rates (e.g., the variance for a certain period) independently of our question how this average value is related to PPP. For more on this point see below Section 7.4, footnotes 65, 66, 67 and Suggested Readings to Chapter 7, No. 3.

rate e depend on the price and interest targets which the central agents have fixed. Both currency communities have to accept the movements of e as the result of fixed target values of prices and interests if the consistency with general equilibrium is to be preserved.

In fact, the independence of national monetary policy of one country from the monetary policy of other countries was one of the main arguments for the introduction of flexible exchange rates. Milton Friedman, the most prominent defender of flexible exchange rates in our time, went even further and hoped simultaneously for an independence of national fiscal policies[27] – an inappropriate hope because of the connection of real interest rates among different currencies which also exists in the case of flexible exchange rates.

We summarize: under the ideal conditions of general equilibrium in a ZTC-world consistent monetary policies in the two currency communities may lead to constant exchange rates over time. By consistent monetary policy we mean here a consistent fixing of price and interest targets in the two currencies. On the other hand, we can imagine that the price targets are fixed independently in the two currency communities in a ZTC-world – "the case of independence of national monetary policies from each other" – provided the currency communities are willing to accept whatever rate of exchange results. In a world *with* transaction costs, a stable development of exchange rates is only possible if the (consistent) price targets relate to goods whose mark- and dollar-prices are closely connected with each other through arbitrage operations on the goods markets (e.g., precious metals). If the price targets refer to goods for which arbitrage operations are not worthwhile or impossible, as it is the case for most goods of daily consumption, the development of stable exchange rates may not come about even if the price and interest targets are consistent.

We shall return to the heatedly discussed subject of fluctuating vs. fixed exchange rates below in Section 7.4.

5.7.2 *Fixed Exchange Rates*

In the case of fixed exchange rates, as understood here, the central agents agree explicitly or implicitly upon a certain exchange rate target (a parity rate of exchange). Its achievement is guaranteed by interventions on the exchange market by the relevant central agents. In our simple example, both e_1 and e_2 are exogenous variables.

The real anchoring of the system may be ensured by one of the central agents (e.g., of currency community 2) having fixed the price target of, e.g., one good for all time. This is a variant of the case of a foreign exchange standard. Exogenously fixed

---

[27] M. Friedman (1953, 199f.). Analogously later H.G. Johnson (1972, 199): "The fundamental argument for flexible exchange rates is that they would allow countries autonomy with respect to their use of monetary, *fiscal* and other policy instruments, consistent with the maintenance of whatever degree of freedom in international transactions they choose to allow their citizens, by automatically ensuring the preservation of external equilibrium." (Italics added).

are e_1, e_2, p_1^2, p_2^{2*}. The free variables are the interest rates for money loans in the various currencies (here i^1, i^2) and the prices of all goods expressed in currency 1: p_1^1, p_2^{1*}. We call the currency, the central agent of which assures the real anchoring of the system, the key currency.

Consider a *stationary* equilibrium of the Pure Futures Economy in a ZTC-world. If the central agent of the key-currency community No. 2 fixes a price target which is constant over time ($p_1^2 = p_2^{2*}$) and if the other community (No. 1) fixes a target of constant exchange rates over time ($e_1 = e_2$), and if these targets are actually realized, then the free variables (the other prices and interest rates) will also be constant: $\rho = i^1 = i^2$, and $p_1^1 = p_2^{1*}$. If, on the other hand, the central agent of the key currency community chooses a target of rising prices ($p_1^2 < p_2^{2*}$), i.e., a positive rate of inflation $v^2 > 0$, and if the central agent No. 1 sticks to his target of constant exchange rates ($e_1 = e_2$), the currency community No. 1 must accept equally rising prices: $v^1 = v^2$. We have here the case which W. Stützel[28] has called the "direct price effect" of *imported inflation* with fixed exchange rates, which is perfect in the ZTC-world.

Currency community No. 1 cannot choose simultaneously its exchange rate target *and* its price target. The nominal rates of interest are, in the two currency communities and in a ZTC-world, equal to each other; they are, however, greater than the real rate of interest by the rate of inflation; roughly speaking we have

$$\rho + v \approx i^1 = i^2 \ ; \qquad v = v^1 = v^2 \qquad \text{(see Section 5.6)} \ .$$

If the central agent of the key-currency community (No. 2) fixes a constant price target ($p_1^2 = p_2^{2*}$) and if the central agent of No. 1 devalues his currency today once and for all, i.e., if he chooses as his exchange rate target $e_1 = e_2$, but on a higher level than before, this is consistent with general equilibrium only if the prices p_1^1, p_2^{1*} are raised in accordance with (5-23), (5-24). In this sense, the devaluation of a currency has an inflationary, and the revaluation a deflationary effect.

In this model in which, in distinction to J.M. Keynes's theory, there is always full employment and in which money is neutral, a devaluation has no real effects. It merely raises domestic prices.

R.A. Mundell (1968, 123) described this fact in the following words: "Devaluation from a position of equilibrium will in fact *induce* a proportionate increase in the price level ...." He continues further on: "It is hardly necessary to point out, of course, that no country would need to devalue if it were already in equilibrium ...." Yet: "Devaluation is a means by which a country, whose prices and costs have got out of line internationally, can restore equilibrium without the less attractive alternatives of deflation or trade exchange controls. Bygones have to be accepted as bygones." (loc. cit. 129). This was the method which was adopted several times, e.g., by the contracting parties of the Bretton Woods Agreement (see below).

M.v.N. Whitman (1975, 494) calls the "small but influential group" of foreign trade theorists "who stand the traditional theory of the balance of payments on its head" "*global monetarists.*" In their most extreme form (according to M.v.N. Whitman) they argue: "A change in the exchange rate will not systematically alter their relative prices of domestic and foreign goods and it will have only a

---

[28] W. Stützel (1960b, 10–41) quoted from the slightly changed excerpt in W. Stützel (1973, 72), where further references can also be found.

transitory effect on the balance of payments ... a change in the exchange rate will have a direct impact on the domestic price level ... ."

The Bretton Woods Agreement is a prominent example of the foreign exchange standard. It determined the world currency order in the years after World War II until the beginning of 1973. The member states of the International Monetary Fund (IMF) had agreed: the key currency is the US-dollar. The dollar parity of the member states was fixed ("dollar standard")[29] and the dollar price for an ounce of fine gold was fixed until December 1971 at dollar 35. The central banks had to ensure that the spot price of their currencies in terms of dollars did not deviate by more than 1% from the parity rate.[30]

The articles of agreement of the IMF state that the parity of the currency of each member state is to be defined either in gold or in terms of US-dollars on the basis of the gold parity of the dollar of July 1, 1944. Almost all countries chose to fix their parities in dollars, rather than directly in gold. (The French franc was an exception). The sections of Article IV of the IMF to which we have implicitly referred in the text are:

Section 1. Expression of par values. – (a) The par value of the currency of each member shall be expressed in terms of gold as a common denominator or in terms of the United States dollar of the weight and fineness in effect on July 1, 1944. (b) ...
Section 3. Foreign exchange dealings based on parity. – The maximum and the minimum rates for exchange transactions between the currencies of members taking place within their territories shall not differ from parity (i) in the case of spot exchange transactions, by more than one percent; and (ii) in the case of other exchange transactions, by a margin which exceeds the margin for spot exchange transactions by more than the Fund considers reasonable.
Section 4. Obligations regarding exchange stability. – (a) Each member undertakes to collaborate with the Fund to promote exchange stability, to maintain orderly exchange arrangements with other members, and to avoid competitive exchange alterations. (b) ...
Section 5. Changes in par values. – (a) A member shall not propose a change in the par value of its currency except to correct a fundamental disequilibrium. (b) A change in the par value of a member's currency may be made only on the proposal of the member and only after consultation with the Fund. (c) When a change is proposed, the Fund shall first take into account the changes, if any, which have already taken place in the initial value of the member's currency as determined under Article XX, Section 4. If the proposed change, together with all previous changes, whether increases or decreases, (i) does not exceed ten percent of the initial par value, the Fund shall raise no objection; ..."[31]

The dollar parity of the mark was changed several times between Germany's adherence to the Bretton Woods Agreement in 1952 and the change to a freely fluctuating mark/dollar-exchange rate on March 19, 1973. There were two revaluations, in 1961 and 1969, a limited suspension of the obligation of the Bundesbank to intervene in the foreign exchange market in 1971 with a subsequent new fixing of the dollar parity, and finally a renewed revaluation when the US-dollar was devalued in terms of gold in February 1973.

---

[29] *De jure* the currencies were tied to gold *or* the US-dollar "of the weight and fineness in effect on July 1, 1944" (Sect. 1, Art. IV of the Statutes of the IMF). H. Möller (1972, 19) comments: "*de facto* the dollar also replaced gold as a 'standard' because afterwards the other countries got used to considering the dollar as the general measure of value for their own currencies as they had gold after the First World War." (Translated by W.F.St.; with the comment: the reason was that the US was the only large economy not destroyed by the war, and so everyone needed dollars to get the goods they wanted.)

[30] There have been many such arrangements before: the sterling standard is the most important. Even today we have a dollar area (in Central America), a French franc zone (mainly in Africa). The European Monetary System, though, is somewhat different.

[31] Articles of Agreement of the International Monetary Fund (July 22, 1944), in: Horsefield, J.K. and de Vries, M.G. (1969), Vol. III, 189f.

Is the purchasing power of the currencies determined and fixed in a system of currency communities whose central agents announce in advance only their exchange rate and interest rate targets? Specifically in our example which requires four price targets: will it be sufficient for the stability of the currency to fix e_1, e_2 and i^1, i^2? Obviously not. Of these four magnitudes, only three are independent of each other. Once e_1, e_2 and i^1 are fixed, i^2 is simultaneously determined. The currency communities have no other choice than to fix in addition one goods price p exogenously. In any case, the price of at least *one* good in *one* currency and for *one* period must be fixed exogenously (the direct or indirect way) for the whole currency system if the purchasing power of all currencies is to be determined in general equilibrium, i.e., if the system is to be anchored in the real economy. With exogenously fixed exchange rates e_1, e_2 we could think, for example, of i^2 and p_1^2 as fixed targets. In this case i^1, p_1^1, p_2^{1*}, and p_2^{2*} are free variables. The real anchoring consists in fixing the dollar price of wheat available and payable today. When applied to the fixing of the exchange rates, we have here the so-called "(*N*-1) *problem of exchange rate policy*." The reason is that for N currencies only N-1 exchange rates may be fixed in each period, or altogether two exchange rates in our two-period example. Two further magnitudes must be fixed exogenously in addition, among them at least one goods price in one currency (e.g., p_1^2). Fixing only the exchange rates is not sufficient to determine the purchasing power of money in the two currency communities.

An example of an international currency agreement without explicit agreement about the real anchoring is the *European Monetary System* (EMS).[32] In this system the exchange rates are not fixed in terms of *one* currency but are multilaterally negotiated. This can be visualized by imagining that the member countries at first agree bilaterally on certain exchange rate goals which they then make compatible with each other in common negotiations. This regulation has the advantage that (as opposed to the Bretton Woods System) changes in the exchange rates are only feasible if all the member states agree. Beyond this, there exists no definition in terms either of a monetary metal or in terms of the currency of another country for which a definite and generally agreed-upon inflation rate is fixed and somehow guaranteed.[33] To this extent it remains open whether the agreed-upon exchange rates may continue without internal contradictions are not.

If the announced rates of inflation of the individual central agents are not the same the exchange rates cannot permanently remain at the same constant agreed-upon level even in a world with transaction costs, in which the law of one price applies only vaguely. The parity rates must be periodically renegotiated (more on this in Section 7.4).

[32] The *European Monetary System* (EMS) exists since March 13, 1979. The member states are the Federal Republic of Germany, Belgium/Luxembourg, Denmark, France, Ireland, Italy, and the Netherlands.

[33] Only very generally formulated agreements exist "to enhance the convergence of economic policies towards greater stability" or that commit the partner countries to "pursue policies conducive to greater stability at home and abroad." The first agreement can be found in the Resolution of the European Council (Dec. 6, 1978) Annex 1, Part B 1. The second is mentioned in the Conclusions of the Presidency of the European Council (July 6/7, 1978) Annex item 5, in: P. Ludlow (1982, 302, 307).

Thus we see: the central agents of the currency communities cannot fix both arbitrary price and arbitrary exchange rate targets independently of each other. If each chooses a certain price target autonomously, the purchasing power of money is determined. But in this case they have no choice but to accept exchange rates as the market determines them which are consistent with their price targets. If they choose only certain agreed-upon exchange rate targets, the purchasing power of money is not determined. The system lacks a real anchoring. In addition, one currency community has to determine a (goods-) price target which is accepted (at least indirectly) by all other currency communities. Stable exchange rates, which are freely determined on the foreign exchange market, may be realized in two ways: either by autonomous choice of price targets or by agreement on exchange rate targets in connection with the price target for one currency community. Both methods work perfectly in the ZTC-world. Goods arbitrage transactions guarantee the stability of exchange rates.

In the real world, though, the law of one price does not work for most goods and financial assets nearly rigidly as we have assumed. Yet, goods arbitrage plays some role in reality and cannot be disregarded completely. That is in particular so if one wishes to design workable currency orders. The PPP is not a good exchange rate theory. But it is a *sine qua non* as an aid for the construction of a theory of the institutional framework of a system of currency communities. In this case, the precise course of the adaptation process is not of interest, only its limits and general aim are. Regarding the latter it is only possible to maintain the price targets of the system of currency communities, assuming fairly free goods and capital movements, if the arbitrage equilibrium conditions of prices, interests and exchange rates are not to be violated systematically. With respect to the limits of the course of the adaptation processes (e.g., the "bands" in which the exchange rates fluctuate freely), the particular commodities chosen as price targets play a role: for instance either a single good for which arbitrage works virtually perfectly, e.g., gold, or different baskets of standard of living goods, the prices of which adapt themselves only slowly, if at all, through arbitrage. In the first case the exchange rate stabilizes itself through commodity arbitrage transactions "automatically", in the second case this cannot be expected, at least not in the short term. In the first case the market clearly determines the "bands" within which exchange rates may fluctuate. This is not so in the second case; serious "overshooting" is to be expected; speculative bubbles may occur. If clearly and narrowly defined bands are desired, interventions on the exchange markets are unavoidable, e.g., agreed-upon interventions by the national central banks. The arbitrage logic illustrated in this chapter is quite simple. It is well-known to practitioners. Its importance, though, is sometimes overlooked by theorists as for example in the great debate on flexible exchange rates in the sixties.[34]

[34] For example, PPP (i.e., the role of commodity arbitrage) does not appear in the index of E. Sohmen's book (1969) and plays no role in his discussion of the stability of flexible exchange rates. The same is true for M. Friedman (1950).

5.8 Neutral Money

The ZTC-world which we have discussed in this chapter does not correspond in every respect to the model world of the classical or neo-classical economists. It is, however, a world for which the best known theorems of the classical and neo-classical economists are valid without restrictions, among them such heatedly contested theorems as

- Say's law,
- Fisher relation,
- purchasing power parity theory.

There is no money illusion. Arbitrage operations make sure that with direct exchanges the negotiated exchange relations and real interest rates are always equal to the corresponding ratios of the goods prices negotiated in purchase or loan transactions, or to the nominal interest rates corrected for inflation. In the ZTC-world, exchanges with or without the use of money have exactly the same final results. Money is neutral. Patinkin (1965, 75) defines "neutral money" as follows:

> "Strictly speaking such neutrality obtains if the mere conversion of a barter economy to a money economy does not affect equilibrium relative prices and interest."

In an analogous manner J.G. Koopmans (1933, 228) writes:

> "According to our terminology money is neutral only, *when all processes in the money economy correspond to the ideal type of the barter economy according to the laws of equilibrium theories.*"[35]

According to Hayek (1931, 93) the concept of neutral money was first used by Wicksell. Hayek refers to the following passage of Wicksell's *Money and Interest* which we have quoted above (Section 5.5):

> "There is a certain rate of interest on loans which is *neutral* in respect to commodity prices, and tends neither to raise nor to lower them. This is necessarily the same as the rate of interest which would be determined by supply and demand if no use were made of money and all lending were effected in the form of capital goods. It comes to much the same thing to describe it as the current value of the *natural rate of interest on capital.*" (K. Wicksell 1936, 102; first emphasis added).

In the later literature the neutrality of money is understood to refer to relative rather than absolute goods prices. The equilibrium values of the real exchange relations are independent of the changes in the purchasing power of money. In the ZTC-world they are even independent of whether money is used or not. Money is merely a "veil." Its use has no economic advantages. For the ZTC-world, the use of money is irrelevant. The situation is, however, quite different as soon as we assume

[35] J.G. Koopmans (1933, 228) (transl. by W.F. St.; italics in the original.). In his second edition of *Prices and Production* Hayek adds some notes on the concept of "neutral money" and refers in particular to the study by J.G. Koopmans (Hayek, op. cit. p. 129). See also F.A. Hayek (1933b).

costs of transaction. In a world with transaction costs, the use of money is advantageous: a money economy is really more efficient than a barter economy. In this case the equilibrium values of the real exchange relations will be altered with the movement from direct exchange to an exchange with the use of money. Niehans (1978, 8) has stressed this point. In addition, the holding of cash becomes worthwhile in a world with transaction costs. The concept of the quantity of money becomes relevant. There arises now the question of the relation between the quantity of money and the level of goods prices. Accordingly, P.A. Samuelson (1968, 3) distinguishes between a *qualitative* and a *quantitative neutrality* of money. In the ZTC-world, money is qualitatively neutral; in the world with transaction costs it is at best quantitatively neutral. In such a case, the quantity theory applies and:

"For given resources and tastes, equilibrium prices would always change in proportion to the exogenous quantity of money." (J. Niehans 1978, 8).

The problem of the neutrality of money is nowadays always discussed in the sense of quantitative neutrality.[36] We shall discuss the world of the quantity theory of money and the conditions for a quantitative neutrality of money in the next chapter.

Suggested Readings to Chapter 5

The concept of *Pure Futures Economy* underlying this chapter derives from *J.R. Hicks* (1946, 136ff.). It must be added, though, that unexpected changes of the (model-) conditions were excluded. In its pure form this world is assumed by *K.J. Arrow* and *G. Debreu* (1954) in a fundamental analysis of the problem of the existence of a general equilibrium; therefore one speaks also of the *Arrow-Debreu model.* The first comprehensive presentation was given by *G. Debreu* (1959) as mentioned already in Chapter 1. He gives also a brief interpretation of goods prices, nominal interest rates and exchange rates (op. cit. pp. 32–35) in the same meaning as they are discussed and interpreted in this chapter.

1 A Pure Book-Money System

The concept of a central accounting system was developed by *J.A. Schumpeter* in a book manuscript (written in German) in which the author deals with "the nature of the social institution of money." He stopped working on it in 1929/30. The manuscript was published after his death: *J.A. Schumpeter* (1970), see there Chapter IX "*Das Wesen des Geldes.*" It was preceded by *J.A. Schumpeter* (1917/18), an article which is translated into English: *J.A. Schumpeter* (1956). A central "Clearing System" is also described vividly by *J.R. Hicks* (1967, 7ff.), or by *E.F. Fama* (1980) who applies "a pure accounting system of exchange" (op. cit. p. 42). On (German) legal aspects of book money see, e.g., *K. Duden* (1968).

[36] See, e.g., D. Patinkin (1965, 8) or S. Fischer (1979a).

2 The Neoclassical Theory of the Nominal Rate of Interest

For a survey see *D. Patinkin* (1965, 366–372; 630–633) as well as *J.W. Conard* (1959, Chapter VIII).

The works in the primary literature to be emphasized are *I. Fisher* (1930) Chapter II and *J.R. Hicks* (1946), Chapters XI, XII. On other theories of the nominal or money interest rate, see *J.W. Conard* (1959). On the Fisher relation, see *I. Fisher* (1926, 55–58), *I. Fisher* (1930, 37–41, 407–451). Later, in the sixties and seventies numerous authors dealt with the empirical support of the hypothesis. For an overview, see *R. Roll* (1972); on more recent works: *W. Gebauer* (1982).

3 The Theory of Commodity Futures Markets

For the first rudiments, see *J.M. Keynes* (1930, Vol. II, 142–144) and *J.R. Hicks* (1946, 135–140). Their theories were criticized by *N. Kaldor* (1939), *G. Blau* (1944) and *L.G. Telser* (1958). On the question why there are so few commodity futures markets and on the historical development of commodity futures, see *H.S. Houthakker* (1959). For an overview and some further development, see *B.A. Goss* (1972). On the organization of futures exchanges, see *R.W. Anderson* (1984).

4 The Term Structure of Interest Rates

For an introduction to the subject, see *J.R. Hicks* (1946, Ch. XI) in connection with *D. Meiselman* (1962, Ch. 1), who provides a very clear introduction to the problem. The (simple) expectations hypothesis, which we have mentioned above, was held and improved, e.g., by I. Fisher, J.M. Keynes, J.R. Hicks, F.A. Lutz; see *F.A. Lutz* (1940/1941) and *J.W. Conard* (1959, Part III). It is supported empirically and defended by *D. Meiselman* (1962). On further developments, see in particular *B.G. Malkiel* (1966).

5 Wicksell's Theory on the Spread Between Real and Nominal Interest Rates

His theory contrasts the equilibrium models expounded above (see Section 5.5). Read the original work *K. Wicksell* (1898/1936) together with *K. Wicksell* (1928/1935).

A good survey and discussion of the Wicksellian theory is provided by, among others, *J.R. Hicks* (1977, 61–72) and *D.E.W. Laidler* (1975). Wicksell's influence on the literature of the twenties and early thirties was remarkable, see, e.g., *J.M. Keynes* (1930) or *F.A. Hayek* (1931) – see also *J.M. Keynes* (1936) (cf. on this point *D.E.W. Laidler* (1975, 115ff.)).

6 The Purchasing-Power-Parity Theory (PPP)

J. Wheatly and D. Ricardo are mentioned as originators with publications in the early 19th century (see *J.A. Frenkel* 1978). The PPP was revived by *G. Cassel* (1916, 1918, 1925) and taken up by *J.M. Keynes* (1923). For a clear discussion of its assumptions and problems see *J. Niehans* (1984). Survey: *L.H. Officer* (1976), *J.A. Frenkel* (1978), *R.M. Levich* (1985, 1002ff.).

The law of one price, which is the basis of the PPP, is in actual fact in international trade "flagrantly and systematically violated by empirical data" (*P. Isard* (1977, 942)). On the consequences for exchange-rate theory see *J.A. Frenkel* (1978, 1981).

Empirical support can be found for PPP as a long run equilibrium condition on which the exchange rate tends to converge; see, e.g., *M.P. Taylor* and *P.C. McMahon* (1988). Note that we treat here the PPP as an arbitrage condition even though it is usually expressed in terms of price indices.

"In fact, PPP should be interpreted as a *comparative-statics* result arising from a monetary disturbance, embodying the essential feature of *monetary neutrality*." (N. Bruce and D.D. Purvis 1985, 839. Emphasis in the original).

7 The Theory of Forward Exchange

One of the first works is *J.M. Keynes* (1923, 115–139). *P. Einzig* (1937, 1962) wrote two important monographs. Of the numerous further contributions are emphasized *S.C. Tsiang* (1959) and *E. Sohmen* (1961, 1969, 1973). On the empirical analysis of forward exchange rates and for a survey of the literature see *W. Gaab* (1983).

8 Fixed versus Flexible Exchange Rates

The debate, after World War II, started with the agreements underlying the International Monetary Fund. On the beginning and functioning of the Bretton Woods System until 1965 see *J.K. Horsefield* and *G.M. de Vries* (1969, Vol I.); for the time span of 1966–1971 see *G.M. de Vries* (1976, Vol. I). On the end of Bretton Woods (also for an overview on the IMF in general) *H. Möller* (1972) is very clear. *M. Friedman* (1953) criticized the Bretton Woods System fundamentally in a memorandum written in 1950. In the same vein *E. Sohmen* (1961, 1973), *H.G. Johnson* (1969).

As representatives of the opposing view (i.e., against flexible exchange rates) *W. Stützel* (1960a, 1983), *Ch.P. Kindleberger* (1969), *H. Möller* (1972) are emphasized.

J.M. Keynes (1923, 154–163) commented on this topic, in a similar debate in the early twenties, with carefully weighed arguments on the problem of "price stability or exchange-rate stability?"

The problem of the stability of flexible exchange rates played an important role in the debate on flexible exchange rates before 1973. It was taken up again in view of the considerable volatility of exchange rates after the final breakdown of the Bretton Woods System. On the relevant literature see Suggested Readings to Chapter 7, No. 4, 5. On the problem of incomplete forward markets for forward exchange transactions under flexible exchange rates see *R.I. McKinnon* (1988).

9 Neutral Money

For an introduction into the more recent debate see *J. Niehans* (1978, 7ff.). Of fundamental importance under the history-of-thought aspects are *F.A. Hayek* (1931b; 1933a, 129–131) with his reference to *K. Wicksell* (1898, 93; 1936, 102) as well as *J.G. Koopmans* (1933). For a critical opinion on this concept see, e.g., *J.A. Schumpeter* (1955, 1088).

P.A. Samuelson (1968) discusses the concept of neutral money in a nice way in a more modern setting. From the point of view of economic policy the question is whether monetary policy may have an influence on real exchange rates (or "relative prices"), assuming that individuals are free of money illusion. This is not the case in the ZTC-world of this chapter in which barter is as efficient as exchange with the use of money. Money is here "qualitatively" neutral. Non-neutrality of money in spite of the absence of money illusion can only be modeled if we consider a world with transaction costs. More on this in Suggested Readings to Chapter 6.

Chapter 6
The Quantity of Money and the Prices of Goods

In the preceding chapter we considered an abstract monetary economy in which the holding of cash balances is not worthwhile. Money (book money) was not used as a "store of value." We are now changing that. We now assume that transaction costs exist; exchange by the use of money is advantageous. In particular we assume costs resulting from the change of money into bonds and bonds into money; the holding of cash balances is now worthwhile. We assume that the currency communities consist of individuals of overlapping generations; in such a world the use of outside money can be justified economically. We keep to the assumption of perfect competition. Precisely what is used as money proper, i.e., means of payment, book money or piece money (coins, bank notes), is irrelevant for the expositions in this chapter. Yet it helps our imagination if we think of money in terms of piece money. We therefore assume that the quantity of money consists only of coins or banknotes.

In the present chapter we assume a very simple relationship between the quantity of money M and the prices of goods p: an increase in the quantity of money leads to a proportional increase in the prices of goods. This is the central theorem of the quantity theory of money. As an explanation of the movement of goods prices the quantity theory is as badly suited as the PPP is as an explanation of the movement of exchange rates. But, for the construction of a theory of the currency order, i.e., of the institutional framework of a currency community, the quantity theory is of vital importance – as is the purchasing power theory and the logic of arbitrage transactions in general. In this book we deal with the theory of currency order. Therefore, we are not interested in how the quantity of money and the prices of goods are related with each other every second or every hour, but – in the present chapter – in how the price target and the supply of means of payment have to be determined in order to be compatible with each other. For that purpose the ideal case of the quantity theory offers a natural point of orientation.

As for the details we proceed in this chapter as follows: first we argue that in a world with transaction costs not only is exchange by means of money preferred to barter, but also money loans to loans in kind or futures transactions. The model of the Pure Futures Economy is replaced, in a simplifying manner, by the model of the Pure Spot Economy in which, by assumption, only spot purchase and money loan transactions are concluded.The course of time is viewed as a sequence of such Pure Spot Economies. In accordance with these assumptions we develop a simple theory of the demand for cash balances which we integrate into neoclassical household theory. Consumers hold part of their financial assets in form of money proper (i.e., as means of payment); an optimal quantity of cash balances exists. We incorporate this extended version of the theory of consumer behavior into an overlapping generations model in which a particular quantity of money M is not only used as means of payment, but also as a store of value which is transferred from one generation to the next. In this connection the meaning of rational expectations is explained and it is shown how prices and interests react in the stationary overlapping generations model to changes of the actual or expected quantity of money. The concept of the "quantitative neutrality" of money is illustrated and the problem of the non-neutrality of money is briefly considered from the point of view of a theory of the currency order.

6.1 A World With Transaction Costs

Assume now a world with transaction costs. Exchange by the use of money is more economic than barter. Money, therefore, loses its qualitative neutrality which we have heretofore assumed. For simplicity's sake we shall assume that in this world *all* transactions are concluded by the use of money. We imagine further that it is cheaper to exchange goods only for cash, and to transfer assets into the future only by means of money loans. There are no forward exchanges. J.R. Hicks (1946, 136) calls this a Pure Spot Economy. In this model world, prices and the amounts of future goods (wheat available tomorrow) are no longer agreed upon today in a legally binding manner, as is the case in the Pure Futures Economy. They are agreed-upon only when the future has become the present. Certain conventions may nevertheless exist within relational contracts but there are no concrete fixed agreements. It would not be rational to negotiate such agreements because of imperfect knowledge of future events which would require revisions, which in turn would entail cost. Under our assumptions the parties prefer to transfer their positive or negative assets into the future exclusively through claims on money and in the form of cash.[1] In the transaction costs world Say's law need not, of course, hold at every moment of time. A person buying less wheat today does not thereby automatically buy more wheat tomorrow.[2] The individual consumption and production plans are no longer matched in every detail and for all time as in the Pure Futures Economy. But we assume here that they are by and large matched in the minds of individuals, otherwise they would not lend or borrow money. They trust Say's law, so to speak, for average values.

Without trust money loan transactions between private persons are not imaginable. This picture is quite consistent with temporary discrepancies between the supply of and the demand for goods which are smoothed out over time. In practice such discrepancies are dealt with by bufferstocks of goods and money etc., and

---

[1] These procedures cause fewer transaction costs than the conclusion and possible later revision of futures contracts. For an illustration, see J.R. Hicks (1946, 135ff.). See also K.J. Arrow (1974, 8). Arrow stresses the problem of futures contracts. "An individual may make a contract which he cannot in fact fulfill. Penalties may indeed be imposed on failure to live up to one's agreement, but they are not a substitute for compliance from the viewpoint of the other party, and there is always a degree of cost in enforcing the penalties. The laws of bankruptcy are a social recognition that complete enforceability is impossible and that it is even socially desirable to set limits on the penalties for failure."

[2] We remind the reader of J.M. Keynes: "... an individual decision to save does not, in actual fact, involve the placing of any specific forward order for consumption, but merely the cancellation of a present order." We cannot, however, accept the subsequent conclusions of Keynes. See J.M. Keynes (1936, 211).

through relational contracts whose precise contents remain flexible (see above Section 3.4).

Future prices and sales are not negotiated in a Pure Spot Economy, or at least not agreed upon in a legally binding manner. The economic units have, however, certain price and sales expectations which play an essential role in determining the individual plans. In the place of the future prices p^* of the Pure Futures Economy, which are agreed upon today, we have now, in the Pure Spot Economy, the (for tomorrow) *expected* spot prices p^+.

For the theorist the question now arises how the formation of expectations is to be explained in this context. The older literature does not, as a rule, deal with the formation of expectations. The p^+ are introduced into the Pure Spot Economy as exogenous variables, as in, e.g., J.R. Hicks[3] and D. Patinkin[4]. The newer contributions, on the other hand, attempt to explain the formation of expectations, following neoclassical tradition, in a rational manner. The rational expectations hypothesis, much quoted and much disputed, will be employed. We will discuss in this chapter both approaches, the older and the newer one. As for transaction costs, we shall take account of them explicitly only in the model of optimal intertemporal planning of consumption, namely as the costs of an exchange of cash against bonds and vice versa. We do this in order to explore the old question of monetary theory, why individuals would prefer to hold money. Otherwise we shall allow transaction costs only implicitly. Since money has ceased to be qualitatively neutral in a transaction-costs world the exchange relations π_{ij} which have been directly negotiated are no longer equal to the relation of the goods prices p_j/p_i. *Mutatis mutandis* this also holds for loan transactions with or without the use of money. Generally, $1 + \rho$ will no longer be equal to

$$\frac{p_t}{\overset{+}{p}_{t+1}}(1 + i_t) \ .$$

We can, however, calculate the real exchange relations which result implicitly in an exchange by means of money. We shall use the superscripts$^+$ to denote those implicit exchange relations. Thus we shall write:

$$\pi_{12}^{+} = \frac{p_1}{p_2} \quad \text{or} \quad 1 + \rho^+ = \frac{p_1}{p_2^+}(1 + i) \ .$$

The second term may also be expressed as

$$1 + \rho^+ = \frac{1 + i}{1 + v^+} \ ,$$

where $p_2^+ = (1 + v^+)p_1$; v^+ denotes the expected rate of change of prices.

[3] "... every individual has a definite idea of what he expects any price which concerns him to be in any future week." J.R. Hicks (1946, 124f., 126).

[4] D. Patinkin (1965, 61).

The concept of the real rate of interest is particularly interesting in this context; we can understand it as an *ex ante*, i.e., expected, magnitude or an *ex post*, i.e., realized, magnitude. The *ex ante* real rate of interest, i.e., the expected rate of interest plays an important role in the formation of individual plans for savings and investments: it can, however, be determined empirically only with great difficulty.[5] The *ex post* real rate of interest is more easily measured and indeed is regularly found in the relevant literature.

In a world with imperfect foresight and with, e.g., price expectations for a particular point of time, there will as a rule not be consistent price expectations.[6] We shall nevertheless follow, for the time being, the older literature which assumed consistent price expectations.[7]

Concerning the *process* of the formation of prices, we remind the reader of the discussions in Section 4.4. To visualize an exchange process by the use of money in a transaction costs world it is necessary to assume that individuals have an idea of the real definition of the unit of account. Accordingly, we assume this to be the case.

In a Pure Spot Economy new (spot) purchase agreements and money loan transactions are concluded at the beginning of each period. We assume, as before, perfect competition. In each period a general equilibrium with given price expectations is realized, a so-called *temporary equilibrium* (J.R. Hicks 1946, 123). Our model economy may be viewed as a sequence of such temporary equilibria. How each single equilibrium is materialized – how the process of price formation looks like – is not of interest to us in this connection. For reasons given we look at the institutional framework or order of our model economy: in particular the currency order. As before we assume that the currency order (or the central agent) determines a price target – not only for "today" but also for "tomorrow" and the foreseeable future. Moreover, a regulation of the supply of means of payment which is consistent with the price target is necessary – not only for "today" but also for "tomorrow" and the foreseeable future. We assume that each single temporary equilibrium is achieved through the price mechanism, i.e., that prices are perfectly flexible. Yet, our considerations would not be changed much if we were to assume temporarily fixed prices (i.e., by a temporary non-price mechanism of the control of demand and supply, e.g., on the basis of relational contracts between buyers and sellers). Only government price fixing and rationing are excluded. Under these conditions we can assume that the parties to the contract will adjust the temporarily fixed prices to the current market situation (for instance, if they are convinced that the change in the quantities demanded or supplied will be permanent). They will do this, – in particular, if there is no doubt that the change in demand is the consequence of a permanent change in the quantity of money.

We summarize: in the Pure Spot Economy there are forward transactions neither for goods nor for money claims. In the single-good world, which we apply here, only the following business transactions are concluded and realized:

---

[5] W. Gebauer (1982, 133ff.).

[6] Consistent in the sense that all individuals expect the same price (J.R. Hicks 1946, 133).

[7] See D. Patinkin (1965, 67) who even speaks of a "'blackout' on the future." In this world there is no trade in shares, a very strong simplification.

1. *A Purchase Agreement in Cash*:
   exchange of wheat available today against money available today at price p_1; and
2. *A Money Loan Contract*:
   the promise to pay money available tomorrow against payment of money available today at the rate of interest i.

No price p_2^* for wheat available tomorrow, payable tomorrow, but *agreed upon today* materializes – at any rate none that is legally binding. Nevertheless, the economic units calculate in their intertemporal optimization with particular prices for tomorrow, in the one-good case by assumption with the expected price p_2^+ for wheat available and payable tomorrow. However, only the price p_1 and the rate of interest i are agreed upon by the market.

6.2 Optimal Cash Balances

We now determine the optimal consumption plan of a household under the assumptions that

(a) all exchange is transacted by the use of money;
(b) all assets are transferred into the future only in the form of money loans (bonds) or cash; and
(c) the exchange of cash against bonds and vice versa has transaction costs.

Money may be bank money or notes. For the present section this makes no difference; though we assume money to consist only of banknotes. The household has a certain endowment with the one good of our model, part of which it consumes and part of which it "saves" by selling it for money. It invests part of the proceeds in bonds and keeps the rest as cash. The amount of the planned cash balances depends on the transaction costs of financial investments. Under certain assumptions on the costs of the transactions consisting of the exchange of money into bonds and back again into money, cash may be held together with bonds. An optimal amount of cash- and bonds-holdings may exist. What are the marginal conditions for the optimal amount of cash balances?

We assume that the transaction costs of the exchange of cash into bonds and vice versa must be paid "today" when the cash-into-loan transaction is concluded. Their real value is C, and they depend on the present real value of bonds $\dfrac{B}{p_1(1+i)}$ the household buys from firms. They increase with an increase in the volume of loans. The law of diminishing marginal returns applies so that the marginal (real) transaction costs, C', increase with the real value of loans.

The yield of a money investment (of bonds) is assumed to be certain in our model. It is made certain through the input of resources by the investors. These are the transaction costs. The relationship between (real) transaction costs and the (real) present value of the money investment is represented by the transaction costs function or curve in analogy to Fig. 3-4. We assume this to be given. The transaction costs include in our case all costs which are connected with granting and administering a money loan:

the costs of the procurement and of the settlement of the loan contract, the supervision of its fulfillment – and, in addition, all internal coordination costs of the household pertaining to a money-loan transaction. Our concept of (real) transaction costs, C, is therefore broader than that of Baumol or Niehans. The marginal (real) cost of transactions, C', may at first decrease with additional invested units of money with increasing volume of investments (all in real terms). Yet, from a certain point onward the marginal real cost of transactions will increase. At least, that is what we believe will be the case and what we assume. Otherwise there would be no optimal size, i.e., no size limits for reasons of efficiency, to financial intermediaries (as, e.g., banks) which we regard as quite implausible. In this book we apply only the "upper branch" of the total transaction costs curve which is concave from below. This is sufficient for our purposes.

In this sense we assume a real *transaction costs function* $C\left(\frac{\hat{B}}{p_1}\right)$, where $\hat{B} \equiv \frac{B}{1+i}$, which satisfies the usual conditions of continuity and twofold differentiability, with $C' > 0$ and $C'' > 0$. As for the rest, the transaction costs function corresponds to the function $C(y_{1U})$ which we have discussed in Section 3.3.[8]

For our overlapping generations model the optimization problem of the *household* and for the case of one good (wheat) and two periods (today and tomorrow) is as follows (see also above Section 2.5.2):

$$\text{Max} \quad U = U(x_1, x_2)$$

$$\text{s.t.} \quad p_1 x_1 + \hat{B} + M + p_1 C\left(\frac{\hat{B}}{p_1}\right) = p_1 \bar{x}_1^1$$

$$p_2^+ x_2 = \hat{B}(1+i) + M$$

$$M \geqq 0\,, \quad \hat{B} \geqq 0\,, \quad \bar{x}_1^1 > 0\,.$$

In words: the household of the young generation maximizes its utility subject to the conditions of the budget equation for its youth and its old age. The transaction costs for the exchange of money into bonds and back into money, $p_1 C$, are accounted for in its youth. The young generation earns its original endowment with wheat, $\bar{x}_1^1$,

---

[8] We have

$$-C = y_{1H} + y_{1U}$$

or since

$$\phi(y_{1H}, y_{1U}) = 0$$

$$-C(y_{1U}) = f(y_{1U}) + y_{1U}\ .$$

The maximum profit $Q'_{t,\max}$ is in this case equal to zero (see Section 2.5), and therefore

$$y_{1U} = \frac{p_2}{p_1} x_2 \qquad \text{(see Appendix to Chapter 3)}$$

or

$$y_{1U} = \frac{\hat{B}}{p_1}\ .$$

by working in the firm belonging to the old generation, i.e., through its original endowment with working time which we do not mention specifically. The maximum profit Q of the firm Robinson is by assumption zero (see Section 2.5). The young generation cannot, by assumption, go into debt ($\hat{B} \geqq 0$). Cash balances cannot be less than zero ($M \geqq 0$).

This is a non-linear programming problem. But, because we are interested only in the case of an interior optimum and assuming twice differentiable functions, the marginal conditions are (see Appendix 1 to this chapter):

$$(6\text{-}1) \qquad \frac{U_1}{U_2} = \frac{p_1}{p_2^+}\,, \quad \text{where} \quad U_j \equiv \frac{\delta U}{\delta x_j}\,, \qquad j = 1, 2$$

and

$$(6\text{-}2) \qquad C' = i\ ; \qquad C' \equiv \frac{dC}{d(\hat{B}/p_1)}\ .$$

The interest on the last mark loaned is exactly used up by the marginal transaction costs. The dimensions are discussed in Appendix 1 to this chapter.

It is in this case not the real rate of interest which determines the interior optimum, but the *opportunity cost of holding cash* with respect both to each type of good (here: wheat), i.e., $\frac{p_1}{p_2^+}\left(=\frac{1}{1+v^+}\right)$ and with respect to the holding of bonds, i.

Both determine *simultaneously* and together with the given real assets $\bar{x}_1$ the consumption plan and the financial investment or loan plan of the household.

Note: a corner solution is generally possible with demand for money $M = 0$. In such a case the household will not hold cash even with positive transaction costs for the exchange of money for bonds and conversely – at least not voluntarily. We shall return to this case in Section 6.4.

The marginal conditions (6-1) and (6-2) may be interpreted in different ways:

Variant 1:
We write equation (6-1) in the form

$$(6\text{-}3) \qquad \left|\frac{dx_2}{dx_1}\right| - 1 = \frac{p_1 - p_2^+}{p_2^+} = \frac{-v^+}{1+v^+}\ ; \qquad \left|\frac{dx_2}{dx_1}\right| \equiv -\frac{dx_2}{dx_1}\ .$$

In words: at an interior optimum the rate of time preference for each good is (for small v^+) approximately equal to the negative value of the expected rate of price change v^+ for this good. Expressed differently, it is approximately equal to the expected rate of deflation $-v^+$ of the relevant good (here wheat). Expressed still differently, it is equal to the expected real rate of interest of cash expressed in terms of the relevant good.[9]

[9] This result corresponds to that of M. Friedman (1969, 21). Note that M. Friedman uses the terms "time preference" and "internal rate of discount for the future" synonymously (op. cit. p. 18).

Theorem (Variant 1): For an interior optimum of the cash holding household and with a given endowment $\bar{x}_1$ the following has to be done *simultaneously*:

1. the intertemporal *consumption of goods* is to be arranged so that the rates of time preference for the individual goods are approximately equal to the expected real rates of interest of cash with respect to the individual goods (here wheat), i.e., the expected rate of deflation $-v^+$ (in terms of wheat)

$$\left|\frac{dx_2}{dx_1}\right| - 1 = \frac{-v^+}{1 + v^+} , \tag{6-3}$$

2. the *financial assets* are to be divided between cash and bonds so that the marginal transaction costs, C', of cash into bonds and bonds into cash are just equal to the opportunity cost of holding cash as related to the individual interest bearing titles, i.e., equal to the money or nominal rate of interest i

$$C' = i . \tag{6-2}$$

The theorem is illustrated by means of a graph and an algebraic example in Appendix 2 to this chapter.

Variant 2:
We now write (6-1) in the form

$$\frac{U_1}{p_1} = \frac{U_2}{p_2^+} .$$

This expression may be interpreted as the intertemporal equalization of the *marginal utilities of spending money* on wheat available today and on wheat available tomorrow. In analogy to Section 5.3 we get the following

Theorem (Variant 2): For an interior optimum and a given endowment $\bar{x}_1$ belonging to the cash holding household we get simultaneously:

1. the marginal utility of money today spent on present goods is equal to the marginal utility of money held as cash until tomorrow and spent tomorrow on future goods

$$\frac{U_1}{p_1} = \frac{U_2}{p_2^+} ,$$

2. the marginal transaction costs of money into bonds and bonds into money are equal to the nominal or money rate of interest

$$C' = i .$$

J. Niehans (1978, 26) calls U_1/p_1, U_2/p_2^+ the "marginal flow utilities of money" and the difference $U_2/p_2^+ - U_1/p_1$ the "marginal stock utility of money." The marginal stock utility, he writes,

"... can be visualized as the benefit from spending a dollar today, minus the sacrifice involved in not spending it yesterday. It is the gain in utility from postponing a dollar's worth of expenditure from one day to the next by holding cash overnight. Whenever cash balances are actually held, their marginal utility will be equalized to their marginal cost, which, in the present model, is zero." "In this way the marginal utility of cash balances is rigorously related to the marginal utility of goods." (J. Niehans 1978, 27).

Variant 3:
We can also interpret variant 2 in the following manner:

Theorem (Variant 3): For an interior optimum and a given endowment $\bar{x}_1$ belonging to the cash holding household the following must be simultaneously true:

1. the intertemporal *comsumption of goods* will be such that the marginal utility of holding cash is zero:

$$\frac{U_2}{p_2^+} - \frac{U_1}{p_1} = 0 \text{ [10]} ,$$

2. the *financial assets* are divided between cash and interest bearing titles (bonds) so that the marginal yields of both forms of investments are equal to each other, i.e., equal to zero in the case under consideration in which there is (no interest bearing cash assumed):

$$C' - i = 0 \ .$$

There is finally a fourth variant for (6-1) and (6-2).

Variant 4:
Since $C' = i$, we can write (6-1) in the form:

$$\frac{U_1}{p_1}(1 + C') = \frac{U_2}{p_2^+}(1 + i)$$

or

$$\left|\frac{dx_2}{dx_1}\right|(1 + C') - 1 = \frac{i - v^+}{1 + v^+}(=\rho^+) \ . \tag{6-4}$$

[10] This refers to the increase in utility which arises from the fact that 1 mark is not spent today but kept in the form of cash until tomorrow and is spent only tomorrow. In the interior optimum this increase in utility is zero.

When writing the equation in this manner we include the marginal transaction costs with the time preference of wheat.

Theorem (Variant 4): For an interior optimum and a given endowment $\bar{x}_1$ belonging to the cash holding household the following must be simultaneously true:

1. the *consumption of goods* is divided intertemporally so that the rates of time preference for each type of good (including the marginal transaction costs) are equal to the expected own rates of interest of the respective types of goods (here: wheat),
2. the *financial assets* are divided between cash and interest bearing titles such that the marginal costs of transaction C' of cash into bonds and bonds into cash are equal to the money interest rate i.

A Note on the History of Thought:

J.M. Keynes (1936, 166) writes appropriately, that the household has to make two decisions: one on the level of its savings and a second on the form in which those savings will be held. He continues, the first decision is determined by the propensity to consume (he does not mention the real rate of interest), the second by "the rate of interest" (Keynes obviously meant the money or nominal rate of interest). He continues: "We shall find that the mistake in the accepted theories of the rate of interest lies in their attempting to derive the rate of interest from the first of these two constituents of psychological time-preference to the neglect of the second; and it is this neglect which we must endeavour to repair."

Keynes does not mention that the supposed mistake in the "accepted theories" disappears if one distinguishes explicitly between the real and the nominal rate of interest.

Because of (6-1) and (6-2), the arguments of the equations determining the optimal consumption plan are,

$$i\ , \quad \frac{p_1}{p_2^+}\ , \quad \bar{x}_1^1 \qquad \text{(see Appendix 2 to this chapter).}$$

Alternatively, they may be written as

$$\frac{p_1}{p_2^+}(1+i)\ , \quad \frac{p_1}{p_2^+}\ , \quad \bar{x}_1^1\ .$$ [11]

Once we know the first two terms we also know the money or nominal rate of interest i.

The general form of the equations determining the optimal consumption plan for the household of the young generation are therefore

[11] In the literature different notations are found: e.g., (v^+, i) in R. Richter, U. Schlieper, W. Friedmann (1981, 373ff.); or (ρ^+, v^+) with S. Fischer (1979a).

$$x_j = x_j\left(\frac{p_1}{p_2^+}(1+i), \frac{p_1}{p_2^+}, \bar{x}_1^1\right), \quad j = 1, 2$$

$$\tilde{B} = \tilde{B}(\cdot), \quad \tilde{B} \equiv \frac{\hat{B}}{p_1},$$

$$\tilde{M} = L(\cdot), \quad \tilde{M} \equiv \frac{M}{p_1}.$$

The demand function for bonds is derived from the second constraint on the household. Its explicit form is:

$$\tilde{B}(\cdot) = \frac{1}{1+i}\left(\frac{p_2^+}{p_1}x_2(\cdot) - L(\cdot)\right).$$

Of course, it is not necessarily true that cash bears no interest. Interest bearing titles may also be used as cash (as, e.g., interest bearing demand deposits). In such a case, the opportunity cost of holding cash compared to goods is (roughly) $v^+ - z$, and compared to bonds is (roughly) $i - z$, where z denotes the interest rate on cash (e.g., on book money). The marginal conditions are correspondingly changed to [12]:

$$\frac{U_1}{U_2} = \frac{p_1}{p_2^+}(1+z), \quad \text{or} \quad \frac{U_1}{U_2} = \frac{1+z}{1+v^+},$$

$$C' = \frac{i-z}{1+z}.$$

If the interest on cash balances z is precisely equal to the expected rate of inflation $v^+ (z = v^+)$, i.e., if the real value of cash balances is not changed by inflation or deflation, we have

$$\frac{U_1}{U_2} = 1$$

and

$$C' = \frac{i - v^+}{1 + v^+}(=\rho^+).$$

The arguments of the equations determining the optimal consumption plan reduce to

---

[12] The formulation is:

$$\begin{aligned} \text{Max} \quad & U = U(x_1, x_2) \\ \text{s.t.} \quad & p_1 x_1 + \hat{B} + M + p_1 C(\hat{B}/p_1) = p_1 \bar{x}_1^1 \\ & p_2^+ x_2 = B(1+i) + M(1+z). \end{aligned}$$

$$\frac{p_1}{p_2^+}(1+i)(=1+\rho^+)\ .$$[13]

The level of real cash balances depends under our assumptions only on the level of the transaction costs C of exchanging cash for bonds and vice versa. A reduction in these transaction costs will result in a reduction in the (positive) optimal level of cash balances, generally associated with an increase in the consumption of present goods and the investment in bonds. The latter leads to an increase in the capital stock and thus of the level of production. For example, the transaction costs C might be reduced by the introduction of financial intermediaries such as banks. J.G. Gurley and E.S. Shaw (1960, 92 ff.) have stressed this aspect. We shall return to this point in Chapter 8.

To repeat: in the preceding analysis the *optimal real cash balances* are determined simultaneously with the optimal intertemporal allocation of goods. The holding of cash balances, even though it yields no direct utility, may be worthwhile because it may save transaction costs. To this extent the holding of cash yields an *indirect* utility.

A Note on the History of Thought:

Cash balances due to the existence of transaction costs have already been explained by W.J. Baumol (1952) and J. Tobin (1956) with the use of the theory of optimal lot size. Their analysis assumed, however, a given level of consumption. P. Bernholz (1965, 1967) was the first to analyze the simultaneous determination of the consumption plans and the cash balances of the household. The analysis of J. Niehans (1975a, 1978) goes in the same direction. Our contribution consists in the simplification of this analysis. In order to explain the simultaneous determination of the optimal level of cash balances and the optimal intertemporal allocation of goods we need only to add the activity "transaction."

Conceptually these ideas are already implicit in the famous article by J.R. Hicks (1935). However, Hicks does not develop them further. He also considers transaction costs ("the cost of transferring assets from one form to another," op. cit. p. 67) less important than the risk factor (p. 68 ff.).

For a long time the discussion of the theory of money was dominated by the three motivations for holding cash which Keynes made famous: the transactions-motive, the precautionary-motive, and the speculative-motive.[14] Keynes attributed particular importance to the last motive as did Hicks.

The precautionary-motive refers to the uncertainty of future cash inflows and outflows. E.L. Wahlen (1966) among others has developed a corresponding model. The speculative-motive relates to the uncertainty about future prices of financial assets, primarily stocks and bonds. One of the most frequently

---

[13] Corresponding formulations apply to the case of the taxation of cash at the tax rate $-z$, or the case of an anticipated rate of deflation $-v^+(=-z)$. An anticipated inflation or deflation has in this case no effect on real cash holdings. We shall return to this point below Section 6.6.

[14] J.M. Keynes (1936, 170). According to Keynes, liquidity preference may be considered to be dependent on:

"(i) the transactions-motive, i.e., the need of cash for the current transactions of personal and business exchanges;
(ii) the precautionary-motive, i.e., the desire for security as to the future cash requirements of a certain proportion of total resources; and
(iii) the speculative-motive, i.e., the object of securing profit from knowing better than the market what the future will bring forth".

cited papers of this type on optimal cash holdings was written by J. Tobin (1958). All these theories are described in sufficient detail in the various text books.[15]

It may be objected to the holding of cash balances for the purpose of minimizing risks that reality knows numerous money-like financial assets which bear interest without burdening the investor with considerable risks of loss. The risk factor is not unimportant, but, as Niehans rightly stresses, it is only of secondary importance.[16] D. Patinkin argues in an anlogous manner.[17] We will not further discuss the risk argument.

Unlike the present chapter, the older neoclassical literature of the theory of money explained the optimal cash balances on the assumption that (real) cash balances have a *direct utility*, e.g., in the sense of the *service d'approvisionnement* of L. Walras (1926, Lect. 29). Real cash balances become in this case an argument in the utility function. For an interior optimum we can write the corresponding optimization problem of the consumer in the following brief form:[18]

$$\text{Max} \quad U = U\left(x_1, \frac{M}{p_2^+}, x_2\right)$$

$$\text{s.t.} \qquad p_1 x_1 + \frac{p_2^+}{1+i} x_2 + \frac{i}{1+i} M = p_1 \bar{x}_1^1 \ .$$

For an interior optimum we get the following marginal conditions:

$$\frac{U_1}{U_2} = \frac{p_1}{p_2^+}(1+i) \ , \tag{6-4}$$

$$\frac{U_{\tilde{M}}}{U_2} = i \ , \qquad U_{\tilde{M}} \equiv U(M/p_2^+) \ . \tag{6-5}$$

This, too, gives a solution for the limiting case of $M = 0$, i.e., for cases in which no cash is held voluntarily.

In place of (6-4) and (6-5) we may also write:

$$\frac{U_1}{p_1} = \frac{U_2}{p_2^+} + i \frac{U_2}{p_2^+} \ , \tag{6-4'}$$

---

[15] For a brief survey, see K. Nagatani (1978, Part I).

[16] J. Niehans (1978, 21).

[17] D. Patinkin (1965, 80): "uncertain price and/or interest expectations are not a sine qua non of a positive demand for money."

[18] In the extended formulation we have now the two budget equations:

$$p_1 x_1 + \hat{B} + M = p_1 \bar{x}_1^1$$

$$p_2^+ x_2 = \hat{B}(1+i) + M \ .$$

We discount the second equation to "today." This results in:

$$p_1 x_1 + \frac{p_2^+}{1+i} x_2 + \frac{i}{1+i} M = p_1 \bar{x}_1^1 \ .$$

(6-5′) $$U_M = i\frac{U_2}{\overset{+}{p}_2} \quad \text{since} \quad U_M = \frac{1}{\overset{+}{p}_2} U_{\tilde{M}} \; .$$

Conditions (6-4′) and (6-5′) are, in words:

1. The marginal utility of money today for present goods is equal to the marginal utility of money tomorrow for future goods plus the loss of interest entailed by the holding of cash balances:

$$\frac{U_1}{p_1} = \frac{U_2}{\overset{+}{p}_2} + i\frac{U_2}{\overset{+}{p}_2} \; .$$

2. The marginal utility of cash balances is equal to the "subjective" opportunity costs of cash balances:

$$U_M = i\frac{U_2}{\overset{+}{p}_2} \; .$$

We consolidate (6-4′) and (6-5′) into

$$\frac{U_1}{p_1} = \frac{U_2}{\overset{+}{p}_2} + U_M \; .$$

In words: the marginal utility of money today is equal to the marginal utility of money tomorrow for future goods plus the (subjective) opportunity costs of holding cash. Note the difference to the law of the equalization of the marginal utilities of money in the first approach without a direct utility of cash balances, where $U_M = 0$.

This does, however, not mean that there are no (subjective) opportunity costs of holding cash balances. However, they do not appear explicitly ("directly"); but they do appear implicitly ("indirectly") by a lower level of consumption of the household. Though the marginal conditions differ for the direct utility approach compared to the previously dealt with transaction costs case, the arguments of the equations of the optimal consumption plan remain the same. As before we shall use the arguments

$$\frac{p_1}{\overset{+}{p}_2}(1+i) \; , \quad \frac{p_1}{\overset{+}{p}_2} \; , \quad \bar{x}_1^1 \; .$$

If one assumes that bonds, too, have "some degree of liquidity," as D. Patinkin (1965, 457ff.) does, one may include real bond holdings in the utility function (see Appendix 3 to this chapter).

We summarize: the assumption of direct utility of cash balances formally simplifies the rational explanation of cash balances. It evades, however, an explicit explanation of these cash balances. The transaction costs approach is in this respect more general. It models explicitly the avoidance of "inconveniences" by the holding of cash balances.

6.3 Cash Balances in General Equilibrium: A Monetary Overlapping Generations Model

In order to be able to explain, at least in principle, why consumers hold cash balances we make three assumptions:

1. all exchanges are made by the use money;
2. the household plans to transfer part of its assets into the future exclusively in the form of money assets (bonds and cash); and
3. the exchange of cash against bonds and vice versa involves costs (transaction costs).

This by itself does not exclude the case in which no cash is held. We shall consider this case further on.

The preceding section dealt with the case of the equilibrium of economic units: households and firms. The present section will develop a suitable general equilibrium model. For this purpose we shall use the overlapping generations model developed in Chapter 2. It is a simple but useful model for the discussion of unsynchronized cash inflows and outflows for the sale or purchase of goods and services.

K. Wicksell's (1936, 56) reasons for non-synchronized cash in- and outflows are partly seasonal variations, partly random events. D. Patinkin (1965, 14, 79) assumes "that payments on the Monday marketing period for commodities are made, not simultaneously at the close of this period, but at randomly determined hours of the ensuing week." J. Niehans (1978, 64ff., 81ff.) assumes a fixed (stationary) cycle of receipts and disbursements from purchase or sales of goods within each year.

All these approaches are arbitrary. So is ours. Our aim is to clarify the point with simple means.

It is important for the construction of a general equilibrium model with the holding of cash balances to clarify whether the received money may be *entirely* exchanged against goods of individual choice in the next period. This is possible in the case of the exclusive use of inside money. It is impossible if outside money is used. Inside money can be understood as being issued in exchange against money loans used for production purposes, so to speak as (real) "investment certificates." To this extent it is a "claim" on a part of the future national product.[19] This is not true for outside money. The typical outside money is definitive paper money. It is issued primarily in exchange against titles of government debt. The actual currency communities of the present time are, on the whole, paper currency communities of this type. In the elementary case, paper money gets into circulation simply through goods purchased by the state and is to be understood as non-interest bearing debt titles of the government with unlimited time of circulation. Such paper money has and keeps its value only in an economy without foreseeable end. Since the individual lives only for a limited time, the overlapping generations model seems to be the appropriate approach. As will be discussed in the following chapter, the overlapping generations model is also suitable to describe an economy in which paper money is redeemable into a money good. It is thus a generally meaningful theoretical approach for our purposes.

---

[19] J.A. Schumpeter (1970, 210).

We start once more with the two-generations model with one good (wheat) which was developed in Chapter 2. There is no forward market for wheat. The generation of tomorrow with which the present generation would have to conclude a contract is not as yet alive. This is a Pure Spot Economy which repeats itself in each period; we have a sequence of temporary equilibria. It is not even possible to talk about the expected prices for tomorrow because the purchaser of tomorrow is not yet born. Price expectations can be formed rationally in the generation model only if a certain stability of the individual behavior pattern is presumed. This includes the presumption of a stable institutional framework, i.e., of an order and its guarantee mechanism. The use of money is a social activity. Its explanation demands more than an individual optimization calculus. This is precisely the fascination and the difficulty of monetary theory.

We shall consider here an economy with production of the Robinson type which we have described in Section 2.5.2. Money loan transactions are added and we assume that the investment of money (paper money) in interest-bearing money claims (bonds) causes transaction costs of $C(\hat{B}/p_t)$. Each generation lives for two periods and plans strictly only for itself (no super-rationality).

This means that the long-run equilibrium level of the real interest rate remains positive in our stationary model (see above Section 2.5). As for the rest, we assume the existence of an interior optimum, i.e., that cash balances are always held voluntarily.

The optimization problem of the *household* of the generation which is young in period t is:

$$\text{Max} \quad U^t = U^t(x_t^t, x_{t+1}^t)$$

$$\text{s.t.} \quad p_t x_t^t + \hat{B}^t + M_t^t + p_t C\left(\frac{\hat{B}^t}{p_t}\right) = p_t \bar{x}_t^t$$

$$p_{t+1}^+ x_{t+1}^t = M_{t+1}^t + \hat{B}^t(1 + i_t)$$

$$\text{where} \quad \hat{B}^t \geqq 0 \,, \quad M_t^t \geqq 0 \,, \quad M_{t+1}^t \geqq 0 \,, \quad \bar{x}_t^t > 0 \,.$$

The young Robinson in period t earns his "endowment" of wheat $\bar{x}_t^t$ by working as a harvester on the farm of the old Robinson in t (see below).

The optimization problem of the *firm* in period $t - 1$ is correspondingly (see above Section 2.5.2):

$$\text{Max} \quad Q^{t-1} = p_{t-1} y_{t-1} + \frac{p_t^+}{1 + i_{t-1}} \bar{x}_t$$

$$\text{s.t.} \quad \phi(\bar{x}_t, y_{t-1}) = Q \,.$$

When Q^{t-1} is related to period t we get

$$Q_0^{t-1} = p_{t-1}(1 + i_{t-1}) y_{t-1} + p_t^+ \bar{x}_t$$

$$= p_t^+ \left(\frac{1 + i_{t-1}}{1 + v_{t-1}^+} y_{t-1} + \bar{x}_t\right) .$$

As already discussed in Section 2.5.2 we implicitly assume a linear homogeneous production function with the factors seed and labor. The quantity of labor used is constant and is paid in real terms $\bar{x}_t^t = \text{const.}$, i.e., with a constant quantity of wheat in each period t. The maximum real profit

$$\tilde{Q}_0^{t-1} = \frac{Q_0^{t-1}}{p_t^+}$$

is in this case

$$\tilde{Q}_0^{t-1} = \bar{x}_t^t \ .$$

The expression

$$-\frac{1 + i_{t-1}}{1 + v_{t-1}^+} y_{t-1}$$

is in real terms the quantity of wheat which the firm has to repay in period t to the old generation $t - 1$ for its loan including interest $[=(1 + \rho_{t-1}^+)y_{t-1}]$.

To explain: each young generation establishes a new firm which is dissolved after one period. The generation $t - 1$ founds in *period* $t - 1$ the firm UN_{t-1} to which it lends out of its given nominal labor income $p_{t-1}\bar{x}_{t-1}^{t-1}$ the sum of $\hat{B}^{t-1}(=\hat{B}^{dt-1})$, for which the firm in turn buys the amount y_{t-1} kg of seed wheat which it sows. In *period* t the firm UN_{t-1} buys the services of the new young generation t which harvests the wheat. The firm pays for these services the sum of $p_t^+\bar{x}_t^t$. Under our assumptions of a linear homogeneous production function in seed and labor, of a given supply of labor, and a given real wage of $\bar{x}_t^t$ (see Section 2.5.2), maximum profit is

$$p_t^+\bar{x}_t^t = Q_0^{t-1} \ .$$

As for the rest, firm UN_{t-1} repays in period t the old generation $t - 1$ its money loan with interest, i.e., the sum of

$$\text{(6-6)} \qquad \hat{B}^{t-1}(1 + i_{t-1}) = -p_t^+ \frac{1 + i_{t-1}}{1 + v_{t-1}^+} y_{t-1} \ , \quad \text{where} \quad p_t^+ = p_t \ .$$

Thereafter, the firm UN_{t-1} is dissolved. The young generation t establishes a new firm UN_t etc.

What happens if the expected and the actual prices differ, i.e., if $p_t^+ \neq p_t$? The purchasing power of the money loan $\hat{B}^{t-1}$ is then smaller or larger than it was planned to be in period $t - 1$. Since, in our example, the old generation is represented by one single person who also owns the firm UN_{t-1} which pays a fixed amount of real wages $\bar{x}_t^t$ in period t, these gains or losses in the purchasing power of the money loan $\hat{B}^{t-1}$ are exactly compensated by its (windfall) losses or profits from deflation or inflation. In other words: an unexpected change in the price level

p_t has no effect on the old generation's real income. If we wish the same to be true in the case of more than one person per generation we have to assume what D. Patinkin (1965, 74) calls a "*neutral distribution effect*" of a price change. It is this case we have in mind in our further considerations.

In case of an inflation, for example, the increase in the amount of wheat demanded by debtors is exactly offset by the decrease in the amount of wheat demanded by creditors.

Now the young generation in each period saves for its old age not only in the form of interest-bearing investments $\hat{B}$, but simultaneously also in the form of a non-interest-bearing paper money M. In the case of the just explained optimum the holding of cash is worthwhile because of the transaction costs which we have discussed above. The quantity of the next wheat harvest (i.e., of the next gross national product) is determined by that part of the income of the young generation in t which has been invested in bonds: $\frac{\hat{B}_t}{\bar{x}_t^t}$. The greater this part (i.e., the smaller the share of cash balances $M_t^t/\bar{x}_t^t$) the greater is the level of total production $\bar{x}_t$ ($=GNP$) in the following period. If, on the other hand, real cash balances decline because, for example, higher prices are expected in the next period (and with them losses in real cash balances due to inflation), total production of the following period $\bar{x}_{t+1}$ will rise. This is the basic idea of the *Tobin effect*.[20]

It follows from the same model that a decline in transaction costs C_t will result in a reduction in real cash balances held and with that in an increase of the stocks of bonds held and of total production $\bar{x}_t$. The level of supply rises if transaction costs fall. It pays, therefore, to lower transaction costs. With an interior optimum and the use of non-interest-bearing paper money ($z = 0$) we get, therefore, for the *household*, the following marginal conditions as the result of (6-1) and (6-2):

$$\frac{U_1^t}{U_2^t} = \frac{p_t}{\overset{+}{p}_{t+1}} \,,$$

$$C'\left(\frac{\hat{B}^t}{p_t}\right) = i_t \;.$$

The firm UN_t maximizes its profit Q^t. With an interior optimum we get for the *firm* the marginal condition

$$\frac{\phi_1}{\phi_2} = \frac{p_t}{\overset{+}{p}_{t+1}}(1 + i_t) \;.$$

In analogy to Section 6.2 we use as arguments of the equations of the conditions for optimal plans in t the terms

$$\alpha_t = \left\{\frac{p_t}{\overset{+}{p}_{t+1}}(1 + i_t), \frac{p_t}{\overset{+}{p}_{t+1}}, \bar{x}_t^t\right\}$$

[20] J. Tobin (1965).

for the cash holding household; and

$$\beta_t = \left\{\frac{p_t}{\overset{+}{p}_{t+1}}(1 + i_t)\right\}$$

for the firm. The symbol $\bar{x}_t^t$ designates the original endowment with wheat of the young household.

The equations of the conditions for optimal consumption plans for the household are then in period t, and on the assumption of an interior optimum:

$$x_t^t = x_t^t(\alpha_t) \ ,$$

$$x_{t+1}^t = x_{t+1}^t(\alpha_t) \ ,$$

$$\tilde{B}_t^{dt} = \tilde{B}_t^{dt}(\alpha_t) \ ,$$

$$L_t = L_t(\alpha_t) \ .$$

The equations of the conditions for optimal production plans of the firm UN_t are

$$y_t = y_t(\beta_t) \ ,$$

$$\bar{x}_{t+1} = \bar{x}_{t+1}(\beta_t) \ .$$

Because of (6-6), $(\tilde{B}^{st} = \tilde{B}^{dt} = \tilde{B}^t)$, $y_t = -\tilde{B}^{st}$ in equilibrium. In addition we get, together with the second budget equation,

$$x_{t+1}^t = -\frac{1 + i_t}{1 + \overset{+}{v}_t} y_t + \frac{M_{t+1}^t}{\overset{+}{p}_{t+1}} \ .$$

In analogy to Section 2.5.2 we write down first the *conditions for a temporary market equilibrium* of the overlapping generations model for period t. We begin with the goods market.

Note that the quantity of money M_t^{t-1} may be changed by the central agent in two ways:

1. *Directly* by purchase or sales of wheat to the extent of $\dfrac{M_t^t - M_t^{t-1}}{p_t}$ (for or from an imagined stock of wheat);
2. *Indirectly* by positive or negative transfer payments to or from the households.

Monetary policy is in the two cases identical with what is normally called fiscal policy.[21] In general, the difference $\dfrac{M_t^t - M_t^{t-1}}{p_t}$ must be substituted into the goods market equation.

[21] M. Friedman (1953, 140) describes this case for a paper standard.

Note further the consumption of the *old generation* is

$$(6\text{-}7)\qquad x_t^{t-1} = \frac{M_t^{t-1}}{p_t} - (1 + \rho_{t-1}^{+})y_{t-1} \ .$$

In analogy to Section 2.5.2 we write the conditions for the *goods market equilibrium* in the sense of "planned capital supply K_t^s of the presently young generation equal to planned demand for capital K_t^d of the firm which the presently young generation has established today," i.e., as

$$K_t^s = K_t^d$$

or

$$\bar{x}_t - x_t^{t-1} - x_t^t - C_t - \frac{M_t^t - M_t^{t-1}}{p_t} = -y_t \ .$$

Using equation (6-7) this becomes

$$(6\text{-}8)\qquad \bar{x}_t + (1 + \rho_{t-1}^{+})y_{t-1} - x_t^t - C_t - \frac{M_t^t}{p_t} = -y_t \ .$$

At an optimum it is also true that

$$(Q_0^{t-1}/p_t^{+}) = \bar{x}_t^t$$

or

$$(1 + \rho_{t-1}^{+})y_{t-1} + \bar{x}_t = \bar{x}_t^t$$

or

$$\bar{x}_t = \bar{x}_t^t - (1 + \rho_{t-1}^{+})y_{t-1} \ .$$

If we substitute this expression for $\bar{x}_t$ into (6-8) we get

$$(6\text{-}9)\qquad \bar{x}_t^t - x_t^t - C_t - \frac{M_t^t}{p_t} = -y_t$$

or written as the *equilibrium condition for the bond market*

$$(6\text{-}10)\qquad \tilde{B}^{dt} = \tilde{B}^{st} \ .$$

The goods- and bond-market equations are equivalent in the one-good model. Furthermore, we must allow for the *equilibrium condition for the money market*:

$$L_t = \frac{M_t^{t-1}}{p_t} + \frac{M_t^t - M_t^{t-1}}{p_t} = \frac{M_t^t}{p_t} \; .$$

Initially we require that only the old generation supplies paper money:

$$M_t^t = M_t^{t-1} \; ,$$

so that we get in this case

$$(6\text{-}11) \qquad L_t = \frac{M_t^{t-1}}{p_t} \; .$$

In this case we have to substitute M_t^{t-1} into equation (6-9) instead of M_t^t.

The assumption $M_t^t = M_t^{t-1}$ means the following: if the central agent changes the amount of money M in period t compared to period $t-1$, this change only affects the cash balances of only the old generation of period t (i.e., the owner of cash balances). If we additionally assume (with several old people) that the cash balances of the old generation change in proportion to M then we have a *neutral change in the quantity of money* (neutral supply of money). The famous "helicopter-drop" example describes such a case.[22]

We now substitute the three conditions for market equilibrium into the equations of the conditions for the optimal values of the freely variable magnitudes x, y, L. We then get the following temporary equilibrium of the overlapping generations model:

$$(6\text{-}12) \qquad \bar{x}_t^t - x_t^t(\alpha_t) - C_t(\alpha_t) - \frac{M_t^{t-1}}{p_t} = -y_t(\beta_t) \quad \rightarrow \textit{goods market}$$

$$(6\text{-}13) \qquad \tilde{B}^{dt}(\alpha_t) = \tilde{B}^{st}(\beta_t) \quad \rightarrow \textit{bond market}$$

$$(6\text{-}14) \qquad L_t(\alpha_t) = \frac{M_t^{t-1}}{p_t} \; ; \quad \text{where} \quad L_t(\cdot) > 0 \quad \rightarrow \textit{money market}$$

endogenous variables: i_t , p_t

exogenous variables: M_t^{t-1} , $\overset{+}{p}_{t+1}$.

In the one-good model the goods and bond market equations are equivalent. We imagine, for example, a solution for i_t, p_t by means of (6-12) and (6-14). This formulation relates the model to the case of the paper standard: the central agent

[22] See M. Friedman (1969, 4). This argument is found in the quantity theoretical writings since D. Hume. See, e.g., D. Patinkin (1965, 244): "Let there now be some external force which, say, suddenly doubles the initial money holdings of each individual of the economy." S. Fischer (1979a) comments on this point: "In general, however, money injections are not neutral . . . ." He therefore prefers the case in which the quantity of money is changed in a non-neutral fashion by government purchases or sales of goods (op. cit. 232 n. 8). *Note*: in our example the old generation consists of only one person. If there are several persons we require that the additional quantity of money is distributed among the individuals *in proportion* to their cash holdings.

determines the quantity of money M_t^{t-1}. The purchasing power of money is determinate if M is exogenously fixed.

The model may be interpreted both in the sense of a paper standard and in the sense of a commodity standard. In both cases the price target p and the chosen quantity of money M_t^{t-1} are determined by equations (6-12) to (6-14). Expressed differently: each given price target p_t is related to a definite quantity of money M_t^{t-1}, independently of whether the latter is fixed actively from the outside or determines itself passively within the system. We limit ourselves in this chapter to the case of an actively fixed quantity of money, the case of a paper standard, in which the price target is pursued the "indirect way." Both the commodity and the paper standard will be dealt with in detail in the next chapter.

6.4 An Illustration of the Monetary Overlapping Generations Model

Before continuing we present a few illustrations of the simple overlapping generations model (6-12) to (6-14) for the case of a paper standard. First, by assumption, there is no money illusion. But do we also have a quantitative neutrality of money, i.e., will p_t change proportionally to M_t^{t-1}? This will depend on the expected value $\overset{+}{p}_{t+1}$ for tomorrow. Suppose that $\overset{+}{p}_{t+1}$ changes by the same multiple as p_t. This will, for example, be the case if we assume with Patinkin that the prices expected for tomorrow are equal to today's prices:

$$\overset{+}{p}_{t+1} = p_t$$

or, generally,

$$\overset{+}{p}_{t+1} = (1 + v_t^+)p_t \ ,$$

where the inflation rate v_t^+ is exogenously given (i.e., Patinkin assumes $v_t^+ = 0$). This was the standard neoclassical assumption before the rational expectations hypothesis appeared. In all such cases the Hicksian elasticity of expectations is equal to one (see J.R. Hicks 1946, 205).

We shall follow the development of economic doctrine by assuming at first that p^+ is given and equal to p (i.e., $p^+ = p$). The *temporary equilibrium system* may then be written briefly as follows

$$\text{(6-15)} \qquad \hat{\hat{x}}(i_t) - \frac{M_t^{t-1}}{p_t} = -y_t(i_t) \ ; \qquad \hat{\hat{x}}_t = \bar{x}_t^t - x_t^t - C_t$$

$$\text{(6-16)} \qquad L_t(i_t) = \frac{M_t^{t-1}}{p_t} \ , \qquad L_t(i_t) > 0 \ ,$$

endogenous variables: i_t, p_t

exogenous variable: M_t^{t-1} (where $M_t^{t-1} = M_t^t$) .

The well-known *theorem of the quantity theory* holds: a change in the quantity of money M leads to a proportional change in the equilibrium prices p; the money or nominal rate of interest i remains unchanged. We get the strict proportional relation between M and p which allows us to state for $L(\cdot) > 0$ that the central agent of the currency community can realize his price target p the "indirect way" by fixing M. The temporary equilibrium (6-15), (6-16) may at the same time be interpreted as a special case of a long term equilibrium of our overlapping generations model. We shall expand on this in the next section.

In this chapter we assume that M is paper money, not book money. Since M_t^t is smaller than the total volume of expenditure of the young generation in period t the question arises as to how one is to conceive of the payments transactions, i.e., the exchange by the use of money. We usually think of a repeated use of the same means of payment within a period, i.e., of the "circulation of money" and of the "velocity of money." The circulation of money, though, is not being modelled here (or elsewhere in neoclassical monetary theory). All we know is that at the beginning of the period the old generation and at the end of the period the young generation, holds the economy's cash balances. It is simplest to imagine that the buyers and sellers initially use abstract money with a certain real definition of the unit of account as a measure of prices.

The delivery and counterdelivery of goods and bonds is agreed upon; money claims and liabilities are mutually cleared. Concrete money (paper money) is used only at the end of the period to settle open balances, i.e., only when the money values of the deliveries and counterdeliveries are not equal.

In our example this is expressed as follows: the old generation buys for the sum M more wheat from the firm than the firm owes to the old generation from the loan of the preceding period. The old generation pays the amount of money M to the firm. The firm delivers to the young generation less wheat (in terms of money) to the extent of M than it owes the young generation as wage payments $p\bar{x}_t^t$. After the payments are cleared the firm pays to the young generation the amount of paper money M. The young generation holds this amount M as cash balances until the next period. The book transactions look as follows:

Old generation $(t-1)$

M $-B_{t-1}$	px_t^{t-1}
px_t^{t-1}	px_t^{t-1}

UN_{t-1}

px^{t-1} px^t pC $-py_t$	M $-B_{t-1}$ $Q_0^{t-1} = p\bar{x}_t^t$
$p\bar{x}_t$	$p\bar{x}_t$

Young generation (t)

$p\bar{x}_t^t$	px_t^t pC $-py_t$ M
$p\bar{x}_t^t$	$p\bar{x}_t^t$

This is one way to visualize the circulation of paper money in this particular model. In this connection it is essential to think in bookkeeping terms. Our considerations follow essentially J.A. Schumpeter's description of the concept of money:

"However we wish to limit the concept of money, it always serves in its property as *means of payment*..., to the provisional settlement of credit relationships which arise from the lack of simultaneity of the payments and counterpayments which enter into economic clearing. The essential phenomena are the credit relationships of the processes of production and consumption or the accounts in which they are shown. These are the logical *prius* for which money, defined in another way than as a credit entry in an account, plays only a subsidiary role. This serving role is understandable only in the context of a system of credit and debit entries."[23]

We can interpret $p\bar{x}$ as the volume of transactions of the current period. The well-known Fisher *equation of exchange* becomes in this case:

$$M_t^t V_t = p_t \bar{x}_t ,$$

where V_t is the *velocity of money* in period t.

The concept simulates a false realism. Despite this, economists became used to applying it as an (imaginary) measure of "payments habits" of individuals defined as

$$V_t = \frac{p_t \bar{x}_t}{M_t^t} .$$

In the case of quantity theory, V and $\bar{x}$ are independent of M; p changes proportionally to M. This also follows from our microeconomic assumptions.

I. Fisher (1911, 15ff.) is content merely to give an illustration of the quantity theory by means of this equation. He writes:

"The quantity theory of money will be made more clear by the equation of exchange, which is now to be explained. The equation of exchange is a statement, in mathematical form, of the total transactions effected in a certain period in a given community." (op. cit., 15f.).

In Fisher's terminology the equation of exchange is

$$MV = \sum pQ ,$$

where Q is the total amount of *one* good purchased at the average price p, and $\sum pQ$ stands for the sum of "price times quantity" for all goods (op. cit. p. 26).

It may, however, also happen that, although the exchange of money against bonds and vice versa does not entail any transaction costs, no cash will be held voluntarily, i.e., in case of a corner solution (see Section 6.2). Even in this case the purchasing power of money as defined by the quantity theory may be determined the "indirect way" (i.e., by an exogenous fixing of the supply of money M) by forcing individuals to hold certain real cash balances, i.e., to demand a certain (real) amount of money L.

In our overlapping generations model, for instance, the assumption might be added that every young generation must hold cash at least equal to the value of the fraction μ $(0 < \mu < 1)$ of its (nominal) wage income $p_t \bar{x}_t^t$. In case of a corner solution the real demand for money is then

$$L_t = \mu \bar{x}_t^t .$$

---

[23] J.A. Schumpeter (1970, 209f.), translated by W.F. St.

The money market equation (6-13) is then changed to

$$\text{(6-13')} \qquad \mu\bar{x}_t^t = \frac{M_t^{t-1}}{p_t} \ , \quad \text{where } L_t(\alpha_t^0) \leqq \mu\bar{x}_t^t \ ; \qquad \alpha_t^0 = \{\alpha_t, \mu\} \ .$$

The parameter μ is then one of the arguments of the equations determining the optimal consumption plan.

E.F. Fama (1980) presents a similar idea in order to demonstrate (a) under what circumstances minimum reserve requirements are needed to ensure the determinacy of the purchasing power of money; and (b) that they need not necessarily be imposed on banks.[24] We shall return to this point in Chapter 8.

In a paper standard there is, however, a price involved when households are forced to hold cash simply to make the purchasing power of money determinate the "indirect way." The levels of supply will, at least in our overlapping generations model, be lower than they would be without cash balances. It is possible that the costs of achieving a price target the "direct way" may be smaller when there is no need to hold cash balances. In such a case it would be irrational to force individuals to hold cash balances merely in order to determine the purchasing power of paper money the "indirect way."

We leave this question open and limit the further discussion to the case in which cash is held voluntarily by the members of the currency community.

6.5 A Simple Stationary Equilibrium With Rational Expectations

The preceding section has discussed the temporary equilibrium of a monetary overlapping generations model with exogenously fixed price expectations. We have forgone an explanation of how the expectations were formed. This is not satisfactory. Why should the expected rate of inflation v^+ be just zero, or for that matter have any particular value? We now turn to this question.

To this end we assume that individuals form their expectations rationally exactly as we assume that they determine their production and consumption plans rationally. This is consistent with the neoclassical approach based on the ideal type of "instrumentally rational" (zweckrational) actions by individuals.[25] A non-rational or irrational explanation of the formation of expectations does not fit this picture. The hypothesis of rational expectations consists in the application of the ideal type of rational behavior of individuals to the acquisition and processing of information

---

[24] Generally: in order to avoid the case in which the equilibrium price of money is zero, we must assume a positive (real) demand for money. The place of minimum reserves may be taken by suitable taxes which have to be paid in money. See R.M. Starr (1980, 261 f.). An early statement of this point is found in A.P. Lerner (1947, 313) in his evaluation of the work of G.F. Knapp: "The modern state can make anything it chooses generally acceptable as money and thus establish its value quite apart from any connection, even in the most formal kind, with gold or with backing of any kind."

[25] M. Weber (1968, 24).

and the formation of expectations thereby implied.[26] The simplest case of the formation of rational expectations is when information about the framework for action is costless and correct. Exogenously given price expectations are replaced by an exogenously given model of the market as expected for tomorrow. We thus "endogenize" the prices expected for tomorrow in the overall model. We now apply this simple approach to the case of a stationary equilibrium in our overlapping generations model.

Assume now that every generation forms its price expectations $p_{t+1}^+, p_{t+2}^+ \ldots$ by utilizing all available information about the demand and supply functions of future generations for and of goods, bonds and money. The prices expected for tomorrow, the day after tomorrow etc. are now no longer exogenously fixed but – going beyond this – all future supply and demand functions including the expected price target and corresponding volume of money M_{t+1}^+ are now given. The system is in stationary equilibrium in period t. Cash is held voluntarily. Generation t knows with absolute certainty that the existing stationary conditions of the model economy (constant population, constant technological knowledge, constant preferences) will continue unchanged into the future. By assumption, only the amount of money can be changed and that only in a neutral manner.

Assume now that the quantity of money expected *tomorrow* and all future time is M^+. The corresponding expected prices p^+ and interest rates i^+ may be calculated in principle using the following stationary model:

$$\text{(6-17)} \qquad \hat{x}^+(i^+) - \frac{M^+}{p^+} = -y^+(i^+)$$

$$\text{(6-18)} \qquad L^+(i^+) = \frac{M^+}{p^+}\,, \qquad L^+(\cdot) > 0$$

endogenous variables: i^+, p^+

exogenous variable: M^+ .

We solve (6-17), (6-18) for i^+, p^+ and thus get the value of the expected price p^+ as the prediction of the "relevant economic theory" (6-17), (6-18).[27] The formation of expectations is rationally explained in this sense.[28]

---

[26] "... rational expectations is the application of the principle of rational behavior to the acquisition and processing of information and to the formation of expectations." R. Maddock and M. Carter (1982, 41).

[27] As formulated by the founder of the REH, J.F. Muth, (1961, 316f.): "... that expectations, since they are informed predictions of future events, are essentially the same as the predictions of the relevant economic theory."

His illustration of the REH may be interpreted to mean that he does *not* assume that the economic units really know the model with all its informations and always make the correct predictions. Rather, it suffices to assume that the economic units behave *as if* they knew the model and that their predictions agreed with those of the model at least with regard to the general direction.

[28] "... the price level we expect to exist tomorrow should depend on the money stock we now expect to exist tomorrow. This is the logic behind the rational expectations approach." S. Fischer (1979a, 227f.).

Today's prices and interest rates are determined [in analogy to (6-12) and (6-14)] as the solution of the temporary equilibrium approach applied for today with the rationally expected price p^+ as an exogenous variable:

$$\hat{\hat{x}}\left(\frac{p}{p^+}(1+i), \frac{p}{p^+}\right) - \frac{M^0}{p} = -y\left(\frac{p}{p^+}(1+i)\right) \tag{6-19}$$

$$L\left(\frac{p}{p^+}(1+i), \frac{p}{p^+}\right) = \frac{M^0}{p}\ ; \qquad L(\cdot) > 0 \tag{6-20}$$

endogenous variables: i, p

exogenous variables: M^0, p^+ .

For $M^0 = M^+$ we have $p = p^+$. We are able to justify rationally, in this manner, our previous assumption concerning p^+, namely an elasticity of expectations of onc. The exogenously given values for tomorrow's prices p^+ are replaced by a model for the market as expected for tomorrow, the equations (6-17) and (6-18), including the stock of money M^+ expected for tomorrow with complete certainty. The expectation about the future quantity of money is itself not rationally explained; but it would be possible to do so with an appropriate extension of the model (see, e.g., S. Fischer (1979a)). The systems (6-17), (6-18) and (6-19), (6-20) together explain i, i^+, p and p^+ with given M^0, M^+.

We need as many pairs of equations as we have different given quantities of money. For $M^0 = M^+ = \cdots = M$ the stationary model reduces to

$$\hat{\hat{x}}(i) - (M/p) = -y(i) \tag{6-21}$$

$$L(i) = M/p\ ; \qquad L(\cdot) > 0 \tag{6-22}$$

endogenous variables: i, p

exogenous variable: M .

We repeat for clarification: we imagine that a "time machine" transports us in discrete steps along the time axis through the stationary model world. In each point of time t, purchase agreements, legally binding for the current period t, are agreed upon and fulfilled; in addition money-loan transactions from t to $t+1$ are concluded, shares in firms are acquired (or else firms UN_t founded), and cash balances are taken over. Period $t+1$ is expected to be in all aspects the same as period t. In particular, it is expected that the same nominal quantity of money will be supplied by the central agent. Therefore

$$M_{t+1}^+ = M_t\ ,$$

so that

$$p_{t+1}^+ = p_t\ .$$

The stationary overlapping generations model (6-21), (6-22) with voluntarily held cash balances will be the basis for our institutional reasoning in the next chapter. The model explains, in a simple manner, the existence of a strict proportional connection between the quantity of money and prices. The theorem of the quantity theory is valid as long as, among other things, the quantity of money is assumed to vary in a neutral manner (see next section). In this model world, the central agent can, with a paper currency, realize his specific price target p the "indirect way" by simply fixing the quantity of money appropriate to his price target.

6.6 Neutrality of Money With Cash Balances

In a world with transaction costs in which exchange by means of money is the rule and the holding of cash balances is worthwhile, the concept of the neutrality of money is only of interest in the quantitative, rather in the qualitative sense. The literature always discusses the question of the neutrality of money in the quantitative sense. In this connection it is irrelevant whether cash balances are held voluntarily or not.

In our simple monetary overlapping generations model, money is always *quantitatively* neutral as long as its quantity is changed in a neutral manner (= simultaneous proportional variation of all cash balances) and, in case of unforeseen changes, a neutral distribution effect prevails. In addition to the qualitative neutrality of money discussed in Section 5.8, quantitative neutrality has further implications:

1. there is a *dichotomy* between the real and the monetary sector of the economy; and
2. the quantity theory applies.

With quantitative neutrality of money the arbitrage logic described in Chapter 5 applies unchanged to a model world with cash balances. The relevant theorems of classical or neoclassical theory are valid, in particular

- the Fisher relation, and
- the (strict) purchasing power parity theory.

This section will deal with the concept of the (quantitative) neutrality of money using our monetary overlapping generations model. In this connection we shall briefly touch upon the subject matter of the non-neutrality of money. In reality money is not neutral. Changes in the quantity of money influence the "real" part of the economy: real exchange rates, real growth of the economy, and employment. For the explanation or determination of a currency order, we draw the conclusion, that caution is necessary regarding changes in the quantity of money, particularly for the paper standard. We doubt that in the long run monetary policy can achieve more than to safeguard the purchasing power of money. We regard the attempt to actively stabilize the price level as a dubious undertaking. If price level changes are caused by the "real" part of the economy, they could hardly be fought effectively by monetary means. If they have monetary causes, the solution to the problem would be achieved by smoothing out the growth of the quantity of money rather than by monetary countermovements. This has been discussed extensively in the monetarism debate. We will do without a further interpretation of our position (see Suggested Readings for this chapter).

The previous section has clarified the role of expectations about the future volume of money. In the discussion of the quantitative neutrality of money, the level of the quantity of money is irrelevant. Only the change in the quantity is of interest: when will a change occur and for how long will it last? Will it be foreseen or not?

Following S. Fischer (1979a), we distinguish four cases.

Case 1: The Unanticipated Permanent Change in the Stock of Money

The quantity of money today M_t is increased (or decreased) unexpectedly and permanently today (period t) by a certain amount, so that the actual quantity of money today M_t is greater (or smaller) than the quantity of money which was expected yesterday for today and all future days M_t^+:

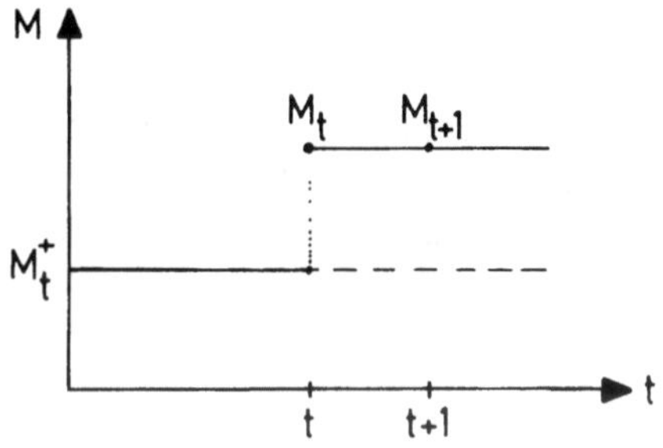

Fig. 6-1. Unanticipated Permanent Change in the Stock of Money

Case 2: The Anticipated Permanent Change in the Stock of Money

The quantity of money M_{t+1}^+ anticipated today for tomorrow with complete certainty is permanently increased (or decreased) only relative to M_t. We refer to this as an anticipated permanent change in the money supply.

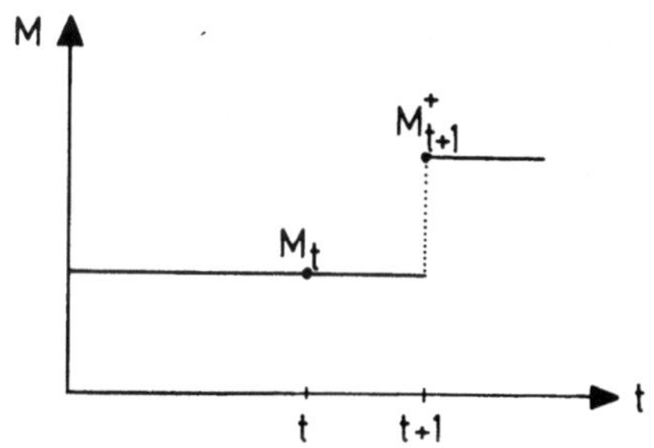

Fig. 6-2. Anticipated Permanent Change in the Stock of Money

Case 3: The Unanticipated Transitory Change in the Stock of Money

The quantity of money today M_t is unexpectedly and temporarily increased, e.g., only for today. Yesterday the quantity M_t^+ was expected for today. The actual quantity M_t is larger. It is expected today with complete certainty that the quantity of money will fall back to its original level tomorrow and stay there forever.

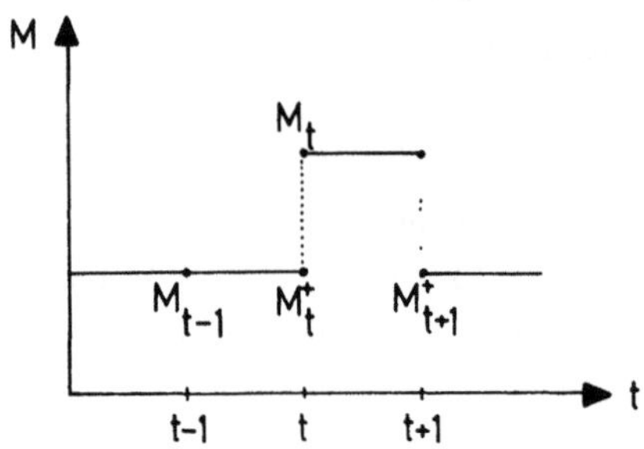

Fig. 6-3. Unanticipated Transitory Change in the Stock of Money

Case 4: The Anticipated Transitory Change in the Stock of Money

The quantity of money expected for tomorrow M_{t+1}^+ is increased or decreased only for tomorrow relative to today. It is expected with certainty that the quantity of money the day after tomorrow ($t + 2$) will fall back to today's level and stay there forever.

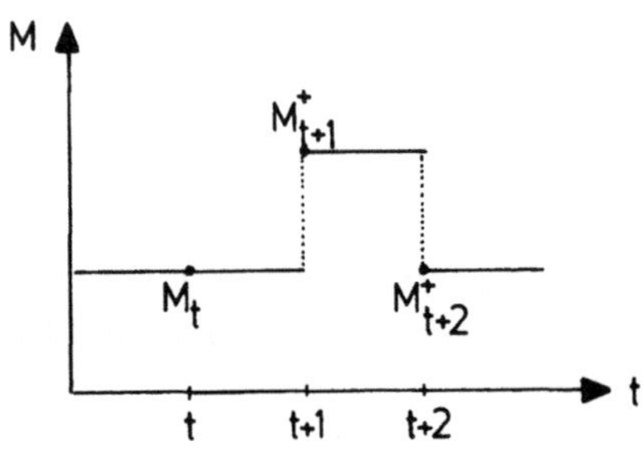

Fig. 6-4. Anticipated Transitory Change in the Stock of Money

On Case 1: The Unanticipated Permanent Change in the Stock of Money

Our overlapping generations model is in stationary equilibrium. At the beginning of period t, the central agent increases the supply of money in a neutral manner without a previous announcement. The increase is permanent. A neutral distribution effect of the unforeseen change in p_t obtains.

Let us assume that the quantity of money is doubled, then

$$M_t = 2M_{t-1}$$

and

$$M_t = M^+_{t+1} = \cdots = M^+ \ .$$

Since today's increase in the quantity of money was not foreseen, rational expectations had led individuals to expect in $t-1$ that $p_t = p^+_{t+1}$ etc.

System (6-21), (6-22) is equally applicable for $t-1$ (with M) and for t (with λM). In both periods it is $\rho = i$.

The level of the nominal or money rate of interest remains the same in both periods if the increase in the quantity of money is permanent and unanticipated. Since it remains true that

$$L_t(i) = L_{t-1}(i)$$

it follows from

$$M_t = 2M_{t-1}$$

that

$$p_t = 2p_{t-1} \ .$$

Prices change proportionally to the quantity of money M and the nominal rate of interest remains unchanged.[29] The theorem of the quantity theory holds.[30]

For prices to rise proportionally to M in this model world we need neither an actual excess demand nor any "transmission mechanism of monetary policy." A credible public announcement of a change in M suffices to produce a corresponding change in p. Milton Friedman (1969, 10) expresses this as follows:

> "A natural question to ask about this final situation is, 'What raises the price level, if all points markets are cleared and real magnitudes are stable?'. The answer is 'Because everyone confidently anticipates that prices will rise!'... If there is widespread agreement, the prices can be marked up or down with little actual trading."

These arguments are based on the concept of perfect commodity arbitrage: imminent excess demand as a result of an unanticipated change in the quantity of money leads to an immediate price adaptation; in the limiting case, an actual excess demand will not be realized. With quantitative neutrality of money, a credibly announced deflation or a reduction in the rate of inflation affects prices or the development of prices immediately, without reductions in employment or a stabilization crisis. There is no "braking distance" for a deflationary policy.

---

[29] J.-M. Grandmont (1983, 40) gives a similar argument for an overlapping generations model in a stationary equilibrium without production.

[30] This is the case described by D. Patinkin (1965, 74f.): "If there is no money illusion and if outstanding debts are revalued (or, alternatively, if there is a neutral distribution effect), then a uniformly introduced increase in the quantity of money causes a proportionate increase in the equilibrium prices of commodities and leaves the equilibrium rate of interest unaffected."

On Case 2: The Anticipated Permanent Change in the Stock of Money

The central agent announces publicly in period t that he will double the quantity of money tomorrow in a neutral manner, i.e., the cash balances of the old generation will be doubled. The announcement is believed without reservation. The stationary *real* cash balances remain unchanged. Hence generation t expects that prices p will also double tomorrow. Moreover, because of the announced neutral manner of the increase in the quantity of money, generation t expects further that the cash balances M_t^t, which it has kept today, will also double tomorrow. Generation t calculates its optimal cash balances in the same manner we have described in Section 6.3.

Changes in the quantity of money in a neutral manner are equivalent to the case in which the interest on cash balances z is precisely equal to the expected rate of inflation v^+ ($z = v^+$), i.e., if the real value of cash balances is not changed by inflation or deflation. As has been shown in Section 6.2 we then have

$$\frac{U_1}{U_2} = 1$$

and

$$C' = \frac{i - v^+}{1 + v^+} \qquad (=\rho^+) \ .$$

The arguments of the equations determining the optimal consumption plan *for period t* reduce in this case to the expected real rate of interest ρ_t^+ or

$$1 + \rho_t^+ = \frac{p_t}{p_{t+1}^+}(1 + i_t)$$

and *for period* $t + 1$ the expected real rate of interest is

$$\rho_{t+1}^+ = i_{t+1}^+ \ .$$

We determine the unknowns p_t, p_{t+1}^+, i_t, i_{t+1}^+ by means of equations (6-17) to (6-20).

In stationary equilibrium the real rate of interest is constant. Hence $\rho_t^+ = \rho$ and the *Fisher relation*

$$i_t = \rho + v_t^+$$

holds.

The change publicly announced today in the quantity of money for tomorrow is certainly neutral today. It will also be neutral tomorrow if the announced change will be actually realized. A correctly anticipated change in the quantity of money is perfectly neutral. Note the fundamental importance of the assumption of a neutral manner of change in the quantity of money for this conclusion to hold: in case of a correctly anticipated neutral injection of new money balances in period t, no losses will result from cash holdings nor from money loans in $t + 1$. The nominal rate of interest increases in t corresponding to the Fisher relation. Today's price level p_t is not affected by the expected change in the quantity of money. We are dealing here with a pure case of a *completely anticipated inflation* (see Section 5.4).

Analogous considerations apply for a deflation. In this case the nominal rate of interest i is smaller than the real rate ρ. It may even be less than zero. With neutral changes in the quantity of money the nominal value of cash holdings M decreases precisely by the rate of deflation (see above). The real value of cash balances remains unchanged. If we assume that the transaction costs of loans in kind are much higher than of money loans, then money-loan contracts will be concluded even if the money rate of interest i is negative. In this case the creditor would be willing to give the debtor today an amount of money which is, e.g., 3 percent higher than the debtor would have to pay back tomorrow, because both parties know with certainty that tomorrow the purchasing power of money will be, e.g., 6 percent higher than today. Effectively, the debtor pays the creditor in this case a *real* rate of interest of (roughly) 3 percent. In the final analysis it is the level of the real rate of interest over which creditor and debtor bargain.

In spite of a rather strong deflation, money loans are, under our assumptions, preferable to cash balances. The real rate of interest on cash holdings is zero because of the assumed neutral manner of changes in the quantity of money.

The situation looks, however, quite different, even with rational expectations, if the change in the quantity of money is anticipated correctly but realized in a *non-neutral* manner. In this case today's price level p_t will not remain unaffected by the change in the quantity of money. In the case of inflation the young generation in t allows for the certain future deterioration of purchasing power in the optimization of its cash balances, and it calculates as shown above in Section 6.2. The young generation knows already in period t that its cash balances saved today will be worth less tomorrow and that it will not be compensated for that loss. It will, therefore, demand less cash today and will wish to buy more consumer goods (wheat) today, as well as to hold more interest-bearing bonds. Thus the price level p_t will rise already in period t. As a result, in period t the old generation will be able to buy fewer goods with its amount of money M_t^{t-1} than it had planned. The presently young generation shifts its expected reduction in its own old age consumption in part onto today's old generation. Because of the higher real savings the input of seed (i.e., the capital stock) increases in period t so that the amount of production in $t + 1$ will rise. The optimal real cash balances of the young generation in period t is now a function:

$$L_t = L_t\left(\frac{p_t}{\overset{+}{p}_{t+1}}(1 + i_t), \frac{p_t}{\overset{+}{p}_{t+1}}\right).$$

The so-called *Tobin effect* becomes relevant: the planned real cash balances for period t, L_t, decline with an expected increasing rate of inflation $\frac{p_{t+1}}{p_t} = 1 + v_t^+$ and, in consequence, the capital stock for period t increases. Total output $\bar{x}_{t+1}^+$ to be expected for period $t + 1$ therefore increases (see Section 6.3). Because the quantity of money has been increased in a non-neutral manner, the Tobin effect is effective despite the rational formation of expectations. Money is *not quantitatively* neutral[31] in spite of rational expectations, costless perfect information about the conditions within which decisions are made, and the absence of money illusion. A change in the stock of money changes not only the purchasing power of money but also the volume of production. Monetary policy has real, if only temporary, effects. Stationary equilibrium will be reestablished only after a certain time, provided the system is stable (see, S. Fischer 1979a). The theorem of the quantity theory, i.e., the quantitative neutrality of money, does not apply in the short and medium run. In the long run it remains valid.

The Tobin effect works in the opposite direction in case of a deflation caused by a non-neutral manner of the change in the quantity of money. With an increase in the expected rate of deflation, the real value of the planned cash balances L_t increases, i.e., today's real savings decrease and so does the amount of production in $t + 1$.

On Case 3: *The Unanticipated Transitory Change in the Stock of Money*

We have a stationary equilibrium in period t. Then the central agent of the currency community changes in the same period the stock of money for a short time in an unexpected manner and without previous announcement. Assume that the quantity of money in t is doubled compared with period $t - 1$. The members of the currency community, however, count firmly on a reduction of the quantity of money tomorrow (in $t + 1$) to its previous level. With a neutral increase in the quantity of money (particularly for period $t + 1$) we have $p_t = 2p_{t-1}$ and $p_{t+1} = 1/2p_t = p_{t-1}$. The money rate of interest i_t is, as shown by the Fisher relation, lower than i_{t-1} by the negative inflation rate v_t^+ (<0). Money is quantitatively neutral.

With a non-neutral increase in the quantity of money the real cash balances in t will increase according to the Tobin effect and p_t will less than double. Money is no longer quantitatively neutral despite rational expectations, correct and costless information concerning the conditions within which decisions have to be made, and the absence of money illusion.[32]

On Case 4: *The Anticipated Transitory Change in the Stock of Money*

We start again with the stationary equilibrium of the overlapping generations model. The central agent announces in period t that he will increase the stock of money in $t + 1$ for one period only and that he will reduce the stock of money in $t + 2$ to its original level. The economic units believe this announcement and accomodate themselves accordingly. Everybody is convinced that the changes in the quantity of money will be realized in a neutral manner. Our discussion of Case 2 applies accordingly. The price p_{t+1}^+ changes in proportion to M_{t+1}^+. The money rate of interest i_t is higher than i_{t-1} by the positive rate of inflation v_t^+. The money rate of interest i_{t+1}^+ is less than the rate of interest i_{t-1} by the negative inflation rate v_{t+1}^+. Thus, the Fisher relation applies twice. Money is quantitatively neutral.

---

[31] S. Fischer (1979a, 228 ff.)

[32] S. Fischer (1979a, 237 f.)

If the change in the quantity of money is non-neutral the Tobin effect will apply twice: the demand for real cash balances declines in t, and the price level p_t increases in t. In period $t + 1$ the demand for real cash balances increases; p_{t+1}^{+} anticipates in part the change in the quantity of money expected for period $t + 2$. At any rate, the strictly proportional connection between M and p is interrupted in t and $t + 1$. Money is no longer quantitatively neutral despite rational expectations, costless perfect information about the conditions within which decisions have to be made, and the absence of money illusion.

We have seen that if all individuals in our model world are free of money illusion, are able to inform themselves about all supplied goods and their prices, and form their expectations rationally, if all prices are perfectly flexible and (general) changes in prices have neutral distribution effects, then anticipated as well as unanticipated changes in the stock of money have no influence on the real values of our model economy – provided that the money stock is changed in a neutral manner. Money is here quantitatively neutral. From this it follows that the non-neutrality of money is compatible with absence of money illusion, rational expectations, perfect information, and flexible prices. Above we dealt with such a type of non-neutrality: the Tobin effect, which is effective under the aforementioned conditions if the anticipated change in the money stock occurs in a non-neutral manner. In such a case unanticipated changes in the money stock are neutral while anticipated changes are not; they have real effects. Other forms of non-neutrality of money can be generated by corresponding changes of the model. In this connection the model of R.E. Lucas (1972) has become famous. In this model all above mentioned assumptions of the neutrality of money are valid, in particular the rational expectations assumption, but not the assumption of perfect price information. Real and monetary shocks influence prices but, because of certain imperfections in information (similar to the type described by E.S. Phelps (1970)), the individuals are not able to judge immediately whether price changes have been caused by real or monetary shocks. In this case unanticipated changes in the money stock have real effects while anticipated changes are neutral. The Tobin effect is here deliberately left out of account (see R.E. Lucas 1975, 1119, n. 7). The proposition of the ineffectiveness of monetary policy (the "policy ineffectiveness" proposition) of the rational expectations "revolution" of the seventies goes back to this consideration. It was among others brought forward by T.J. Sargent and N. Wallace (1975) using a simple ad hoc macroeconomic model which consists essentially of an IS-LM model together with the aggregate supply schedule proposed by R.E. Lucas (1972, 110; 1973), the so-called Lucas-supply function. We are not going to describe the model here. A simple version together with a critique can be found, e.g., in the excellent introductory article by R. Maddock and M. Carter (1982).

Such models are only applicable to the case of the paper standard in which the price target of the central agent remains more or less unclear. We may, therefore, conclude from the viewpoint of the theory of the currency order of a paper standard: monetary disturbances in the "real part" of the economy can be neglected if one avoids unforseeable changes in the money stock, that is, if one takes care, e.g., of a steady supply of means of payment. But this is exactly why Wicksell prefers a paper standard to the gold standard: the regulation of prices would constitute the prime purpose of monetary policy (in Wicksell's model equivalent to discount-rate policy) "which would no longer be subject to the caprices of the production and consumption of gold or of the demand for the circulation of coins" (K. Wicksell 1936, 194). Finally, non-neutrality of money can also be produced by assuming inflexible prices, i.e., in a Keynesian world in which exchange takes place at disequilibrium prices. Here, involuntary unemployment can be the consequence of wage and price rigidities. As S. Fischer (1977a) has shown for this family of models, the monetary authority may be able to stabilize output if it wants to do so, even in the absence of money illusion, the presence of rational expectations, and all other conditions of the neutrality of money (except perfect price flexibility). Fischer illustrates this point with a rational expectations model in which money wages are fixed for a certain period of time. Because the money stock can be changed by the monetary authority more frequently than labor contracts are renegotiated, monetary policy has the ability to affect the short-run behavior of output under Fischer's assumptions, though it has no effects on output in the long run.

The assumptions of wage and price stickiness and exchange at disequilibrium prices play an important role both in the critique and in the further development of the quantity theory of money. The critique has its basis in Wicksell's theory and can be found in the General Theory of J.M. Keynes.[33] Various attempts at a rational explanation of temporarily inflexible prices or wages have been made. One important approach to the explanation of temporarily rigid money wages is the so-called *theory of implicit contracts* which is primarily connected with the name of C. Azariadis (1975).[34] Wage contracts are not simply viewed as sequential spot contracts but as complicated long-term agreements. The amount of work to be done is negotiated within the framework of insurance contracts. The risk-neutral firms insure the risk-averse workers against random variations in the marginal product of labor.

More general but in the same direction is the concept of relational contracts discussed above in Section 3.4. The significance of this hypothesis cannot be estimated too highly; for its application to price rigidity see, e.g., A.A. Alchian (1970) or A.M. Okun (1981).

Whatever the economic explanation of rigid prices, which explains in turn why monetary policy may be regarded to be effective in the short term even under rational expectations, the argument has to be taken seriously that a discretionary monetary policy, aiming at greater stability of employment, may in effect destabilize the economy. The argument has also to be seen in connection with the fact that even an independent central bank may be subject to political pressures and thus contribute to a "political business cycle" (see below, Section 8.).

To summarize: money is not neutral. A number of reasons lead to that conclusion. In particular, aspects of the theory of public choice suggest doubts about a monetary stabilization policy. Yet the non-neutrality of money appears to be too thin an argument in favor of an active monetary policy. Rather, it seems to be appropriate to dispense with anticyclical variations in the quantity of money as a means of stabilization policy and, in the case of a growing economy, to allow for a

[33] See, e.g., K. Wicksell (1898, 97, 108) and J.M. Keynes (1936, Ch. 21, particularly p. 295f.).

[34] See also C. Azariadis and J. E. Stiglitz (1983).

steady growth of the money supply in accordance with a price target. Beyond that, we believe that our observations regarding the currency order are not affected by the non-neutrality of money. In the long run, money may be considered to be neutral. If this is assumed, as we do, the model developed in this chapter may be a useful tool for the analysis of currency orders.

Thus, within the framework of this book the non-neutrality of money is only a side issue. For the construction of a workable currency order we are interested primarily in the condition under which a proportional connection exists between the quantity of money and prices, given the existence of positive cash balances. In this case the price target and the supply of money are interrelated in a simple manner. The central agent needs only to fix the present and future quantity of money which is appropriate for the price target announced for the present and the future. Given perfect competition and price flexibility, everything else is accomplished by the interaction of supply and demand on the goods and bond markets. A workable currency system must function at least in such a world. Since we here understand monetary theory as the theory of currency orders, this ideal case is the natural basis for our considerations. This will allow us to work out the framework for the most important currency systems, to describe them in toto, and to compare them to each other. This is the subject matter of the next chapter.

Appendix to Chapter 6

1. *The Dimension of the Marginal Costs of Transaction*

Consider the following optimization problem:

$$\text{Max} \quad U = U(x_1, x_2)$$

$$\text{s.t.} \quad p_1 x_1 + \hat{B} + M + p_1 C\left(\frac{\hat{B}}{p_1}\right) = p_1 \bar{x}_1^1 \; ; \qquad \bar{x}_1^1 = \tilde{Q}_0$$

$$p_2^+ x_2 = \hat{B}(1+i) + M$$

$$M \geqq 0 \, , \qquad \hat{B} \geqq 0 \, .$$

Determination of the interior optimum according to Lagrange:

$$L = U(x_1 x_2) - \lambda_1 (p_1 x_1 + \hat{B} + M + p_1 C(\cdot) - p_1 \bar{x}_1^1) - \lambda_2 (p_2^+ x_2 - \hat{B}(1+i) - M) \, .$$

L has the dimension of "units of utility" ("utils"), i.e.,

$$\dim[\lambda_1] = \frac{\text{utils}}{\text{mark today}} \, ,$$

$$\dim[\lambda_2] = \frac{\text{utils}}{\text{mark tomorrow}} \, .$$

Cash today has the dimension:

$$\dim[M] = \text{mark today (more precisely } M_1) \ ,$$

cash tomorrow

$$\dim[M] = \text{mark tomorrow (more precisely } M_2) \ .$$

The nominal or money rate of interest i has the dimension

$$\dim[1+i] = \frac{\text{mark tomorrow}}{\text{mark today}} \ .$$

The necessary conditions for an interior optimum are:

1. $U_1 - \lambda_1 p_1 = 0$
2. $U_2 - \lambda_2 p_2^+ = 0$
3. $-\lambda_1 - \lambda_1 C' + \lambda_2(1+i) = 0$
4. $-\lambda_1 + \lambda_2 = 0$.

Regarding the third necessary condition we have:

$$\dim[\lambda_1 C'] = \frac{\text{utils}}{\text{mark today}} \frac{\text{kg wheat today}}{\text{kg wheat today}} = \frac{\text{utils}}{\text{mark today}}$$

and

$$\dim[\lambda_2 i] = \frac{\text{utils}}{\text{mark tomorrow}} \frac{\text{mark tomorrow}}{\text{mark today}} = \frac{\text{utils}}{\text{mark today}} \ ;$$

Referring to the fourth necessary condition we have:

$$\dim[\lambda_1 \cdot 1] = \frac{\text{utils}}{\text{mark today}} \cdot \text{mark today} = \text{utils} \ ,$$

$$\dim[\lambda_2 \cdot 1] = \frac{\text{utils}}{\text{mark tomorrow}} \cdot \text{mark tomorrow} = \text{utils.}$$

From the four necessary conditions it follows that

$$\frac{U_1}{U_2} = \frac{p_1}{p_2^+} \ ,$$

$$C' = i \ .$$

The dimension of $C' = i$ may be interpreted as

either: $$\dim[\lambda_1 C'] = \dim[\lambda_2 i] = \frac{\text{utils}}{\text{mark today}}$$

or: $$\dim[C'] = \dim\left[\frac{\lambda_2}{\lambda_1} i\right] = [1] \ .$$

2. *The Optimal Consumption and Investment Plan of the Household: An Example*

For purposes of graphic illustration and to clarify the optimization considerations it is useful to reduce the two constraints to *one* equation. We, therefore, write the optimization problem in the following form:

$$\text{Max} \quad U = U(x_1, x_2)$$

$$\text{s.t.} \quad p_1 x_1 + \frac{p_2^+}{1+i} x_2 + \frac{i}{1+i} M + p_1 C(\hat{B}/p_1) = p_1 \bar{x}_1^1$$

$$\text{where} \quad \hat{B}/p_1 = \frac{p_2^+}{p_1} \frac{1}{1+i} x_2 - \frac{1}{1+i} \frac{M}{p_1} \geqq 0$$

$$\text{and} \quad M \geqq 0 \ .$$

We now discuss the *budget equation* for the special case $C = (\hat{B}/p_1)^2$. Solved for x_1, the budget equation is:

$$x_1 = \bar{x}_1^1 - \frac{i}{1+i}\tilde{M} - \left(\frac{1}{1+i}\right)^2 \tilde{M}^2 - \left(\frac{1}{1+\rho^+} - \frac{2}{1+\rho^+}\frac{1}{1+i}\tilde{M}\right)x_2 - \left(\frac{1}{1+\rho^+}\right)^2 x_2^2 \tag{1}$$

where $\tilde{M} \equiv \dfrac{M}{p_1}$.

The cross section in the (x_1, x_2) plane at any point $\tilde{M}$ is a parabola concave to the origin. For $\tilde{M} = 0$, the vertex S of the parabola is to the left of the x_1-axis (Fig. 6-5). For $\tilde{M} > \dfrac{1+i}{2}$, S is to the right of the x_1-axis.

For the cross section in the $(x_2, \tilde{M})$ plane at any point x_1 we get an ellipse with a maximum B for $x_1 = 0$ (Fig. 6-6).

As the complete three-dimensional budget plane with the $\left(x_2, \dfrac{M}{p_1}, x_1\right)$ axes, we get Figure 6-7.

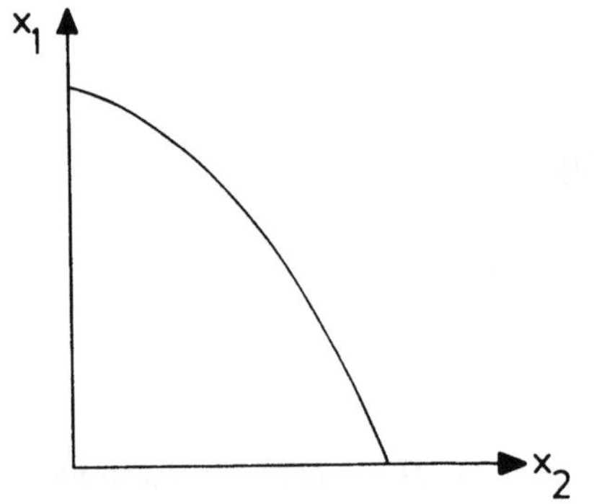

Fig. 6-5. The Cross Section in the (x_1, x_2) Plane at M

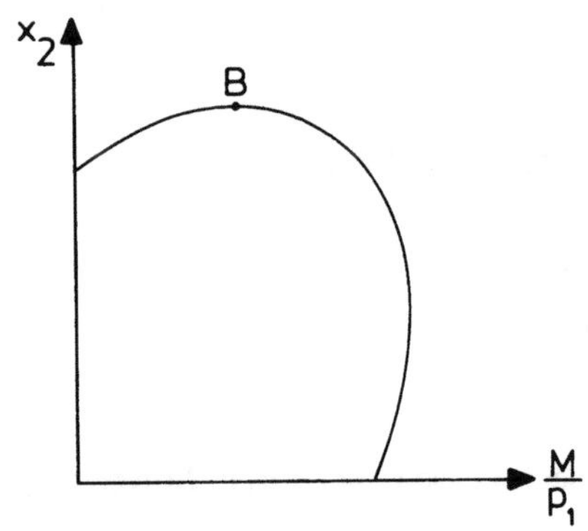

Fig. 6-6. The Cross Section in the $(x_2, \tilde{M})$ Plane at x_1

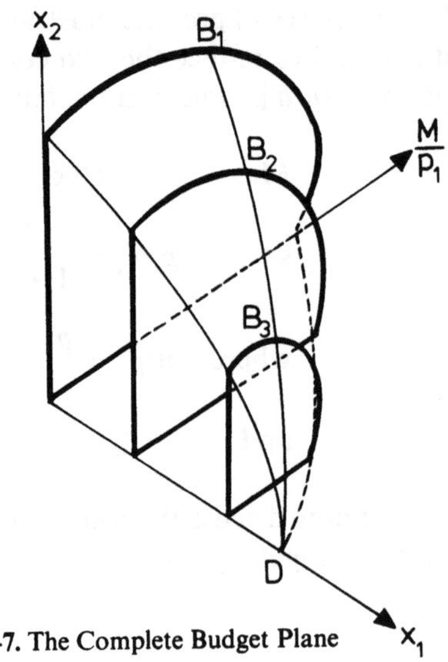

Fig. 6-7. The Complete Budget Plane

The cross section in the $\left(x_2, \dfrac{M}{p_1}\right)$ plane have increasing maxima B_1, B_2, B_3 etc. as x_1 increases. The graphic solution of the optimization problem is shown by the points where the highest possible (x_1, x_2) indifference curves (which we have not drawn in) are tangent to the budget plane in the $(x_2, M/p_1, x_1)$ diagram (Fig. 6-7). With indifference curves convex to the origin it is plausible that with an interior optimum the tangent point will be the maximum of a $(x_2, M/p_1)$ cross section, e.g., at point B_2. The coordinates of this point designate in this case the optimal consumption and investment plan of the household $\left(x_1^0, \dfrac{M^0}{p_1}, \hat{B}^0/p_1\right)$.[35] Corner solutions for the optima may exist, i.e., cases without cash balances. They would in this case lie on the part of the curve which is in the (x_1, x_2) plane.

[35] With $\hat{B}^0/p_1 = \dfrac{p_2^+}{p_1}\dfrac{1}{1+i}x_2^0 - \dfrac{1}{1+i}\dfrac{M^0}{p_1}$.

Whatever the final outcome, the choice of the optimal consumption and investment plan is here always made *simultaneously*.

We now discuss the budget plane of our example in order to determine the locus of the maxima B_1, B_2 etc. To this end, we partially derive the budget equation in both directions with respect to M/p_1, set the derivatives equal to zero and thus determine the function of the $(x_2, M/p_1)$ values of the maxima B. It is $\frac{\delta x_1}{\delta \tilde{M}} = \frac{\delta x_2}{\delta \tilde{M}}$. We thus get the function

$$x_2 = \frac{1}{2}\frac{1+i}{1+v^+}i + \frac{1}{1+v^+}\frac{M}{p_1} \; . \tag{2}$$

In our three-dimensional diagram, the picture of equation (2) is the A-plane of Fig. 6-8.

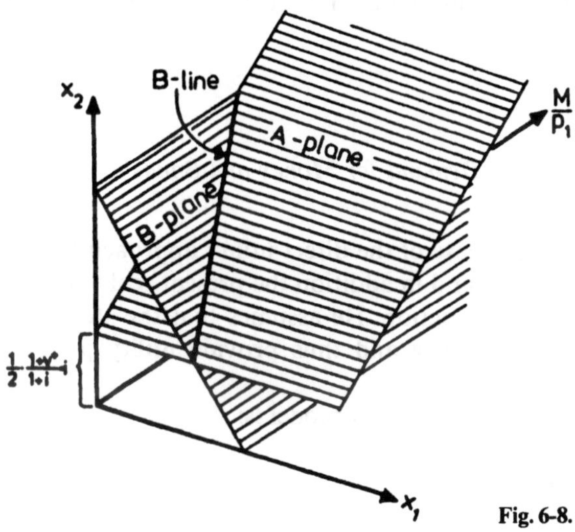

Fig. 6-8. The Crest of the Budget Plane: the B-Line

We now substitute the real cash balances M/p_1, by substituting equation (2) into the budget equation (1). We thus receive the function of the (x_1, x_2) values of the maxima B:

$$x_1 = \bar{x}_1 + \frac{i^2}{4} - (1 + v^+)x_2 \; . \tag{3}$$

The graph of this function is represented by the B-plane in Fig. 6-8. The curve of intersection of the A- and B-plane – the B-line – is the *crest* of the budget plane in our example. According to our first marginal condition the marginal rate of substitution is $\left|\frac{dx_1}{dx_2}\right| = 1 + v^+$ for all points on the crest.

Equation (2) can be also written in the form

$$i = 2\left(\frac{1+v}{1+i}x_2 - \frac{1}{1+i}\frac{M}{p_1}\right)$$

or

$$i = 2(\hat{B}/p_1) \; ,$$

which is equivalent to our marginal condition

$$i = C' \; .$$

The parameters $\bar{x}_1$, i, v^+ of equation (3) are the arguments of the three functions which determine the optimal consumption and investment plan of the household.

3. *On the Direct Utility Approach to the Demand for Money and Bonds*

D. Patinkin (1965, 457 ff.) includes in the case of the direct utility approach to the demand for money the real cash balances and in addition the present real value of bond holdings in the household's utility function. He assumes that the stocks of bonds also "possess some degree of liquidity and thus provide utility *per se*" (op. cit. 113, 464).

Patinkin's optimization procedure applied to our model is:

$$\begin{aligned} \text{Max} \quad & U = U(x_1, M/p_2^+, B/p_2^+, x_2) \\ \text{s.t.} \quad & p_1 x_1 + (B/1+i) + M = p_1 \bar{x}_1 \\ & p_2^+ x_2 = B + M \\ & B \geqq 0 \; , \quad M \geqq 0 \; . \end{aligned}$$

The marginal conditions are

$$\text{(1)} \qquad \frac{U_1}{U_{\tilde{B}} + U_2} = \frac{p_1}{p_2^+}(1+i) \; ; \quad \tilde{B} \equiv \frac{B}{p_2^+}$$

$$\text{(2)} \qquad \frac{U_1}{U_{\tilde{M}} + U_2} = \frac{p_1}{p_2^+} \; ; \quad \tilde{M} \equiv \frac{M}{p_2^+}$$

(see Patinkin 1965, 458 f.).

Suggested Readings to Chapter 6

Introductory Remarks

The core of this chapter is the neoclassical quantity theory applied to the overlapping generations model. The quantity of money and the prices of goods are strictly proportionally interrelated. Money is quantitatively neutral both in the short and in the long run. As an introduction, the reader should consult the two essays of *David Hume* (1752, reprinted 1952) "Of Money" and "Of the Balance of Trade" as well as *P.A. Samuelson* (1968) and *J. Niehans* (1978, particularly Ch. 1). A survey on the history of economic thought is found, e.g., in *T.M. Humphrey* (1974).

1 Temporary Equilibrium

The idea is, following Lindahl and Myrdal, extensively described by *J.R. Hicks* (1935, 1965) and intensively applied for monetary theory by *D. Patinkin* (1956, 1965). Patinkin's work plays an important role in the discussions of monetary theory around *J.M. Keynes* particularly in the 1960s (see, e.g., *H.G. Johnson* 1962). On expectations in the older temporary equilibrium analysis, see the survey in *K. Nagatani* (1978, Ch. 9).

The mathematical economic theory of temporary equilibrium was intensively developed in the second half of the 1960s and particularly during the 1970s. An excellent introduction to these approaches with a survey of the literature is found in *R. Radner* (1974). The survey by *J.-M. Grandmont* (1977, particularly pp. 548–556) is more inclusive though shorter. A non-technical description of this development is found in *K. Nagatani* (1978, 175ff.). He concludes with the sentence:

> "While none of the temporary equilibrium models studied so far has gone very far in terms of positive results, these studies give us an idea as to of what sort of difficulties we must face when we move from a full equilibrium to a temporary equilibrium." (p. 187).

2 Optimal Cash Balances

The holding of cash balances due to transaction costs was first modelled by *W.J. Baumol* (1952) and *J. Tobin* (1956). Here the *given* money assets are investigated with respect to their distribution between cash balances or interest bearing investments. This does not, however, integrate completely the optimization of cash balances into the theory of the individual consumer. The older literature dealt with this problem by assuming the real cash balances to be part of the utility function in the sense of Walras's "service d'approvisionnement" (*L. Walras* 1926, English translation 1954). For a discussion, see *D. Patinkin* (1965, Note C, 541 ff.) and on further developments of the marginal utility theory of money (ibid., Note D, 573 ff.). A modern formulation of the theory of the direct utility of cash balances is found in *D. Patinkin* (1965) Ch. V. Our approach of assuming an indirect utility of cash balances, i.e., of assuming costs in the exchange of cash for bonds and vice versa, is more elegant. An earlier approach in this direction is due to *P. Bernholz* (1965). Cash is held as a store of value because its storage costs are less than the storage costs of goods (interest bearing money claims are not considered). Fomally this corresponds to the later approaches by *K. Sontheimer* (1972) and *R.M. Starr* (1972), whose explanation of the holding of cash is, however, the transactions-motive: it is cheaper to trade by means of money (cash) than directly. If credits are disallowed, cash balances must not become negative in any period. The place of the constraint of a single budget equation for the whole planning horizon, as, e.g., in the Arrow-Debreu model, is taken by the constraint of a *sequence of budget equations* subject to the condition that there must be no negative cash balances in any period. For an interpretation, see *D. Gale* (1983). *J. Niehans* (1978, Ch. 2) offers a particularly lucid and intensive discussion on this point. A first approach to the inclusion of interest-bearing claims *and* cash into the constraints of the utility maximization problem of the household was presented by *P. Bernholz* (1967). The first extensive model is due to *J. Niehans* (1975a; 1978, Ch. 4).

We have listed only the literature for part of the theory of the demand for money. For a general survey of the theory of the demand for money, see, e.g., *E.-M. Claassen* (1980, Part II) or *K. Nagatani* (1978, Part I).

3 Once More: The Model of Overlapping Generations (See also the Suggested Readings to Chapter 2)

The analysis of temporary equilibrium of the type listed under point 1 raises the problem of the planning horizon when outside money is used. *P.A. Samuelson*'s (1958) overlapping generations model gives a natural answer. *N. Wallace* (1980), among others, considers the overlapping generations model the ideal basic model for monetary theory. A survey of this approach is found in *B.T. McCallum* (1982). For a proof of the existence of the equilibrium of monetary overlapping generations models, see *J.-M. Grandmont* and *G. Laroque* (1973), *J.-M. Grandmont* (1983).

4 Rational Expectations

The rational expectations hypothesis (REH) is due to *J.F. Muth* (1961) whose presently much cited article was hardly noticed for a decade. Its later fame is due to the work of *R.E. Lucas Jr.* (1972, 1973, 1975, 1976) who had already recognized the fundamental importance of Muth's hypothesis in the sixties (see *R.E. Lucas Jr.* and *T.J. Sargent* (1981, Chs. 4, 5). The REH has many applications. Its special popularity is due to the so-called "policy ineffectiveness" proposition, i.e., the assertion of the ineffectiveness of systematic monetary stabilization policy. On this point, see, besides *R.E. Lucas* op. cit., in particular *T.J. Sargent* and *N. Wallace* (1975) and *R.J. Barro* (1976). A very lucidly written and easily understood introduction to this subject matter can be found in *R. Maddock* and *M. Carter* (1982). With a suitable change in assumptions (price and wage rigidities) it may, however, be shown that even with rational expectations a systematic monetary policy may be effective, if only temporarily. On this point, see *S. Fischer* (1977a), and critically *R.J. Barro* (1977). Temporary real effects of a generally known change in the quantity of money result also if the dependence for cash holdings on the rate of inflation is allowed for. This is done in *S. Fischer* (1979a). A prominent critic of the ineffectiveness proposition and the "New Classical Macroeconomics", as he has christened it, is *J. Tobin*

(1980b), particularly Ch. II. For an opposite view read the review article of *R.E. Lucas, Jr.* (1981). *B.T. McCallum* (1979, 244) doubts whether the question of the extent to which the ineffectiveness proposition is applicable can ever be settled convincingly. However, he continues by noting that the influence of the Lucas-Sargent-Barro school on present views of monetary policy is remarkable:

> "Just over a decade ago, Milton Friedman's suggestion that unemployment could be kept low only by accelerating inflation seemed radical; now even many activists doubt that it can be kept low by *any* monetary policy."

A systematic overview of the main arguments and counterarguments of the rational expectations "revolution" is given by *B.T. McCallum* (1980). *J. Niehans* (1987) analyzes the application of the rational expectations hypothesis by *R.E. Lucas* et al., into the context of the history of economic thought.

A survey of the REH at an advanced level is found in *R.E. Lucas* and *T.J. Sargent* (1981, Introduction, XI, XL); for a typical contribution to the current debate see *S. Fischer* (1980).

5 The Problem of the Non-Neutrality of Money

The simplest way to model the non-neutrality of money is by assuming temporarily inflexible money wages, goods prices or interest rates. *K. Wicksell* (1936, 105f., 117) assumed inflexible goods prices and money rates of interest which react with a lag. *J.M. Keynes* (1936, 247) assumes inflexible money wages. The IS-LM system due to *J.R. Hicks* (1937) is based on the assumption of inflexible money wages and goods prices with a flexible rate of interest. The so-called *disequilibrium analysis* assumes inflexible money wages, prices and in part even inflexible money rates of interest, see, e.g., *R.J. Barro* and *H.I. Grossman* (1971) or *E. Malinvaud* (1977).

The rational explanation of inflexible money wages or goods prices and with it the non-neutrality of money has really been discussed only since the 1970's. A well-known approach is, the so-called "New Microeconomics in Employment and Inflation Theory" which is based, among others, on *E.S. Phelps* et al. (1970). The concept of the *natural rate of unemployment* of *M. Friedman* (1968) plays an important role in this connection. The paradigm of an auction market is replaced in this case by a *search model* which may also be applied in an analogous manner to goods markets. See, e.g., *A.A. Alchian* (1970) or *A.M. Okun* (1981, 138ff.). Another approach to the microeconomic explanation of inflexible money wages is found in the literature on *implicit contracts*: *M.N. Baily* (1974), *D.F. Gordon* (1974), *C. Azariadis* (1975). For a survey, see *H.J. Ramser* (1978), *C. Azariadis* and *J.E. Stiglitz* (1983). Money may, however, not be neutral even with the assumption of perfectly flexible (money) wages, prices and interest rates when cash balances are held. As *S. Fischer* (1979a) has shown, the Tobin effect may in such a case produce a temporary non-neutrality of money.

The rational expectations hypothesis is also relevant to the subject matter of the neutrality or non-neutrality of money. For a discussion of the REH and the "neutrality" proposition, see above No. 4. For the disequilibrium analysis with the assumption of rational expectations, see *H.I. Grossman* (1983).

6 The Monetarism Debate

A central theme of this debate is the problem of the non-neutrality of money and with it the possibility of a monetary employment policy. It is a theme of unchanged contemporary relevance. Should an activist monetary or fiscal stabilization policy be pursued or not? *M. Friedman* (1959, 1968) denies, *J. Tobin* (1972) defends the possibility. *S. Fischer* (1977a, 1980) considers a monetary policy for the purpose of stabilizing employment as a possibility. *T. Sargent* and *N. Wallace* (1975) show that the opposite is also possible. A more recent exchange of opinion is found in *J. Tobin* (1980) and *R.E. Lucas* (1981) which we have already cited above under No. 4.

For a survey of the monetarist theories, see *D.D. Purvis* (1980) or sympathizing *D.E.W. Laidler* (1981). A critical comment of these surveys is found in *J. Tobin* (1981). As a kind of retrospective see *Th. Mayer* (1985).

Chapter 7
Safeguarding the Value of Money: Some Basic Institutional Solutions

This chapter will complete our theory of the currency order in the simplest possible manner. We shall discuss the last point of the elementary currency order, namely the regulation of the supply of the means of payment, and we shall do this on the basis of the stationary overlapping generations model with cash balances which we have developed in the preceding chapter. We will do this for the two basic types of currency orders, the commodity and the paper standard, illustrated by the example of a redeemable and a non-redeemable paper currency, for the case of one currency and of two currencies (of a "national" and an "international" currency order). Each currency community has a central agent, the central bank. There are no other banks or financial intermediaries. We shall introduce them in the next chapter.

Money is assumed to be quantitatively neutral in this chapter. The world of quantitatively neutral money is the ideal reference system for a theory of the currency order.[1] In any case that is true for a concise exposition of our theory: in order that a currency constitution guarantees the value of money, it must be able to do so under ideal conditions at least. The problems which will arise under less than ideal conditions will be illustrated in brief insertions.

In Chapter 5, we left open the manner in which the target values of prices, interest or exchange rates fixed by the central agent or the constituent assembly, are guaranteed. We shall deal with this question now. In a world with cash balances the central agent (or the currency order) must see to it that the quantity of money is consistent with the previously fixed price target.

In case of a commodity standard the price target is determined the "direct way." Paper money is redeemable into a money good; the central agent has to provide the quantity of paper money demanded by the money users. In this sense, the quantity of money M is an endogenous variable. In the case of a paper standard the central agent has to fix the quantity of money M exogenously such that the aimed-at price target will be realized. The price target is here determined the "indirect way." In both, the commodity and the paper standard, we now deal with currency systems in which the means of payment are not only used for the purpose of payment (as in Chapter 5) but also as a store of value in the form of cash balances. The paper standard, in particular, presupposes the advanced planning of certain long-run cash balances in real terms. Otherwise the purchasing power of paper money would be indeterminate. The holding of such cash balances would have to be required if they are not held voluntarily.

---

[1] Thus Schumpeter argues in a manner reminiscent of M. Weber's ideal type: "... the concept of a state of equilibrium, although no such state may ever be realized, is useful and indeed indispensable for purpose of analysis and diagnosis, as a point of reference. Actual states can conveniently be defined by their distance from it." (J.A. Schumpeter 1939, I, 69).

Regardless of whether we assume redeemable or non-redeemable paper money, the central agents of the currency communities must now determine not only the accounting units, means of payment and price targets but must also see to it that the supply of money is consistent with these targets. All four elements of the elementary currency order must now be considered to be taken care of.

We shall proceed as follows: we first deal with the commodity standard for the case of one currency community and then of two currency communities. We assume, to simplify, that only paper money (redeemable into the money commodity) is used as a means of payment. The case of a pure gold coin standard (in which only gold coins circulate as means of payment) is briefly touched upon. The arbitrage logic, as presented in Chapter 5, is applied. Occasionally, we leave our reference system, the strictly elaborated stationary overlapping generations model, to deal in an interpretative manner with more complex cases. For the purpose of illustration historical examples will be given. The paper standard will be dealt with afterwards in an analogous fashion – again, at first, for one "country," next for two "countries." The significance of the Friedman rule and the old controversy of "fixed versus flexible exchange rates" are discussed with reference to a theory of the currency order. In a final section we shall discuss the advantages and disadvantages of a commodity standard compared to a paper standard.

7.1 Safeguarding the Value of Money With a Redeemable Paper Currency: The Case of a Single Currency

Consider the case of a commodity standard in which the sole means of payment is paper money that is redeemable at a fixed rate into the money commodity. The central bank has determined the unit of account (mark) and the means of payment, namely central bank notes. The regulation of price targets and of the money supply appears as follows:

1. *The Regulation of the Price Target*: The precise number of units of account which will buy a unit-by-weight of the money commodity is fixed for today and the future. That is, the exchange relation "accounting units per unit of money commodity" is fixed. The term "standard of coinage" (in German "*Münzfuß*") is used when the money good is also used as a means of payment. We shall use this expression also.

Example: At the time of the German Reich gold standard (1876–1914) the standard of coinage was 1395 mark per 500 g of fine gold, or 0.358423 g fine gold per mark.[2]

2. *The Regulation of the Supply of Means of Payment*: The central agent must at any time buy the uncoined money commodity against notes at the fixed price, and redeem notes at the fixed price against the money good.[3] In the case of gold, this means that the central agent must buy and sell gold on demand at a fixed price.

---

[2] Law about the Minting of Reich Gold Coins of December 4, 1871, see R. Koch (1885).

[3] Corresponding, e.g., to D. Ricardo's detailed proposition for using paper money within a currency community, while using gold bars in international transactions for the settlement of payments balances. D. Ricardo (1816/1951, 65ff.).

Example: At the time of the German Reich gold standard the Reichsbank was

1. obliged according to Art. 14 of the Banking Law (Bankgesetz) of March 14, 1875[4] to exchange gold ingots at the fixed rate of 1392 mark per pound (of 500 g) against its notes. According to Art. 16 the Bank was entitled to issue bank notes "according to the needs of the economy" ("nach den Bedürfnissen des Verkehrs"),
2. obliged according to Art. 18 of the Banking Law to redeem its notes
   (a) immediately when presented at its main office in Berlin; and
   (b) to redeem against *German gold coins* the notes presented at branch offices to the extent to which it had gold coins on hand permitted.[5]

The price target is "automatically" realized through the obligation of the central agent to buy or sell the money commodity at a fixed price. This regulation assumes the existence of transaction costs, in particular of costs of controlling the central agent by the money users. The organization of the control is here very simple: everybody can check during office hours whether the central agent really observes his price target. Furthermore: the central agent has to pay attention to his liquidity (here: his ability to supply the money commodity on demand) exactly as all other firms. For that purpose he needs credit with other economic units which have sufficient access to the money commodity. Credit together with comparatively small reserves of the money commodity (of "cash") should actually be sufficient. Yet, to avoid a run on the central agency the money users have to be sufficiently convinced of the agent's credit. Information costs (or transaction costs) play in this connection a vital role. To hold comparatively large reserves of the money commodity was possibly, at the time of commodity standards, the least expensive method of convincing the money users of the central agent's liquidity, as well as of the agent's ability to observe the announced price target. At any rate, the gold-cover ratio of the notes in circulation was closely watched at the time of the gold standard. It played a central role in the public regulation of the currency.

Example: As for the *cover ratio*, the Reichsbank was limited in its issue of bank notes by the so-called "*one third coverage*" rule: the Reichsbank was obliged to hold other kinds of money (i.e., gold coins) or gold ingots, for at least one third of its circulating notes. The average values of the actual gold-cover ratio of the Reichsbank during these years was as follows:[6]

1876–1880	26.5%	1896–1900	36.3%
1881–1885	26.7%	1901–1905	37.9%
1886–1890	40.5%	1906–1910	34.1% .
1891–1895	41.0%		

For simplicity's sake we shall assume in this chapter the strictest form of the convertibility rule: paper money is issued only in exchange against the money good, and vice versa.

---

[4] As formulated by the amendments of December 18, 1889, June 7, 1899, and June 1, 1909; reprinted in E. Heilfron (1911).

[5] The *purchase price* for the pound of ingot gold was 3 mark per 500 g below the standard of coinage of 1395 mark per 500 g of fine gold. This was the *mintage fee*. The redemption requirement was in force until August 4, 1914.

[6] See J. Plenge (1913, 77).

The complete modeling of a redeemable paper currency requires, of course, the assumption of more than one good. However, the guarantee of the value of (paper) money of a commodity standard can also be described within the framework of our elementary overlapping generations model with only a single good. We therefore continue to work within our simple wheat economy. The fixing of the standard of coinage as a price target is in this case the legal fixing of the wheat prices

$$p_t = \overset{+}{p}_{t+1} = \cdots = p \ .$$

For two periods this becomes

$$\frac{p_t}{\overset{+}{p}_{t+1}}(1 + i_t) = 1 + i_t \ .$$

As we assumed in Chapter 5 the price target is fixed the "direct way." The consistency of the price target with cash balances is guaranteed by the convertibility rule of wheat into paper money. The quantities of money corresponding to the fixed prices p_t, $\overset{+}{p}_{t+1}$ are

$$M_t^t \ , \quad M_{t+1}^t \ .$$

They are achieved under our assumption according to business needs, i.e., "automatically." Hence, in *stationary equilibrium* of our overlapping generations model [cf. (6-20), (6-21)] we have:

(7-1) $\quad \hat{x}(i) - M/p = -y(i)$

(7-2) $\quad L(i) = M/p$

endogenous variables: i, M

exogenous variable: p .

By assumption, these conditions are fulfilled at every moment of time, hence also in t and $t + 1$. Every equilibrium rate of interest i is according to (7-1) associated with a particular distribution of real income of the young generation between their consumption x_t^t, their investments in bonds $-y_t$, and the transaction costs C_t of their bonds investments and their real cash holdings L_t (see above equation (6-9)). The demand for paper money is determined according to (7-2) as $pL(i) = M$, given the exogenously fixed standard of coinage p. The quantity of paper money M is, therefore, an *endogenous* quantity in the case of a commodity standard with redeemable paper money. The quantity of paper money is automatically determined. The older literature therefore talks appropriately of an *automatic currency.*[7]

[7] J.H.G. Olivera (1970, 805) uses the term "passive money."

In stationary equilibrium M is constant. If for some reason an unexpected once-and-for-all real shock occurs in period t, e.g., an increase in productivity, and if the generation which is young in period t demands more paper money $\Delta M_t^t = M_t^t - M_t^{t-1}$ than the old generation in t offers, they can get the additional amount of paper money ΔM_t by the sale to the central agent of the increased amount of wheat (or gold) which is available as the result of the real shock.

The central agent is legally obliged to buy the money commodity with its notes. While, as we assumed before, an individual cannot store wheat the central agent can do so indefinitely. If the demand for money of the young generation in t declines by $-\Delta M_t^t$ the old generation in t will offer their superfluous notes to the central agent which must sell wheat from its wheat reserve at the guaranteed price p. This is a case of a money market with a *fixed price policy* that is consistent with the working of the market. Any positive or negative excess demand for paper money is made good by a reserve holding authority, in this case the central bank, in exchange against the money commodity.

If we assume stochastic real shocks with an expectational value of 0 the reserve holding authority must hold sufficient buffer stocks of wheat (or gold) in order to be able to guarantee $p =$ constant. This does not require a 100% reserve of paper money.[8]

Model (7-1), (7-2) can also be interpreted as a pure gold standard by assuming an exogenously given stock of gold coins and no demand for gold for other purposes. In this case M is the quantity of gold coins, expressed in abstract accounting units ("mark") at the coinage standard p_2 per 500 g of fine gold which generation t demands in period t (M has the dimension "gold mark in coins available in t"). $\hat{B}$ is the demand for money of generation t, also expressed in terms of gold mark. The agreed upon rate of interest i is in this case also the own rate of interest of gold. The price of wheat available today, p_1, is also expressed in gold mark. The real value of cash balances is calculated in units of the consumption good, wheat. The stationary equilibrium value of the wheat price p_1, expressed in gold mark, results from solving

(7-3) $$\hat{x}_1(i) - M/p_1 = -y_1(i)$$

(7-4) $$L(i) = M/p_1$$

endogenous variables: i, p_1

exogenous variable: $M(=p_2\bar{x}_2)$ ($\bar{x}_2$ is the given amount of minted gold) .

The quantity of money ($\equiv$quantity of gold) is an exogenous quantity. The quantity theory applies here in the manner described by D. Hume (1955, 41):

"It seems a maxim almost self-evident, that the prices of everything depend on the proportion between commodities and money, and that any considerable alteration of either has the same effect, either of heightening or lowering the price."

---

[8] For an early contribution on this point, see K. Wicksell (1936, 57).

Hume, in his further argumentation, thought only of the neutral kind of change in the quantity of money. His version of the "helicopter drop" is:

"..., suppose that all the money of Great Britain were multiplied fivefold at night, must not ..." [the price of all labour and commodities rise in proportion]?[9]

If gold is held not only as cash and if we also consider its production, then the proportional (quantity theoretical) connection between the quantity of gold and (wheat etc.) prices no longer holds. J. Niehans (1978, 142ff.) has made this crystal clear.

We now return to a paper currency redeemable into a money commodity but with *two* goods, e.g., wheat (good 1) and gold (good 2). Wheat and gold are used both for consumption and for productive purposes. Wealth is held exclusively as money wealth: bonds or paper money. The old generation now uses its stock of paper money, M, both to purchase wheat and gold for consumption purposes. We leave the distribution between the two open by including the real cash holdings M/p_2, expressed in the money commodity, with the excess demand function of the households (in analogy to Chapter 1, equations (1-12)ff.). We now have

$$\hat{x}_1\left(\frac{p_1}{p_2}, i, \frac{M}{p_2}\right) = -y_1\left(\frac{p_1}{p_2}, i\right) \tag{7-5}$$

$$\hat{x}_2\left(\frac{p_1}{p_2}, i, \frac{M}{p_2}\right) = -y_2\left(\frac{p_1}{p_2}, i\right) \tag{7-6}$$

$$L\left(\frac{p_1}{p_2}, i\right) = \frac{M}{p_2} \tag{7-7}$$

endogenous variables: i, p_1, M

exogenous variable: p_2 .

We substitute L into (7-5), (7-6) and solve for p_1/p_2, i. Next we determine M by means of (7-7). Since p_2 is given we also know p_1 once we get p_1/p_2.

The purchasing power of money is measured by the monetary value P of the commodity basket $Wk = \{x_1^*, x_2^*\}$ (see Section 1.3). We now have

$$P = p_1 x_1^* + p_2 x_2^*$$

or

$$P/p_2 = p_1/p_2 x_1^* + x_2^* = T_2 \ .$$

T_2 is the real value of the commodity basket Wk in kg gold. In stationary equilibrium, $T_2 = \text{constant}$. Hence $P = \text{constant}$ with a given constant standard of

[9] D. Hume (1955, 63).

coinage p_2. If the real cash balances are not expressed in terms of gold but of the commodity basket Wk, we have

$$L^*(p_1/p_2, i) = M/p$$

or since

$$P = p_2 T_2$$

$$L^*(p_1/p_2, i) = \frac{M}{p_2 T_2} \,. \tag{7-7'}$$

We solve as before: we first substitute L^* into (7-5), (7-6) and solve for p_1/p_2, i. This gives us the equilibrium value of the real cash balances L^* and the real value T_2 of the commodity basket Wk. The price p_2 is given. We can determine M by (7-7′).

Because of $P = p_2 T_2$ the purchasing power of money $1/P$ is proportional to the purchasing power of gold $1/T_2$. Both are "stable" (i.e., constant) in the stationary case.

We leave now our stationary model and assume a changing purchasing power of money or gold. This means in our case, at the same time, a changing real exchange rate of gold into wheat p_1/p_2. The changes are not foreseeable with certainty. Some investors speculate in gold others in wheat. Assuming rational expectations, all profitable opportunities which are known today will be exploited immediately. If an increase in the gold/wheat exchange rate is expected with certainty for tomorrow, then the demand for wheat and with it the gold/wheat exchange rate will increase today to the level expected for tomorrow. The present real exchange rates perfectly reflect all available information. We have an efficient market before us: the future movements of the real exchange rate p_1/p_2 cannot be predicted. Given today's exchange rate, the rate of tomorrow may increase or decrease with equal probability, or (what amounts to the same in this context) the purchasing power of gold $1/P$ follows a "random walk." Inflation, or more precisely, the change in the costs of living $(P_t - P_{t-1})/P_{t-1}$, are white noise in this case, a presumption which is supported by R. Barsky (1987) with data of the USA and Great Britain for the relevant period before 1914.

How much did the purchasing power of money vary in the heyday of the international gold standard before 1914? For a long period and for several countries we have to make do with wholesale price indices whose development is pictured in Fig. 7-1 for the German Reich, Great Britain and the USA for the period 1877–1914. As one would expect the three time series look pretty similar. They give the impression that there was a deflation until the nineties and afterwards an inflation. Yet, random walk series can generate such movements.

The average values of the inflation rates were comparatively small in the long term and quite substantial in the short run. In the long term, over 30 years and more, the average inflation or deflation rate in the German Reich, in Great Britain and the USA were less than ± 1 percent p.a. (see Table 7.1).

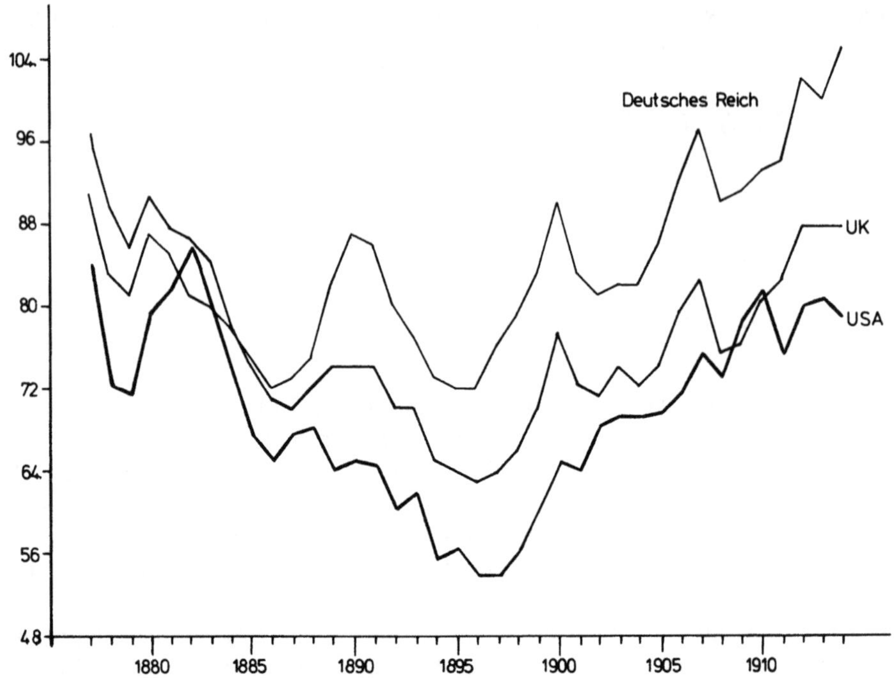

Fig. 7-1. Wholesale-price Indices German Reich, UK and USA 1877–1914

Table 7.1 Long-Term Inflation Rates at the time of the International Gold Standard[10]

Country	Period	Average Annual Inflation Rate in % p.a.[a]
German Reich	1877–1914	+0.8
Great Britain	1821–1914	−0.2
USA	1879–1914	+0.4

[a] Measured by the wholesale price index. The cost of living index for food and rentals for the German Reich rose during the same period on the average by 0.8% p.a.[11]

In the medium term (15–30 years), however, the picture looks quite differently. The average inflation or deflation rates were larger. There were long periods of "inflation" of the order of magnitude of 1–3% p.a., which were interrupted by periods of "deflation" of more or less equal orders of magnitude and durations (Table 7.2).

[10] The sources for the data are
- for the German Reich: Deutsche Bundesbank (1976a, Table 1.02, p. 6),
- for Great Britain and the United States: R.W. Jastram (1977, 32–33 and 145–146).

[11] Calculations by J. Kuczynski, in: Deutsche Bundesbank (1976a, 6).

Table 7.2 Medium Term Rates of Inflation During the Period of the International Gold Standard[12]

Country	Period	Average Annual Rate of Inflation in % p.a. (Wholesale Prices)
German Reich	1877–1896	−1.28
	1897–1914	3.03
	1877–1914	0.76
Great Britain	1821–1849	−1.23
	1850–1873	1.68
	1874–1896	−2.49
	1897–1914	1.97
	1821–1914	−0.18
USA	1879–1897	−1.39
	1898–1914	2.35
	1879–1914	0.38

The annual rates of inflation showed even greater fluctuations. The fluctuations during the period under consideration vary considerably:

German Reich	between −8.8% and 9.3%
Great Britain	between −15.6% and 21.8%
USA	between −14.2% and 11.4%[13]

We have thus fairly substantial price changes around a constant long-term trend.

Notes on the History of Thought:

Given the fluctuations of the money value in the short and medium term it is not surprising that economic theorists concerned themselves with the problem of the stabilization of commodity prices even during the heyday of the international gold standard. This required, first, developing the concept of the purchasing power of money and its measurement. W.St. Jevons (1884, 13) worried in 1863 about a "serious fall in the value of gold" – the rate of inflation of the British pound averaged at the time 6.67% p.a. – and he considered the use of a commodity basket to measure the value of money.[14] A. Marshall (1926, 10) in his testimony before the Royal Commission on the Depression of Trade and Industry in 1886 argued that "... the Government should publish tables showing as closely as may be the changes in the purchasing power of gold, and should facilitate contracts for payments to be made in terms of units of fixed purchasing power."

[12] The sources for the data are
- for the German Reich: Deutsche Bundesbank (1976a, Table 1.02, p. 6),
- for Great Britain and the United States: R.W. Jastram (1977, 32–33 and 145–146).

[13] The coefficients of variation were in these years (rounded off):

Deutsches Reich:	+5.0
Great Britain:	+17.8
USA:	+4.0 .

For the inflation rates in the German Reich, measured by the consumer price index, the coefficient of variation was, however, substantially smaller, viz. 1.1.

[14] W.S. Jevons (1875/1898, 318 ff.) sees the difficulties involved in introducing a "tabular standard," but judges the advantages of its eventual application very positively. "Such a standard would add a wholly new degree of stability to social relations, ... " (op. cit. 325).

K. Wicksell (1898, English translation 1936) dedicates his famous work "*Interest and Prices*" (Geldzins und Güterpreise) to the problem of price fluctuations. He visualized a change to a non-redeemable "international paper standard" as the ideal solution, a standard, which he believed could be manipulated so as "to stabilize the general level of world prices" (op. cit. 1936, 194).

I. Fisher (1911) in his book "*The Purchasing Power of Money*" examines carefully the stabilization of the purchasing power of money and he discusses different stabilization procedures including one of his own.[15] The first step for a reform for the monetary system would, however, have to be "to persuade the public, and especially the business public, to study the problem of monetary stability and to realize that at present contracts in money are as truly speculative as the selling of futures, – are, in fact merely a subdivision of future selling." (op. cit., 348).

Fisher is probably right with respect to the "speculative" character of investments in terms of money. Yet, it is difficult to believe that the business community was too "stupid" or unobserving to see the problem. The business community may have calculated in gold and exploited, with respect to gold, all profitable opportunities immediately such that the remaining "inflation" or "deflation" was only "white noise."

The situation changed fundamentally only after the First World War. The restoration of the gold standard was indeed attempted, but in most cases without redeemability of paper into gold coins, but only into gold ingots or another gold currency.[16] The international gold standard finally collapsed with the world economic crisis. J.M. Keynes (1924, 172ff.) criticized the situation during the debate about whether to return to the gold standard or not in the well-known words: "In truth, the gold standard is already [1924] a barbarous relic. All of us, from the Governor of the Bank of England downward, are now primarily interested in preserving the stability of business, prices, and employment, and are not likely, when the choice is forced on us, deliberately to sacrifice these to the outworn dogma, which had its value once, of £3 : 17 : $10\frac{1}{2}$ per ounce."

To summarize: with a commodity standard of the redeemable paper currency type there exists a uniquely defined price target, as a rule related to one particular commodity (e.g., gold), which is maintained throughout. The price target is realized by clearly regulated control of the quantity of paper money: paper is at all times convertible into gold at a fixed rate and vice versa. The quantity of money which is consistent with the "directly" fixed price target is "automatically," i.e., endogenously determined. Given the existence of a general equilibrium, the equilibrium value of the purchasing power of money is determined via the goods markets as the real rate of exchange of the money good into the other goods, and with it into any chosen commodity basket. Its stability is independent of the stability of the demand-for-money function. However, it is "subject to the caprices of the production and consumption of gold or of the demand for the circulation of coins." (K. Wicksell 1936, 194). An ad hoc policy of stabilizing the value of money through interventions in the gold market with the aim to stabilize the purchasing power of gold is theoretically conceivable, but does not really conform to the basic idea of the gold standard. At the time of the pre-1914 gold standard the purchasing power of money was more or less constant only over very long periods. In the medium term of 10 to

---

[15] I. Fisher summarizes as follows: "One such method was to make inconvertible paper the standard money, and to regulate its quantity. Another was to regulate the supply of metallic moneys by a varying seigniorage charge. Still another was to issue paper money, redeemable on demand, not in fixed amounts of the basic precious metal, but varying amounts, so calculated as to keep the level of prices unvarying. Lastly was considered the proposal of the writer, – to adopt the gold-exchange standard combined with a tabular standard." (I. Fisher 1911, 348).

[16] E.W. Kemmerer (1944, 118ff.).

20 years, which is the relevant term for investments and loans, the observed rates of inflation are of the order of magnitude of $\pm 3\%$, and the annual fluctuations of the purchasing power of money were, as we have seen, substantially larger. However, no systematic inflation occured. Inflation (or deflation) during the time of the gold standard, may be understood as "white noise." Apparently, the investors were not much disturbed by that. In any case, the pre-1914 gold standard was generally trusted. This trust was, among others, based on the expectation that the central banks would *not* sacrifice the dogma "which had its value ..., of £3 : 17 : 10½ per ounce," i.e., the defense of the price target with regard to the money commodity (and with that the defense of the external value of money).

7.2 Safeguarding the Value of Money With Redeemable Paper Currencies: The Case of Two Currencies

We begin with the case of an international commodity standard. There are now two currency communities. Both use the same money commodity, but different units of account and means of payment:

- as accounting units: "mark" (currency 1) and "dollar" (currency 2);
- as means of payment: "mark central bank notes" and "dollar central bank notes."

The regulation of the price target and of the supply with means of payment looks as follows:

1. *Regulation of the Price Target*: The standard of coinage is determined autonomously for each currency: for the mark currency p^1 and the dollar currency p^2.

Example: at the time of the pre-1914 international gold standard,
1 mark = 0.3584 g fine gold;
1 US dollar = 1.50463 g fine gold.

2. *The Regulation of the Supply of Means of Payment*: Both central agents are obliged to buy and sell the money commodity at the fixed price p^1 and p^2 respectively for their notes. In this case, public regulation of the monetary system on a "national" basis suffices, provided the central banks abided by the convention not to intervene in the gold market. This convention was not strictly adhered to even during the heyday of the international gold standard.

The regulation is limited to the enactment of a national bookkeeping and value safeguarding order and to ensuring that it is obeyed. With regard to the cover ratio of the notes in circulation the same considerations as in the preceding section apply. For simplicity's sake we assume a 100% cover for bank notes. The central banks have no liquidity problem. The exchange rate e, i.e., the rate of exchange of dollar notes for mark notes, is freely determined on the foreign exchange market. The exchange rate is a purely "mercantile phenomenon," as G.F. Knapp (1924, 217) says. It is "flexible" and not "fixed" by treaties and the like. If the money commodity is a precious metal, e.g., gold, for which arbitrage transactions are comparatively quick and cheap, the exchange rate e, freely arrived at on the exchange market, stays "automatically" within a narrow band of either side of the so-called mint par of exchange:

$$e^0 = \frac{p^1}{p^2} .$$

For Example: for the mark/dollar rate of exchange, the mint par was before 1914 $e^0 = 4.19792$ mark/dollar.

In a world without transaction and transport costs $e = e^0$. When the currency communities occupy different areas (German Reich – USA), a difference between the purchase and the selling prices of the money commodity against the individual paper money arises which depends, among other things, on the transport costs (including insurance premiums and fees) of shipping the money commodity from one currency area to the other. In the case of the international gold standard, one speaks of a "gold import" and "gold export point" respectively. The exchange rate of two currencies tied to gold can fluctuate freely only within the limits given by the gold points.[17]

Example: Before 1914, the gold points for the mark vis-à-vis the dollar were, as seen from New York:

gold export point: 4.1680 mark/US-dollar
gold import point: 4.2185 mark/US-dollar.

More precisely, even the gold points are variable because they also depend on the variable losses of interest for the period required to ship gold. Nevertheless, it seems as if at that time only fixed values were quoted. In fact, T.A. Clark (1984) has shown that the US/British gold points including interest losses were violated for several successive months. Thus, there was not a quick adaptation. Clark also found that gold moved occasionally in the unprofitable direction. He explained these observations by governmental interventions on the gold market which had previously been reported by A.I. Bloomfield.[18] Another reason might be that not all costs were allowed for in the calculation of the gold points. The profit possibilities calculated by Clark might therefore be the result of errors in measurement.

In this case, no international public regulation of the exchange rate is necessary, e.g., in order to stabilize the exchange rate. It suffices that both central banks stick to their own fixed price targets vis-à-vis gold *and* to the convention not to intervene in the gold market. Whether they stick to their price targets can easily be checked by everybody during business hours. The costs of the gold standard (the allegedly "useless" holdings of national gold reserves) have to be compared with the costs of the international public regulation of a system of "fixed" exchange rates (in the sense that they fluctuate within a narrow band).

---

[17] For an explanation, see, e.g., E. Sohmen (1964, 105f.) or K. Rose (1981, 111f.).

[18] Under the heading "*Manipulation of the Goldpoints*" namely with the aim of defending or improving national gold reserves; see A.I. Bloomfield (1959, 52ff.).

Note:

Actual movements of gold may be avoided by a suitable foreign exchange policy of the central agents of the currency communities.[19] For this purpose, the central agents hold not only gold but also foreign exchange reserves. They intervene on the foreign exchange market with purchases or sales of foreign exchange so that no actual gold movements occur. Such a policy works, however, only if all central agents maintain their gold holdings and do not try to increase their gold reserves at the expense of the other central agent through foreign exchange sales. In fact, there were in this respect problems even before the First World War, and even more so after the war. J.M. Keynes (1924, 167f.) stresses this point:

"Gold itself has become a "managed" currency. The West as well as the East has learned to hoard gold ..."

"The actual value of gold will depend, therefore, on the policy of three or four of the most powerful Central Banks, whether they act independently or in union."

The institutional construction of the safeguarding of the value of paper money of two paper currencies tied to the same money commodity may be modeled as in the preceding section by means of our elementary overlapping generations model with one type of good, wheat. The fixing of the standard of coinage as price target for the mark or the dollar corresponds to the fixing of

$$p_t^1 = p_{t+1}^{1+} = \cdots = p^1 \ ,$$
$$p_t^2 = p_{t+1}^{2+} = \cdots = p^2 \ .$$

As in Chapter 5, we imagine that the two currency communities coexist in the same area. The members of the mark community hold only mark notes, the members of the dollar community only dollar notes. Initially there is *no "currency substitution"* (i.e., no "mixed" cash balances). (For further discussion see below Section 7.4).

As before, we assume for each currency community a real cash balance function $L(i)$. As far as investments in bonds are concerned, we assume indifference between the two currencies: in this sense we assume *perfect capital mobility*. Formally, this means that we have only one bond market equation.

According to the logic of arbitrage described in Section 5.7 it is clear that under these assumptions the stationary equilibrium values of the rates of interest for mark and dollar loans will be equal:

$$i^1 = i^2 \ ,$$

and that the stationary equilibrium value of the exchange rate will be constant over time:

$$e_t = e_{t+1} = e \ .$$

The latter will also be equal to the mint parity p_1/p_2.

Our stationary overlapping generations model consists now of an expansion of (7-1), (7-2):

---

[19] A.I. Bloomfield (1959, 55f.) reports on this point.

$$(7\text{-}8) \qquad \hat{x}(i^1) - \frac{M^1 + eM^2}{p^1} = -y(i^1)$$

$$(7\text{-}9) \qquad L^1(i^1) = M^1/p^1$$

$$(7\text{-}10) \qquad L^2(i^2) = M^2/p^2$$

$$(7\text{-}11) \qquad i^1 = i^2$$

$$(7\text{-}12) \qquad e = p^1/p^2$$

endogenous variables: i^1, i^2, e, M^1, M^2

exogenous variables: p^1, p^2 .

Equation (7-8) describes the distribution of the real income of the young generation among their consumption, their seed inputs, the transaction costs of their bond investments, and their real cash balances in mark and dollar L^1, L^2. (See Section 6.3). The demand for mark notes is determined according to (7-9) as

$$p^1L^1(i^1) = M^1 \ ,$$

that for dollar notes according to (7-10) as

$$p^2L^2(i^2) = M^2 \ .$$

The stationary equilibrium values of the quantity of paper money M^1, M^2 are, therefore, endogenous variables in the case of a commodity standard. They are "automatically" determined. Similarily, the quantity of world money

$$(7\text{-}13) \qquad M^{(2)} = \frac{1}{e}M^1 + M^2$$

is an endogenous variable. Its distribution between mark and dollar cash holdings depends on the demand for real cash holdings, i.e., on the two money market equations (7-9), (7-10). Because of perfect and costless goods arbitrage, the exchange rate e is equal to the mint parity p^1/p^2. For the money commodity, purchasing power parity applies without restriction, whether the system is in equilibrium or not. In the present case it is valid also for all other goods (see above Section 5.6.).

Few if any actual arbitrage transactions are needed for the adaptation of prices. It suffices that they are possible. D.N. McCloskey and J.R. Zecher (1976) have stressed this point for the case of the international gold standard:

"A flow of gold is by no means a necessary part of this process of arbitrage. In fact, the mere *threat* of arbitrage may be sufficient to bring a nation's prices and interest rates into line with the world's, without flows of anything."[20]

As a matter of fact, the price levels of the German Reich, Great Britain and the USA 1877 – 1914 moved in a very similar fashion (see above Fig. 7-1). David Hume's price-specie flow-mechanism which

[20] D.N. McCloskey and J.R. Zecher (1976, 365).

postulates that the current accounts in the balance of payments are kept in equilibrium by means of changes in relative prices at home and abroad and the corresponding gold movements cannot explain this. As P.A. Samuelson (1980) showed, it is also theoretically incorrect. We shall deal with this now.

The Monetary Approach to the Balance-of-Payments Theory

We now look at the case of two pure gold coin currencies (only gold coins are used as means of payment) within the framework of our world without arbitrage cost. In analogy to the preceding section, M^1 and M^2 denote the amounts of the circulating money (here gold coins) expressed in abstract accounting units, both calculated at the respective standards of coinage p_2^1 and p_2^2; x, y are the amounts of wheat; p_1^1 is the freely variable wheat price in terms of gold mark, p_1^2 the same price in gold dollar. As previously assumed, there is no "currency substitution" of gold coins here. However, the melting down and re-minting of gold coins is a way to achieve substitutability. In both currency communities there exists the *right of free coinage*. The variables of the stationary equilibrium model (7-8) to (7-12) described above, and of the equation defining the world quantity of money (7-13) (now to be interpreted as world *gold* quantity $M^{(2)}$) are to be correspondingly re-interpreted, with

endogenous variables: $i^1, i^2, p_1^1, p_2^2, M^1, M^2$; and

exogenous variables: $M^{(2)}, e\ (=p_2^1/p_2^2)$.

The distribution of the world gold quantity $M^{(2)}$ between the two currency communities, i.e., the national supply of money M^1, M^2, is here determined endogenously. This means that the central agents have no influence on the level of the national stocks of money. The result corresponds to D. Hume's (1752/1955, 63) reasoning:

"All water wherever it communicates, remains always at a level."

Under our assumptions, however, the process of adaption is not a *price*-specie-flow-mechanism, for the prices adapt themselves directly through goods arbitrage. The law of one price always holds, even in disequilibrium on the goods and money markets. In equilibrium there is in this case no trade between the two currency communities. The members of each currency community consume annually exactly as much wheat as they produce. The national gold stocks M^1, M^2 are constant. The balance of trade balances are zero.

Assume now that the distribution of the constant world gold stock $M^{(2)}$ between the two currency communities is disturbed by one single intervention from the outside. Because of the law of one price we have

$$p_1^1 = ep_1^2 \ .$$

For simplicity's sake we assume that the p^i remain the unchanged equilibrium prices. Immediately after the disturbance, let

$$M^1 > p_1^1 L^1(\cdot)\ ,$$
$$M^2 < p_1^2 L^2(\cdot)\ .$$

In this case, the members of the mark currency community will wish to reduce their excess cash balances by demanding more wheat than they produce. They demand wheat in the dollar currency community in exchange for their excess gold. A temporary deficit in the trade balance results which in this case is also a *balance-of-payments deficit*. The opposite is true for the dollar-currency community. Under the assumptions made, the latter accepts the excess gold of the mark community in exchange for wheat exports. The adaptation does not occur indirectly via temporary price differences, as Hume imagined, but directly via real cash balance effects. We deal here with a *specie-flow mechanism.*[21]

The same consideration can be carried out for the case of a fractional gold standard with bank notes as means of payment.

H.G. Johnson (1972, 230) argues in an analogous manner in his presentation of the *monetary approach to the balance of payments theory*:

"... the new approach to the balance of payments theory, while basically Humean in spirit, places emphasis not on relative price changes but on direct influence of excess demand for or supply of money on the balance between income and disposal of funds whether through production and consumption or through borrowing and lending, and therefore on the overall balance of payments."

If the production of gold is allowed for, the strictly proportional quantity-theoretical connection between the quantity of gold and wheat (etc.) prices does not obtain. If in both currency communities there are both gold coins *and* paper money redeemable into gold (the two being regarded as perfect substitutes) the sum of coins and paper money of both currencies, $M^{(2)}$, must be considered an endogenous variable whose value is *automatically* determined with free coinage and unlimited convertibility, and assuming that paper money had got into circulation only in exchange against gold. (Further discussion of the monetary approach to the balance of payments theory is found below, Section 7.4).

On the Basic Conception of the Gold Exchange Standard

Thus far we have considered the case of an international currency order in which *all* currencies (here two) are directly anchored in the money commodity through the standard of coinage. Following 5.7 we may, however, also consider an international currency order in which only *one currency* is directly anchored in the money commodity through the standard of coinage, the so-called *reserve* or *key currency*, e.g., the dollar (currency 2). The other currencies (here currency 1) are tied to the reserve currency by a fixed exchange rate *e*, i.e., they are indirectly anchored in the money commodity. This is the construction of the gold exchange standard, the

[21] P.A. Samuelson (1980, 147); J. Niehans (1984, 38ff.).

logic of which leeds to the explicit creation of an international currency community together with an explicitly negotiated international currency order and the creation of an international central agency. The following magnitudes must be determined:

- the international unit of account (dollar),
- the international means of payment [dollar credit or debit entries with the central agency of the reserve-currency community ("chartal" means of payment in the wider sense) or gold ingots ("natural" means of payment)],
- the price target of the international unit of account (the standard of coinage of the dollar in gold) and the price targets of the member currencies (i.e., their exchange rates vis-à-vis the key currency), and finally
- the manner in which international means of payment are created, e.g., the gold convertibility of the dollar in both directions.

The Bretton Woods Agreement in general, though not in detail, was based on this principle of construction.

The institutional regulation of the safeguarding of the value of money must look as follows (we deal only with the case of two currencies):

1. *Regulation of the Price Target*: A standard of coinage p^2 is fixed for the reserve or key currency (dollar). For the other currencies, here the mark, the exchange rate e is fixed.

Example: The dollar was the reserve currency in the Bretton Woods System. The dollar price of fine gold was $35.00 per ounce. The parity rate of exchange for the other currencies was fixed in gold or the US dollar according to the mentioned gold parity. It was changed repeatedly. For the mark the following values obtained from the adherence of the Federal Republic of Germany to the International Monetary Fund in 1952 to the final abandonment of fixed exchange rates of mark/dollar on March 19, 1973:

Dollar Parity of the Mark	*US Dollar/Mark*	*Rate of Revaluation*
Time of adherence to the IMF, August 14, 1952	0.238	
Revaluation, March 6, 1961	0.250	+5.0%
Revaluation of Oct. 27, 1969	0.273	+9.3%
New fixed exchange rate, Dec. 21, 1971	0.310	+13.6%
Revaluation of Feb. 14, 1973 as consequence of the devaluation of the dollar vis-à-vis gold on Feb. 12, 1973	0.345	+11.1%

2. *Regulation of the Supply of Means of Payment*: The central agents of each currency community are obliged:

(a) in the case of the key or reserve currency (dollar) to buy and sell the money commodity at any time at the fixed price against dollar notes (gold convertibility of the dollar);
(b) for the other currency (mark): to exchange at any time mark notes against dollar and vice versa (foreign exchange convertibility of the mark).

Example: In the Bretton Woods System, there existed no strict gold or foreign exchange convertibility.

Ad (a) The convertibility of the *dollar against gold* was limited to the obligation of the American Treasury to buy or sell gold at dollar35.00 per ounce in unlimited quantities from or to the governments or the currency authorities of the IMF member countries.

Ad (b) The convertibility of the other *member currencies into dollar* was not agreed-upon. The other countries were only generally obliged somehow to maintain the dollar exchange rate of their currencies within a band of $\pm 1\%$ of their declared dollar parity. However, for the Federal Republic of Germany the mark was practically freely convertible after 1958. The other member countries, in parts, realized the official dollar parity of their currency by considerable restrictions of foreign exchange convertibility, particularly with respect to capital transfers.

Our overlapping generations model (7-8) to (7-12) illustrates the gold exchange standard for the case of two redeemable paper currencies in a simple manner. Determination of the variables occurs as follows:

endogenously: i^1, i^2, p^1, M^1, M^2

exogenously: p^2, e .

The monetary approach to the balance of payments theory applies here as in the case of the international gold standard: the quantities of money M^1, M^2 are now endogenous variables. The central agents of the individual currency communities cannot pursue independent monetary policies as long as they adhere strictly to the rules outlined above. The functioning of the gold exchange standard is thus very similar to that of the gold standard. Its advantage is that it requires less monetary gold than the international gold standard; its disadvantage is that carried to its logical conclusion it requires an effective international public regulation of the monetary system. Yet this appears to be rather difficult if the national states are not prepared to transfer parts of their sovereignty to a supranational administration. The text of the Bretton Woods Agreement and the history of this agreement illustrate these problems.

Example: Because there were no strict convertibility requirements

- of the dollar into gold and
- of the other currencies into the dollar

the Bretton Woods System lacked the necessary and clear direct or indirect real anchoring. It was possible to pursue a national monetary policy which was incompatible with the Bretton Woods System and such policies in fact were pursued by the central banks of the member states. The USA did provide the reserve currency; the Federal Reserve System pursued, however, a monetary policy as if the dollar were an inconvertible paper currency. The Federal Reserve System made no serious monetary policy efforts to maintain the gold price at \$35.00 per ounce.[22] The reserve currency country, the USA, very soon had an experience similar to that of Great Britain after the suspension of the convertibility of the pound sterling in 1797. After a few calm years, the "paper dollar" was devalued vis-à-vis gold. The free gold price passed the upper limit of \$35.00 per ounce for the first time in 1960. At first, the gold parity of the dollar was defended by interventions on the gold market, though not directly by the

[22] See M.R. Darby and J.R. Lothian (eds.) (1984).

USA but indirectly by the Bank of England in conjunction with the central banks of the other Western industrial nations. The interventions on the free gold market had to be finally given up in March, 1968.[23] In August 1971, the limited redemption of the dollar into gold was suspended. The other member countries of the IMF finally ceased to defend the fixed dollar parity in March, 1973.[24]

In historical perspective, the international gold standard of the half century before the first world war approximated most closely the ideal form of an international commodity standard. The centuries old competition between gold and silver had been decided in favor of gold. During the Middle Ages the silver standard predominated in Europe, though gold coins were also minted in some cases and simultaneously used within the same currency community. Now we consider several theoretical aspects on this matter.

Two Currencies, Two Money Commodities

We extend our model to the case in which the two currency communities use different money goods. The only means of payment is redeemable paper money. Currency 1 (mark) is redeemable at the fixed price p_1^1 into gold; currency 2 (dollar) is redeemable at the fixed price p_2^2 into silver. We discuss here only that part of the currency order which deals with the safeguarding of the value of money. For this purpose we use an appropriately extended stationary overlapping generations model with two goods instead of equations (7-5) to (7-7). We now get:

$$\text{(7-14)} \qquad \hat{x}_1\left(\frac{p_1^1}{p_2^1}, i^1, \frac{M^1}{p_1^1}, \frac{M^2}{p_2^2}\right) = -y_1\left(\frac{p_1^1}{p_2^1}, i^1\right)$$

$$\text{(7-15)} \qquad \hat{x}_2\left(\frac{p_1^1}{p_2^1}, i^1, \frac{M^1}{p_1^1}, \frac{M^2}{p_2^2}\right) = -y_2\left(\frac{p_1^1}{p_2^1}, i^1\right)$$

$$\text{(7-16)} \qquad L^1\left(\frac{p_1^1}{p_2^1}, i^1\right) = \frac{M^1}{p_1^1}$$

$$\text{(7-17)} \qquad L^2\left(\frac{p_1^2}{p_2^2}, i^2\right) = \frac{M^2}{p_2^2}$$

$$\text{(7-18)} \qquad i^1 = i^2$$

$$\text{(7-19)} \qquad \frac{p_1^1}{p_1^2} = \frac{p_2^1}{p_2^2}$$

$$\text{(7-20)} \qquad e = \frac{p_1^1}{p_1^2}$$

endogenous variables: $p_2^1, p_1^2, i^1, i^2, e, M^1, M^2$

exogenous variables: p_1^1, p_2^2.

---

[23] See H. Mayer (1983).

[24] A.J. Schwartz (1984) gives a good brief survey for the period of the Bretton Woods Agreement until its breakdown.

The quantities of paper money M^1, M^2 are, as before, endogenous variables. However, the exchange rate is now not fixed simultaneously with p_1^1, p_2^2. It will now be determined by the exchange ratio of gold for silver. In stationary equilibrium it is also constant. In general this cannot be expected to be the case. The exchange rate, therefore, will be less stable as if both currency communities choose the same commodity for their price target.

Curiously enough, the exchange ratio of the relevant two money commodities, silver and gold, was quite stable over extended periods. Thus A. Soetbeer (1879, 120) writes: "For the approximately twenty centuries before the discovery of America for which we have information about the relative value of the two precious metals, and except for a few initial exceptions in the Orient and in antiquity, the value of gold did not rise above twelve time the value of silver. In the Middle Ages it was frequently even lower. For the first century after the discovery of America this ratio did not change appreciably. Later gold rose substantially in value. This was particularly true for the years 1621–1650, and then again in our days since 1873." (Translated from the German by W.F. St.).

We have reliable data on the relative value of gold and silver after 1687 in the form of regular quotations of the silver and gold price on the Hamburg and London exchanges. According to annual averages of the exchange quotations the relative value of the metals fluctuated according to Soetbeer about $3\frac{1}{3}\%$ around an average value which remained fixed over many years. An absolutely fixed exchange rate thus did not exist (see Fig. 7-2). This was probably the reason why the bigger trading nations oriented themselves towards the same money commodity: gold; i.e., the money commodity which was used by the biggest trading nation of the day: England. The exchange rate of silver to gold deteriorated increasingly in the second half of the last century.

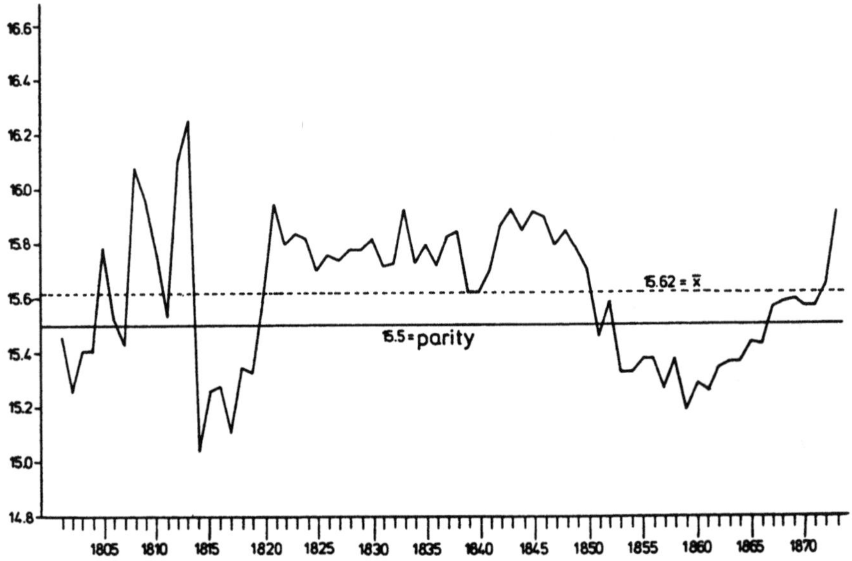

Fig. 7-2. Exchange Ratio Silver/Gold 1801–1873

On the average, the *relative value of silver to gold* was

1687–1790 approximately 15.00 kg silver per kg gold[25]
1801–1873 approximately 15.62 kg silver per kg gold.

[25] A. Soetbeer (1879, 128ff.).

Between 1874 and 1914, the relative value rose steadily above 16 : 1. It was

1880	18.05
1890	19.75
1900	33.33
1910	38.22
1914	37.37.[26]

England changed from a silver to a gold standard in 1774 (with an interruption during the Napoleonic wars). The four other European powers and the USA followed about a century later. France changed to gold in effect in 1878; in Germany the transition occurred in 1873 after the founding of the German Reich; Austria-Hungary had a gold standard de facto after about 1900,[27] Russia after 1897, the USA after 1834, with an interruption of the Greenback period 1862–1879.[28]

The Scandinavian countries, as well as Holland, Belgium, Switzerland, Italy, Japan and others also went onto a gold standard or adhered to it de facto. The institutional arrangements, however, varied from country to country.

"Broadly speaking, ... one might distinguish countries on a "full" gold standard, such as England, Germany, and perhaps the United States; countries on a socalled "limping" gold standard (legal convertibility of notes into gold or full legal-tender silver coins at the option of the authorities), such as France, Belgium and Switzerland; and countries on a wide variety of forms of "gold exchange standard," such as Russia, Japan, Austria-Hungary, the Netherlands, most of the Scandinavian countries, Canada, South Africa, Australia, New Zealand – all of which held a substantial part or the bulk of their external reserves in foreign exchange ..."[29]

Each country adhered strictly to its own fixed standard of coinage and thus to the announced parity rates.

One Currency, Two Money Commodities

Why should not a currency community, which is organized according to the principles of a commodity standard, choose for its price targets the prices of two commodities instead of one? Consider the case of two money commodities: silver and gold. Two variants of this case were applied which we will illustrate briefly by use of our model (7-8) to (7-12). Money commodity 1 is gold, money commodity 2 is silver; M^1 is the quantity of gold coins in terms of abstract units of account, M^2 the quantity of silver coins respectively; x, y denote the quantities of wheat etc. as above.

1. *Parallel Standards*: The currency order determines two units of account, e.g., the thaler and the friedrichsdor; two means of payment, e.g., silver and gold coins; two price targets, one for silver, the other for gold; and it fixes a suitable

[26] Lexis and Terhalle, Article "Silber und Silbergeld" Handwörterbuch der Staatswissenschaft, 4th ed., Jena 1926, p. 483. The devaluation of silver is traced by the contemporary literature to the changeover to the international gold standard.

[27] "... until the disruption of the Habsburg monarchy the standard remained legally what is usually called a paper standard since the Austro-Hungarian Bank was not obliged to redeem its own notes, which were legal tender to any amount. Nevertheless, from 1900 to 1914 Austria-Hungary really possessed a gold standard or gold-exchange standard, for the Bank did in fact readily provide gold for commercial requirements." L. v. Mises (1953, 58).

[28] See "The Gold Standard: Its History and Record Against Inflation," A Study Prepared for the Use of the Subcommittee on Monetary and Fiscal Policy of the Joint Economic Committee, Congress of the United States, Sept. 18, 1981, Washington, 1981, p. 4.

[29] A.J. Bloomfield (1959, 14).

regulation of the supply of means of payment. The development of the relative value of silver in terms of gold, i.e., the exchange rate e between the two means of payment, is left to the free market.

Under the conditions of our model

$$e = \frac{M^1}{M^2}\,\frac{L^2(i^2)}{L^1(i^1)} .$$

The dimension of e is "friedrichsdor per thaler." In stationary equilibrium $e =$ const. It is irrelevant whether contracts are concluded in thaler or friedrichsdor. Not so in the real world. Individuals would therefore only use one of the two types of coins – probably that one of which the larger amount exists.

Examples: England after the coinage reform of 1663. The previously existing fixed relationship between gold and silver coins was given up. A new gold coin was introduced, the guinea, which had to be accepted by government offices at the existing market price.

"The success of this trial was so discouraging that the parallel currency had to be abandoned after a short while. It was never again tried [in England]. In practice, there were two currencies which were as separate as the currencies of two different countries. It was constantly necessary to take account of the fluctuating quotations even within the country, and complicated calculations had to be undertaken."[30] (Translated by W.F. St.)

Prussia had *de facto* a parallel currency after the coinage edict of Frederic the Great of July 14, 1750 and *de jure* after the patent of February 2, 1787.[31] In Prussia the parallel currency ended with a practically exclusive circulation of silver until the founding of the German Reich.

2. *Fixed-ratio Mintage, Bimetallism*: The currency order fixes *one* unit of account (franc), two kinds of means of payment (silver and gold coins), two price targets, one for silver the other for gold but both expressed in the same unit of account, the franc. It also fixes a suitable regulation of the supply of means of payment. The silver/gold ratio, i.e., the exchange rate between the two means of payment, is here also fixed. This presupposes that, first, with constant price targets the value of silver compared to gold fluctuates only within a narrow range on the world market. It presupposes, secondly, that the price targets correspond to the exchange ratios of the two metals on the free market. If that exchange ratio deteriorates systematically for one of the metals over a long period, as was the case for silver, and if the price targets remain fixed, the relatively cheaper metal will be coined and issued in increasing amounts and the more expensive metal will more or less quickly disappear from circulation, depending on the difference in value. Gresham's law will apply:[32] "cheap money will drive out dear money"[33] – a simple consequence of the logic of arbitrage transactions.

---

[30] O. Veit (1969, 386f.).

[31] K. Helfferich (1923, 120f.).

[32] O. Veit (1969, 385).

[33] I. Fisher (1911, 113).

Notes on the History of Thought and the Economic History:

Some theorists of the bimetallism idea, such as M. Wolowski, thought that the value ratio of gold/silver could be stabilized by governmental decree if in all countries of the world the two metals "would be made money materials in the same ratio ...." In such a case "the artificially enforced relation would gain such power from this international agreement that it would be equivalent to a natural relation based on the objective circumstances."[34] But this could work only if the most important currency communities would intervene continuously and in a coordinated fashion on the international gold and silver markets – a difficult and costly undertaking. As for the rest, such interventionistic ideas do not fit into the system of order of a free (world-) market economy.

In fact the opposite happened in the relevant period (the second half of the 19th century): all the governments of the industrialized nations tried hard to enlarge their gold reserves with, as A. Marshall commented, "little reference to international interests."[35,36]

There are many instances of bimetallism before the epoch of the international gold standard; e.g., England in the 18th century, France in the 18th and 19th century until 1878; the United States between 1792 and 1873. The value of gold in terms of silver was astonishingly stable over long periods (see above). There were nevertheless even then extended periods in which the value of silver deteriorated systematically with the result that the legally fixed ratio of silver/gold had to be changed or that silver coins supplanted gold as Gresham's law predicted. For a particular case, see the French coinage law of 1803.[37] The silver/gold ratio was listed as 15.5 : 1, and the standard of coinage was

1 kg gold, 9/10 fine = 3100 frcs.
1 kg silver, 9/10 fine = 200 frcs.

The posted ratio 15.5 : 1 was set too low. The actual average value was during the relevant period (1803–1873) 15.62. As Fig. 7-2 shows, the average annual values fluctuated until 1873 within a narrow range of this value (the coefficient of variation was 0.03). With a more appropriate posted price French bimetallism might therefore have worked better than it actually did, at least until 1873. Thus French bimetallism did not succeed in keeping gold and silver coins in circulation on an even footing. The founding of the *Latin Mint Union* between France, Belgium, Italy and Switzerland in 1865 did not do much good. The member states, which were joined by Greece in 1868, limited the private coinage of silver coins in 1873 and in 1878 the coinage of silver was terminated all together. The five countries changed over to the gold standard.

One of the economic arguments made in favor of bimetallism was that it would lead to a more stable "standard of value" than a monometallic currency. That would be correct to the extent to which the fluctuations in the purchasing power of gold

[34] M. Wolowski, cited after O. Veit (1969, 704f.).

[35] A. Marshall (1926, 24) writes: "The real question is, then, not what governments *could* do, but what they *would* do if the inducement to scramble for gold were much increased?" Marshall illustrates the reason why a fixed-ratio mintage would develop into a silver monometallism: "Fixed-ratio mintage would attract capital and labour to the production of whichever metal was being most easily mined, and therefore most plentiful supplied." (p. 27). He therefore prefers a parallel currency.

[36] I. Fisher (1911, 123) has an extensive and pertinent discussion of a fixed-ratio mintage.

[37] G.F. Knapp (1921, 299ff.), K. Helfferich (1923, 124ff.), O. Veit (1969, 391f.).

and silver might compensate for each other. This was not so and in actual fact the bimetallic currencies tended to develop into monometallic ones. A somewhat better solution would be the one suggested by A. Marshall (1926, 28f.) to create a paper currency which had to be redeemed into appropriate composed metal bars. In general terms this later so-called *symmetallism* becomes a question of defining the unit of account with respect to a particular commodity basket. The target variable is the monetary value P of a particular commodity basket Wk of money goods, consisting, e.g., of a definite amount of good 1 (gold) and of good 2 (silver), where

$$P = p_1 x_1^0 + p_2 x_2^0$$

with, e.g., $x_1^0 = 1$ kg gold (9/10 fine), and $x_2^0 = 15.5$ kg silver (9/10 fine). The fixed standard of coinage P refers to a unit of the commodity basket Wk, with the quantities (x_1^0, x_2^0). The p_i are the freely variable market prices of gold and silver expressed in abstract units of account. The obligation to redeem paper in gold at a fixed price p_1 is replaced by the obligation to redeem paper in commodity basket units (in our case composed of linked bars of gold and silver in the ratio of 1 : 15.5) at the fixed price of P per unit of Wk. This is reminiscent of the proposals for a commodity reserve currency by, e.g., B. Graham in 1937, which was supported by, among others, W. Eucken (1952, 261f.). For the so-called Graham Plan, see above Section 4.4. Milton Friedman (1951/1953) has criticized these plans in a convincing manner.

We summarize: when several commodity standards coexist it is understandable that with increasing economic relationships the different currency communities will go over to the same money good purely out of self interest,[38] i.e., without international agreement. This will be a particularly marketable or saleable good with relatively low arbitrage cost in trade, i.e., cost that will stay within a relatively narrow band, such that the exchange rate of, say mark/dollar is stabilized "automatically" in this sense. The transition to a single currency metal, gold, and the development of the international gold standard may be understood in this manner. Once a definite standard of coinage is fixed in each country, a precisely defined parity exchange rate (mint parity) follows even without international agreement, around which the spot exchange rates will fluctuate within precisely defined, and in the case of gold, narrow limits. An internationally agreed-upon public regulation is unnecessary provided the currency communities stick to the convention not to intervene on the international gold market and to stick to the gold standard. In the final analysis, this means that they must tacitly agree to defend only their own standard of coinage and protectionist measures to leave the steering of the economy to market forces. This in turn means that they must forego not only interventions on the international gold market but also an autonomous policy of determining the value of money, an autonomous business cycle policy of stable prices in international trade and capital transactions, etc. The international gold standard works "automatically" only as long as the member currency communities

[38] C. Menger (1909, 558).

do not interfere with the competitive formation of prices. In that case, it works very well as historical experiences demonstrate. In fact, the international gold standard may be understood as a successful result of the application of free market principles to the monetary system.[39]

Unlike the gold standard, the logic of the gold exchange standard demands more than just an implicit agreement among the currency communities on the money commodity and the defense of the price target. It requires the explicit establishment of a superior ("world") currency community together with the solution of the associated practical problems – including the establishment of effective international supervision of the agreement. Thus its advantage in saving gold reserves is possibly bought at a very high price. For the rest, it works just like the gold standard. In particular, the gold exchange standard works in the long run only if the participating currency communities adhere to the principles of competitive formation of prices and refrain from pursuing autonomous monetary and business cycles policies, or beggar-thy-neighbor policies, e.g., counteracting unemployment by devaluation, etc. The preconditions of the gold exchange standard are thus equally incompatible as those of the gold standard with the limited market ideologies and the still dominant nationalism of our time. The final breakdown of the Bretton Woods System illustrates this point. Also Bretton Woods was only to a limited extent a gold exchange standard; it tried to come to terms with the nationalistic desires for independent monetary policy etc. and tried to preserve convertibility by regulating the conditions of exchange adjustments.

7.3 Safeguarding the Value of Money With an Inconvertible Paper Currency: The Case of a Single Currency

We proceed now to discuss paper standards. The means of payment consists of non-redeemable paper money. In this case, too, price targeting may consist of fixing the price p of a single good, say, gold. However, for lack of a convertibility rule, the quantity of money M is no longer "automatically" determined. It must be exogenously (administratively) fixed so that it is compatible with the price target p. Ricardo mentions this case of a paper standard related to gold as a possibility. He writes:

"... it is not necessary that paper money should be payable in specie to secure its value; it is only necessary that its quantity should be regulated according to the value of the metal which is declared to be the standard."[40]

However, Ricardo was sceptical about how well such a system would work. In his famous pamphlet, *The High Price of Bullion. A Proof of the Depreciation of Bank Notes* (1810), he therefore advocated obliging the central agent to redeem notes into gold:

---

[39] F.A. Lutz (1936/1962).

[40] D. Ricardo (1951, I, 354).

"The only legitimate security which the public can possess against the indiscretion of the bank is to oblige them to pay their notes on demand in specie...."[41]

Yet the problem that the gold standard (and the paper standard with the price of gold as a price target) has experienced is the volatility of the cost of living in the short and medium term. With the paper standard the money value *P* of a commodity basket *Wk* of cost-of-living goods may be directly chosen as a price target. This makes it possible, at least in principle, to eliminate the problem of fluctuations in the value of money. Thus K. Wicksell (1936) argued for the creation of an international paper standard for that very reason. In this case, he stated (op. cit. 194), commodity prices would

"no longer be subject to the caprices of the production and consumption of gold or of the demand for the circulation of coins. It would be perfectly free to move, governed by the deliberate aims of the banks."

But how should the problem of the control or regulation of the paper standard be solved? In any case by a suitable regulation of the central agent. It does not matter in our simple model world where the central agent is tied down by a fixed rule – directly at the price target or indirectly at the supply of means of payment. In the ideal case, which we consider here, both are determined by the currency order.

We assume the unit of account (mark) and the means of payment (central bank notes) have been fixed. With reference to the safeguarding of the value of money, the currency order determines the following:

1. *Regulation of the Price Target*: The money value of *P* of a particular commodity basket *Wk* of cost-of-living goods is to have a determinate value.[42]

Example: We can't find real-life examples which fit exactly. The Deutsche Bundesbank is, however, obliged, according to Art. 2 of the Deutsche Bundesbank Act "to regulate the amount of money in circulation and of credit supplied to the economy, ..., with the aim of safeguarding the currency...." This can be understood at least as the safeguarding of the stability of the value of money within the country, a weak form of the regulation proposed by H.C. Simons (1936). Regulation of the price target in the literal sense of the word does therefore not exist. The Bundesbank did, however, publish for a while its ideas of a target of regulating the future

[41] D. Ricardo (1951, III, 99).
For illustration:
The redemption requirement of the Bank of England was suspended in 1797 with the result that the price of gold in terms of pounds rose gradually by about 15% til 1809. In this year, D. Ricardo wrote a letter to the Morning Chronicle (dated August 29, 1809 and reprinted in D. Ricardo (1951). A year later his pamphlet "The High Price of Bullion" appeared. There he wrote: "If the Bank directors had kept the amount of their notes within reasonable bounds; *if they had acted up to the principle which they have avowed to have been that which regulated their issues, when they were obliged to pay their notes in specie, namely, to limit their notes to that amount which should prevent the excess of the market above the mint price of gold, we should not have been now exposed to all the evils of a depreciated, and perpetually varying currency.*" (op. cit., 95. Italics in the original.)

[42] See above Section 1.4.2.

price level by publishing the "unavoidable" price increase for the next year (1974–1984); see Table 7.4[43]

2. *The Regulation of the Supply of Means of Payment*: The quantity of paper money M is fixed "exogenously" by the central agent of the currency community so that under the given conditions the announced price target P is realized.

Example: The Deutsche Bundesbank attempts to keep to definite monetary targets announced for the following year.[44] Until 1984, it also allowed for "unavoidable" price increases in calculating the money supply targets (see below Table 7.4).

In the stationary overlapping generations model with a single good, the non-redeemable paper money may be modeled as follows:

(7-1) $\hat{x}(i) - M/p = -y(i)$

(7-2) $L(i) = M/p$

endogenous variables: i, p

exogenous variable: M .

In the terminology of Tinbergen's theory of economic policy, M is an instrument variable, and p is a target variable. M is fixed by the central agent so that p will be equal to its target value. J.H.G. Olivera (1970, 805ff.) calls this an *active-money model.*

In the case of many goods, the purchasing power of money is determined by the money value P of a commodity basket Wk. This is described in Section 1.4.

An exact legal requirement for the central agent to observe a certain monetary target presents no problem under the conditions of our model: in stationary general equilibrium there exist no instabilities in the demand for money (of the income

[43] Behind the concept of an "unavoidable price increase" is among other things the idea that inflationary developments should be gradually moderated in order to avoid calamitous declines in employment. On this point we quote several statements of the Bundesbank: "It also had to be borne in mind that, even with a stability-oriented economic policy, price increases could not be completely eliminated in 1976 but could only be reduced; the virtually unavoidable rise in the price level was put at 4 to 5%." (Report of the Deutsche Bundesbank for the Year 1976, p. 13).

"... the Bundesbank furthermore assumed that the rate of price rises will continue to slow down in 1977, but without the desirable aim of complete price stability being achieved." (Monthly Report of the Deutsche Bundesbank, January 1977, p. 5).

"... allowance was made for a new (albeit moderate) rise in prices, which will be unavoidable in spite of further stabilisation efforts." (Monthly Report of the Deutsche Bundesbank, January 1979, p. 6).

"... if all ... behave in a stability-oriented manner, the ... increase in prices ... can be limited to about 4% ... in favourable circumstances. This objective rather represents the lower limit of the inflation rate that from the present perspective looks likely ... However, when deriving its monetary policy target the Bundesbank must assume that the monetary scope for raising prices will be kept as small as possible so that nobody can expect inflationary tendencies to be financed." (Monthly Report of the Deutsche Bundesbank, December 1979, p. 7).

[44] The Deutsche Bundesbank (1987, 91 ff.) (Special series No. 7, 2nd ed.).

velocity of money), and no price rigidities. We don't face the problem of which concept of M should serve as a monetary target, and whether the relevant stock of money (or its rate of increase) is to be kept on a fixed level in the short term (by the minute or hour or on a daily or weekly basis) or only in the long run (e.g., as an annual average). We shall now leave our reference model and briefly discuss some of these problems.

Note on Monetary Rules in Case of a Paper Standard

To determine a price target is one thing; it is another to guarantee it by committing the central agent to a certain monetary rule. The guarantee could be imagined to be an abstract instruction (simply: the central agent is obliged to observe a certain price target – however it is done) or it could be a concrete direction of action (e.g., the redeemability of bank notes into gold coins). Now we must distinguish whether the price target refers to a certain commodity, e.g., gold, or a certain financial asset, e.g., the money of another currency community (dollar). The guarantee can be realized in either of two ways – through active intervention of the central bank in the gold or foreign exchange market, or through passive observation of the redeemability obligation. In both cases the price target is realized "the direct way." However, matters are more complicated if the price target refers to the money value P of a basket Wk of cost-of-living goods. Of course, the observation of the price target can be demanded here too by a legal requirement (e.g., "to safeguard the currency"). Yet the central bank can no longer realize this requirement the "direct way." The central bank cannot directly intervene in the markets of goods that are in daily use. What it can do is to try to realize the price target the "indirect way" by determining a certain quantity M, defined by a certain concept of "the stock of money." A suitable rule for the central agent would be directed towards the quantity of money M. Now, as we know, there is no strict relationship between M and P. Still, if one makes the plausible assumption that the rate of increase of the trend of M/P is roughly equal to the rate of increase of the real GNP,[45] it is possible to conceive of a rule for the growth of money which requires that the stock of money M be increased at the average growth rate of real GNP (of, say, 3 percent) possibly corrected by a certain amount to allow for a secular decrease in the income velocity. The proposal by M. Friedman (1960) aims in this direction. How should one treat seasonal

[45] For West Germany and for the period 1973–1985 we get the following regression:

$$\hat{M}_3 - \hat{Y}_{G,\text{real}} = \underset{(0,6)}{0.97} + \underset{(2,6)}{1.00}\, \hat{P}_{\text{GNP-Index}}$$

$$R^2 = 0.38\ , \quad DW = 2.06$$

(values in brackets are the t-values)

where

$\hat{M}_3$ = rate of growth of M_3
$\hat{Y}_{G,\text{real}}$ = rate of growth of the Gross National Product (in 1980 prices)
$\hat{P}_{\text{GNP-Index}}$ = rate of growth of the GNP-price index, 1980 = 100

Data in or calculated from: Sachverständigenrat zur Begutachtung der gesamtwirtschaftlichen Entwicklung, Jahresgutachten 1985/86, Tables 27, 33, 40. Data for 1985 from Monthly Report of the Deutsche Bundesbank, June 1986, Tables I.2, VIII.1, VIII.7.

movements in the demand for money? M. Friedman (1960, 92) suggests they be disregarded

"to dispense with seasonal adjustments and to adopt the rule that the actual stock of money should grow month by month at the predetermined rate."

What should be done in a financial crisis? Exceptions from the rule should be possible in such cases. But when do we have the *casus ultimus*? Finally, which concept of "the stock of money" is to be applied for the money growth rule? In this chapter M is identical with the amount of central bank money. In actual fact there are many such concepts. M. Friedman (1960, 91) has a rather broad concept in mind which at least includes demand deposits in addition to currency. But how are we to mark off demand deposits in the face of the many changes in the banking business? Would it not be better to leave it at the central bank money stock? In either case, which corrections are to be made? We cannot deal with these questions in greater detail in this book. The general problem of a money growth rule will be taken up again in the next chapter, in particular in Section 8.7.1.

Table 7.3 Money Growth Targets and Their Realization in West Germany

Year	Growth Target of the Central Bank's Money Stock		Actual Development	
	Percent in the course of the year[1]	Percent annual average	Percent in the course of the year	Percent annual average
1975	8	–	9.9	(7.6)
1976	–	8	(9.0)	9.3
1977	(6–7)[2]	8	(9.5)	9.0
1978	(5–7)[2]	8	(11.7)	11.4
1979	6–9	–	6.4	(9.1)
1980	5–8	–	4.8	(4.8)
1981	4–7	–	3.5	(4.4)
1982	4–7	–	7.0	(4.9)
1983	4–7	–	7.0	(7.3)
1984	4–6	–	4.5	(4.8)
1985	3–5	–	4.5	(4.5)
1986	3.5–5.5	–	7.7	(6.4)
1987	3–6	–	8.1	(8.05)
1988	3–6[3]	–	6.7[p]	(6.4)[p]
1989	5[3]	–		

[1] From the fourth quarter of the previous year to the fourth quarter of the current year, respectively; 1975: Dec. 1974 to Dec. 1975.

[2] With this rate of growth in the course of the year the desired annual average would have been reached.

[3] Since 1988 the Deutsche Bundesbank uses M3 as money growth target.

[p] Provisional.

From: The Deutsche Bundesbank, Its Monetary Policy Instruments and Functions, Deutsche Bundesbank Special Series No. 7, October 1987 and

Reports of the Deutsche Bundesbank for the Years 1982 1983, 1984, 1985, 1986, 1987, Frankfurt/Main.

Table 7.4 The "Unavoidable Price Increases" Published by the German Bundesbank[a]

1975:	about 5–5.5% from: Jahreswirtschaftsbericht der Bundesregierung 1975, *TZ* 6, p. 6. The Bundesbank itself points to the agreement of its figures with those of the Bundesregierung (federal government).
1976:	4–5% annual average from: Report of the Deutsche Bundesbank for the Year 1976, p. 13.
1977:	prices of all goods produced: 3.5%; consumer prices: 4% from: Monthly Report of the Deutsche Bundesbank, January 1977, p. 6.
1978:	3.5% or less from: Monthly Report of the Deutsche Bundesbank, January 1978, p. 6.
1979:	about 3% annual average from: Jahreswirtschaftsbericht der Bundesregierung, 1979, *TZ* 6, p. 6.
1980:	4% or slightly less from: Monthly Report of the Deutsche Bundesbank, December 1979, p. 7.
1981:	3.5–4.0% from: Monthly Report of the Deutsche Bundesbank, December 1980, p. 8.
1982:	3.5% measured by the GNP price deflator from: Monthly Report of the Deutsche Bundesbank, December 1981, p. 8.
1983:	3.5% from: Monthly Report of the Deutsche Bundesbank, December 1982, p. 9.
1984:	3% from: Monthly Report of the Deutsche Bundesbank, December 1983, p. 8.
1985:	2%[a] from: Monthly Report of the Deutsche Bundesbank, December 1984, p. 8.

[a] The Bundesbank publishes no specific value for 1985. However, the Monthly Report of the Deutsche Bundesbank of Dec. 1984, p. 8, permits the calculation of the "unavoidable increase in prices" for 1985 of 1–3% from the growth in the volume of central bank money (1–5%) and the growth of the productive potential of "at least 2%."

In this chapter we ignore all doubts and objections regarding money growth rules. For our model we assume the central agent of the currency community to be obliged by the currency order to determine a certain quantity M of the stock of money which is compatible with the price target of the currency order.

Money Growth Targets and Price Targets of the Deutsche Bundesbank: How does the Deutsche Bundesbank proceed? There is no legal obligation to set a money growth target. The publicly announced money growth targets can be understood as self-imposed obligations of the Bundesbank. They are determined only for the following year; from 1979 until 1988 they have not been announced in form of a single number. (On the development until 1989, see Table 7.3).

In calculating its quantity-of-money targets the Bundesbank allows for the following influences on the real cash holdings of the private sector:

(a) the expected growth of the productive potential of the economy,
(b) the desirable change in total capacity utilization,
(c) the "unavoidable price increases"; this consideration was abandoned in 1985, and
(d) the expected development in the velocity of circulation of money (this was abandoned as well in 1985).

On the "unavoidable price increase"[46] see Table 7.4. As of 1988, the target of the Bundesbank refers to M3 instead of central bank money stock.

Point (b) means that the Bundesbank also pursues business cycle policy purposes when fixing the supply of money. The Bundesbank also seems to be convinced of the effectiveness of ad hoc policies to stabilize

[46] See (The) Deutsche Bundesbank (1987, 93).

the business cycle and prices. On the whole the Bundesbank pursues three targets with its monetary policy: a price target, a business cycle target and an exchange rate target.[47]

Main Arguments in the Literature on Binding Rules for the Central Bank

"In a free-enterprise system we obviously need highly definite and stable rules of the game, especially as to money." H.C. Simons (1936/1951, 349).

Simons finds a money supply rule to be attractive though he discards this idea because it could only be realized if wages and prices were perfectly flexible. Otherwise a policy of, e.g., a constant money supply would lead to fluctuations of employment as a consequence of changes in the demand for money. Yet prices and wages are not perfectly flexible. Furthermore financial crises cannot be excluded, given the present organization of the banking system. For both reasons Simons regards a money supply rule as inapplicable. He argues in favor of a price rule as a second-best solution:

"If price-level stabilization is a poor system, it is, still from a liberal viewpoint, infinitely better than no system at all." H.C. Simons (1951, 358).

For a currency authority, this is, as we have already argued, a rather loose requirement. Simons would like to impose it on the treasury:

"Ultimate control over the value of money lies in fiscal practices – in the spending, taxing, and borrowing operations of the central government. Thus, in an adequate scheme for price-level stabilization, the Treasury would be the primary administrative agency; and all the fiscal powers of Congress would be placed behind (and their exercise religiously limited by) the monetary rule." (op. cit. 359).

The idea behind it is that in the final analysis the creation of money is in the hands of the Treasury – this possibility can be avoided by a suitable central bank law. In any case: the problem of the "distance" between the price rule and the grip of the administration remains, whether or not the Treasury is included in the responsibility.

M. Friedman (1960, 87), in criticizing the price rule, argues that there is only a rather vague relationship between the quantity of money and the price level in the short term (for example one year):

"... the key difficulty is that the link between price changes and monetary changes over short periods is too loose and too imperfectly known to make price level stability an objective and reasonably unambiguous guide to policy. The Federal Reserve System does not control the price level. It controls the volume of its own earning assets.... But the link [between M and P] is not direct and rigid, nor is it fully understood. While the stock of money is systematically related to the price level on the average, there is much variation in the relation over short periods of time...."

---

[47] In (The) Deutsche Bundesbank (1987, 97) it is stated: the Bundesbank insists that "... it seemed appropriate to give monetary policy over the course of a year scope for reacting to unexpected disruptions of economic activity, prices and exchange rates without jeopardising the credibility of monetary targeting." (op. cit. 98).

Furthermore, non-monetary influences on the price level which must be known in order to orient monetary policy on the price level raise problems. M. Friedman (1960, 88) concludes:

"A satisfactory policy guide or rule should be connected more directly with the means available to the monetary authority than its price level. We will, I believe, further the ultimate end of achieving a reasonably stable price level better by specifying the role of monetary authorities in terms of magnitudes they effectively control and for whose behavior they can properly be held responsible than by instructing them solely to do the right thing at the right time when there is no clear and accepted criterion even after the event whether they have done so."

The money stock is the most important variable. The currency authority is able to control it effectively and it should be responsible for doing so (loc. cit, 89). In this connection Friedman has a wider concept in mind than the stock of central bank money. The links between financial assets of the central bank and some wider concept of the money supply would be sufficiently close, so that reasonably close control over the money supply would be feasible. But Friedman does not believe it is vital which particular concept is chosen as long as

"first, it is at least as broad as currency plus adjusted demand deposits; second, a definite and clear-cut choice is made; and third, the rate of increase chosen is adapted to the concept" (loc. cit. 91).

The rate of increase should be chosen so that on the average the price level remains approximately stable in the long term. Friedman (1960, 100) arrives in this manner at what was later called the *Friedman rule*:

"Instruct the System ... to produce a 4% per year rate of growth in total currency held by the public and adjusted deposits in commercial banks. The System should be instructed to keep the rate of growth as steady as it can week by week and month by month and to introduce no seasonal movement in the money stock."

The advantages of this rule are, according to Friedman, quite modest; they would prevent the central bank from making mistakes:

"The first and most important lesson that history teaches about what monetary policy can do – and it is a lesson of the most profound importance – is that monetary policy can prevent money itself from being a major source of economic disturbance." (M. Friedman, 1968, 12).

One cannot say in general theoretically, that the rule of a fixed money growth rate is preferable to discretionary monetary policy. J.J. Rotemberg (1983), e.g., constructed feedback rules which dominate the simple Friedman rule. F.E. Kydland and E.C. Prescott (1977), on the other hand, showed, using a different model, that the application of rules leads to better results than a discretionary policy.

Dynamic models may furnish any result and S. Fischer (1980, 226) is certainly right when he remarks: "After all, we do not know the optimal activist policy." Still, Fischer argues in favor of a discretionary monetary policy and against the Friedman rule because he considers it impracticable for two reasons:

1. There should be "some agency in a position to deal with potential panics in the financial markets. The most natural agency for this purpose would be the Fed [in general: the central bank] which should have left open to it the possibility of discounting freely and/or conducting large-scale open market operations."
2. The central bank should be able to react to business cycle developments. "The argument would be that there might be business cycle developments to which the Fed should react and that the details are too subtle to spell out in legislation." S. Fischer (1980, 231).

It can be argued against Fischer's first point that financial crises (general runs on banks) are rather improbable with the kind of deposit insurance that exists in the USA. In answer to point 2 one may say that monetary employment policy is ineffective in the longer run. Yet, both arguments leave doubts open. S. Fischer (1980, 234) argues:

"The conservative course is not to immobilize monetary policy when it might be useful in a recession or panic."

Finally, with regard to a legally required growth rule for a particular monetary aggregate, it should be realized that a fixed growth rule can be hardly applied forever, or for a very long period of time. It would have to be amended as the financial system evolved. Changes in the rule might also have to be made in the short run. Therefore, S. Fischer (1980, 230) argues, a monetary rule would have to be subject to the same legislative process as tax changes. The suggestion that the rule should be embodied in a constitutional amendment reflects excessive confidence (or hybris).

So much for the determination of the purchasing power of money "the indirect way" by fixing M exogenously. Of course, this kind of purchasing power determination works only if goods' prices are flexible at least in the medium term – flexible in the sense that they are determined by demand and supply. In actual fact this is not the case for quite a number of prices which are fixed "exogenously", e.g., by the government.

In the case of West Germany about 30% of the prices which enter the cost-of-living index are administered prices.[48]

Now, the purchasing power of money can also be determined "the direct way" in a paper standard: by fixing exogenously the price of a good (or a bundle of goods) which is legally enforced together with a suitable adaptation of the money supply M (an accommodating monetary policy). The extreme case is the centrally planned economy in which all (official) prices are fixed by the state. The money stock has to be adapted accordingly.[49] If this is not done disequilibrium situations inevitably

[48] See Sachverständigenrat zur Begutachtung der gesamtwirtschaftlichen Entwicklung, Jahresgutachten 1976/77, appendix VIII, p. 210f. We limit ourselves to three partial indices of "directly administered" prices (transport and communications prices etc.), "partially administered" prices (public utility rates, rents etc.), and "indirectly administered" prices (food stuffs).

[49] For East Germany, see S.J. Flätgen (1985, 79ff.).

result. The same applies if the price of only one good is fixed exogenously. An accommodating monetary policy is necessary to avoid a disequilibrium. Suppose the ministry of agriculture fixes the prices of certain agricultural products and the central bank determines the money stock. The ministry of agriculture determines the purchasing power of money if the central bank pursues an accommodating monetary policy. Yet if the central bank declares beforehand that it will strictly follow a certain money growth rule, then the ministry of agriculture has to consider whether or not it should take the lead and risk causing an economic disequilibrium. Assume the ministry of agriculture leads the way with, say, a 10 percent increase of prices of agricultural goods, then the question arises whether or not the central bank will yield to the political pressure to which it is exposed. But even if it gave in, would the disequilibrium necessarily disappear, viz. if agricultural prices are raised again with the argument that production costs are growing etc.? This cost-price spiral would end only when the interested groups realized that they gain next to nothing that way in real terms. An accommodating monetary policy would be inappropriate.

The same considerations can be applied regarding the wages negotiated between employers and unions. They can determine the purchasing power of money provided the central bank adapts the money stock M accordingly. If this is not done unemployment would be the consequence (provided the general level of negotiated wages is too high at the given money stock M). If the central bank yields to political pressure and accommodates its money stock to excessively raised money wages a long-term equilibrium cannot be expected to prevail either. The (real) income expectations of the employees would soon be disappointed and result in new and higher wage demands. The result would be a wage-price spiral. As in our other example an accommodating monetary policy would be inappropriate.

These two possible ways of determining the purchasing power of money "the direct way" may somewhat ironically be called the "agricultural standard" or the "labor standard."[50] Central in both cases are redistributional interests of specific pressure groups and not the safeguarding of the value of money of the currency community.[51] An accommodating monetary policy contradicts the redistributional interests. The adoption of a constant, legally required, money growth rule could here afford relief. It could dampen the high spirits of pressure groups insisting on excessively raised prices of agricultural products, of wages or whatever else in the hope that their possible mistakes will be repaired by the currency authority. The concept of the "clear distribution of roles in business cycle policy" with flexible

[50] J.R. Hicks (1955, 391) speaks, e.g., of a "Labour Standard."

[51] M.W. Reder (1948, 55ff.) clarifies the mentioned problem of the autonomous determination of the value of money by the central bank in the presence of powerful trade unions and employers' organizations. He talks of a trilateral monopoly: "There would be, in effect, three monetary authorities – the *de jure* authorities, the labour union and the employers' organisation." It would be difficult to say how in such a case price stability and full employment could be guaranteed. It might even be best to encourage the formation of big trade unions and employers' organizations "... in order to enable them to bargain in real terms with the consequences of the decisions clearly before them, in the hope that they will assume their responsibilities and make their demands compatible in real terms of their consequences for employment and prices."

exchange rates can be understood in this sense, as suggested by G. Fels, H. Giersch and others, and that is also shared by the West German Council of Economic Experts (Sachverständigenrat zur Begutachtung der gesamtwirtschaftlichen Entwicklung) in its experience on the macroeconomic developments of the economy.[52] G. Fels, H. Giersch et al. write:

"The more firmly the Bundesbank commits itself to a particular strategy, the more the responsibility for a high level of capacity utilization and employment shifts to the entrepreneurs and the unions to the extent to which they have sufficient market power to force certain increases in prices or wages. If, on the other hand, the Bundesbank appears uncertain or undecided, it will itself become the target of the joint pressure of the autonomous groups to adapt instead the other way round." (G. Fels et al. 1971, 6, translated by W.F. St.)

Whether or not the pressure groups are willing or can be forced to accept disciplinary measures of the currency authority is an open question. In the final analysis we may say that in a free society whose currency is organized according to the principles of a paper standard, only such a development of the purchasing power of money can be realized for which there is a social consensus.[53]

We summarize this section: in case of a paper standard the central agent is not obliged to redeem its bank notes. As a price target the price of a specific good can be chosen and realized "the direct way" by interventions of the central agent in the market of the specific good. Yet typically, the money value P of a basket Wk of standard of living goods is chosen as a price target of a paper standard community. It can only be realized "the indirect way" by steering the money stock M accordingly. In our model this can be done with the utmost precision. In reality it can not. Even though there is a clear relationship between M and P in the long run, the relationship is too vague in the short term to be able to stabilize a consumer price index by variations of M. What one can try to do is to see to a fairly steady development of the money stock M. In principle a legally binding rule for the central agent can be formulated in this sense. Yet it would be problematic in view of the danger of financial crises and deep recessions. On the other hand, without clear legal requirements the central agent of a paper standard community could possibly be the victim of the political influence of pressure groups. In a world in which prices, wages and interest rates are not only determined by competing market forces but also by the government or through private interest groups monetary policy alone cannot safeguard the value of money. The influence of pressure or interest groups on prices and thus on the purchasing power of money in a paper standard cannot be disregarded. One can try to narrow the influence of the state or of interest groups on prices through privatization, deregulation, antitrust policy, free trade policy etc. Yet the problem can hardly be done away with. If the value of a definite paper money

[52] G. Fels, H. Giersch, H. Müller-Groeling and K.D. Schmidt (1971); Sachverständigenrat zur Begutachtung der gesamtwirtschaftlichen Entwicklung, Jahresgutachten 1974/1975, Chapter 4.

[53] B.T. McCallum (1983) investigated this question for the rates of inflation only for the industrial nations and for the seventies. His results: "The evidence is rather dramatically consistent with the hypothesis that the degree of social consensus as proxied by a measure of long run strike activity was the key factor accounting for intercountry differences in inflation in the seventies." (op. cit. 802).

should remain stable, administered prices, which *nolens volens* have the function of a real anchor (W. Stützel 1983, 34ff.), have to remain stable as well.

7.4 Safeguarding the Value of Money With Inconvertible Paper Currencies: Two Currencies

We now turn to the international paper standard. There are two currency communities. The units of account and the means of payment of the respective currency communities are determined as follows:

- "D-mark" (currency No. 1) and "dollar" (currency No. 2),
- "D-mark central bank notes" and "dollar central bank notes."

7.4.1 *The System of Flexible Exchange Rates*

The regulation of the price target (defined as a cost-of-living index) and of the supply with means of payment now proceeds as follows:

1. *Regulation of the price targets*: The central agent of each currency community fixes autonomously a price target in the form of the money value P of a commodity basket Wk, which will be designated P^1 for the mark currency, and P^2 for the dollar currency.

Example: The price-increase expectations of the Bundesbank were given above in Table 7.4. The Federal Reserve System announces no price target. Nor is the Federal Reserve System legally obliged "to safeguard the currency." But the course of the rate of inflation is, to put it mildly, "observed." During the early eighties the Federal Reserve had tried successfully to reduce the rate of inflation.

2. *Regulation of the supply with means of payment*: The central agent of each currency community fixes autonomously its quantity of paper money M^1 and M^2 so that under the existing circumstances the announced price targets P^1 and P^2 are realized "the indirect way."

Example: The quantity-of-money targets of the Deutsche Bundesbank (Table 7.3) and of the Federal Reserve System (Table 7.5). The multiplicity of targets of the Federal Reserve System, though, seem to be more confusing than clarifying.

There exists a foreign exchange market where, in our model, mark notes are exchanged against dollar notes at the exchange rate e. The exchange rate is in the ideal case completely flexible. There is no government intervention in the foreign exchange market nor is there any international coordination of monetary policies. Public regulation of the monetary system is limited to the "national currency."

We now turn to the ideal case of a strict proportionality between the quantity of money and prices. We also assume the validity of purchasing power parity: the

Table 7.5. Quantity-of-Money and Credit-Volume Targets of the USA, 1980–1985

	IV/1979 to IV/1980	IV/1980 to IV/1981	IV/1981 to IV/1982	IV/1982 to IV/1983	IV/1983 to IV/1984
M1A[a]	3.5–6	3–5.5	–	–	–
M1B[a]	4–6.5	3.5–6	2.5–5.5	4–8[b] 5–9[b]	4–8
M2	6–9	6–9	6–9	7–10	6–9
M3	6.5–9.5	6.5–9.5	6.5–9.5	6.5–9.5	6–9
CBC[c]	6–9	6–9	6–9	8.5–11.5	8–11

	IV/1984 to IV/1985	IV/1985 to IV/1986	IV/1986 to IV/1987	IV/1987 to IV/1988
M1A[a]	–	–	–	–
M1B[a]	4–7[b] 3–8[b]	4–7[b] 3–8[b]	3–8[e]	–
M2	6–9	6–9	5.5–8.5	5–8
M3	8–11	6–9	5.5–8.5	5–8
CBC[c]	9–12			
Debt[d]	–	8–11	8–11	7.5–10.5

All data in percent. For the definition of the individual aggregates, see Federal Reserve Bulletin 66, Feb. 1980, p. 149.

[a] The series for M1A was discontinued in 1981. The later series M1 corresponds to the old series M1B; see Federal Reserve Bulletin 68, Feb. 1982, p. 108.

[b] The original anouncements were revised in the middle of the year, the upper value gives the original anouncement, the lower the corrected range.

[c] Commercial Bank Credit.

[d] Total domestic nonfinancial debt.

[e] The M1 target range was given up in mid '87; see Federal Reserve Bulletin, April 1987, p. 241: "The *FOMC* elected not to establish a specific target range for M1 at this time because of uncertainties about its underlying relationship to the behavior of the economy and its sensitivity to a variety of economic and financial circumstances and assumptions at particular points in time. With the deregulation of deposit rates and the attendant changes in the compositions of M1, the narrow money measure has become much more responsive in the short run to changes in interest rates, and possibly to other factors affecting the portfolio decisions of households."

freely fluctuating foreign exchange rate e is kept within the immediate neighborhood of purchasing power parity through goods arbitrage transactions. Finally, we assume for the time being, as we did in Section 7.2, that there is *no currency substitution*; the members of the mark currency community hold only mark notes, those of the dollar community only dollar notes. In addition *capital is perfectly mobile* so that there is only a single bond market equation in our model.

In the stationary overlapping generations model with constant money stocks M^1, M^2 the exchange rate e is also constant over time and equal to the purchasing power parity. In case of one good it is

$$e = \frac{p^1}{p^2} ,$$

the interest rates for mark and dollar loans are equal:

$$i^1 = i^2 \ .$$

The corresponding stationary overlapping generations model of the one-good case with two definitive paper currencies and flexible exchange rate is represented by the following system of equations:

$$\text{(7-8)} \qquad \hat{x}(i^1) - \frac{M^1 + eM^2}{p^1} = -y(i^1)$$

$$\text{(7-9)} \qquad L^1(i^1) = M^1/p^1$$

$$\text{(7-10)} \qquad L^2(i^2) = M^2/p^2$$

$$\text{(7-11)} \qquad i^1 = i^2$$

$$\text{(7-12)} \qquad e = p^1/p^2 \quad \text{(purchasing power parity)}$$

endogenous variables: i^1, i^2, p^1, p^2, e

exogenous variables: M^1, M^2 .

The price targets of the two currency communities refer here to the same good, wheat.

We substitute equations (7-9) to (7-12) into (7-8) and solve first for i^1. Next we determine the stationary equilibrium value of the exchange rate e by means of (7-9) to (7-12):

$$\text{(7-21)} \qquad e = \frac{L^2(i^1)}{L^1(i^1)} \frac{M^1}{M^2} \ .$$

Equation (7-21) is the reduced form of the so-called *monetary approach to the theory of foreign exchange rates.*

The exchange rate is determined by the relative supply of and demand for cash balances, here the paper money of the two currencies.[54]

The exchange rate e is on the assumption of our model constant over time, provided the two money stocks remain constant or are changed proportionally. The money demand functions are stable by assumption. What happens if there is a change in the stock of money of one of the currency communities, say No. 2? The answer to this question depends, among other things, on the types of the change in the money stock: whether it is anticipated or not and whether it is permanent or transitory. In the following we shall disregard transitory changes in the quantity of money.

[54] "... exchange rates are best thought of as relative prices of different national moneys ..."; M.L. Mussa (1976, 230).

Case 1: An unanticipated permanent change in the quantity of money in currency community 2

In this case, the theorem of the quantity theory applies for currency 2 and also for certain non-neutral kinds of the change in the quantity of money (see above Section 6.6). An unanticipated permanent doubling of M^2 will immediately double p^2. The rates of interest i^2 and i^1 and the price p^1 remain unchanged. The exchange rate e is halved according to (7-21), i.e., the mark/dollar rate, is revalued by 100 percent.

Case 2: An anticipated permanent change in the quantity of money in currency community 2

Our reasoning follows that explained in Section 6.6. Money is quantitatively neutral only if the quantity of money is changed in a neutral manner. A doubling of M_2^2 tomorrow ($t = 2$), which is expected today with certainty, has, under our stationary assumptions, no influence on the equilibrium values of today's ($t = 1$) prices p_1^1, p_1^2, today's exchange e_1 and today's mark rate of interest i_1^1. Today's dollar rate of interest i_1^2 roughly doubles according to the Fisher relation:

$$i_1^2 = \rho + v_1^{2+}$$

(see above Section 6.6). Also, tomorrow's prices p_2^2 will be doubled and e_2 halved, the latter because of

$$\text{(7-21')} \qquad e^2 = \frac{L^2(\cdot)M_2^1}{L^1(\cdot)M_2^2} \, .$$

The money rate of interest i_2^2 will return tomorrow to its original level. The equilibrium conditions for the interest arbitrage equilibrium are

For period $t = 1$:

$$\text{(7-11')} \qquad 1 + i_1^1 = \frac{e_2}{e_1}(1 + i_1^2)$$

(see above Section 5.6). Alternatively, because of (7-21) and (7-21') we can also write:

$$\text{(7-22)} \qquad \frac{1 + i_1^1}{1 + i_1^2} = \frac{M_1^2}{M_2^2} \cdot \frac{M_2^1}{M_1^1} \, .$$

For period $t = 2$ the interest rate arbitrage equilibrium is

$$\text{(7-11'')} \qquad i_2^1 = i_2^2 \, .$$

What happens in the case of currency substitution? The same as above if money is changed in a neutral manner. In this case there are no gains or losses through deflation or inflation.

In general we may therefore say: under the assumptions of our model, including the assumptions of the PPP, of quantitatively neutral money and neutral manner of changes in the money stock the following formulation of M. Friedman (1953, 200) will be true:

"In effect, flexible exchange rates are a means of combining interdependence among countries through trade with a maximum of internal monetary independence; they are a means of permitting each country to seek for monetary stability according to its own lights, without either imposing its mistakes on its neighbors or having their mistakes imposed on it."

Matters are, however, quite different as soon as the assumption of neutral changes in the quantity of money is dropped. In that case the Tobin effect may occur: the change in the quantity of dollar affects all currency communities through a temporary change in the equilibrium value of the real rate of interest, hence also on the mark rates of interest and mark-goods prices (Section 6.6).[55] Friedman's proposition is not true. If in addition we allow currency substitution[56] (assuming non-neutral changes in the money stock), another effect is added to the Tobin effect which further restricts Friedman's proposition about the independence of national monetary policies in a world with flexible exchange rates. If currency substitution is to be possible and the exchange of dollar for mark and vice versa entails no costs, a non-neutral change in money stocks will lead to the holding of cash balances in the more stable currency only – regardless of the currency required to make payments. Thus we get only corner solutions. If, on the other hand, the exchange of mark for dollar and vice versa entails transaction costs, it is conceivable that cash will be held in both currencies even if there is a difference in the rates of inflation of the two currencies ($v^1 - v^2 \neq 0$).[57] The money demand functions must in this case be supplemented by the variable $\frac{v^1 - v^2}{1 + v^2} (\equiv \varepsilon)$, or approximately by $(v^1 - v^2)$. The more the opportunity costs of holding mark increase, the fewer mark and the more dollar will be held. We get then:

$$L^1(i^1, v^1 - v^2) \; ; \qquad \frac{\partial L^1}{\partial(v^1 - v^2)} < 0 \; ,$$

$$L^2(i^2, v^1 - v^2) \; ; \qquad \frac{\partial L^2}{\partial(v^1 - v^2)} > 0 \; .$$

---

[55] Note that we assume *perfect foresight*. Thus tomorrow's volumes of money M_2^1, M_2^2 are, among others, perfectly known.

[56] On the concept of *currency substitution* and the relevant publications, see E. Baltensperger and S. Böhm (1982, 36ff.).

[57] Example: "Multinational corporations have strong incentives to diversify the currency composition of their cash balances in order to facilitate their endeavors in various countries. Even individuals and businesses that are clearly domiciled in a particular country often have transactions or precautionary or even speculative motives for diversifying the currency composition of their money holdings." M.A. Miles (1978, 428).

The smaller the costs of currency substitution the greater the absolute value of the partial derivatives of $L^1(\cdot)$, $L^2(\cdot)$ with respect to the opportunity costs $(v^1 - v^2)$.

Thus, with a non-neutral change in the quantity of money, even with currency substitution, a permanent deterioration of the value of the mark (currency 1) anticipated for tomorrow with permanent stability of the purchasing power of the dollar expected (i.e., $v^1 > 0$, $v^2 = 0$) may cause a devaluation of the spot rate of exchange e and an increase in prices today. The effect of currency substitution on the rate of exchange is greater the smaller the transaction costs of the currency substitution.[58]

If the relevant transaction costs converge towards zero we get only corner solutions. Cash holdings will consist in this case only of the more stable money, in our example the dollar. Today's price level p^1 and the exchange rate e are indeterminate.[59] (There exist any number of equilibrium values of the price level p^1 and the exchange rate e.)

Note the crucial importance of the assumption of the neutrality of the change in the quantity of money. With a neutral change in the quantity of money, the argument of an autonomous national monetary policy with flexible exchange rates is correct for our model, even with currency substitution.[60] We have already shown this.

Notes on the Monetary Approach to the Exchange Rate Determination:

The monetary approach to the theory of foreign exchange rates is, as is the PPP condition (7-12), nothing more than an equilibrium condition under extremely simple assumptions. Absolute validity of the PPP and the quantity theory are assumed. As we know, the propositions of both theories are not confirmed by the facts in the short and medium term. Equilibrium conditions do not describe any process of adaptation; but we are not considering such processes in this book. Yet we can learn this about the formation of the framework of an international currency order from our elementary considerations: if we organize the safeguarding of the value of money of two (open) currency communities according to the principles of a paper standard with some consumer price indices as price targets we get (unlike with the international gold standard) only a vague institutional limitation of the possible movements of the price targets and the exchange rate. The equilibrium conditions of the general equilibrium model may be conceived as the interior axes

---

[58] So also L. Girton and D. Roper (1981, 16).
They write, currency substitution (CS) "... will cause exchange rate 'instability' in the sense that shifts in the anticipated rate of change of the exchange rate lead to larger exchange movements with greater degrees of CS."

[59] "..., perfect CS implies that the exchange rate is indeterminate." L. Girton and D. Roper (1981, 16).

[60] The assumption that changes in the stock of money occur in a neutral manner is decisive. It is, therefore not possible to say that with flexible exchange rates non-substitutability on the demand side must also be assumed "in order that the monetary authority has complete control over the domestic volume of money." E. Baltensperger and S. Böhm (1982, 133, transl. by W.F. St.).

With perfect competition and perfect foresight the critical assumption is the *neutrality* of the manner in which the volume of money is changed. Without this assumption the national currency authority does not have "complete control" over prices even without currency substitution.

of a "soft", imprecisely defined system of valves. Even if the movements of the money stocks M^1, M^2 are coordinated and parallel to each other, and the money demand functions are stable the time series of the exchange rate e may move in wide swings around its parity level.

This is so because in the real world, goods arbitrage frequently works poorly or not at all. The picture of a commodity exchange applies only to relatively few internationally traded goods, so-called "auction goods." It does not apply to goods which are not internationally traded. Hence we cannot assume a prompt use of arbitrage opportunities for most goods in the manner of a commodity exchange. Larger deviations from any calculated purchasing power parity must thus be expected, i.e., the "overshooting" of the exchange rates which are formed on the free market may be very substantial, as experience shows (Fig. 7-3).

As to the autonomy of the central banks with flexible exchange rates we may only say with certainty that they are the master of their own (central bank) money stock. A closer look shows that with flexible exchange rates central banks cannot determine their individual currency community's price level independently of each other. If the stock of money is changed in a non-neutral manner (and this would be the case in reality) national inflations may "spill over" to other countries even if all other assumptions of quantitative neutrality of money are given (see above Section 6.6). In any case, we observe between 1973 and 1985 a significant relationship between rates of inflation in the USA and its most important European trade partners (see Table 7.6). Furthermore one cannot speak of an independent national fiscal policy – as was assumed by supporters of flexible exchange rates (e.g., H.G. Johnson 1972, 199). An increase in the budget deficit of one nation (in particular of the *économie dominante*) causes an increase in the level of the real rate of interest everywhere. The corresponding crowding-out effect has to make itself felt somewhere although not necessarily in the deficit country itself. An increase of the level of the world real-rate-of-interest will cause an increase in the level of the national nominal interest rates – even if a policy of stable money is pursued. In the final analysis, coordination of fiscal policy is therefore absolutely necessary.

Table 7.6. Relationship Between Rates of Inflation Under Flexible Exchange Rates

Endogenous Variable	Intercept	*P* USA	R^2
P Japan	5.95	0.23	0.19
	(4.51)	(1.61)	
P France	−2.82	1.01	0.65
	(1.18)	(4.49)	
P W. Germany	2.56	1.10	0.33
	(1.13)	(2.35)	
P Italy	−2.13	0.64	0.50
	(0.71)	(3.30)	
P Great Britain	3.19	0.36	0.43
	(1.89)	(2.88)	

t-values in brackets; 1st order autocorrelation in the residuals was allowed for in all regressions.
Data from IMF, International Financial Statistics, 1986 Yearbook.

Coordination of monetary policy would seem desirable. Flexible exchange rates in their pure form, "chemically pure" clean floating, cannot be realized because of the non-neutrality of money. They were understood as an international monetary system with absolutely no international cooperation on national monetary or fiscal policy. Friedman (1953, 199) wanted to clarify matters:

"Really effective 'co-ordination' would require essentially either that nations adopt a common commodity monetary standard like gold and agree to submit unwaveringly to its discipline or that some international body control the supply of money in each country, which in turn implies control over at least interest-rate policy and budgetary policy."

It should be clear that such a strict cooperation would neither be realizable nor desirable under today's political conditions. It would require a democratic world government. But if cooperation is absolutely necessary the states have no other choice than to adapt somehow. The problem of monitoring and enforcing international agreements does not confront governments only in the field of economic activity. Under the present conditions, though, there is as little hope to realize a perfect international currency order as it is feasible to achieve a perfect world peace order.

Example: During the great debate about flexible exchange rates before 1973 the supporters of this idea counted on a fairly stable movement of exchange rates. That is not what we have observed since the definite collapse of the Bretton Woods System in March 1973. Small movements aside, we have observed between 1973 and 1987 a long down-up-and-down again movement between a trough in Jan. 3, 1980 of 1.7062 mark/dollar, a peak of 3.4690 mark/dollar in Feb. 26, 1985 and after that again a downswing which up to now (March 1st, 1989) reached its minimum at 1.5815 mark/dollar in Dec. 31, 1987.

Fig. 7-3 shows in addition to the daily values of the spot rate, the monthly values of the consumer-price parity (Verbrauchergeldparität) between West Germany and the USA as calculated by the West German Statistische Bundesamt, in relation to an American and a German commodity basket. We pictured, at the same time, the average values of these two parities. Consider simplistically the average consumer price parity as a measure of the purchasing power parity between the two countries. The actual exchange rate differs for long periods considerably from this "PPP."

From 1973 to 1981 the actual exchange rate was markedly lower than the "PPP"; between the end of 1983 and 1985 it was considerably higher; and since 1987 it has been much lower again. Only in the rather short period between 1981 and mid 1983 and during the first half of 1986 were the actual rates in the neighborhood of our estimated PPP values. The phenomenon is called "overshooting" or "undershooting" in the literature. The deviation of the actual rate from the PPP (however calculated) are considerable because the feedback via the goods markets is, after all, very weak. One cannot expect more in the case of two paper standards with quite vague price targets which, if they exist at all, aim at the money value of consumer goods baskets which are not even composed of identical elements.

Did official interventions on the foreign exchange markets end after the floating of the dollar exchange rate in 1973? They did not. They were not quite as frequent as in the seventies (until 1984) but most central banks continued to intervene consistently and sometimes considerably.[61] This was in particular so after the Louvre Accord of the Group of Seven (U.S.A., Canada, Great Britain, France, Italy, Japan, West Germany) of February 22, 1987.

---

[61] "Major countries have intervened frequently and heavily in the exchange markets, and at certain times have accorded exchange rate considerations a high priority in the conduct of domestic economic policies." See P. Jurgensen (1983, 1).

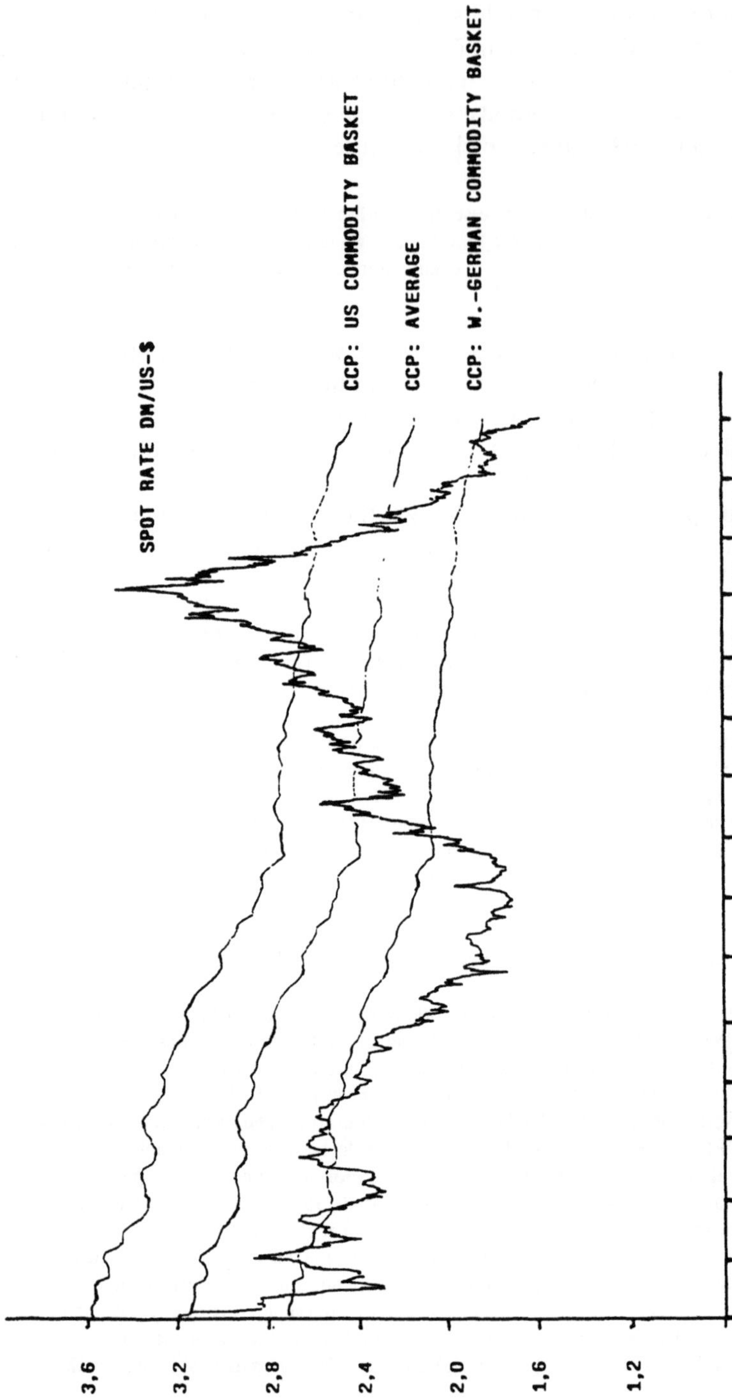

SPOT RATE DM/US-$
CCP: US COMMODITY BASKET
CCP: AVERAGE
CCP: W.-GERMAN COMMODITY BASKET
3,6
3,2
2,8
2,4
2,0
1,6
1,2
1973
1974
1975
1976
1977
1978
1979
1980
1981
1982
1983
1984
1985
1986
1987

The officially announced intervention targets ranged all the way from limited objectives to smooth out short term fluctuations (e.g., "countering disorder") via attempts to influence exchange rate levels over intermediate periods (e.g., "leaning against the wind") to attempts to influence exchange rate levels over long periods (e.g., "resisting apparent overshooting").[62] In all these cases the question is whether the official interventions did in fact have a stabilizing influence on the exchange rate or not.[63] We must also remember the (N − 1) problem: of N currency communities, only $N - 1$ can pursue an independent currency target. For this reason there must be an international agreement on the exchange market among the intervening central banks. Such agreements do exist, though with the vagueness usual in such cases.[64] The Louvre Accord of the G-7 is one more recent example.

But even if they were more precise, the system would still lack real anchoring. We made this clear in Section 5.7 and shall again take up this problem in the present section.

"The Case for Flexible Exchange Rates": Comments on M. Friedman (1953)

The debate over the question "should we have fixed or flexible exchange rates?" belongs to the grand economic discussions of the period following World War II. In the USA the advocates of flexible exchange rates were led by M. Friedman and G. Haberler, in West Germany the leading names were E. Sohmen and H. Giersch. The leading representatives of the opposing view were, in the USA, C.P. Kindleberger and H. Wallich, and in West Germany H. Möller and W. Stützel. We shall make here only a few comments on the position of Friedman.

M. Friedman (1953) opened his memorandum ("The Case For Flexible Exchange Rates" which had been written in 1950) with the assertion that the recently enacted Bretton Woods System was "ill suited to current economic and political conditions." And he continues:

> "These conditions make a system of flexible or floating exchange rates ... absolutely essential for the fulfillment of our basic economic objectives: the achievement and maintenance of a free and prosperous world community engaging in unrestricted multilateral trade." (loc. cit. 157).

For Friedman as for W. Eucken (1952, 254ff.) and other great advocates of a free market economy, a stable value of money is a basic precondition for such an economic order. This aim can only be realized in a system of fixed exchange rates,

---

[62] P. Jurgensen (1983, 9f.).

[63] See, e.g., J.A. Levin (1977, 57–62); J. Niehans (1984, 271ff.).

[64] The International Monetary Fund initially proposed to its members that they observe certain "Guidelines for the Management of Floating Rates." An amendment to the Articles of Agreement of the IMF was finally adopted. Article IV "Obligations Regarding Exchange Arrangements," Section 1 notes as follows:

"In particular, each member shall:

(i) endeavor to direct its economic and financial policies toward the objective of fostering orderly economic growth with reasonable price stability, with due regard to its circumstances;
(ii) seek to promote stability by fostering orderly underlying economic and financial conditions and a monetary system that does not tend to produce erratic disruptions;
(iii) avoid manipulating exchange rates or the international monetary system in order to prevent effective balance of payments adjustment or to gain an unfair competitive advantage over other members; and
(iv) follow exchange policies compatible with the undertakings under this Section."

such as a gold exchange standard, if all partner countries cooperate. That means that the national governments have to subordinate their internal economic policies to the goal of balance-of-payments equilibrium. Effective cooperation would be only conceivable if nations adopted a common commodity standard like the international gold standard ("and agree to submit unwaveringly to its discipline") or by the establishment of an international authority which controlled the supply of money in each country ("which in turn implies control over at least interest-rate policy and budgetary policy") (loc. cit. 199). A return to the international gold standard is, according to Friedman, neither currently feasable nor particularly desirable. As to the second alternative Friedman wonders whether "such far-reaching powers [should] be surrendered to any authority other than an effective federal government democratically elected and responsible to the electorate?" (loc. cit. 199). And he continues:

"A system of flexible exchange rates eliminates the necessity for such far-reaching co-ordination of internal monetary and fiscal policy in order for any country separately to follow a stable internal monetary policy." (loc. cit., 199).

There will certainly be changes in the exchange rate. Yet the major aim of policy was not, according to Friedman, to prevent such changes from occurring "but to develop an efficient system of adapting to them" (loc. cit., 202). Friedman is convinced that a system of flexible exchange rates would remain relatively stable, provided the national central banks pursue stable money growth rates.

"... advocacy of flexible exchange rates is *not* equivalent to advocacy of unstable exchange rates. The ultimate objective is a world in which exchange rates, while *free* to vary, are in fact highly stable. Instability in exchange rates is a symptom of instability in the underlying economic structure. Elimination of this symptom by administratively freezing of exchange rates cures none of the underlying difficulties and only makes adjustment to them more painful." (loc. cit., 158).

The movement of the mark/dollar exchange rate as we have observed it since 1973 may quite possibly be a symptom of the "instability in the underlying economic system": the effect of two oil price shocks (in 1974 and 1980), and the emerging inflation which has roots in the time of the Vietnam War and its abatement in the eighties. During the same period the Deutsche Bundesbank tried, though without complete success, to reduce the inflation rate of the mark which had increased until 1973 (see Fig. 7-4). But even if in both the American and the West German economies the money supply had grown steadily and in accordance with a stable purchasing power of money one could not expect highly stable rates in a system of flexible exchange rates. Of that, however, Friedman was convinced. He believed that profitable foreign exchange speculation stabilizes the exchange rate. This proposition provoked a debate that has not yet ended.[65] Without speculation we would

[65] For an early review, see E. Sohmen (1969, Ch. III). Sohmen illustrates the point and then writes: "Both purchases and sales would therefore tend to bring the exchange rate at any time closer to its long-run average" (op. cit. 61). A few pages later, though, he adds: "The case for flexible exchange rates should not be misunderstood to stand and fall on the hypothesis that speculation will always be stabilizing. If this hypothesis should turn out to be wrong, as it occasionally might, the authorities have at their disposal all the traditional means of correcting excesses and are free to use them as they see fit." (op. cit. 74). On the more recent literature, see R. Dornbusch (1982/1986), K. Singleton (1987).

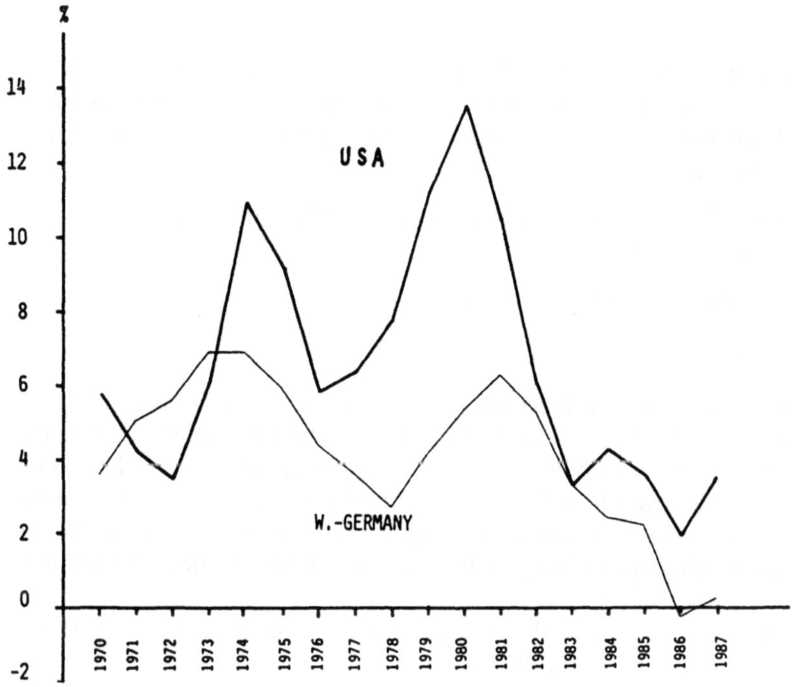

Fig. 7-4. Inflation Rates USA and W. Germany 1970–1987

probably have sudden and extreme movements in the foreign exchange rate which we do not observe in fact. On the other hand speculation is not sufficient to stabilize the *level* of foreign exchange rates. In the meantime the view has been generally accepted that foreign exchange rates are determined in the same manner as prices of real or financial assets. That means expectations play an important role and

"... that there is an exchange rate indeterminancy because financial policies, which supposedly anchor the system, are in fact endogenous and may be substantially caused by movements in the exchange rate."[66]

We confined ourselves here to the description of the general line of argument for flexible exchange rates as presented by M. Friedman (1953) and as they were later elucidated by H.G. Johnson (1972). This is more important for a general understanding of the role of the order or institutional framework of an international currency system than detailed technical comments.

[66] R. Dornbusch (1982, 574). That view had already been advanced by R. Nurkse (1944), whom Dornbusch quotes as follows: "... anticipations are apt to bring about their own realization. Anticipatory purchases of foreign exchange tend to produce or at any rate to hasten the anticipated fall in the exchange value of the national currency, and the actual fall may set up or strengthen expectations of a further fall.... Exchange rates in such circumstances are bound to become highly unstable, and the influence of psychological factors may at times be overwhelming." (R. Nurkse 1944, 118).

7.4.2 *The System of Fixed Exchange Rates*

One can imagine different institutional arrangements for an international paper standard with mutually agreed upon fixed exchange rates.[67] All have in common that the central agencies of the co-operating currency communities must explicitly agree about two matters:

- the level of the exchange rate targets, i.e., the parity of exchange; and
- the real anchoring of the system.

We shall look at two cases for illustration.

(I) Fixed Exchange Rates Type A:

Consider first the case in which the central agency of one currency community (of the key currency) provides the real anchoring of the system as a whole by keeping the supply of its money nominally fixed. The other central agencies link their currencies to the key currency by fixing and guaranteeing an exchange rate vis-à-vis the key currency. The only non-convertible paper money is in this case the money of the key currency. The paper money of the other currencies can be redeemed into the key currency at fixed rates.

Assuming two currencies with the dollar as the key currency, the price target and the supply of money would ideally be as follows:

1. Regulation of the Price Target:

(a) The currency order or central agent of the mark community in agreement with the central agent of the dollar community fixes a definite target for the exchange rate, i.e., a mark/dollar parity rate e. This exchange rate is to be constant over time.
(b) The central agent of the dollar community in agreement with the central agent of the mark community fixes a price target in form of the money value P^2 of a commodity basket Wk.

2. Regulation of the Supply of Means of Payment:

(a) The central agent of the mark community is obliged or else obliges itself to redeem at the parity rate e at any time mark notes into the notes of

[67] We have here only the case in mind in which two or more currency communities *explicitly* agree mutually upon a particular level of their exchange rates. Of course, exchange rates can be pegged without any explicit agreement, e.g., when one (usually smaller) currency community pegs its currency to that of a bigger one, as for instance Austria vis-à-vis West Germany after 1973. An implicit agreement might be assumed also in this case. Or an exchange rate can be pegged temporarily by a big currency community vis-à-vis another one. Thus the British pound was pegged with respect to the mark for about one year in 1987/88 within a band of mark 2.93 and mark 3 (see Wall Street Journal, March 8, 1988). Managed floating is also a form of temporarily pegged exchange rates with mutual agreement as, e.g., in the Louvre Accord of February 22, 1987 among the Group of Seven (USA, Canada, England, France, Federal Republic of Germany, Italy and Japan). In this case target zones were not officially agreed upon, allegedly not even secretely. Still, the interventions of the central banks on the foreign exchange markets were coordinated among the central banks of the G-7. (See G. Haberler 1987, 378 ff.).

the key currency (here the dollar). The dollar is freely convertible in both directions: the mark-central agent is obliged to buy and sell dollars freely upon demand.

(b) The central agent of the key currency (the dollar community) fixes the world quantity of money $M^{(2)}$ so that the price target P^2 is realized "indirectly."

We have here a special case of the ideal type of an exchange standard, the so-called *dollar standard.*[68]

Such a system causes considerable transaction costs. Unlike the case of the international gold standard, it is now necessary to negotiate an international currency agreement between the central agencies (or the states) and to monitor its observance, which is not unproblematic. We mentioned this point already. (Still, it may involve lower transaction costs than the system of managed floating after the Louvre Accord of February 1987).

We disregarded the problem of monitoring such an agreement in our simple model. For the case of the stationary overlapping generations model and of a single good, the dollar standard may then be modeled as follows:

(7-8) $\hat{x}(i^1) - (M^1 + eM^2)/p^1 = -y(i^1)$

(7-9) $L^1(i^1) = M^1/p^1$

(7-10) $L^2(i^2) = M^2/p^2$

(7-11) $i^1 = i^2$

(7-12) $e = p^1/p^2$ (PPP)

(7-13) $M^{(2)} = (1/e)M^1 + M^2$

endogenous variables: $i^1, i^2, p^1, p^2, M^1, M^2$

exogenous variables: $M^{(2)}, e$.

What we have called here the world quantity of money, $M^{(2)}$, is identical with the world quantity of gold in Section 7.2. $M^{(2)}$ is the total amount of "paper gold" in the world. The term $\frac{1}{e}M^1$ in (7-3) designates the stock of dollar notes (currency 2) which has been converted into mark notes and is kept as a reserve by the central agent of currency 1.

The system is solved as follows. We first calculate the equilibrium values of $i^1(=i^2)$ by means of (7-8) to (7-11). From (7-9), (7-10) and (7-13) we get

(7-23) $L^1(\cdot) + L^2(\cdot) = M^{(2)}/p^2$.

[68] A.K. Swoboda (1978) analyzes such a case, though not within the framework of a general equilibrium model.

The money stock of the world $M^{(2)}$ is (exogenously) fixed by the dollar-central agent. This determines the stationary equilibrium value of p^2. Because of purchasing power parity (7-12) and the fixed exchange rate e, p^1 is determined together with p^2. The quantities of money M^1 and M^2 are finally calculated by means of (7-9), (7-10). A variation in $M^{(2)}$ will lead to adjustment through the specie flow mechanism which we have described above (in Section 7.2); in an analogous manner the monetary approach to the balance of payments applies. Unlike the case of flexible exchange rates the central agent of currency 1 is here unable to determine its money stock M^1 autonomously. Strictly speaking the central agent of currency 2 is also unable to determine its (national) money stock M^2 on its own. What it is able to determine autonomously is the (paper) money stock of the world $M^{(2)}$.

The described dollar standard is asymmetrically constructed. Only the dollar community is able to produce paper "gold." Only it can change the world quantity of money $M^{(2)}$ and thus influence the price levels p^1, p^2. The standard may nevertheless work, provided the currency communities agree on a particular course of growth of the money stock of the world $M^{(2)}$ and the level of the exchange rates as well as on a way to effectively supervise the agreement. The latter would be difficult without a supranational authority.

The Bretton Woods System was towards its end a dollar standard though no agreement existed about movements of the quantity of world money $M^{(2)}$, or about the inflation rate of the USA. As a result there were, again and again, unilateral changes in the dollar parity rate of exchange until the "fixed" dollar rate was finally abandoned in spring of 1973.

(II) Fixed Exchange Rates Type B:

If the mark and the dollar are equally important currencies – which is not the case – and if the members of both currency communities have similar living habits – which is only very approximately the case – the asymmetry of the dollar standard could be avoided by the following regulations, which correspond approximately to those agreed upon in the European currency system:

1. *Regulation of the Price Target*: The central agents of the two currency communities agree explicitly on a fixed exchange rate target e and implicitly on the price targets p^1, p^2 which are consistent with purchasing power parity:

(7-24) $$p^1 = ep^2 \; .$$

We may think of the price targets as cost-of-living targets or, as, e.g., R.I. McKinnon (1984) does, of wholesale price indices of tradeable goods with identical commodity baskets.

Example: Both currency communities agree implicitly to aim at an inflation rate, expressed by a common price index, of 1 percent per annum.

2. *Regulation of the Supply of Means of Payment*: The central agents of the two currency communities agree to fix their respective money stocks M^1, M^2 so that the

agreed rate of exchange e is realized according to

$$e = \frac{L^2(i^2)}{L^1(i^1)} \frac{M^1}{M^2} . \tag{7-21}$$

For that purpose the regulation of the supply of means of payment is to be specified as follows: there have to be agreements about

(a) compatible money-stock targets M^1, M^2;
(b) rules about interventions, e.g., the obligations of all central agents to buy or sell the currency of the partner country in unlimited quantities at predetermined intervention points.[69]

Enforcement of the agreed-upon money-stock targets is in this case problematic. Such a regulation works perfectly only if the currency communities establish an international office and authorize it accordingly. But perhaps not everything needs to be organized as perfectly as Friedman or Johnson believed to be necessary. Why shouldn't the voter demand the observance of a stable value of money? Why should not the elected politicians find that it would be in their best interests to act according to the will of their voters? In this case one could imagine that it is sufficient to agree explicitly upon the exchange rates in connection with a tacit orientation of the parties to the contract with respect to the most stable currency community. That is possibly how the European Monetary System works. The exchange rates are explicitly agreed upon, the tacit "stability leader" is the Federal Republic of Germany. Still, since the foundation of the EMS in March 1979 until the end of 1985 there were eight appreciations of the mark.[70] Whether it is possible to expand the EMS to an "Atlantic Currency System" remains to be seen. At any rate the stability leadership would in such a case pass over to the USA as the dominant economy. But would the USA really rank the goal of safeguarding the value of money as highly as the Federal Republic of Germany does?

To summarize this section: what characterizes the international paper standard in comparison with the international gold standard? Two things: the applicability of definitive paper money as an international means of payment and

[69] This is the case with the European Monetary System (EMS) Art. 2 para 2, Agreement about the Working of the European Currency System of 13 March 1979. For a survey see "The European Monetary System, Structure and Operation," Deutsche Bundesbank, Monthly Report, March 1979, p. 11f.

[70] The subject matter of the harmonization of monetary policy within the European Monetary System is discussed in the Sachverständigenrat, Jahresgutachten, 1976/77, p. 179f. There it is proposed that partner countries enter into obligations with each other to intervene in the foreign exchange markets with only the proviso that countries do not deviate substantially and permanently in their monetary policy from a commonly agreed-upon monetary path.

For the EMS this would point to the origin of the problem. "For its cause is the monetary policy, and the obligation to intervene in the foreign exchange markets is the point where, in a particular case, the solidarity of the partners is required." The Sachverständigenrat recommends agreement on a monetary policy target (volume of central bank money) and its changes over time. It would be important to agree on a precise definition of the target volume and to determine the deviations from the target volume to be tolerated. If the target volumes fall outside the tolerated deviations, the obligations of every member country to intervene vis-à-vis the country in question are automatically suspended.

the impossibility of stabilizing the exchange rate between different paper standards purely through the market mechanism, i.e., purely by following one's self-interest. With regard to the exchange rate two institutional arrangements present themselves in principle in the case of an international paper standard: "flexible" and "fixed" exchange rates. Flexible exchange rates permit the central agent to autonomously fix its money supply M. This is not possible with fixed exchange rates where no independent money value policy exists. It does exist, however, with flexible exchange rates in its pure form and under strongly idealized assumptions: the assumption of quantitative neutrality of money *and* of neutral money-stock changes. Still, the law of one price with respect to real interest rates also holds in this ideal case. That means that an independent fiscal policy is impossible even under these ideal conditions. Fiscal policy influences the level of the capital stocks of all currency communities via the (world) real interest rate. Therefore, it would be sensible with flexible exchange rates, even under our strongly idealized assumptions, for the currency communities (or national economies) to co-operate in their fiscal interest rate policies. With fixed exchange rates, co-operation in the field of monetary policy would be always necessary. In this case the coordination of the money value policy of the individual economies would have to be relatively detailed. It may be left open whether it is really necessary to establish an international authority to enforce the agreement between the currency communities. It could be imagined that one of the currency communities assumes the role of the "stability leader" without an explicit contractual agreement. With an international paper standard with flexible or fixed exchange rates, the behavior of the dominant economy is decisive for its functioning.

7.5 Gold or Paper? A Retrospective of This Chapter

In this chapter we have discussed the two basic types of a currency order, the paper and the commodity standard. The two types were illustrated mainly by the examples of a redeemable and a non-redeemable paper currency. The theoretical model was the stationary overlapping generations model with cash holding, i.e., a special case of the theory of general equilibrium. Under the assumption that changes in the quantity of money occur in a neutral manner the model leads to a strict proportional relation between the quantity of money and prices.

The central question of the chapter was: what has to be the nature of the order to safeguard the value of money, in the two cases of redeemable and non-redeemable paper currencies particularly with respect to the regulation of the quantity of money? We have treated this problem both within the theoretical model of our stationary overlapping generations model and also in an interpretative style with respect to its possible institutional arrangements.

In this section we will summarize the main results of the present chapter and at the same time contrast the commodity and paper standard. We start with a single currency community.

With the commodity standard (here the case of redeemable paper money) the unit of account is clearly defined by an exogenously fixed standard of coinage. If the standard of coinage is kept at a constant level, which during the period of the international gold standard was always the case, then the movement of the purchasing power of money (= of the money commodity) is left to the "caprices of the production and consumption of gold or the demand for the circulation of coins." This results in unsystematic fluctuations of the purchasing power of money which can be quite considerable in the short term (during one year). They can be also quite substantial in the medium term (during ten or twenty years).

On the other hand, with the commodity standard it is comparatively easy to realize the guarantee of the safeguarding order of money.[71] This is particularly true for a commodity standard with a 100% cover of paper money in circulation. The currency order stipulates for the central agent the following: the unit of account, the kinds of the means of payment, the price target, and the regulation of the supply of means of payment (the central agent is obliged to exchange any time during business hours paper money into the money commodity or vice versa at a fixed price). Whether the central agent observes its obligations can be easily verified by anybody at any time.

With the paper standard (the case of an unredeemable paper money) one does without a definite real anchoring of the unit of account. The money value P of a commodity basket Wk of standard of living goods is chosen as the price target; the actual composition of this commodity basket is unknown to most money users. Attempts are made to realize the price target "the indirect way" by fixing appropriately the money stock M. In the short term and possibly also in the medium term (say during a couple of years) this can be done only very inexactly. In reality fine tuning of P via M would therefore be impossible. It is advisable to aim at a steady growth of the money stock M which is known in advance by the money users. In our model, though, the aforementioned problems are not of importance. The price target can here be determined precisely even if it relates to a commodity basket and it can be controlled exactly via M.

With the paper standard the guarantee of the safeguarding of the money value is problematic. Rules to be observed by the central agent can at best refer to a money-stock concept, say: the quantity of central bank money. Yet, considering the danger of financial crises and catastrophic business downswings it is not advisable to demand an absolutely strict observance of a specific money-stock target (which may even be embodied in the constitution). On the other hand a central bank which is not obliged to observe certain rules may be pushed from the path of virtue by the strong influence of pressure groups and seduced to an inflationary policy. What is decisive in the end is, at least in an open society, the ranking stable money assumes in the opinion of the general public. Rational reasons speak for stable money – but also emotional reasons. In view of the delicateness of money it is impossible to tell clearly one from the other; but it is really not necessary. If the voters rate a stable money very highly, it can be realized in a modern constitutional state even for a paper standard, without a strict obligation of the central agent to observe the

---

[71] On the central bank policy before 1914, see G. Stolper: "The handling of this mechanism had become a matter of routine, so simple that it could be learned and successfully handled by men who rarely cared to give much thought to economic or social theories. One learned central banking as today one learns to drive a motorcar ...." G. Stolper (1942, 9).

money-stock target. One should not expect, though, a precise observance of a certain inflation rate. This could not be achieved in a paper standard, as has been shown, for reasons of the organizational technique of this type of currency order. But with the gold standard this would be even less so. Whether a commodity reserve standard (an organizational monster) would be better in this respect may be doubted. Why not, then, trust in the victory of reason and leave it with the paper standard without placing narrow restrictions on the central agent? We think that this is advisable with certain qualifications which will be dealt with in the next chapter. To what extent the paper standard is "less expensive" than a commodity standard is difficult to say. Of course, the cost of the commodity reserves disappear. But the costs of regulation increase.

We now turn to the case of two currency communities, i.e., to the consideration of international currency problems, and begin with the *international commodity standard.* If both currency communities use the same money good (e.g., gold) then the exchange rate fluctuations remain in a narrow neighborhood of the parity rate which is equal to the ratio of the two standards of coinage. This is ensured by arbitrage on the market for the money good (e.g., gold arbitrage). For that purpose actual arbitrage transactions are not or at least not on a large scale necessary. The purchasing power of money (i.e., of the money good) moves similarly in the two currency communities. It depends, however, to a high degree "on the caprices of the production and consumption of gold or the demand for the circulation of coins."

The members of each primary currency community have more or less close economic relations with each other. With regard to exchange with the use of money *between* constituent primary currency communities, the question arises again: what should be the general unit of account and what the corresponding means of payment? The answer is that world money will evolve from habit and with it a *world currency order*. For the international commodity standard, the international currency order is as a rule constituted in an "autometallic" fashion.[72]

Example: The world currency order of the international gold standard before 1914 was characterized by particularly simple and stable rules. The accounting unit was a certain amount of gold; the means of payment were gold ingots of certain fineness; there were only "natural" definitive means of payment in international trade; accordingly the price target was 1 (see Section 4.4); the means of payment were supplied exclusively by the gold market.

Such a world currency order is determined purely by self-interest. Its rules are simple; they are understandable by everyone and easily controllable. This is true also for the national currencies, in particular also for the size of the band within which floating exchange rates may fluctuate freely. Its limits are determined by the possible commodity arbitrage transactions with the money good. The export and import points of the money good as well as its mean value, the fixed parity rate, are easily calculated by everybody and hence generally known. Stable exchange rates are guaranteed in this world without greater organizational efforts. On the other

[72] This is the terminology of G.F. Knapp (1924).

hand one must be prepared to accept fluctuations in the value of money as a result of fluctuations in the prices of precious metals relative to other goods.[73] As for the rest the automatism of the international gold standard would seem to work perfectly only if prices are determined freely on all markets. F.A. Lutz (1935/1962, 22) rightly characterized the gold standard as "the" currency system of a free market economy. Model-like perfect market economies are not necessary in order for the gold standard to work, but certainly the clear dominance of prices, wages, and interest rates as the control mechanisms of the market is required.

We now turn to the *international paper standard* considering first two currency communities of the paper standard variety with a freely floating exchange rate. Under the ideal conditions of quantitatively neutral money, i.e., that the PPP is valid, and by assuming that money stock changes occur in a neutral manner so that the movements of prices and interest rates of each single currency community are independent of the changes of the money stocks of the other currency community, a perfectly autonomous national money value policy is possible. The exchange rate of the two currencies is in our model constant if the money stocks of the two currency communities remain constant or, more generally, if they are changed proportionally. But since in reality money stocks are not changed in a neutral manner and indeed the other conditions of quantitative neutrality of money are not fulfilled, one cannot expect that in a world with flexible exchange rates the national money policies are perfectly independent of each other. Since, in addition, goods arbitrage doesn't function so perfectly that the conditions of PPP are always met, more or less large deviations of the exchange rate from PPP are to be expected. The international paper standard with flexible exchange rates will also work if – as is the case today – a comparatively large number of goods prices are not controlled by market forces. Also, the central banks are, in this case, free to try a monetary employment policy. In fact, the international paper standard with flexible exchange rates corresponds more to the philosophy of interventionism of the Keynesian type than the international gold standard. J.M. Keynes (1924), after all, supported flexible exchange rates.

The world currency order consisting of a system of paper standards with flexible exchange rates is itself a special case of the paper standard. It, too, may develop in an "organic" manner in the sense of C. Menger, i.e., without explicit agreement or legal enforcement. The members of the international currency community agree implicitly to use few, or in the limiting case, one currency as the world currency. In the latter case the world currency order is identical to the currency order of the community whose money is used as international money. Consider, for purposes of illustration, the present (1989) international currency situation. Since the beginning of the 1970's we have had, for the first time in the history of humanity, an international paper standard. The US-dollar (itself an unredeemable paper money) is, if

[73] Adherents of the gold standard like C. Menger (1909, 59f.) argue on this point: "Variations in the money prices of the precious metals seem to me the lesser danger compared to the regulation of the intrinsic exchange value of money by governments or social and political parties. In particular the difficulties of coming to an international regulation of a matter of such importance should not be overlooked." (transl. by W.F. St.).

not the sole, at least the most important "world money."[74] The dollar serves:

- as a *unit of account* on the international foreign exchange markets, frequently also in international commodity trade, e.g., gold, petroleum, coal, other raw materials; frequently in the international capital markets (e.g., consider the importance of the Euro-dollar market),
- as a *means of payment*, frequently for the settlement, or clearing of balances, particularly in the international foreign exchange markets.

Even during the years of high dollar inflation rates after 1973 the international users of the dollar did not switch to more stable money such as the Swiss franc or the Deutsche mark, as Hayek's theory of currency competition suggests. The reasons may lie in the cost of transactions. Once an existing paper currency is generally used as world money it will continue to be used in the case of limited inflationary tendencies. The country whose currency supplies the world money will see to it in its own interest that the inflationary developments stay within limits.

We can imagine the further development of the international paper standard in the style of Menger's theory of evolution as follows: one currency will be used as world money (the US-dollar). The supplier of the world money can finance part of its government debt free of interest. It wants to keep this advantage and therefore pursues a policy of safeguarding the value of money. The central agents of the other currency communities proceed by themselves in their own interst without agreements or difficult to enforce international treaties, to stabilize the exchange rate vis-à-vis the world money. The mark-central agent, e.g., chooses the mark/dollar-exchange rate as price target. It announces its price target clearly and defends it within a certain range, which also has been clearly announced, by intervening on the foreign exchange market. The dollar currency community accepts the dollar exchange rate aimed at by the mark-central agent and refrains from counteracting interventions. If the market trusts the announcement of the exchange rate target and the refraining from counteracting measures by the dollar currency community, then the actually necessary interventions on the mark/dollar market will remain within limits.

Can we expect such a development? The international gold standard of the last century developed roughly in this manner. The world money was in those days the British pound, that had a fixed price in gold which was guaranteed by the Bank of England's promise of redemption. Most other states were at first on silver. Their gradual change to gold came about in response to England, the dominant economy of that time.

In today's era of an international paper standard matters are somewhat more complicated. Difficulties may arise for the more important trading partners of a country if it tries to link up with the dollar. It is therefore probably not reasonable

---

[74] This was probably the reason why the US-dollar remained the most important reserve currency even after the transition to floating dollar exchange rates, though theoretically no currency reserves of central banks are necessary with flexible exchange rates. See. A.J. Schwartz (1983, 33): "Although other currencies have increased their role as reserve currencies in recent years, the dollar had continued to serve as the main reserve currency, accounting for about 80% of the world's official foreign reserves."

to expect the process of the Mengerian invisible hand, propelled purely by self-interest to work. Explicit negotiations between the central agents will be necessary to avoid contradictory foreign exchange interventions and to convince the market that the central agents are agreeing with each other and that the upper and lower points of intervention will really be observed. In the terminology of C. Menger (1909, 574) we deal in this connection with a "perfecting of the monetary system by the state [more precisely: "by the states"]."

The meeting of the Group of Seven (G-7) leading industrial nations (of the U.S.A., Canada, Great Britain, Federal Republic of Germany, France, Italy and Japan) in February, 1987 points in this direction. The new course is a "managed float" in which coordinated actions are taken to keep exchange rates within prescribed, but undisclosed, target zones. As such, it is a reform of the monetary system without a formal international agreement, relying strongly on each nation's self-interest in cooperation. (For its description, criticism and for further ideas see Suggested Readings to this chapter, item 5).

Our considerations have led us to an international paper standard with fixed exchange rates. Such a standard makes an autonomous monetary policy impossible. Since, therefore, the central agents must necessarily cooperate, a development of the international currency order towards fixed exchange rates appears plausible. Such a system will last as long as the practical operation of the supplier of the world money is stablizing the value of its money. It would hardly be possible to establish an international control of the monetary policy of the world money supplier. Will it not exploit its monopoly position, particularly if it is strengthened by international agreements, and start an inflationary policy? There are reasons to believe that it might. We shall deal with them in the next chapter. Would it be therefore necessary to establish an international public regulation of the world currency monopoly? Certainly in an ideal well ordered world. This problem of regulation did not exist in the pre-1914 international gold standard. Gold or paper? We shall briefly take up again this question at the end of the next chapter.

Suggested Readings for Chapter 7

For an introduction discussing the amount of money in the context of general equilibrium theory with redeemable and non-redeemable paper currencies see *J.H.G. Olivera* (1970). On the advantages of a commodity standard with redeemable paper money, see *D. Ricardo* (1816/1951, 65ff.). For reasons to prefer a paper standard, see *K. Wicksell* (1936, 193f.). About the question whether a binding rule is desirable for a redeemable paper currency and to what extent it is practicable, see *M. Friedman* (1948, 1960). For the general problem of a currency constitution, see *J.M. Buchanan* (1962) and *H.G. Brennan* and *J.M. Buchanan* (1981). For the influence of the currency constitution on the development of the value of money, see *P. Bernholz* (1983). For the history of the international currency order from the pre-1914 gold standard to present and for the "rules of the game," see *K.W. Dam* (1981).

1 The Gold Standard

For the history of the German currency order, see *O. Veit* (1969) pp. 481–632; *K. Borchardt* (1976). For the relevant legal provisions of the German Reich before

1914, see *E. Heilfron* (1911). For a simple historical survey of the USA and Great Britain including developments since 1914, see *M.D. Bordo* (1981). For a more thorough discussion which also includes all big Western industrial nations after 1914, see *L.B. Yeager* (1976) Part II, and *M.D. Bordo* and *A.J. Schwartz* (1984). For the general theory of commodity money, see *J. Niehans* (1978, Ch. 8); *R.J. Barro* (1979). The classical contribution to the redeemable paper currency is *D. Ricardo*, "The High Price of Bullion" (1810/1951) and *D. Ricardo* (1817/1951) Ch. XXVII "On Currency and Banks." The historic background to Ricardo's pamphlet was the suspension of the redeemability of pound sterling between 1797 and 1821. This is briefly and vividly described in *E. Cannan* (1925), Introduction.

For the price-specie-flow mechanism, see *D. Hume*, "Of the Balance of Trade" (1752/1955) together with the correction by *P.A. Samuelson* (1980), supplemented by *D.N. McCloskey* and *J.R. Zecher* (1976).

For the gold exchange standard, see the previously given literature about the IMF in Chapter 5. See also the historical survey of the development of the international monetary system after the second world war by *A.J. Schwartz* (1983, 14–32).

2 The Paper Standard

The principle of safeguarding the purchasing power of a non-redeemable paper currency was described by, among others, *D. Ricardo* (1817/1951, Ch. XXVII) for the case of a specific price target, in his case a fixed price of gold. On the determination of the purchasing power of non-redeemable paper currency in general equilibrium, see *D. Patinkin* (1961, 116).

A suggestive comparison of the natures of the commodity and the paper standards is found in *J.A. Schumpeter* (1970, 219 ff.) using his concept of a "critical number." For normative criteria for the paper standard and its institutional realization, see *P. Dittus* (1987).

The central problem of the non-redeemable paper currency is whether the currency authorities are to be bound to "simple and stable" rules or not. *K. Wicksell* (1936) requires no obligations to follow specific rules. On the other hand, e.g., *H.C. Simons* (1936), *W. Eucken* (1952, 261 ff.), and *M. Friedman* (1960, 1968) demand such a clear obligation to follow specific rules.

For the basic monetarist position, see *K. Brunner* (1970). For the determination of the value of money "the direct way" for a non-redeemable paper currency ("labour standard"), see *J.R. Hicks* (1955), together with the excellent contribution of *M.W. Reder* (1948).

3 Balance of Payments Theories

The subject matter of the balance of payments theory as understood in the present context is the question of what determines the changes in the currency reserves in open economies with full-bodied coins or *redeemable paper currencies*: the international gold standard, the gold exchange standard, the exchange standard (e.g., the dollar standard). The presently predominant theory, which is also used in this chapter, is the so-called monetary approach to the balance of payments theory which goes back, among others, to *D. Hume* (1752/1955) "On the Balance of Trade." *H.G. Johnson* (1972, 230) states this approach clearly (see above Section 7.2).

See also, *R.A. Mundell* (1968), in particular Chapters 11, 16, 18 and Chapter 9. For a survey, see *E.M. Claassen* (1980), *J.A. Frenkel* and *H.G. Johnson* (1976, 21–45).

According to this view, in a system of fixed exchange rates, no independent national monetary policy for stabilizing the value of money is possible. The transfer of inflation occurs through the "direct price connection." In the discussion about the transmission of inflation during the period of the Bretton Woods Agreement, *W. Stützel* (1960b) pointed this out very early. See also *O. Issing* (1967/68), *G. Fels* (1969). For a survey, see *E.-M. Claassen* (1980, 354–357).

In a world of non-redeemable currencies, the factors determining exchange rates pose a major problem. There are several approaches to this problem. In this chapter we deal only with the simple *monetary approach to the theory of foreign exchange rates* with perfect foresight. It is principally the same theory as the monetary approach to the balance-of-payments theory. The only difference is that the variable to be explained is now the exchange rate, rather than the change in foreign exchange reserves. *R.A. Mundell* (1968, Ch. 8) and *H.G. Johnson* (1972, Ch. 9) have drawn attention to this explanatory possibility. The first model of this type is due to *J.A. Frenkel* (1976) and *M.L. Mussa* (1976), see also *J.A. Frenkel* and *M.L. Mussa* (1985, 716ff.).

The objection that, at least in the short term, the purchasing power parity theory does not apply is met in a simple manner by *R. Dornbusch* (1976). An explanation of this approach is found in *J.F.O. Bilson* (1979, 13). This model explains the "overshooting" of actual exchange rates compared to the purchasing power parity. *J. Niehans* (1975b) argued earlier in the same direction. See also *J. Niehans* (1984, 218ff.) where a theoretical discussion of conceivable processes of adaptation of interest, exchange rate and prices in response to a change in the quantity of money can also be found (op. cit. 219ff.).

For a survey of the various newer exchange rate theories, see *J.F.O. Bilson* (1979), *E. Baltensperger* and *S. Böhm* (1982), *G. Hacche* (1983). For a survey of empirical studies of exchange rates, see *R.M. Levich* (1985). The major econometric problem is modeling the formation of expectations:

"The inherent unpredictability of new informations explains much of the difficulty of forecasting exchange rate changes." (G. Hacche 1983, 10).

4 The Problem of the Stability of Flexible Exchange Rates

The problem of the stability of flexible exchange rates played an important role in the debate before 1973. The assertion by *M. Friedman* (1953, 187f.) that private speculation will more likely be stabilizing than government intervention (because destabilizing private speculators would make losses and therefore be eliminated from the market) provoked a debate that has not yet ended. For an early review, see *E. Sohmen* (1969, Ch. III). The proponents of Friedman's thesis did not discuss or even mention the problems which might arise because of the missing feed-back through goods arbitrage.

In view of the considerable volatility of foreign exchange rates after the final breakdown of the Bretton Woods System the debate on the stability of flexible exchange rates shifted finally to the applicability of the theory of speculative bubbles (as developed, among others, by *O.J. Blanchard* (1979) and *J. Tirole* (1982)) to the explanation of the volatility of exchange rates. See, e.g., *R. Dornbusch* (1982) and *K. Singleton* (1987).

The problem of "overshooting" has been mentioned by *M. Friedman* (1953, 183) but a precise discussion of the actual path of adjustment of the exchange rates was not considered essential by Friedman in this connection. The order of size and length of time of the over- and undershootings were not foreseen by the advocate of flexible exchange rates. E. Sohmen, e.g., referred to the stable freely floating Canadian dollar during the fifties (op. cit. 247f.). This is amazing in view of the French experiences of the twenties and the conclusions drawn by *R. Nurkse* (1944, 118) which we quoted above in footnote 66.

Looking somewhat further back in history one can find more examples of unstable exchange rates as *P. Bernholz* (1982) has pointed out.

On the possible reasons for the incompleteness of the forward foreign exchange markets, see *R.I. McKinnon* (1988, 88ff.)

5 Arguments and Proposals for an International Coordination of Exchange Rate Policy

On the political level a new phase of international coordination of exchange rate policy started with the agreement of the Group of Five (G-5) ministers of finance (of the U.S.A., England, the Federal Republic of Germany, France and Japan) of September 1985. The agreement aimed at an orderly revaluation of the most important currencies (mainly Deutsche mark and Japanese yen) vis-à-vis the US-dollar. New arrangements were made according to which this aim was to be achieved. For a survey of this problem, see *J. Sachs* (1986). At the Louvre meeting in February 1987 the Group of Seven (G-5 plus Canada and Italy) declared that the exchange rates of their currencies then were "broadly consistent with the underlying fundamentals" (see *G. Haberler* 1987). Coordinated actions were taken to keep exchange rates within prescribed but undisclosed target zones. Among the practical proposals for an improvement of the coordination of national paper standards three ideas or plans should be particularly mentioned: the idea of PPP-based monetary guidelines as suggested by the OPTICA group of experts set up by the *Commission of the European Communities* (1977) (for a critical survey, see *J. Niehans* 1984, 277ff.); the plan for monetary integration under rigidly fixed exchange rates – "a gold standard without gold" – by *R.I. McKinnon* (1974, 1984, 1986, 1988); and the plan to introduce target zones. For proposals of the latter type, see, e.g., *J. Williamson* (1985, 1986) and *D. Lebèque* (1986). A broad view at the experience with flexible rates since 1973 and at proposed alternatives is taken by *R. Dornbusch* and *J. Frankel* (1987).

For the actual interventions of central banks, see *J. Niehans* (1984, Ch. 13) and *P. Jurgensen* (1983). For the historical development of managed floating, see *A.J. Schwartz* (1983, 32–45). On recent developments of the international monetary system, see *G. Haberler* (1987).

6 Gold or Paper?

The economically serious debate on this issue began under the general heading of "Stable Gold Price or Stable Purchasing Power of Money?". The first comprehensive work on this subject was *I. Fisher* (1911). He was sceptical about the possibility of achieving stable prices by a correspondingly "manipulated" paper standard (op. cit., 329). Even at the time of the pre-1914 gold standard, he favored a paper money redeemable into gold at a standard of coinage that varied with an index (op. cit., 331, 337ff.). *K. Wicksell* (1936), on the other hand, was optimistic about the possibility of stabilizing the purchasing power of money with an international paper standard (op. cit., 176f.). Following the collapse of the international gold standard after the first world war, *J.M. Keynes* (1924) argued strongly against a return to gold. Keynes favored a policy of purchasing power stabilization through flexible exchange rates and the abandonment of a fixed gold cover, the redemption into gold, and a fixed standard of coinage (op. cit., 177ff.). In essence he pleaded for a paper standard though he did not wish to do without gold reserves being held by the central bank (op. cit., 197). *L.v. Mises* (1924, English translation 1953) and other authors doubted that the target of a money with constant purchasing power could be achieved (English translation p. 236). He prefers commodity money with a fixed standard of coinage, because of its "freedom from State influence" (op. cit. 238). *W. Eucken* (1952) preferred a currency order which has a "stabilizer of the value of money" and is at the same time as automatic as possible (op. cit., 257). Following *B. Graham* (1937) he pleaded for a commodity reserve currency (op. cit., 261f.). *M. Friedman* (1951) had correctly criticized these plans. He himself advocates a paper standard with flexible exchange rates bound to fixed rules (see *M. Friedman* (1951, 241f.) and (1950)). *F.A. Lutz* (1935/1962) had worked out the connection between the economic and the currency order for the gold standard which was emphasized by *W. Eucken* (1952, 264) for the commodity-reserve currency. For the possible conflicts between interest groups and the central bank with a paper standard, see *M.W. Reder* (1948) and *P. Dittus* (1987). For a critical retrospective on the classical gold standard, see the NBER conference issue edited by *M. Bordo* and *A.J. Schwartz* (1984). The reviewer writes: "Anyone who still believes that the gold-standard was an autonomous money supply process should read it." (*J.B. Van Huyck* (1987, 455)).

Chapter 8
Money and Banks

The two preceding chapters dealt with primary currency communities. We assumed the central agent of each currency community realizes the bookkeeping part of his elementary currency order by issuing paper money as a means of payment. He realizes the value safeguarding part of his elementary currency order in the case of a commodity standard by promising to redeem his bank notes into the money good and keeping a one hundred percent cover for them; or in the case of a paper standard without any obligation to redeem his notes, by issuing definitive paper money. However, paper money and book money may also be "created" (issued) in exchange for money claims on private parties. This is typically done by commercial banks, which in turn may be understood as the central agents of secondary currency communities. Commercial banks issue book money which is redeemable into the money of a primary currency community. However, the central agents of the primary currency communities also issue money in exchange for money claims on private parties, e.g., by purchasing trade bills.

This chapter will consider "two-tiered" currency communities. Such communities consist of a number of secondary currency communities which are attached to a primary community. The central agents of the secondary currency communities, i.e., the commercial banks, issue redeemable money (inside money) exclusively. The central agents of the primary currency communities, i.e., the central banks, issue only non-redeemable money (outside money) which we assume to be bank notes.

We now ask: what institutional problems arise when solving the problem of safeguarding the value of money of "two-tiered" currency communities? In answering this question we shall expand our stationary overlapping generations model to include commercial banks (to be referred to simply as "banks"). This expansion essentially requires two additional considerations. First we need a theory of the banking firm which explains the volume of deposits which a profit maximizing bank plans to issue and how many loans it plans to give. Second, we need an expanded theory of household behavior which explains the amount of bank deposits a household plans to keep in addition to paper money and bonds. We start with the simplest formulation of these two problems. Then we will consider the problems of safeguarding the value of money in a world in which the central agents of both the primary and the secondary currency communities are banks. Next we will survey the relevant literature. Finally, we will deal with public regulation of the central banks and the commercial banks and its problems.

8.1 The Theory of the Banking Firm: Preliminary Considerations

In the two preceding chapters we have assumed that the only means of payment are the notes issued by the central agent of the primary currency community. Payments may, of course, also be made by the transfer of interest bearing claims (i.e., "bonds"), or even simply by the exchange of goods. Consider the case of a transfer (cession) of money claims. We assume three households. Household 1 sells mark 100 worth of wheat to household 2 payable today. Household 2 "pays" by transferring a money claim against household 3, payable tomorrow. Exchange by the use of money in this particular sense presupposes that household 1 is willing to accept the money claim on household 3 instead of paper money. It will do so only if it considers household 3 to be sufficiently creditworthy. This in turn presupposes that household 1 has sufficient information about household 3.

The cooperation of household 3 may pose problems. A cession of claims without the cooperation of the borrower has been gradually permitted in German law since the 15th century. Only the German Civil Code (BGB) of 1900 brought the development to a conclusion (BGB Articles 398–413).[1]

Merchant practice developed the *bill of exchange* which may be transferred by endorsement. This involves a security which is strictly defined by law. The strict definition facilitates its use as a means of payment.[2]

Whoever pays with or acquires a good in exchange for a money claim on a third party must be informed about two markets: the relevant goods market and the market for the money claims offered in exchange. Both markets allow for intermediation by specialized firms: commodity traders on the goods markets, and financial intermediaries on the market for money loans. On the one side, financial intermediaries give money loans to the ultimate borrower, i.e., they buy "primary" money claims or "primary securities;"[3] on the other side, they accept loans from "investors," i.e., they sell "indirect" money claims or "indirect securities."[3] Such indirect money claims are, for example, bank deposits. One of their advantages consists in the fact that the exchange of wheat for a bank deposit is easier to realize than for a primary money claim. The payee knows, as a rule, where he stands. He will, as a rule, already maintain business relations with a bank in which he has confidence, and he will have a checking account with it. Banks specialize in executing the payments of their depositors. As a result, bank deposits are more liquid than primary money claims such as bonds.

The supply of marketable indirect money claims (the "production" of bank deposits) is a typical banking business. In American terminology, a (commercial or deposit) bank has even been defined as a financial firm whose debits include deposits payable on demand, i.e., deposits for which no term or period of notice has been arranged. German terminology is in this respect broader.[4]

---

[1] "It is likely that the requirement of the debtor's agreement was abandoned only under the influence of the unilateral right of disposal by the money lender." K. Luig (1966, 10f., translated by W.F. St.).

[2] "The strictness of the bill of exchange which is its legal characteristic, is not its own purpose but the necessary precondition if the bill of exchange is to fulfill its task as a short run means of circulation ..." "The apparent disadvantages of the strict characteristics of the bill of exchange are in reality its advantages ..." A. Baumbach and W. Hefermehl (1967, 20, translated by W.F. St.).

[3] J.G. Gurley's and E.S. Shaw's (1960, 4) concepts.

[4] In West Germany all credit institutions may call themselves "banks" which are permitted by the Bundesaufsichtsamt to enter into banking businesses in the sense of Article 1 KWG (Kreditwesengesetz). The law enumerates nine kinds of businesses, among them the deposit business.

Thus banks have two activities of interest to us: they perform

- Payments services, in Germany primarily by transfers (of deposits) and
- Financial intermediation through their deposit and credit business.

Banks are thus at the center of both a payments and a credit community whose members may be largely the same as the customers of commercial banks, but may also be different as is the case with postal savings banks. A substantial coincidence of the members of a payments and a credit community is advantageous for the relevant central agent (a bank) because its knowledge of current payments is also an excellent source of information about the business practices of potential or actual borrowers.

We suppose a bank to consist of two divisions: a *portfolio division* and a *transactions division*:

> "The portfolio division receives deposits and holds as its assets capital in good-producing firms and loans to the transactions division, for which it charges the market interest rate.... The transactions division in turn rents capital and high-powered money to make transactions, and repays the portfolio division out of the proceeds of its charges." (S. Fischer 1983, 6).

We assume that the costs of the transactions division calculated in relation to the volume of deposits, decrease with increases in deposit volume. If so, it pays to expand the transactions division of a bank without limits. In practice this is done by cooperation of commercial banks, e.g., in the (German) giro-transfer business.

This is not true for the portfolio division. It performs the financial intermediation services of the bank. As the concept of a "portfolio division" is here understood, this involves the deposit and credit business. The portfolio devision is a "transactions firm" as defined in Section 3.2. Unlike the transactions division it runs into decreasing returns to scale after a certain point. The portfolio division of a bank undertakes specific coordination functions of the market: the search for the ultimate lenders and borrowers; the estimation of the credit-worthiness of the borrowers and thus of the risk of defaults; the closing of appropriate loan agreements; the monitoring of the business activities of the lenders and the fulfilment of the performance obligations of the loan agreement, etc. The bank exercises these activities more efficiently than the individual investor could do via the market with the help of independent specialists. The bank "produces" for the ultimate lender a mixture of investments with different risks which may suit the various risk preferences of the individual investors. The individual depositor can, as a rule, mix the various risks less well than the bank can. In addition, the bank performs what is called in German "Fristentransformation" ("transformation" of short-term bank deposits into longer term bank loans) which provides considerable facilities to the individual investors. The purchaser of a bank deposit saves himself the closure of numerous individual contracts. He receives instead a standardized claim with or without an agreed-upon period of notice, which is more liquid than other forms of investment and which saves the depositor substantial transaction costs. The existence of transaction costs is thus an essential reason for the existence of banks:

"The raison d'être for this industry is the existence of transaction costs." (G.J. Benston and C.W. Smith, 1976, 215)

Notes on the History of Thought:

The newer literature emphasizes the intermediation between creditors and debtors as the essential function of banks, see, e.g., J.G. Gurley and E.S. Shaw (1960), or J. Tobin (1963/1967). Tobin writes (op. cit. p. 3):

"The essential function of financial intermediaries, including commercial banks, is to satisfy simultaneously the portfolio preferences of two types of individuals or firms. On one side are borrowers who wish to expand their holdings of real assets ... beyond the limits of their own net worth. On the other side are lenders who wish to hold part or all of their net worth in assets of stable money value with negligible risk of default."

In the older literature, A. Wagner (1857, 30) argues more simply but in a similar manner:

"The most important principle which is the very basis for our whole modern banking system is that the banks which we are considering here, are *trading firms, traders*. The banks *trade*, i.e., they buy and sell, and do so with the essential characteristic of trade: to make a profit."

Wagner continues: the commodities in which banks trade are "abilities to purchase in the form of money and its surrogates ... they draw abilities to purchase denominated in money from all circles and sell them to those who need help with abilities to purchase." (op. cit. 45, translated by W.F. St.)

O. Hübener (1854) argues in a similar manner. So does later F. Leitner (1920) who writes:

"Just as the trade in goods mediates between the producers and customers of goods, so the bank mediates among a great number of transactions. With typical bank transactions it mediates between the supply of money capital and the demand for money capital, between those who need credit and those who look for investments." (F. Leitner 1920, 18, translated by W.F. St.).

For demand deposits the analogy between a bank and a trading firm applies, however, only when the activity of the portfolio division is seen to be connected with the transactions division. The depositors hand over to the bank demand deposits in order to be able to use them for payments. They do not do so, or at least not primarily so, in order to make a loan to the bank. Demand deposits are to be understood as part of a relational contract, as was discussed above in Section 4.6 (see also Suggested Readings to this chapter).

8.2 The Banking Firm as a Financial Intermediary: A Simple Model

In this section we limit ourselves to modeling the portfolio division of a bank. We assume that no optimization problem exists for the transactions division. Only the portfolio division of the bank has an optimization problem. That is, the optimization problem is assumed to exist for the bank only in its function as a financial intermediary. In reality uncertainty exists in this as in all other respects. We assume that the bank transforms this uncertainty into certainty, in the case under consideration into certainty about its lending. The resources employed for this purpose are expressed as transaction costs and modeled by a transactions function.

We apply the model of a transactions firm to the bank in the simplest possible manner. The bank buys one-period primary securities, i.e., it gives loans; and it sells indirect one-period securities, i.e., it accepts bank deposits. This happens in "equal step," so to speak each Monday of the Hicksian week. We neglect for the time being the problem of bank reserves.

The planned volume of deposits is treated by the bank as an input into the transactions function. Thus it has a negative sign. We denote the real value of the planned deposit volume as of today $\tilde{D}^s$ (<0). The planned volume of bank loans appears in the transactions function as an output, i.e., as a positive magnitude. The real value as of today is denoted as $\tilde{B}_B$ (>0). The implicit form of the transactions function is then:

$$\varphi(\tilde{D}^s, \tilde{B}_B) = 0 \ .$$

The rate of interest on deposits is d, and that for bank loans is i. D^s and B_B are nominal deposits and loans respectively as of tomorrow so that:

$$\tilde{D}^s \equiv \frac{D^s}{p_1(1+d)} \ , \qquad \tilde{B}_B \equiv \frac{B_B}{p_1(1+i)} \ .$$

P_1 is today's price of today's good ("wheat today") or the money value of a corresponding basket of goods.

The bank profit as of tomorrow is in this case:

$$QB = D^s + B_B \ .$$

Numerical example: Given $p_1 = 1, d = 0.02, i = 0.10$. The bank accepts deposits today of mark 100 and lends today mark 95. The difference of mark 5 equals transaction costs. The bank will be repaid tomorrow mark 104.50. In turn it must repay its depositors tomorrow mark 102. The bank profit tomorrow is thus QB = mark 2.50.

The bank will choose the transactions plan $(\tilde{D}^s, \tilde{B}_B)$ which maximizes its profits QB. Thus, its optimization problem reads as follows:

$$\begin{aligned} &\text{Max} \quad QB = p_1(1+d)\tilde{D}^s + p_1(1+i)\tilde{B}_B \ , \qquad \tilde{D}^s \leqq 0 \ , \qquad \tilde{B}_B \geqq 0 \\ &\text{s.t.} \qquad \varphi(\tilde{D}^s, \tilde{B}_B) = 0 \ . \end{aligned}$$

All quantities are in real terms because the real transaction costs necessary to search for a borrower, to examine its credit-worthiness, to supervise its business activities etc. depend on the real, not the nominal level of the loans. At first there may be increasing returns to scale. But sooner or later returns to scale will decline. For simplicity's sake we assume, however, diminishing returns to scale from the beginning (above p. 191 f.). As in Fig. 3-3, the returns to scale are convex from above:

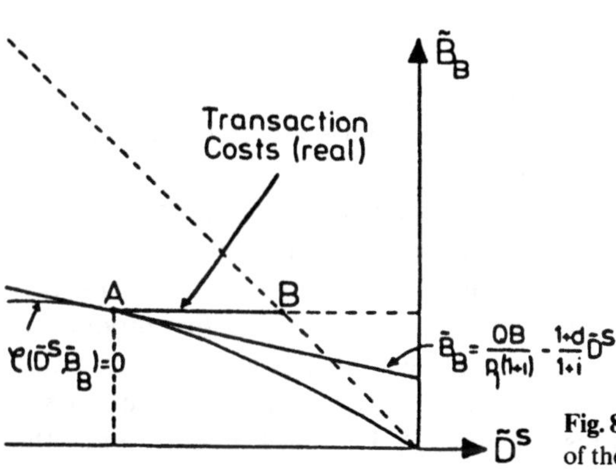

Fig. 8-1. The Profit Maximizing Transactions Plan A of the Banking Firm

The (real) present value of the bank's optimal transactions plan $(\tilde{D}^s, \tilde{B}_B)$ is point A in Fig. 8-1 where the isoprofit line is tangent to the transactions curve. The marginal condition is:

$$-\frac{d\tilde{B}_B}{d\tilde{D}^s} = \frac{1+d}{1+i} < 1 ,$$

or its inverse

$$\text{(8-1)} \qquad -\frac{d\tilde{D}^s}{d\tilde{B}_B} = \frac{1+i}{1+d} > 1 .$$

The left side of (8-1) is the gross marginal rate of transformation of bank loans into bank deposits, in real terms. The *net marginal rate of transformation* is

$$\text{(8-2)} \qquad -\frac{d\tilde{D}^s}{d\tilde{B}_B} - 1 = \frac{i-d}{1+d} > 0 .$$

In words: for an interior optimum of the banking firm the net marginal rate of transformation of bank loans into bank deposits is equal to the interest differential discounted at the interest rate of the depositors. The precondition for the existence of an interior optimum is $i > d$. An expansion of the real supply of bank deposits or bank money pays for the bank only as long as the net marginal rate of transformation of bank loans into bank deposits is greater than the present value of the interest differential. It can thus be seen that credit creation by banks (i.e., the production of bank money) is, under the assumptions made, limited in real terms, and independent of the reserves maintained by the bank which, for simplicity's sake, we have here assumed away.

The equations determining the bank's (real) demand for primary securities $\tilde{B}_B$ (= supply of bank loans) and the bank's (real) supply of secondary securities $\tilde{D}^s$ (= demand for bank deposits) are in this case (written in general form):

$$\tilde{D}^s = \tilde{D}^s(i, d) ,$$
$$\tilde{B}_B = \tilde{B}_B(i, d) .$$

With given interest rates i, d, the bank will demand a certain (real) volume of "bonds" (i.e., it is prepared to give a certain volume of bank credits), and the bank supplies a certain (real) volume of bank deposits.

We may now interpret the bank as a central agent of a secondary currency community as discussed in Section 4.5. He uses the accounting unit of the primary currency community, but he offers his own means of payment (bank money) which he issues and redeems at par against the basic money. In our simplified model this may be imagined as follows: every young generation establishes a bank with which it keeps part of its savings from labor income (why not the whole? See Section 8.3) in the form of deposits with the real present value $\tilde{D}$. The bank in turn lends the amount $\tilde{B}_B$ to the production firm Robinson. In the next period the now aged generation buys wheat out of the current production of the production firm Robinson and pays for part of it with its bank deposit plus the bank profit $D + QB$. The production firm Robinson repays with these revenues its bank debt B_B. The old generation pays for its remaining wheat purchases with the paper money M of the primary currency community and with its money claims B_H which now become due (see Section 8.3).

With this construction of our example the bank needs no reserves at all in the stationary case. To be sure, it promises redemption into central bank money, but the depositors make no use of this. Their demand over the deposits are in the form of checking accounts not in the form of cash. As we have seen, this is irrelevant to the determination of the real value of the bank money supplied.

Now, how can we introduce bank reserves into our considerations? Consider first the definition of bank profit as of tomorrow. In our model this is the equivalent to the liquidation profit of the banking firm. If the bank keeps reserves R, tomorrow's "revenue" will be $B_B + R$. The "cost" due tomorrow is D^s. The bank profit valued as of tomorrow is then the sum

$$QB = D^s + B_B + R \ .$$

We now "stretch" the simultaneity of market transactions somewhat by assuming that the old generation exhausts its bank account tomorrow before the firm Robinson repays its bank debts. It withdraws part of its deposits in cash; for the rest it writes checks. In addition we assume that the bank can get cash tomorrow only at a cost. In such a case, it pays for the bank to keep reserves. Let the cash withdrawal "tomorrow" be X, where X is a random variable. The bank does not know today what value X will have tomorrow. It knows, however, the probabilities $\pi(X)$ whereby we for simplicity's sake calculate with discrete probabilities instead of a probability function or density function.

We follow in this the well-known article by D. Orr and W.G. Mellon (1961): if bank withdrawals X are bigger than reserves R, the bank can raise central bank money at the price s mark per mark. The expected value EK of the cost to the bank from obtaining reserves from the central bank (i.e., central bank money) tomorrow is equal to

$$EK = s \sum_{\tilde{X}_j > \tilde{R}} (\tilde{X}_j - \tilde{R})\pi(\tilde{X}_j) \ .$$

The value of bank profit "tomorrow" is now reduced by EK. The optimization problem of the bank can then be formulated as follows:

$$\begin{aligned} \text{Max} \quad & QB = p_1(1 + d)\tilde{D}^s + p_1(1 + i)\tilde{B}_B + p_1\tilde{R} \\ & \qquad - p_1 s \sum_{\tilde{X}_j > \tilde{R}} (\tilde{X}_j - \tilde{R})\pi(\tilde{X}_j) \\ \text{s.t.} \quad & \varphi(\tilde{D}^s + \tilde{R}, \tilde{B}_B) = 0 \\ & \tilde{D}^s \leqq 0 \ , \quad \tilde{R} \geqq 0 \ , \quad \tilde{B}_B \geqq 0 \ , \end{aligned}$$

where $\tilde{R}$ and $\tilde{X}$ are the real values of the bank reserves and withdrawals. Bank deposits are no longer completely lent but only to the extent $\tilde{D}^s + \tilde{R}$. (Example: $\tilde{D}^s = -100$, $\tilde{R} = 5$, $\tilde{D}^s + \tilde{R} = -95$.) The sum $\tilde{D}^s + \tilde{R}$ is the "input" into our transactions function φ; the expression $\tilde{B}_B$ is read as an output. Otherwise the transactions function looks exactly as in Fig. 8-1.

The marginal conditions are:

$$(8\text{-}1) \qquad -\frac{d\tilde{D}^s}{d\tilde{B}_B} = \frac{1+i}{1+d}$$

or

$$(8\text{-}1') \qquad d = -\frac{d\tilde{B}_B}{d\tilde{D}^s}(1+i) - 1 \ .$$

In words: for an interior optimum the bank's marginal costs d of borrowing money from the public are equal to the marginal yield of the additional bank loan resulting from the additional deposit (the term on the right hand side of the equation (8-1')).

In addition we get the marginal condition

$$(8\text{-}3) \qquad d = s \sum_{\tilde{X}_j > \tilde{R}} \pi(\tilde{X}_j)$$

or because of (8-1')

$$(8\text{-}3') \qquad -\frac{d\tilde{B}_B}{d\tilde{D}^s}(1+i) - 1 = s \sum_{\tilde{X}_j > \tilde{R}} \pi(\tilde{X}_j) \ .$$

In words: for an interior optimum the expected value of the marginal costs to the bank of obtaining central bank money is equal to the marginal yield which results from the reduction of the bank reserves by one mark and the corresponding increase in bank loans (given the volume of deposits).

Furthermore, the expected value of the marginal costs to the bank of obtaining central bank money is equal to the interest rate d on deposits at an interior optimum of the total model of the banking firm (see equation (8-3)). We assume $d > 0$.

For $-\frac{d\tilde{B}_B}{d\tilde{D}^s} = 1$, i.e., for transaction costs of zero (and therefore $i = d$), we get

$$(8\text{-}3'') \qquad i = s \sum_{\tilde{X}_j > \tilde{R}} \pi(\tilde{X}_j) \ .$$

(The derivation is found in Appendix 1 of this chapter.)

Equation (8-3'') corresponds to the marginal condition which is found in the bank reserve models of the Orr and Mellon type (though there only for the case of a continuous density function, see, e.g., E. Wagner (1982, 113)).

The bank now plans a bundle of three magnitudes: the volumes of deposits, reserves and loans – all in real terms discounted to the present: $\tilde{D}^s$, $\tilde{R}$, $\tilde{B}_B$. We get in this case three equations with the loan interest i, the deposit interest d and the parameters s and $\pi(\tilde{X}_j)$ (which we will write from now on as $s\pi$) of the expected value of the cost of obtaining central bank money as arguments. We get:

$$\tilde{D}^s = \tilde{D}^s(i, d, s\pi) \ ,$$
$$\tilde{R} = \tilde{R}(i, d, s\pi) \ ,$$
$$\tilde{B}_B = \tilde{B}_B(i, d, s\pi) \ .$$

Remember: we have modeled here only the portfolio division of the banking firm. That means, the deposit interest rate d is here the interest rate which the portfolio division has to pay to the transactions division (see S. Fischer (1983, 6) as quoted above in Section 8.1). It will be equal to some market rate, e.g., the rate for overnight money. We disregard the calculation of the transactions division. If its costs are zero then the rate d may actually be paid to the depositor. Otherwise, if its costs are positive, the depositors get a rate smaller than d or they get nothing or even have to pay some fee for each transfer as, e.g., in West Germany. The difference between d and what the depositors actually receive will be paid out, e.g., as wages or as profits. The resulting distributional problems are also ignored in our model. If we assume that only the old Robinson works for the bank then he gets, in effect, the rate d which the portfolio division of the bank paid to its transactions division: because he is the only worker *and* the 100 percent owner of the bank.

8.3 The Demand for Bank Money

We assume that cash (central bank notes) and bank money (bank deposits) are not perfect substitutes for each other.

Thus it does not suffice to determine the demand for the sum of the two kinds of money. We need two demand-for-money functions, one for cash and another for bank money. The easiest way to model these functions is a direct utility function of the type:

$$\text{Max} \quad U = U\left(x_1, \frac{M}{p_2^+}, \frac{D}{p_2^+}, x_2\right)$$

$$\text{s.t.} \quad p_1 x_1 + M + \frac{D}{1+d} + \frac{B_H}{1+i} = p_1 \bar{x}_1^1$$

$$p_2^+ + x_2 = M + D + B_H + QB$$

$$M \geqq 0 \ , \quad B_H \geqq 0 \ , \quad D \geqq 0 \ , \quad \bar{x}_1^1 \geqq 0 \ , \quad QB \geqq 0 \ ,$$

where QB is the bank profit due "tomorrow" which goes 100% to the household of "tomorrow's" old Robinson who owns the bank.

This formulation allows us to determine simultaneously the optimal inter-temporal consumption and investment plans of the household. For an interior optimum we get analogously to Section 6.2 the marginal conditions:

$$\frac{U_{x_1}}{U_{x_2}} = \frac{p_1}{p_2^+}(1+i) \ ,$$

$$\frac{U_{\tilde{\tilde{M}}}}{U_{x_2}} = i \ , \quad U_{\tilde{\tilde{M}}} \equiv U_{(M/p_2^+)} \ ,$$

$$\frac{U_{\tilde{\tilde{D}}}}{U_{\tilde{\tilde{M}}}} = \frac{i-d}{i(1+d)} \ , \quad U_{\tilde{\tilde{D}}} \equiv U_{(D/p_2^+)} \ .$$

For the derivation see Appendix 2 of this chapter.

Under the usual convexity assumptions about the utility function the marginal conditions are sufficient to maximize utility. The third marginal condition is new, compared to Section 6.2. It concerns the marginal rate of substitution between bank deposits and cash balances of the household. If the household were indifferent between the two kinds of money this marginal rate would be equal to 1. We assume, however, that the marginal rate of substitution of bank money for cash is declining. That is, we assume that the $\left(\frac{M}{p_2^+}, \frac{D}{p_2^+}\right)$-indifference curves have a curvature to the left as in Fig. 8-2. The optimum is reached when the relevant budget line is tangent to the indifference curve, i.e., if

$$\operatorname{tg} \alpha = \frac{i(1+d)}{i-d} \quad \text{(see Fig. 8-2)} \ .$$

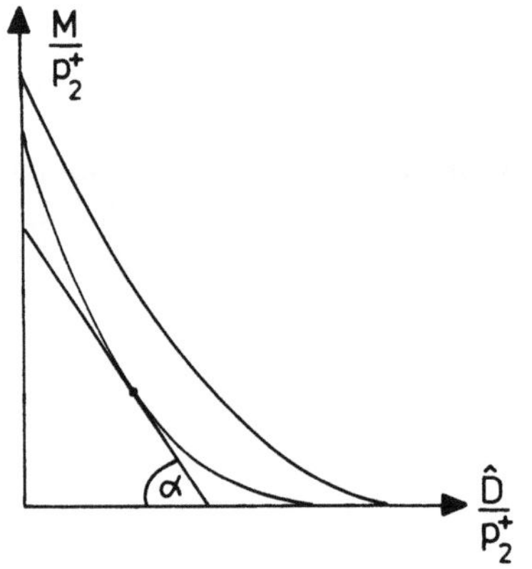

Fig. 8-2. The Optimal Cash and Bank-money Holdings of the Household

The arguments for the equations for the optimal consumption and investment plans of the household are

$$i, d, \frac{p_1}{p_2^+}, \bar{x}_1^1 \ .$$

The bank profit QB is itself also a function of i and d. For that reason we need not write it separately as an argument (see above Section 8.2).

The equations for determining the optimal consumption and investment plan of the household are now:

$$x_j = x_j\left(i, d, \frac{p_1}{p_2^+}, \bar{x}_1^1\right) ; \quad j = 1, 2$$

$$\tilde{B}_H = \tilde{B}_H(\cdot) , \quad \tilde{B}_H \equiv \frac{B_H}{p_1(1+i)}$$

$$\tilde{D} = \tilde{D}(\cdot) , \quad \tilde{D} \equiv \frac{D}{p_1(1+d)}$$

$$\tilde{M} = L(\cdot) , \quad \tilde{M} \equiv \frac{M}{p_1} .$$

We have now, what is relevant here, two separate demand functions for money: one for cash $L(\cdot)$ and one for bank money $\tilde{D}(\cdot)$.

The demand functions for cash and bank money may also be derived in a different manner. We may, for example, assume that transaction costs of an intertemporal transfer of assets are different for the two types of investments. We reason analogously to Section 6.2. We now have two real transaction-costs functions $CB\left(\frac{\hat{B}_H}{p_1}\right)$ and $CD\left(\frac{\hat{D}}{p_1}\right)$ with positive first and second derivatives. It is

$$\hat{B}_H = \frac{B_H}{1+i} \quad \text{and} \quad \hat{D} = \frac{D}{1+d} .$$

We have given reason in Section 6.2 why the marginal transaction costs of converting paper money into bonds rise (i.e., why $CB'' > 0$). In the present case transaction costs comprise also the costs of supervising banks which, from a certain point onward, increase with additional invested units of money (all in real terms). Therefore, an analogous argument as in Section 6.2 applies to transactions of cash into bank money.

The utility maximizing household will choose that mixture of the three investment possibilities in which the marginal returns (= interest less marginal transaction costs) of the three investments are equal to each other. When non-interest bearing paper money is used, they will be zero.

Table 8.1

Investment	Interest	minus	Marginal Transaction Costs	= Marginal Revenue of Investment
cash	0	–	0	= 0
deposits	d	–	CD'	= 0
bonds	i	–	CB'	= 0

The corresponding optimizing problem of the household can now be written as follows (this is analogous to our procedure in Section 6.2):

$$\text{Max} \quad U = U(x_1, x_2)$$

$$\text{s.t.} \quad p_1 x_1 + \hat{B}_H + \hat{D} + M + p_1 CB\left(\frac{\hat{B}_H}{p_1}\right) + p_1 CD\left(\frac{\hat{D}}{p_1}\right) = p_1 \bar{x}_1^1$$

$$p_2^+ x_2 = \hat{B}_H(1 + i) + \hat{D}(1 + d) + M + QB$$

$$M \geqq 0 , \quad \hat{B}_H \geqq 0 , \quad \hat{D} \geqq 0 , \quad \bar{x}_1^1 \geqq 0 , \quad QB \geqq 0 .$$

The transaction costs for bonds and bank deposits of Robinson are accounted for "today" (in his "youth"). The young generation has no debts and no negative cash balances M. The conditions for an interior optimum are:

$$\frac{U_1}{U_2} = \frac{p_1}{p_2^+} ,$$

$$CB' = i ,$$

$$CD' = d .$$

(For a derivation see Appendix 3 to this chapter.)

As in Chapter 6, the marginal conditions may be interpreted in different ways. We choose the interpretation corresponding to variant 3 in Section 6.2.

Theorem: At an interior optimum of the household and a given original endowment $\bar{x}_1^1$ the following hold simultaneously:

1. The intertemporal *consumption of goods* will be such that the marginal utility of cash balances will be zero:

$$\frac{U_2}{p_2^+} - \frac{U_1}{p_1} = 0$$

2. The *money assets* will be distributed among the three investment possibilities M, $\hat{D}$, $\hat{B}_H$ such that the marginal returns on each investment possibility are equal to each other; in our example they will be equal to zero (cash holdings are non-interest bearing):

$$CB' - i = 0 ,$$

$$CD' - d = 0 .$$

The arguments in the equations determining the optimal consumption and investment plans of the household are the same as before. The equations themselves have an analogous form.

For the purposes of this chapter it suffices to assume that as a rule cash and bank deposits are only imperfect substitutes for each other. This is the reason why we need two demand functions for money, one for cash and one for demand deposits. We see: the transaction costs approach can also be used to explain economically the two demand functions, though it is in the present context perhaps overtaxed. The direct utility approach does not provide an economic explanation but suffices for the modeling of the problem.

8.4 The Banking Firm as the Central Agent of a Primary Currency Community: The Commodity Standard

We have not yet dealt in any detail with the central agents of currency communities. We shall do so now. We consider them to be banks both in the cases of the primary and the secondary currency communities. This section will consider the bank as the central agent of a (closed) primary currency community with a commodity standard. It issues claims against itself, which we assume to be only bank notes, in exchange for a money commodity or a money loan. In Chapter 7 we postulated for simplicity's sake that the central agent of the primary currency community (the "central bank") issues or repays only paper money in exchange for a money commodity. We also assumed, in the case of a stationary overlapping generations model with a single good "wheat", that an individual cannot store the perishable good indefinitely while the central agent of the primary community can. The circulating volume of money M is confronted, as it were, by the stock of wheat x of the central agent valued at the fixed (and given) price p; i.e., $M = px$. With a fixed p, M can only increase if the wheat stocks of the central agent increase correspondingly. In such a case the central agent of the currency community is more like a government stock authority than a bank.

This greatly simplified approach is useful when, as in Chapter 7, the central agent of the primary currency community is only of secondary importance in the considerations entertained. If, however, we wish to analyze the central agent itself we must use a different approach. We must now consider that the central agent will, as a rule, issue paper money not only against a money good but also against financial assets. The model of a bank developed in Section 8.2 must be appropriately applied if these financial assets consist wholly or in part of loans to private parties. We must also drop the implicit assumption that the central bank can store an otherwise non-storable good.

For these reasons we now assume an overlapping generations model with two goods: an indefinitely storable good "gold" and a perishable good "wheat." Only the perishable good wheat can be produced; the amount of gold on the other hand is given and fixed, specifically in the form of coins. We used this construction already briefly in Section 7.1. In the present model, GM denotes the amount of existing gold coins which is also demanded by the young generation. It is expressed in accounting units, say "mark." M is the nominal amount of paper money demanded by the young generation. R is the gold reserve, expressed in accounting units which the central bank holds, and $\hat{B}_N$, $\hat{B}_H$ are the nominal present values of the demand for bonds by the central bank and the young generation respectively. Again we consider only the bank's portfolio division which pays the rate d to its transactions division (see S. Fisher 1983, 6 as quoted above in Section 8.1). The latter prints the notes and takes care that they are used. Because of transaction costs no interest will be paid on notes.[5] But there are costs involved to make the use of the issuer's notes sufficiently attractive (see, e.g., L.H. White 1984a, 7f.), though we otherwise disregard this part of the bank. As has been argued at the end of Section 8.2 the old Robinson receives, in effect, under the conditions of our model as the owner of the central bank, the positive rate d on his deposits D or (here) on his cash M_N. The central bank is privately owned and maximizes tomorrow's profit QNB, subject to its transactions function. The optimization problem can then be formulated as follows (in analogy to Section 8.2):

$$\text{Max} \quad QNB = p_1 \tilde{M}_N^0(1+d) + p_1(1+i)\tilde{B}_N + p_1 \tilde{R} - p_1 s \sum_{\tilde{X}_j > \tilde{R}} (\tilde{X}_j - \tilde{R})\pi(\tilde{X}_j)$$

$$\text{s.t.} \quad \varphi(\tilde{M}_N^0 + \tilde{R}, \tilde{B}_N) = 0 \ , \quad \tilde{M}_N^s \equiv -\tilde{M}^s \leqq 0 \ , \quad \tilde{R} \geqq 0 \ , \quad \tilde{B}_N \geqq 0 \ .$$

$\tilde{M}_N^s$ $(= -\tilde{M}^s)$ is the volume of bank notes offered by the central bank; X_j is the loss of gold coins (analogously to the loss of cash in Section 8.2); s are the cost of getting cash for gold mark; p_1 is the price of wheat today. The tildes above the symbols refer to the real values (in kg of wheat). The marginal conditions are again:

$$-\frac{d\tilde{M}^s}{d\tilde{B}_N} = \frac{1+i}{1+d} \ , \tag{8-1'}$$

$$d = s \sum_{\tilde{X}_j > \tilde{R}} \pi(\tilde{X}_j) \ . \tag{8-3}$$

Note that the stock of gold reserves is now as a rule smaller than the stock of notes in circulation. In other words, we are dealing with the case of fractional gold reserves. The optimal transactions plan of the central bank is here a bundle of three magnitudes: the volume of paper money, of gold reserves and of loans, *all* calculated in real terms ("wheat") and referring to today: $(\tilde{M}^s, \tilde{R}, \tilde{B}_N)$. Thus we get three equations determining the optimal plan of the central bank, with three arguments: the loan interest i, the deposit rate d charged by the portfolio division, and the parameters of the costs of getting gold coins whose vector is denoted by $s\pi$. We have therefore:

$$\tilde{M}^s = \tilde{M}^s(i, d, s\pi) \ ,$$

$$\tilde{R} = \tilde{R}(i, d, s\pi) \ ,$$

$$\tilde{B}_N = \tilde{B}_N(i, d, s\pi) \ .$$

[5] "To collect interest for the holding of a bank note would require going through a bothersome procedure such as having the date of original issue stamped upon it and having the accumulated interest calculated with each paying over the note." (L.H. White 1984a, 8).

With regard to the dispositions of the household of our model world we reason analogously to Section 8.3 with $d = 0$. (The income from interest of the transactions division, which charges the rate d, is in our simple example part of QNB.) The optimization approach of the household is then as follows (using the direct utility approach):

$$\text{Max} \quad U = U\left(x_1, \frac{GM^d}{p_2^+}, \frac{M^d}{p_2^+}, x_2\right)$$

$$\text{s.t.} \qquad p_1 x_1 + GM^d + M^d + \frac{B_H}{1+i} = p_1 \bar{x}_1^1$$

$$p_2^+ x_2 = GM^d + M^d + B_H + QNB \ .$$

The household Robinson owns the central bank 100% and receives, therefore, tomorrow the total profit of the central bank QNB. GM, the fixed amount of minted gold, is passed from generation to generation. Every generation holds the whole amount of gold coins GM (= the stock of gold times the standard of coinage) which it gives to the next generation for wheat.

Analogously to Section 8.3 we have the following marginal conditions:

$$\frac{U_{x_1}}{U_{x_2}} = \frac{p_1}{p_2^+}(1+i)$$

$$\frac{U_{\widetilde{\widetilde{GM}}}}{U_{x_2}} = i \ ; \qquad \widetilde{\widetilde{GM}} \equiv \frac{GM}{p_2^+}$$

$$\frac{U_{\tilde{\tilde{M}}}}{U_{\widetilde{\widetilde{GM}}}} = 1 \ ; \qquad \tilde{\tilde{M}} \equiv \frac{M}{p_2^+} \ .$$

The third marginal condition expresses the following facts: at an interior optimum the household holds those amounts of each kind of money such that the marginal utility of holding bank notes is equal to the marginal utility of holding coins (point B on Fig. 8-3). Only in the optimum is the household indifferent whether to hold bank notes or gold coins.

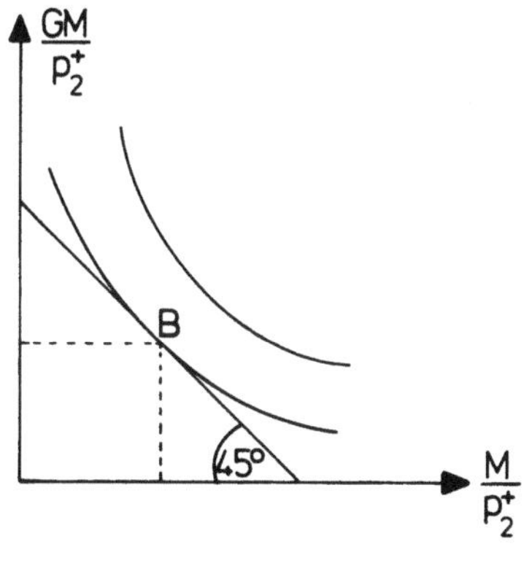

Fig. 8-3. The Optimal Holdings of Bank Notes and Gold Coins

The equations determining the optimal consumption and investment plans of the household $(x_1, x_2, \widetilde{GM}, \tilde{M}, \tilde{B}_H)$ are:

$$x_j = x_j\left(i, \frac{p_1}{p_2^+}, \bar{x}_1^1\right) \; ; \quad j = 1, 2$$

$$\tilde{B}_H = \tilde{B}_H\left(i, \frac{p_1}{p_2^+}, \bar{x}_1^1\right)$$

$$\widetilde{GM} = \widetilde{GM}\left(i, \frac{p_1}{p_2^+}, \bar{x}_1^1\right) \; ; \quad \widetilde{GM} \equiv \frac{GM}{p_1}$$

$$\tilde{M} = \tilde{M}\left(i, \frac{p_1}{p_2^+}, \bar{x}_1^1\right) \; ; \quad \tilde{M} \equiv \frac{M}{p_1} \; .$$

In the stationary case GM = const. and hence $p_1 = p_2^+ = p$. Neglecting parameters $\bar{x}_1^1$ and $s\pi$ the stationary overlapping generations model of a commodity standard with fractional reserves of the bank of issue is now as follows:

$$\hat{x}_1(i) - \frac{GM}{p} = -y(i) \tag{8-4}$$

$$\widetilde{GM}^d(i) + \tilde{R}(i, d) = \frac{GM}{p} \tag{8-5}$$

$$\tilde{M}(i) = \tilde{M}^s(i, d) \tag{8-6}$$

endogenous variables: i, p

exogenous variables: GM, d (GM = standard of coinage times stock of gold).

The system is overdetermined. Of course, we could have assumed d to be an endogenous variable as well, but where is the corresponding loan market? There is no market for the "deposits" which the transactions division holds with the portfolio division of the bank of issue. So we have to assume, in our simple example, that d is determined by an administrative act of the bank's management which, in the formal language of our model, means d is "given exogenously." We could imagine the model to be extended to include various banks of issue which compete with each other – the case of "free banking." A market for interbank loans of short duration may develop, e.g., of overnight money with d as the interest rate. We would then have one more market equation and one more endogenous variable, d. Yet the system would still be overdetermined, i.e., it would still have more equations than variables. So, we may as well go ahead and discuss the simple model (8-4) to (8-6).

Overdeterminacy means that it is (generally) impossible to make all the assumptions simultaneously; something has to give. We could, for example, assume that the users of money consider gold coins and bank notes perfect substitutes. In this case the demand for money consists of the sum of the demand for gold coins and bank notes. Hence, equations (8-5) and (8-6) must be added. We get

$$(8\text{-}7) \qquad L^0(i) + \tilde{R}(i,d) = \frac{GM}{p} + \tilde{M}^s(i) \ .$$

The new system (8-4) to (8-7) is no longer overdetermined. The greater the (real) supply of paper money $\tilde{M}^s$, i.e., the greater the business activity of the central bank in its function as financial intermediary, the higher will be the price of wheat p. Safeguarding the purchasing power of money would require in this case an exogenous limitation of the volume of central bank credit or notes.

The assumption, however, that the users of money consider gold coins and bank notes to be perfect substitutes for each other is not plausible – certainly not if strictly interpreted. The two means of payment not only look differently, but are used for different purposes. Individuals might perhaps distinguish a wheat price expressed in gold coins and a wheat price expressed in paper money, and paper money may in fact have an agio or disagio in terms of gold coins.

Another possibility for eliminating the overdeterminacy of the system (8-4) to (8-6) consists in the assumptions that, first, the rate of interest i^* which satisfied equations (8-4) and (8-5) results in a real supply of bank notes $\tilde{M}^s$ which is larger than the real demand for bank notes $\tilde{M}$; and, secondly, that the central bank acts like a "rationed seller" (E. Malinvaud 1977, 15). The central bank purchases according to its transactions function φ that real amount of $\tilde{B}_N$ which corresponds to the real amount of the demand for bank notes $\tilde{M}$. Under these assumptions equations (8-4) to (8-6) are changed as follows:

$$(8\text{-}4) \qquad \hat{\tilde{x}}_1(i) - \frac{GM}{p} = -y(i) \ ,$$

$$(8\text{-}5) \qquad \widetilde{GM}^d(i) + \tilde{R}(i,d) = \frac{GM}{p} \ ,$$

$$(8\text{-}6') \qquad p\tilde{M}(i) = M \ ;$$

endogenous variables: i, p, M

exogenous variables: GM, d .

We may suppose that the equilibrium values of i and p are found by a process of trial and error (tâtonnement) on the market for goods (8-4) and for gold coins (8-5). This determines simultaneously the real demand for bank notes $\tilde{M}$ and the corresponding nominal value M. The volume of bank notes M of the commodity standard therefore becomes an endogenous variable – as was assumed in Section 7.1. The market for bank notes is a buyers' market. The central bank supplies precisely the amount of notes M demanded. In this view, the central bank cannot supply more bank notes than the public wants. And we can add that the goods prices p no longer depend on the circulating amount of bank notes M, but the other way 'round: the circulation of money is determined by the level of goods prices.[6]

---

[6] As is immediately evident, the purchasing power of money $1/p$ may with a fractional gold standard be influenced through exogenous variations in the gold reserve of the central bank (see J. Niehans 1978, 152f.). This presupposes a closed economy or the case of a (very) big open economy. For a small country, p is given. Variations in the gold reserves are ineffective.

These are the two central assertions of Thomas Tooke, the leading representative of the banking school. In the concluding summary of his pamphlet Tooke (1844, 122) writes that he has shown, among other things,

"that it is not in the power of Banks of Issue, including the Bank of England, to make any direct addition to the amount of notes circulating ... however disposed they may be to do so."

"That the prices of commodities do not depend upon the quantity of money indicated by the amount of bank notes, nor upon the amount of the whole of the circulating medium; but that, on the contrary, the amount of the circulating medium is the consequence of prices."[7]

The second part of the quoted assertion can be reconciled with the results of our model if we write the total of the means of circulation as the sum

$$M^0 = GM + p\tilde{M}(\cdot)$$

with GM exogenously given, and $\tilde{M} > 0$.

Whether Tooke understood this half-sentence in precisely this manner and considered gold coins and bank notes to be imperfect substitutes for each other is another question. The half-sentence is not tenable if the money users are assumed to consider gold coins and bank notes to be perfect substitutes for each other (equation (8-7)). But, as we saw, this case is not plausible.

In our model, the central bank issues paper money by buying bonds $\hat{B}_N$. These are one-period loans which are given for productive purposes. There is no risk of default. All bank notes flow back to the central bank on the next market day; some are used to repay cash (gold coin) reserves; some are used to repay money loans financed by the central bank (interest payments are included with bank profits). The repayment of bank loans, as construed here, corresponds to the well-known *reflux principle* of the banking school. In principle it allows a perfect adaptation of the stock of bank notes at any one moment of time to the demand for paper money. The repayment or reflux principle does not, however, guarantee the liquidity of the central bank (i.e., bills of exchange may default) nor does it prevent the overissue of paper money ($M > p\tilde{M}(i)$) as the banking school asserted. In order to understand this we take another look at our model. It is based on the assumption, which is not further discussed here, that for the paper-money price of wheat p^p and the gold price of wheat p^g the law of one price, or PPP, holds

$$p^p = ep^g \ ,$$

implying that the rate of exchange of paper money for gold coins is always equal to 1 ($e = 1$). The latter is guaranteed by the obligation of the central bank to redeem paper money into gold and vice versa. The validity of the PPP follows from the logic of arbitrage.

[7] L. Robbins calls this a "most startling" assertion of Tooke's (L. Robbins 1958, 124) and F.W. Fetter (1965, 189) writes, that this is a very complex and unclear argument which only confused the debate. We believe, however, as we shall presently show, that the argument is tenable with a suitable choice of assumptions.

The model may then be reformulated as follows:

$$(8\text{-}4') \qquad \hat{x}_1(i) - \frac{GM}{p^g} = -y(i) \ ,$$

$$(8\text{-}5') \qquad \widetilde{GM}(i) + \tilde{R}(i,d) = \frac{GM}{p^g} \ ,$$

$$(8\text{-}6'') \qquad \tilde{M}(i) = \frac{M}{p^p} \ ,$$

$$(8\text{-}7) \qquad e = \frac{p^p}{p^g} \ .$$

If $e = 1$ is not guaranteed by appropriate measures we have as

endogenous variables: i, p^p, p^g, e

exogenous variables: GM, M, d .

Even if the reflux principle is valid the purchasing power of bank notes may be arbitrarily high or low, depending on the value of M chosen by the central bank. The reflux principle does not prevent the central bank from choosing a value of M at which the purchasing power of bank notes is, e.g., substantially lower than the purchasing power of gold coins.

The equality of the purchasing power of paper money and gold coins may be brought about in two ways. The central bank may use its discretionary power to fix M in particular so that $e = 1$ or it may strictly follow an automatic rule, viz. the promise to redeem its notes into gold and vice versa at a fixed rate. In the first case we have a paper standard, in the second a commodity standard. Yet, in both cases we have in our model as

endogenous variables: i, p^p, p^g, M

exogenous variables: $GM, e = 1, d$.

With the paper standard, the target variable is e, and M is the instrument variable in the sense of Tinbergen's theory of economic policy. The commodity standard may be understood in the same manner with the difference, though, that the instrument variable M is now determined "automatically," i.e., by the demands of the money users. The guarantee of a fixed exchange rate $e = 1$ is achieved for the commodity standard in a "market conforming" manner, through the obligation of the central bank to redeem its notes at a fixed price, and not as in the paper standard purely administratively. If the central bank is obliged to redeem its notes into gold and vice versa an overissue will lead to a loss of gold reserves, or else the central bank will have to buy gold on the market at a higher price than the price at which it is obliged to sell gold. In these circumstances it must reduce its supply of notes and *mutatis mutandis* increase it in the opposite case. The decisive measures which in the case of a commodity standard will avoid an excessive note issue are therefore regulations which deal with the proper adjustment of M, and not the reflux principle so strongly stressed by the banking school.[8] The banking school thus came into close proximity of the *real bills doctrine* which claims that the issue of bank notes against trade bills (short-term loans made for "productive purposes") will not be inflationary.[9] If this doctrine were correct, $e = 1$ could be achieved even without a special guarantee to supply the correct amount of M. But we have shown that this is not possible.

We assume in our simple model that, given a certain demand for money, there is a strictly proportional relation between GM and p^g, and between M and p^p. But we also know that this relation is in reality not very strict. With fractional reserves this has necessary consequences for the determination of M. With fractional reserves the volume of M is regulated primarily by variations in the supply of central bank credits ($\hat{B}_N$). In practice this was in turn achieved by variations in the discount rate of the central bank. Since there is only a loose connection between M and p^p, an overissue of M will be felt only with a lag by reserve losses of the bank of issue, possibly by an increase of e, the price of gold expressed in paper money. The central bank then cuts back the note issue too late and possibly too much. After a while it must once more pursue an expansionary path etc. So, it stimulates business activity by, say, lowering the discount rate, then puts on the brakes again. The interest-rate policy of the central bank may thus exaggerate business fluctuations and it may even cause fluctuations in this manner. Financial crises could be the consequence.

How can all this be avoided? As far as the regulation of M is concerned this would be very simple: the currency order obliges the central bank not only to redeem notes into gold, but also to issue notes only against gold and vice versa. The central bank need not keep a 100% gold reserve to do this. It suffices to keep an appropriate amount of reserves to smooth out fluctuations in the circulation of bank notes by redemption of notes into gold and vice versa. A certain minimum amount of bank notes will always remain in circulation and can be brought into circulation by a constant amount of money loans to the government. Peel's Bank Act of 1844 was based on this idea.

A second method of supplying the appropriate amount of M may consist of free banking, i.e., the freedom to establish banks of issue. With competing private banks of issue, which accept notes of their competitors and then clear them against their own notes, an excessive issue of one bank will lead to losses in its reserves and will do so much quicker with competing banks than with a monopoly bank. L.H. White (1984a, 18) argues in this vein:

"Under a free banking system of multiple competing note issues, the check against overissues by any single bank is more rapid and direct. Because the single bank's customers comprise only a small fraction

---

[8] See on this point the argument by J. Fullarton (1845, 67): "Perfect convertibility is no doubt one essential condition of every sound and efficient system of currency. It is the only effectual protection against internal discredit, and the best preventive of any violent aberrations of the exchange with foreign countries. But it is not so much by convertibility into gold, as by the regularity of the reflux, that in the ordinary course of things any redundance of the bank-notes is rendered impossible."

[9] The real bills doctrine was already criticized early by, among others, H. Thornton (1802/1962, 244).

of the money-using members of the regional economy, holders of its excess notes in depositing them with their favorite banks will place all but a small fraction in other banks. Adverse clearings will consequently approach the size of the overissue rapidly. The bank in a multiissuer system that has mistakenly overissued immediately experiences negative feedback telling to reverse course to protect its viability. The excess notes may be promptly withdrawn before the bank creates a major monetary disturbance."

This idea was made more precise by G.A. Selgin (1987). It contradicts, among other things, V.C. Smith's (1936, 156) assertion that with free banking the volume of money would fluctuate more wildly than with only one issuing bank.

Note on the History of Thought:

The currency-banking school controversy centered on the question of the public regulation of note issue with a gold standard. Both sides wanted the bank of issue to be obliged to redeem their money into gold at a fixed rate. The banking school believed this obligation to be sufficient to maintain the gold standard. The currency school did not think so. Its general theoretical framework was the price-specie-flow mechanism of David Hume. In addition it insisted that with a "mixed" circulation of money the sum of gold coins and bank notes should be made to behave exactly as it would with a 100% gold cover.[10] This is achieved very simply – the bank of issue may vary its note circulation only with its gold stock in the ratio 1 : 1 (E. Wood 1939, 111).

The banking school had a different idea of how balance of payments equilibrium was achieved. In its view gold imports or exports were regulated by interest differentials and not by commodity price differentials. For this reason it did not agree with the currency school which demanded the regulation of note issue. In addition it pointed out that not only bank notes but also bank deposits, bills of exchange, etc. were used as means of payment. The definition of the volume of money as the sum of gold coins and bank notes is arbitrary.

Samuel Johns Lloyd, George Ward Norman and Robert Torrens were the leading representatives of the currency school. Thomas Tooke, John Fullarton and James Wilson were the leading representatives of the banking school. The best known representatives were Torrens and Tooke respectively.

That David Hume's price-specie-flow mechanism needed correction, has been known at least since P. Samuelson (1980) (see Section 7.2). In fact, gold movements were during the period of the international gold standard relatively insignificant. They are not needed to establish an arbitrage equilibrium on the goods markets, as D.N. McCloskey and J.R. Zecher (1976, 370ff.) have pointed out. The required adjustments of the quantity of money were evidently achieved through variations in interest rates just as Tooke (1844, 124) surmised. To this extent Tooke was right, that the assurance of the convertibility of paper money at a fixed rate and the liquidity of the bank was "the most important consideration in the regulation of our banking system."

Tooke and other representatives of the banking school were, however, wrong in believing that the reflux principle would prevent the overissue of bank notes, provided they were issued only against short term loans to (productive) firms. We have already explained this point. The overissue of notes becomes noticeable only well after it has occurred (L. Robbins 1958, 128), i.e., after an outflow of gold.

The representatives of the currency school feared that the lagged regulation of note circulation would magnify, as we would say today, the amplitude of the business fluctuations (E. Wood 1939, 113).

They were convinced that a strict control of note circulation would mitigate price fluctuations. It is difficult to say whether this presumption is correct. It is, however, probably correct that the regulation of note circulation is less clearcut with a fractional gold standard than with a gold coin standard. The regulation of the supply of money of Peel's Bank Act of 1844, however, turned out to be much too rigid.

---

[10] The *currency principle* in R. Page's formulation (1826, 258) is: "That only is a sound and well regulated state of things, when no greater numerical amount of paper is in circulation than would have circulated of the precious metals if no paper had existed."

There were several financial crises in which the regulation of note circulation had to be suspended until the Bank of England changed to a more flexible policy.

The essential provisions of the Peel's Bank Act of 1844 were the following: the Bank of England was set up with two departments, the issue department and the banking department. Only the issue department issued bank notes. It could issue up to £14 million of notes against government bonds, the so-called fiduciary issue. The rest had to be covered by gold or silver, though the share of silver was limited to a maximum of one fifth of the total. The issue department had to buy gold at the fixed price of £3:17:9 per ounce, and to sell it at the price of £3:17:10. At the same time, the bank notes served as reserves of the banking department which dealt with the deposit and loan business of the Bank of England. The founding of new banks of issue was forbidden and the transaction volume of the existing banks of issue was limited to the existing volume of bank notes (see Encyclopaedia Britannica, Vol. 3, 1962, 98).

We summarize: with a commodity standard the value of bank notes in terms of gold may also be safeguarded when the notes are issued by a profit maximizing bank of issue, *provided* that the bank of issue must redeem its notes upon request at a fixed price into the money good. No particular reserve requirement or limitation of the lending business is required to safeguard the purchasing power of bank notes. The regulation of the issue business as in Peel's Bank Act of 1844 may stabilize fluctuations of purchasing power, though this cannot be asserted with certainty. The guarantee of the price target is with the commodity standard achieved in the simplest possible manner by the requirement that the notes must be redeemable into the money good at a fixed price. Due to the obligation to redeem the notes the bank of issue remains like any other private firm within the realm of civil or common law. Like any other economic unit it can be held to its promise. It has to perform or else it will be declared bankrupt. In other words, it has to obey to the same rules as any other economic agent of a free market economy. With a commodity standard, private banks may, therefore, fulfill the role of a central agent of a currency community.[11] It is conceivable that free banking stabilizes the supply of money.

8.5 The Banking Firm as the Central Agent of a Primary Currency Community: The Paper Standard

With a paper standard the means of payment issued by the central agent of a currency community are not redeemable. The central agent makes no promises of redemption when he issues his notes. The owner of a bank note cannot force the central agent to fulfill an outstanding debt, for example, through bankruptcy proceedings, because no such debt exists. As far as debts are concerned, the central agent stands outside the network of claims and obligations from exchange transactions which are characteristic of a market economy. Other legal obligations must take the place of enforcement by writ or bankruptcy. Thus, we must first of all clarify precisely

[11] Historical developments support this presumption. M. Friedman and A.J. Schwartz write on this point: "Many examples can be cited on fairly long-continued and successful producers of private moneys convertible into specie. We do not know, however, of any example of the private production of a purely inconvertible fiduciary money (except as temporary expedients, e.g., wooden nickles, clearing house certificates)..." M. Friedman and A.J. Schwartz (1986, 45).

what it is that the central agent promises with a paper standard. In general it promises to regulate payments and to assure the value of money. As far as safeguarding the value of money is concerned, it seems reasonable to introduce rules which limit the amount of the means of payment issued by the central agent directly or indirectly. The legal determination of a rule about the quantity of money is a "hard" regulation. Yet whatever the actual procedures, the required restrictions are inconsistent with the idea of competition among private firms: control by the incentive of making profits and the disincentives of enforcement by writ or bankruptcy.

In this section we shall assume from the beginning that we deal with a governmental bank of issue which issues non-redeemable bank notes. To simplify we do not consider bank deposits. The governmental bank of issue lends to the state and to private parties. Since in this case economic market considerations are of secondary importance we shall neglect credits from the bank of issue to private parties. With credits to the state there are in our case no diminishing returns to scale. The transactions function φ does not apply.

We start with a closed currency community. There are no competing suppliers of money. The governmental bank of issue is a perfect monopoly. The purchasing power of paper money is determined once the bank of issue fixes the nominal amount of paper money. Assume now that the bank of issue is initially obliged (in $t = 0$) to issue a certain amount of money M_0 in exchange for an interest free loan to the government. Will it subsequently as an institution of the Treasury leave the quantity of money unchanged? It would be able to make profits through a continuous expansion of the circulation of money. Why should the Treasury as the claimant of the profits of the bank of issue forego such a source of revenue? Such a course might be tolerable if, for example, the rate of inflation were stabilized at a certain low level. This might be the case if there were a rate of inflation which would maximize the bank of issue's profits and which were not too high. We shall discuss several aspects of this using our stationary overlapping generations model.

We ask first: what is the real profit of the bank of issue (= the state) from an increase of the quantity of money which is announced for tomorrow, if tomorrow the money is handed over exclusively to the state and not to the old generation, and if the state buys wheat with it out of current production?

The state profits tomorrow in real terms exactly as much as the old generation loses, i.e., the reduction in the amount of wheat which it experiences tomorrow for its nominally unchanged cash holdings M that it gave today.

The old generations loses:

$$\frac{M}{p_1} - \frac{M}{p_1(1+v)} = \frac{M}{p_1}\frac{v}{1+v} \tag{8-8}$$

or approximately (for small values of v)

$$\frac{M}{p_1}v \; .$$

We have here a kind of tax on real cash holdings. The rate of inflation is the tax rate, the real cash holdings are the tax base (M.J. Bailey, 1956). The real inflation profit in this connection can also be called "seigniorage"[12] (in German "Schlagschatz"), a concept, that was applied originally to the difference between the real and the nominal values of the newly issued coins by the state.[13] Now, the real cash holdings are a function of the money rate of interest i which in the present case is approximately higher by the rate of inflation v than the real rate of interest:

$$i = \rho + v \ .$$

If we neglect the Tobin effect the equilibrium value of ρ is in our model world constant. Hence the demand for real cash balances is solely a function of the rate of inflation v; thus it can be read in the form $L(v)$. With an increasing rate of inflation the planned real cash balances L decline as $L_v < 0$ (see Fig. 8-4).

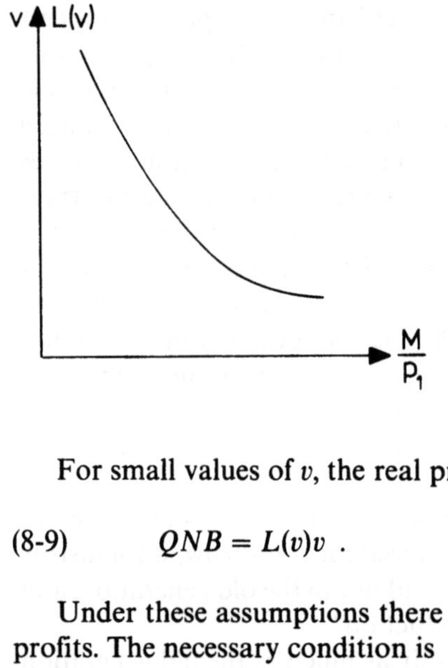

Fig. 8-4. The Demand for Real Cash Balances as a Function of the Inflation Rate

For small values of v, the real profit of the bank of issue is

$$QNB = L(v)v \ . \qquad (8\text{-}9)$$

Under these assumptions there exists a rate of inflation v which will maximize profits. The necessary condition is

$$v = -\frac{L}{L_v}$$

or

$$L_v \frac{v}{L} = -1 \ . \qquad (8\text{-}10)$$

[12] French "seigneurage": the mint privilege.

[13] In addition the central bank also earns interest which by analogy is counted also as part of the seigniorage of the monopolistic supplier of money (see R. Vaubel 1977, 440).

In words: the bank of issue, which under the given assumption wishes to maximize its real inflation profit or seigniorage chooses and announces in advance that rate of inflation v at which the elasticity of demand for money is -1 (M.J. Bailey 1956, 105). Mutatis mutandis this is also true for each succeeding period.

The level of the rate of inflation depends on the shape of the demand function for money $L(v)$. Here we leave the problem of the level of the rate of inflation and turn briefly to another important problem: will the bank of issue stick to its announced profit maximizing rate of inflation? Given the assumptions of our model the answer is: no! The bank of issue has no incentive to keep its word: rather it will be profitable to break its word at least from time to time and to expand the quantity of money faster than originally announced. This has been pointed out by L.A. Sjaastad (1976) among others. G.A. Calvo (1978) goes further. He shows that the standard solution of the optimal seigniorage problem is *time inconsistent*: it pays the bank of issue to announce today a certain finite rate of inflation. But as of tomorrow the old optimization considerations have become irrelevant. It now becomes profitable to realize the presently possible optimizing rate of inflation. However, with rational expectations and perfect information the users of money will already today count on this behavior of the bank of issue and hold correspondingly smaller cash balances. As G.A. Calvo (1978) shows, there is in this case only one possible solution: the bank of issue determines immediately the highest possible rate of inflation. If the currency order does not envisage any maximum rate of inflation the problem of an optimal inflation rate has no solution. This means, at least in the case of our model world, with a paper standard there exists no tendency toward the stabilization of the rate of inflation without a strict rule to which the bank of issue is tied. If both an upper as well as an lower limit to the allowed growth in the quantity of money are announced in advance, the rate of increase will eventually reach the upper limit.

We have thus far dealt with the case of a currency monopoly. How would competition among several government banks of issue help matters? Would competition among currencies contribute to stabilizing the value of money? In order to analyze this problem consider two governmental currency communities competing for their users. Following F.A.v. Hayek (1977, 1) we might, for example, imagine that both the French franc and the Deutsche mark are used equally in France and the Federal Republic of Germany as accounting units and as means of payment. Every person living in France or West Germany is free to use either currency for all purposes. Cartel agreements between the two banks of issue are precluded by effective international legislation. The ffr. and the mark are perfect substitutes. In this case the banks of issue have an incentive to solve the problem of time inconsistency. This they can achieve only by gaining the confidence of their prospective money users in their announced price targets. This is impossible without some use of real resources. Confidence is not a free good. With a commodity standard, for example, the confidence of the users of money is achieved by the promise of the central authority to redeem its notes at fixed rates and by keeping its promise. Keeping a reserve of the money good may be understood also as an investment in confidence building. With a paper standard the confidence must be guaranteed differently: by the particular form of the currency constitution, by a convincing public regulation of money, by the appointment of responsible persons to run the bank of issue – most of all by the bank of issue keeping its word promptly. B. Klein (1974) talks in connection with private currency competition of an investment in "brand name capital." This idea may be mutatis mutandis applied also to governmental central agents of currency communities.

We shall now discuss the competition of two governmental currency communities by means of the stationary overlapping generations model discussed in Section 7.4 assuming flexible exchange rates. Assume initially *perfect currency substitution*:[14] the currency with the greater announced rate of inflation will not be used. The central agents of the two currency communities will in this case – in analogy to the Bertrand-duopoly case – competitively reduce their rates of inflation to zero (not beyond zero because then they would make losses). This applies also to more than two currency communities.

May we, therefore, conclude that currency competition will safeguard the stability of the purchasing power of money? Such a conclusion would be premature. The actual purchasing powers of the two monies are not yet determined, only their rates of change ($=0$). With a single currency it suffices to assume that initially the quantity of money has a certain value $M = M_0$. This is not enough in the case of several currency communities under the assumption of perfect currency substitution. As stated, if the rates of inflation differ, only one currency will be used. This case reduces to the case of a single currency community. With equal rates of inflation we must reason as follows:

To start with, perfect currency substitution does not mean that the means of payment of different currencies are perfectly homogeneous and could not be distinguished. It means only that with equal rates of inflation individuals are indifferent in what proportions of the different currencies their cash holdings are kept. Even though the two monies are denominated in two different currencies, we can, with equal rates of inflation, specify only the total real demand function for money L, not the two functions L^1, L^2.

$$\hat{x}(i^1) - \left(\frac{M_0^1}{p^1} + \frac{M_0^2}{p^2}\right) = -y(i^1) \; , \tag{8-11}$$

$$L(i^1) = \frac{M_0^1}{p^1} + \frac{M_0^2}{p^2} \; , \tag{8-12}$$

$$i^1 = i^2 \; , \tag{8-13}$$

$$e = \frac{p^1}{p^2} \; . \tag{8-14}$$

Hence, we have with an unchanged number of variables one equation less than in the case of imperfect currency substitution discussed in Section 7.4; the system is underdetermined. Given the quantities of money M_0^1, M_0^2, this means that the prices p^1, p^2 and with them the rate of exchange e are not determined (L. Girton and

[14] Perfect substitution of the means of payment of different currencies.

D. Roper, 1981, 16). In words: the Bertrand-duopoly equilibrium previously described lacks any real anchoring. Result: with a paper standard, currency competition with perfect currency substitution (perfect substitution of the means of payment of different currencies) does not solve the problem of the indeterminancy of the purchasing power of money. Currency competition cannot in this case assure the stabilization of the purchasing power of money.[15]

We now turn to currency competition with *imperfect currency substitution.* We explain this heterogeneity of the two currencies by assuming that each bank of issue offers its means of payment jointly with different packages of services. As before, their local uses are identical. Even with equal rates of inflation the users of money will no longer be indifferent as to the two currencies. With different rates of inflation cash in both currencies will be held. There will, therefore, as a rule be two demand functions for money L^1, L^2 (above Section 7.4).

The two banks of issue are now a heterogeneous duopoly. Several solutions are possible, among them the Launhardt – Hotelling solution which we re-interpret as follows: the two banks of issue react to each other's rates of inflation by choosing alternatively that rate of inflation of their currency which maximizes their profit under the assumption that the announced rate of inflation of their opponent remains constant. They continue their adaptations until a pair of inflation rates v^{1*}, v^{2*} is reached at which both, acting autonomously, maximize their seigniorage. They now act to realize these rates of inflation which, incidentally, need not be the same.

In this case a stabilization of the rates of inflation consistent with self-interest of the individual banks is conceivable and perhaps also the competitive reduction of the equilibrium rates of inflation with an increasing number of competing currency communities. As for the rest, oligopoly theory also suggests other models, e.g., the model of price leadership. Competition with rates of inflation is probably more dangerous for the competing currencies than "quality competition," e.g., with different packages of services.

We have not yet dealt with two important aspects or problems. First, uniform currency areas are profitable and will arise even if governmental currencies compete freely with each other. Secondly, the connection between M and p is by no means as strict as assumed thus far.

Ad 1. Uniform currency areas are economically advantageous because money is a natural monopoly good. As a rule such areas will coincide with areas of the same legal order.

---

[15] If the means of payment of the two currency communities are indistinguishable, the well-known argument applies that with a paper standard currency competition will produce inflation without limit. See, e.g., M. Friedman (1960, 7), who writes on this point: "So long as the fiduciary currency has a value greater than its cost of production – which under conditions can be compressed close to the cost of the paper on which it is printed – any individual issuer has an incentive to issue additional amounts. A fiduciary currency would thus probably tend through increased issue to degenerate into a commodity currency – into a literal paper standard – there being no stable equilibrium price level short of that at which the money value of currency is no greater than that of the paper it contains. And in view of the negligible cost of adding zeros, it is not clear that there is any finite price level for which this is the case."

would be a buyer's market, with the banks offering that amount of deposits which is demanded. Our model changes, in this case, to:

(8-15) $$\hat{x}(\cdot) - \frac{M}{p} = -y(\cdot) ,$$

(8-16) $$L(\cdot) + \tilde{R}(\cdot) = \frac{M}{p} ,$$

(8-17′) $$\tilde{D}(\cdot) = \frac{\hat{D}}{p^s} , \quad \left(\hat{D} \equiv \frac{D}{1+d}\right) ,$$

(8-18) $$e = \frac{p^s}{p} .$$

The endogenous variables now look somewhat different in the commodity and the paper standard:

a) *Commodity standard*
   endogenous variables: $i, p^s, M, \hat{D}$
   exogenous variables: $p, d, e = 1$

b) *Paper standard*
   endogenous variables: $i, p^s, p, \hat{D}$
   exogeneous variables: $d, M, e = 1$.

It makes no difference whether we assume this or the preceding equilibrium case. In both cases the volume of deposits D is an endogenous variable. In analogy to Section 8.4 we can say that the deposit bank cannot create more deposits (= bank money) than its customers want to hold. This corresponds to the positions of the so-called "*New View*" of the theory of credit creation, such as that of J. Tobin (1963/1967). Banks are no different from other financial intermediaries. They equalize the portfolio preferences of two types of economic units: the final debtors who wish to expand their real resources beyond their monetary wealth and the final lenders who wish to hold their wealth in the form of money claims, including bank deposits. The banks are subject to the same limits of scale as the other financial intermediaries.

"Neither individually nor collectively do commercial banks possess the widow's cruse." (J. Tobin 1967, 5)

The argument reminds us of the position of Th. Tooke (above Section 8.4) applied to the volume of bank deposits. If the deposit rate of interest d is exogenously fixed at too low a level, bank deposits will lead to exactly the same problems of regulation as bank notes. The automatic reflux of deposits does not guarantee the purchasing power of bank money. The obligation of the banks to redeem deposits into central bank money is decisive. Steered by losses or gains of reserves they must try to find the equilibrium value of their deposits D. But since the connection between

D and p is not particularly close, the bank will have considerable room for play. An overexpansion of deposits may become evident only with a considerable lag. High deposit rates of interest and even financial crises may result. Mutatis mutandis this is true for too low rates of interest on deposits. The simplest solution consists in making the interest rate d flexible by insuring competition among the banks. (We do not model this case). If this is not done the following second-best solutions are conceivable:

1. The 100% *reserve requirement proposal*: the currency order prescribes for the banks a 100% reserve requirement on their deposits. In this case bank money can be issued only in exchange for central-bank money and vice versa. In principle we have here a solution which is analogous to the Peel's Bank Act. The 100% reserve requirement proposal was first made by H.C. Simons (1934). He justified it, however, in a different manner from ours. This proposal has so far not been applied.
2. The *minimum reserve proposal*: the currency order prescribes that the banks keep reserves equal to a fixed proportion r of their volume of deposits. In this case we have

$$\hat{D} = \frac{R}{r} \tag{8-19}$$

or, on the assumption of a fixed currency ratio c (the non-banks use currency in a fixed ratio c of currency in circulation (here central bank money) plus bank deposits:

$$\hat{D} = \frac{1-c}{c + r(1-c)} M \ . \tag{8-20}$$

The quotient on the right side of the equation is the "deposit multiplier", a variant of the well-known money multiplier. The central bank controls directly its volume of central bank money M and indirectly the volume of deposits $\hat{D}$ through the deposit multiplier. This practice was first introduced by the American Federal Reserve System, though for different reasons from the ones we have described, viz. in order to avoid bank failures through inadequate maintenance of reserves. Later, minimum reserve requirements were justified with the argument that in their absence banks could create unlimited amounts of bank credit or bank money. To safeguard the value of money, the bank would have to be required to keep minimum reserves. This is the "*Old View*" of the theory of credit creation.

Most modern central banks adhere to the minimum reserve proposals, although this is not without problems. The money multiplier is not the fixed magnitude, which we have assumed. If central-bank money and bank money are not perfect substitutes, which is probably the case, the regulation of the volume of bank deposits by means of a flexible deposit rate of interest d is probably the simplest and best solution.

The "*Old View*" assumes, however, that central bank and commercial bank monies are at the very least close substitutes, so that they can be viewed practically as a *single* money. Let us pursue this idea. For greater clarity we assume that central bank and commercial-bank money are perfect substitutes. The purchasing power of the two means of payment is in this case always the same, i.e., $p = p^s$. Thus, equation (8-18) disappears. Our initial model then looks as follows:

$$\text{(8-15)} \qquad \hat{x}(i,d) - \frac{M}{p} = -y(i)$$

$$\text{(8-21)} \qquad \begin{aligned} &L^0(i,d) + \tilde{R}(i,d) = \frac{M}{p} + \tilde{D}^s(i,d) \;; \\ &L^0(i,d) \equiv L(i,d) + D(i,d) \;. \end{aligned}$$

We now have only two equations for three variables i, d, M in the case of the commodity standard; and i, d, p with the paper standard. One of the variables must now be exogenously fixed. In this case the most reasonable choice is the deposit rate of interest d. If central bank and commercial bank monies are perfect substitutes their rates of interest must also be equal to each other, i.e., in this case equal to zero, since interest on cash is uneconomic. In a pure book money economy, however, a positive central bank rate of interest would be conceivable though it would have to be exogenously fixed.

With a *paper standard* we have thus

endogenous variables: i, p

exogenous variables: $M, d = 0$.

We shall consider only this case. If a solution exists, then for $\tilde{D}^s < L^0$ the values of i and p will be determinate. For $\tilde{D}^s > L^0$ difficulties arise. We argue as follows: since there is no reason to hold central-bank money, $M = R = 0$. The banks (assuming there are more than one as has been modeled here) will now offer as many deposits as are demanded. We have:

$$\text{(8-15')} \qquad \hat{x}(i) = -y(i)$$

$$\text{(8-21')} \qquad p\tilde{D}(i) = \hat{D} \;.$$

The price p can be determined only if the deposit volume $\hat{D}$ is nominally fixed exogenously. This can also be achieved indirectly by requiring minimum reserves. The banks are obliged to hold central-bank money in the volume

$$R = r\hat{D}$$

or to demand it respectively. The central bank offers the amount of central-bank money $R = M$. Hence

$$(8\text{-}22) \qquad \hat{D} = \frac{M}{r} .$$

The money market equation (8-21′) is then changed to

$$(8\text{-}21'') \qquad p\tilde{D}(i) = \frac{M}{r} .$$

The equilibrium value of i is then calculated with the equation for the goods market; the associated equilibrium value of p is calculated with the money market equation with a given M. Equation (8-22) corresponds to the elementary money multiplier without loss of currency (here of commercial bank money). We are now in the world of the "*Old View*" of the money creation theory, more precisely the "very old view" in the sense of the early theory of the creation of money of C.A. Phillips (1921) without loss of currency of the banking system.[16] If the central bank increases its supply of money by ΔM the banking system as a whole, here modelled as a single bank, will increase the volume of commercial bank money, which is here the total volume of money in the economy, by a multiple, namely

$$\Delta\hat{D} = \frac{1}{r}\Delta M .$$

$1/r$ is the money multiplier. The consequence is that when central-bank money and commercial-bank money are perfect substitutes it is not "superficial and irrelevant" (J. Tobin 1967, 5) to distinguish between banks and other intermediaries. A special public regulation of the banks, e.g., through minimum reserve requirements, is indictated.

The question whether minimum reserve requirements or other methods of regulating the banking system are needed in order to guarantee the value of money of a two-tiered currency community of the paper standard type continues to be discussed (see Suggested Readings to this chapter). Which regulation is preferred depends on one's view of how close substitutes central-bank money and bank money are. A comparatively close relationship between the two means of payment certainly does exist particularly when deposits are insured by the state. Therefore it makes a difference how we approach the problem. If we deal with it using a strictly microeconomic approach the New View is more plausible. With a macroeconomic approach it seems more appropriate to argue in the manner of the Old View. This may be the reason why the Old View of the theory of money creation continues to be used in textbooks on macroeconomics, despite all the criticisms. We tend more to the position of the New View.

The assumption of perfect substitutability between central-bank and bank money does not allow for the fact that each currency community must have a definite

[16] The usual assumption made by the theory of money creation of a currency ratio is inconsistent with the assumption of perfect substitutability of central bank and bank money. If there is a currency ratio both kinds of money would have to be non-homogeneous means of payment which again leads back to the "New View" of the theory of money creation.

money whose payment settles definitely all claims from a transaction. Definitive money is only the money of a primary currency community; bank deposits (secondary money) are redeemable money. This legal distinction requires at the same time a particular technical form of definitive money; the payment with definitive money must be suitable to settle a money claim "definitively" the moment the payment is made. With a payment in redeemable money, e.g., by check, this is not the case. The payee still has a money claim after the check has been credited to his account, viz. against his bank. In a futuristic electronic-data processing world there might be a definitive money in the form of deposit money. For example, each individual maintains an account with the central bank, which can be instantaneously transferred in the central bank's books by microwave transmission, the transfer being instantaneously confirmed by radio. Instead of central bank notes we now have individual accounts with the central bank. The central bank continues to be able to regulate the volume of money, i.e., the volume of deposits kept with it, and thus to determine the value of money – provided that money is actually kept in these accounts. Because of transaction costs it probably will be. If individuals still do not keep a certain amount on their central-bank accounts they may be obliged by law to do so. Such minimum reserve requirements need not, however, be required of banks. The requirements might be applied to any or all private households or firms. E.F. Fama has worked out this idea in a nice example:

> In a futuristic cashless world people know that there are many potential candidates for minimum reserve requirement: "In the end, the government imposes the reserve requirement on spaceship owners. Every spaceship owner has to keep a reserve of X 'units' with the central 'unit' authority. Since most citizens of the society desire the transportation services of private spaceships, the reserve requirement creates a real demand for 'units'. The government then renders the price of the 'unit' determinate by fixing the interest rate paid on 'units', perhaps at zero, and controlling the supply of 'unit' reserves." (E.F. Fama 1980, 56)

Thus far we do not live in such a perfect electronic data processing world. Even today definitive money with a paper standard consists of central-bank notes for which a specific demand exists which is clearly distinguishable from the demand for bank money. In order to safeguard the purchasing power of money in a two-tiered currency community with a paper standard the requirement of redeemability of bank money into central bank money is sufficient. Minimum reserves are unnecessary for this purpose. Neither are minimum reserves necessary to stabilize the development of the deposit volume of the banks. Flexible deposit rates of interest may be more suited to achieve this end than minimum reserve requirements combined with special measures of monetary policy. On this view it would suffice to keep the volume of central-bank money ("high-powered money") scarce and to regulate only its rate of growth. A quantity-of-money rule, if it is considered at all necessary, refers then to a concept of central-bank money.[17] The question, "Which

[17] A limitation of the nominal amount of central bank notes in circulation is theoretically sufficient. See on this point E.F. Fama (1983, 7): "... because currency and deposits are not perfect substitutes, there are simplified financial systems in which control of the supply of currency – either direct control of the supply of a fiduciary currency or passive control through the exchange policy of a commodity standard – is sufficient to control the price level."

monetary aggregate?" – which is posed with the technical development of payment transactions and the increasingly difficult distinction between the major money aggregates – disappears. But as already pointed out, we prefer the New View and its results which have a strong microeconomic orientation.

Typical macroeconomists, as, e.g., S. Fischer, who is no monetarist, differ.[18] M. Friedman (1959, 90) advocates basing monetary policy on a broader concept of the stock of money which includes, at the very least, cash and demand deposits of private non-banks.

Remarks on the History of Economic Thoughts:

First the theory of credit creation: it is opposed to the classic theory of credit intermediation (A. Wagner 1857, 30). According to the theory of credit creation banks are not merely credit intermediaries but credit, or deposit producers. H.D. Macleod (1863) is considered the father of this theory. In this view banks are in the position to *create* a multiple of the amounts deposited with them. The bank deposits function like money. "Deposits are nothing but bank notes in disguise." (Macleod quoted from V.F. Wagner (1937, 149)). The identification of central-bank and bank monies, which is not unimportant for the further development of the discussion, thus goes back to the beginnings of the theory of credit creation. C.A. Phillips (1921, 38f.) later made clear that with more than one bank the theory of credit creation applies only to the banking system as a whole, and not to individual banks. If the individual bank acquires additional reserves ΔR_i it can lend only $\Delta X_i = (1 - r)\Delta R_i$. With a constant reserve requirement r the banking system as a whole may create in addition

$$\Delta X = \frac{1-r}{r}\Delta R .$$

The stock of bank money increases in this case by

$$\Delta \hat{D} = \frac{1}{r}\Delta R .$$

The (bank) money multiplier is under these circumstances maximally equal to the reciprocal of the reserve requirement.

Philipps's distinction between credit creation by a single bank and by the banking system as a whole and his later multiplier formula are fundamental to most of the later contributions concerning the problem of multiple bank credit expansion, or money creation. J.H. Rogers (1933) and J.E. Meade (1934) first introduced the leakage of currency (the currency ratio) into the credit creation multiplier. The generally known present formula of the rigid money creation multiplier which E. Schneider (1962) for example derives in detail dates back to this period. The microeconomic foundation of the theory of the multiple creation of bank credit and bank deposits leads much later to the development of the modern theory of the bank as a firm. This approach is worked out in detail by D. Orr and W.G. Mellon (1961) whose

[18] S. Fischer (1983, 9) writes: "If other classes of assets were close substitutes for high-powered money, and if the composition of the aggregate of those assets and high-powered money fluctuate, it would be more stabilizing for the price level to target the aggregate than the stock of high-powered money. Such a monetary rule is an efficient way of adjusting the nominal supply of high-powered money for shifts in real demand."

central propositions we have explained in Section 8.2. The theory of the credit-creation multiplier becomes a theory of the supply of money, a new research field in the theory of money in which particularly K. Brunner (1961) has become widely known. See also A.J. Meigs (1962) and G.R. Morrison (1966). In the course of developing the theory of the bank as a firm it was attempted to show that the volume of business of a bank, as that of any other financial intermediary, was limited by diminishing returns to scale. *All* financial assets including demand deposits are faced with demand and supply functions which have interest rates as arguments. With the aid of these supply functions of and demand functions for financial assets the equilibrium rates of interest are simultaneously determined with the equilibrium prices on the goods markets. These considerations amount to the very old theory of credit intermediation (not to be confused with the Old View) which J.G. Gurley and E.S. Shaw (1960), J. Tobin and W.C. Brainard (1963/1967) among others have again put into the forefront. Tobin speaks of the "New View" of the theory of money creation. In clarifying Gurley and Shaw, D. Patinkin (1961, 116) writes: "... the necessary conditions for rendering a monetary system determinate are that there be an exogenous fixing of (1) some nominal quantity and (2) some rate of return."

The theory of multiple creation of bank credit and bank money as developed in the twenties and thirties raised at the same time the question of the possibilities of influencing the creation of bank money. J.M. Keynes (1930) puts this question at the beginning of his great work "A Treatise on Money" and emphasizes the possibility as well as the necessity of controlling the creation of bank money by the central bank (Vol. I, 29 f.). He advocates the introduction of legal minimum reserve requirements in Great Britain (Vol. II, 77) and pleads for the idea, which was new at that time, of monetary policy by changes in reserve requirements (Vol. II, 260). For Germany, F.A. Lutz (1936/1962, 100) demanded "a fixed proportion of cash holdings by the banks on which the central bank can rely" in order to enable it to influence the volume of deposit money. In common with the older authors, Lutz (1962, 29) considers central-bank and bank monies to be perfect substitutes. "The basic problem of the monetary order" consists for him in leaving the credit side of the banking system to competition among private banks; the money side, on the other hand, should be guided and guaranteed "from above." (F.A. Lutz 1962, 32)

Cash and bank deposits are also treated as equivalent in later discussions including M. Friedman (1960) and H.G. Johnson (1969). The turn comes with the cited works by Gurley and Shaw, Tobin and more recently E.F. Fama (1980, 1983). R.E. Hall (1982a) speaks in this connection of the "New Theory of Money." Strangely enough, none of these authors points out the need for a definitive money in order to ensure an automatically working "stop rule" in a market economy.

To summarize this section: a two-tiered currency community consists of a primary currency community to which a number of secondary currency communities have attached themselves. The means of payment of the secondary currency communities ("bank money") are redeemable into the definitive means of payment of the primary currency community ("central-bank money"). It is assumed that central-bank money and bank money are not perfect substitutes. The redemption requirement of bank into central-bank money is therefore probably sufficient to safeguard the purchasing power of bank money. Minimum reserve requirements are not necessary for that purpose. They are also not necessary for movements in the stock of bank deposits. It probably suffices to have flexible deposit rates of interest to achieve this end, which means competition among the individual banks on the "deposit side." It follows that with a paper standard the exogenous determination of the stock of central-bank money together with the requirement of redemption of bank money into central-bank money is sufficient to safeguard the value of the currency. Reserve requirements would be needed only if in the course of the automatization of payment transactions practically no central-bank money were used. The reserve requirements need not, however, necessarily be imposed on banks. From this point of view no special public regulation of commercial banks is necessary in order to safeguard the value of money.

8.7 Comments on the Public Regulation of Money and Banking

In this section we deal with some aspects of the public regulation of money and banking. We base our discussion on our preceding considerations. We deal first with primary, and then with secondary currency communities.

8.7.1 Public Regulation of the Central Agents of Primary Currency Communities (Central Banks)

Not only goods and services are produced, but also institutions. In each of these cases we may have natural monopoly goods. Such goods are characterized not only by decreasing average costs of production but also by decreasing user costs with an increasing number of users. In Section 4.6 we argued that primary currency communities are natural monopolies. They are also characterized by long-term business relationships (or relational contracts) between the users of money among each other and between the users of money and the central agent.

Both the natural monopoly of a primary currency community and the long-term business relationships of its members with the central agent suggest that public regulation of the monetary order is appropriate. In addition, the natural monopoly speaks for a public ordering of the monetary system.

The government supplies a uniform accounting and payment system (C. Menger 1909, 576) by determining, among other things, the unit of account and the issue of the means of payment (coins, bank notes etc.), but primarily by an appropriate shaping of civil law as far as money debts are concerned. Furthermore, the state takes care for the safeguarding of the money value by an appropriate money – guaranteeing part of the currency order.

This does not, however, require a perfect currency monopoly. The inhabitants of a currency area could and should be free to decide, in which currency they wish to conclude sales, labor, rental, loan and other contracts with other inhabitants of the same community. Currency competition is to some degree possible, even desirable, with governmental currency monopolies.

Moreover, governmental regulation of the monetary order and of the central agent does not mean that the central agency of the currency community must be run by the government. Quite to the contrary: here too the role of the state should be strictly limited. To illustrate our opinion we look now first at the commodity and then at the paper standard.

(a) With a *commodity standard* with a chartal constitution two extreme possibilities are conceivable:

- As means of payment are used full-bodied coins in addition to paper money etc.;
- As means of payment only token coins and paper money are used both redeemable into the money commodity (example: gold ingot standard).

We shall consider here only the first variant. Only full-bodied coins are definitive money. They are minted in a governmental mint. With a fully developed commodity standard, e.g., the gold standard of the German Reich before 1914, a mint law limits the minting of full-bodied and token coins.[19] The mint must adhere strictly to the mint law. The interest of the Treasury in seigniorage is here kept within strictly circumscribed limits. The mint is run like a public office. Under these conditions full-bodied coins become like natural monopoly goods. A mint working under governmental supervision which adheres to definite and easily controlled regulations is probably the economically best solution.

However, not only full-bodied coins are used with a commodity standard, but also bank notes without a 100% cover. May the issue of bank notes be left to private competing banks of issue? Can free banking be defended? In principle yes. First, banks of issue are, with a commodity standard, subject to the same stop rules as all other economic units. They promise to deliver something, namely to redeem their notes upon demand into full-bodied coins, and they are legally obliged to keep this promise. Second, the issue of notes of a bank, provided it takes place, in exchange for money debt claims against private parties, sooner or later runs into diminishing returns to scale. The real supply of bank notes of an individual bank of issue is therefore also limited with free banking (L.H. White 1984a, 14). This is certainly true for a commodity standard.

In the case we have just described, a bank of issue may, in analogy to a deposit bank, be considered as the central agent of a secondary currency community (see Section 8.6), provided that it applies the unit of account and the price target of another currency community already in existence. In contrast to the issue of deposits, there exists no direct market regulation for the issue of bank notes. The rate of interest for bank notes used as cash is fixed and equal to zero. Regulation works through the in- and outflow of reserves which may occur with considerable lags. Greater fluctuations of interest rates or prices and even financial crises may result.

Defenders of free banking such as L.H. White (1984a, 18) believe that with free competition of the note issuers the lags in adaptation will be less than with a note monopoly. Opponents of free banking, such as V.C. Smith (1936, 156), believe the contrary.[20] It is difficult to say who is generally right.

Historical examples suggest that free banking is not necessarily unstable.[21] It may also be argued that with free banking clearing houses fulfill important functions of the central bank. This at least has been said of the American clearing houses before the founding of the Federal Reserve System:

[19] See, e.g., the German Mint Law of 1. June 1909. (E. Heilfron 1911, 3ff.).

[20] V.C. Smith (1936, 155ff.) gives three reasons to oppose free banking:

1. Difficulties arising from the note circulation of banks that have defaulted.
2. The fluctuations in the quantities of money are bigger with free banking than with a note monopoly, and thus the business cycles more violent.
3. A financial crisis cannot be contained.

[21] L.H. White (1984a) and A. Rolnick and W. Weber (1983, 1984) argue in this manner. They refer to the Scottish and American free banking systems of the last century respectively. A. Rolnick and W. Weber (1983, 1984) and R. King (1983) also point out that only very few bank failures of the free banking period in the USA can be traced back to "wildcat banking."

"They admitted, expelled, and fined members; they imposed price ceilings, capital requirements, and reserve requirements; they audited members and required the regular submission of balance sheet reports. Finally, they issued money and provided a form of insurance during panics." (G. Gorton 1985b, 283)

It is conceivable that private central banks with a de facto note issue monopoly within a region develop out of clearing houses. This is the argument of Ch. Goodhart (1985, 76). In fact, however, central banks have not been the result of spontaneous market developments but of legislation. G.A. Selgin and L.H. White (1986, 25) stress this point:

"We find no market forces leading to the spontaneous emergence of a central bank, in contrast to the view of Charles Goodhart."

This may be so and probably applies also to the unification of the mint order over an area. In analogy to C. Menger's argumentation we are inclined to view the establishment of a central bank with note issue monopoly as a kind of "perfecting of the money and mint order by the state" (C. Menger 1909, 574f.).

With the establishment of a note issue monopoly the state must also limit the issue of notes. With a commodity standard it prescribes by law the price target (i.e., the standard of coinage) and obliges the central bank to redeem on demand and during business hours their notes into the money good at a fixed price. In such a system it is very simple for the public to see whether the currency authority has adhered to the price target. Normally no great reserves of the money good will be necessary. They are, however, advisable as measures for building confidence. An individual bank of issue may help itself, e.g., in case of an unusually high demand for gold, if it shows strength and in case of need refinances itself through other banks of issue. We shall return to this point further on when discussing the Bagehot rule. A completely rigid adherence to a rule such as envisaged by Peel's Bank Act has turned out not to be feasible.

Notes on the Free Banking Principle:

About free banking, particularly the free issue of notes, there are wildly different opinions, ranging from "free trade in banking is synonymous with free trade in swindling" to free trade in banking is natural and just (see A. Wagner 1857, 2). The view prevailed that the issue of coins and notes should be reserved for a governmental monopoly. M. Friedman (1960) has proposed and justified this view. More recently doubts have arisen both for theoretical and empirical reasons. We emphasize in this connection the works of L.H. White (1984a) and A. Rolnick and W.E. Weber (1983, 1984). White deals with the Scottish experiences with free banking which were extraordinarily good. The American experiences in this field were for a long time viewed as extraordinarily bad. Rolnick and Weber have shown that this is mistaken. In this connection the experiences with the American clearing houses which were reported in some detail by the contemporaries, e.g., J.G. Cannon (1910), are extraordinarily interesting. This literature has recently been rediscovered and been worked on (G. Gorton 1985a, R.H. Timberlake, Jr. 1984). As already mentioned the clearing houses did take over important functions of a central bank. Authors like R.H. Timberlake, Jr. (1984) question whether the Federal Reserve System really needed to be established. Did the Federal Reserve system actually contribute to stabilizing the American banking system? Experiences during the Great Depression do not indicate this (see M. Friedman and A.J. Schwartz 1963). However, the open market policy of the Fed seems to have at least contributed to dampening seasonal fluctuations of money market rates (J.A. Miron 1986).

Free banking was extensively practiced in Scotland and England in the 18th and 19th century and in the USA in the 19th century. As for the good experiences in Scotland, M. Friedman and A.J. Schwartz (1986, 50) point to the special circumstances which then obtained. Except for three specially privileged banks, the private banks of issue were institutions with unlimited liability of the partners. In addition, in a small and stable society such as Scotland the partners of the banks of issue were well-known personalities. For the rest, the system had access to the London financial market which performed central-bank functions for the Scottish banks of issue.

(b) With *a paper standard* the central agent of the primary currency community always occupies an exceptional position: it can now produce its own liquidity. Enforcement of judgement, or worse, bankruptcy proceedings cannot affect it. For this reason it must be subjected to another stop rule, e.g., a quantity of money rule. Such a requirement is incompatible with the idea of freely competing banks of issue. We therefore will not discuss this idea further. Public regulation of the bank of issue is unavoidable with a paper standard. This does not necessarily mean that the bank of issue has to be a government bank. Quite the contrary: as with the mints of the commodity standard, the incentives of property rights, particularly the profit motive, interfere with the organization of the monetary system, regardless of whether these rights are lodged in the state or in private parties. As we have shown in Section 8.5, unanticipated inflations may raise the profits of the bank of issue. The optimal plan of a bank of issue is, with a paper standard, dynamically inconsistent. The law must therefore ensure that the owner of the right to the residual profit of the bank of issue can make no or at least only a very minor profit by an inflationary expansion of the note circulation. This might be ensured by a strict rule to which the bank of issue must adhere, e.g., in analogy to the minting law under the commodity standard. A weaker rule would be merely to ensure the independence of the bank of issue from the state, i.e., from the demands of the government, of parliament or of its private share owners, without however tying the bank of issue to a strict rule. Neither the one nor the other is found in reality in pure form. There are no strict rules to which the bank of issue is tied with a modern paper standard, nor is there perfect independence of the bank of issue from the government or the parliament.

One reason why perfect independence is not granted to the bank of issue lies in the idea of the trade-off of the Phillips curve, i.e., in the ideal that there could be at least a temporarily successful employment policy.[22] In this view the central bank

[22] In this context a "conflict of targets," namely a stable currency vs. full employment, is regularly mentioned. K.v. Bonin (1979, 195f.) in a legal study of the independence of the Deutsche Bundesbank writes: monetary policy could never be neutral. The question really would be which social group would suffer more from unemployment, and which from inflation? Which group can influence monetary policy? Which group is powerless to influence it? With a politically independent central bank which in cases of conflict decides over the currency policy targets and thus exercises political power, it therefore would become necessary to enquire after the constitutional authority to exercise such governmental power (op. cit., 196). Bonin concludes that a politically independent central bank could not be justified constitutionally in any of the countries investigated: the Federal Republic of Germany, England, France. In the case of the Deutsche Bundesbank he thinks of the introduction of an absolute veto as can be exercised vis-à-vis the Banque de France by the French Government (op. cit., 240), i.e., to give up its independence. The author fails to see the problem that the government could in this manner realize inflation profits, otherwise he would have mentioned other ways of preventing a "governmental exercise of power" by the central bank: the legal or constitutional setting of fixed rules for the supply of means of payment. Bonin's contribution is a frightening example of the dubiousness of looking at economic problems from a purely legal point of view.

and the government should collaborate in their employment policies. Among other things this implies that the government might improve its chances for reelection by a mildly inflationary policy. This would be acceptable were it not for the possibility that the policy might raise prices but not employment.[23] On this supposition, which a model could formulate precisely, rests M. Friedman's famous argument:

Monetary policy "cannot peg the rate of employment for more than a very limited period" (M. Friedman 1968, 5).

There are, therefore, problems with limiting the independence of the central bank. But this is also true for complete independence, even if it were compatible with a democratic constitution. Also an independence guaranteed by the constitution could be abolished, in some countries, again by parliament. A central bank trying to defend its status might find itself compelled to friendly behavior vis-à-vis a qualificd majority of parliament.[24] Still easier is it to threaten the actual independence of the central bank if only a simple majority of parliament is required.[25]

"One strategy to survive can be, in this case, to induce the directors of the central bank to "voluntarily" transfer its profits to the government as in the case of the Fed (see W.F. Shugart and R.D. Tollison 1983). Political pressure may induce the central bank to levy an inflation tax – hidden by the demand for tolerable levels of the rate of interest which have risen through the need to finance budget deficits by credits (R.E. Weintraub, 1978, 356–362). Or it might be induced to use its instruments to produce a political business cycle." (P. Dittus 1987, 187; translated by W.F. St.).

In the final analysis everything depends on what importance the public places on the independence of the bank of issue. If it is viewed as quite important, a government interested in being reelected will not put any (obvious) pressure on the central bank. In such a case the safeguarding of the value of money will have priority. Such behavior might be supported by currency competition with imperfect currency substitution which we have described in Section 8.5. The fact must not be overlooked that even with a paper standard there is such a thing as a "key currency" (a world money) whose central agent decisively determines the general atmosphere of monetary policy. How strongly the aim of safeguarding the value of money is pursued with an international paper standard depends decisively on the behavior of the central bank of the international key currency (today the Federal Reserve Board in Washington). Its behavior is not only determined by the degree of independence from the government but also by the freedom of action of its managers and their preferences. No general answer can be given about the behavior of management. But if the behavior of the management cannot be predicted with some

---

[23] A theoretical model of these arguments is found in F.E. Kydland and E.C. Prescott (1977). In the meantime an extensive literature has arisen on this point. See P. Dittus (1987, Section 8.4), A. Cukierman (1986).

[24] P. Dittus (1987, Section 10.1) with a reference to A. Downs.

[25] The independence of the central bank is not a subject of discussion in the Federal Republic of Germany, at least not in public.

degree of assurance, at least their freedom of action should be strictly circumscribed.[26] A strict and thus clear tying to a rule is therefore preferable to a great latitude if only for this reason.

We summarize the preceding discussion: a uniform regulation of accounting and payments is for a primary currency community economically meaningful. So is a governmentally guaranteed order for safeguarding the value of money.

With a commodity standard the governmental guarantee is relatively easily done: the price target (the standard of coinage) is legally prescribed and the central bank is obliged to redeem its notes on demand into the money good.

There are some problems with the cover of the notes in circulation. Daily transactions need no great reserve requirements, though they may be advisable as a means to build confidence. A strict tying of the central bank to a strict note cover has not worked in practice. But it is not necessary in order to safeguard the value of money. The legal determination of the price target and the obligation to redeem the notes is with a commodity standard a sufficient regulation of the central bank.

With a paper standard there is no strict price target. However, the limitation of the quantity of notes that may be issued by the central bank remains (more generally: a limitation of the issue of the central-bank money). The following considerations suggest the desirability to limit the bank of issue rather strictly:

- The dynamic inconsistency of the optimal plan of the bank of issue;
- The possibility of putting pressure even on an independent bank of issue to gain an advantage (higher central-bank profits, or simply political advantages which may, however, have inflationary consequences);
- Uncertainty about the behavior of the managers;
- Constitutional doubts about the independence of a central bank with great freedom of action of its directors.

The rules to which the central bank is subject may be formulated more or less strictly. A very strict rule might look as follows: the bank of issue is obligated to change its volume of bank notes plus deposits lodged with it (the central bank) by an average weekly rate of $n \geqq 0$. With flexible exchange rates this is not impossible. If the bank of issue wants to, it can keep its volume of money literally hourly or at least daily at a certain level. In this case, however, it cannot simultaneously stabilize the money market rates in the short run. If the central bank wants to stabilize interest rates it must be satisfied with a less strict rule to control the volume of money fixed at an average annual rate (without time limitation).[27]

In the absence of clear-cut price targets the arbitrage transactions described in Section 4.3 may become profitable. If so they will tie down resources. This might be acceptable in order to stabilize the supply of money. This procedure, however, makes the monetary stabilization of the business cycle impossible, which in view

[26] "If one cannot predict well how administrators will exercise authority delegated to them, it is sensible to try to delegate as little as possible." (R. Schmalensee 1979, 62).

[27] This need not mean "for ever and ever." One could imagine the determination for a minimum number of years (say five or ten years), after which a special commission would investigate whether and, if so, how the quantity-of-money target should be corrected.

of the present discussion is not necessarily a disadvantage. The role of the central bank as a lender of last resort with which we will deal in the next section, must, however, not be interfered with. The management of the central bank must have an appropriate freedom of action.

The working of the international paper standard is still terra incognita. As we have shown in Chapter 5, its real anchoring is unavoidable. If a return to the international gold or gold exchange standard is not contemplated then there is no choice but to ensure the credibility of the real anchoring of the paper standard. An individual nation may have unlimited confidence in its own politically independent central bank. An analogous worldwide confidence into the currency authority of a world money (today the Federal Reserve Board in Washington) is not conceivable without tying it to a clear rule. But worldwide confidence in the world money is essential if free trade and free international capital movements are to be maintained. The domestic economy cannot be uncoupled from the world economy simply by flexible exchange rates, particularly not from the effects of the monetary (and fiscal) policy of the dominant economy.

8.7.2 Public Regulation of the Central Agents of Secondary Currency Communities (Commercial Banks)

Unlike primary currency communities, secondary currency communities are not natural monopolies. The latter are characterized by competing commercial banks which fill the spaces left by the currency order of the primary currency community to which they are attached. The value of their money is safeguarded by their promise to redeem their money into central-bank money at a fixed rate of exchange $e = 1$ together with the self-interest of a sound business policy. Each commercial bank chooses a bundle of deposit, reserve and loan volumes which maximizes its profit with the given goods prices p, and the loan and deposit rates of interest i and d (see Section 8.2). Beyond this, the banking firm meets its special credit losses and interest risks by an appropriate capital reserve, possibly expanded to a personal liability of the business partners. If we assume nothing else then we have, in Bagehot's words, a "natural banking system,"

"... that which would have sprung up if Government had let banking alone." (W. Bagehot 1873/1962, 32)

The "natural banking system" consists of many banks with the same or not too different volumes of business. Each bank keeps its own (gold) reserve

"with the penalty of failure before them if they neglect it" (Bagehot 1873/1962, 160).

There is no central bank to which the commercial banks leave the holding of gold reserves as under a gold standard. Bagehot believed that in such a banking system substantial bank failures would be unlikely (op. cit. 53).

Unlike Bagehot we believe as already indicated, that there are "natural" reasons why a bank of issue develops.[28] This is our starting point. We assume further that only the central bank is allowed to issue notes, regardless of whether we deal with a commodity or paper standard.

There are several reasons given for the public regulation of commercial banks. Our interest is directed particularly to the problem of safeguarding the purchasing power of central-bank money and of bank money. We shall deal primarily with these problems in the rest of this section.

(a) The Relationships Between the Central Bank and the Commercial Banks

The question of how the relation between commercial banks and the central bank is to be regulated requires an answer to the following question: how close is the substitution between the means of payment of the two institutions? If central-bank and commercial-bank money are, for all practical purposes, perfect substitutes, then the safeguarding of the purchasing power of central-bank money justifies fixing the deposit rate of interest d exogenously and requiring the commercial banks to keep minimum reserves with the central bank (see above Section 8.6). If, however, they are not perfect substitutes no particular decisive limitation of free banking can be justified. Quite the contrary: instead of limiting free banking, competition among the banks should be stimulated. The question to what extent central-bank and commercial-bank money are substitutes can be answered by our every day experience: they are not *perfect* substitutes. If they were perfect substitutes the potential payee would be indifferent whether he is paid in cash or not. This is not the case universally. With a paper standard the two means of payment are not even approximately equal; the one is definitive money, the other is not – an essential qualitative difference.

We believe that the possibilities for an institutional solution of the problem of ensuring the purchasing power of money must be thought through on a micro-economic level, and that for this reason the demands for cash and for bank money should be clearly distinguished. The guarantee of the purchasing power of money does not require minimum reserves. But neither is it necessary to require the banks to keep only deposits consisting of money claims redeemable into cash. It is irrelevant for the purchasing power of bank money how the banks finance the volume of their loans, whether by money debts or by shares (analogously to the shares of mutual funds).[29]

---

[28] With non-interest bearing reserves it pays in general to pool the reserves if the assumption is reasonable that the individual deposits and withdrawals of the individual banks are stochastically independent of each other. (P. Dittus 1987, Section 4.2 n. 30).

[29] The West German credit law (Kreditwesengesetz) on the other hand obliges the banks in its Article 3 no. 3 to pay in cash. The offical justification (see N. Juchem 1983, 42) argues along the lines of the Old View of the theory of money and credit creation. The justification speaks of a prohibition of a "misuse of the possibility of pure book keeping transactions to grant credits." If entrepreneurs were not obliged to hold some liquid reserves against their obligations, they would have "a particularly high expansion multiplier" (= credit creation multiplier). However, the justification continues rather strangely: "The minimum reserve requirements do not guarantee that these particular dangers to monetary policy can be neutralized. For the reserve requirements are formulated for credit institutions with the usual business in mind ..." (But, if one wanted to follow this train of thought, this would really require higher reserve requirements for mutual funds rather than the prohibition of this new form of deposit).

If bank money exists, there will as a rule also be a problem of a cash reserve. If the commercial banks can, as we assume, refinance themselves at any time with the central bank, then they will need a relatively small cash reserve. But they must in this case be able to rely on the central bank furnishing them with cash upon demand.

It is in this connection important to see that no classical individual contracts were concluded between the central bank and the commercial banks, but instead relational contracts which are part of longterm business relationships (see above Section 3.4). It is characteristic of relational contracts that numerous points of the contract remain open. Not all future eventualities are specified. The parties agree however on the general framework (the "constitution") of their business relationships. In this connection general rules of behavior play a role such as, for example, the so-called Bagehot rule which characterizes the relational contract between the central bank and the commercial banks. This rule refers to the behavior of the central bank and is: "lend freely" during a panic (W. Bagehot 1873/1962, 23). More generally, it is the obligation of the central bank to ensure orderly markets by being the lender of last resort. In this manner it can prevent the indefinite fall of the quotations for fixed interest bearing long term papers.[30] According to the Bagehot rule the central bank buys or sells only such assets which are normally safe.[31] The monopoly position of the central bank, however, suggests that the Bagehot rule does not become "self-enforcing" simply through the self-interest of the contracting parties. Public regulation in the interest of all money users including the public at large is indicated. For this reason we shall return to this topic in the next section which deals with the relation between commercial banks and the public.

The newer literature has a broader interpretation of the concept of the lender of last resort than Bagehot. The extreme interpretation is that the central bank has the tacit responsibility to provide all commercial banks in difficulties with central-bank money under all circumstances. This, however, raises the problem of moral hazard: the commercial banks will be induced to make particularly risky loans with chances for great profits and keep their own capital at a relatively low level.[32] Public regulation of commercial banks is inescapable.

[30] See P. Dittus (1987, Section 4.4): "It is the task of the lender of last resort to buy otherwise good assets during a run at a price which lies above the quoted price ..." (translated by W.F. St.).

[31] See W. Bagehot (1873/1962, 25): "A panic, in a word, is a species of neuralgia, and according to the rules of science you must not starve it. The holders of the cash reserve must be ready not only to keep it for their own liabilities, but to advance it most freely for the liabilities to others. They must lend to merchants, to minor bankers, to 'this man and that man,' *whenever the security is good.* In wild periods of alarm, one failure makes many, and the best way to prevent the derivative failures is to arrest the primary failure which causes them." (Italics added).

[32] Thus D.W. Diamond and P.H. Dybvig (1983, 417) write: "If the lender of last resort were *always* required to bail out banks with liquidity problems, there would be perverse incentives for banks to take on risk, even if bailouts occurred only when many banks fail together. For instance, if a bailout is anticipated, all banks have an incentive to take on interest rate risk by mismatching maturities of assets and liabilities, because they will all be bailed out together." (Italics in the original).

(b) The Relationships Between Commercial Banks and the Public

There are also long term business relationships between the commercial banks and the public of the sort we have termed "relational contracts." Unlike the central bank, however, commercial banks are not monopolies. Nor is it particularly difficult or expensive for the customers of a commercial bank to change banks. Why then is a public regulation of commercial banks necessary? The literature gives numerous answers. J. Welcker (1978, 18f.) lists, e.g., protection of the depositors, ensuring the working of the credit business, protection of the consumers, promoting the sale of government bonds, structural policy, enforcing of central bank policy, ensuring the continued existence of the banks, prevention of abuses of the credit economy which might make the ordinary banking business more difficult or which might bring about considerable disadvantages for the economy as a whole. However, all these arguments may be, *mutatis mutandis* applied equally well to all other businesses. There is perhaps just one exception which is not included in the list just given but is implied in it. The problem is to prevent a general run on the banks with its high social cost in the wake of refusing the renewal of loans and interrupting the course of production.

Manufacturing enterprises and other non-banks may also experience a run of their creditors. Banks however are distinguished from non-banks because they are subject more than others to a "me-first" behavior of their creditors. (D.R. Fischel, A.M. Rosenfield and R.S. Stillman (1987))

The manner in which the run on one bank might spread to others can be imagined as follows. There is a run on one bank. As a result, non-banks keep more cash reserves. If the central bank does not supply the additional cash demanded the money rate of interest will rise. This will lead to an increase in the medium and long-term rates of interest. The stock exchange quotations of bank assets decline, with the result that there are further bank insolvencies, etc. The increasing number of bank failures will affect not only the immediately affected bank users. There will be a general collapse of production with the consequence of further bank failures. This may be imagined as follows: with the increase in the demand for cash by banks and non-banks, the supply of money, i.e., of cash plus bank deposits decreases ceteris paribus. The unexpected decline in the supply of money leads to an increase in unemployment and a reduction of total economic output.

A run on the banks is the result of self-fulfilling expectations. It can be avoided only by measures which ensure that the depositors will not fear a run. Contrary to Bagehot's ideas no bank can do this by itself even with the most conservative management. A simple supervisory authority doesn't do much good either.[33] The

[33] Banking supervision is worthless against runs because a run may also occur for reasons which have nothing to do with the situation of a particular bank or banks as such. On this point D.W. Diamond and P.H. Dybvig (1983, 410) write: "This could be a bad earnings report, a commonly observed run at some other bank, a negative government forecast, or even sunspots. It need not be anything fundamental about the bank's condition. The problem is that once they have deposited, anything that causes them to anticipate a run will lead to a run. This implies that banks with pure demand deposit contracts will be very concerned about maintaining confidence ..."

Bagehot rule and deposit insurance, among other things, have been successful in this direction.

Thus the Bagehot rule may be viewed as an implicit contract between the central bank and the commercial banks. The central bank undertakes to see to orderly money markets especially in critical times; the commercial banks undertake to keep an adequate amount of "eligible" assets suitable for rediscounting at the central bank, and to keep an adequate amount of capital. But is this implicit contract likely to be realized?

Some doubt is in order. On the one hand there is a strong central bank which can afford to disregard the Bagehot rule. Its own existence is not threatened by a general banking crisis. On the other side there are many commercial banks. The quality of their assets and the extent of their capital basis is subject to the free rider problem. Some form of regulation is indicated, be it private or public. R.G. Holcombe and L.P.H. Holcombe (1986) hypothesize that (private) regulation will appear wherever it is needed. The American example of clearing houses might fit this picture. Private regulation of commercial banks might possibly be sufficient, but it would be difficult to make it consistent with a monopolistic central bank. Regulation through a governmental central bank might also be sufficient, but at critical times commercial banks might doubt its willingness to help out, thus leading to a general run.[34] Nor is it necessarily true that the public regulation of banks has a beneficial influence on their business activities.[35]

Unlike the Bagehot rule, *deposit insurance* requires more than merely a relationship between banks and their customers. It requires cooperation of the otherwise competing commercial banks, i.e., the formation of solidarity communities among banks (Solidargemeinschaften) or the founding of private or public insurance firms. This raises considerable problems of information, which may be the reason why there is no private deposit insurance. Besides, it is doubtful whether private deposit insurance, deposit guarantee funds or solidarity communities can prevent a bank collapse in serious cases. They are themselves part of the endangered system. Depositors might therefore not be completely convinced. The state with its taxing power is more likely to be in the position to stabilize the expectations of the depositors. Note: in both cases problems of competition policy arise which for a public deposit insurance can be handled by legal means – at least on a national plane. On an international scale appropriate international agreements concerning competition among banks are required.

---

[34] See D.W. Diamond and P.H. Dybvig (1983, 417): "A run can even occur in response to expectations about the general willingness of the lender of last resort to rescue failing banks, as illustrated by the unfortunate experience of the 1930s when the Federal Reserve misused its discretion and did not allow much discounting."

[35] For whatever reasons, the own capital ratio to all assets of German banks has steadily fallen. They were:

1872	45%
1900	34%
1927	10%
1960	4%
1975	3%

(see J. Welcker 1978, 67).

From the standpoint of competitive policy solidarity agreements among banks aimed at assuring their mutual deposits are obviously questionable. This is true, e.g., for the Federal Republic of Germany with its various insurance arrangements of the credit unions, saving banks and the private banking business. (For a survey, see H. Bieg 1983, 108 ff.). Public deposit insurance does not exist in the Federal Republic of Germany. Private banks, e.g., have agreed upon the institution of deposit insurance fund with the *Bundesverband Deutscher Banken e.V.* However, "the deposit insurance fund works like a market access cartel" (V. Ronge 1979). The dangers to competition are obvious. W. Möschel (1975, 1029) regrets for this reason that the legislator has declined a legal regulation.

From the point of view of stabilizing expectations, public deposit insurance may have an advantage over the Bagehot principle. For the depositors the quality of the bank assets becomes irrelevant. The disadvantage is that deposit insurance or other deposit guarantee systems raise the moral hazard problem: the commercial banks will accept greater risks. The moral hazard problem may be reduced by public regulation but it cannot be eliminated altogether. It consists in financial intermediaries being specialists in the field of initiating and supervising loan contracts. A public authority might not be in the position to acquire as good information about the debtors of the commercial banks as the banks themselves. It will hardly be in a position to examine the specific information of the commercial banks of their customers, particularly as part of this information consists in "personal knowledge" of bank employees which is difficult to transmit even with the best of intentions. This is a special case of "specific information" (O.E. Williamson 1985b, 53).

We repeat: the specific problem with banks is the danger of a general banking crisis. The ensuing collapse in production has high social cost.[36] The only public interest in a special regulation of banks is the avoidance of this danger. On the other hand the social aspects of deposit insurance are not specific to banks. In a social market economy it can be dealt with in other ways, e.g., by guarantees adressed directly to economically weaker persons. There exists no "birth right" of the citizen in the absolute guarantee of his deposits (J.H. Kareken 1983, 198).

Whatever the method of stabilizing the expectations of the depositors, competition among commercial banks should not thereby be limited, or any limitation should be minimized. This is particularly true for the deposit business. The flexibility of the deposit rate of interest, whose importance for the guarantee of the value of money in an economy with commercial banks we have learned in Section 8.6, should be preserved. But competition is necessary not only for its regulating function but for its incentives as the stormy development of financial innovations shows, which the individual national banking systems will hardly be able to avoid for ever. Finally the banking system should not be excepted from the distributional effects of competition.[37] A national banking system which is protected from foreign

[36] On this point, see B.S. Bernanke's (1983) study on the connection between financial crises and aggregative economic activity. His basic hypothesis is: "... because markets for financial claims are incomplete, intermediation between some classes of borrowers and lenders requires nontrivial market-making and information gathering services. The disruption of 1930–33 ... reduced the effectiveness of the financial sector as a whole in performing these services. As the real costs of intermediation increased, some borrowers (especially households, farmers and small firms) found credit to be expensive and difficult to obtain. The effects of this credit squeeze on aggregate demand helped convert the severe but not unprecedented downturn of 1929–30 into a protracted depression." (op. cit., 257)

[37] For a survey, see R.A. Posner (1974).

competition such as that of the Federal Republic of Germany is incompatible with the increasing internationalization of economic life. It is also incompatible with an adequate development of national financial markets. All this requires a thorough rethinking.

Notes on Banking Regulation in the Federal Republic of Germany:

The history of public regulation of the German banking system reads like a textbook example of the "economic theory of public regulation" in the version of G. Stigler (1971, 3).

At first, regional interest-rate cartels developed. In 1884 the first interest-rate cartels among private banks were organized in Berlin. This was followed by other regional agreements in Cologne in 1908, Mannheim 1909, Munich 1909 and elsewhere. In 1913, a cartel about all bank conditions was founded which covered the whole area of the Reich (see W. Möschel 1972, 329f.). "The agreement regulated the acceptance of last day of month money, the level of the acceptance and credit provisions and the percentage of the value of shares that would be required as security. In addition the agreement dealt primarily with interest conditions." (op. cit. 330f; translated by W.F. St.)

Bank supervision was introduced in Germany by emergency decree only in 1931 after the banking crisis. Among other things the credit business was obligated to come to agreements about debit and credit rates of interest and other loan conditions. In January 1932 the top organizations of the credit institutions agreed upon an umbrella agreement which referred to agreements about debit rates of interest, credit rates of interest and so-called agreements about competition. These cartels were subject to several changes and finally abolished in 1967.

The abolition of the forced cartels has, however, not led to commercial banks competing for depositors as in the USA with interest rates on deposits while charging no or neglible fees for paper work. There is an exemption for banks in the German antitrust law (see Article 102 of the Gesetz gegen Wettbewerbsbeschränkung). We have already pointed to the access limitations inherent in the collective deposit selfinsurance of banks in Germany.[38]

The Reichsgesetz über das Kreditwesen (KWG) (Reich law concerning the credit business) of Dec. 15, 1934 became law Jan. 1, 1935. The KWG of 1961 took over large parts of its basic ideas. This has been justified by the argument of the susceptibility of confidence peculiar to the banking business as we have pointed out. W. Möschel (1972, 233) writes on this point:

"The law does not in principle interfere directly with the business decisions of the credit institutes and the forms of the individual bank transactions. It works rather by specifying, on the one hand, general conditions for the internal structure and business practices of credit institutions, corresponding obligations to publicize their conditions and actions and, on the other hand, possibilities for the supervising authority to intervene. This means that with the regulation of capital and liquidity principles according to Articles 10, 11 KWG, which can be understood as the allocation of specific quotas and business volumes, one of the most important questions of substantive bank supervision has been transferred to an administrative level. Probably the most important intervention into the business policy of the credit institutions has been made possible by legislative regulation by the authority of Article 23.1 KWG about the regulation of interest and commission rates since 1971. This authority has not been exercized since 1967. The Bundesbank has become involved in many ways with the supervision of banks. The Federal Minister of Economics may issue specific legal orders which serve the general order of the credit business. This power has been partly transferred to the Federal Office for Credit Supervision (Bundesaufsichtsamt für das Kreditwesen). In the event of catastrophes of the order of the banking crisis of 1931, the Federal Government has legal power to take remedial action (Articles 47, 48, KWG: moratorium, closure of banks and stock exchanges, regulations of renewed openings.)" (translated by W.F. St.)

---

[38] W. Möschel (1972, Chapter 4) offers a detailed theoretical analysis on competitive assumptions. He analyzes the economic workability of competition for the different banking activities (credits, investment opportunities for money, money transactions and other service functions) from the standpoint of regulatory, incentive, and distributional functions of competition and concludes that they would work.

As of Jan. 1, 1985, an amendment to the credit business law has become law (Gesetz über das Kreditwesen as reformulated of Dec. 20, 1984, BGB I.I, p. 1693). The central points of this amendments are the expansion of the regulations concerning capital, the introduction of credit consolidation, changes in the area of large credits and changes about the limitation of borrowers (W. Werner 1985, 237).

We summarize our considerations about the public regulation of commercial banks: in order to safeguard the value of money no special regulation of banks is needed. There is a clear distinction between the demand for central-bank and commercial-bank money. Minimum reserve requirements cannot be justified for this reason. This is also true for all other direct intervention by the central bank into the business activities of the banks (example: security of credits). Neither must banks be required to issue only claims redeemable into cash. Safeguarding the value of money does not justify limitations on free banking. On the contrary free banking should be encouraged. Of all the other arguments in favor of the public regulation of banks only one argument is tenable: that a general run on the banks with its consequent social cost must be avoided under all circumstances. However, bank regulation does not suffice for this purpose. The primary requirements are measures which will stabilize expectations as the institutionalization of the Bagehot rule or the creation of governmental deposit insurance. In this case bank regulation becomes a supporting actor.

One should not overestimate in this connection the possibilities open to a bank supervisory authority. It cannot get a complete view into the information of the banks about their borrowers, let alone acquire better information. The banks therefore have considerable elbow room for opportunistic behavior. The informed public knows this and will remain sceptical.

Finally, the effect of bank regulations restricting competition among banks has its own problems. In contrast to traditional wisdom, the limitation of competition among commercial banks does not contribute to safeguard the value of money; quite the contrary. Nor is limitation of competition needed to prevent a general run. It uncouples the domestic banking system unnecessarily from technical and organizational progress which develops on international financial markets and gives away chances of growth. A national banking system isolated from the rest of the world is incompatible with the increasing internationalization of economic life.

* * *

We have come to the end of our discussion of monetary theory. Models of general equilibrium theory served us as a reference system. We used the approach of the new institutional economics to describe the world of exchange with the use of money. The concepts of a currency community and a currency order played a central role in this.

We developed the concept of a *currency order* in its two basic forms, the commodity and the paper standard, and in three steps: for a world

- Without transaction costs and thus without cash (Chapter 5);
- With transaction costs and cash but without commercial banks (Chapter 7);
- With cash and bank money (Chapter 8).

We used the concept of a *currency community* in two variants: the primary and the secondary currency community. Currency competition among secondary currency communities such as commercial banks is without exeption economically justified. Currency competition among primary currency communities is, on the other hand, not justifiable without some limitations. A primary currency community is a "natural monopoly." Public regulation is indicated and practiced. We deal therefore in general with governmental money. Just the same, some competition among national currencies exists and is desirable. It provides an incentive for individual governments to try to maintain orderly currency conditions. There is also some tendency to develop a world money, i.e., an "ultimate" primary currency community. At the time of the gold standard the ultimate money was gold by weight (a natural means of payment). Today, with an international paper standard and largely flexible rates of exchange, it is on many markets the US dollar.

With an international commodity or paper standard with fixed exchange rates there arises the problem of a lender of last resort and with it that of the public regulation of the international monetary order. This is not so for the international paper standard with flexible exchange rates provided we live in a world of perfectly neutral money. But this is not the case. The national commodity communities therefore cannot completely isolate themselves by flexible exchange rates from the rest of the world as far as goods prices and money rates of interest are concerned. This is particularly true about isolating themselves from a dominant economy whose money is as a rule also the world currency. Since the national central banks of open economies must cooperate if they wish to maintain stability, an international paper standard with fixed exchange rates is preferable to the present system of flexible dollar rates. It would help to establish a clear-cut economic relationship. However a truly effective international regulation of the producer of the world money, the Fed, is not feasible. Creations like the ECU or the special drawing rights of the International Monetary Fund can hardly drive out a world money which has developed in a "natural" way. How well an international paper standard with fixed exchange rates works depends therefore on how clear and firm the rules are to which a world currency authority is tied. If a return to the international gold or gold exchange standard is not desired (with an unlimited obligation of the world money producer to redeem its money) there is no other choice but to insist on a credible limitation of the quantity of world money. One way might be, for example, to announce a target for the growth of central-bank money which is sure to be adhered to for several years. The disadvantage of this system is that it is very abstract and politically difficult to realize. Its advantage is the independence from the accidents of the international gold market.

Gold or paper? We incline toward the latter. The urge towards the international paper standard corresponds to our urge to control our own lives, to our wish to dominate nature, to the pecularities of our social life and, ironic though it may sound, to our desire for greater security. In theory the paper standard is superior to the gold standard. What is true in theory should also be true in practice given the right way of going at the problem. As for the necessity of international cooperation in case of an international paper standard Knut Wicksell's final sentences of his "Interest and Prices," first published in 1898, still apply today: viz. "That its realization [of an international paper standard] depends on international co-operation, which would have to be both permanent and somewhat thorough in nature, is to my mind a positive recommendation. I joyfully welcome every fresh step towards the uniting of nations for economic or scientific ends, for it adds one more safeguard for the preservation and strengthening of that good on which the successful attainment of all other goods, both material and immaterial, ultimately depends – international peace." (K. Wicksell 1936, 196).

Appendix to Chapter 8

1 *Profit Maximization of the Bank Assuming Cost of Obtaining Reserves (Section 8.2)*

The optimization problem is:

$$\text{Max} \quad QB = p_1(1+d)\tilde{D}^s + p_1(1+i)\tilde{B}_B + p_1\tilde{R} - p_1 s \sum_{\tilde{X}_j > \tilde{R}} (\tilde{X}_j - \tilde{R})\pi(\tilde{X}_j)$$

$$\text{s.t.} \quad \varphi(\tilde{D}^s + \tilde{R}, \tilde{B}_B) = 0\,;$$

$$\tilde{D}^s \leqq 0\,, \quad \tilde{R} \geqq 0\,, \quad \tilde{B}_B \geqq 0\,.$$

We take the derivatives of the Lagrange equation with respect to $\tilde{D}^s$, $\tilde{R}$, $\tilde{B}_B$ and get the following necessary conditions:

$$(1) \qquad p_1(1+d) - \lambda\varphi_1 = 0$$

$$(2) \qquad p_1(1+i) - \lambda\varphi_2 = 0$$

$$(3) \qquad p_1 + p_1 s \sum \pi(\tilde{X}_j) - \lambda\varphi_1 = 0\,.$$

Division of (2) into (1) results in:

$$(8\text{-}1) \qquad \frac{\varphi_2}{\varphi_1} = \frac{1+i}{1+d} \quad \left(= -\frac{d\tilde{D}^s}{d\tilde{B}_B}\right).$$

Division of (3) and (1) results in:

$$(8\text{-}3) \qquad d = s \sum_{\tilde{X}_j > \tilde{R}} \pi(\tilde{X}_j)\,.$$

2 *Determination of the Optimal Intertemporal Consumption and Investment Plans of the Consumer: The Direct Utility Approach (Section 8.3)*

The real values of cash and bank money holdings of the consumer enter the utility function. The optimizing problem is

$$\text{Max} \quad U = U\left(x_1, \frac{M}{p_2^+}, \frac{D}{p_2^+}, x_2\right)$$

$$\text{s.t.} \qquad p_1 x_1 + M + \frac{D}{1+d} + \frac{B_H}{1+i} = p_1 \bar{x}_1^1$$

$$p_2^+ x_2 = M + D + B_H + QB \ .$$

We simplify by consolidating the restrictions:

$$p_1 x_1 + \frac{p_2^+}{1+i} x_2 + \frac{i}{1+i} M + \frac{i-d}{(1+d)(1+i)} D = p_1 \bar{x}_1^1 + \frac{QB}{1+i} \ .$$

Taking the derivatives of the Lagrange equation with respect to x_1, x_2, M, D yields as necessary conditions:

$$(1) \qquad U_{x_1} - \lambda p_1 = 0$$

$$(2) \qquad U_{x_2} - \lambda \frac{p_2^+}{1+i} = 0$$

$$(3) \qquad \frac{1}{p_2^+} U_{(M/p_2^+)} - \lambda \frac{i}{1+i} = 0$$

$$(4) \qquad \frac{1}{p_2^+} U_{(D/p_2^+)} - \lambda \frac{1-d}{(1+d)(1+i)} = 0 \ .$$

Division of (1) by (2) results in:

$$\frac{U_{x_1}}{U_{x_2}} = \frac{p_1}{p_2^+}(1+i) \ .$$

Division of (3) by (2) results in:

$$\frac{U_{\tilde{\tilde{M}}}}{U_{x_2}} = i \ .$$

Division of (4) by (3) results in:

$$\frac{U_{\tilde{\tilde{D}}}}{U_{\tilde{\tilde{M}}}} = \frac{i-d}{i(1+d)} \ .$$

3 Determination of the Optimal Intertemporal Consumption and Investment Plan of the Consumer: The Transaction Costs Approach (Section 8.3)

There are two real transaction costs functions: one for the exchange of cash into bonds, $CB\left(\frac{\hat{B}_H}{p_1}\right)$, and another one for the exchange of cash into bank deposits $CD\left(\frac{\hat{D}}{p_1}\right)$. Both have positive first and second derivatives.

The optimization problem of the household is:

$$\text{Max} \quad U = U(x_1, x_2)$$

$$\text{s.t.} \quad p_1 x_1 + \hat{B}_H + \hat{D} + M + p_1 CB\left(\frac{\hat{B}_H}{p_1}\right) + p_1 CD\left(\frac{\hat{D}}{p_1}\right) = p_1 \bar{x}_1^1$$

$$p_2^+ x_2 = \hat{B}_H(1 + i) + \hat{D}(1 + d) + M + QB \ .$$

We differentiate the Lagrange equation with respect to x_1, x_2, $\hat{B}_H$, $\hat{D}$, M and obtain the necessary conditions:

(1) $$U_1 - \lambda_1 p_1 = 0 \ ,$$

(2) $$U_2 - \lambda_2 p_2^+ = 0 \ ,$$

(3) $$-\lambda_1(1 + CB') + \lambda_2(1 + i) = 0 \ ,$$

(4) $$-\lambda_1(1 + CD') + \lambda_2(1 + d) = 0 \ ,$$

(5) $$-\lambda_1 + \lambda_2 = 0 \rightarrow \lambda_1 = \lambda_2 \ .$$

We get the following marginal conditions:

$$\frac{U_1}{U_2} = \frac{p_1}{p_2^+} \ ,$$

$$CB' = i \ ,$$

$$CD' = d \ .$$

Suggested Readings to Chapter 8

The central topic of Chapter 8 is the determination of the purchasing power of money in a model world with outside money and banks. For an introduction, see *S. Fischer* (1983). On transaction costs and financial intermediaries, see the survey article by *G.J. Benston* and *C.W. Smith* (1976). For an introduction particularly to the theory of the bank as a firm, see *J. Niehans* (1978, Ch. 9).

1 The Theory of the Banking Firm

For a critical survey, see *E. Baltensperger* (1980), *A.M. Santomero* (1984); on more recent advances in the theory of financial intermediation, see *S.D. Williamson* (1987). Unlike with the neoclassical theory of the production firm, there is no single neoclassical theory of the banking firm. There are, however, several approaches in the general neoclassical manner. The existing theories of the banking firm may be classified as "models of production techniques or models of portfolio selection" (see *E. Wagner* 1982). Within the group of production models the literature presents different views concerning the actual services of the bank that are to be considered bank outputs and what are to be considered bank inputs. For *B.P. Pesek* and *T.R. Saving* (1968) the bank is a producer of deposits. The bank inputs are real factors as well as excess reserves of banks (thus *T.R. Saving* 1977). For *G.J. Benston* (1972) as well as *C.W. Sealey* and *J.T. Lindley* (1977) the bank is on the other hand a producer of credit. The bank inputs are real factors and bank deposits. For *R.T. Stillson* (1974) the bank is a producer of intermediation services. *F. Ritzman* (1973) sees the bank as a producer of risk transformation services. However, what is to be considered a bank input and a bank output is according to *E. Baltensperger* (1978, 2, No. 3) a "purely semantic problem without operational significance."

The advocates of the portfolio model of the banking firm deal with the question of the rational dispositions with measurable uncertainties. The risk of loss of deposits is considered. The theory explaining the optimal reserves by *D. Orr* and *W.G. Mellon* (1961) has become famous, a theory which itself goes back to an idea of *F.Y. Edgeworth* (1888). *R.C. Porter* (1961) among others allows for the risks of changes in interest rates and credit losses. See also on this point the more extensive study by *G.R. Morrison* (1966). *J. Niehans* (1978) combines the production and portfolio approaches to the theory of the banking firm (more detailed in this direction *E. Baltensperger* and *H. Milde* (1987)). We follow in this book the approach of the transactions firm (Section 3.3) with the risk of loss of deposits.

2 The Currency-Banking Debate

For a concise and clear survey, see *A. Feaveryear* (1963, 261–269). A more detailed survey is found in *F.W. Fetter* (1965, 165–197).

The debate goes back to the 1830's in pamphlets and newspaper articles. The well-known books date back to the time when Peel's Bank Act was passed. As original contributions we recommend

- On the position of the currency theory: *R. Torrens* (1844/1858) combined with *L. Robbins* (1958);
- On the position of the banking theory: *Th. Tooke* (1844) combined with *D.E.W. Laidler* (1975b).

In Germany, *A. Wagner* (1857) sympathized with the currency theory. The newer literature overwhelmingly follows the currency school. See *T.E. Gregory* (1928), *J. Viner* (1937, 220–289), *L. Robbins* (1958). For a different view, see *F.W. Fetter* (1965, 193f.).

In retrospect it can be said that the leading representative of the banking school, Thomas Tooke, understood the monetary system of his time by and large better than the representatives of the currency school, and that his proposals were more reasonable than those of his opponents.

This is also the view of *D.E.W. Laidler* (1975), with the proviso that Tooke in the heat of the controversy came close to accepting the false conclusion of the real bills doctrine, though perhaps less so than his fellow fighter *J. Fullarton* (1845, 67).

3 The Real Bills Doctrine

The real bills doctrine goes back to *A. Smith* (1776/1976, 304). On the present view of Adam Smith's position about monetary theory see *D.E.W. Laidler* (1981, 195f.). As Laidler stresses (op. cit. 195ff.). Adam Smith did not commit the error of later proponents of the real bills doctrine of stating that the doctrine showed that a convertibility of notes into gold was not necessary. On the history and the criticism of the real bills doctrine, see *L.W. Mints* (1945). *H. Thornton* (1802/1962) is a much quoted early critic of the doctrine. For a survey, see *W.F. Fetter* (1965, 40ff.). On the "real bills fallacy" in the context of general equilibrium theory, see *D. Patinkin* (1965, 309f.). *T.J. Sargent* and *N. Wallace* (1982) have undertaken an interesting attempt to rehabilitate the real bills doctrine.

4 Maximization of Seigniorage

This topic belongs to a more subtle approach to the possibilities for the government to finance its budget by means of printing money. In this connection the dependence of the holding of real cash balances on the expected rate of inflation plays an important role. *M. Friedman* (1953) and *P. Cagan* (1956) made early contributions to this topic. *M.J. Bailey* (1956) discusses the hypothetical case of a perfectly anticipated inflation in a stationary economy with fixed real incomes which we have explained in Section 8.4. He dealt, among other things, with the optimizing approaches and welfare losses of such a public financing. The classic contributions to the problem of the optimal seigniorage from the point of view of welfare economics are by *M. Friedman* (1969) and *P.A. Samuelson* (1968, 1969) ("full liquidity rule"). *J. Tobin* (1965) was one of the first to discuss the related problem of interest on cash holdings in order to realize the golden rule, using simple growth models. *L.H. Summers* (1981) has combined the Friedman/Samuelson and the Tobin/Marty approaches. *E.S. Phelps* (1972, 1973) was the first to deal with the welfare maximizing rate of interest on cash holdings in a second-best world. This formulation was generalized by *A. Drazen* (1979). *L.A. Sjaastad* (1976) points out that the rate of seigniorage may be increased by unannounced variations in the rate of inflation. *G.A. Calvo* (1978) shows that the standard solution of the optimal seigniorage problem is not time consistent. *M.F. Hellwig* (1985, 579ff.) has shown the importance of this result for currency legislation using competing outside monies as an example.

5 The Theory of Credit Creation

On the development of the "Old View," see the article by *H.D. Macleod* (1863) in the Dictionary of Political Economy. Also *C.A. Phillips* (1921, Ch. III), *J.E. Meade* (1934). *E. Schneider* (1962, Ch. II) has an extensive and clear exposition of the Old View. For a survey of the older discussion, see *V.F. Wagner* (1937, Ch. 6).

On the origin of the "New View," see *J. Tobin* (1963/1967) and the detailed study by *J. Tobin* and *W.C. Brainard* (1963/1967). The New View does not hold that banks have a widow's cruse which assures them that credit expansion will at the same time expand their deposits equally. Supply and demand determine the volume of bank money in precisely the same manner as the amounts supplied by other production enterprises (*J. Tobin* 1967, 10f.). *H.G. Johnson* (1970/1972, 37–41) gives a concise survey of the New View of monetary theory and policy.

On the use of the multiplier concept in the theory of the supply of money, see *K. Brunner* (1961), *A.J. Meigs* (1962), *K. Brunner* and *A.H. Meltzer* (1964), *R.L. Teigen* (1964), *G.R. Morrison* (1966), *U. Westphal* (1970). On the behavior of credit institutions in the Federal Republic of Germany in particular, see *R. Richter* and *R.L. Teigen* (1982). For a survey of the specifically American circumstances concerning the multiplier concept, see *A.E. Burger* (1971). Burger's article is based on the article by *K. Brunner* and *A. Meltzer* (op. cit.)

6 Minimum Reserves

Minimum reserve requirements have remained an important part of present currency orders, despite the criticisms by the representatives of the New View. For a theoretical justification, see the theory of the money multiplier. About the level of minimum reserve requirements, there is first the extreme view of a 100% reserve by *H.C. Simons* (1934), *J.W. Angell* (1935), *A.G. Hart* (1935). The newer literature deals with the accuracy of influencing the quantity of money by minimum reserves. See among others *W. Poole* (1976), *E.F. Sherman, C.M. Sprenkle* and *B.E. Stanhouse* (1979). On the destabilizing effect of minimum reserves on the national product or prices, see *R. Richter* (1968), *A.M. Santomero* and *J.E. Siegel* (1981) and *E. Baltensperger* (1982).

On the method of calculating the minimum reserves several ways have been proposed: the volume of deposits of the current period; of a preceding period; of a future period. The minimum reserve requirements applied in the Federal Republic of Germany are a mixture of the first two magnitudes. On the discussion of the various proposals and their appropriateness to regulate minimum reserve requirements, see, e.g., *W.L. Coats* (1973, 1976), *B. Gehrig* (1980), *D.E. Laufenberg* (1976, 1977, 1979), *R.D. Laurent* (1979, 1981a, 1981b, 1983).

7 The New Monetary Economics

As new means of payment develop it becomes ever more difficult to say just what the volume of money of an economy is. What must be done with pure book money to safeguard the purchasing power of money? The most influential and at the same time evenhanded contribution to this topic is due to *E.F. Fama* (1980). *F. Black* (1970) has an extreme view. The term "new monetary economics" is due to *R.E. Hall* (1982a). The following contributions deserve to be specially listed (in addition to Fama's contribution): *R.E. Hall* (1982b), *R.L Greenfield* and *L.B. Yeager* (1983). For an overview, see above Appendix to Chapter 4.

The concept of pure book money is not new. *K. Wicksell* (1898) has used it in the first formulation of his theory. *J.R. Hicks* (1967) has used it too. *J.A. Schumpeter* (1970) explains the "nature of money" on the basis of a system of national accounts (see above Chapter 5).

L.H. White (1984b) and *B.T. McCallum* (1985) discuss critically the contributions of F. Black, E.F. Fama, R.E. Hall, R.L. Greenfield and L.B. Yeager. *S. Fischer* (1983) deals with this problem in a simple model of an economy consisting of households, firms, and banks.

Fama opposes a special public regulation of banks with the sole aim of safeguarding the value of money. This is made clear once more in *E.F. Fama* (1983).

8 The Rational Justification of a Central Bank: Free Banking or Central Banking?

The debate over this topic goes back to the time of the gold standard. The questions at issue are: (1) Should the issue of bank notes be limited to one bank or left to any bank? (2) Should banks of issue be subject to special limitations or not? For a survey of the history of central banking, see *K.E. Born* (1980). *V.C. Smith* (1936) gives a detailed history of "free banking vs. central banking" illustrated by the development of banking in England, Scotland, France, the USA and Germany. The topic has recently been revived. *L.H. White* (1984a) investigated anew the experiences with free banking in Scotland up to 1845. He concludes that these experiences speak for the deregulation of banks (op. cit. 148).

H. Rockoff (1975), *A.L. Rolnick* and *W.E. Weber* (1983, 1984, 1988) and *R.G. King* (1983) have reexamined the American experiences for the period before the Civil War and have come to results similar to those of White. The Scottish experiences with free banking were, however, the best. For a criticism of White, see the review article by *G. Gorton* (1985a), as well as *M. Friedman* and *A.J. Schwartz* (1986, particularly pp. 50ff.). In this context see also the discussions about currency competition and the new monetary theory (see above Section 4.6 and Suggested Readings to Chapter 4, No. 6). *P. Dittus* (1987) investigates the normative criteria and their institutional realization for the national paper standard. Dittus also gives further important references, particularly about the politico-economic perspectives of the topic.

9 The Theory and Practice of Central Bank Constitutions

The discussion about the constitution of the central bank is characterized by two great debates: the *Currency-banking Debate* and the *Monetarism-keynesianism Debate* (see Suggested Readings to Chapter 6, No. 6). The first relates to the central bank constitution at the time of the gold standard; the second to the bank of issue constitution with a paper standard. In both cases the advocates of a strict rule and of less strict rules oppose each other. There are similarities in the argumentation, but the analogies should not be carried too far.

(a) Gold Standard

Numerous publications have dealt with the theory and practice of English central bank policy, e.g., *E.V. Morgan* (1965), or *R.G. Hawtrey* (1962). On the history of the theory, see *F.W. Fetter* (1965). The Bagehot principle was important for the effective functioning of English central banking. See *W. Bagehot* (1873/1962) and *F.W. Fetter* (1965, Ch. IX).

On the situation in the German Reich, see *K. Borchardt* (1976). On the monetary policies of the great industrial nations at the time of the gold standard, see *A.I. Bloomfield* (1959).

(b) Paper Standard

There is no doubt that the purchasing power of paper money is determinate only if the quantity of paper money is kept scarce. The remaining question is only whether variations in the quantity of money can stabilize fluctuations in employment. *M. Friedman* (1960, 1968) denies this possibility. *J. Tobin* (1972) and others are of the opposite opinion. So, e.g., also *S. Fischer* (1977a, 1980). The contribution of *F.E. Kydland* and *E.C. Prescott* (1977) has led to interesting models which try to show that an employment stabilizing monetary policy leads to stagflation. For a survey, see *A. Cukierman* (1986). For a later debate, see *P. Dittus* (1987). Another important problem in the context of the quantity of money rule is whether the banking system needs a lender of last resort. For references, see below. See also the literature mentioned in the preceding sections. On the influence of monetarist ideas on the policy of the Deutsche Bundesbank, see *O. Emminger* (1984).

The present bank-of-issue laws of the most important West European countries are expounded in Bank for International Settlements (1963). *H. Aufricht* (1965) provides a comparative survey of central bank law. For a comparative legal analysis of central banks, see also *O. Hahn* (1968). On the Bundesbank law, see *W. Möschel* (1972, Ch. 2). On the legal problem of the independence of the Deutsche Bundesbank, see, e.g., *O. Lampe* (1971), *K.v. Bonin* (1979). Strangely enough neither of these two authors even mentions the heated economic debate over this topic.

10 Bank Regulation

Bank regulation is a special case of the general problem of regulation. See Suggested Readings to Chapter 3, No. 3e. *E. Baltensperger* and *J. Dermine* (1987) provide a concise survey on the discussion on bank regulation on a cross country, comparative perspective. *Ch.P. Kindleberger* (1978) gives a systematic survey of international experience with financial crises. On the German bank crisis of 1931, see *K.E. Born* (1967). On the history of American bank crisis, see *M. Friedman* and *A.J. Schwartz* (1963). *J.J. Merrick* and *A. Saunders* (1985) give a survey of the historical experiences in America and the theoretical discussion of this topic. Of fundamental importance on the role of the central bank as a lender of last resort is *W. Bagehot* (1873/1962). *Ch.P. Kindleberger* (1978) emphasizes the necessity of a lender of last resort. On the theoretical background of panics, see *J. Bryant* (1980), and particularly *D.W. Diamond* and *P.H. Dybvig* (1983).

Diamond's and Dybvig's contribution plays a considerable role in the current discussion about banking regulation. The authors come out against the principle of a lender of last resort (the Bagehot rule) and for a governmental deposit insurance. Critical on this point *D.R. Fischel*, *A.M. Rosenfield* and *R.S. Stillman* (1987). On the organization of a deposit insurance, see *J.J. Merrick* and *A. Saunders* (1985, 704 ff.). A systematic exposition of the traditional ideas about the aims and purposes of bank regulation is found in *W. Möschel* (1985).

On bank regulation in Germany from an economic point of view, see *J. Welcker* (1978); from the standpoint of the economics of the individual firm, particularly the accounting aspects, see *H. Bieg* (1983); for an English survey of the legal framework and bank supervision in West Germany see *H.-H. Francke* and *M. Hudson* (1984, 63ff.). On the legal aspects of West German bank regulation, see the extensive treatment of *W. Möschel* (1972). On the major points of the proposed legislation of the West German credit-business law (*Kreditwesengesetz*) of 1985, see *W. Werner* (1985).

W. Stützel's (1964) idea of a "depositor-protection-balance sheet" (*Einlegerschutzbilanz*) plays a considerable role in the German discussion, for criticism of the idea, see among others *W.A. Müller* (1981).

On bank regulation in the USA, see *F.S. Mishkin* (1986, Ch. 9), with a list of references particularly on the American circumstances (op. cit., 196). Critical of American bank regulation, and very stimulating, is *D.R. Fischel, A.M. Rosenfield* and *R.S. Stillman* (1987). A systematic description of the regulation of banks in the member states of the EEC is provided by *J. Welch* (1981). A brief overview of national regulatory arrangements including Canada, Hong Kong, Japan, Singapore, Switzerland, and the United States can be found in *R. Dale* (1982).

On the problem of regulation of international banking from an economic point of view, see *Ch.P. Kindelberger* (1978), *E.-M. Claassen* (1985). On the growth of multinational banking and its regulation, see the extensive study by *R. Dale* (1984). For a general survey of international banking including the problems of regulation, see *R.Z. Aliber* (1984). On the law of international supervision, see *K. Wagner* (1982), *K.-A. Bauer* (1985).

Bibliography

Adams, M. 1981. *Ökonomische Analyse des Zivilprozesses*, Königstein/Taunus: Athenaeum.

Albach, H. 1980. "Vertrauen in der ökonomischen Theorie," *Zeitschrift für die gesamte Staatswissenschaft*, 136, 2–11.

Alchian, A.A. 1970. "Information Costs, Pricing and Resource Unemployment," in: *Microeconomic Foundations of Employment and Inflation Theory*, eds. E.S. Phelps et al., 27–52, New York: Norton.

Alchian, A.A. 1977, "Why Money?," *Journal of Money, Credit and Banking*, 9, 133–140.

Alchian, A.A. and Richter, R. (eds.) 1985. "Views and Comments on Contractual Relations", *Zeitschrift für die gesamte Staatswissenschaft/Journal of Institutional and Theoretical Economics*, 141, 539–611.

Aliber, R.Z. 1984. "International Banking", *Journal of Money, Credit and Banking*, 16, 661–678.

Allen, R.G.D. 1975. *Index Numbers in Theory and Practice*, London: Macmillan.

Andel, N. 1977. "Nutzen-Kosten-Analysen," in: *Handbuch der Finanzwissenschaft*, eds. N. Andel, H. Haller and F. Neumark, Vol. I, 475–518, Tübingen: Mohr.

Anderson, R.W. (ed.) 1984. *The Industrial Organization of Futures Markets*, Lexington/Mass.: Lexington Books.

Angell, J.W. 1935. "The 100 Percent Reserve Plan," *Quarterly Journal of Economics*, 50, 1–35.

Arrow, K.J. 1969. "The Organization of Economic Activity: Issues Pertinent to the Choice of Market Versus Nonmarket Allocation," in: *The Analysis and Evaluation of Public Expenditures: The PBB-System*, Joint Economic Committee, 91st Congress, 1st Session, Vol. 1, 47–64, Washington/ D.C.: U.S. Government Print Office.

Arrow, K.J. 1971. "Political and Economic Evaluation of Social Effects and Externalities," in: *Frontiers of Quantitative Economics*, ed. M.D. Intriligator, 3–31, Amsterdam-London: North-Holland.

Arrow, K.J. 1973. *Essays in the Theory of Risk Bearing*, Chicago: Markham Press.

Arrow, K.J. 1974. "Limited Knowledge and Economic Analysis," *American Economic Review*, 64, 1–10.

Arrow, K.J. 1978. "The Future and the Present in Economic Life," *Economic Inquiry*, 16, 157–169.

Arrow, K.J. and Debreu, G. 1954. "Existence of an Equilibrium for a Competitive Economy," *Econometrica*, 22, 265–290.

Aufricht, H. 1965. *Comparative Survey of Central Banking Law*, New York-Washington/D.C.: Praeger.

Azariadis, C. 1975. "Implicit Contracts and Underemployment Equilibria," *Journal of Political Economy*, 83, 1183–1202.

Azariadis, C. and Stiglitz, J.E. 1983. "Implicit Contracting and Fixed Price Equilibria," *Quarterly Journal of Economics*, 48, Supplement, 1–22.

Bagehot, W. 1873/1962. *Lombard Street. A Description of the Money Market*, 1873, New York: Scribner, Armstrong; 1962 Homewood/Ill.: Irwin.

Bailey, M.J. 1956, "The Welfare Cost of Inflationary Finance," *Journal of Political Economy*, 64, 93–110.

Baily, M.N. 1974. "Wages and Employment under Uncertain Demand," *Review of Economic Studies*, 41, 37–50.

Balasko, Y. and Schell, K. 1981. "The Overlapping Generations Model II. The Case of Pure Exchange With Money," *Journal of Economic Theory*, 24, 112–142.

Baltensperger, E. 1978. "*Alternative Approaches to the Theory of the Banking Firm*," Paper presented at the Konstanzer Seminar on Monetary Theory and Monetary Policy.

Baltensperger, E. 1980. "Alternative Approaches to the Theory of the Banking Firm," *Journal of Monetary Economics*, 6, 1–37.

Baltensperger, E. 1982. "Reserve Requirements and Economic Stability," *Journal of Money, Credit and Banking*, 14, 205–215.

Baltensperger, E. and Böhm, P. 1982. "Stand und Entwicklungstendenzen der Wechselkurstheorie – Ein Überblick," *Außenwirtschaft*, 37, 109–157.

Baltensperger, E. and Dermine, J. 1987, "The Role of Public Policy in Ensuring Financial Stability: A Cross Country, Comparative Perspective," in: R. Portes and A. Swoboda (eds.), Threats to International Financial Stability, Cambridge: Cambridge University Press.

Baltensperger, E. and Devinney, T.M. 1985. "Credit Rationing Theory: A Survey and Synthesis," *Zeitschrift für die gesamte Staatswissenschaft/Journal of Institutional and Theoretical Economics*, 141, 475–502.

Baltensperger, E. and Milde, H. 1987. *Theorie des Bankverhaltens*, Berlin-Heidelberg et al.: Springer.

Banfield, E.C. 1985. *The Moral Basis of Backward Society*, Glencoe/Ill.: Free Press.

Bank for International Settlements (ed.) 1963. *Eight European Central Banks. Organization and Activities*, London: Allen & Unwin.

Barro, R.J. 1974. "Are Government Bonds Net Wealth?", *Journal of Political Economy*, 82, 1095–1117.

Barro, R.J. 1976. "Rational Expectations and the Role of Monetary Policy," *Journal of Monetary Economics*, 2, 1–32.

Barro, R.J. 1977. "Long-Term Contracting, Sticky Prices and Monetary Policy," *Journal of Monetary Economics*, 3, 305–316.

Barro, R.J. 1979. "Money and the Price Level Under the Gold Standard," *Economic Journal*, 89, 13–33.

Barro, R.J. 1982. "United States Inflation and the Choice of Monetary Standard," in: *Inflation, Causes and Effects*, ed. R.H. Hall, 99–110, Chicago-London: University of Chicago Press.

Barro, R.J. and Grossman, H.I. 1971. "A General Disequilibrium Model of Income and Employment," *American Economic Review*, 61, 82–93.

Barsky, R.B. 1987. "The Fisher Hypothesis and the Forecastability and Persistence of Inflation," *Journal of Monetary Economics*, 19, 3–24.

Bauer, K.-A. 1985. *Das Recht der Internationalen Bankenaufsicht*, Baden-Baden: Nomos.

Baumbach, A. and Hefermehl, W. 1967. *Wechselgesetze und Scheckgesetz*, 9th ed., München-Berlin: Beck.

Baumol, W.J. 1952. "The Transaction Demand for Cash: An Inventory Theoretic Approach," *Quarterly Journal of Economics*, 66, 545–556.

Bendixen, F. 1908. *Das Wesen des Geldes. Zugleich ein Beitrag zur Reform der Reichsbankgesetzgebung*, Leipzig: Duncker & Humblot.

Benston, G.J. 1972. "Economies of Scale of Financial Institutions," *Journal of Money, Credit and Banking*, 4, 312–341.

Benston, G.J. and Smith, C.W. 1976. "A Transactions Cost Approach to the Theory of Financial Intermediation," *Journal of Finance*, 31, 215–231.

Bernanke, B.S. 1983. "Nonmonetary Effects of the Financial Crisis in the Propagation of the Great Depression," *American Economic Review*, 73, 257–276.

Bernholz, P. 1965. "Aufbewahrungs- und Transportkosten als Bestimmungsgründe der Geldnachfrage," *Schweizerische Zeitschrift für Volkswirtschaft und Statistik*, 101, 1–15.

Bernholz, P. 1967. "Erwerbskosten, Laufzeit und Charakter zinstragender Forderungen als Bestimmungsgründe der Geldnachfrage der Haushalte," *Zeitschrift für die gesamte Staatswissenschaft*, 123, 9–24.

Bernholz, P. 1978. "Hayek, F.A.: Denationalisation of Money," *Kyklos*, 31, 136–139.

Bernholz, P. 1982. "*Flexible Exchange Rates in Historical Perspective*," Princeton Studies in International Finance, 49.

Bernholz, P. 1983. "Inflation and Monetary Constitutions in Historical Perspective," *Kyklos*, 36, 397–419.

Bernholz, P. 1986. "The Implementation and Maintenance of a Monetary Constitution," *Cato Journal*, 6, 477–511.

Bernholz, P., Faber, M. and Reiss, W. 1978, "A Neo-Austrian Two-Period Multisector Model of Capital," *Journal of Economic Theory*, 17, 38–50.

Bieg, H. 1983. "*Bankbilanzen und Bankenaufsicht*," Schriften des Instituts für Arbeits- und Wirtschaftsrecht der Universität zu Köln, München: Beck.

Bilson, J.F.O. 1979. "Recent Developments in Monetary Models of Exchange Rate Determination," *International Monetary Fund Staff Papers*, 26, 201–223, Washington/D.C.: IMF.

Black, F. 1970. "Banking and Interest Rates in a World Without Money," *Journal of Bank Research*, 1, 8–20.

Blanchard, O.J. 1979. "Speculative Bubbles, Crashes and Rational Expectations," *Economic Letters*, 3, 386–389.

Blau, G. 1944. "Some Aspects of the Theory of Futures Trading," *Review of Economic Studies*, 12, 1–30.

Bliss, C.J. 1975. *Capital Theory and the Distribution of Income*, Amsterdam: North-Holland.

Bloomfield, A.I. 1959. *Monetary Policy Under the International Gold Standard*, 1880–1914, New York: Federal Reserve Bank of New York.

Böhm, S. 1980. "Austrian Economics – Geschichte und philosophische Wurzeln," *Wirtschaftspolitische Blätter*, 28, 119–129.

Böhm-Bawerk, E.v. 1921a. *Kapital und Kapitalzins* I. Geschichte und Kritik der Kapitalzinstheorien, 4th ed. (1st ed. 1884), Jena: Fischer.

Böhm-Bawerk, E.v. 1921b. *Positive Theorie des Kapitals*, Vol. 1, 4th ed. (1st ed. 1888), Jena: Fischer.

Böhm-Bawerk, E.v. 1891/1930. *The Positive Theory of Capital*, translation of Böhm-Bawerk (1921b) (translated by William Smart), New York: G.E. Stechert & Co.

Böhm-Bawerk, E.v. 1891/1959. *Capital and Interest*, translation of Böhm-Bawerk (1921a) (translated and edited by G.D. Huncke and H.F. Sennholz), Vol. I "History and Critique of Interest Theories" and "Recent Literature on Interest," South Holland/Ill.: Liberation Press.

Bössmann, E. 1977. "Information," in: *Handwörterbuch der Wirtschaftswissenschaft*, eds. W. Albers et al., 4, 184–200, Stuttgart: Fischer

Bössmann, E. 1981. "Weshalb gibt es Unternehmungen? Der Erklärungsansatz von Ronald H. Coase," *Zeitschrift für die gesamte Staatswissenschaft/Journal of Institutional and Theoretical Economics*, 137, 667–674.

Bössmann, E. 1982. "Volkswirtschaftliche Probleme der Transaktionskosten," *Zeitschrift für die gesamte Staatswissenschaft/Journal of Institutional and Theoretical Economics*, 138, 664–679.

Bofinger, P. 1985. *Währungswettbewerb. Eine systematische Darstellung und kritische Würdigung von Friedrich A. von Hayeks Plänen zu einer grundlegenden Neugestaltung unserer Währungsordnung*, Köln: Heymann.

Bonin, K.v. 1979. *Zentralbanken zwischen funktioneller Unabhängigkeit und politischer Autonomie, dargestellt an der Bank von England, der Bank von Frankreich und der Deutschen Bundesbank*, Baden-Baden: Nomos.

Bonus, H. 1986. "The Cooperative Association as a Business Enterprise: A Study in the Economics of Transactions," *Journal of Institutional and Theoretical Economics/Zeitschrift für die gesamte Staatswissenschaft*, 142, 310–339.

Borchardt, K. 1976. "Währung und Wirtschaft," in: *Währung und Wirtschaft in Deutschland* 1876–1975, ed. Deutsche Bundesbank, 3–55, Frankfurt/Main: Knapp.

Bordo, M.D. 1980. "The Effects of Monetary Change on Relative Commodity Prices and the Role of Long Term Contracts," *Journal of Political Economy*, 88, 1088–1109.

Bordo, M.D. 1981. "The Classical Gold Standard: Some Lessons for Today," *The Federal Reserve Bank of St. Louis Review*, 63, No. 5, 1–17.

Bordo, M.D. and Schwartz, A.J. (eds.) 1984. *A Retrospective on the Classical Gold Standard* 1821–1931, Chicago-London: University of Chicago Press.

Born, K.E. 1967. *Die deutsche Bankenkrise* 1931. *Finanzen und Politik*, München: Piper.

Born, K.E. 1980. "Notenbanken, I: Geschichte," in: *Handwörterbuch der Wirtschaftswissenschaft*, eds. W. Albers et al., 5, 329–334, Stuttgart: Fischer.

Brennan, H.G. and Buchanan, J.M. 1981. "*Monopoly in Money and Inflation. The Case for a Constitution to Discipline Government*," Hobart Paper, 88, London: Institute of Economic Affairs.

Bruce, N. and Purvis, D.D. 1985. "The Specification and Influence of Goods and Factor Markets in Open-Economy Macroeconomic Models," in: *Handbook of International Economics*, eds. R.W. Jones and P.B. Kenen, Ch. 16, 807–857, Amsterdam: North-Holland.

Brunner, K. 1961. "A Schema for the Supply Theory of Money," *International Economic Review*, 2, 79–109.

Brunner, K. 1970. "The 'Monetarist Revolution' in Monetary Theory," *Weltwirtschaftliches Archiv*, 105, 1–30.

Brunner, K. and Meltzer, A.H. 1964. "Some Further Investigations of Demand and Supply Function for Money," *Journal of Finance*, 19, 240–283.

Brunner, K. and Meltzer, A.H. 1971. "The Uses of Money: Money in a Theory of an Exchange Economy," *American Economic Review*, 61, 784–805.

Bryant, J. 1980. "A Model of Reserves, Bank Runs, and Deposit Insurance," *Journal of Banking and Finance*, 4, 335–344.

Buchanan, J.M. 1962. "Predictability: The Criterion of Monetary Constitutions," in: *In Search of a Monetary Constitution*, ed. L.B. Yeager, 155–183, Cambridge/Mass.: Harvard University Press.

Buchanan, J.M. 1975. "A Contractarian Paradigm for Applying Economic Theory," *American Economic Review, Papers and Proceedings*, 65, 225–230.

Buiter, W.H. 1979. "Government Finance in an Overlapping Generations Model with Gifts and Bequests," in: *Social Security versus Private Saving*, ed. G.M.v. Fürstenberg, 395–429, Cambridge/Mass.: Ballinger.

Buiter, W.H. and Tobin, J. 1979. "Debt Neutrality: A Brief Review of Doctrine and Evidence," in: *Social Security versus Private Saving*, ed. G.M.v. Fürstenberg, 39–63, Cambridge/Mass.: Ballinger.

Bureau of Labor Statistics (ed.) 1972. *Handbook of Methods for Surveys and Studies*, U.S. Department of Labor, Washington/D.C.: Government Office.

Burger, A.E. 1971. *The Money Supply Process*, Belmont/Calif.: Wadsworth.

Burmeister, E. 1974. "Synthesizing the Neo-Austrian and Alternative Approaches to Capital Theory: A Survey," *Journal of Economic Literature*, 12, 413–456,

Cagan, P. 1956. "The Monetary Dynamics of Hyperinflation" in: *Studies in the Quantity Theory of Money*, ed. M. Friedman, 25–117, Chicago-London: University of Cicago Press.

Calvo, G.A. 1978. "Optimal Seignorage from Money Creation. An Analysis of the Optimum Balance of Payments Deficit Problem," *Journal of Monetary Economics*, 4, 503–517.

Cameron, V.L. 1877. *Across Africa*, Vol. 1, 5th ed., London: Daldy, Isbister & Co.

Cann, E. 1925. *The Paper Pound of* 1797–1821. *A Reprint of the Bullion Report and Resolutions Proposed to the House of Commons*, 2nd ed. (1st ed. 1919), London: P.S. King & Son.

Cannon, J.G. 1910. *Clearing Houses*, Publications of the National Monetary Commission, Vol. 6, United States Congress. 61, Session 2, Document No. 491, Washington/D.C.: Government Printing Office.

Cass, D. 1965. "Optimum Growth in an Aggregate Model of Capital Accumulation," *Review of Economic Studies*, 32, 233–240.

Cassel, G. 1916. "The Present Situation of the Foreign Exchanges," *Economic Journal*, 26, 62–65.

Cassel, G. 1918. "Abnormal Deviations in International Exchanges," *Economic Journal*, 28, 413–415.

Cassel, G. 1922. *Money and Foreign Exchange after* 1914, London: Constable; New York: Macmillan.

Chalmovsky, L.E. 1984. *Der internationale Zahlungsverkehr und die Devisenmärkte in der betrieblichen Praxis. Eine kritische Würdigung des Problemeinstiegs ausgewählter Zahlungsbilanz- und Wechselkurstheorien*, Frankfurt/Main: Lang.

Claassen, E.-M. 1980. *Grundlagen der Geldtheorie*, 2nd ed., Berlin-Heidelberg et. al.: Springer.

Claassen, E.-M. 1985. "The Lender-of-Last-Resort Function in the Context of National and International Financial Crisis," *Weltwirtschaftliches Archiv*, 121, 217–237.

Clark, T.A. 1984. "Violations of the Gold Points, 1890–1908," *Journal of Political Economy*, 92, 791–823.

Coase, R.H. 1937. "The Nature of the Firm," *Economica*, N.S., 4, 386–405, or in: *Readings in Price Theory* (1953), eds. G.J. Stigler and K.E. Boulding, 331–351, Homewood/Ill.: Allen & Unwin.

Coase, R.H. 1960. "The Problem of Social Cost," *Journal of Law and Economics*, 3, 1–44.

Coats, W.L. 1973. "Regulation *D* and the Vault Cash Game," *Journal of Finance*, 28, 601–607.

Coats, W.L. 1976. "Lagged Reserve Accounting and the Money Supply Mechanism," *Journal of Money, Credit and Banking*, 8, 167–180.

Coleman, J.S. 1984. "Introducing Social Structure into Economic Analysis," *American Economic Review, Papers and Proceedings*, 74, 84–88.

Commission of the European Communities (ed.) 1977. *Inflation and Exchange Rates: Evidence and Policy Guidelines for the European Community*, OPTICA Report 1976, Brussels.

Commons, J.R. 1934. *Institutional Economics. Its Place in Political Economy*, New York: Macmillan.

Conard, J.W. 1959. *An Introduction to the Theory of Interest*, Berkeley: University of California Press.

Congress of the United States 1981, "The Gold Standard: Its History and Record Against Inflation," A Study Prepared for the Use of the Subcommittee on Monetary and Fiscal Policy of the Joint Economic Committee, Sept. 18, 1981, Washington.

Cornwall, J. 1979. "Economic Growth: Two Paradigms," *Journal of Post Keynesian Economics*, 1, 69–90.

Courchene, T.J. 1970. "General Equilibrium Models and the World Payments System," *Southern Economic Journal*, 36, 309–322.

Cukierman, A. 1986. "Central Bank Behavior and Credibility: Some Recent Theoretical Developments," *The Federal Reserve Bank of St. Louis Review*, 68, 5–17.

Dahlman, C.J. 1979. "The Problem of Externality," *Journal of Law and Economics*, 12, 144–162.

Dale, R. 1982. Bank Supervision Around the World, Group of Thirty: New York.

Dale, R. 1984. The Regulation of International Banking, Cambridge: Woodhead-Faulkner; Englewood Cliffs/N.J.: Prentice-Hall.

Dam, K.W. 1983. *The Rules of the Game: Reform and Evolution in the International Monetary System*, Chicago: University of Chicago Press.

Darby, M.R. and Lothian, J.R. (eds.) 1983. *The International Transmission of Inflation*, National Bureau of Economic Research monograph, Chicago et al.: University of Chicago Press.

Debreu, G. 1959. *Theory of Value. An Axiomatic Analysis of Economic Equilibrium*, New York – London: Chapman & Hall.

Demsetz, H. 1968a. "The Cost of Transacting," *Quarterly Journal of Economics*, 82, 33–53.

Demsetz, H. 1968b. "Why Regulate Utilities?", *Journal of Law and Economics*, 11, 55–66.

(The) Deutsche Bundesbank 1976a. *Deutsches Geld- und Bankwesen in Zahlen* 1876–1975, Frankfurt/Main: Knapp.

(The) Deutsche Bundesbank 1976b. *Währung und Wirtschaft in Deutschland* 1876–1975, Frankfurt/Main: Knapp.

(The) Deutsche Bundesbank 1977/1983/1984/1985/1986. *Report of the Deutsche Bundesbank for the Year* 1976/1982/1983/1984/1985, Frankfurt/Main: Deutsche Bundesbank.

(The) Deutsche Bundesbank, *Monthly Report of the Deutsche Bundesbank* April 1971, Jan. 1977/1978/1979, March 1979, Dec. 1979/1980/1981/1982/1983/1984, June 1986.

(The) Deutsche Bundesbank 1982. "*Geldpolitische Aufgaben und Instrumente*," Sonderdrucke der Deutschen Bundesbank, Nr. 7, Frankfurt/Main: Deutsche Bundesbank.

(The) Deutsche Bundesbank 1987. "*Its Monetary Policy Instruments and Functions*," Deutsche Bundesbank Special Series, No. 7, 2nd ed., Frankfurt/Main: Deutsche Bundesbank.

(The) Deutsche Bundesregierung 1975. Jahreswirtschaftsbericht, BT-Drucksache, Bonn.

Dewey, D. 1963. "The Geometry of Capital and Interest: A Suggested Simplification," *American Economic Review*, 53, 134–139.

Dewey, D. 1965. *Modern Capital Theory*, New York-London: Columbia University Press.

Diamond, D.W. and Dybvig, P.H. 1983. "Bank Runs, Deposit Insurance, and Liquidity," *Journal of Political Economy*, 91, 401–419.

Diamond, P.A. 1965. "National Debt in a Neoclassical Growth Model," *American Economic Review*, 55, 1126–1150.

Diamond, P.A. 1971. "Political and Economic Evaluation of Social Effects and Externalities: Comment," in: *Frontiers of Quantitative Economics*, ed. M. Intriligator, 30–32, Amsterdam: North-Holland.

Dittus, P. 1987. "*Die Wahl der Geldverfassung*," Schriftreihe Annales Universitatis Saraviensis (Rechts- und Wirtschaftswissenschaftliche Abteilung), Vol. 121, Köln et al.: Heymann.

Dorfman, R. 1958/1959, "A Graphical Exposition of Böhm-Bawerk's Interest Theory," *Review of Economic Studies*, 26, 153–158.

Dorfman, R. 1959. "Waiting and the Period of Production," *Quarterly Journal of Economics*, 73, 351–372.

Dornbusch, R. 1976. "Expectations and Exchange Rate Dynamics," *Journal of Political Economy*, 84, 1161–1176.

Dornbusch, R. 1982. "Equilibrium and Disequilbrium Exchange Rates," *Zeitschrift für Wirtschafts- und Sozialwissenschaften*, 102, 573–599, or in: *Dollars, Debts and Deficits* (1986), ed. R. Dornbusch, 31–58, Leuven: Leuven University Press; Cambridge/Mass.: The MIT-Press.

Dornbusch, R. and Fischer, S. 1987. *Macroeconomics*, 4th ed., New York: McGraw Hill.

Dornbusch, R. and Frankel, J. 1987. The Flexible Exchange Rate System: Experience and Alternatives, National Bureau of Economic Research, Working Paper Series No. 2464 (forthcoming in a book of the International Economic Association, Macmillan: London).

Drazen, A. 1978. "Government Debt, Human Capital and Bequests in a Life-Cycle Model," *Journal of Political Economy*, 78, 505–517.

Drazen, A. 1979. "The Optimal Rate of Inflation Revisited," *Journal of Monetary Economics*, 5, 231–248.

Duden, K. 1968. "*Der Gestaltwandel des Geldes und seine rechtlichen Folgen*," Juristische Studiengesellschaft Karlsruhe, Schriftenreihe Heft 86, Karlsruhe: C.F. Müller.

Edgeworth, F.Y. 1881. *Mathematical Physics*, London: Paul.

Edgeworth, F.Y. 1888. "The Mathematical Theory of Banking," *Journal of the Royal Statistical Society*, 51, 113–127.

Ehrlicher, W. 1981. "Geldtheorie und Geldpolitik, III: Geldtheorie," in: *Handwörterbuch der Wirtschaftswissenschaft*, eds. W. Albers et al., Vol. 3, 374–391.

Ehrlicher, W. and Becker, E.-D. (eds.) 1978. "*Die Monetarismus-Kontroverse. Eine Zwischenbilanz*," Beihefte zu Kredit und Kapital, Heft 4, Berlin: Duncker & Humblot.

Ehrlicher, W. and Richter, R. 1984. "*Devisenmarktinverventionen der Zentralbanken*," Schriften des Vereins für Socialpolitik, Gesellschaft für Wirtschafts- und Sozialpolitik, N.F., Vol. 139, Berlin: Duncker & Humblot.

Einzig, P. 1937. *The Theory of Forward Exchange*, London: Macmillan.

Einzig, P. 1951. *Primitive Money. In its Ethnological, Historical, and Economic Aspects*, London: Eyre & Spottiswoode.

Einzig, P. 1962. *A Dynamic Theory of Forward Exchange*, London: Macmillan.

Emminger, O. 1976. "Deutsche Geld- und Währungspolitik im Spannungsfeld zwischen innerem und äußerem Gleichgewicht (1948–1975)," in: *Währung und Wirtschaft in Deutschland* 1876–1975, ed. Deutsche Bundesbank, 485–554, Frankfurt/Main: Knapp.

Emminger, O. 1984. "Deutsche Geldpolitik im Zeichen des Monetarismus," in: *Friedman contra Keynes*, ed. P. Hampe, 43–66, München: Olzog.

Encyclopaedia Britannica 1962. "Banking", 3, 98, Chicago et al.: W. Benton.

Encyclopaedia Britannica 1982. "Futures", 7, 816–818, Chicago et al.: Helen Hemingway Benton.

Endemann, W. 1863. "Die nationalökonomischen Grundsätze der canonischen Lehre," *Jahrbücher für Nationalökonomie und Statistik*, 1, 26–48, 154–181, 310–367, 537–576, 679–730.

Engels, W. 1977. "Notenemissionen als Bankgeschäft," in: *Der Bankbetrieb zwischen Theorie und Praxis*, ed. J. Süchting, 193–204, Wiesbaden: Gabler.

Engels, W. 1981. *The Optimal Monetary Unit*, Frankfurt/Main: Campus.

Eucken, W. 1940/1950. *Die Grundlagen der Nationalökonomie*, 1st ed. 1940, Jena: G. Fischer; 6th ed. 1950, Berlin-Heidelberg et al.: Springer.

Eucken, W. 1950. *The Foundations of Economics. History and Theory in the Analysis of Economic Reality*, translation of Eucken (1940) (translated by T.W. Hutchinson), Chicago: University of Chicago Press, London: W. Hodge.

Eucken, W. 1952. *Grundsätze der Wirtschaftspolitik*, Tübingen: Mohr.

Faber, M. 1979. *Introduction to Modern Austrian Capital Theory*, Berlin-Heidelberg et al.: Springer.

Fama, E.F. 1980. "Banking in the Theory of Finance," *Journal of Monetary Economics*, 6, 39–58.

Fama, E.F. 1983. "Financial Intermediation and Price Level Control." *Journal of Monetary Economics*, 12, 7–28.

Fama, E.F. and Miller, M.H. 1972. *The Theory of Finance*, New York: Dryden Press.

Feaveryear, A. 1963. *The Pound Sterling. A History of English Money*, 2nd ed. rev. by E.V. Morgan, Oxford: Clarendon Press.

Fels, G. 1969. "*Der internationale Preiszusammenhang*," Schriftreihe Annales Universitatis Saraviensis, Vol. 46, Köln et al.: Heymann.

Fels, G., Giersch, H., Müller-Groeling, H. and Schmidt, K.D. 1971. "Neue Rollenverteilung in der Konjunkturpolitik," *Die Weltwirtschaft*, 1, 5–8.

Ferguson, C.E. 1971. *The Neoclassical Theory of Production and Distribution*, Cambridge: University of Cambridge Press.

Fetter, F.W. 1965. *Development of British Monetary Orthodoxy* 1797–1875, Cambridge/Mass.: Harvard University Press.

Fischel, D.R., Rosenfield, A.M. and Stillman, R.S. 1987. "The Regulation of Banks and Bank Holding Companies," *Virginia Law Review*, 73, 301–338.

Fischer, S. 1977a. "Long-Term Contracts, Rational Expectations and the Optimal Money Supply Rule," *Journal of Political Economy*, 85, 191–205.

Fischer, S. 1977b. "Long-Term Contracting, Sticky Prices and Monetary Policy: Comments," *Journal of Monetary Economics*, 3, 317–323.

Fischer, S. 1979a. "Anticipations and the Nonneutrality of Money," *Journal of Political Economy*, 87, 225–252.

Fischer, S. 1979b. "Besprechung von J. Niehans, The Theory of Money, Baltimore-London 1978," *Zeitschrift für die gesamte Staatswissenschaft*, 135, 285–288.

Fischer, S. 1980. "On Activist Monetary Policy with Rational Expectations," in: *Rational Expectations and Economic Policy*, ed. S. Fischer, 211–247, Chicago: University of Chicago Press.

Fischer, S. 1981. "Towards an Understanding of the Costs of Inflation: II," *Carnegie-Rochester Conference Series on Public Policy*, 15, 5–42.

Fischer, S. 1982. "Relative Price Variability and Inflation in the United States and Germany," *European Economic Review*, 18, 171–196.

Fischer, S. 1983. "A Framework for Monetary Stability," *Economic Journal, Supplement*, 1–16, Conference Papers from the Annual Conference of the Royal Economic Society and the Association of University Teachers of Economics, Guildford/Surrey, 1982.

Fischer, S. 1986. "Friedman verus Hayek on Private Money," Review Essay, *Journal of Monetary Economics*, 17, 433–439.

Fischer, I. 1896. *Appreciation and Interest*, New York: Macmillan.

Fisher, I. 1907. *The Rate of Interest*, New York: Macmillan.

Fisher, I. 1911. *The Purchasing Power of Money. Its Determination and Relation to Credit, Interest and Crises*, New York: Macmillan.

Fisher, I. 1912. *The Nature of Capital and Income*, New York: Macmillan.

Fisher, I. 1926. *The Purchasing Power of Money. Its Determination and Relation to Credit, Interest and Crises*, new and rev. ed., New York: Macmillan.

Fisher, I. 1930, *The Theory of Interest. As Determined by Impatience to Spend Income and Opportunity to Invest It*. New York: Macmillan.

Fisher, I. 1973. "Lost and Found: I discovered the Phillips Curve," *Journal of Political Economy*, 81, 496–502.

Flätgen, S.J. 1985. *Monetary Stability in a Centrally Planned Economy. The Case of GDR*, Ph.D. diss. manuscript, Florenz, March 1985.

Fögen, H. 1969. *Geld- und Währungsrecht*, München: Beck.

Foley, D.K. 1970. "Economic Equilibrium with Costly Marketing," *Journal of Economic Theory*, 2, 276–291.

Francke, H.-H. and Hudson, M. 1984. *Banking and Finance in West Germany*, London-Sydney: Croom Helm.

Frenkel, J.A. 1976. "A Monetary Approach to the Exchange Rate: Doctrinal Aspects and Empirical Evidence," *Scandinavian Journal of Economics*, 78, 200–224, or in: *The Economics of Exchange Rates: Selected Studies* (1978), eds. J.A. Frenkel and H.G. Johnson, Ch. 1., Reading/Pa.: Addison-Wesley.

Frenkel, J.A. 1978. "Purchasing Power Parity. Doctrinal Perspective and Evidence from the 1920s," *Journal of International Economics*, 8, 169–191.

Frenkel, J.A. 1981. "Flexible Exchange Rates, Prices and the Role of News: Lessons from the 1970's," *Journal of Political Economy*, 89, 665–705.

Frenkel, J.A. and Johnson, H.G. 1976. "The Monetary Approach to the Balance of Payments – Essential Concepts and Historical Origins," in: *The Monetary Approach to the Balance of Payments*, eds. J.A. Frenkel and H.G. Johnson, 21–45, London: Allen & Unwin.

Frenkel, J.A. and Mussa, M.L. 1985. "Asset Markets, Exchange Rates and the Balance of Payments," in: *Handbook of International Economics*, eds. R.W. Jones and P.B. Kenen, Vol. 2, 679–747, Amsterdam: North-Holland.

Fried, J. and Howitt, P. 1983. "The Effects of Inflation on Real Interest Rates," *American Economic Review*, 73, 968–980.

Friedman, M. 1948. "A Monetary and Fiscal Framework for Economic Stability," *American Economic Review*, 38, 345–364, or in: see *M. Friedman* (1953), 133–156.

Friedman, M. 1950. "The Case for Flexible Exchange Rates," in: *Essays in Positive Economics* (1953), ed. M. Friedman, 157–203, Chicago-London: University of Chicago Press.

Friedman, M. 1951. "Commodity-Reserve Currency," *Journal of Political Economy*, 59, 203–232, or in: see *M. Friedman* (1953), 204–250.

Friedman, M. 1953. *Essays in Positive Economics*, Chicago-London: University of Chicago Press.

Friedman, M. 1960. *A Program for Monetary Stability*, New York: Fordham University Press.

Friedman, M. 1968. "The Role of Monetary Policy," *American Economic Review*, 58, 1–17.

Friedman, M. 1969. *The Optimum Quantity of Money and Other Essays*, Chicago-London: Aldine.

Friedman, M. 1977. "Nobel Lecture: Inflation and Unemployment," *Journal of Political Economy*, 85, 451–472.

Friedman, M. and Schwartz, A.J. 1963. *A Monetary History of the United States*, Princeton/N.J.: University Press.

Friedman, M. and Schwartz, A.J. 1986. "Has Government Any Role in Money," *Journal of Monetary Economics*, 17, 37–62.

Fullarton, J. 1845. *On the Regulation of Currencies. Being an Examination of the Principles, on Which it is Proposed to Restrict, Within Certain Fixed Limits, the Future Issues on Credit of the Bank of England, and of the Banking Establishments of Throughout the Country*, 2nd ed. with corrections and additions (1st ed. 1844), London: J. Murray.

Furubotn, E.G. and Pejovich, S. 1972. "Property Rights and Economic Theory: A Survey of Recent Literature," *Journal of Economic Literature*, 10, 1137–1162.

Furubotn, E.G. and Pejovich, S. 1974. *The Economics of Property Rights*, Cambridge/Mass.: Ballinger.

Furubotn, E.G. and Richter, R. 1984. "The New Institutional Economics," Editorial Preface, *Zeitschrift für die gesamte Staatswissenschaft/Journal of Institutional and Theoretical Economics*, 140, 1–6.

Furubotn, E.G. and Richter, R. (eds.) 1988. "Some Perspectives on Contractual Relations," *Journal of Institutional and Theoretical Economics/Zeitschrift für die gesamte Staatswissenschaft*, 144, 1–5.

Gaab, W. 1983. *Devisenterminmärkte und Wechselkurse. Eine theoretische und empirische Analyse*, Berlin-Heidelberg et al.: Springer.

Gale, D. 1982. *Money: In Equilibrium*, Welwyn-Cambridge-New York: Nisbet.

Gebauer, W. 1982. *Realzins, Inflation und Kapitalzins. Eine Neuinterpretation des Fischer-Theorems*, Berlin-Heidelberg et al.: Springer.

Gehrig, B. 1980. *Geldpolitik unter alternativen institutionellen Voraussetzungen. Die Bedeutung der Refinanzierungs-, Mindestreserven- und Depositenvorschriften für die Steuerbarkeit der Geldmenge*, Bern-Stuttgart: Paul Haupt.

Gerloff, W. 1944. "Ursprung und Sinn des Geldes," *Weltwirtschaftliches Archiv*, 60, 240–254.

Gerloff, W. 1947. *Die Entstehung des Geldes und die Anfänge des Geldwesens*, Frankfurt/Main: Klostermann.

Girton, L. and Roper, D. 1981. "Theory and Implications of Currency Substitution," *Journal of Money, Credit and Banking*, 13, 12–30.

Goldberg, V.P. 1976a. "Toward an Expanded Theory of Contract," *Journal of Economic Issues*, 10, 45–61.

Goldberg, V.P. 1976b. "Regulation and Administered Contracts," *The Bell Journal of Economics*, 7, 426–448.

Goldberg, V.P. 1980. "Relational Exchange, Economics and Complex Contracts," *American Behavior Scientist*, 23, 337–352.

Goodhart, C. 1985. *The Evolution of Central Banks: A Natural Development*? London: Suntory-Toyota International Centre for Economics and Related Disciplines/London School of Economics and Political Science.

Gordon, D.F. 1974. "A Neoclassical Theory of Keynesian Unemployment," *Economic Inquiry*, 7, 431–459.

Gorton, G. 1985a. "Banking Theory and Free Banking History, A Review Essay," *Journal of Monetary Economics*, 16, 267–276.

Gorton, G. 1985b. "Clearinghouses and the Origin of Central Banking in the United States," *Journal of Economic History*, 45, 277–283.

Goss, B.A. 1972. *The Theory of Futures Trading*, London-Boston: Routledge & Kegan Paul.
Graham, B. 1937. *Storage and Stability*, New York: McGraw-Hill.
Graham, F.D. 1930. *Exchange, Prices, and Production in Hyperinflation: Germany* 1920–1923, Princeton/N.J.: University Press.
Grandmont, J.M. 1977. "Temporary General Equilibrium Theory," *Econometrica*, 45, 535–572.
Grandmont, J.M. 1983. *Money and Value. A Reconsideration of Classical and Neoclassical Monetary Theories*, Cambridge et al.: Cambridge University Press.
Grandmont, J.M. and Laroque, G. 1973. "Money in the Pure Consumptions Loan Model," *Journal of Economic Theory*, 6, 382–395.
Gravelle, H. and Rees, R. 1981. *Microeconomics*, London-New York: Longman.
Greenfield, R.L. and Yeager, L.B. 1983. "A Laissez-Faire Approach to Monetary Stability," *Journal of Money, Credit and Banking*, 15, 302–315.
Greenwald, B. and Stiglitz, J. 1986. "Externalities in Economies with Imperfect Information and Incomplete Markets," *Quarterly Journal of Economics*, 101, 229–264.
Gregory, T.E. 1928. *An Introduction to Tooke and W. Newmarch's 'A History of Prices,'* London School of Economics and Political Science.
Grossman, H. 1983. "The Natural-Rate Hypothesis, the Rational-Expectations Hypothesis, and the Remarkable Survival of Non-Market-Clearing Assumptions," in: *Variability in Employment, Prices, and Money*, eds. K. Brunner and A.H. Meltzer, Carnegie-Rochester Conference Series on Public Policy, Vol. 19, 225–246, Amsterdam: North-Holland.
Gurley, J.G. and Shaw, E.S. 1960. *Money in a Theory of Finance*, Washington/D.C.: Brookings.

Haavelmo, T. 1960. *A Study of the Theory of Investment*, Chicago: University of Chicago Press.
Haberler, G. 1927. *Der Sinn der Indexzahlen*, Tübingen: Mohr.
Haberler, G. 1948. *Prosperität und Depression. Eine theoretische Untersuchung der Konjunkturbewegung*, Bern: Francke.
Haberler, G. 1958. *Prosperity and Depression. A Theoretical Analysis of Cyclical Movements*, translation of Haberler (1948), 4th ed. (new revised and enlarged), London: Allen & Unwin.
Haberler, G. 1987. "The International Monetary System: Recent Developments in Historic Perspective," *Außenwirtschaft. Schweizerische Zeitschrift für internationale Wirtschaftsbeziehungen*, 42, 373–385.
Hacche, G. 1983. "*The Determinants of Exchange Rate Movements*," OECD Economics and Statistics Department Working Papers, No. 7, Paris: OECD.
Hahn, F.H. 1965. "On Some Problems of Proving the Existence of an Equilibrium in a Monetary Economy," in: *The Theory of Interest Rates*, eds. F.H. Hahn and F.P.R. Brechling, Proceedings of a Conference held by the International Economic Association, London: Macmillan.
Hahn, F.H. 1971. "Equilibrium with Transaction Costs," *Econometrica*, 39, 417–439.
Hahn, F.H. 1973. "On Transaction Costs, Inessential Sequence Economics and Money," *Review of Economic Studies*, 40, 449–461.
Hahn, F.H. and Matthew, R.C.D. 1964. "The Theory of Economic Growth: A Survey," *Economic Journal*, 74, 779–902.
Hahn, O. 1968. *Die Währungsbanken der Welt*, Vol. I: Institutionen und Organe, Vol. II: Die Abhängigkeiten der Zentralbankleitung, Stuttgart: Poeschel.
Hall, R.E. 1982a, "Monetary Trends in the United States and the United Kingdom: A Review from the Perspective of New Developments in Monetary Economics," *Journal of Economic Literature*, 20, 1552–1556.
Hall, R.E. 1982b. "Explorations in the Gold Standard and Related Policies for Stabilizing the Dollar," in: *Inflation: Causes and Effects*, ed. R.E. Hall, 111–122, Chicago: University of Chicago Press.
Hansen, A.H. 1941. *Fiscal Policy and Business Cycles*, London: Allen & Unwin.
Hansen, B. 1966. *Lectures in Economic Theory*, Part I: General Equilibrium Theory, Lund: Student literatur.
Hart, A.G. 1935. "The 'Chicago Plan' of Banking Reform," *Review of Economic Studies*, 2, 104–116.
Hawtrey, R.G. 1962. *The Art of Central Banking*, Liverpool-London: Cass.
Hayak, P.R. 1980. "Efficiency of Non-Walrasian Equilibria," *Econometrica*, 48, 127–134.
Hayek, F.A. 1931a. *Preise und Produktion*, Wien: Springer.
Hayek, F.A. 1931b. *Prices and Production*, translation of Hayek (1931a), London: Routledge & Kegan Paul (reprinted 1951).

Hayek, F.A. 1933a. "The Trend of Economic Thinking," *Economica*, 40, 121–137.

Hayek, F.A. 1933b. "Über neutrales Geld," *Zeitschrift für Nationalökonomie*, 4, 659–661.

Hayek, F.A. 1945. "The Use of Knowledge in Society," *American Economic Review*, 35, 519–530.

Hayek, F.A. 1961. *The Pure Theory of Capital*, London: Routledge & Kegan Paul.

Hayek, F.A. 1976a. *Law, Legislation and Liberty*, Vol. 2: The Mirage of Social Justice, London: Routledge & Kegan Paul.

·Hayek, F.A. 1976b. "*Choice in Currency: A Way to Stop Inflation*," Occasional Paper, 48, London: Institute of Economic Affairs.

Hayek, F.A. 1976c. *Denationalization of Money. An Analysis of the Theory and Practice of Concurrent Currencies*, Hobart Paper Special, No. 70, London: Institute of Economic Affairs.

Hayek, F.A. 1977. *Entnationalisierung des Geldes. Eine Analyse der Theorie und Praxis konkurriender Umlaufsmittel*, translation of Hayek (1976c) (translated by W.v. Klinckowstroem), Tübingen: Mohr.

Hayek, F.A. 1978. "Towards a Free Market Monetary System," *Journal of Libertarian Studies*.

Heilfron, E. 1911. *Die Gesetzgebung über Geld-, Bank- und Börsenwesen*, Berlin: Speyer & Peters.

Helfferich, K. 1923. *Das Geld*, 6th ed., Leipzig: Hirschfeld.

Hellwig, M.F. 1985. "What do we Know About Currency Competition?", *Zeitschrift für Wirtschafts- und Sozialwissenschaften*, 105, 565–588.

Helmstädter, E. 1969. *Der Kapitalkoeffizient*, Stuttgart: Fischer.

Henderson, J.M. and Quandt, R.E. 1980. *Microeconomic Theory. A Mathematical Approach*, 3rd ed. (1st ed. 1958), New York-London: McGraw-Hill.

Hester, D.D. and Tobin, J. (eds.) 1967. *Financial Markets and Economic Activity*, Cowles Foundation for Research in Economics at Yale University, Monograph 21, New York-London-Sydney: Wiley.

Hicks, J.R. 1935. "A Suggestion for Simplifying the Theory of Money," *Economica*, N.S.Z., 2, 1–19, or in: *Readings in Monetary Theory* (1951), eds. F.A. Lutz and L.W. Mints, 13–32, Philadelphia/Pa.: Blakiston.

Hicks, J.R. 1937. "Mr. Keynes and the 'Classics,'" *Econometrica*, 5, 147–159.

Hicks, J.R. 1946. *Value and Capital. An Inquiry into Some Fundamental Principles of Economic Theory*, 2nd ed., Oxford: Clarendon Press.

Hicks, J.R. 1955. "Economic Foundations of Wage Policy," *Economic Journal*, 65, 389–404.

Hicks, J.R. 1962. "Liquidity," *Economic Journal*, 72, 787–802.

Hicks, J.R. 1965. *Capital and Growth*, Oxford: Clarendon Press.

Hicks, J.R. 1967. "The Two Triads," Lecture I, in: *Critical Essays in Monetary Theory*, ed. J.R. Hicks, 1–16, Oxford: Clarendon Press.

Hicks, J.R. 1973. *Capital and Time. A Neo-Austrian Theory*, Oxford: Clarendon Press.

Hicks, J.R. 1974. "Capital Controversies: Ancient and Modern," *American Economic Review, Papers and Proceedings*, 64, 307–316.

Hicks, J.R. 1977. *Economic Perspectives. Further Essays on Money and Growth*, Oxford Clarendon Press.

Hildenbrand, W. and Kirman, A.P. 1976. *Introduction to Equilibrium Analysis. Variations on Themes by Edgeworth and Walras*, Amsterdam et al.: North-Holland.

Hippel, E.v. 1963. *Die Kontrolle der Vertragsfreiheit nach anglo-amerikanischem Recht*, Frankfurt/Main: Klostermann.

Hippel, F.v. 1936. *Das Problem der rechtsgeschäftlichen Privatautonomie*, Tübingen: Mohr.

Hirschman, A.O. 1987. "Interests," in: *The New Palgrave: A Dictionary of Economics in four Volumes*, eds. J. Eatwell, M. Milgate and P. Newman, Vol. 2, 882–887, London: Macmillan.

Hirshleifer, J. 1959. "On the Theory of Optimal Investment Decision," in: *The Management of Corporate Capital*, ed. E. Solomon, 205–228, Glencoe/Ill.: Free Press.

Hirshleifer, J. 1970. *Investment, Interest and Capital*, Englewood Cliffs/N.J.: Prentice-Hall.

Hirshleifer, J. 1973. "Where are We in the Theory of Information?", *American Economic Review, Papers and Proceedings*, 63, 31–39.

Hirshleifer, J. 1975. "Speculation and Equilibrium: Information, Risk, and Markets," *Quarterly Journal of Economics*, 89, 519–542.

Hirshleifer, J. and Riley, J.G. 1979. "The Analytics of Uncertainty and Information – An Expository Survey," *Journal of Economic Literature*, 17, 1375–1421.

Holcombe, R.G. and Holcombe, L.P.: 1986. "The Market for Regulation," *Journal of Institutional and Theoretical Economics/Zeitschrift für die gesamte Staatswissenschaft*, 142, 684–696.

Honkapohja, S. 1978. "On the Efficiency of a Competitive Monetary Equilibrium with Transaction Costs," *Review of Economic Studies*, 45, 405–416.

Horsefield, J.K. and de Vries, M.G. 1969. *The International Monetary Fund* 1945–1965. *Twenty Years of International Monetary Cooperation*, Vol. I: Chronicle, Vol. III: Documents, Washington/D.C.: International Monetary Fund.

Houthakker, H.S. 1959. "The Scope and Limits of Futures Trading," in: *The Allocation of Economic Resources*, eds. M. Abramovitz et al., 134–159, stanford/Calif.: University Press.

Hübner, O. 1854. *Die Banken*, Leipzig: Hübner.

Hume, D. 1752/1955. *Writings on Economics*, ed. E. Rothwein (1955), London-Edinburgh et al.: Nelson.

Humphrey, T.M. 1974. "The Quantity Theory of Money: Its Historical Evolution and Role in Policy Debates," *Economic Review, Federal Reserve Bank of Richmond*, Richmond/Virginia.

(The) International Monetary Fund 1969. 1945–1965. *Twenty Years of International Monetary Cooperation*, Vol. III: Documents, Washington/D.C.: International Monetary Fund.

Isard, P. 1977. "How Far can we Push the 'Law of One Price,'" *American Economic Review*, 67, 942–948.

Issing, O. 1968. "Die Theorie des direkten internationalen Preiszusammenhangs," *Jahrbücher für Nationalökonomie und Statistik*, 181, 289–303.

Jastram, R.W. 1977. *The Golden Constant. The English and American Experience*, 1560–1976, New York et al.: Wiley.

Jensen, M.C. 1983. "Organization Theory and Methodology," *Accounting Review*, 58, 319–339.

Jensen, M.C. and Meckling, W.H. 1976. "Theory of the Firm, Managerial Behavior, Agency Costs and Ownership Structure," *Journal of Financial Economics*, 3, 305–360.

Jevons, W.S. 1875. *Money in the Mechanism of Exchange*, London-New York: King.

Jevons, W.S. 1884. *Investigations in Currency and Finance*, (first published 1863), London: Macmillan.

Johnson, H.G. 1962. "Monetary Theory and Policy," *American Economic Review*, 52, 335–384, or in: *Essays in Monetary Economics* (1967), ed. H.G. Johnson, Ch. I., London: Allen & Unwin.

Johnson, H.G. 1968. "Problems of Efficiency in Monetary Management," *Journal of Political Economy*, 76, 971–990.

Johnson, H.G. 1969. "The Case for Flexible Exchanges Rates, 1969," in: *UK and Floating Exchanges*, eds. H.G. Johnson and J.E. Nash, 9–37, London: Institute of Economic Affairs, or in: *Further Essays in Monetary Economics* (1972), ed. H.G. Johnson, 198–222, London: Allen & Unwin.

Johnson, H.G. 1970. "Recent Developments in Monetary Theory – a Commentary," in: *Money in Britain*, 1959–1969, eds. D.R. Crome and H.G. Johnson, Ch. III, 83–114, Oxford: University Press, or in: *Further Essays in Monetary Economics* (1972), ed. H.G. Johnson, 21–49, London: Allen & Unwin.

Johnson, H.G. 1972. *Further Essays in Monetary Economics*, London: Allen & Unwin.

Jones, R.A. 1976. "The Origin and Development of Media of Exchange," *Journal of Political Economy*, 84, 757–775.

Joskow, P.L. and Noll, R.C. 1981. "Regulation in Theory and Practice: An Overview," in: *Studies in Public Regulation*, ed. G. Fromm, Cambridge/Mass.: MIT-Press.

Joskow, P.L. and Schmalensee, R. 1983. *Markets for Power. An Analysis of Electric Utility Deregulation*, Ch. 9, Contractual Relationships: Theoretical and Empirical Issues, 109–113, Cambridge/Mass.: MIT-Press.

Juchem, N. 1983. *Geldschöpfung privater Banken: Ein Grundproblem der Geldverfassung*, Ph. D. diss. Saarbrücken.

Jurgensen, P. 1983. *Report of the Working Group on Exchange Market Intervention* (March 1983), sine locus.

Jurgensen, P. 1984. "Bericht der Arbeitstagung über Interventionen an den Devisenmärkten," in: *Devisenmarktinterventionen der Zentralbanken*, eds. W. Ehrlicher and R. Richter, Schriften des Vereins für Socialpolitik N.F., 139, 83–113, Berlin: Duncker & Humblot.

Kaldor, N. 1939. "Speculation and Economic Stability," *Review of Economic Studies*, 7, 1–27, or in: *Essays on Economic Stability and Growth* (1960), ed. N. Kaldor, 17–58, London: Duckworth.

Kareken, J.H. 1983. "The First Step in Bank Deregulation: What About the FDIC?", *American Economic Review, Papers and Proceedings*, 73, 198–203.

Kareken, J.H. and Wallace, N. (eds.) 1980. *Models of Monetary Economics*, Federal Reserve Bank of Minneapolis.

Katzenstein, D. 1982. "Verfassungsrechtlicher Schutz der Rentenansprüche nach dem gegenwärtigen Stand der Rechtssprechung des Bundesverfassungsgerichts," *Deutsche Rentenversicherung*, 38, 177–190.

Kemmerer, E.W. 1944. *Gold and Gold Standard*, New York-London: McGraw-Hill.

Keynes, J.M. 1923. *A Tract on Monetary Reform*, (reprinted 1924), London: Macmillan.

Keynes, J.M. 1930. *A Treatise on Money*, Vol. I: The Pure Theory of Money, Vol. II: The Applied Theory of Money, London: Macmillan.

Keynes, J.M. 1932. *Vom Gelde*, translation of Keynes (1930) (translated by C. Krämer), München-Leipzig: Duncker & Humblot.

Keynes, J.M. 1936. *The General Theory of Employment, Interest and Money*, London: Macmillan.

Kindleberger, C.P. 1969. "The Case for Fixed Exchange Rates, 1969," in: *The International Adjustment Mechanism*, Conference Series, No. 2, Proceedings of the Monetary Conference, Melvin Village/N.H., 8–10 October 1969, 93–108, or in: *International Money. A Collection of Essays* (1981), ed. C.P. Kindleberger, 169–182, London-Boston: Allen & Unwin.

Kindleberger, C.P. 1978. *Manias, Panics, and Crashes. A History of Financial Crises*, London-Basingstoke: Macmillan.

King, R.G. 1983. "On the Economics of Private Money," *Journal of Monetary Economics*, 12, 127–158.

Klanberg, F. and Prinz, A. 1983. "Anatomie der Sozialhilfe," *Finanzarchiv*, N.F., 41, 281–311.

Klein, B. 1974. "The Competitive Supply of Money," *Journal of Money, Credit and Banking*, 6, 421–453.

Knapp, G.F. 1921. *Staatliche Theorie des Geldes*, 3rd ed. (1st ed. 1905), München-Leipzig: Duncker & Humblot.

Knapp, G.F. 1924. *The State Theory of Money*, translation of Knapp (1921) (translated by H.M. Lucas and J. Bonar), London: Macmillan.

Knight, F. 1944. "Diminishing Returns from Investment," *Journal of Political Economy*, 52, 26–47.

Koch, R. 1885. *Die Reichsgesetzgebung über Münz- und Bankwesen, Papiergeld, Prämienpapiere und Reichsanleihen*, Berlin-Leipzig: Guttentag.

Koopmans, J.G. 1933. "Zum Problem des neutralen Geldes," in: *Beiträge zur Geldtheorie*, ed. F.A. Hayek, Wien: Springer.

Koopmans, T.C. 1957. *Three Essays on the State of Economic Science*, New York-London: McGraw-Hill.

Koopmans, T.C. 1960. "Stationary Ordinal Utility and Impatience," *Econometrica*, 28, 287–290.

Koopmans, T.C. 1963. "*On the Concept of Optimal Economic Growth. The Econometric Approach to Development Planning*," Cowles Foundation for Research in Economics, Discussion Paper No. 163, New Haven/Conn.

Koopmans, T.C. 1967. "Intertemporal Distribution and 'Optimal' Aggregate Economic Growth," in: *Ten Economic Studies in the Tradition of Irving Fisher*, eds. W. Fellner et al., 95–126, London-New York: Wiley.

Koopmans, T.C., Diamond, P.A. and Williamson, R.E. 1964. "Stationary Utility and Time Perspective," *Econometrica*, 32, 82–100.

Krispis, E. 1967. "Money in Private International Law," *Recueil des Cours I, Tome* 120 *de la collection, Académie de Droit International*, 195–311, Leyde (1968): A.W. Sijthoff.

Kurz, M. 1974a. "Equilibrium with Transaction Cost and Money in a Single Market Exchange Economy," *Journal of Economic Theory*, 7, 418–452.

Kurz, M. 1974b. "Equilibrium in a Finite Sequence of Markets with Transaction Cost," *Econometrica*, 42, 1–20.

Kydland, F.E. and Prescott, E.C. 1977. "Rules Rather than Discretion: The Inconsistency of Optimal Plans," *Journal of Political Economy*, 85, 473–491.

Laidler, D.E.W. 1975a. "On Wicksell's Theory of Price Level Dynamics," in: *Essays on Money and Inflation*, ed. D.E.W. Laidler, 101–119, Chicago: University of Chicago Press.

Laidler, D.E.W. 1975b. "Th. Tooke on Monetary Reform," in: *Essays on Money and Inflation*, ed. D.E.W. Laidler, 211–227, Chicago: University of Chicago Press.

Laidler, D.E.W. 1981a. "Adam Smith as a Monetary Economist," *Canadian Journal of Economics*, 14, 185–200.

Laidler, D.E.W. 1981b. "Monetarism: An Interpretation and Assessment," *Economic Journal*, 91, 1–28.

Laidler, D.E.W. and Parkin, M. 1975. "Inflation: A Survey," *Economic Journal*, 85, 741–809.

Laidler, D.E.W. and Rowe, N. 1980. "Georg Simmel's Philosophy of Money: A Review Article for Economists," *Journal of Economic Literature*, 18, 97–105.

Lampe, O. 1971. *Die Unabhängigkeit der Deutschen Bundesbank. Eine verfassungsrechtliche und verwaltungsrechtliche Untersuchung*, 2nd ed., München: Beck.

Lampert, H. 1985. *Sozialpolitik*, Berlin-Heidelberg et al.: Springer.

Lange, O. 1942. "Say's Law: A Restatement and Criticism," in: *Studies in Mathematical Economics and Econometrics*, ed. O. Lange, 49–68, Chicago: University of Chicago Press.

Larenz, K. 1982. *Lehrbuch des Schuldrechts*, Vol. I: Allgemeiner Teil, 13 th ed., München: Beck.

Laufenberg, D.E. 1976. "Contemporaneous Versus Lagged Reserve Accounting," *Journal of Money, Credit and Banking*, 8, 239–245.

Laufenberg, D.E. 1977. "*Legal Reserve Requirements: An Instrument of Monetary Control?*", Special Studies Paper, No. 96, Washington/D.C.: Federal Reserve Board.

Laufenberg, D.E. 1979. "Optimal Reserve Requirement Ratios Against Bank Deposits for Short-Run Monetary Control," *Journal of Money, Credit and Banking*, 11, 99–105.

Laughlin, J. 1903. *Principles*, New York: C. Scribner's sons.

Laum, B. 1924. *Heiliges Geld. Eine historische Untersuchung über den sakralen Ursprung des Geldes*, Tübingen: Mohr.

Laurent, R.D. 1979. "Reserve Requirements: Are They Lagged in the Wrong Direction?", *Journal of Money, Credit and Banking*, 11, 301–310.

Laurent, R.D. 1981a. "Reserve Requirements, Deposit Insurance and Monetary Control," *Journal of Money, Credit and Banking*, 13, 314–324.

Laurent, R.D. 1981b. *A Comprehensive Proposal for Accurate Money Control Through Reserves*, Staff Memoranda (81-1), Chicago: Federal Reserve Bank of Chicago.

Laurent, R.D. 1983. *Comparing Alternative Replacements for Lagged Reserves: Why Settle for a Poor Third Best?* Staff Memoranda (83-2), Chicago: Federal Reserve Bank of Chicago.

Lebègue, D. 1985. "Pour une réforme du système monétaire internationale," in: *Economie prospective internationale*, No. 24, 7–18, Paris: Centre d'Etudes Prospectives et d'Informations Internationales.

Leitner, F. 1920. *Das Bankengeschäft und seine Technik*, 4th ed., Frankfurt/Main: Sauerländer.

Leontief, W. 1958. "Theoretical Note on Time – Preference, Productivity of Capital, Stagnation and Economic Growth," *American Economic Review*, 48, 105–111.

Lerner, A.P. 1947. "Money as a Creature of the State," *American Economic Review*, 37, 312–317.

Levich, R.M. 1985. "Empirical Studies of Exchange Rates: Price Behavior, Rate Determination and Market Efficiency," in: *Handbook of International Economics*, eds. R.W. Jones and P.B. Kenen, Vol. II, 979–1040, Amsterdam: North-Holland.

Levin, J.A. 1977. "Speculation and the Crawling Peg," *Economica*, 44, 57–62.

Lexis, W. 1893. "Papiergeld," in: *Handwörterbuch der Staatswissenschften*, eds. J. Conrad, L. Elster, W. Lexis and E. Coening, Vol. 5, 96–117, Jena: Fischer.

Lexis, W. and Terhalle, F. 1926. "Silber und Silbergeld," in: *Handwörterbuch der Staatswissenschaften*, eds. L. Elster, A. Weber and F. Wieser, 4th ed., Vol. 7, 469–488, Jena: Fischer.

Lindahl, E.R. 1929. "The Place of Capital in the Theory of Price," in: *Studies in the Theory of Money and Capital* (1939), ed. E.R. Lindahl, 271–350, London: Allen & Unwin.

Lippman, S.A. and McCall, J.J. 1976. "The Economics of Job Search: A Survey," *Economic Inquiry*, 14, 155–189 and 347–368.

Lucas, R.E., Jr. 1972. "Expectations and the Neutrality of Money," *Journal of Economic Theory*, 4, 103–124.

Lucas, R.E., Jr. 1973. "Some International Evidence on Output-Inflation Tradeoffs," *American Economic Review*, 63, 326–334.

Lucas, R.E., Jr. 1975. "An Equilibrium Model of the Business Cycle," *Journal of Political Economy*, 83, 1113–1144.

Lucas, R.E., Jr. 1976. "Econometric Policy Evaluation: A Critique," *Journal of Monetary Economics*, 2, *Supplement*, Carnegie – Rochester Conference Series, Vol. 1., 19–46.

Lucas, R.E., Jr. 1981, "Tobin and Monetarism: A Review Article," *Journal of Economic Literature*, 19, 558-567.

Lucas, R.E., Jr. and Sargent, T.J. (eds.) 1981. *Rational Expectations and Econometric Practice*, London et al.: Allen & Unwin.

Ludlow, P. 1982: *The Making of the European Monetary System*, London et al.: Butterworth.

Luig, K. 1966. *Zur Geschichte der Zessionslehre*, Köln-Graz: Bohlau.

Lutz, F.A. 1935. "Goldwährung und Wirtschaftsordnung," *Weltwirtschaftliches Archiv*, 41, 224–251, or in: see *F.A. Lutz* (1962), 1–27.

Lutz, F.A. 1936. *Das Grundproblem der Geldverfassung*, Stuttgart – Berlin: Kohlhammer, or in: see *F.A. Lutz* (1962), 28–102.

Lutz, F.A. 1940/1941. "The Structure of Interest Rates," *Quarterly Journal of Economics*, 55, 36–63, or in: *Readings in the Theory of Income Distribution* (1946), ed. American Economic Association, Philadelphia/Pa.: Blakiston.

Lutz, F.A. 1962. *Geld und Währung. Gesammelte Abhandlungen*, Tübingen: Mohr.

Lutz, F.A. 1963. "The Essentials of Capital Theory," in: *The Theory of Capital*, eds. F.A. Lutz and D.C. Hague, 3–17, London: Macmillan.

Macauly, S. 1963. "Non-contractual Relations in Business: A Preliminary Study," *American Sociological Review*, 28, 55–69.

Macleod, H.D. 1863. "Credit," "Bank," "Capital" and "Currency," in: *Dictionary of Political Economy*, Vol. I, London.

Macneil, J.R. 1974. "The Many Futures of Contract," *Southern California Law Review*, 47, 691–816.

Macneil, J.R. 1978. "Contracts: Adjustment of Long-term Economic Relations under Classical, Neoclassical, and Relational Contract Law," *Northwestern University Law Review*, 72, 854–905.

Macneil, J.R. 1980. *The New Social Contract: An Inquiry Into Modern Contractual Relations*, New Haven/Conn.: Yale University Press.

Macneil, J.R. 1983. "Values and Contracts: Internal and External," *Northwestern University Law Review*, 78, 340–418.

Maddock, R. and Carter, M. 1982. "A Child's Guide to Rational Expectations," *Journal of Economic Literature*, 20, 39–51.

Malinvaud, E. 1953. "Capital Accumulation and Efficient Allocation of Resources," *Econometrica*, 21, 233–268.

Malinvaud, E. 1961. "The Analogy Between Atemporal and Intertemporal Theories of Resource Allocation," *Review of Economic Studies*, 28, 143–160.

Malinvaud, E. 1977. *The Theory of Unemployment Reconsidered*, Oxford: Blackwell.

Malkiel, B.G. 1966. *The Term Structure of Interest Rates. Expectations and Behavior Patterns*, Princeton/N.J.: University Press.

Mann, F.A. 1960. *Das Recht des Geldes. Eine rechtsvergleichende Untersuchung auf der Grundlage des englischen Rechts*, Frankfurt/Main-Berlin: Metzner.

Mann, F.A. 1971. *The Legal Aspect of Money*, 3rd ed., Oxford: Clarendon Press.

Marshall, A. 1926. *Official Papers*, London: Macmillan.

Mayer, H. 1932. "Der Erkenntniswert der funktionellen Preistheorien," in: *Die Wirtschaftstheorie der Gegenwart*, ed. H. Mayer, Vol. 2, 147–239, Wien: Springer.

Mayer, H. 1983. "Auf verlorenem Posten: Die Geschichte der Goldpool-Vereinbarungen," in: *Geld- und Währungsordnung*, eds. W. Ehrlicher and R. Richter, 219–241, Berlin: Duncker & Humblot.

Mayer, T. 1985. "The Status of the Monetarist Debate in the United States: An Evaluation," in: *Öffentliche Finanzen, Kredit und Kapital*, Festschrift für Werner Ehrlicher zur Vollendung des 65. Lebensjahres, eds. D. Cansier and D. Kath, 357–375, Berlin: Duncker & Humblot.

McCallum, B.T. 1979. "The Current State of the Policy-Ineffectiveness Debate," *American Economic Review, Papers and Proceedings*, 69, 240–245.

McCallum, B.T. 1980. "Rational Expectations and Macroeconomic Stabilization Policy. An Overview," *Journal of Money, Credit and Banking*, 12, 716–746.

McCallum, B.T. 1982. "*The Role of Overlapping-Generations Models in Monetary Economics*," National Bureau of Economic Research, Working Paper, No. 989, Cambridge/Mass.: NBER.

McCallum, B.T. 1983. "Inflation and Social Consensus in the Seventies," *Economic Journal*, 93, 784–805.

McCallum, B.T. 1985. "Bank Deregulation, Accounting Systems of Exchange, and the Unit of Account: A Critical Review," in: *The 'New Monetary Economics,' Fiscal Issues and Underemployment*, eds. K. Brunner and A.H. Meltzer, Carnegie – Rochester Conference Series on Public Policy, Vol. 23, 13–45, Amsterdam: North-Holland.

McCloskey, D.N. and Zecher, J.R. 1976. "How the Gold Standard Worked, 1880–1913," in: *The Monetary Approach to the Balance of Payments*, eds. J.A. Frenkel and H.G. Johnson, 357–385, London: Allen & Unwin.

McKinnon, R.I. 1974. "*A New Tripartite Monetary Agreement on a Limping Dollar Standard?*", Essays in International Finance, No. 106, International Finance Section, Department of Economics, Princeton University, Princeton/N.J.

McKinnon, R.I. 1979. *Money in International Exchange: The Convertible Currency System*, New York: Oxford University Press.

McKinnon, R.I. 1981. "The Exchange Rate and Macroeconomic Policy: Changing Postwar Perceptions," *Journal of Economic Literature*, 19, 531–557.

McKinnon, R.I. 1984. "*An International Standard for Monetary Stabilization*," Policy Analysis in International Economics, 8, Ch. 5, Washington/D.C.: Institute for International Economics.

McKinnon, R.I. 1986. *Monetary and Exchange Rate Policies for International Financial Stability: A Proposal*, manuscript, September 1986, Stanford University.

McKinnon, R.I. 1988. "Monetary and Exchange Rate Policies for International Financial Stability: A Proposal," *The Journal of Economic Perspectives*, 2, 83–103.

Meade, J.E. 1934. "The Amount of Money and the Banking System," *Economic Journal*, 44, 77–83, or in: *Readings in Monetary Theory* (1956), ed. American Economic Association, 54–62, Philadelphia/Pa.: Blakiston, London: Allen & Unwin.

Meigs, A.J. 1962. *Free Reserves and the Money Supply*, Chicago: University of Chicago Press.

Meiselman, D. 1962. *The Term Structure of Interest Rates*, Englewood Cliffs/N.J.: Prentice-Hall.

Menger, C. 1883. *Untersuchungen über die Methoden der Socialwissenschaften und der Politischen Ökonomie insbesondere*, Leipzig: Duncker & Humblot, or in: *Gesammelte Werke* (1969), ed. F.A. Hayek, 2nd ed., Vol. II, Tübingen: Mohr.

Menger, C. 1892. "On the Origin of Money," *Economic Journal*, 2, 239–255.

Menger, C. 1909. "Geld," in: *Handwörterbuch der Staatswissenschaften*, eds. J. Conrad, L. Elster, W. Lexis and E. Loening, 3rd ed., Vol. 4, 555–610, Jena: Fischer.

Menger, C. 1934. *The Collected Works of Carl Menger*, Vol. I (Grundsätze der Volkswirtschaftslehre), No. 17 in Series of Reprints of Scarce Tracts in Economic and Political Science, ed. The London School of Economics and Political Science.

Menger, C. 1963. *Problems of Economics and Sociology*, translation of Menger (1883) (translated by F.J. Nock), ed. L. Schneider, Urbana/Ill.: University of Illinois Press.

Merrick, J.J. and Saunders, A. 1985. "Bank Regulation and Monetary Policy," *Journal of Money, Credit and Banking*, 17, 691–717.

Metzler, L.A. 1951. "Wealth, Saving, and the Rate of Interest," *Journal of Political Economy*, 59, 93–116.

Meyer, E. 1910. "Münzwesen," in: *Handwörterbuch der Staatswissenschaften*, eds. J. Conrad, L. Elster, W. Lexis and E. Loening, 3rd ed., Vol. 6, 824–832, Jena: Fischer.

Meyer, W. 1983. "Entwicklung und Bedeutung des Property-Rights-Ansatzes in der Nationalökonomie," in: *Property Rights und ökonomische Theorie*, ed. A. Schüller, 1–44, München: Vahlen.

Miles, M.A. 1978. "Currency Substitution, Flexible Exchange Rate, and Monetary Independence," *American Economic Review*, 68, 428–436.

Mints, L.W. 1945. *A History of Banking Theory in Great Britain and the United States*, Chicago: Chicago Press.

Miron, J.A. 1986. "Financial Panics, the Seasonality of the Nominal Interest Rate, and the Founding of the Fed," *American Economic Review*, 76, 125–140.

Mises, L.v. 1924. *Theorie des Geldes und der Umlaufsmittel*, 2nd ed., München-Leipzig: Duncker & Humblot.

Mises, L.v. 1953. *The Theory of Money and Credit*, translation of Mises (1924) (translated by H.E. Batson), New Haven/Conn.: Yale University Press.

Mishkin, F.S. 1986. *The Economics of Money, Banking and Financial Markets*, Boston-Toronto: Little River.

Modigliani, F. 1978. "Die Monetarismuskontroverse. Eine Zwischenbilanz," in: *Beihefte zu Kredit und Kaptial*, eds. W. Ehrlicher and E.-D. Becker, Heft 4, 246–276, Berlin: Duncker & Humblot.

Möller, H. 1972. *Das Ende der Währungsordnung*?, München: Piper.

Möschel, W. 1972. *Das Wirtschaftsrecht der Banken. Die währungs-, bankaufsichts-, kartell- und EWG-rechtliche Sonderstellung der Kreditinstitute*, Frankfurt/Main: Athenaeum.

Möschel, W. 1975. "Bankenrecht und Wirtschaftsordnung," *Betriebsberater, Zeitschrift für Recht und Wirtschaft*, 30, 1025–1030.

Möschel, W. 1985. "Eine Systematik von Bankenregulierungszielen," in: *Festschrift für Walter Stimpel zum 68. Geburtstag*, ed. Marcus Lutter, 1065–1085, Berlin-New York: de Gruyter.

Möschel, W. 1986. "Dogmatische Strukturen des bargeldlosen Zahlungsverkehrs," *Archiv für civilistische Praxis*, 186, 187–236.

Moldofsky, N. 1982. "Market Theoretical Framework – Which One?" *Economic Record*, 58, 152–168.

Morgan, E.V. 1965. *The Theory and Practice of Central Banking* 1793–1913, New York: A.M. Kelley.

Morrison, G.R. 1966. *Liquidity Preferences of Commercial Banks*, Chicago: University of Chicago Press.

Müller, W.A. 1981. *Bankenaufsicht und Gläubigerschutz*, Baden-Baden: Nomos.

Müller-Graff, P.-C. 1973. *Rechtliche Auswirkungen einer laufenden Geschäftsverbindung im amerikanischen und deutschen Recht*, Ph.D. diss. Tübingen, Karlsruhe: Verlag für Versicherungswirtschaft.

Mundell, R.A. 1961. "A Theory of Optimum Currency Areas," *American Economic Review*, 51, 657–665.

Mundell, R.A. 1968. *International Economics*, New York: Macmillan.

Musgrave, R.A. 1959, *The Theory of Public Finance*, New York-London: McGraw-Hill.

Musgrave, R.A. 1969. "Cost-Benefit Analysis and the Theory of Public Finance," *Journal of Economic Literature*, 7, 797–806.

Mussa, M.L. 1976. "The Exchange Rate, the Balance of Payments and Monetary and Fiscal Policy Under a Regime of Controlled Floating," *The Scandinavian Journal of Economics*, 78, 229–248.

Muth, J.F. 1961. "Rational Expectations and the Theory of Price Movements," *Econometrica*, 29, 313–335.

Nagatani, K. 1978. *Monetary Theory*, Amsterdam et al.: North-Holland.

Negishi, T. 1962. "The Stability of a Competitive Economy: A Survey Article," *Econometrica*, 30, 635–669.

Nelson, C.R. 1972. *The Term Structure of Interest Rates*, New York-London: Basic Books.

Niehans, J. 1969. "Money in a Static Theory of Optimal Payment Arrangements," *Journal of Money, Credit and Banking*, 1, 706–726.

Niehans, J. 1975a. "Interest and Credit in General Equilibrium with Transaction Costs," *American Economic Review*, 65, 548–566.

Niehans, J. 1975b. "Some Doubts About the Efficacy of Monetary Policy under Flexible Exchange Rates," *Journal of International Economics*, 5, 275–281.

Niehans, J. 1978. *The Theory of Money*, Baltimore-London: Johns Hopkins University Press.

Niehans, J. 1984. *International Monetary Economics*, Oxford: Allan.

Niehans, J. 1987. "Classical Monetary Theory. New and Old," *Journal of Money, Credit and Banking*, 19, 409–424.

North, D.C. 1986. "The New Institutional Economics," *Journal of Institutional and Theoretical Economics/Zeitschrift für die gesamte Staatswissenschaft*, 142, 230–237.

Nurske, R. 1944. *International Currency Experience: Lessons of the Interwar Period*, Geneva-Princeton/N.J.: League of Nations.

Nussbaum, A. 1925. *Das Geld in Theorie und Praxis des deutschen und ausländischen Rechts*, Tübingen: Mohr.

Nussbaum, A. 1950. *Money in the Law, National and International. A Comparative Study in the Borderline of Law and Economics* (A completely revised English edition of A. Nussbaum 1925), Brooklyn: The Foundation Press.

Officer, L.H. 1976. "The Purchasing-Power-Parity Theory of Exchange Rates: A Review Article," *International Monetary Fund Staff Papers*, 23, 1–60, Washington/D.C.: International Monetary Fund.

Okun, A.M. 1981. *Prices and Quantities. A Macroeconomic Analysis*, Oxford: Blackwell.

Olivera, J.H.G. 1970. "On Passive Money," *Journal of Political Economy*, 78, 805–814.

Orr, D. and Mellon, W.G. 1961. "Stochastic Reserve Losses and Expansion of Bank Credit," *American Economic Review*, 51, 614–623.

Page, R. 1826. *Letters to the Editor of "The Times" journal, On the affairs and conduct of the Bank of England; the introduction of British silver money into the colonies; and generally on the Currency of the United Kingdom, both paper and metallic: with notes and appendix*, London: printed for Richard Long.

Pareto, V. 1927. *Manuel D'Economie Politique*, 2nd ed., Paris: Giard.

Pareto, V. 1971. *Manual of Political Economy*, translation of Pareto (1927) (translated by A.S. Schwier and A.N. Page), New York: Kelley.

Patinkin, D. 1948. "Relative Prices, Say's Law, and the Demand for Money," *Econometrica*, 16, 135–154.

Patinkin, D. 1949. "The Indeterminancy of Absolute Prices in Classical Economic Theory," *Econometrica*, 17, 1–27.

Patinkin, D. 1961. "Financial Intermediaries and the Logical Structure of Monetary Theory. A Review Article," *American Economic Review*, 51, 95–116.

Patinkin, D. 1965. *Money, Interest, and Prices. An Integration of Monetary and Value Theory*, 2nd ed. (1st ed. 1956), New York: Harper & Row.

Peltzman, S. 1976. "Toward a More General Theory of Regulation," *Journal of Law and Economics*, 19, 211–240.

Pesek, B.P. and Saving, T.R. 1968. *The Foundations of Money and Banking*, London – New York: Macmillan.

Phelps, E.S. 1961. "The Golden Rule of Accumulation. A Fable for Growthmen," *American Economic Review*, 638–643.

Phelps, E.S. 1967. *Golden Rules of Economic Growth – Studies in Efficient and Optimal Investment*, Amsterdam – New York: North-Holland.

Phelps, E.S. et al. 1970. *Microeconomic Foundations of Employment and Inflation Theory*, New York: Norton.

Phelps, E.S. 1972. *Inflation Policy and Employment Theory. The Cost-Benefit Approach to Monetary Planning*, London-Basingstoke: Macmillan.

Phelps, E.S. 1973. "Inflation in the Theory of Public Finance," *Swedish Journal of Economics*, 175, 67–82.

Phillips, C.A. 1920. *Bank Credit. A Survey of the Principles and Factors Underlying Advances Made by Banks to Borrowers*, New York: Macmillan.

Picot, A. 1981. "Transaktionskostentheorie der Organisation," in: *Beiträge zur Unternehmensführung und Organisation*, ed. A. Picot, Schriftreihe der Universität Hannover.

Picot, A. 1982. "Transaktionskostenansatz der Organisation: Stand der Diskussion und Aussagewert," *Die Betriebswirtschaft*, 42, 267–284.

Plenge, J. 1913. *Von der Diskontpolitik zur Herrschaft über den Geldmarkt*, Berlin: Springer.

Poole, W. 1976. "A Proposal for Reforming Bank Reserve Requirements in the United States," *Journal of Money, Credit and Banking*, 8, 137–147.

Porter, R.C. 1967. "A Model of Bank Portfolio Selection," in: *Risk Aversion and Portfolio Choice*, eds. D.D. Hester and J. Tobin, 12–54, New York-London: Wiley.

Posner, R.A. 1974. "Theories of Economic Regulation," *The Bell Journal of Economics and Management Science*, 5, 335–358.

Purvis, D.D. 1980. "Monetarism: A Review," *Canadian Journal of Economics*, 13, 96–122.

Putterman, L. 1986. "The Economic Nature of the Firm: Overview," in: *The Economic Nature of the Firm*, ed. L. Putterman, 1–29, Cambridge: Cambridge University Press.

Radford, R.A. 1945. "The Economic Organization of a Prisoner of War Concept," *Economica*, 12, 189–201.

Radner, R. 1974. "Market Equilibrium and Uncertainty: Concepts and Problems," in: *Frontiers of Quantitative Economics*, eds. M.D. Intriligator and D.A. Kendrick, Vol. II, 43–90, Amsterdam et al.: North-Holland.

Rae, J. 1905. *The Sociological Theory of Capital*, New York: Macmillan.

Ramser, H.J. 1978. "Die Kontrakttheorie als Beitrag zu einer ökonomischen Theorie des Arbeitsmarktes," *Zeitschrift für die gesamte Staatswissenschaft*, 134, 628–659.

Ramsey, F.P. 1928. "A Mathematical Theory of Saving," *Economic Journal*, 38, 543–559.

Reder, M.W. 1948. "The Theoretical Problems of a National Wage-Price Policy," *Canadian Journal of Economics and Political Science*, 14, 46–61.

Ricardo, D. 1810/1951. "The High Price of Bullion. A Proof of the Depreciation of Bank Notes," London 1810, in: *The Works and Correspondence of David Ricardo* (1951), ed. P. Sraffa, Vol. III, Pamphlets and Papers, 1809–1811, Cambridge et al.: Cambridge University Press.

Ricardo, D. 1811. *The High Price of Bullion. A Proof of the Depreciation of Bank Notes*, 4th corrected ed., London: J. Murray.

Ricardo, D. 1816/1951. "Proposals for an Economical and Secure Currency; with Observations on the Profits of the Bank of England, as They Regard the Public and the Proprietors of Bank Stock," London 1816, in: *The Works and Correspondence of David Ricardo* (1951), ed. P. Sraffa, Vol. IV, 43–141, Cambridge et al.: Cambridge University Press.

Ricardo, D. 1817/1951. "On the Principles of Political Economy and Taxation," London 1817, in: *The Works and Correspondence of David Ricardo* (1951), ed. P. Sraffa (with collaboration of M.H. Dobb), Vol. I, Cambridge et al.: Cambridge University Press.

Richter, R. 1968. "The Banking System Within Macro-Economic Theory," *German Economic Review*, 6, 273–293.

Richter, R. 1978. "Der Multiplikatoreffekt bei Interventionskosten," *Zeitschrift für die gesamte Staatswissenschaft*, 134, 197–202.

Richter, R. (ed.) 1981. "Meinungsäußerungen und Stellungnahmen zum Thema 'Das Wesen der Unternehmung,'" *Zeitschrift für die gesamte Staatswissenschaft/Journal of Institutional and Theoretical Economics*, 137, 665–732.

Richter, R. 1987. "*The New Institutional Economics Applied to Monetary Economics*," Working Paper Series of the Center for the Study of the New Institutional Economics, No. 1, Department of Economics, Universität des Saarlandes, Saarbrücken (W.-Germany), published in the Journal of Institutional and Theoretical Economics/Zeitschrift für die gesamte Staatswissenschaft, 144 (1988), 208–224.

Richter, R. (ed.) 1988. "A Collection of Views and Comments on the Problem of Order in Economics," *Journal of Institutional and Theoretical Economics/Zeitschrift für die gesamte Staatswissenschaft*, 144, 208–224.

Richter, R., Schlieper, U. and Friedmann, W. 1981. *Makroökonomik. Eine Einführung*, 4th ed., Berlin-Heidelberg et al.: Springer.

Richter, R. and Teigen, R.L. 1982. "Commercial Bank Behavior and Monetary Policy in an Open Economy: West Germany 1960–1980," *Journal of Monetary Economics*, 10, 383–405.

Ritzmann, F. 1973. *Die Schweizer Banken*, Bern – Stuttgart: Paul Haupt.

Robbins, L. 1958. *Robert Torrens and the Evolution of Classical Economics*, London: Macmillan.

Rockoff, H. 1975. *The Free Banking Era: A Reexamination*, New York: Arno Press.

Rogers, J.H. 1933. "The Absorption of Bank Credit," *Econometrica*, 1, 63–70.

Roll, R. 1972. "Interest Rates on Monetary Assets and Commodity Price Index Changes," *Journal of Finance*, 27, 251–277.

Rolnick, A.J. and Weber, W.E. 1983. "New Evidence on the Free Banking Era," *American Economic Review*, 73, 1080–1091.

Rolnick, A.J. and Weber, W.E. 1984. "The Causes of Free Banking Failures: A Detailed Examination," *Journal of Monetary Economics*, 14, 267–292.

Rolnick, A.J. and Weber, W.E. 1988. "Explaining the Demand for Free Bank Notes," *Journal of Monetary Economics*, 21, 47–71.

Ronge, V. 1979. *Bankpolitik im Spätkapitalismus – Politische Selbstverwaltung des Kapitals?*, Starnberger Studien, Vol. 3, ed. by Max-Planck-Institut zur Erforschung der Lebensbedingungen der wissenschaftlich-technischen Welt, Frankfurt/Main: Suhrkamp.

Rose, K. 1981. *Theorie der Außenwirtschaft*, 8th ed., München: Vahlen.

Rotemberg, J.J. 1983. "Monetary Policy and Costs of Price Adjustment," *Journal of Economic Dynamics and Control*, 5, 267–288.

Sachs, J. 1986. "The Uneasy Case for Greater Exchange Rate Coordination," *American Economic Review, Papers and Proceedings*, 76, 336–341.

Sachverständigenrat zur Begutachtung der gesamtwirtschaftlichen Entwicklung, *Jahresgutachten* für die Jahre 1974/75, 1976/77, 1985/86, BT-Drucksache, Bonn: Heger.

Samuelson, P.A. 1947. *Foundations of Economic Analysis*, Cambridge/Mass.: Harvard University Press.

Samuelson, P.A. 1958. "An Exact Consumption-Loan Model of Interest With or Without the Social Contrivance of Money," *Journal of Political Economy*, 66, 467–482.

Samuelson, P.A. 1967. "Irving Fisher and the Theory of Capital," in: *Ten Economic Studies in the Tradition of Irving Fisher*, eds. W. Fellner et al., 17–37, New York: Wiley.

Samuelson, P.A. 1968. "What Classical and Neoclassical Monetary Theory Really Was," *Canadian Journal of Economics*, 1, 1–15.

Samuelson, P.A. 1969. "Nonoptimality of Money Holding Under Laissez-Faire," *Canadian Journal of Economics*, 2, 303–308.

Samuelson, P.A. 1980. "A Corrected Version of Hume's Equilibrating Mechanism for International Trade," in: *Flexible Exchange Rates and the Balance of Payments*, eds. J.S. Chipman and C.P. Kindleberger, 141–158, Amsterdam et al.: North-Holland.

Samuelson, P.A. 1982. "Schumpeter as an Economic Theorist," in: *Schumpeterian Economics*, ed. H. Frisch, 1–27, Eastbourne – New York: Praeger.

Samuelson, P.A. and Nordhaus, W.D. 1985. *Economics*, 12th ed., New York: McGraw Hill.

Santomero, A.M. 1984. "Modeling the Banking Firm: A Survey," *Journal of Money, Credit and Banking*, 16, 576–602.

Santomero, A.M. and Siegel, J.E. 1981. "Bank Regulation and Macro-Economic Stability," *American Economic Review*, 71, 39–53.

Sargent, T.J. and Wallace, N. 1975. "'Rational' Expectations, the Optimal Monetary Instrument, and the Optimal Money Supply Rule," *Journal of Political Economy*, 83, 241–254.

Sargent, T.J. and Wallace, N. 1982. "The Real-Bills Doctrine versus the Quantity Theory: A Reconsideration," *Journal of Political Economy*, 90, 1212–1236.

Saving, T.R. 1977. "A Theory of the Money Supply with Competitive Banking," *Journal of Monetary Economics*, 3, 289–303.

Schmalensee, R. 1979. *The Control of Natural Monopolies*, Lexington/Mass.: Heath.

Schmidtchen, D. 1984. "German 'Ordnungspolitik' as Institutional Choice," *Zeitschrift für die gesamte Staatswissenschaft/Journal of Institutional and Theoretical Economics*, 140, 54–70.

Schneider, E. 1952. *Einführung in die Wirtschaftstheorie*, III. Teil: Geld, Kredit, Volkseinkommen und Beschäftigung, Tübingen: Mohr.

Schneider, E. 1962. *Money, Income and Employment*, translation of Schneider (1952) (translated by Kurt Klappholz), 6th ed., London: Allen & Unwin.

Schotter, A. 1981. *The Economic Theory of Social Institutions*, Cambridge et al.: Cambridge University Press.

Schüller, A. (ed.) 1983. *Property Rights und ökonomische Theorie*, München: Vahlen.

Schultz, D. 1967. *Der Vertrag als privatrechtliches Ordnungselement des wirtschaftlichen Geschehens: Grundfragen im Lichte moderner Entwicklungen in Wirtschaft und Recht*, Darmstadt: Technische Hochschule Darmstadt (Vortrag anläßlich der Feier der Rektoratsübergabe).

Schumpeter, J.A. 1912. *Theorie der wirtschaftlichen Entwicklung*, Leipzig: Duncker & Humblot.

Schumpeter, J.A. 1917/1918. "Das Sozialprodukt und die Rechenpfennige. Glossen und Beiträge zur Geldtheorie von heute," *Archiv für Sozialwissenschaften und Sozialpolitik*, 44, 627–715, or in: *Aufsätze zur ökonomischen Theorie* (1952), ed. J.A. Schumpeter, 29–117, Tübingen: Mohr.

Schumpeter, J.A. 1939. *Business Cycles. A Theoretical, Historical, and Statistical Analysis of the Capitalist Process*, 2 Vols., London-New York: McGraw Hill.

Schumpeter, J.A. 1951. *The Theory of Economic Development. An Inquiry into Profits, Capital, Credit, Interest, and the Business Cycle*, translation of Schumpeter (1912) (translated by R. Opie), Cambridge/Mass.: Harvard University Press.

Schumpeter, J.A. 1955. *History of Economic Analysis*, edited from manuscript by Elizabeth Boody Schumpeter, New York: Allen & Unwin.

Schumpeter, J.A. 1956. "Money and the Social Product," in: *International Economic Papers*, No. 6, ed. by A.T. Peacock, W.F. Stolper, R. Turvey and E. Henderson, London-New York: Macmillan.

Schumpeter, J.A. 1961. *Konjunkturzyklen. Eine theoretische, historische und statistische Analyse des kapitalistischen Prozesses*, translation of Schumpeter (1939) (translated by Klaus Dockhorn), 2 Vols., Göttingen: Vandenhoeck & Ruprecht.

Schumpeter, J.A. 1970. *Das Wesen des Geldes*, ed. and introduced by F.K. Mann, Göttingen: Vandenhoeck & Ruprecht.

Schwartz, A.J. 1983. "The Postwar Institutional Evolution of the International Monetary System," in: *The International Transmission of Inflation*, eds. M.R. Darby and J.R. Lothian, 14–45, Chicago: University of Chicago Press.

Schweizer, U. 1988. "Externalities and the Coase Theorem: Hypothesis or Result?", *Journal of Institutional and Theoretical Economics/Zeitschrift für die gesamte Staatswissenschaft*, 144, 245–266.

Scott, W.R. 1981. Organizations. Rational, Natural, and Open Systems, Englewood Cliffs/N.J.: Prentice-Hall.

Sealy, C.W. and Lindley, J.T. 1977. "Inputs, Outputs and a Theory of Production and Cost at Depository Financial Institutions," *Journal of Finance*, 32, 1251–1266.

Selgin, G.A. 1987. "The Stability and Efficiency of Money Supply Under Free Banking," *Journal of Institutional and Theoretical Economics/Zeitschrift für die gesamte Staatswissenschaft*, 143, 435–456.

Selgin, G.A. and White, L.H. 1986. "The Evolution of a Free Banking System," Department of Economics, George Mason University and New York University, manuscript, or in: *Economic Inquiry*, 1987, 25, 439–457.

Seyfert, W. 1985a. *Zins und wirtschaftliche Entwicklung*, Köln et al.: Heymann.

Seyfert, W. 1985b. "A Weberian Analysis of Economic Progress: The Case of Resource Exporting LCD's," *Zeitschrift für die gesamte Staatswissenschaft/Journal of Institutional and Theoretical Economics*, 141, 170–183.

Sherman, E.F., Sprenkle, C.M. and Stanhouse, B.E. 1979. "Reserve Requirements and the Control of Money Supply," *Journal of Money, Credit and Banking*, 11, 486–493.

Shubik, M. 1983. *Game Theory in the Social Sciences*. Concepts and Solutions, Cambridge/Mass.: MIT-Press.

Shugart, W.F. II and Tollison, R.D. 1983. "Preliminary Evidence on the Use of Inputs by the Federal Reserve System," *American Economic Review*, 73, 291–304.

Simmel, G. 1907. *Die Philosophie des Geldes*, München: Duncker & Humblot.

Simmel, G. 1978. *The Philosophy of Money*, translation of Simmel (1907) (translated by Tom Bottomore and David Frisby), London: Routledge & Kegan Paul.

Simons, H.C. 1934. "*A Positive Program for Laissez-Faire*: *Some Proposals for a Liberal Economic Policy*," Public Policy Pamphlets, No. 15, Chicago: University of Chicago Press.

Simons, H.C. 1936. "Rule Versus Authorities in Monetary Policy," *Journal of Political Economy*, 44, 1–30, or in: *Readings in Monetary Theory* (1951), ed. American Economic Association, 337–368, New York et al.: Blakiston.

Singleton, K. 1987. "Speculation and the Volatility of Foreign Currency Exchange Rates," *Carnegie-Rochester Conference Series on Public Policy*, 26, 9–56.

Sjaastad, L.A. 1976. "Why Stable Inflation Fail: An Essay in Political Economy," in: *Inflation in the World Economy*, eds. M. Parkin and G. Zis, 73–86, Manchester: Manchester University Press.

Smith, A. 1776/1976. *An Inquiry into the Nature and Causes of the Wealth of Nations*, General eds. R.H. Cambell and A.S. Skinner, Textual ed. W.B. Todd, Vol. 2, Oxford: Clarendon Press.

Smith, V.C. 1936. *The Rationale of Central Banking*, London: P.S. King & Son.

Soetbeer, A. 1879. *Edelmetall-Produktion und Wertverhältnis zwischen Gold und Silber seit der Entdeckung Amerikas bis zur Gegenwart*, Gotha: J. Perthes.

Sohmen, E. 1961/1969. *Flexible Exchange Rates*, 1st and 2nd (revised) edition, Chicago-London: Chicago University Press.

Sohmen, E. 1964. *Internationale Währungsprobleme. Eine Einführung*, Frankfurt/Main: Knapp.

Sohmen, E. 1973. *Wechselkurs und Währungsordnung*, Tübingen: Mohr.

Sohmen, E. 1976. *Allokationstheorie und Wirtschaftspolitik*, Tübingen: Mohr.

Sommerlad, T. 1911. "Zinsfuß im Mittelalter," in: *Handwörterbuch der Staatswissenschaften*, eds. J. Conrad, L. Elster, W. Lexis and E. Loening, 3rd ed., 1023–1029, Jena: Fischer.

Sontheimer, K. 1972. "On the Determination of Money Prices," *Journal of Money, Credit and Banking*, 4, 489–508.
Starr, R.M. 1972. "The Structure of Exchange in Barter and Monetary Economies," *Quarterly Journal of Economics*, 86, 290–302.
Starr, R.M. 1980. "General Equilibrium Approaches to the Study of Monetary Economics: Comments on Recent Developments," in: *Models of Monetary Economics*, eds. J.H. Kareken and N. Wallace, 261–263, Minneapolis/MN: Federal Reserve Bank of Minneapolis.
Starret, D.A. 1973. "Inefficiency and the Demand for 'Money' in a Sequence Economy," *Review of Economic Studies*, 40, 347–448.
Stigler, G. 1961. "The Economics of Information," *Journal of Political Economy*, 69, 213–225.
Stigler, G. 1971. "The Theory of Economic Regulation," *The Bell Journal of Economics and Management Science*, 2, 3–21.
Stillson, R.T. 1974. "An Analysis of Information and Transaction Services in Financial Institutions," *Journal of Money, Credit and Banking*, 6, 517–535.
Stolper, G. 1942. *This Age of Fable. The Political and Economic World we Live in*, 2nd ed. (1st ed. 1941), New York: Reynal & Hichcock.
Streissler, E. and Streissler, M. 1984. *Grundzüge der Volkswirtschaftslehre für Juristen*, Wien: Manz.
Stützel, W. 1954. "Kapital und Zins," in: *Evangelisches Soziallexikon*, ed. F. Karrenberg, 631–640, Stuttgart: Kreuz.
Stützel, W. 1958. *Volkswirtschaftliche Saldenmechanik*, Tübingen: Mohr.
Stützel, W. 1959. "Liquidität," in: *Handwörterbuch der Sozialwissenschaften*, eds. E.v. Beckerath et al., Vol. 6, 622–629, Stuttgart: Fischer.
Stützel, W. 1960a. "Währungspolitik und Wirtschaftsverfassung – zurück zum monetären Nationalismus?", Beilage zu den "Mitteilungen" der Industrie- und Handelskammer, Dortmund, 7, Oktober 1960, or in: *Währung in weltoffener Wirtschaft. Lehrstücke der Währungspolitik – unter der Herausforderung des Tages* (1973), ed. W. Stützel, 84–99, Frankfurt/Main: Knapp.
Stützel, W. 1960b. "Über Notenbankpolitik und importierte Inflation," *Beihefte zur Konjunkturpolitik, Zeitschrift für angewandte Konjunkturforschung*, Heft 7, 10–41.
Stützel, W. 1964. *Bankpolitik heute und morgen*, Frankfurt/Main: Knapp.
Stützel, W. 1969. *Über einige Währungstheorien*, Walter-Eucken-Institut, Vorträge und Aufsätze, Nr. 23, Tübingen: Mohr.
Stützel, W. 1973. *Währung in weltoffener Wirtschaft. Lehrstücke der Währungspolitik – unter der Herausforderung des Tages*, Frankfurt/Main: Knapp.
Stützel, W. 1979. *Das Mark-gleich-Mark-Prinzip und unsere Wirtschaftsordnung. Über den sogenannten Nominalismus, insbesondere im Schuld- und Steuerrecht*, Baden-Baden: Nomos.
Stützel, W. 1983. "*Über unsere Währungsverhältnisse. Zehn Jahre Floating: Verheißung und Erfahrung*," Walter-Eucken-Institut, Vorträge und Aufsätze, Nr. 91, Tübingen: Mohr.
Summers, L.H. 1981. "Optimal Inflation Policy," *Journal of Monetary Economics*, 7, 175–194.
Swan, T.W. 1956. "Economic Growth and Capital Accumulation," *Economic Record*, 32, 334–361.
Swoboda, A.K. 1978. "Gold, Dollars, Euro-Dollars, and the World Money Stock Under Fixed Exchange Rates," *American Economic Review*, 68, 625–642.

Takayama, A. 1974. *Mathematical Economics*, Hinsdale/Ill.: Dryden Press.
Taylor, J.B. 1981. "On the Relation Between the Variability of Inflation and the Average Rate," *Carnegie-Rochester Conference Series on Public Policy*, 15, 57–86.
Taylor, M.P. and McMahon, P.C. 1988. "Long-Run Purchasing Power Parity in the 1920s," *European Economic Review*, 32, 179–197.
Teigen, R.L. 1964. "Demand and Supply Functions for Money in the United States: Some Structural Estimates," *Econometrica*, 32, 476–509.
Telser, L.G. 1958. "Futures Trading and the Storage of Cotton and Wheat," *Journal of Political Economy*, 65, 233–255.
Thorn, R. 1966. *Monetary Theory and Policy. Major Contributions to Contemporary Thought*, New York: Random House.
Thornton, H. 1802/1939. *An Enquiry into the Nature and Effects of the Paper Credit of Great Britain*, ed. F.A.v. Hayek, London: Allen & Unwin.

Thornton, H. 1802/1962. *An Enquiry into the Nature and Effects of the Paper Credit of Great Britain*, ed. F.A.v. Hayek, London: Frank Cass; New York: Kelley.

Timberlake, R.H. 1984. "The Central Banking Role of Clearinghouse Associations," *Journal of Money, Credit and Banking*, 16, 1–15.

Tirole, J. 1982. "On the Possibility of Speculation under Rational Expectations," *Econometrica*, 50, 1163–1181.

Tobin, J. 1956. "The Interest-Elasticity of Transactions Demand for Cash," *Review of Economics and Statistics*, 38, 241–247.

Tobin, J. 1958. "Liquidity Preference and Behavior Towards Risk," *Review of Economics and Statistics*, 40, 65–86.

Tobin, J. 1963. "Commercial Banks as Creators of 'Money,'" in: *Banking and Monetary Studies for the Controller of the Currency*, ed. D. Carson, 408–419, U.S. Treasury, Homewood/Ill.: R.D. Irwin, or in: *Financial Markets and Economic Activity* (1967), eds. D.D. Hester and J. Tobin, 1–11, New York-London: Wiley.

Tobin, J. 1965. "Money and Economic Growth," *Econometrica*, 33, 671–684.

Tobin, J. 1972. "Inflation and Unemployment," *American Economic Review*, 62, 1–18.

Tobin, J. 1980a. Comments in: *Models of Monetary Economics*, eds. J.H. Kareken and N. Wallace, 83–90, Federal Reserve Bank of Minneapolis.

Tobin, J. 1980b. *Asset Accumulation and Economic Activity. Reflections on Contemporary Macroeconomic Theory*, Chicago: University of Chicago Press.

Tobin, J. 1981. "The Monetarist Counter-Revolution Today. An Appraisal," *Economic Journal*, 91, 29–42.

Tobin, J. and Brainard, W.C. 1963. "Financial Intermediaries and the Effectiveness of Monetary Controls," *American Economic Review, Papers and Proceedings*, 53, 383–400, or in: *Financial Markets and Economic Activity* (1967), eds. D.D. Hester and J. Tobin, 55–93, New York-London: Wiley.

Tooke, Th. 1844/1959. *An Inquiry into the Currency Principle. The Connection of the Currency with Prices and the Expediency of a Separation of Issue from Banking*, London 1844: Longman, Brown, Green, and Longmans; London 1959: The London School of Economics and Political Science (Series of Reprints of Scarce Works on Political Economy, No. 15).

Torrens, R. 1848/1858. *The Principles and Practical Operation of Sir Robert Peel's Act of* 1844, *Explained and Defended*, London (1848): Longman, Brown, Green, and Longmans; 3rd ed. (1858), Revised and Enlarged: *Comprising Critical Examinations of the Report of the Lord's Committee of* 1848 *upon National Distress, of the Novel Principles of Currency Propounded by Mr. Tooke and Mr. Wilson, and of the Chapter on the Regulation of Currency in Mr. J.S. Mill's 'Principles of Political Economy,'* London (1858): Longmans.

Tsiang, S.C. 1959. "The Theory of Forward Exchange and Effects of Government Intervention on the Forward Exchange Markets," *International Monetary Staff Papers*, 7, 75–106, Washington/D.C.: *IMF*.

Ulph, A.M. and Ulph, D.T. 1975. "Transaction Costs in General Equilibrium Theory – A Survey," *Economica*, 42, 355–372.

Van Huyck, J.B. 1987. "A Retrospective on the Classical Gold Standard, 1821–1931: A Review Essay," *Journal of Monetary Economics*, 19, 451–456.

Varian, H. 1984. *Microeconomic Analysis*, New York: Norton.

Varian, H. 1987. Intermediate Microeconomics, New York: Norton.

Vaubel, R. 1977. "Free Currency Competition," *Weltwirtschaftliches Archiv*, 113, 435–461.

Vaubel, R. 1978. *Strategies for Currency Unification: The Economics of Currency Competition and the Case for a European Parallel Currency*, Tübingen: Mohr.

Vaubel, R. 1985. "Competing Currencies: The Case for Free Entry," *Zeitschrift für Wirtschafts- und Sozialwissenschaften*, 105, 547–564.

Veit, O. 1969. *Grundriß der Währungspolitik*, 3rd rev. ed., Frankfurt/Main: Knapp.

Viner, J. 1937. *Studies in the Theory of International Trade*, New York: Harper; London 1955: Allen & Unwin.

de Vries, G.M. 1976. *The International Monetary Fund 1966–1971. The System Under Stress*, Washington/D.C.: International Monetary Fund.

Wachter, M.L. and Williamson, O.E. 1978. "Obligational Markets and Mechanism of Inflation," *The Bell Journal of Economics*, 9, 549–571.

Wagenführ, H. 1959. *Der Goldene Kompaß*, Stuttgart: Schuler.

Wagner, A. 1857. *Beiträge zur Lehre von den Banken*, Leipzig: Voss.

Wagner, E. 1982. *Theorie der Bankunternehmung. Eine Analyse von Bankverhaltensmodellen unter dem Aspekt der Transaktionskosten*, Frankfurt/Main – Bern: Lang.

Wagner, K. 1982. *Die internationale Tätigkeit der Banken als aufsichtsrechtliches Problem*, Baden-Baden: Nomos.

Wagner, V.F. 1937. *Geschichte der Kredittheorien. Eine dogmenkritische Darstellung*, Wein: Springer.

Wahlen, E.L. 1966. "A Rationalization of the Precautionary Demand for Cash," *Quarterly Journal of Economics*, 80, 314–324.

Wallace, N. 1980. "The Overlapping-Generations Model of Fiat Money," in: *Models of Monetary Economics*, eds. J.H. Kareken and N. Wallace, 49–82, Federal Reserve Bank of Minneapolis.

Walras, L. 1872. *Eléments d'Economie Politique Pure*, Lausanne: Rouge; 4th ed. (1900) Lausanne: Rouge; Paris: Pichon.

Walras, L. 1926/1954. *Elements of Pure Economics or the Theory of Social Wealth*, translation of Walras (1872) (translated by W. Jaffé), London: Allen & Unwin; Homewood/Ill.: Irwin.

Weber, M. 1949. *The Methodology of the Social Sciences* (translated by E.A. Shils and H. Finch), Glencoe/Ill.: Free Press.

Weber, M. 1968. *Economy and Society. An Outline of Interpretative Sociology*, ed. by G. Roth and C. Wittich, 3 Vols., New York: Bedminster Press.

Weber, M. 1980. *Wirtschaft und Gesellschaft. Grundriß der verstehenden Soziologie*, 5th rev. ed., Tübingen: Mohr.

Webster's Deluxe Unabridged Dictionary 1983, 2nd ed. New York: World.

Weintraub, R.E. 1977. "The Microfoundations of Macroeconomics: A Critical Survey," *Journal of Economic Literature*, 15, 1–23.

Weintraub, R.E. 1978. "Congressional Supervision of Monetary Policy," *Journal of Monetary Economics*, 4, 341–362.

Weizsäcker, C.C.v. 1962. "Investitionsoptimum in einer wachsenden Wirtschaft," in: *Optimales Wachstum und optimale Standortverteilung*, ed. E. Schneider, Schriften des Vereines für Socialpolitik, N.F., Vol. 27, 60–76, Berlin: Duncker & Humblot.

Weizsäcker, C.C.v. 1971. *Steady State Capital Theory*, Berlin – Heidelberg et al.: Springer.

Weizsäcker, C.C.v. 1972. "The Temporal Structure of the Production Process and the Problem of Distribution of Income between Capital and Labour," *German Economic Review*, 10, 289–309.

Weizsäcker, C.C.v. 1982. "Staatliche Regulierung – Positive und normative Theorie," *Schweizerische Zeitschrift für Volkswirtschaftslehre und Statistik*, 118, 325–343.

Welch, J. (ed.) 1981. The Regulation of Banks in the Member States of the EEC, 2nd ed., The Hague/Boston/London: Martinus Nijhoff Publishers; London: Graham & Trotman Ltd.

Welcker, J. 1978. *Neuordnung der Bankenaufsicht*, Frankfurt/Main: Knapp.

Werner, W. 1985. "Schwerpunkte der Novellierung des Kreditwesengesetzes," *Zeitschrift für Handelsrecht und Wirtschaftsrecht*, 149, 236–260.

Westphal, U. 1970. *Theoretische und empirische Untersuchungen zur Geldnachfrage und zum Geldangebot*, Kieler Studien, Nr. 110, Tübingen: Mohr.

White, L.H. 1984a. *Free Banking in Britain: Theory, Experience, and Debate*, 1800–1845, Cambridge: Cambridge University Press.

White, L.H. 1984b. "Competitive Payments Systems and the Unit of Account," *American Economic Review*, 74, 699–712.

Whitman, M.v.N. 1975. "Global Monetarism and the Monetary Approach to the Balance of Payments," *Brookings Papers on Economic Activity*, 3, 419–536.

Wicksell, K. 1898. *Geldzins und Güterpreise. Eine Studie über die den Tauschwert des Geldes bestimmenden Ursachen*, Jena: Fischer.

Wicksell, K. 1901. *Föreläsningar i nationalekonomi*, Lund: Berlingska; Stockholm: Fritze.

Wicksell, K. 1928. *Vorlesungen über Nationalökonomie auf der Grundlage des Marginalprinzips*, Theoretischer Teil, Zweiter Band: Geld und Kredit, translation of Wicksell (1901) (translated by M. Langenfeldt), 2nd ed., Jena: Fischer; reprint (1969) Aalen: Scientia.

Wicksell, K. 1934. *Lectures on Political Economy*, translation of Wicksell (1901) (translated from the Swedish by E. Claassen), *Vol.* 1: *General Theory*, London: Routledge & Kegan Paul.

Wicksell, K. 1935. *Lectures on Political Economy*, translation of Wicksell (1901) (translated from the Swedish by E. Claassen), *Vol.* 2: *Money*, London: Routledge & Kegan Paul.

Wicksell, K. 1936. *Interest and Prices. A Study of the Causes Regulating the Value of Money*, translation of Wicksell (1898) (translated by R.F. Kahn), London: Macmillan.

Williamson, J. 1985. *The Exchange Rate System, Policy Analysis in International Economics*, 5, 2nd ed, Washington/D.C.: Institute for International Economics; Cambridge/Mass.: MIT-Press.

Williamson, J. 1986. "Target Zones and the Management of the Dollar," *Brookings Papers on Economic Activity*, 1, 165–175.

Williamson, O.E. 1975a. *Markets and Hierarchies: Analysis and Antitrust Implications. A Study in the Economics of Internal Organization*, New York-London: Free Press.

Williamson, O.E. 1975b. "Understanding the Employment Relation: The Analysis of Idiosyncratic Exchange," *The Bell Journal of Economics*, 6, 250–280.

Williamson, O.E. 1976. "Franchise Bidding for Natural Monopolies – In General and With Respect to *CATV*," *The Bell Journal of Economics*, 7, 73–104.

Williamson, O.E. 1979. "Transaction-Cost Economies: The Governance of Contractual Relations," *Journal of Law and Economics*, 22, 233–261.

Williamson, O.E. 1980. "The Organization of Work," *Journal of Economic Behavior and Organization*, 1, 5–38.

Williamson, O.E. 1981. "The Economics of Organization: The Transaction-Cost Approach," *American Journal of Sociology*, 87, 548–577.

Williamson, O.E. 1984. "The Economics of Governance: Framework and Implications," *Zeitschrift für die gesamte Staatswissenschaft/Journal of Institutional and Theoretical Economics*, 140, 195–223.

Williamson, O.E. 1985a. "Reflexions on the New Institutional Economics," *Zeitschrift für die gesamte Staatswissenschaft/Journal of Institutional and Theoretical Economics*, 141, 187–195.

Williamson, O.E. 1985b. *The Economic Institutions of Capitalism*, New York-London: Macmillan.

Williamson, S.D. 1987. "Recent Developments in Modeling Financial Intermediation," *Federal Reserve Bank of Minneapolis, Quarterly Review*, 11, 19–29.

Wolff, M. 1917. "Das Geld," in: *Handbuch des gesamten Handelsrechts*, ed. V. Ehrenberg, Vol. IV, 563–648, Leipzig: Reisland.

Wood, E. 1939. *English Theories of Central Banking Control* (1819–1858), Cambridge/Mass.: Harvard University Press.

Yeager, L.B. 1976. *International Monetary Relations: Theory, History, and Policy*, 2nd ed., New York et al.: Harper & Row.

Name Index

Subject Index

Numbers in *italics* indicate on which page the definition or illustration of the respective subject is given.

MIX
Papier aus verantwortungsvollen Quellen
Paper from responsible sources
FSC® C105338

If you have any concerns about our products,
you can contact us on
ProductSafety@springernature.com

In case Publisher is established outside the EU,
the EU authorized representative is:
Springer Nature Customer Service Center GmbH
Europaplatz 3, 69115 Heidelberg, Germany

Printed by Libri Plureos GmbH
in Hamburg, Germany